50TH *Anniversary Edition*

The Art of Eating

M.F.K. FISHER

WITH AN INTRODUCTION BY
CLIFTON FADIMAN

AN APPRECIATION BY
JAMES A. BEARD

AND A RETROSPECTIVE ESSAY BY
JOAN REARDON

WILEY

Wiley Publishing, Inc.

Published by Wiley Publishing, Inc., Hoboken, New Jersey

A compilation of the works of M. F. K. Fisher first published in book form separately under the titles: *Serve It Forth; Consider the Oyster; How to Cook a Wolf; The Gastronomical Me;* and *An Alphabet for Gourmets.*

For general information on our other products and services or to obtain technical support please contact our Customer Care Department within the U.S. at 800-762-2974, outside the U.S. at 317-572-3993 or fax 317-572-4002.

Wiley also publishes its books in a variety of electronic formats. Some content that appears in print may not be available in electronic books.

Library of Congress Catologing-in-Publication Data

Fisher, M. F. K. (Mary Frances Kennedy), 1908–
    The art of eating / by M. F. K. Fisher ; with an introduction by Clifton Fadiman, an appreciation by James Beard, and a biographical essay by Joan Reardon.—50th anniversary ed.
        p. cm.
Includes index.
    ISBN-10: 0-7645-4261-3 (paperback : acid-free paper)
    ISBN-13: 978-0-7645-4261-9 (paperback : acid-free paper)
    1. Gastronomy. I. Title.
    TX633.F515 2004
    641'.01'3—dc22

                                        2003026124

Manufactured in the United States of America

10 9

Contents

THE ART OF EATING: IN CELEBRATION   x

THOUGHTS ABOUT M. F. K. FISHER AND HER WORK   xvi

ONE MORE TIME   xxvi

APPRECIATION   xxviii

INTRODUCTION   xxx

Serve It Forth

To Begin	5
When a Man Is Small	7
Greek Honey and the Hon-Zo	12
3000 B.C.–100 A.D.	
Egypt, the Orient, and Greece	
The Curious Nose	17
Let the Sky Rain Potatoes	22
Borderland	26
Garum	29
100 A.D.–400 A.D.	
Rome	
Fifty Million Snails	34
Meals for Me	40
Dark Ages and the Men of God	45
1000 A.D.–1400 A.D.	
Europe	
I Arise Resigned	47
In Sinistra Parte, Johannus Baptista	52
1100 A.D.–1450 A.D.	
England	
Pity the Blind in Palate	57
A Pigges Pettie Toes	60
Elizabethan England	

The Standing and the Waiting 64

Catherine's Lonesome Cooks 75
    1533 A.D.–1810 A.D.
    France

Two Birds Without a Branch 80

The Pale Yellow Glove 83

The Brothers 89

Set-piece for a Fishing Party 91
    1810 A.D.–1900 A.D.
    France

On Dining Alone

Sing of Dinner in a Dish 100

Shell-Shock and Richard the Third 107
    1900 A.D.– –
    Europe and America

The Social Status of a Vegetable 111

Cesar 116

To End 121

Consider The Oyster

Love and Death Among the Molluscs 125

A Supper to Sleep On 129

R is for Oyster 135

The Well-dressed Oyster 139

Take 300 Clean Oysters 144

A Lusty Bit of Nourishment 146

Pearls Are Not Good to Eat 160

Those Were Happy Days 166

Soup of the Evening, Beautiful Soup 170

Love Was the Pearl 175

My Country, 'Tis of Thee 178

As Luscious as Locusts 181

How To Cook A Wolf

Introduction to Revised edition	187
How to Be Sage Without Hemlock	189
How to Catch the Wolf	195
How to Distribute Your Virtue	198
How to Boil Water	207
How to Greet the Spring	223
How Not to Boil an Egg	229
How to Keep Alive	240
How to Rise Up Like New Bread	245
How to Be Cheerful Though Starving	252
How to Carve the Wolf	257
How to Make a Pigeon Cry	277
How to Pray for Peace	286
How to Be Content with a Vegetable Love	296
How to Make a Great Show	300
How to Have a Sleek Pelt	305
How to Comfort Sorrow	310
How to Be a Wise Man	320
How to Lure the Wolf	323
How to Drink to the Wolf	329
How Not to Be an Earthworm	335
How to Practice True Economy	343
Conclusion	350

The Gastronomical Me

Foreword	353
The Measure of My Powers	354
A Thing Shared	356
The Measure of My Powers	359
The Measure of My Powers	364
The First Oyster	368
The Measure of My Powers	378
The Measure of My Powers	382
Sea Change	385
The Measure of My Powers	393
To Feed Such Hunger	408
The Measure of My Powers	419
Noble and Enough	427
The Measure of My Powers	435
The Measure of My Powers	446
Sea Change	455
Sea Change	463
Sea Change	469
Define This Word	474
The Measure of My Powers	483
Once I Dreamed	501
I Remember Three Restaurants	502
Sea Change	510
The Lemming to the Sea	518
The Flaw	526
The Measure of My Powers	536
Feminine Ending	552

An Alphabet For Gourmets

Foreword   575

A is for dining *Alone*   577

B is for *Bachelors*   584

C is for *Cautious*   589

D is for *Dining* out   594

E is for *Exquisite*   600

F is for *Family*   605

G is for *Gluttony*   613

H is for *Happy*   618

I is for *Innocence*   623

J is for *Juvenile* dining   628

K is for *Kosher*   634

L is for *Literature*   640

M is for *Monastic*   645

N is for *Nautical*   650

O is for *Ostentation*   658

P is for *Peas*   663

Q is for *Quantity*   670

R is for *Romantic*   678

S is for *Sad*   682

T is for *Turbot*   687

U is for *Universal*   693

V is for *Venality*   701

W is for *Wanton*   706

X is for *Xanthippe*   713

Y is for *Yak*   720

Z is for *Zakuski*   727

From A to Z: The Perfect Dinner   736

INDEX OF RECIPES   745

The Art of Eating: In Celebration

DURING HER LIFETIME M. F. K. Fisher was no stranger to introductions. She wrote them for well-known authors and for community cookbooks and for friends and fans—or she dashed one off because the subject of the book interested her. During her fallow periods she welcomed requests to introduce books on tea, on wine, on Japanese cooking, and on "road food" simply to keep her name in the mainstream of gastronomical publishing. Fisher also introduced her own books with clarifying forewords although she seldom warmed to introductions to her work penned by others. In a letter to *Esquire's* Arnold Gingrich, she indicated that she found "[W. H.] Auden's little essay [for *The Art of Eating*] very wandering and foggy." She even revisited the introductions she had written, and revisionist that she was, she reintroduced the "introductions and conclusions and forewords and afterwords" to her major works in the slender volume called *Dubious Honors*.

So, is another introduction to M. F. K. Fisher necessary? Yes, because celebrating the 50th anniversary of the publication of *The Art of Eating* mandates placing this seminal work into the context of twenty-first century gastronomy.

The volume heralded in 1954 as the *Collected Gastronomical Works of M. F. K. Fisher* has not only been in continuous print for fifty years, but it has also become a benchmark for all that is original and memorable in America's culinary writing during the first half of the twentieth century. Fisher brought to the nutrition-oriented and commercial-centered culinary landscape a fresh vision, and she was uniquely positioned to do so. Exposed to French wines and food and steeped in the rich tradition of Continental gastronomical writing while studying in Dijon in the early 1930s, nurtured in the California tradition of fresh and seasonal ingredients, mentored by a succession of variously trained cooks in her family's kitchen, and more than a little intrigued by the language and lore of culinary history, Fisher found the perfect medium to display her journalistic skill, a legacy from her father and grandfather, and, as James Beard said, "her deeply personal thoughts and experiences that resound in one's emotions." And in each book, beginning with *Serve It Forth* in 1937, Fisher became more adept at creating her glorious mix of subjectivity and history, legend and lore.

Fisher said of her first book, *Serve It Forth*, "It will be about eating and about what to eat and about people who eat. And I shall do gymnastics by trying to fall between the three fires, or by straddling them all." The book ranges from Egypt, the Orient, and Greece (3000 B.C.–100 A.D.) to twentieth-century America in a sequence of vignettes highlighting amusing and sober events in the history of food. Woven among the historical essays are personal tales of secret indulgences, restaurants visited, two friendly recipes, and Fisher's thoughts about an ideal kitchen. The focus of each piece is food—tangerines toasting on a radiator, a perfect waiter spilling the soup, the smell of cabbage denoting class distinction, steak as a masculine prerogative, and diplomate au kirsch at a Sunday family feast. Overlaid with multiple connotations, food becomes a metaphor for our basic human hungers.

In *Consider The Oyster* (1941), Fisher ranged more freely, adding the fascinating maritime habits and scientific information of the bisexual bivalve to the aphrodisiac lore and personalities famous for generating the legends defining the oyster. From Antoine's in New Orleans to a tavern in Connecticut, she collected those recipes that traditionally attracted the aficionados of both raw and cooked preparations. She also drew on fond memories of childhood Sunday suppers of comforting oyster stew, and her mother's reminiscences of boarding school oyster loaves. The result was less studied than her first book and an interesting blend of facts and personal experiences. That she wrote it to distract her second husband, Dillwyn Parrish, from the debilitating pain of Buerger's disease accounts for the wit and lighthearted tone that permeates the book; but she was also sharing stories, memories of stories told to her, and recipes the same way she would share a tureen of oyster stew, ladling out "a lusty bit of nourishment."

The progress of World War II in Europe, the tragedy of Dillwyn Parrish's illness and death, and the advent of America's involvement in war with the Axis powers mandated Fisher's third book be aptly called

How To Cook A Wolf. Having seen blackout curtains, and experienced food shortages and curfews in Switzerland, she was in a unique position to recommend strategies for Americans intent on living agreeably in a world of constraints. Published in 1942 when shortages and rationing were rampant, she used what was a dire but temporary situation to discuss current fallacies regarding what people should eat, singling out the "balanced meals" touted by popular home and garden magazines for particular criticism. Every chapter in this book is a how-to guide. "How to: Greet the Spring, Be Sage Without Hemlock, Keep Alive, Rise Up Like New Bread, Be Cheerful Though Starving, and Be Content with a Vegetable Love." And there are a few "How Not to . . ." chapters as well. She proposes breakfasts of heaps of toast, an all-vegetable lunch of soup or salad, steak or a cheese soufflé for dinner, and juice or fruit for a between-meal pick-up. If the entire day, rather than each meal, balances out nutritionally, fine. The important thing is awakening the palate to the pleasures at hand whether they be starches or proteins. She draws on memories of her mother's gingerbread, French food, and canned foods and arranges the seventy-three recipes into traditional categories like appetizers, egg dishes, poultry, meat, and desserts, adding, with a wink and a nod, tips to ensure the survival of the dog Butch and cat Blackberry during wartime shortages.

The centerpiece of *The Art of Eating*, and the most oblique book in the collection, is the autobiographical *The Gastronomical Me* (1943). Written during her first pregnancy, Fisher used memorable meals and food experiences to tell her own story and assess her career before she assumed the role of a single mother. The people she wrote about were "with me then, [with] their other deeper needs of love and happiness"—Grandmother Holbrook making jam in the Whittier kitchen; her father Rex and sister Anne dining on fresh peach pie and thick cream by a stream when the three drove home from her aunt's ranch; her first husband Al Fisher and Mary Frances celebrating their first-month anniversary at the Aux Trois Faison restaurant in Dijon; Dillwyn and she returning to the States on the *Normandie*, their last trans-Atlantic voyage together; and her brother David's strange fascination with Juanito's mariachi band in Lake Chapala. The happy days of Fisher's youth and romantic days of honeymooning with her first husband become complicated in the ménage à trois in Vevey,

Switzerland, where Al Fisher exits the scene and Dillwyn Parrish and Mary Frances live their short-lived idyll at Le Paquis. Present in her stories also are the ocean crossings, resettling in California, tragedy, death, and Fisher taking the measure of her personal and professional powers against the cosmopolitan backgrounds of Europe, Hollywood, and Mexico. Through the revisiting of her shared sequences of meals and events, Fisher learns "her place in the world."

By 1945, Fisher had married her third husband—the former publisher, literary agent, and writer Donald Friede. He quickly began orchestrating her career, introducing her to Henry Volkening, her agent until 1978, and his former partner Pat Covici, an editor at Viking. In what would prove to be the most productive decade of her long career, Fisher wrote a novel, translated Brillat-Savarin's *Physiology of Taste* that critics hailed as the King James version of Savarin's Bible, compiled an anthology of literary pieces on eating and drinking, and wrote articles for a spectrum of quality magazines. In 1948 she completed a series of twenty-six articles based on the alphabet, which were to run consecutively in *Gourmet* magazine. Revised and expanded, the pieces were then published as a book called *An Alphabet For Gourmets*. The sequence forms a kaleidoscopic image of Fisher's life in the 1940s. From "*A* is for dining *Alone*," a thoughtful essay on living in a studio apartment and making quality but limited meals, to "*Z* is for *Zakuski*," a piece derived from Donald Friede's memories of his boyhood in St. Petersburg, Fisher revisits meals savored, draws on Brillat-Savarin's sage advice, and considers food as an aphrodisiac—all with a light touch. She offers, as one critic wrote, "a merry, sometimes biting, often passionate defense of the lover's approach to food—any kind of food."

Although he was by then divorced from Fisher, Donald Friede proposed what he called an omnibus of his ex-wife's first five gastronomical books in 1953, and he was able to command a generous advance from World Books, where he worked with Mary Frances's successor in marriage, Eleanor Kask, whom he wed in 1951. Together they produced a volume with illustrations—called decorations—by Leo Manso and an Introduction by the respected author Clifton Fadiman. Although Fisher resisted the idea initially, saying in a letter to her friend Larry Bachman that the collected edition would make her feel like "a minor Somerset Maugham of Sulphur Springs Avenue . . .

or a Colette of California . . . ant-size, of course," she soon saw the advantage of keeping her name and reputation before the public during a period when she was actively involved with the education of her daughters, Anna and Kennedy, and not writing as much as she would have liked. The critics proved her right and hailed the omnibus as "a refreshing breeze flowing from the twin sources of sense and sensibility. She writes, in short, as one intelligent adult to another—practically, often profoundly, and always beautifully." So said the *San Francisco Chronicle*. Collecting her five earlier gastronomical books into one volume dramatically enhanced her culinary reputation, because as Fadiman said, "It was the work of the most interesting philosopher of food now practicing in our country."

Fisher was living at Madame Lane's boarding house in Aix-en-Provence with her two daughters when *The Art of Eating* arrived in the fall of 1954. Writing to friends and family, she said that she felt quite detached from the glowing reviews. In response, some of them wrote that they hoped that publishing the collection of her early gastronomical books would free her from culinary magazine deadlines and "the hot stove of cookery bookery." For her part, Mary Frances felt that there were other things—folk remedies and old age; other places—Aix and Marseille; and other people—waiters, friendly doctors, and taxicab drivers to write about whenever time would permit.

But *The Art of Eating* had made its mark in the ever-growing number of books about the pleasures of the table, and Fisher's audience grew. The popularity of Fisher's book propelled an impressive publication history both in the United States and abroad. In 1963 Faber & Faber brought out a British edition of *The Art of Eating* without the inclusion of *How To Cook A Wolf*, apparently because Duell, Sloan and Pearce, the copyright-holding publisher of the book, refused permission. W. H. Auden wrote the Foreword, and it contained the oft-quoted statement, "Mrs. Fisher is as talented a writer as she is a cook. Indeed, I do not know of anyone in the United States today who writes better prose. If a reader wishes to test this assertion, let him read the first three pages of the section in *An Alphabet For Gourmets* entitled '*I* is for *Innocence*.'" Auden also launched into an elaborate theory about women who developed a passion for cooking, proposing that their animus, or unconscious masculine side, was stronger than normal. Although he did not apply his conclusions directly to Fisher, he did suggest that her preoccupation with wine and food was cerebral as well as creative. Twenty years later, the British publisher Pan Books reissued *The Art of Eating*, including *How To Cook A Wolf*, with the same W. H. Auden foreword.

On this side of the Atlantic, the Macmillan Company acquired the rights from World and republished *The Art of Eating* in 1971 with the original Leo Manso illustrations throughout and the Fadiman introduction. This edition also included an "Appreciation" written by James Beard in which he emphasized that Fisher "has been a rarity in American gastronomy." While this country has countless numbers of cookbook writers, he maintained, there have been precious few writers in the European tradition of Brillat-Savarin, Maurice des Ombiaux, or George Saintsbury. Fisher successfully and incomparably joined memory and the word. "She writes about fleeting tastes and feasts vividly, excitingly, sensuously, exquisitely. There is almost a wicked thrill in following her uninhibited track through the glories of the good life. What pleasure awaits the reader who has not known the five volumes that make up *The Art of Eating*." In 1990 Macmillan published a paperback with an added Introduction by M. F. K. Fisher, "as my one and only fan letter to myself." Whether in hardcover or paperback, during the past fifty years, the omnibus has lost none of its impact or relevance as a contribution to the art of writing.

Some books are meant to be read and passed on; others require a permanent place in one's personal library for frequent savoring, for delight in what "oft was thought, but ne'er so well express'd." *The Art of Eating* contains those intimate moments recollected in tranquillity when eating, drinking, and conversing was as good as it could ever be; when freshly picked, simply cooked, happily eaten green peas symbolized the satisfaction of our deepest needs; and when a father and his two young daughters discovered the depth of their relationship while picnicking on freshly baked peach pie garnished with thick cream. "This is M. F. K. Fisher's special genius." [Publisher's copy, 1954]

—JOAN REARDON

Thoughts about M. F. K. Fisher and Her Work

⌁ Julia Child, cookbook author and teacher:

"How wonderful to have here in my hands the essence of M. F. K. Fisher whose wit and passionate opinions on food and those who produce it, comment upon it, and consume it are as apt today as they were several decades ago, when she composed them. Why did she choose food and hunger she was asked, and she replied, 'When I write about hunger, I am really writing about love and the hunger for it, and warmth, and the love of it . . . and then the warmth and richness and fine reality of hunger satisfied.' This is the stuff we need to hear, and to hear again and again."

⌁ Alice Waters, owner of Chez Panisse:

"This comprehensive volume should be required reading for every cook. It defines in a sensual and beautiful way the vital relationship between food and culture."

⌁ Dr. Maya Angelou, poet, author, friend:

"During some golden days in the 1970s I moved to Sonoma, California, in the wine country. I had come to know the town by visiting with my friends David Bouverie and M. F. K. Fisher who lived there.

"My stove and refrigerator were working but my pots and pans were still in moving boxes. I went to the local cookery shop and bought good kitchenware that I knew I would continue to use even after mine was liberated from its holding prison. I told the shop owners that I had invited M. F. K. Fisher for dinner. They paled with shock and asked me: 'You mean you are going to cook for Mary Frances in pots you haven't tried out?'

"The invitation had gone out so I had no choice. We spent a wonderful evening together and although we lived only three miles apart, she sent me a letter thanking me for the splendid evening. Her postscript was typical of the M. F. K. Fisher I knew and who I still miss. It was, 'P. S. That was the first honest cassoulet I have eaten in years.'"

Ruth Reichl, editor in chief, Gourmet *magazine:*

"In the mid-seventies, when I was a contributing editor at *New West* magazine, one of my editors announced that he was about to ask M. F. K. Fisher to write something for us. What, he wanted to know, should he read to familiarize himself with her work? In response I handed him my very worn copy of *The Art of Eating* with this note:

> '*Mary Frances has the extraordinary ability to make the ordinary seem rich and wonderful. Her dignity comes from her absolute insistence on appreciating life as it comes to her. You'll see.*
>
> '*Read in this order:*
>
> > *Foreword, p. 353*
> > *Conclusion, p. 350*
> > *Define This Word, p. 474*
> > *Feminine Ending, p. 552*
> > *Pity the Blind in Palate, p. 57*
> > *A is for dining Alone, p. 577*
>
> '*After that you're on your own, but if I were you I'd read all of* The Gastronomical Me, *just because I wouldn't be able to stop myself. I can't tell you how much I envy you the joy of reading Mary Frances for the first time. It will change your life.*'

"In the almost thirty years that have passed since then, my feelings about this have not changed one bit."

Jacques Pépin, chef, cookbook author, cooking show host:

"M. F. K. Fisher's writing is always amusing, smart, and sharp but especially accurate and current. In '*T* is for *Turbot*' she is the apologist for steaming turbot in a copper wash boiler, a method created by Brillat-Savarin on the spur of the moment to accommodate the size of that large fish. With a gibe toward Escoffier techniques, she explains the process of the 'professor' in mouthwatering detail and, furthermore, gives a simple but elegant recipe for preparing trout in aspic that appears to come straight from the lexicon of nouvelle cuisine."

Betty Fussell, food historian:

"Reading M. F. K. Fisher never made me as hungry for food as it made me hungry for the company of one who was so tartly witty and wise, so provocative and persuasive, so artful and contradictory that, like Shakespeare's Cleopatra, 'she makes hungry where most she satisfies.'"

To read little is to want more and to read much is to want all. Thank god she wrote a lot. Fisher is truly a fisher of men, a master seducer with words as her medium and food as the bait. Whether this is your first taste of Fisher or a lifelong addiction, don't try to escape. She has anticipated your every move."

 James Villas, cookbook author, food writer, friend:

"When people ask me how Mary Frances Fisher influenced my career and life, no doubt they expect me to relate still another sugary anecdote about a lunch with her at the ranch in Sonoma, or some special dish she cooked for me, or advice she offered regarding my work. All of that I could do with great love and affection for this gentle but complex woman, but no personal experience with Mary Frances over the years could ever equal the indelible impact that one particular passage from *The Gastronomical Me* had on me when I first began writing about food.

"The episode pertains to an invocation of a beloved husband slowly dying of cancer during a voyage on the *Normandie* back in the late 1930s:

> *We got up late, and went after bathings and shavings to the Lounge, where we sat in soft chairs by the glass wall and looked out past the people sunning themselves to the blue water. We drank Champagne or sometimes beer, slowly, and talked and talked to each other because there was so much to say and so little time to say it.*
>
> *Even when New York loomed near us, we felt outward bound. I bit gently my numb fingers. I seemed beautiful, witty, truly loved . . . the most fortunate of all women, past sea change and with her hungers fed.'*

"The passage, for me, is not only one of the most heartbreaking that Mary Frances ever composed but the finest example I know of her unique art. In just a few sentences, every sense comes into play as she juxtaposes highly charged emotion with tragic resignation and transforms a wretched experience into a positive philosophical phenomenon. The tension and ambiguity of human relations, the absence of self-pity and honest acceptance of Fate, the quiet desperation to feed a hunger that far surpasses that of the stomach, the determination to confront Time and defeat its onslaught—only a poet like Mary Frances could reduce such complexities to a few well-chosen words. It doesn't matter whether Champagne or beer is drunk or whether it's good or bad; what matters is that it's sipped slowly and relates to the drama. Other food writers would wax endlessly and stodgily over flavors and textures and impressions; with Mary Frances, such secondary details are useless unless they contribute to the pathos of an event or sensation. Here, as elsewhere, she manages to transcend the subject so that the art of living takes supreme precedence over the more subordinate act of nourishing our bodies, and in doing so, she elevates 'food writing' to a level that is both noble and extremely difficult to imitate.

"And such, I am convinced, is the true art of M. F. K. Fisher, an art that is so deceivingly simple and unpretentious but one that imparts a dynamic message that lingers a lifetime. Today, still, I never drink Champagne or beer (especially on my crossings aboard *QE 2*) without recalling Mary Frances's powerful story—her 'sea change.' And I still struggle to write sentences like those in this exquisite passage."

✐ *Amanda Hesser, cookbook author, food writer (New York):*

"As a reader I feel I know M. F. K. Fisher like a friend. Who can deny me this? Why, I know her family and friends! I can picture her father vividly: the calm, thoughtful newspaper editor who sent her to the dictionary to look up words she did not know. I could draw her small adobe house, piled with books, in Glen Ellen. Madame Rigoulot's dining room in Dijon, where she and Al, her first husband, were overfed in *The Gastronomical Me*. And, in the same book, the snowy windowsill where she chilled dried tangerines.

"I can't find a single passage where what follows is described, but I can nonetheless see her with her hair pulled back from her round face. She is sitting in an armchair, stroking a cat on her lap while talking to visitors over cocktails. She is at a café in Aix with her daughters, fat square ice cubes melting at the bottom of their emptied glasses of *citron presse*. I have shared so many meals with her. She made me, everyone who read her, feel so close.

"I fell in love with the emotional, social Mary Frances. She is the sensualist I wanted to become. She is the woman who cried after revisiting M. Ribaudot's restaurant, her old haunt; who swept her children off to France for no other reason than that she was drawn back to Aix. And she is the diner who never said 'No' to that last glass of marc.

"Food came alive for her in a social context; the table was where everything that mattered happened. It was where she, Al, and Norah ate papayas, 'cold and smooth as butter,' and drank Champagne on their voyage from France to California. And where she learned, by observing a diner across the room, how to eat Burgundian snails, tipping the garlicky juice from the shell into her mouth and then swabbing the shell, 'with a morsel of her crusty bread.'

"But there is one place where I have never felt quite as if I could peer over her shoulder, or listen to her thoughts and worries: the kitchen.

"Certainly Mary Frances's skills as a cook and as an observer are at work in many of her recipes. Explaining how to make her Aunt Gwen's fried egg sandwiches, she wrote: 'Heat the drippings in a wide flat-bottomed skillet until they spit and smoke. Break in the eggs, which will immediately bubble around the edges, making them crisp and indigestible, and break their yolks with a fork and swirl them around, so that they are scattered fairly evenly through the whites. This will cook very quickly, and the eggs should be tough as leather.'

"And in *How To Cook A Wolf,* there are dozens of cooking tips, including a great one for purifying and saving cooking fat. (Pour it into a jar and cover with water. The burned bits will be absorbed into the water and the pure fat will rise to the top and harden.)

"When I look back now at *How To Cook A Wolf,* I am surprised by how much specific cooking advice it contains. And I can only guess that the reason it didn't stick with me was that it was more didactic than sensual. It is a cooking manual written from the perspective of a woman in the know, not a woman discovering—and not the woman who let us in on so many other parts of her emotional life.

"Mary Frances admits to overcooking eggs, and confesses to keeping a mirror in the kitchen, so that if 'the Prince of Wales or Charles Boyer' comes to the door, she could be forewarned of the smudge on her nose, but she doesn't readily relive any cooking dramas or leave us with any vivid fascination or joy with the kitchen.

"For her, process was process. She was not leaning into her oven, sweating as she chopped onions, licking her fingers, wishing her husband would stop standing in her way. Well, she was, probably, but she wasn't telling us about it. I can barely picture a single pan that she owned. Nor can I imagine where the window was, if there was one, in any of her kitchens.

"She addressed only lightly the questions that obsess today's food lovers. What kind of knives did she have? How did she arrange her refrigerator? Did she make her own mayonnaise? Did she ever lose sleep over a dinner party? Cookware fetishes were not yet born. Good cooking skills were not yet a social asset like being well-read or witty.

"Mary Frances left other voids in her writing, as well. Though she writes that her mother disapproved of her open enjoyment of food as a child, calling it 'unseemly,' Mary Frances never explores the possibility that her profession may have begun as a rebellion. And when she and Al split up, you never witnessed a single fight.

"Though she may not have specifically explored her relationship with her mother in print, she definitely fleshed out her long rebellion. Through her writing, she told a public steeped in Puritan values that it was okay to treat eating as an act of pleasure rather than an act of duty and restraint.

"It's an issue that continues to test people, and this is one of many reasons that Mary Frances's work holds up so well today. Her early life—taking long overseas voyages to Europe, living through war rations, and being a single mom in Aix—may now require a good deal of imagination to embrace. But people still come of age, get in bad relationships, suffer, rejoice, and move on. So *The Art of Eating* could not be more current.

"Yet we readers are selfish—we can never get enough from people we love. For me, her life as a cook will always feel like a missing piece. Mary Frances grew up in an upper-middle-class family, where the kitchen was not likely a place that anyone gathered but the help. Maybe she found that expressing pleasure at the table was amply progressive, while self-revelation in the kitchen remained shameful.

"Or perhaps the explanation for her self-abnegation in the kitchen can be found in a short passage in *Serve It Forth*, slipped in there subtly, like butter into a sauce. In the passage, she goes into great detail about what her ideal kitchen would look like. There are open shelves, a window or two, and space enough to prepare a meal for six. And one last thing, she writes: 'Most of all I need to be let alone. I need peace.' And no hungry readers peeking over her shoulder."

∽ *Susan Herrmann Loomis, author,* On Rue Tatin *and other books:*

"As I turn the pages of Mary Frances Kennedy Fisher's works—*The Art of Eating*, or *Boss Dog*, or *Two Towns in Provence*, or others—I find myself alongside her. She paints a picture so deftly, with strokes of such natural and living hues, that it is possible to smell the marc she sips, the chocolate she orders for her girls, the faint wisps of perfume and cigarette smoke that cloak nearly any French situation, anywhere in France. I feel the cloth of her characters' clothing, smell the rich aromas of food they put on the table, receive their whispered comments as does she. Even when she has just finished a hike on a hill near Les Laumes-Alésia of the Côte d'Or in Burgundy and is breathing hard, she makes me feel and smell the cold thin air ' . . . which felt like heavy fire before it thawed,' with the same sensuality as the subsequent chocolate she put in her mouth, which 'broke at first like gravel . . . then . . . grew soft, and melted voluptuously into a warm stream down my throat.' (*Serve It Forth*)

"In her writings, M. F. K. Fisher introduces me to a cast of characters around her, few of whom are intimates, yet whom she reveals intimately through her keen, lush observation and undoubtedly lively yet ever-so-slightly dark sense of life. She describes her own manner so well in the following description of a dining room, taken from *The Gastronomical Me*, 'The room was so intimate and yet so reassuringly impersonal. . . .' This is her key, I believe, beyond a voluptuous sense of life and adventure— she writes of everything and airs her opinions without emotionally embroiling the reader. She wraps her observations in food and eating, yet it seems to me her true concern is physical desire and satiation, and she turns her wit and intelligence to the subjects with great style.

"M. F. K. Fisher's writing, her life, and her attitudes are endlessly fascinating and succulent, and ever-inspiring."

Jack Shoemaker, one of Fisher's publishers and friends:

"I learned so much from Mary Frances—that pleasure is serious business and the consequences of not having a sufficient amount of pleasure are dire, that daily life is where life happens and we should treat daily life as a sequence of moments granted us as sacred gifts. She taught and practiced a philosophy of living inside those moments to the fullest degree possible, and she would have sounded like a Zen teacher, 'a perfectly realized master,' in a different culture. She thought the English language, if carefully used, had the potential to be one of the world's great languages, and when poorly used was uglier than nearly every other language on the planet. 'She's a nice enough person,' I can hear her say, 'but I wish she would learn to write a sentence!' And she thought life was the process of acquiring age with grace and enthusiasm, not something to endure. I think she thought the literary depressives, neurasthenics, and professional existentialists were rather pitiful. Reading her prose is like listening to her talk, and listening to her talk for a long afternoon was as glistening and exciting as an evening spent with Beethoven's piano sonatas."

Marsha and Patrick Moran, Fisher's assistant and friends:

"The *Art of Eating* is a fine book, which both of us continue to pick up to remember not only our friend Mary Frances, but also just to remind ourselves about how good sentences are constructed. In reading through it, we are also reminded of Mary Frances's ability to turn a phrase on itself so that it most often surprises and delights her readers, and always nourishes them. Her hunger to put her own self into her words is revealed from the very first writings in her journals, which spring off the page as fully formed, mature creations, even though they were inked from the pen of a teenager. And, from that point forward, it seems her greatest appetite was to reveal the humanity in each of us, or lack of it, through the portal by which we sustain ourselves physically, through the food we eat."

Jeannette Ferrary, author, M. F. K. Fisher and Me: A Memoir of Food and Friendship *and six cookbooks:*

"'When shall we live if not now?' So begins *Serve It Forth,* one of the five books in the collection of M. F. K. Fisher's works called *The Art of Eating.* In it she writes of the preciousness of time, especially time spent at the table. She begins with lofty invocations about the 'honor and sanctity in eating together,' but it isn't long before she gets down to brass tacks. She doesn't waffle about her specific preferences for everything from the height of the chairs and the size of the plates to the optimal number of guests and how they should be chosen (they should be able to sit and eat for five or six hours before a 'meal of soup and wine and cheese as well as one of twenty fabulous courses'). She also counsels not to invite people who are in the first 'tremors of love' because it's simply, as she puts it, 'a waste of good food.' Just as you're thinking of finding a pencil to make a checklist of these imperatives so you don't get it wrong, you realize that's not her point.

"What she's telling you is that you're not alone if you obsess a bit about these same sorts of things. If you're the kind of person who can make a ceremony out of eating a sandwich or a pickle or a few tiny pearls of caviar, you're not so crazy after all.

"At least that's how I felt when I first read M. F. K. Fisher almost thirty years ago.

"Until I discovered her writings, I had serious doubts about my sanity. And for good reason. I couldn't help noticing that other people could eat an entire meal and not utter a word about it. There were those who actually didn't begin musing about their dinner choices before they brushed their teeth in the morning. I could name quite a few friends who never memorized *Gourmet* magazine, who didn't have cookbooks piled ceiling high on their night tables. I had occasionally wondered if this behavior was entirely normal.

"All that changed when I was introduced to the work of M. F. K. Fisher. In *The Art of Eating*—all five books of it—I found a soulmate. Visiting these pages, I could drift off to Dijon (where I'd never been) and breathe in the French gingerbread called *pain d'epice* with its 'smell as thick as a flannel curtain.' I curled up with her book-length observations of the oyster and its 'dreadful but exciting life.'

"I chuckled—and humor is one of her often overlooked attractions—with such commentary as: 'One way to horrify at least eight out of ten Anglo-Saxons is to suggest their eating anything but the actual red fibrous meat of a beast.' I tasted the salad 'made in a bowl you used to see in Venice, the cooked and the raw entwined in an easy marriage.' I was right there with her when she spoke of her 'belief that unexpectedness and a modicum of astonishment enliven any good dinner.'

"On her honeymoon in Paris—her very first visit as a young woman—I imagined sitting with her watching the Seine flow past as we sipped hot chocolate and nibbled croissants on the Quai Voltaire. I felt myself tremble with the rapture that enveloped her as she shared with Dillwyn Parrish, the love of her life, the wine that 'was like music on our tongues.'

"Her writing helped me understand that food is a valid and fascinating world to explore as a writer, which ultimately changed my life. It was the kind of experience known to many who become Alices in her wonderland, enchanted by her sensual renderings. It was both transformation and confirmation. In M. F. K. Fisher, I found permission to be myself."

Norah Barr, Fisher's sister and coeditor of Fisher's letters:

"Mary Frances was the person closest to me from 1917 to 1991—very difficult to reduce to a paragraph or two. But I am very sure that she would welcome this anniversary edition of *The Art of Eating*. This is a wonderful gift for all of us, but especially so for people born in the past fifty years who may not have yet read Fisher. These books are so young, so sensitive and aware of the power of her experience that readers will fall in love with this writer as her contemporaries did. And they will find that her books only deepened and became more enjoyable as Mary Frances grew older."

Anna Parrish, Fisher's older daughter:

"I remember the sound of the typewriter at odd hours and that sound can still put me right to sleep. I felt safe and knew that sound meant my mother was doing what made her happiest. Her cooking? Simple, unfashionably simple and good. (She would serve salami, prosciutto and melon, a big salad of romaine, crisp sourdough, and good wine. Maybe some grapes or ice cream for dessert. My friends were baffled, but always came back for more.) Her writing has the same effect on me that it probably does on her other readers: she weaves a very complex spell of words, beautiful, resonant English. The language I heard spoken as I grew up and the language I love to read. When I put down one of her books, I have been to her world, and I am refreshed. Oh, and usually hungry."

Kennedy Friede Golden, Fisher's younger daughter:

"I was eight years old when *The Art of Eating* was first published, and appropriately oblivious to my mother's profession. I was engaged in being a child, playing with my older sister, enjoying family get-togethers, and moving away from the family home in Whittier to new frontiers in northern California and Aix-en-Provence. M. F. K. Fisher was my mother, and I have no sense of knowing her as anything else. She no doubt prepared our meals and gathered us at table with family and friends, but to me she was my mother, and no more.

"Now, fifty years later, rereading *The Art of Eating* has been a wonderful experience. I am pleased that this anniversary edition will give today's readers access to her stories, to experience her love of people and enjoy her artful use of the English language. From the sad story of Charles in 'The Standing and the Waiting' to her discussion of the art of eating alone in '*A is for dining Alone*,' this book is filled with stories of passion, compassion, love and loss. It is sad for me that I never appreciated her written words during her life, but I have certainly enjoyed reading them now.

"The connection I feel between *The Art of Eating* and my experience of forty-six years of life with my mother is as complex as I believe she was. In her life and her writing, her passion was always for simplicity and goodness in both food and people. In this volume she shares that passion, bringing to life her intense personal connections with waiters, cooks, vendors in outdoor markets, men, women, children, and elders. In her stories I believe that readers will experience a richness of life seldom committed to paper, in her case, typed in the early morning hours while the rest of the world slept.

"From the sex life of the oyster to the complexities of loss and death, *The Art of Eating* gives an intimate view into the many facets of being alive. Each story is brought within easy reach of the reader with food as the common element, whether it be the 'twenty-six or -seven quarts an hour' drunk by the tiny oyster or the peach pie eaten together under a canyon oak by a father and his seven-year-old daughter. In life's most simple plan, we must all eat to stay alive.

"*The Art of Eating* has aged well and is a book to be enjoyed by today's busy cooks, parents, travelers, lovers, and anyone who has a love of life and a desire to live it to the fullest."

Family picnic, California, 1950. *Left side, front to back:* David Barr (nephew); John Barr, Jr. (nephew); M. F. K. Fisher; John Barr, Sr. (brother-in-law); Matthew Barr (nephew); Norah Barr (sister). *Right side, front to back:* Kennedy Friede (daughter); Anna Friede (daughter); Donald Friede (husband); Rex Kennedy (father).

Photo courtesy of Kennedy Friede Golden

One More Time

I NEVER DID LIKE to write introductions, especially to my own stuff, although I find now that three good men have tried their hands at explaining why the first five books I wrote have been collected into this one volume called *The Art of Eating*.

The original collection was brought out by The World Publishing Company about forty years ago, and Clifton Fadiman was already well known as an important literary critic when he wrote the introduction to it. His agent asked a fee of five hundred dollars. This was appalling to me, and it was only after a month of trying to do something myself about me that I grudgingly agreed to borrow half the fee from my father, if World would come up with the other half. Of course, this all seems puny now, but it was a real problem to me when it happened, for various reasons connected with my aversion to debts and my completely penniless condition as a divorced woman with two small children and no monies at all, either patrimonial or alimonial. (Much later on, Kip Fadiman was, of course, horrified by my small tale when he heard it, but he is amused as I am by now, because we are good friends forever.)

Then the book was sold to Macmillian, and later to Vintage, and I think it was for Alfred Knopf that James Beard wrote a little introduction/preface for that edition to go along with the original by Clifton Fadiman.

Meanwhile, in England the book had been bought by Faber & Faber, which was fine except that because of some political or publishing snafu, the one section that should have been printed for the hungry limeys, *How To Cook A Wolf,* was omitted. The book was introduced by W. H. Auden, though, which made it well worth the price of admission to the British scene, and in later printings, the *Wolf* was included, for reasons quite beyond my comprehension.

The book has been published by other people in other countries as well as here, and now finally settled with one of its original owners, Macmillan. The best thing about the forty-odd years of its comings and goings is that it has had three of the finest men I've ever known write generously and well of it, and whether their interests were purely

pecuniary or were based on compassion and even kindness, they happen to have been people I both respect and love. Fortunately, they've all known this, but it does me good to have a chance to repeat it here.

It seems almost ridiculous to add that I myself find it impossible to read anything that I have written, once it is in print. I admit that a while ago, I asked a young man to read me a chapter from another book I'd written, mainly to see if he could indeed read and therefore qualify as a literate college graduate. He managed fairly well to stumble through the chapter about my cat Blackberry in *A Cordial Water*, and I found it fairly well written and indeed enjoyable. At least I could understand why it had been pointed out to me as a good bit of writing by several people I admire for other reasons.

The mean cold, cold fact remains, though, that on page one of the chapter, there is a use of one word which I shall never point out to anyone but which offends me gravely. It is the only thing I can remember now about the whole story, I'm so sorry to say, and I'll regret until the day I die that I know it is there.

This fault in my behavior is a foolish one, as I'm the first to admit, and I fear that it is too late to remedy it. I know that I should ask someone to read parts of *The Art of Eating* to me, and indeed I plan to do so before much longer. I shall try to enjoy the words because I know that much better people than I have done so. Many of them have written to me and I am proud of anything they have told me that is good, although I can honestly accept it only in the name of M. F. K. Fisher. As Mary Frances, I am incapable of believing what they say with such grace and generosity, so I shall read it and think long about it, as something written by Fisher for me.

And perhaps some day I may consider this introduction as my one and only fan letter to myself.

M. F. K. Fisher
Glen Ellen, California
September 1989

Appreciation

THE FIRST OF M. F. K. Fisher's Books to fall into my hands was *How To Cook A Wolf*, published during World War II. I was a cryptographer in the Army at that point, and I reveled in her brilliant approach to wartime economics for the table. (I later actually tried that life-saving recipe for the "Sludge," so intent was I on fighting the wolf.) Like so many readers before me, I was hooked. I quickly searched out her earlier books, *Serve It Forth* and *Consider The Oyster*. Oddly enough, though we eventually moved in the same professional sphere, corresponded, talked by telephone long-distance, and shared a number of friends, it took twenty-five years more for us to meet. By then I had long since been a captive to her prose, her charm, and her taste for the better things of this planet.

On rereading *The Art of Eating*, which contains the core of her work, I find it amazing that so much of these five books has lingered in the mind and the feelings—not just witty and sensible passages about eating, but deeply personal thoughts and experiences that resound in one's emotions. M. F. K. Fisher has the effect of sending the reader away with a desire to love better and live more fully.

Mrs. Fisher is a woman who has had many gifts bestowed on her—beauty, intelligence, heart, a capacity for pleasures of the flesh, of which that art of eating is no small part, and the art of language as well. Though she can write with a silver attelet dipped in sauce of Carême or Montagne, her palate goes beyond ortolans and rare vintages. She can also write about eating and drinking with a pure, primitive enjoyment. I think of that intoxicating description, in *Alphabet For Gourmets*, of a family meal in Switzerland, *al fresco*, highlighted by the ritual of eating peas fresh from the garden, cooked right on the spot. This celebration—it could be called nothing less—supports my thesis that good simple food, even rudimentary food, can give the same delight as the most elaborately prepared dishes.

M. F. K. Fisher has been a rarity in American gastronomy. This country has produced quantities of cookbook writers—all too many who write without personality or originality—but few writers in the

great European tradition of Brillat-Savarin, Maurice des Ombiaux, or George Saintsbury. The first of American gastronomes to gain recognition was George Ellwanger, from my home state of Oregon. Ellwanger's initial book, published in 1898, was called *Meditations on Gout: With a consideration of its cure through the use of wine*. This was followed by the far more explicit and fascinating volume *The Pleasures of the Table*, first published in 1902 and now available in a facsimile edition. Ellwanger was an esthete who counted gastronomy among his favorite arts and who was ahead of his time in the appreciation of good eating and fine wines. He was succeeded by a few others, such as Theodore Child and Percival Z. Didsbury, who wrote briefly on those subjects, but the field was empty for many years until the advent of M. F. K. Fisher.

For an art as transitory as gastronomy there can be no record except for a keen taste memory and the printed word. *The Art of Eating* reminds me again that in M. F. K. Fisher memory and word are joined incomparably. She writes about fleeting tastes and feast vividly, excitingly, sensuously, exquisitely. There is almost a wicked thrill in following her uninhibited track through the glories of the good life. What pleasure awaits the reader who has not known the five volumes that make up *The Art of Eating*. And for those of us who have already known and loved the work of M. F. K. Fisher, the perpetuation of this great omnibus brings back old delights and comforts.

JAMES A. BEARD

Introduction

LET THACKERAY provide our text: "Next to eating good dinners, a healthy man with a benevolent turn of mind, must like, I think, to read about them." Amen.

I have been addicted to eating for half a century and to date show no sign of breaking the habit—or its kindred one of devouring food by courtesy of Gutenberg. I do not speak of recipe books, which are part of the literature of knowledge, but of those belonging to the literature of power, those that, linking brain to stomach, etherealize the euphoria of feeding with the finer essence of reflection. "He who does not mind his belly will hardly mind anything else." I will out-dogmatize Dr. Johnson: He minds his belly all the better who is learned in belly lore.

We Americans, however, do not as a rule take gladly to the literature of gastronomy. Perhaps a native Puritanism is at fault. Though things are on the mend, we still plump ice cream into carbonic acid gas, rank steak and potatoes just below the Constitution, and contrive the cafeteria. How explain such things except as forms of self-punishment, stern reproofs to the rampant flesh? And, by the same token, to judge from its small audience, we must feel something vaguely licentious or censorable about the literature of food.

Indeed we will not even discuss it. In Anglo-Saxon countries, as Ford Madox Ford one remarked, food is no more talked of than love or heaven. The tantrums of cloth-headed celluloid idols are deemed fit for grown-up conversation, while silence settles over such a truly important matter as food.

Now good eating itself is of course the nub of the matter. But good books about good eating have their own noble uses. While the most exquisitely balanced dinner can never be relived, a book may evoke its graceful ghost. I own a small volume called *Tables of Content* by the dean of oenophiles, André Simon. It merely records some lunches and dinners he was lucky enough to get outside of during the late twenties and early thirties. But the menus, the names of the wines, the notes are enough to start glowing the second imagination that dwells in the palate.

A writer as good as Simon can set a table in your mind—but he must be good. Part of his goodness flows from the relation he bears to his subject, the relation of love and respect. Much of the literature of gusto is in fact well written. A man who is careful with his palate is not likely to be careless with his paragraphs. You will hurl Thoreau at me—Thoreau, who would as lief eat raw chipmunk. You will bring up Shaw, who lived on weeds, water and liver pills. But both these exceptions would have written even better had they collaborated with a good French cook. I am persuaded that poor Thoreau died at forty-five partly of malnutrition, and that Shaw would not have hurried off at the (for him) absurd age of ninety-four had he not progressively weakened himself with his lethal vegetarian messes.

A good book about food informs us of matters with which we are to be concerned all our lives. Sight and hearing lose their edge, the muscles soften, even the most gallant of our glands at last surrenders. But the palate may persist in glory almost to the very end. Indeed the greatest gourmets alive are elderly men and, less frequently, elderly women. Where is the tongue, the palate that is truly grown-up before thirty? The ability to enjoy eating, like the ability to enjoy any fine art, is not a matter of inborn talent alone, but of training, memory and comparison. Time works for the palate faithfully and fee-lessly.

Furthermore, the alimentary canal contains the only stream that flows through all history and geography, laving banks on which cluster those works that mark man at his most civilized.

Finally, gastronomical writing at its best is almost as much touched with the spirit as the bread and meat and wine with which it deals. There are no gross foods, only gross feeders; and by the same token even the homeliest prose about food, provided it be honest, can penetrate to the heart as do all words that deal with real things. A lordly dish of terrapin—or good bread and cheese—can be as uplifting as any landscape, and more so than many workers of art at which we are bid to "Oh!" and "Ah!" I have yet to meet that man who, with a good *tournedos Rossini* inside him, was not the finer for it, the more open to virtuous influences. "Asparagus," Charles Lamb says softly, "inspires thoughts," and even to read about such things cannot fail to purify our spirits.

All such pleasures may be savored in this volume, the work of the most interesting philosopher of food now practicing in our country.

The term philosopher has been chosen after due thought. Writes Mrs. Fisher: "There is a communion of more than our bodies when bread is broken and wine is drunk. And that is my answer, when people ask me: Why do you write about hunger, and not wars or love." Anyone who can set down such a sentence is no recipe monger, no writer of magazine pieces exploiting gastronomy's *dernier cri*, no boring apostle of standardization's sleekest product, "gracious living." She is a philosopher, one who believes that "it is impossible to enjoy without thought," that "when we exist without thought or thanksgiving [for food] we are not men, but beasts."

Her subject is hunger. But only ostensibly so. Food is her paramount but not her obsessive concern. It is the release-catch that sets her mind working. It is the mirror in which she may reflect the show of her existence. For, despite her denials, there is much in these five volumes about wars and love, much about death and joy and sorrow and indeed many of the major concerns of men and women. For all her awesome learning and authority, Mrs. Fisher writes not as a specialist, but as a whole human being, spiky with prejudices, charming, short-tempered, well-traveled and cosmopolitan, yet with her full share of intolerances. She is a person, not a gourmet masked as a writer. Her passion comes from inside her, and it is a passion, not an enthusiasm or a hobby.

Here then is a witty, well-furnished mind roving over the field of food, relating it to the larger human experience of which dining, while a miracle, is still but a part. Yet I would not have you think Mrs. Fisher always or only the philosopher. As the index to this book demonstrates, she is as practical as she is inspiring. She never loses sight of the fact that we struggle to gastronomy's altitudes only through the foothills of pots and pans and kitchen stoves and meats and vegetables and many tastings and humiliating failures.

So that if you are in quest of recipes only, here is a treasure trove; and if you seek something beyond recipes, this is no less your book. It can be thrice blessed, this book, blessing him that keeps it for himself, him that gives, and him that takes. For what better gift can there be for anyone still in firm possession of a palate, whether it be your weekend hostess, or the new-vintaged bride, or the matron of the mellower years, or the popinjay bachelor who fancies himself a Prosper Montagné, or just anyone fit to savor a personality as candid and polychrome as Mrs. Fisher's?

Of the five volumes here reprinted in classic form the most down-right useful is *How To Cook A Wolf.* Originally published in 1942, it was intended as a kind of culinary guide for bedeviled housewives suffering under the burden of wartime shortages. It has lost little of its point. Indeed, accompanied by the notes and glosses that the author added in the 1951 edition, it becomes more useful than ever—even though I can hardly agree that a recipe for roast pigeon can be of much value to economy-minded households. But, if you are hay-poor, how inspiriting to learn from Mrs. Fisher how to cook in a haybox; or, if you are plain poor, How To Be Cheerful Though Starving. Here too is the conclusive word on How To Boil An Egg.

Since Lewis Carroll no one had written charmingly about that indecisively sexed bivalve until Mrs. Fisher came along with her *Consider The Oyster.* Surely this will stand for some time as the most judicious treatment in English of a mollusc whose life career is matched in improbability only by our rash decision in the distant past to use it as a food.

An equally curious volume is *An Alphabet For Gourmets.* Of the recipes that act as tailpieces to these twenty-six miniature essays I am no great judge. The rest of the pert and pertinent matter, with its sly pokes at the fops and cultists of gastronomy, should divert anyone. I refer the reader particularly to several paragraphs on the complex relation between eating and making love. These include the details of a dinner warranted to satisfy one appetite while blunting another. The literature of venereal cookery, by the way, is vast, ancient and probably harmless. The only dependable aphrodisiacs, my worldly friends tell me, are not to be found in books. They are two in number, the first being the presence of a desirable woman, the second her absence.

Every man, it has been said, has in him an autobiographical novel. It has been even better said that in most cases it should be kept in him. However that may be, all of us surely house within ourselves another unwritten book. This would consist of an account of ourselves as eaters, recording the development of our palates, telling over like beads of a rosary the memories of the best meals of our lives.

In *Serve It Forth* and *The Gastronomical Me* Mrs. Fisher has done just this, though the first-named also contains a good deal of purely historical information. In these strange volumes, sometimes funny, sometimes sorrowful, always full of rich juices of keenly felt life, the kitchen, the dining room, the restaurant, the café, the transatlantic steamer, and the bedroom mingle in a flavorous *hochepot* of memories. Some of the stories are works of art—I shall leave it to the reader to make his own selection. Rereading these volumes after many years I found I had forgotten few details of the story of Papazi and snails, or the count of the delights of eating tangerines *á la* radiator, or the anecdote about the last virgin woman truffle-hunter in France.

The number of writers on food who are both artists and honest men or woman is limited. Among them must be placed M. F. K. Fisher, wise and witty spokesman for

> ". . . .the race
> *Of those that for the Gusto stand.*"

Of this race it is commonly agreed Brillat-Savarin stands at the head. It so happens that Mrs. Fisher has translated to perfection his great *Physiology of Taste*. This circumstance alone would entitle her to rank high among gastronomer-scholars. But her own original work gives her claim to an even nobler eminence. Of all writers on food now using our English tongue she seems to me to approach most nearly, in range, depth, and perception, the altitude of Brillat-Savarin himself. And, with that said the treasury of praise is exhausted.

CLIFTON FADIMAN
MARCH 8TH, 1954

The Art of Eating

1937

Serve It Forth

FOR R.B.K. AND E.O.H.K.

"Of course," concluded
Robert Kilburn Root, sitting crosslegged
and contemplating his Shashlik—
"of course if this book is well larded
with anecdotes, it will of necessity
be short."

To Begin

THERE are two kinds of books about eating: those that try to imitate Brillat-Savarin's, and those that try not to. The first substitute whimsy for his wit, and dull reminiscences for his delightful anecdotes. The second are gross where he would be delicate, and choose blunt statistics rather than his piercing observations.

And books about what to eat: they too are twins from one source, the first written recipes in our world. They are stodgy, matter-of-fact, covered very practically with washable cloth or gravy-coloured paper, beginning with measurements and food values and ending with sections on the care of invalids—oddly enough for books so concerned with hygiene! They are usually German, or English or American.

Or, on the other hand, they are short, bound impractically in creamy paper or chintz, illustrated by woodcutters *à la mode*. They begin with witty philosophizing on the pleasures of the table, and end with a suggested menu for an intimate dinner given to seven gentlemen who know his wife, by a wealthy old banker who feels horns pricking up gently from his bald skull. These books are usually French. They are much more entertaining, if less useful, than their phlegmatic twins.

To make one into two yet again, there are two painful variants of one most interesting subject: those who eat. The first, foisted upon us at least semiannually by enthusiastic publishers, is listed under *Memoirs* in book catalogues. Its pages totter and crumple under a weight of well-known names, and from each chapter rises a reek, a heady stench of truffles, Château Yquem, and quails *financière*. You sit, pompously nonchalant, on a balcony at Monte Carlo, *tête-à-tête* with three princes, a millionaire, and the lovely toast of London, God bless her! Or, in a Georgian dining-room filled

5

with quietly munching Cabinet ministers, you exchange quips which grow by repetition into *fin-de-siècle* epigrams. It is all very enervating —and it sells well, they say.

Its partner, that other kind of book about people who eat, is at times even more objectionable. It is usually written by two self-styled gourmets, or three. It shows pictures of its authors standing beside a quaint old inn near Oxford or a quaint old inn near Cannes. It discusses seriously and with firm authority the problem of Bordeaux *versus* Burgundies or when to drink Barsac, and settles with a fine confidence all questions of vintage, *pourboires*, and the barbaric horrors of the cocktail. It is perhaps needless to say that its authors are young and full of intellectual fun and frolic, and that they are making a gastronomic tour on bicycles.

Now I am going to write a book. It will be about eating and about what to eat and about people who eat. And I shall do gymnastics by trying to fall between these three fires, or by straddling them all.

The first, that great ghost born in Belley who ate like a fat parson and wrote consummately on eating with delicate art, I shall very humbly recognize.

The second—was it a Sicilian cooking for Cæsar or a Norman chef in old England who first wrote our plans for dishes, or was it perhaps a round monk in Touraine?—the second I shall avoid. Recipes in my book will be there like birds in a tree—if there is a comfortable branch.

The third I can most easily miss. I am not old and famous, with friends whose names sound like the guest-lists of all the diplomatic receptions held in all the world capitals since 1872. Nor am I young and intellectually gastronomic on a bicycle.

So my book, hopefully evading each of the three fires, will be singed by all. Brillat-Savarin will haunt it, and very probably show himself in an inevitable aphorism. *The Settlement Cook Book* and Paul Reboux will peer shyly and with little recognition at their ancestors *The Harleian Manuscript* and Mrs. Glasse and Carême and Roselli. And people I know will talk a little and eat more, not with prime ministers in Geneva, perhaps, nor with munitions-makers at Menton. But they are really very nice people, most of them.

I serve it forth.

When a Man Is Small

WHEN a man is small, he loves and hates food with a ferocity which soon dims. At six years old his very bowels will heave when such a dish as creamed carrots or cold tapioca appears before him. His throat will close, and spots of nausea and rage swim in his vision. It is hard, later, to remember why, but at the time there is no pose in his disgust. He cannot eat; he says, "To hell with it!"

In the same way, some foods are utterly delicious, and he thinks of them and tastes them with a sensuous passion which too often disappears completely with the years.

Perhaps there are little chocolate cookies as a special treat, two apiece. He eats his, all two, with an intense but delicate avidity. His small sister Judy puts one of hers in her pocket, the smug thing. But Aunt Gwen takes a bite from each of her cookies and gives what is left of one to Judy, what is left of the other to him. She is quite calm about it.

He looks at her with dreadful wonder. How can she bear to do it? He could not, *could* not have given more than a crumb of his cooky to anyone. Perhaps even a crumb would be too big. Aunt Gwen is wonderful; she is brave and superhuman. He feels a little dizzy as he looks at the bitten cooky in his hand. How could she do it?

By the time a man is ten or twelve he has forgotten most of his young passions. He is hungry and he wants to be full. It is very simple.

A few more years and he is at his life's peak of energy. His body is electric with young muscle, young blood, a new-found manhood, an awakening mind. Strangely enough, it is now that he whips himself up to greater speed. He drinks strong raw spirits and countless cups of coffee, hot and black. He devours such mild aphrodisiacs as chili, tamales, and rare beef drowned in bottled sauces. He pours salt and pepper over everything except desserts.

At this age, eighteen or nineteen, gastronomic perceptions are non-existent, or at the most naïve. I remember that when I was a college freshman my nearest approach to *la gourmandise* was a midnight visit to *Henry's*, the old *Henry's* on Hollywood Boulevard which all the world said that Charlie Chaplin owned secretly.

There I would call for the head waiter, which probably awed my escort almost as much as I hoped it would. The waiter, a kindly soul except on Saturday nights, played up to me beautifully, and together we ordered a large pot of coffee and a German pancake with hot apple-sauce and sweet butter. ("Salted butter ruins the flavor," I would add in a nonchalant aside to my Tommy or Jimmy.)

When the pancake appeared, after an impressive wait, it was big as a tabletop, with curled edges. Two waitresses fussed over it, while people stared at us and I made sure that the apple-sauce was spread on *after* the melted butter, and that plenty of lemon juice and cinnamon were sprinkled about.

I always looked away while the monstrous thing was rolled: the waitresses were too nervous and stuck out their tongues. And I cannot remember ever finishing even my half of the pancake, when it was sliced and powdered and laid before me. Nor can I imagine ordering one now.

It is, however, these innocent experiments with food, mixed though they may be with snobbishness and "showing off," that indicate what kind of older person a young one may become. And he had two choices, the two oft-quoted oft-abused alternatives of eating to live and of living to eat.

Any normal man must nourish his body by means of food put into it through the mouth. This process takes time, quite apart from the lengthy preparations and digestions that accompany it.

Between the ages of twenty and fifty, John Doe spends some twenty thousand hours chewing and swallowing food, more than eight hundred days and nights of steady eating. The mere contemplation of this fact is upsetting enough!

To some men it is actively revolting. They devise means of accomplishing the required nourishments of their bodies by pills of condensed victuals and easily swallowed draughts which equal, they are told, the food value of a beefsteak or a vegetable stew.

To others, the stunning realization of how much time is needed to feed themselves is accepted more philosophically. They agree with La Rochefoucauld's aphorism: To eat is a necessity, but to eat intelligently is an art.

Critics of the resulting scheme of life are easily led to accuse its practicants of substituting a less pleasant word for "intelligent." So, indeed, do many of us. We sink too easily into stupid and over-fed sensuality, our bodies thickening even more quickly than our minds. We sharpen one sense at the cost of losing many others, and call ourselves epicures, forgetting that Epicurus himself employed the same adjective as La Rochefoucauld when he advocated our finding an agreeable use for our faculties in "the intelligent enjoyment of the pleasures of the table."

Whichever school a man may adhere to, the protestant or the philosophical, he continues to eat through the middle years of life with increasing interest. He grows more conscious of his body as it becomes less tolerant.

No longer can he dine heavily at untoward hours, filling his stomach with the adolescent excitations of hot sauces and stodgy pastries—no longer, that is, with impunity. No more can he say with any truth: "Oh, I can eat anything. I can drink without showing it. I am made of iron."

He is confused by strange aches and rumblings, and shudders at the thought of being forced by old age to return to the pap and pabulum of his infancy.

Most of us, unhappily, shudder and ache and rumble as secretly as possible, seeming to feel disgrace in what is but one of the common phenomena of age: the general slowing of all physical processes. For years we hide or ignore our bodily protests and hasten our own dyspeptic doom by trying to eat and drink as we did when we were twenty.

When we are past fifty, especially if we have kept up this pathetic pose of youth-at-table, we begin to grow fat. It is then that even the blindest of us should beware. Unfortunately, however, we are too used to seeing other people turn heavy in their fifties: we accept paunches and double chins as a necessary part of growing old.

Instead, we should realize this final protest of an overstuffed system, and ease our body's last years by lightening its burden. We should eat sparingly.

It is here that gastronomy, or an equivalent, can play its most comforting rôle. Even in crude form the desire for a special taste or sensation has often helped an old man more than his critical family can know. They may call him heartless; he in his turn may as logically be acting with good sense, like the ancient sailor whose much-loved son was lost at sea. When at last some one mustered courage to tell the father this tragic news, the old man looked at him coldly for a minute, glanced out the window at the blown sea, and then snapped: "Dad blast it, where's my dish of tea? I want my tea!"

For many old people, eating is the only pleasure left, as were the "endless dishes" and "unceasing cups of wine" to the aged Ulysses. And between gobbling down an indistinguishable mess of heavy meat and bread, or savouring a delicate broiled trout or an aspic full of subtle vegetable flavours, how few of us would choose the distressful insomnia that follows the first for the light easy rest of the second?

But men are thoughtless and they are habit-followers. They have eaten meat and starches for years: they see no reason for stopping when they are old, even when they think enough to realize that every function of their bodies is carried on more slowly and with more effort than ever before.

They go on whipping up their blood with "well-done" roasts, which travel haltingly through the system to the final colonic decay that makes one of the great foes of senescence—constipation.

They are floated to their coffins on a river of "stimulating" infusions of beef-extract and iron, usually fed to them surreptitiously by well-meaning daughters.

They plump out their poor sagging paunches for years with the puffed richness of such "nourishing" desserts as the typical English sweet which a friend described to me: "cake soaked with bad port, smothered in boiled custard stained a purple-brown with blackberry juice, which is in turn top-layered with warm ill-beaten white of egg tinted fuchsia pink, the whole garnished with small dirty-brown buttons of granite that are reported by us hardier Britons to be macaroons. This particular foul concoction is called 'Queen o' Puddings'!"

No wonder old people are dubbed "quaintly crabbed and testy" by sentimental novelists, and "plain hell to live with" by their less idealistic offspring!

But we must grow old, and we must eat. It seems far from unreasonable, once these facts are accepted, for a man to set himself the pleasant task of educating his palate so that he can do the former not grudgingly and in spite of the latter, but easily and agreeably because of it.

Talleyrand said that two things are essential in life: to give good dinners and to keep on fair terms with women. As the years pass and fires cool, it can become unimportant to stay always on fair terms either with women or one's fellows, but a wide and sensitive appreciation of fine flavours can still abide with us, to warm our hearts.

Greek Honey and the Hon-Zo

3000 B.C.—100 A.D.

Egypt, the Orient, and Greece

TWENTY-EIGHT hundred years before Jesus broke bread for his children, a wise emperor in China thought of his. Shennung was his name, and before he died he had compiled a great cookbook, the *Hon-Zo*. In forty-seven centuries we have not learned much more about food than it can tell.

While Shennung's millions died and lived, humans all over this world were eating according to their fashions, but principally because they had to. From the north still came a faint snarl of hungry blond men gnashing at raw meat, and an occasional whiff of carrion, that sweet wild sickening smell. But all around the Mediterranean and to the east, a ring of good things was sprouting. Gradually fig trees were planted, and then grapes, and wheat grew because men made it. New pleasures were born for the warm brown people.

In Egypt they ate quite simply. Every-day bread was made from *spelt*, the dried pounded centers of the sacred lotus plants, and for feasts fine wheaten flour in loaves. They caught fish and spread them in the sun to dry, thick with salt.

All the Egyptians ate leeks and onions with some impunity, but tried to hide their passion for garlic from the priests, who most fastidiously denounced it as an unclean abomination.

Ox meat was roasted or boiled, but many kinds of little birds, and even quails and ducks, were salted and eaten raw. And melons in increasing variety made fine the poorest fare, with grapes and figs and dates, and barley beer, and sweet wine in great pottery vases glazed with blue.

Honey from the richly flowered delta had already in those far days been changed into a hundred kinds of sweetmeats, or baked into the breads, or simmered with the flesh of melons and fruits to make the same heavy voluptuous confitures that travellers eat today in Alexandria.

Then, as now, the Egyptians were temperate and frugal, but always hospitable. They welcomed strangers as well as kin to their meals, where men and women ate together, and where, for the most part, the lowest *fellahin* and members of the royal family ate much the same simple food.

It was in the tools for eating, and the dining-rooms, that caste difference most clearly showed itself. The peasants and the artisans used pottery, glazed blue or red, perhaps, but always simple, and they sat on benches in their low mud houses.

The palaces of the wealthy people, the nobles and scientists, were airy and beautiful, surrounded by pools and arboured gardens, and built with carved painted columns to hold the canopies that made their walls.

Everywhere, on the stone pillars and the embroidered linens, and in the faïence, and the gold that was "plentiful as dust," the sacred lotus and the date frond curved and lifted.

At feasts guests sat upon wooden armchairs, heavily inlaid with gold and stones, and made more comfortable by soft cushions of leather and silky Egyptian linen. They ate from delicate spoons of carved wood or ivory, and drank from lotus-cups of blue glaze or, later, of iridescent glass. Bowls, no matter how simple their contents, were of the common gold, or rarer silver, or the most valuable bronze.

Unlike the Greeks and Romans, who barred women from all banqueting, and only invited the hetæræ to come in with the final wines for philosophic dalliance, the Egyptians dined easily together. While the lords and ladies tarried over their cool courses of melons and sweet wine, dancers entertained them with slow gay rhythms, or more highly educated singers, usually women, chanted to the ancient plaintive sounds of lutes and pipes.

At more vulgar feasts, girls or young men in female dress performed much the same obscene dances that can still be seen in Cairo or any Egyptian port, but they were rare. In general, the amusement of the Nile people was like their nourishment—delicate, fresh, wholesome.

While the Greeks across the sea were still free of any Egyptian finesse, and lived simply on boiled fish and black broth, with "running, fatigue, hunger, and thirst" for seasoning, things to eastward had taken quite a different turn. There natural indolence and sensuality, and enormous wealth, and climate, and viciousness bred with years of intermarriage, made feasting the chiefest recreation of the nobles.

It is hard to find what the poor people ate, but easy to imagine. Their time was too full to make food anything but a necessity, or something seen on the king's board as fantastic and intangible as the mounds of caviar in a Hollywood movie.

They heard and saw strange things, but dully. They saw Xerxes ruin two cities for a single feast, and heard how Belshazzar of Babylon caused a most luxurious banquet to be spread for all his thousand wives and concubines, with music and revelry and the rarest foods.

They whispered with passive amazement after Darius finished one of his famous saturnalia. They knew that King Solomon kept twelve stewards for his table, and that eleven of them travelled constantly, spying out new wines and the strangest viands.

And for many years they remembered Ahasuerus' carnival. It lasted fourscore and one hundred days. Fine folk from all that part of the world came to it and for seven days at the end of it came all the king's subjects, both great and small. They slept on mammoth gold and silver pillows laid on beds of black marble and yellow and scarlet and white stone. All the pillars were of marble, too, and from their silver rings hung purple and linen cords to hold up the white and green and blue tent-walls. And every man could drink his fill of the king's own wine, in a golden goblet different from any other's.

Whispers and odours and the tantalizing noises of banqueting floated swiftly westward. Greece heard and smelled and was fascinated. Gastronomy nourished itself on rumour, and from the Spartan black broth was born a refined and decadent philosophy of eating.

In their love for fresh vegetables and native fruits, however, the Greeks kept their cuisine basically simple. Honey they used for all sweetening, leaving the cane sugar brought from China to the medicine-makers. Chestnuts were roasted, as they had been for centuries, and eaten after meals with dried fruits.

But now delicate little cakes of sesame and honey were served at the same time, and cities became rivals in varying their shapes and flavours. Athens grew famous for its fine breads and honey-biscuits, and villages waxed haughty over cheeses whose special tastes they had tried to disguise only a few years before.

Locusts were still roasted a light golden hue, and meats spitted over coals, but with a new, investigating fervour. Peacocks were served in their feathers. Pork, long the favourite viand, was found to have over fifty different flavours!

And fish, that long-known flesh for soups and stews, emerged from monotony with a whole complex science of its own. Sole was the king of all the dishes, but almost every swimming creature was cooked at one time or another.

The Greeks drank their own wines, and those not naturally sweet they flavoured to cloying heaviness with honey and aromatic herbs and spices. Their *hippocras*, which was just such a syrupy punch, became after several centuries the favourite drink of France's four-teenth Louis.

As the art of eating grew in Greece, men began to write about it. Artimidorus Aristophanius left recipes, some of them very strange to us and as often generous of good suggestions. More than one modern cook has tried his method of using sour young grapes in-stead of vinegar, and has been well pleased.

Athenæus, too, gave in his *Banquet of the Learned* several good ideas to present-day chefs. His recipes, however, are more literary than practical—or even appealing. Few of us save the most precious would enjoy his voluptuous dish of bird brains, eggs, wine, and spices, pounded with very fragrant roses and cooked in oil. When the cover was lifted from this dish, its sweet excessive perfume, diffused throughout the supper-room, made all the guests drop their eyelids with pleasure. And one of them quoted poetry.

It was Athenæus who wrote sternly of the duties of a good cook. For the most part the Greeks were not unusually gifted in cookery. Housewives managed to provide plain, wholesome food for their establishments, and for special occasions imitated the aristocrats and called in professional chefs. Of these, Sicilians were the most famous. Their services were rented at enormous fees, and they were recognized as an important part of the increasingly complex Greek culture.

Dinners grew daily more luxurious, with menus to be read first by the guests, who no longer sat in chairs except at the houses of such ascetic hosts as Socrates. Instead they lay on soft couches brought from sensual Asia, and fed themselves languidly with perfumed fingers.

Great men grew concerned over their tables, and literary gourmets became didactic. Athenæus was their leader.

A good cook, he said, must know the time and the place for supper. That in itself is obvious enough, but further he must ascertain who are the guests, and who the entertainers! He must know what fish to buy, as well as where to buy it. And, most demanding requisite of all, "his mind must comprehend all facts and circumstances."

Another Greek writer (was it Nichomachus?) was even more unrelenting. Any cook, according to him, can take a piece of meat that some one else has bought, and dress it up tolerably well. A perfect cook, however, is quite a different thing. He must be a thorough master of many admirable arts—first of all a smattering of painting, and then others in their due importance. It is easy to see why good cooks were so sought after in Athens!

And it is equally easy to understand that, with such niceties considered necessary, rebellion might fume in some minds and stomachs. The good Archestratus, traveller and gourmet, wrote final quiet damnation of all ornate trickeries of the kitchen when he said:

> *Many are the ways, and many the recipes*
> *For dressing a hare, but this is best of all:*
> *To place before a set of hungry guests*
> *A slice of roasted meat fresh from the spit,*
> *Hot, seasoned only with plain simple salt,*
> *Not too much done. And do you not be vexed,*
> *At seeing blood fresh trickling from the meat,*
> *But eat it eagerly. All other ways*
> *Are quite superfluous, such as when cooks pour*
> *A lot of sticky clammy sauce upon it.*

The restrained fury of that last sentence betrays Archestratus as the universal martyr, ageless and omnipresent, to centuries of over-seasoned sauces and ridiculous conceits of flavour. His is a mutual bond with us all.

The Curious Nose

CENTRAL heating, French rubber goods, and cookbooks are three amazing proofs of man's ingenuity in transforming necessity into art, and, of these, cookbooks are perhaps most lastingly delightful. Many an old belly has been warmed by the reading of them, and for one secret from them, steaming ruddy brown on plate, how many youthful pleasures have been counted well lost!

However, cooking in itself is, for most women, a question less of vocation than of necessity. They are not called to the kitchen by the divine inner voice of a Vatel or an Escoffier. Rather are they lured there, willy-nilly, by the piping of their husbands' empty stomachs.

They cook doggedly, desperately, more often than not with a cumulative if uninspired skill. Occasionally one gathers about herself a local renown for tarts or bonbons or meat pies. More rarely she builds up a reputation for epicurean appreciation—this last with the help of an ample purse, of course, and a good cook in her kitchen. Finally she writes a cookbook, and often it is a good one, in spite of Dr. Sam'l Johnson's dictum that such a thing is impossible from any female. It is eminently practical, like Mrs. Simon Kander's perennial volume which points "the way to a man's heart" between its oilclothed boards. Or it is very faintly literary and much more expensive to follow, compiled, say, by Mrs. William Vaughan Moody or the delightful author of *La Cuisine de Madame*.

Definitely in the limbo, or to be passed by quickly with a shudder of recognition, are cooking-school manuals and those hideous pamphlets sold by ladies' aid societies in small towns. The former are dangerously perfect, and if followed with the care their editors advise, would reduce all cooking to a standard of horrible monotony. The latter, whose broken covers and limp yellow pages clutter every

American cookbook shelf of decent age, are utterly useless unless you know some of the women whose prize recipes are printed in them. Then, if you are feeling ill-tempered, you can curl your lip at Mrs. Sophia Jamison's prune whip, and surreptitiously steal Cousin Annie Fink's little trick of stirring three chopped marshmallows into the —

But if you are in a bad temper you should not be thinking of food at all. Close that ugly book. Hurl it out of the window, or keep it for a curiosity. And avert your eyes from the baleful hygienic correctness of school manuals. There are good cookbooks to read, that other women have written.

One of the best-known collections of recipes of the last century was *Common Sense in the Household: A Manual of Practical Housewifery*.

It was the kind of cookbook that, always suitably inscribed, young husbands gave to wives, and older brothers to their marriageable sisters. My grandmother's copy, the small green edition of 1873, is very spotted and yellow now, but on the flyleaf are still legible her name and her brother's, with his formal order in quotation marks—"Improve each shining hour."

Common Sense was made by Marion Harland, a kindly, sensible woman if her book is true indication. She wrote of everything, almost, that might puzzle a student of "housewifery."

In her index, neatly alphabetical, she lists all the plain tricks like Bread, Ice Cream, Pork, Puddings. But there are others less usual and equally difficult to manage: Catsups, Clean-to-etc., Corn-bread in the C's; farther down Familiar Talk and Fritters; Nursery—the, Pancakes, Pickles; in the S's Sauces, Servants, Sick-room, Shellfish, and Soaps and Soups and Sundries, with Tarts to follow.

Towards the close of the century, Marion Harland's sensible attitude was weakened slightly, perhaps by too many decades of adoring disciples. She permitted several Queen Anne editions of her eminently Mary Anne masterpiece to be sold to *fin-de-siècle* brides. One, lavishly larded with instructive photographs, illustrates the correct way to serve dinner rolls, each tied with satin ribbon and a red, red rose!

But by 1900 the good lady must have felt very tired. It is in the earlier editions that we find her at her best, the American housewife of the nineteenth century. There her prose is straightforward, occasionally anecdotal, with short bits of Dickens stuck in like raisins in a bun.

She herself was probably a teetotaller, but with motherly tolerance she gives recipes for home-made drinks, always ending them with some such comment as the one for Cranberry Wine: "This is said to be very good for scrofula."

At the end of a recipe for Preserved Green Corn she writes, with the determined optimism of a good *hausfrau,* "Green corn is difficult to can, but I *know* it will keep if put up in this way. . . . Should the top layer be musty, dig lower still, and you will probably be rewarded for the search."

Her cautiousness, a self-protective virtue, is very obvious. She never commits herself on the outcome of a recipe, unless it is in the following safe statement: "Any cook with a moderate degree of judgment and experience can undertake it with a reasonable expectation of success"!

About some things, however, she allows herself to grow heated. Read in her introduction to Pork. "We feed the hog with the off-scourings of house, garden, and table; bed him in mire, and swell him with acetous fermentation, not to say active decomposition, and then abuse him for what we have made him—Let us treat Bristles well—I do not say philosophically, but sensibly and kindly."

And sensible and kind she remains, although in her directions for Roast Pig she betrays some of that tenderness for sucklings which is even more noticeable in large men. My father, for instance, who flees sentimentality like the black pox, confesses that one of the loveliest things he has ever seen was—not a sunrise, not a sweet lass naked—was a litter of new piglets, pink and dainty. And in Roast Pig, Marion Harland stops her measurements of salt and dripping long enough to write: "If your pig is large, you can cut off his head and split him down the back before sending to table. Do this with a sharp knife, and lay the backs together. But it is a pity! I have before me now the vision of a pig I once saw served whole on the table of a friend, that forbids me ever to mutilate the innocent before the guests have a chance to feast their eyes upon the goodly picture. He was done to a turn—a rich even brown, without a seam or crack from head to tail, and he knelt in a bed of deep green parsley, alternately with branches of whitish-green celery tops (the inner and tender leaves); a garland of the same was about his neck, and in his mouth was a tuft of white cauliflower surrounded by a setting of curled parsley. Very simple, you see; but I never beheld a more ornamental roast."

Other women as good and wise as Marion Harland have written books on cookery, and long before her, too. In England Mrs. Ellet, Mrs. Rundel, and many another wrote standard handbooks of the early nineteenth and eighteenth centuries, and Mrs. Glasse's classic collection, *The Art of Cookery Made Plain and Easy*, certainly helped as many housewives as it hindered with its syllabubs and "Darling Dainties."

But in 1754 household cookery was so much the rage that even Mrs. Glasse's book had a greater public than it deserved. Cookbooks had freed themselves from the French that was thought necessary to all recipes until well into the seventeeth century, and a veritable rash of such collections broke out.

Some of them were good. Many of them were pompous, quite impractical. Often they were written by men in female fashion, signed or left cravenly anonymous.

It was Gervaise Markham who wrote what will probably remain the most thorough English treatise on the subject. His book, the thinly veiled copy of several less popular works like *The Widdowes Treasure*, which was published in 1625, itself had hundreds of imitators after its publication in London in 1675. They had little left to say; Markham's title page proves that:

"The English housewife; containing the inward and outward Vertues which ought to be in a Compleat Woman; as to her skill in Physick, Chirurgery, Cookery, Extraction of Oyls, Banquetting stuff, Ordering of great Feasts, Preserving of all sorts of Wides, conceited Secrets, Distillations, Perfumes, Ordering of Wool, Hemp, Flax: Making Cloth and Dying; the Knowledge of Dayries: Office of Malting; of Oats, their excellent uses in Families: of Brewing, Baking, and all other things belonging to an household.—A Work generally approved, and now the Eighth time much augmented, Purged, and made most profitable and necessary for all men, and the general good of this Nation."

Of the housewife herself, Markham decided thus: "First she must be cleanly both in garment and body, she must have a quick eye, a curious nose, a perfect taste, and ready ear (she must not be butter-fingered, sweet-toothed, nor faint-hearted); for the first will let everything fall; the second will consume what it should increase; and the last will lose time with too much niceness."

Markham's dicta increase in amusing pomposity, and at the same pace seem almost revolutionary, when we remember that only a few years before he uttered them, Ladies kept clear of the kitchen. Women cooked, but Ladies never.

They knew well enough the polite usages of knives and fingers at table, but how that table was loaded was not for their wits to ponder on.

One brave tutor had suggested, years before, that the ladies of at least the lower upper classes might profit by some knowledge of cookery, but his counsel went unheeded.

"The daughters of Knights, Judges, Physicians, or others of similar conditions," he said, "had better learn the art of cooking, though possibly circumstances will not call upon them to put it into practice."

It took three hundred years for Barberino's advice to become acceptable. Then it was a man again, all-knowing Markham, who made it stylish. And since that day he and all his followers, both male and female, have instructed the world's woman in what she rarely escapes and sometimes never learns, *Common Sense in the Household.*

Let the Sky Rain Potatoes

—The Merry Wives of Windsor

THERE are two questions which can easily be asked about a potato:
What is it, and Why is it?

Both these questions are irritating to a true amateur. The answers
to the first are self-evident: a potato is a food, delicious, nourishing,
and so on. The second question is perhaps too impertinent even to
be answered, although many a weary housewife has felt like shouting it to the high heavens if her family has chanced to be the kind
that takes for granted the daily appearance of this ubiquitous vegetable.

A dictionary will say that a potato is a farinaceous tuber used for
food. An encyclopædia will cover eight or nine large pages with a
sad analysis of its origins, modes of cultivation, and diseases, some
of which are enough in themselves to discourage any potato enthusi-
ast who might read them carefully.

Between these two extremes of definition is a story interesting
even to one who is not overly fond of potatoes as a food. There are
romance and colour, and the fine sound of brave names in its telling.

In Peru, the Spanish found *papas* growing in the early 1500's, and
the monk Hieronymus Cardán took them back with him to his own
people. The Italians liked them, and then the Belgians.

About that time, Sir Walter Raleigh found a potato in the American South, and carried it back to his estate near Cork. Some say it
was a yam he had, thought strongly aphrodisiac by the Elizabethans.
Some say it was a white potato. A German statue thanks Raleigh
for bringing it to Europe. On the other hand, the Spanish claim
recognition for its European introduction.

No matter what its origin, eat it, eat it, urged the British Royal
Society. But for many decades its cultivation made but little progress.

By the time it had become important as a food, especially for poor people, its diseases also had matured, and in 1846 potato blight sent thousands of hungry Irishmen to their graves, or to America.

Warts and scabs and rusts and rots did their work, too, and men worked hard to breed new varieties of potatoes before newer plagues seized them. Great Scott, the Boston Comrade, Magnum Bonum, Rhoderick Dhu and Up-to-Date, Ninetyfold: these and many hundreds more filled pots around the world, and still do.

But no matter the name; a spud's a spud, and by any other name it would still be starchy, and covered with dusty cork for skin, and, what's worse, taken for granted on every blond-head's table.

If the men are darker, it is pastes in slender strings they'll eat, or tubes, always farinaceous, as the dictionary says; but more often on Anglo-Saxon fare the potato takes place before any foreign macaroni or spaghetti.

It is hard sometimes to say why. A potato is good when it is cooked correctly. Baked slowly, with its skin rubbed first in a buttery hand, or boiled in its jacket and then "shook," it is delicious. Salt and pepper are almost always necessary to its hot moist-dusty flavour. Alone, or with a fat jug of rich cool milk or a chunk of fresh Gruyère, it fills the stomach and the soul with a satisfaction not too easy to attain.

In general, however, a potato is a poor thing, poorly treated. More often than not it is cooked in so unthinking and ignorant a manner as to make one feel that it has never before been encountered in the kitchen, as when avocados were sent to the Cornish Mousehole by a lady who heard months later that their suave thick meat had been thrown away and the stones boiled and boiled to no avail.

"Never have I tasted such a poor, flaccid, grey sad mixture of a mess," says my mother when she tells of the potatoes served in Ireland. And who would contradict her who has ever seen the baked-or-boiled in a London Lyons or an A.B.C.?

The Irish prefer them, evidently, to starvation, and the English, too. And in mid-western Europe, in a part where dumplings grow on every kitchen-range, there are great cannon balls of them, pernicious as any shrapnel to a foreign palate, but swallowed like feathery egg-whites by the natives.

They are served with goose at Christmas, and all around the year. They are the size of a toddling child's round head. They are grey, and exceedingly heavy. They are made painstakingly of grated raw potato, moulded, then boiled, then added to by moulding, then boiled again. Layer after layer is pressed on, cooked, and cooled, and finally the whole sodden pock-marked mass is bounced in bubbling goose broth until time to heave it to the platter.

Forks may bend against its iron-like curves, stomachs may curdle in a hundred gastric revolutions; a potato dumpling is more adamantine. It survives, and is served to ever-renewing decades of hungry yodelling mouths.

In itself, this always fresh desire for starch, for the potato, is important. No matter what its form, nor its national disguise, the appetite for it is there, impervious to the mandates of dictators or any other blight.

Perhaps its most insidious manifestation is that Anglo-Saxons take it for granted. A meal for them includes potatoes in some form; it always has, therefore it always will. And no revolt, no smouldering rebellion of the meal-planner, can change this smug acceptance.

Most important, however, is the potato's function as a gastronomic complement. It is this that should be considered, to rob it of its dangerous monotony, and clothe it with the changing mysterious garment of adaptability.

Although few realize it, to be complementary is in itself a compliment. It is a subtle pleasure, like the small exaltation of a beautiful dark woman who finds herself unexpectedly in the company of an equally beautiful blonde. It is what a great chef meant once when he repulsed a consolation.

He was a Frenchman, summoned to London when King Edward VII found that his subjects resented his dining more in Paris than at home.

This great cook one day prepared a dish of soles in such a manner that the guests at Edward's table waited assuredly for a kingly compliment. He was summoned. Their mouths hung open in sated expectation.

"The Château Yquem," said Edward VII, "was excellent."

Later the master chef shrugged, a nonchalance denied by every muscle in his pleased face.

"How could my dish have had a greater compliment?" he demanded, calmly. "His Majesty knows, as I do, that when a dish is perfect, as was my sole to-night, the wine is good. If the dish is lower than perfection, the wine, lacking its complement, tastes weak and poor. So—you see?"

Although there are few ways of preparing potatoes to make them approach the perfection of a royal plate of fish, and none I know of to make them worth the compliment of a bottle of Château Yquem, they in their own way are superlative complements. And it is thus, as I have said, that they should be treated.

If, French fried, they make a grilled sirloin of beef taste richer; if, mashed and whipped with fresh cream and salty butter, they bridge the deadly gap between a ragôut and a salad; if, baked and pinched open and bulging with mealy snowiness, they offset the fat spiced flavour of a pile of sausages—then and then alone should they be served.

Then they are dignified. Then they are worthy of a high place, not debased to the deadly rank of daily acceptance. Then they are a gastronomic pleasure, not merely "tubers used for food."

Borderland

ALMOST every person has something secret he likes to eat. He is downright furtive about it usually, or mentions it only in a kind of conscious self-amusement, as one who admits too quickly, "It is rather strange, yes—and I'll laugh with you."

Do you remember how Claudine used to crouch by the fire, turning a hatpin just fast enough to keep the toasting nubbin of chocolate from dripping off? Sometimes she did it on a hairpin over a candle. But candles have a fat taste that would taint the burnt chocolate, so clean and blunt and hot. It would be like drinking a Martini from silver.

Hard bitter chocolate is best, in a lump not bigger than a big raisin. It matters very little about the shape, for if you're nimble enough you'll keep it rolling hot on the pin, as shapely as an opium bead.

When it is round and bubbling and giving out a dark blue smell, it is done. Then, without some blowing all about, you'll burn your tongue. But it is delicious.

However, it is not my secret delight. Mine seems to me less decadent than Claudine's, somehow. Perhaps I am mistaken. I remember that Al looked at me very strangely when he first saw the little sections lying on the radiator.

That February in Strasbourg was too cold for us. Out on the Boulevard de l'Orangerie, in a cramped dirty apartment across from the sad zoo half full of animals and birds frozen too stiff even to make smells, we grew quite morbid.

Finally we counted all our money, decided we could not possibly afford to move, and next day went bag and baggage to the most expensive *pension* in the city.

It was wonderful—big room, windows, clean white billows of

curtain, central heating. We basked like lizards. Finally Al went back to work, but I could not bear to walk into the bitter blowing streets from our warm room.

It was then that I discovered how to eat little dried sections of tangerine. My pleasure in them is subtle and voluptuous and quite inexplicable. I can only write how they are prepared.

In the morning, in the soft sultry chamber, sit in the window peeling tangerines, three or four. Peel them gently; do not bruise them, as you watch soldiers pour past and past the corner and over the canal towards the watched Rhine. Separate each plump little pregnant crescent. If you find the Kiss, the secret section, save it for Al.

Listen to the chambermaid thumping up the pillows, and murmur encouragement to her thick Alsatian tales of *l'intérieure*. That is Paris, the interior, Paris or anywhere west of Strasbourg or maybe the Vosges. While she mutters of seduction and French bicyclists who ride more than wheels, tear delicately from the soft pile of sections each velvet string. You know those white pulpy strings that hold tangerines into their skins? Tear them off. Be careful.

Take yesterday's paper (when we were in Strasbourg *L'Ami du Peuple* was best, because when it got hot the ink stayed on it) and spread it on top of the radiator. The maid has gone, of course —it might be hard to ignore her belligerent Alsatian glare of astonishment.

After you have put the pieces of tangerine on the paper on the hot radiator, it is best to forget about them. Al comes home, you go to a long noon dinner in the brown dining-room, afterwards maybe you have a little nip of *quetsch* from the bottle on the *armoire*. Finally he goes. Of course you are sorry, but——

On the radiator the sections of tangerines have grown even plumper, hot and full. You carry them to the window, pull it open, and leave them for a few minutes on the packed snow of the sill. They are ready.

All afternoon you can sit, then, looking down on the corner. Afternoon papers are delivered to the kiosk. Children come home from school just as three lovely whores mince smartly into the *pension's* chic tearoom. A basketful of Dutch tulips stations itself by the tram-stop, ready to tempt tired clerks at six o'clock. Finally the soldiers stump back from the Rhine. It is dark.

The sections of tangerine are gone, and I cannot tell you why they are so magical. Perhaps it is that little shell, thin as one layer of enamel on a Chinese bowl, that crackles so tinily, so ultimately under your teeth. Or the rush of cold pulp just after it. Or the perfume. I cannot tell.

There must be some one, though, who knows what I mean. Probably everyone does, because of his own secret eatings.

Garum

WHILE Greece exchanged black broth and its accompanying simplicity for that more complex kitchen science nurtured by her new esthetes, Rome shadowed her some years behind, mimicking with fantastic exaggeration each of her calm inevitable developments.

For her Spartan pottage, Romans had a gruel of lentils. They too ate chestnuts and cheeses and fruits and green vegetables, with honey to sweeten and wine to gladden. Then when refinement, sure arbiter of a decadent civilization, crept into the Grecian cuisine, her tardy shadow Rome leaped feverishly in a grotesque and fascinating imitation.

As had happened in Greece, town and villages vied for culinary honours. Certain cakes, cheeses of a special smell, and even fish from a named lake or river began to cause small feuds among the gourmets. Gradually shadow out-leaped self, and in their furious delicacy of palate and heavy-handed subtlety of selection the wealthy Romans left Greeks far behind.

Are *pâtés de foie gras* better made from cygnets than from milk-white geese? Of course! Not at all! Well, perhaps if the geese are nourished solely on green figs—But on the other hand, a diet of almonds——

Senators cut important electors in the streets; sons quarrelled with fathers, boys with their tutors. Even the philosophers considered such questions weightily, and uttered decisions which had but temporary effect.

When Cleopatra melted her pearl and six million sesterces into the world's most expensive recipe, she set a tantalizingly high mark. Until Rome fell, gourmets tried to outdo her. Undoubtedly the results were more palatable—but never more costly.

Rigid snobbism precluded all but the most extravagant citizens, and thus most plutocratic, from the inner circles of fine eating.

Juvenal drew the portrait of all Roman *bon vivants* when he wrote of one of the greatest, the General Lucullus:

> Stretched on the unsocial couch, he rolls his eyes
> O'er many an orb of matchless form and size,
> Selects the fairest to receive his plate,
> And at one meal devours a whole estate.

Lucullus, perhaps the truest epicure as we now think of one, was undoubtedly the most refined. He set the pace. Other Romans, like Trimalchio's vulgar prototype, might give banquets whose success depended upon the leaping of three naked virgins from a great crusted tart. It was Lucullus who gave his carefully chosen guests the exquisite compliment of letting them watch their next course die!

Mullets bred in the mountain lake he had transplanted to his estates, or trout brought living from one certain stream in all Italy, expired slowly in beautiful glass jars placed before the diners. Each throe was judged. Lucky the guest whose dying fish leaped highest and longest! The flavour would be unforgettable.

It was Lucullus who sorted his friends into different rooms, rather like the various restaurants in a large German railroad station. In some rooms, a meal cost only one or two hundred dollars for each person. Decoration there was relatively simple. More expensive surroundings showed that here Lucullus spent more on his food.

And finally, in the Apollo Room, where only his very intimate or important guests were invited, he spent one thousand dollars for each person.

Here he entertained most frequently, with the most precious foods laid upon tables now solid ivory, now silver or carved tortoise shell. For ordinary guests goblets of inlaid gold did well enough, but in the Apollo Room glasses hollowed from great gems were used with nonchalance.

Other men blinked at their own banquet bills, or complained bitterly, like Julius Cæsar when he found he had spent five millions sterling, one Roman summer, on suppers for his friends—and on barley water mixed with wine, for his favourite charger to drink from a golden trough!

Sometimes there was a suicide, nor was it from remorse for unpaid debts. Apicius, when he found he had squandered over a million pounds on banquets, and had but a tenth of that sum left, died as exquisitely as one of the mullets he had watched.

As Rome festered and decayed, the fever for fine eating mounted. What had been precious became vicious. Mark Antony's largesse of a town of thirty-five thousand souls for his chef's fine paste of flamingo brains changed to Heliogabalus' trick of fattening his prized conger eels on living slave-meat.

As much money was spent on perfumes as on food. It was the usual thing now to have rare aromatic essences blown into the air between the twenty-four courses of daily banquets, as in Nero's famous Domus Aurea, from whose revolving walls flowers and sweet distillations showered down upon the guests.

Indeed, such strange behaviour was necessary. Satiety, that monster behind pleasure, breathed into the stuffed bellies of the Romans. Excitants to their palates were prerequisite—those palates by now so ill-treated that some of the gourmets were forced to wear little tongue gloves to protect their delicate taste-glands from all but the most exotic flavours.

And where could they find new foods? They searched desperately. They had eaten every fish in the earth's waters, except Triton's sacred dolphin and perhaps a mermaid. They had sucked the bones of every bird and birdling in—But wait!

"Send hunters to Lydia," Heliogabalus ordered, "and pay two hundred gold pieces to the one who brings us back a Phœnix!"

But none came.

The fretful ruler tried colours. Perhaps they might whip up his dulled taste. For awhile Roman tables bloomed with shades as violent but not so harmless as those in a modern seed-catalogue. They soon faded.

Les Tables Volantes, which Louis XV of France proudly called his own invention, rose first for Heliogabalus. Laden with dishes resolutely emptied, these tables sank, to the strains of young boys' voices, into the marble floor. New perfumes from Araby spiced the air. Strange dances, increasingly erotic, occupied the dulled eyes of the diners. Then the beautiful boys raised their voices in mock amazement, and fell squealing back. From the floor lifted boards new-decked, like the Phœnix the king yearned for—each time with new plumes.

As the feasts grew longer and more extravagant, the guests lost gradually those stately good manners they had aped from the earlier Greek gourmands. Licence of the senses begot loose behaviour.

If the goblets seemed too small, or the wine-supply stingy or of poor vintage, banqueters howled until they were satisfied. If the dishes displeased them, they hurled food and vessel against a pillar or a serving-man. The host apologized.

Emetics were served with the beginning courses of any longer dinner—as they had been indeed in Greece, because of the difficulty of digestion in the reclining position assumed on the banqueting-couches. Now, however, the Romans found the capacity of their sated stomachs infinitely enlarged by the trick. By the time one dish appeared, its predecessor was well out of the way. Twice as much could be eaten!

This wholesale catharsis necessitated certain architectural changes. And suddenly these changes, luxurious privies to begin with, were metamorphosed once more. *Vomitoria* came into being.

They had a fine name, like a California real-estate development. Little boys still hear it with fascination and disgust, in first-year Latin. Girls still invent other verbs, to avoid its nauseous root. Only one ever used it in public with the proper reverence: Colette, when she described an *éclair si vomiteusement chocolateux*.

Romans, however, their minds less on future derivatives of the word than on their next course, used their *vomitoria* with appreciation.

Their insides heaved too often. Quacks and honest physickers could not help. Rome grew dyspeptic, and heard clearly old Seneca's wry comment, "Are you astonished at the innumerable diseases?—Count the number of our cooks!"

We are inclined to agree with him. One course of a Roman meal would lay us very low, probably, and strip our palates for many days of even the crudest perceptions of flavour.

Look for a minute, hand over nose and a piece of ice on tongue, at the recipe for *garum*:

"Place in a vessel all the insides of fish, both large fish and small. Salt them well. Expose them to the air until they are completely putrid. In a short time a liquid is produced. Drain this off."

And "this" is *garum*, most highly prized and used of all seasonings. In Cochin-China there is something like it, in these days, called *nuocman*—and of course we have our English meat sauces.

Romans, though, used *garum* not as a condiment in itself, but combined with a startling variety of spices. Dill, anise, hyssop, thyme; pennyroyal and rue; cummin, poppy seed, shallots and onions and garlic and leeks—almost every known savour except our parsley, which they wore in garlands on their heads, made the simplest banquet dish a mess of inextricable flavours.

Inextricable to us, that is. It is doubtful if even a professional taster, today, would be able to describe the sauce Apicius recommends for a boiled chicken:

"Put the following ingredients into a mortar: anise-seed, dried mint, and lazar root which is a kind of asafœtida; cover them all with vinegar. Add dates and pour in garum and oil and a small quantity of mustard-seeds. Reduce all to a proper thickness with red wine warmed, and then pour this same over your chicken.

"The chicken," Apicius adds as an afterthought, "should of course be boiled previously in strong anise-seed water."

To cool your enraged palate after this strange dish you would most probably be served a goblet of red wine mixed with spices and sea water.

Then, while pretty slave children imitated worn-out lechers for your eyes' amusement, you would pretend to eat hungrily at a bowl of red mullet seasoned with pepper, rue, onion, dates, mustard, and the flesh of a sea-hedgehog pounded to a jelly.

With this, a fine cup of *vin rosé*, thickened to syrup with honey, myrrh, and spikenard. And after this, a piglet, soaked in——

A good old Roman custom—*vomitoria!*

Fifty Million Snails

I HAVE eaten several strange things since I was twelve, and I shall be glad to taste broiled locusts and swallow a live fish. But unless I change very much, I shall never be able to eat a slug. My stomach jumps alarmingly at the thought of it.

I have tried to be callous about slugs. I have tried to picture the beauty of their primeval movements before a fast camera, and I have forced myself to read in the *Encyclopædia Britannica* the harmless ingredients of their oozy bodies. Nothing helps. I have a horror, deep in my marrow, of everything about them. Slugs are awful, slugs are things from the edges of insanity, and I am afraid of slugs and all their attributes.

But I like snails. Most people like snails.

Once in Dijon I was very dizzy for two days because I ate so many that inside me they changed into old rubber boiled in garlic. I still like them; and in France people eat some fifty million every year.

On a bush they are beautiful, unless you are the gardener who planted the bush. They are beautiful on plates, too, each one in its little dent, shell full of hot green butter like a magic cup.

In Burgundy they are most beautiful, piled in baskets in the stores, the shells one of the most luminous gentle browns in the world, like the hair of a Leonardo Virgin. The round holes are filled very full and smooth with the butter, cold now, firm, and a tender green.

One shop in Dijon sold nothing else, and the window, banked firm against the glass with the finest samples, had from a distance the texture of a heavy glimmering silk. When the door opened, you could taste that peculiar smell of cold cooked snails, not quite like garlic, not quite like rubber tires.

Once I saw a woman eat seven dozen. It was *chez Crespin*, so she had already eaten more than that many oysters. She turned a purplish red. I have often wondered about her.

We lived for two years or so with the Rigagniers in Dijon. The grandfather, Papazi, lived with them too—or did we all live with Papazi?

He was a militant old fellow who mourned lustily every 14th of July that he had been too young to see battle in '71, too old in '14. Instead, he had become one of the most famous candy-makers in all the provinces. Retired from bonbon service, he kept his palate agile by cooking fine dishes for his grandchildren.

And thanks to him, the three of them, in spite of a shared age of less than thirty-five, were seasoned gourmets all. It was very amusing to see Plume, the little boy like a monkey, taste a sauce with the slow tongue-rollings of an old Parisian epicure. The others were just as reverently fussy. Every meal *chez* Rigagnier smacked somewhat of professional gastronomy.

Each spring we were worked subtly and completely into a frenzy for snails by Papazi's sure suggestion. As soon as burgeons darkened the bare branches he began speculating mildly on the possible time for the annual snail-hunt.

The weeks went by and leaves burst out on all the trees, and Papazi brought little twigs to the table and rubbed them between his thick dexterous fingers.

"Quite crisp," he would remark, ruminatively. "Yes, I really do think, in fact I am almost sure, that the snails this year will be finer, sweeter, plumper, truly more delicious than ever before."

He looked calmly at his delighted listeners.

The children were almost beside themselves.

"When can we go, Papazi? How about next Sunday? How about tomorrow? Will we get enough?"

"Calm yourselves, my dears! This excitement will ruin the taste of your mother's delicious *quenelles*!"

Plume and Doudouce subsided like pricked popovers, and Dédé smacked his lips more loudly than ever over a fresh bite, to show his mature appreciation. Papazi ate silently for a minute.

"No, not next Sunday," he continued, finally. "Not next Sunday, but perhaps the Sunday after. That is," he added, hastily, before the children could open their mouths to shout great glee, "*if* the day is fine, and *if* the snails have fed well enough, and *if* there are not too many noxious weeds for them to ruin themselves on, this year! And of course, after we have gathered them, something may happen to spoil them. It is a long and difficult business, the preparing of snails!"

The first time I heard Papazi say this I was fool enough to demand, "Why not buy them, then, all ready to eat?"

There was a shocked silence. The children stared at me. Papazi grew pink and haughty. Finally his daughter rebuked me, very gently:

"Oh, but Madame! Nobody can prepare snails like Papazi. These store snails are good, yes—but to fix them as my father does is an art! It is an achievement!"

I never acted so thoughtlessly again, but we were glad when the hunting-time came to end, we hoped, the daily speculations.

That nightfall we returned from the woods, with most of our snails unescaped from the sacks we carried them in. It had been a pleasant day.

The next morning we noticed a large packing-box in the courtyard. It was covered with a sheet of glass, and on the glass were glued the bottoms of what seemed a thousand snails, warming themselves upside down.

At night it was still there, and the next day.

"They must purify themselves," Papazi explained. "They must get rid of any poisonous food in them. They must, you might say, starve to death!"

"How long will it be, then?"

"A few days—a week, perhaps: these are very sturdy snails."

Indeed they were. For a day or two more they stayed, bottoms up, on the glass. Then they began to drop off. Nights were punctuated by the thumps of snails fainting in their little Black Hole. We lost sleep, feeling very sick for them, waiting for the hunger swoon to overcome another and another.

Every morning we counted the survivors, and hoped they would loosen their hold before dark, and let us sleep.

At last Papazi began his work, most of which I missed watching. There were parboilings to get the emaciated little creatures from their shells, and individual operations to remove their less delectable portions. There were endless scrubbings of each lovely shell, with little curved brushes made especially in Paris. Then the cadavers

were tucked into their coffins again, and Papazi and Madame Rigagnier made an extra trip to market for the parsley, the garlic, and
the sweet butter.

The last scene I caught through the dining-room door: Plume
and Doudouce bent gravely over a lighted table, pouring the hot
sauce into each up-ended snail shell. Their hands trembled very
slightly, and Plume's tongue stuck out.

And when we finally ate them, *les escargots d'or*, sizzling hot and
delicately pungent on our little curved forks, it was clear that
"store snails" were only for those unhappy people who did not live
with Papazi—or those fools too impatient to wait for his slow
perfection.

That was quite awhile ago. I had forgotten about snails, almost.
Then, last month, I heard that a woman in our town was raising
them. She had contracted to send them to good restaurants, at a
very stiff figure. It seems they were blooded stock!

Last weekend she went away, and left all her animals in the
charge of our friend Eric. He had just read all about snail-culture in
a magazine.

"You simply feed them cornmeal," he explained, easily. "It
makes them plump—gives the meat a delightful flavor, too!"

But the snails grew too plump, and then too fat, and then they
blew up, all in a few hours! Eric is devastated, and the restaurants
threaten to sue for broken contracts.

Perhaps it is better to buy store snails, after all. There are few
Papazis, and almost as few recipes, if you can find any escargots
alive and edible, which seems doubtful. However, here is one set
of directions, from *Le Menagier de Paris*:

> "Snails, which are called escargots, should be caught in the
> morning. Take the young small snails, those that have black
> shells, from the vines or elder trees; then wash them in so much
> water that they throw up no more scum; then wash them once
> in salt and vinegar, and set them to stew in water. Then you
> must pick these snails out of the shell at the point of a needle
> or a pin; and then you must take off their tail, which is black,
> for that is their turd; and then wash them and put them to
> stew and boil them in water; and then take them out and put
> them in a dish to be eaten with bread. And also some say that

they are better fried in oil and onion or some other liquid, after they have been cooked as above said; and they are eaten with spice and are for rich people."

This recipe differs quite plainly from Papazi's method, but of course it is older. *Le Menagier de Paris* was first published about 1394.

A POSTSCRIPT ABOUT SNAILS

This made Dillwyn remember more. In a letter he wrote:

"In Hyère, in the middle of summer, I closed the latticed shutters of my room to keep out the dry, blistering sun, but it got through the chinks of the shutters and marked the dusty carpet with a row of white-hot blades. Naked on the bed, I sweated and dozed and imagined myself going to hell in the tropics.

"Once I could not stand the feeling of being cooped up, and went for a walk in the middle of the day. The hotel force watched me go, shrugging shoulders and tapping foreheads. *Fou!*—he walks himself in the sun.

Queer world I walked into! The sun made me squint as one squints walking out of a dark theatre into the bright of day. The heat was something more than heat: it had the dry hurting feeling that radiates from an electric grill.

"Outside of the town there were trees and bushes, vines and grass—but every leaf, blade, stem was coated with plaster-white dust, a dust that night dews had turned to fast-clinging stucco.

"The scorching earth hurt my feet through the thick soles of my shoes.

"I marvelled that men and women would work out in the open under such conditions. There they were, the peasants harvesting grapes for wine, bending under the weight of filled baskets. They were brown as wood. Even the children looked old.

"The incredible sun was in the middle of the sky. The workers in the vineyards stopped to rest and eat. They burned a stretch of grass at the edge of the vineyards along the roadside, and from the black ashes gathered in their hats the snails that had been roasted in the flames. Into cups, carried at their belts, they squeezed with their two hands the juice of half-rotted grapes. It tasted much like wine; it was not wasting the good grapes.

"Roasted snails! Raw wine!

"I noticed that they crossed themselves before eating, gratefully."

Meals for Me

"WHEN shall we live, if not now?" asked Seneca before a table laid for his pleasure and his friends'. It is a question whose answer is almost too easily precluded. When indeed? We are alive, and now. When else live, and how more pleasantly than supping with sweet comrades?

Perhaps Landor, a little later, meant more than he said (but more than Seneca?) when he decided, "I shall dine late, but the dining-room will be well lighted, the guests few and selected."

Whatever his imputations, his tastes are mine. I too dine late by preference, and I too like my room clear and beautiful, and above all, my guests very few and even more selected.

It is true that in the beginnings of all cultures meals were served early in the day, as indeed they are now among simple folk. A banquet at noon leaves long waking-hours for digestion, conversation, and the easing and refilling of the body. It is practical, and early Greeks and Romans, as well as modern peasants, have appreciated the double festival of a day spent far from the fields before tables tottering under the rare dishes of a marriage or a birthday.

Not until ancient men leave their pastures and their vineyards for the vitiated air of cities; not until they stretch days longer with the false light of burning wax or electricity, and then sleep wastefully in artificial darkness when the sun is high; not until they have grown far away from simplicity do they leave their daytime feastings.

Then, as in old Rome and our own towns, we dine later. For us it is a comparatively recent progression; as few years ago as the early eighteenth century Alexander Pope stabbed scornful couplets at the dissolute Londoners who put off banqueting until well past three o'clock.

We soon grow used to the slow signs of corruption, so surrounded by them are we. In the beginning of the nineteenth century we dined at six, and today a good meal is wasted on most people unless the sun has long set.

What is more tedious for us than an early supper? It thrusts itself into the gathering speed of a day's life like a stick into the spokes of a turning wheel. It forces a pause, a stop, which acts as a kind of disequilibrium to the fine balance of the remaining hours of consciousness.

If the days are short, an early evening meal seems to cut them in two, leaving the second part hanging lifeless on the hardly realized beginning. And if the days are long, they are made twice as monotonously hot by the tired interruption of cooked food.

An early evening meal—a long evening. A long evening—what to do with it? There is a fairly good play, a passable movie, a game of bridge—surely *some* way to kill a few hours.

But an evening killed is murder of a kind, criminal like any disease, and like disease a thorough-going crime. If Time, so fleeting, must like humans die, let it be filled with good food and good talk, and then embalmed in the perfumes of conviviality.

Let us kill it in slow parley, over the leisured savourings of fare both simple and elaborate, in the tempered colour of a room lighted softly, clearly, by living fire of wax or oil or wood, or by the most artful disguises of electricity.

Let the death-chamber itself be airy, intimate, free of thick odours and the sensual distraction of high colour. It should be warmed by a fire in winter, cool with moving air in summer; and in summer too the soft comfortable rugs should be taken away, leaving the shadows of chair legs spidering, reflecting, into the polished floor.

The chair should be comfortable, not low and soft enough to slow digestion, as did the Roman couches, not hard as Cornish rocks, but well fitted to the average body. The best I ever sat in were wide, generous, solid, with high backs, made of ash, brought from England and polished in a log-cabin long before they ever set leg on a hardwood floor.

The table should be ample, and above all solid, with no squeaks and shiverings. Plates, too, should be large, and the silver heavy rather than light, with smooth simple lines to it. Plain linen, ample as the table, plain colours in the flowers and the fruits, glasses no more ornamented than the bubbles they imitate—all should be simple, and adequate as the food and drink served there.

The guests, "few and selected," are most important to Landor and to me, as they were to Archestratus long ago. He wrote, in a fragment of his lost poem on "Gastronomy":

> *I write these precepts for immortal Greece,*
> *That round a table delicately spread,*
> *Or three, or four, may sit in choice repast,*
> *Or five at most. Who otherwise shall dine,*
> *Are like a troop marauding for their prey.*

I would add one more person to his dictum, though, and say that six can dine well at a table. More, even one or two, are dangerous, and beyond ten deadly.

What is worse than the rigid right-left conversational etiquette of a formal banquet, unless it be the forced jollity of an annual feast of some modern "service" club, thick with the noise of too many people eating too much food cooked in too large quantities? In either case there is more than a faint likeness to Archestratus' "troop marauding for their prey."

Too few of us, perhaps, feel that the breaking of bread, the sharing of salt, the common dipping into one bowl, mean more than satisfaction of a need. We make such primal things as casual as tunes heard over a radio, forgetting the mystery and strength in both.

Very simple men still know that if you injure the food another leaves, you can thus injure him. The bones from his plate, the rice from his bowl, can be moulded into a little figurine, and then decay will eat into his own flesh as into the mannequin's. Or poison can be dropped into the bowl.

But it is obvious that none who plans to harm a man through food will himself partake of that same food. Thus, there is honour and sanctity in eating together, when you are simple.

So it should be now, although we have civilised ourselves away from the first rules of life. Sharing our meals should be a joyful and a trustful act, rather than the cursory fulfilment of our social obligations.

I know one man, however, the opposite of what I mean, who has so simplified his concept of human hunger and its quelling that he considers the act of taking food as necessary and intimate as any other function, like defecation or sexual play, and no more to be shared with several other beings. For him it is disgusting to eat even with his dear friends.

His viewpoint is exaggerated, and to my mind unhealthy. For me, there is no more agreeable relaxation than a quiet sharing of food with my few friends. My only approximation of his feeling is the irritation and revolt that rise in me at the thought of obligatory feeding with unknown or uncongenial people.

To such a lewd exhibition I should prefer Plato's solitary bowl of olives, but for neither of these would I forego a slow meal with three or four—or six at most, sitting in "choice repast."

What six persons may consider choice is delicate to decide. Six tastes, six appetites, must be known, and fused by one memory and one skill into a mutually exciting whole. Old preferences must be converted into new. New flavours must be linked with old.

From this fusion should result meals as stimulating to the tongue as to the gastric fluids, meals to be remembered with pleasure, evocative of future delights.

And to concoct such meals and serve them is one of the most satisfying of all civilised amenities, I think. Nothing is much sweeter than the sincere gratification—and admiration—of a friend.

When Horace succoured a storm-bound traveller, he fed him a good chicken, a fat kid roasted, grapes, figs and nuts, and sweet Roman wine.

When we went to sup with Nell Coover, the small old etcher, often hungry in her rooms filled with Whistler's cushions and Heppelwhite's beautiful chairs and cupboards, she gave us a strange lovely salad of sea mosses and jewelled ice-plants from the cliffs, and a bowl of green wild spinach. It was all she had, but it was served forth with no apology, nor did it need one. Our eyes and our stomachs were pleased, and Miss Coover too, I think, sure in the pleasure of well-treated guests.

For my own meals I like simplicity above all. I like newness in what I serve, perhaps because any interest I may thus stir in my fellow-diners is indirect flattery of myself. I like leisure.

I like a mutual ease. For this reason I prefer not to have among my guests two people or more, of any sex, who are in the first wild tremours of love. It is better to invite them after their new passion has settled, has solidified into a quieter reciprocity of emotions. (It is also a waste of good food, to serve it to new lovers.)

I do not agree with the Greeks and Romans, that women should be reserved for the end of a meal and served with the final wines and music, nor do I think that Frenchman was right who stated that there are no blue eyes, no curls and dimpled shoulders, which can replace for a true gourmet the charms of a black truffle.

It is, though, very dull to be at a table with dull people, no matter what their sex.

Dining partners, regardless of gender, social standing, or the years they've lived, should be chosen for their ability to eat—and drink! —with the right mixture of abandon and restraint. They should enjoy food, and look upon its preparation and its degustation as one of the human arts. They should relish the accompanying drinks, whether they be ale from a bottle on a hillside or the ripe bouquet of a Chambertin 1919 in a great crystal globe on finest damask.

And above all, friends should possess the rare gift of sitting. They should be able, no, eager, to sit for hours—three, four, six—over a meal of soup and wine and cheese, as well as one of twenty fabulous courses.

Then, with good friends of such attributes, and good food on the board, and good wine in the pitcher, we may well ask, When shall we live if not now?

Dark Ages and the Men of God

1000 A.D.–1400 A.D.

Europe

THE decline of Rome, that "period of insatiable voracity and the peacock's plume," came to its sure end. Rome fell.

Then the Dark Ages cast their mysterious silent gloom over all the arts of Europe. Gastronomy, with the others, dwindled, tottered, tapered into ignorance. Men ate in those countries, certainly: porridge for the lowly, roast meats for the rich. But as far as we know, they did not care.

Food was only a necessity again, like sleep and sweating. There were no more investigating palates, no more keen nostrils trembling with sensuous fine delight at the perfume of a cold melon drenched with wine, or the heady aroma of a succulent piglet, well basted with its own juices and stuffed full of chestnuts and green almonds. *La gourmandise* was dead.

No, not quite. A faint light still glowed, a little flame in the darkness, well hidden behind holiness and the convent walls. The good monks, never more wisely, remembered the spiritual importance of physical well-being.

Helped by a hundred fast-days, whose strict observance would have reduced every priest in Europe to a stringy skeleton, the plump brothers spent much time and thought on making delicious dishes appear frugal.

The best ecclesiastical brains on the continent studied the egg, and discovered the formulae for making it appear on Lenten boards as a rose, a cabbage, or a roasted duck. And roasted ducks, and kids and pigs and even tender bulls, were made to look like nothing that ever breathed and walked about under the All-Seeing Eye. Juices dripped from every convent spit, and were metamorphosed into the best of all disguises, sauces infinitely elaborate.

So abstinence begot kitchen trickery, and good eating survived with holy blessings through the Dark Ages.

I Arise Resigned

Roasted hares, though eaten, are thought to nourish melancholie.
—Elizabethan cookbook.

SABRI, the homesick Turkish lawyer, invited us for tea. We drank too much of it, and ate, ravenously or discreetly, according to our nationalities, at a large cake like a macaroon. Sabri had made it, and he told us how.

"Cook finest vermicelli thoroughly," he instructed, a cold polite smile on his face and his eyes very warm and melancholy. "Then when it is done spread it in a large shallow baking-dish and drip honey and sweet oil upon it until the dish brims.

"Throw slivers of pistachio nuts upon it, as many as you like—I like very many. And then bake it slowly. It will shrivel down to a brown crusty cake with a moist inside, like the one you did not eat much of."

"Sabri, it's—we———"

"I know. It's too sweet for you, eh, Al?"

"Yes. It makes every tooth in my head quiver like a stricken doe." Sabri almost smiled.

"For myself," he remarked, distantly, "it is barely sweet. And these icings and bonbons you eat! They are tasteless as dust to a Turk.

"Of course, in our world, the Near East, we like anything with starch in it, too. There is a good reason." He looked glumly and perhaps a little maliciously at me.

"Yes, a very good reason—for us, that is. We Easterners eat viscous, sticky foods to make ourselves more virile!

"Perhaps that's what ails us," he added, austerely. Then he grinned, and broke the last chunk of cake in his fat, too-sensitive hands. "Young men try to increase what they have; old men look for what they've passed by—but is it only in Turkey?"

47

II

No. Cooks, even before Anthippus', were turning their tricks to physical excitation. His, in ancient Athens, boasted of such skill:

> *Insensible the palate of old age,*
> *More difficult than the soft lips of youth*
> *To move, I put much mustard in their dish;*
> *With quickening sauces make their stupor keen,*
> *And lash the lazy blood that creeps within.*

It was Louis the Fourteenth, however, tired and honing for lost pleasure, whose senile throat was first cheered by the hot pungency of a cordial. He took slow sips of the new liquor, distilled for him at some thoughtful courtier's command, and from that day his temper was sweeter and his old body less obviously damned. Cordials comforted him.

In his land, then, and on the globe everywhere for many centuries, sweet distillations and the sharp taste of spiced vinegars have warmed old men and young, in the armchair or the marriage bed. Bowls of meat, soaked for days in cordials and hot condiments (Cold pudding settles one's love, says an old English proverb!) are still served at wedding feasts in distant European villages.

And then there are truffles, those mysterious growths which spring seedless and rootless from the oaky soil, which may or may not be as good as they are rare and dear, and which even Brillat-Savarin names aphrodisiac.

People tell me that only virgins have the true nose for truffle-hunting: virgin sows, virgin bitches. I cannot vouch for this, as I have never hunted truffles—but I do know a man who once saw the last human hunter in all the Périgord country.

Franz Mayen is the man. He has Napoleon's rippled lips, the vaguely authentic mannerisms of an important *agent provocateur,* and a friend named Buô Dinh Ngo who is the son of an Annamite official.

It was one of the many nights in Strasbourg when Mayen, Buô Dinh, Al, and I sat comfortably filled with fine food. We had eaten a *pâté de foie gras en brioche* (which at the time made me think of Carême's dictum, "To become a perfect cook, one must first be a distinguished pastry-maker." This plate is, however, more of a *tour de force* than a true delicacy, for the unctuous salve of a good Strasbourg *pâté* is not well complemented by the short and sweet flavour of *brioche*. Dry toast with a *pâté* moulded in wine aspic is certainly more fortunate a combination. But—) we had dined marvellously well on a *pâté de foie gras en brioche* among other things, and now we sat complacently at our ease.

Buô Dinh crouched behind a huge cigar and fingered a jade bead in his pocket. Al and I shared a glass of Alsatian *quetschwasser*, harsh and clear. Franz Mayen, very sardonic and entertaining, peered at us and talked ceaselessly, as always.

"Yes," he was saying, "I have seen the last virgin woman trufflehunter in all France! I am probably—no, certainly—unique, for I was but five or six when it happened, and a little boy among old men. It was a secret hunt——"

"By moonlight, of course?" one of us enquired, smoothly.

"Ah no!" Mayen was unruffled as a bowl of cream. "Naturally it was held in the white sunlight of the south—a van Gogh sun, a French Midi sun. And we had gathered secretly because the Church was opposed to women truffle-hunters. The idea of an old virgin sniffing over the hills, with a pack of men hot at her heels—it is disgusting to the Church, it is—you understand me?—pagan!

"So this was to be the last hunt, with the only woman left alive who had the truffle nose. She was old, very old, and she was—yes, unquestionably—she was a virgin! And, *mon Dieu, mon Dieu*, but what a nose! It was long, most pointed, red at the tip. It quivered.

"We started off at a hill far from the church, I lagging behind on my little legs, but very curious. We walked until I was panting.

"The old maid went ahead. Finally she stopped. She lifted her formidable nose, red and quivering, into the hot air. We all watched.

"Then she was off, and it was hard to follow her, I can tell you. She ran like a demented soul straight through the underbrush, over ditches, up a steep hill. There she stopped, in a barren clearing around an old oak tree.

"She pointed to the ground at her feet. The men dug with their blunt forks. Sure enough, truffles! She started away, stopped suddenly and pointed down. More truffles! And all the time she was trembling and sniffing like a sick dog.

"Finally she stood still, and her nose grew pale. She stopped shivering, and looked very old and weary. The hunt was over.

"When we got home, the best truffles were sent to Lyons, and the rest we chopped up and cooked with eggs into a kind of omelette."

Mayen pulled at his cigarette, and added disgustedly: "Of course it is too bad! My one chance to eat enough truffles to see if they really are exciting—and I was only six!"

"But is that all true, Franz, about the old woman? Are you telling the truth? Is he, Buô Dinh?"

But Franz was calling for more *quetsch*, and when we looked at the little Indo-Chinese he relit his cigar and hummed a phrase or two of the "Marseillaise."

III

"You may serve me with two roast pigeons for dinner," said the old Maréchal de Mouchy when he returned home from his best friend's funeral. "I have noticed that after eating a brace of pigeons I arise from the table feeling much more resigned."

Oddly enough, it was not until the eighteenth century that Europeans became conscious of the subtle relations between the soul, on whose existence they spent so much thought, and the human stomach, on whose subsistence they spent even more time.

Then, although the king, Louis XVI, paid small attention to any food so long as it filled him without too much discomfort, his courtiers followed the example of such staunch gentlemen as Mouchy, and enquired into many pseudo-magical refinements of eating.

Many of their remedies for lovesickness, melancholy, and the like, were unproved fantasy. Most of them, arrived at with the usual scientific air of discovery, were nostrums older than the altars of Greece. Warm milk soothes jaded nerves, and brings slumber to the insomniac: no new thing this, although the sated Frenchmen seized with surprise on its ancient simplicity, and on many another like it.

They experimented with strange brews, and although most psychic cures may have been due more to the powers of suggestion than to a mixture of wild herbs, fermentation also helped to warm their tired bodies and thus cheer their souls.

Since the earliest days of what is called civilization men have drunk wines made from the juice of grapes or apples or berries; juice which has been "spoiled," had its sugar changed into alcohol and carbon monoxide by a natural process.

Men have been made foolish, or vicious, or even lifeless, by the fumes of wine, but more often they have been succoured. Gaiety and love have seemed easier to attain, and with wine have flowed the wit of great men and the beauty of women. They are resigned; life has been made acceptable.

Death, too, appears less fearful if a man meets it warmed and relaxed by some spiritous cup. Indeed, so often have dying souls been helped to their fate by a last drink that it is the signal for mourning-cards to be printed when the doctor prescribes champagne for his patient. Poor uncle is as good as dead—let him die happy, with all he can drink for once in his life!

And men to be killed for crimes they may have committed are often thus mercifully treated, as much, probably, to salve the punisher's conscience as to ease the victim's fears. For them, however, a harsher opiate is needed, brandy or rum.

There is a recipe in one of Paul Reboux's entertaining cookbooks which explains this custom of pre-lethal drinking not too inappropriately. He is discussing the preparation of a rabbit for execution.

"Many people," he says, "whose stomachs are more demanding than their hearts are tender, raise rabbits only to eat them.

"This is in itself an act of human energy which I would not know how to accomplish. Intimate family life with a rabbit, strengthened by our daily relations, would make me no more capable of devouring my little animal than I would be of eating one of my friends.

"However, if your sense of realism be strong enough, and if you want your rabbit to be even better than your neighbour's, take care to nourish it——"

Monsieur Reboux tells with his own detached care the schedule for feeding: warm milk while the beastie is still nursing from its mother, tender lettuce and meadow salads as it grows older, a few succulent carrots and grains of corn. And herbs, of course, to perfume its flesh before it is cooked rather than after.

It will enjoy leek soup, he advises, and rich hot potato broth with bread. And even, on Sundays, a little bowl of *café au lait*!

"Finally, the day of the execution, give him a glass of good *marc* to drink. Rum, although traditional for such occasions, will render him less careless of his fate. After this, you will without scruple be able to give to his little neck the final and decisive blow. Your rabbit will already be in such a state of anæsthesia that nothing can matter to him.

"Thus you are assured of having given him a beautiful life, and a beautiful death!"

In Sinistra Parte, Johannus Baptista

1100 A.D.–1450 A.D.

England

IN ENGLAND, things had stayed fairly simple. Barbaric snarlings and pouncings had, of course, been curbed to that state of repressed ferocity which even now marks the hungry Britisher at table. The Romans had come and gone, leaving more roads than recipes.

Druidic laws laid strict *taboos* on certain foods: hares, poultry, fish. Oil and lard were much preferred to cow's butter. Mortars were busy in every house and hovel, replacing the greater part of all our kitchen paraphernalia. Unleavened cakes of oat or wheaten flour, and the ubiquitous stew, were common fare in all the island's homes.

Things had stayed fairly simple.

Then a vision of the Holy Sepulcher, raped by the foul infidel, flashed over western Europe. England followed, mighty and beautiful. Her bravest soldiers, her wiliest dreamers, the sturdiest folk from all her fields went southward and eastward in those stupendous migrations called the Crusades. Gain and the Holy Grail!

Many of the Englishmen died, in battles or storms or in the heathen's tents. Some of them stayed on in the strange lands, took wives, and raised tall blue-eyed sons with dark skins. A few of them went back to England.

They brought rich brocaded silks in many colours, and jewels, and strange heavy perfumes. These were for their women. Also for the women, they said, were the spices in boxes and sacks—and to please the women, nothing more, they showed how to blend seven powders into a hot paste on meat and eggs, or throw magical pinches of this and that into the daily soup, and so transform it that it steamed like incense.

Then, while their wives watched with polite curiosity, the generous Crusaders ate heartily. Their eyes watered with nostalgic delight.

They taught the spicy secrets to underlings. Apprentices were initiated slowly, and rivalries sprang up between the kitchen staffs of different English castles, which were matched only during the French eighteenth century.

Finally a cookbook was written; then several appeared in the libraries of great houses. We can read one of them (with some stumbling, it is true) in what are known now as *The Harleian Mss. 279.*

In these we see how much men could hold, seven hundred years ago. Purveyance lists, made for every visit of a ruler or nobleman, show us incredible pages of supplies. This is only a part of the poultry listed for one of Richard's weekends in 1387:

> "Fifty swans, a hundred and ten geese, fifty capons 'of hie grece' and eight dozen other capons, sixty dozen hens, five herons, six kids and seven dozen rabbits (strange place here for such lively fourlegged wingless little beasts!), five dozen pullets for jelly and some eleven dozen to roast, a hundred dozen peacocks, twenty dozen cranes and curlews, and 'wilde fowle ynogh.'"

Besides the strange meats of crane and peacock and swan, seal was very popular, and whale and porpoise made any meal delicious. Marrow and almond milk were used in almost every recipe, whether with fish, meat, or dainty custard. Puddings of swans' and capons' necks, little birds and oxen salted whole, sweet soups of cinnamon and rose water with the roasts—it all sounds strange now. In as many centuries, our American salads of marshmallow and pink jelly, and our chocolate sodas, will undoubtedly seem even queerer.

Wines, especially a thin red Gascon mixed with honey and spices and called *claré*, were drunk indiscriminately with all foods. More often they were poured over game and puddings and soups.

But Englishmen, even then, drank ale with greater ease, and used it, moreover, in many of their dishes. They soured it in the sun for vinegar; they soaked fish in it as a preservative, and put it in many sauces. Best of all, they quaffed cock-ale, a spiced brew in which one lusty rooster had ended his days and lain for many more.

"To make Cock Ale," instructs one ancient recipe reprinted in 1736 in Smith's *Compleat Housewife*, "take ten gallons of ale and a large cock, the older the better. Parboil the cock, flea him, and stamp him in a stone mortar until his bones are broken. You must craw and gut him when you flea him. Put him into two quarts of sack, and put to it 3 pounds of raisins of the sun stoned, some blades of mace, and a few cloves.

"Put all these into a canvas bag, and a little while before you find the ale has done working, put the ale and bag together into a vessel. In a week or 9 days' time bottle it up, fill the bottles but just above the necks, and leave the same to ripen as other ale."

Recipes in *The Harleian* cookbook are vaguer than this bizarre proof of British strength. In only one or two of them are definite measurements given. "Take sugar enough," says one direction. "Take clean fresh brawn," says another, "and seethe it, but not enough." No step-by-step procedure for young brides here! It is rather the terse understatement of one expert to another.

The directions for thickening sauces and soups leave even more to the reader's foreknowledge. "Let it not be too thick nor too thin, but as *potage* should be . . . make it somewhat running and somewhat standing."

The old cook's English is very pleasant to read. He describes the making of a sauce: "Boil it, and when it cometh on high, ally it and set it a-down—and look that you stir it well!" And for pie shells to fill with meat and birds, he says—most aptly!—"Take and make fair little coffins ——"

Meals were hearty then, as well as plentiful. The several main dishes of a course were bound together with a froth, a fluff, of what were called *light plates*. A typical one directs: "Mince pork and dates, add egg yolks and green cheese and ginger and cannel, mix all, and bake with a covering of hard-baked yolks." This hors-d'œuvre would, no doubt, keep the diners occupied until some real food came their way, something to sink their teeth into!

Here, then, is a recipe for Beef y-Stewed:

"Take fair beef of the ribs of the forequarters, and smite a fair piece, and wash the beef into a fair pot. Then take the water that the beef was soaking in, and strain it through a strainer, and seethe the same water and beef in a pot and let them boil together. Then take cannel, cloves, mace, grains of parise, quibibes, and onions minced, parsley and sage, and cast thereto and let them boil together. And then take a loaf of bread, and steep it with broth and vinegar, and then draw it through a strainer, and let it be still; and when it is near enough, cast the liquor thereto, but not too much; and then let boil and cast saffron thereto, a quantity. Then take salt and vinegar, and cast thereto, and look that it be poignant enough, and serve forth."

As a decoration for this stew, primroses might be tossed upon it, less beautifully than yellow melon-flowers upon the roasted duck of China, but with the same desire.

Flowers were often used thus by the Middle English, sometimes most fortunately. What could be more ludicrously lovely than a tiny crackled piglet all garlanded with lilies and wild daffodils? Or a baked swan in its feathers, with roses on its proud reptilian head?

The three main courses of a banquet were heralded by spectacular puddings and tarts called *warners*. These, more often than not, were eaten in spite of the silk, wire, wood, gilt, and feathers that decorated them.

The biggest set-pieces marking the end of each course, however, were seldom eaten. Instead, after the guest of honour had duly inspected them, they were paraded slowly around the banquet-hall, sometimes carried on long stretchers by the strongest servants and sometimes wheeled cumbersomely on carts.

Subtleties they were called, and in no uncertain style they indicated the character or activities of the honoured diner.

A Templar home from Jerusalem saw sugar heretics bowed down before a Holy Sepulcher of paste and cake, with a Red Sea of jelly shimmering near it.

A sporting nobleman recognized his own hunting-party, reduced to candy, galloping across a custard moor.

When John Stafford was made Archbishop of Canterbury toward the middle of the fifteenth century, he nodded with benign pleasure at the three subtleties composed for him. First he saw Saint Andrew, sitting on a high altar of state, with beams of gold; before him kneeling, John Stafford himself in his pontifical robes, with his crozier crouched behind him, coped.

Then after dishes of crane and venison and many other meats and birds and finally fish and fruit and a great tart, the second subtlety appeared. It was the Trinity showing a Son of gold, with a crucifix in His hand. Saint Thomas sat on one side, Saint Austin on the other, and John Stafford knelt again, still in his bishop's robes. Behind him was his crozier, coped with the arms of Rochester. Behind the crozier, on one side, knelt a black monk of Christ's Church, and on the other the Abbot of Saint Austin's.

The third course came to its end, after fourteen separate dishes. The last great subtlety was trundled before the banqueters, and a clerk described it:

> "A godhede in a son of gold glorified above, in the son the holy giste voluptable. Seint Thomas kneling a-for him, with ye poynt of a swerd in his hede, & a Mitre there-uppon, crowning s.T. in dextera parte, Maria tenens mitram; in sinistra parte, Johannus Baptista; et in iiij partibus, iiij Angeli incensantes."

And with this the banquet ended.

Pity the Blind in Palate

FREDERICK the Great used to make his own coffee, with much to-do and fuss. For water he used champagne. Then, to make the flavour stronger, he stirred in powdered mustard.

Now to me it seems improbable that Frederick truly liked this brew. I suspect him of bravado. Or perhaps he was taste-blind.

Almost all people are born unconscious of the nuances of flavour. Many die so. Some of these unfortunates are physically deformed, and remain all their lives as truly taste-blind as their brother sufferers are blind to colour. Others never taste because they are stupid, or, more often, because they have never been taught to search for differentiations of flavour.

They like hot coffee, a fried steak with plenty of salt and pepper and meat sauce upon it, a piece of apple pie and a chunk of cheese. They like the feeling of a full stomach. They resemble those myriad souls who say, "I don't know anything about music, but I love a good rousing military band."

Let the listener to Sousa hear much music. Let him talk to other music-listeners. Let him read about music-makers.

He will discover the strange note of the oboe, recognize the French horn's convolutions. Schubert will sing sweetly in his head, and Beethoven sweep through his heart. Then one day he will cry. "Bach! By God, I can hear him! I can hear!"

That happens to the taste-blind in just some such way. He eats apple pie, good or bad, because he has always eaten it. Then one day he sees a man turn his back upon the cardboard crust and sodden half-cooked fruit, and eat instead some crisp crackers with his cheese, a crisp apple peeled and sliced ruminatively after the crackers and the yellow cheese. The man looks as if he knew something pleasant, a secret from the taste-blind.

"I believe I'll try that. It is—yes, it is good. I wonder ——"

And the man who was taste-blind begins to think about eating. Perhaps he talks a little, or reads. All he really need do is experiment.

He discovers that cream is good in coffee in the morning, but that after dinner black coffee is better. He looks for the first time at soup, and pushes it away if it is too pale, too thick or thin.

Potatoes become more to him than the inevitable companion of meat, and he finds unsuspected tastes in the vegetables he has been gulping since his infancy.

He is pleased. He is awakened. At last he can taste, discovering in his own good time what Brillat-Savarin tabulated so methodically as the three sensations: (1) direct, on the tongue; (2) complete, when the food passes over the tongue and is swallowed; and most enjoyable of all (3) reflection—that is, judgment passed by the soul on the impressions which have been transmitted to it by the tongue.

Yes, he can taste at last, and life itself has for him more flavour, more zest.

Of all the present nations, France has the simplest school of cooking, in spite of the complicated subtleties of her great chefs—simplest in the sense of primitive and natural. Herbs, much sweet butter, cream, and long heating in pots of earthenware, give the Gallic cuisine its characteristic flavours, and the juices from boiled and roasted meats are the base of almost every one of its sauces.

It has been said that the foundation of all of French cookery is butter, as that of the Italian is olive oil, German lard, and Russian sour cream. In the same way water or drippings may be designated, unfortunately, as the basis of the English cuisine, and perhaps the flavour from innumerable tin cans, of American!

France today possesses what is probably the most intelligent collective palate. I do not mean that her crudest ragamuffin can name each nuance in *Fruits aux Sept Liqueurs*, or give the year of a vintage wine from its bouquet. Indeed, there are many Frenchmen as callous to the harmonies of taste as any American hotdog-gobbler or English connoisseur of teashop Cornish pasties.

In general, though, France eats more consciously, more intelligently, than any other nation. It may be quails *financière*, or it may be a stew concocted from the rabbit that Papa Jacques caught yesterday under the hedge. Whichever France eats, she does it with a pleasure, an open-eyed delight quite foreign to most people.

The quails are an artful lure to the most refined of palates, and the rabbit stew, steaming, aromatic, is made just as tempting with an onion or two, pepper freshly ground, a little bacon, and a dash of cheap pure wine.

In Paris the gourmets eat with quiet deliberation, rolling each mouthful slowly toward their gullets. In Jacques' little cottage three or four friends inhale the stew's rich fumes, and eat it down like the hungry workingmen they are. In Paris and in the village there is a gusto, a frank sensuous realization of food, that is pitifully unsuspected in, say, the college boarding-house or corner café of an American town.

In America we eat, collectively, with a glum urge for food to fill us. We are ignorant of flavour. We are as a nation taste-blind.

Cautiously we blink at a faint glimmer in the gloom. It seems, just now, that we have become conscious of a few subtleties. There is a faddish demand for roomy salad bowls, for pepper-mills, which may bring permanent light to our national palate. Already an occasional shamefaced protest is heard against calling a California wine "dry" Sauterne, or a mild titter over some such synthetic gastronomy as prompted an advertisement saying, "This is a vintage year for maple syrup."

These feeble but encouraging signs must survive as best they may, however, while ten million men rush every noontime for their ham-on-white and cherry coke. Those ten million men may die taste-blind as well as stomach-ulcered, unless they are shocked into recognition of their own powers of enjoyment.

It might be good if you could go to them, quietly, and say, "Please, sir, stop a minute and listen to me. Can you imagine eating bananas and Limburger cheese together? You have never thought about it? Then think. Taste them separately in your mind, the banana, the Limburger. Taste them together. Ah! It is horrible? Then now about mutton chops with shrimp sauce? And try herring soup with strawberry jam, or chocolate with red wine."

Some of those ten million men would listen. Some of them would eat with their minds for the first time. You would be a missionary, bringing flavour and light to the taste-blind.

And that is a destiny not too despicable.

A Pigges Pettie Toes

Elizabethan England

EVEN in the lusty days of Elizabeth's long reign, when England's blood ran, perhaps, at its fastest and finest, there were melancholy observers of what seemed signs of weakening in the nation's appetite.

Who could tell where things would end, when already the most reputable of rich merchants were copying an effeminate Italian mannerism, and carrying their silver and gold forks about with them instead of eating with their fingers and knives as good Englishmen had been glad to do for centuries?

And the ladies, lying in bed until six o'clock in the morning! When they arose, they breakfasted like babies, thinking they could start the day decently on a pot of ale and but one meager pound of bacon.

The Queen, God be thanked, paid no attention to the new-style finicking, and made her first meal of the day light but sustaining: butter, bread (brown, to stay in the stomach longer and more wholesomely than white), a stew of mutton, a joint of beef, one of veal, some rabbits in a pie, chickens, and fruits, with beef and wine to wash all down in really hygienic fashion.

It is true that Elizabeth could more easily command a full breakfast than most of her subjects, even in that prosperous age. They lived in simpler style, and made their dinners the day's biggest meal. They dined early, at about eleven in the morning, and unless guests had been invited their meals were much like the diet-list of one well-to-do London bachelor who, on May 11, 1589, was served in his lodgings in Warwick Lane with the following plain fare:

A pece of bief	xviijd.
A loyne of veale	ijs.
2 chickens	xiiijd.
Orenges	ijd.
For dressings ye veale &	
chickens & sauce	xijd.

For supper that same day the gentleman ate more lightly, as was the general custom:

A shoulder of mutton	xvjd.
2 rabbettes	xd.
For dressinge ye mutton, rabbettes	
& a pigges pettie toes	viijd.
Colde bief	xiijd.
Cheese	ijd.

But even a bachelor grows tired of the purely animal pleasure of eating, and wishes occasionally to change it by conversation with his friends into the even more purely human pleasure of gastronomy. So, on June 20th of the same year, the Elizabethan Londoner invited a few cronies to dine with him. His cook spared no pennies, and served forth a very agreeable dinner:

Butter	iiijd.
A pece of bief	xiiijd.
A legg of mutton	xviijd.
A loyne of veale	xiipd.
2 pecks of pescodes	viijd.
3 rabbettes	ijs.
A quart of creame	vjd.
3 quarts of strawberies	xvjd.
2 li. of cheries	xxd.
Di: li. of muske confectes	xd.

Di: li. of violett confectes	xjd.
Orenges	iijd.
2 lemans	vjd.
Bred	viijd.
Beare	ixd.

Either this gentleman was a moderate drinker, or his cook did not follow the usual rule of adding beverage prices to the daily lists. There are few such entries: an occasional pint of claret or Rhenish, and sometimes beer for dinner.

In most establishments, however, enormous quantities of wines were drunk on ordinary days as well as festivals, and this in spite of the rising prices, which had jumped from the penny-a-gallon of two hundred years before, to an average of one shilling twopence for the same quantity in 1590.

Sack, alicant, claret, muscadine, Rhenish, and a port-like charneco, brown bastard, cider: all these were drunk as well as ales and beers, and most of them were mixed, according to the host's taste, with sugar, hot spices, and even the prized seasoning ambergris.

Queen Bess herself called mead her favourite tipple, and wherever she went had jugs of it carried with her, in case what was provided by her subjects was not spiced to her taste. And indeed, it was a difficult task to add to each brew of honey and water the same amount of herbs and lemon peel and ground spices, although from there on the procedure was the same for the Queen and the kitchen maid: three months in the keg and six weeks in the bottles before the sweet heady stuff could be drunk.

Perhaps such cloying wines made palates insensible to unsweet-ened fare; perhaps the great quantities of meat that were eaten made Elizabethan stomachs demand more stimulus. Whatever the reason, Englishmen then, as now, sucked greedily on candies, and counted as a failure any feast whose table did not include large bowls of "sugared meats" and sweet Naples biscuits, and marchpane, with eringo the candied root of sea holly, and kissing comfits to end the meal and sweeten the hot breath.

Even when we know that it was the fashion, in Elizabeth's days, to serve much more food for each course than could possibly be eaten—a fashion always co-existent with periods of prosperity—it is hard not to feel that the social observers were probably too pessimistic. Granted that appetites had dwindled from earlier Gargantuan size, that forks were turning the Britishers into a race of "foppish fursifers," that men ate like women and women like lazy infants. We cannot but be thankful that we are spared the critical eye of such carpers, as we sit down to our balanced lunches of orange juice and salad, free perhaps from the gout and dropsy that stood like evil fiends behind every dining-bench in old England.

But are we so thankful that we are free also from fine furious Elizabethan life?

The Standing and the Waiting

IT WAS at the top of the stairs that I first felt something wrong. Until then all had been as I last knew it: the archway, the irregular honey-coloured courtyard, the rounded trees in tubs. The stairs, too, were the same, bending round and back over themselves in several shallow flights; and at the top was the familiar glass box with trout, a plate of mushrooms, and some steaks laid carelessly across the cold-pipes that made its bottom.

We looked for a moment into the box, Chexbres with the hurried, timid appraisal of a man who is in a strange place and conscious of being watched for his reactions to it by another person to whom it is familiar, I with the proud worry of a woman who fears she has too much boasted.

Would the dishes be as exciting, as satisfying? Would the wine still be the best wine? And I, would I be accepted, a loving admirer, or would I now be long forgotten?

Well, the glass box was the same. Chexbres flipped me a quick smile of reassurance. We went along the ugly tiled corridor, past the water-closets where I felt a sudden hilarious memory of my mother's consternation when she had first entered them and found them full of men all chatting, easing themselves, belching appreciatively.

I started to tell Chexbres of her face, puckered in an effort to look broad-minded. We turned the first abrupt corner of the hall, the corner where the kitchens started.

One of the doors opened. A rat-like boy darted out, ducking his head and grinning shyly as he passed us. I refused to look at Chexbres, for I knew that he had smelled, as I had, as alas! I had, that

64

faint trail of bad air following after the scullion like the silver of a snail, bad air rising noxiously from the hidden dirty corners of the kitchens.

I finished the story of my mother's dauntless face, as we hurried on down the long dim corridor.

"There are two dining-rooms for the *pensionnaires,*" I chattered foolishly, "and the *pensionnaires* are everybody—like the mayor and the rich brothel-keepers and carpenters and Chinese students.

"And here is Ribaudot's office."

I was trying to sound casual, but I felt very nervous. Oh, to have talked so much of the restaurant, to have boasted! And then that little ominous whiff! Or had Chexbres noticed it?

I tapped nonchalantly on the half-open glass door of the small, incredibly disordered room.

"Come in, then!" The voice was cross and muffled.

We pushed into the office. By the dim window two cooks in very tall hats sat with their bare arms leaning on a table covered with empty dishes. A cradled bottle lay in front of them. They smiled impersonally.

Ribaudot stood clumsily with one leg still half under the table, his hands leaning on his tall desk.

"Come in, come in," he said, more pleasantly. He wiped his mouth, and peered politely at us.

"How do you do—good afternoon, Monsieur Ribaudot. I am sure you don't remember me: Madame Fischer, who used so often to dine here? I used to come here with ——"

"Oh, of course! Why of course!" He smiled warmly, but I could see that he did not remember. I shrugged inside, and while I introduced Chexbres as a fervent student of gastronomy, and we all chattered and assured each other of remembrance and good will, I looked for change.

If the whiff, the faint bad trail, had caught Ribaudot, it was not yet evident. His office was filled with the conglomerate cooling odours of a good meal, and he himself with the first leisurely torpor of perfect digestion. Yes, of course he looked older, perhaps thinner, uncombed as ever, though, and still modestly sure of being a great *restaurateur.*

"And Charles, little Charles?" I asked, suddenly.

Several looks crossed in the air. Chexbres looked at me, warmly,

smiling at my nostalgic probings and at what I had told him of the
waiter Charles. I looked first at Chexbres, thanking him for recognizing the name, and assuring him that even if Charles were long
dead, he had still been the ultimate, the impeccable peak of all
waiters. Then I saw Ribaudot look swiftly at the two silent cooks
and they at him, a look—a look—I felt very sad and puzzled.

Ribaudot interrupted me.

"The little Charles?" he asked, blandly. "Ah, you remember the
little old Charles?" His voice was noncommittal. "But certainly he
is here. We will call him."

Through my half-hearted protestations he walked majestically the
three paces to the door, and disappeared. The air was still full of
crossed meaningful looks. I wondered very much, and watched
Chexbres' impassive interest in the framed diplomas on the walls. I
tried to feel impassive, too.

Chexbres turned. Charles stood in the doorway, breathing quickly,
a rumpled napkin over one arm. Oh, I had forgotten how small—
but hadn't he been fatter? Yes, old, the little *old* Charles.

I went quickly toward him, watching his pouchy face lighten
quickly from peevish bewilderment to pleasure.

"Howdedo, Charles. I don't know if you remember ———"

"O my God! Oh, pardon, pardon, but it is the little American student, the little lady!"

Behind me, Chexbres laughed to hear me called little as I peered
down on Charles, he up at me, timidly still, but recognizing me.

"And you, Madame? And how long is it? And you, are you well?
Has it been two years? *Six?* Impossible! But it is good, pardon me
for saying so, but it is good to see you!"

He stopped suddenly, looking confusedly at the two silent cooks,
and then at Ribaudot. He seemed to shrink even smaller.

"Monsieur Ribaudot," I said, "would it be possible to command
a dinner for this evening, and ask for the services of Charles?"

"But certainly, certainly!" He pulled a pad of paper toward him,
and started to make squiggles on it.

"Until eight tonight, then, Charles. And the old table in the corner—was it Number Four?"

I turned to Ribaudot again. He seemed to know me at last, and
to be trying to comfort me, to soften life for me. And all the time
we discussed food so pleasantly I wondered at Charles' quick, poign-

ant, wet look of—of gratitude—as he hurried back to his work.

I felt sad, but said nothing to Chexbres. Instead, we talked of Burgundian architecture, not even mentioning the Burgundian meal we had so long planned.

At eight o'clock the small dining-room was full, except for our waiting table. As we sat down I saw in one easy glance that the people were no different after six years. There was the old woman with a dog and a dancing-boy on her way to Cannes, and the table of American schoolteachers eating from a guide-book. And there were the two big young Englishmen in brown and grey, looking embarrassed before their larks on toast.

At the table under the mirror sat a college professor; the College Professor, twirling a glass of Corton, the pedagogic connoisseur, sipping alone in solemn appreciation, sure that his accent was as refined as his taste.

There were two tables of French people, gay and hungry. I remembered that their faces would grow red, later on.

A Chinese eating truffled *pâté* in a trance of philosophical nausea, two Lesbians drinking Vichy, three silent *pensionnaires*, a priest— the hard white lights burned down on all of us, the mirror reflected our monotonous gestures, the grey walls picked out our pale natures and the warmth of colour and odour and taste before us on the white tables.

"This is a good room," Chexbres murmured, lowering his eyelids and straightening a straight fork. "I like small rooms. Small rooms, for eating—or mountain-sides."

"Good evening! Ah, 'sieur-'dame, you are here!"

Charles stood by the table, breathing fast. His minute moustache was newly stiff with wax, and his hair was plastered in a thin replica of the debonair curlicues he used to wear. He beamed anxiously at us.

"Does—is everything as you wished?"

"Everything is perfect, Charles!" I wondered if my voice were too fervent. "Now we will start with a little glass of Dubonnet, please."

When he had gone, Chexbres said: "You are known, my dear! You should be much flattered—or I for being with you."

He smiled, the sweet-tongued self-mocker, at me and at the table, and I looked with less haste at the tall crystal tulips to hold wine, at the napkins folded like pheasants, at the inky menu big as a newspaper, and our own little typewritten one on top of it, at the flowers ——

Flowers *chez* Ribaudot, Ribaudot who hated any foreign odours near his plates? Never before—no, we were the only diners with flowers on our table.

On the little serving-board beside us, Charles fussed clumsily with a new bottle of Dubonnet. Finally it was open. He poured it with a misjudged flourish. Purple spread on the cloth. I looked quickly, without meaning to, at Chexbres, but he was watching the quiet colour in his glass. Perhaps he had not seen, had not realized, the fumblings of my perfect waiter?

He raised his *apéritif*. His eyes were wide and candid.

"I drink to our pasts—to yours and mine. And to ours. The wine is strong. Time is strong, too." He bowed slightly. "I grow solemn— or sententious."

I laughed at him. "I'm not afraid of time."

"Don't boast."

"I'm not boasting. Really, I'm glad six years—oh, it's too complicated. But this tastes good. I'm hungry."

"And this will be a good meal, worth waiting even longer than six years for. Do you know," he asked naïvely, "that I've never before had a menu written just for me? It's very exciting."

I felt my self-confidence sweep back, as he meant it to.

"And flowers," he went on. "I've had flowers on my table, but never the only ones, in a room of such important people."

We looked vaguely, amicably, at the stiff little bouquet, mimosa and a purplish rosebud and a short twig of cypress.

Charles steamed beside us, with a tall pitcher of soup. While he served it, it spilled from the trembling cups into the saucers. I felt a flash of intense irritation: wet saucers, God! how they irritate me! I looked straight into his eyes.

They were not wet and grateful now. They were desperate eyes, bloodshot, frantic, desperate. I cringed away.

"Oh, Chexbres," I whispered, "don't mind the spilling! Don't! It's that he's nervous. His hand's shaking because of that, I know."

You are lying to save your own boastful face, too, I said inside. You know Charles is drunk. Yes, Charles, the perfect waiter, spilling soup and drunk, and it hurts your pride.

"Maybe his feet hurt him," I went on very fast. "I know you hate soup in saucers. But you know I've heard that waiters do stranger things than most criminals, simply because their feet hurt."

"Yes, I'm sure," Chexbres agreed, vaguely. "This is really delicious, my dear.

"You know," he said, in a suddenly direct voice, "I can't understand why most people are put off at first by the coloured tiles on the roofs of Burgundy. It seems to me they're a definite outcropping of the plebeian in architecture, like the frescoes of Swiss interiors during the same period."

For a moment I felt rebuffed. But almost at once I knew he was right. Six years—six hundred years . . . architecture was better.

We talked, and well, and all the dinner was most excellent, and the wine was like music on our tongues. Time was forgotten, and its signals, too. But I noticed, with a kind of fifth eye, that Charles' hand grew steady, and his own eye clear, until by the end of the meal I dared preen myself upon his delicate sure touch.

"Have you ever seen that better done?" I asked Chexbres.

"No. No, he is wonderful. He is an artist."

We watched as in a blissful dream the small fat hands moving like magic among bottles and small bowls and spoons and plates, stirring, pouring, turning the pan over the flame just so, just so, with the face bent keen and intent above.

"It's like a brain operation," Chexbres said, "—the hard light, the excitement, the great surgeon. Thank you for bringing me here. It's worth ——"

It was done. We tasted. We nodded silently, and smiled at Charles, and he looked almost like the old Charles again, very self-sure. I felt happy.

After coffee, I laughed to think of us sitting there almost the last, and at what I was going to do.

"Chexbres, you think I've shown off, but that was only the beginning! Now I really do show off, and all for your benefit."

We smiled at each other, very effortless and calm.

"Charles," I called, warning Chexbres quickly, "You have never tasted the local *marc*, remember!

"Charles, what do you think has been the sad experience—but first, are we keeping you too late?"

I waved my hand at the now empty room, dim in every corner but ours, and at a scullery boy scrubbing the hall. I felt expansive, warm from the wine, at ease in Time.

"Oh, but what an idea!" Charles exploded. "Excuse me for chiding you, Madame, but what an idea! Madame, you must know that for you to have another good meal *chez* Ribaudot, and go away remembering it and me, I would gladly stay here until morning—no, until tomorrow night, by God!"

Chexbres and I bowed courteously. Charles did, too.

"And the sad experience, Madame?"

"Oh, thank you for recalling me. I had almost forgotten. Charles, last night we had a stroke of luck that was unfortunate—I should say almost desolating. I, who wished to introduce our good friend Monsieur Chexbres to the famous *marc* of Burgundy, was served with a glass of some strange liquid—thank God I had the good sense to taste it before letting Monsieur come near it!—some strange liquid, pale, cut, rank, which could never ——"

"Ah, but I know! I know where!" Charles beamed, flourishing his napkin with glee.

"Oh, but naturally I would not be so indiscreet as to mention the name of the miserable restaurant," I protested, rhetorically. I glanced at Chexbres exultantly: the scene was beautiful.

"No need, no need, Madame! A restaurant serving the good *marc* so insultingly, and to you, a connoisseur" (here I bowed graciously) "and to this poor gentleman a sure amateur having his first taste (here Chexbres lowered his eyes modestly)—"ah, such poisonous conduct, my God! could only be at" (and here Charles leaned very close to us in the empty room and hissed) "could only be at *La Tour!*"

He stood off, triumphant. I pressed a little line into the tablecloth with my thumb nail, smirking, murmuring, "Of course I say nothing, no names!" in complete agreement. I could feel Chexbres' appreciation all round me.

"But, *but* 'dame, we must rectify that infected, that—pardon me—that stinking behaviour!"

I sighed faintly. It had worked!

"Yes, my idea, too. But no ordinary *marc*, Charles, no liqueur served on any one's order. This must be ——"

"Yes, very special," he finished for me. "Trust me, Madame. It may take a few extra minutes. A little more *filtre*, perhaps, while I am gone?"

Chexbres and I sat wordless, looking mildly and somnolently at each other. We sipped at the bitter black coffee. A rickety old ventilator whirred in the ceiling, and the boy cleaning the hall bumped his bucket against the tiles. Lights went out, except over our table.

Charles tiptoed back, wheezing, but his face full of life. He held a filthy old green bottle, not picturesquely crusted, but filthy. Silently he poured a little dark brown liquid into a large glass. He swirled it round. Chexbres reached for it.

"Permit me, sir," Charles halted him, "permit me to suggest that Madame taste it."

I winked slightly at Chexbres, and took up the glass. I tried to look like a connoisseur, a little pompous probably. I sipped, and then I could only look beatifically delighted, for it was the cleanest, smoothest distillation that I had ever met.

"Ah!"

Charles sighed. I had told him. He poured the glass almost half full, at least twice as full as he should have, and with a jubilant look disappeared into the wet dark hall.

"Chexbres, now *I* shall be solemn. But I have never been served such *marc*! Not even Ribaudot would serve that to his best friends, to anyone less than the mayor or maybe the Holy Ghost. Where did Charles get it?"

Chexbres let it run under his tongue, and sat nodding ecstatically at me. I could almost see it seeping through his head, in and around in a hot tonic tide, and then down his throat.

"Dear sweet gentle Jesus!" he remarked, softly.

"Oh, I'm glad we came, Chexbres. After all, I mean."

We both drank at the one glass, and talked peacefully under the one white light. Finally the *marc* was gone. Charles appeared, carrying the filthy bottle.

"Oh, no more, no more! Really, we couldn't ——"

He stopped very still, and looked at me.

"Madame, you must drink one glass. Please!" he said, in a quiet voice, almost muttering. "Please drink this glass from me. It is I, Charles, who offer it to you and to Monsieur Chexbres."

"But—it is so late, and—" The thought of swallowing one more mouthful closed my throat, almost.

"I have said I would stay until tomorrow for you. I would stay until the end of the world, truly." He looked at me calmly, standing between us and the dark doorway. Beyond him I could see nothing, and there was not a sound anywhere, except the three of us breathing rather cautiously.

"Thank you," Chexbres said, warmly. "Madame was afraid only of detaining you too long, Charles. Otherwise we could sit for ever, too, drinking this miraculous liqueur."

He held out the glass. With a hand steady as oak, Charles poured it to the brim, a good half-pint of strong *marc*.

"Thank you, Charles," I said. "I want never to leave, here where I have so often been happy. It may be six years again. Will you prepare the bill, please?"

We knew we must drink it all. It was like smouldering fire, wonderful still, but hard now to swallow. We sat without moving, conscious suddenly of exhaustion, and of being perhaps too full of food, with all the heady wine-life gone out of us.

Charles came back, with the little sheet of flimsy paper on a plate. I wondered about the tip: in a way I felt like not leaving one, because he seemed more than a waiter now. But when he brought back change, I left it all on the plate.

"Thank you, Madame," he said, and did not pick it up. He stood watching us sip resolutely at the *marc*. Finally I looked up at him.

"Madame, thank you, thank you for coming again."

I wanted not to be personal, so I said, "But why not? All people who love good food come to Ribaudot's again."

"Yes," he stuttered slightly, "but—pardon me—but I mean thank you for asking for me. You don't know ——"

"Oh, Charles, it is we who are fortunate, to have your services." I felt very polished and diplomatic, but at the same time sincere, sincere as hell under the weariness and all the *marc*.

"No, no—I mean, you will never know what it meant, tonight, to have you ask for me, little old Charles. And now, good evening."

Chexbres asked, quickly, "But we will pass this way again, and soon we hope, and then of course ——?"

"Ah, who knows?" Charles raised his eyebrows toward his thinning curlicue of hair, restrained a gesture to stroke his little whiff of moustache, smiled debonairly at us, and disappeared finally into the black corridor.

"I thought he said he would wait until tomorrow night," I murmured, flippantly. Then I felt rather ashamed, and apologized. "He'll probably be waiting at the end of the hall, the top of the stairs, to help us with our coats."

Chexbres said nothing, but slowly drank down the rest of the *marc*.

The chairs squawked wildly as we stood up. The sound was almost good in that silent room.

In the corridor we saw a dim light, and as we went by Ribaudot's office, his silhouette was sharp against the frosted glass, bent over his high desk.

"I know where the coats are," I whispered, and we tiptoed down the hall.

"Is it Madame Fischer?" His voice came muffled through the door. He opened it, blinking at us, with his hair mussed.

"Oh, I'm sorry! I do hope we haven't kept you," I said, in confusion.

He looked very tenderly at us. "No. And have you dined well? I am glad. I have your coats in here."

We stood awkwardly in the doorway while he crossed the little room to the table where the two cooks had sat in the afternoon. Our coats were piled on it, to one side, and a stiff ugly bouquet of mimosa and two purplish rosebuds and a twig of cypress stood by them. I looked dully at it, wishing I were home in bed, very tired.

"It was good of you to remember Ribaudot," he said.

"It was very natural. Who does not?"

"Ah, things nowadays—the affairs—" but he bowed, acceptance calm on his face.

"And the poor old Charles. It was especially good for him. I see you and I shared the honour of flowers from him." He looked impersonally at the ugly bouquet. "Yes, I fired Charles today, just before your first visit. He is on his way to the South by now.

"Permit me to help you with your scarf. It was sad—a fine waiter once, a brave little man always—but what will you do? Everything changes. Everything passes.

"Good-night. Good-night, sir, and Madame, and thank you. And good-bye."

"Au revoir, we hope," I called as we walked away from him towards the dark.

"Who knows?" He shrugged, and closed the glass door.

In the long hall corruption hung faint and weakly foul on the still air. The stairs were deep, with the empty glass box like a dark ice cube, and we breathed freely once out in the courtyard.

It was filled with moonlight. The trees in tubs were black, and through the archway the tower of the palace gleamed and glowed against the black sky.

Chexbres took my hand gently, and pointed to the roofs, coloured tiles, Burgundian, drained of their colour now, but plainly patterned. I began to cry.

Catherine's Lonesome Cooks

1533 A.D.–1810 A.D.

France

UNTIL well into the sixteenth century French cooking developed little. Lordly kitchens aped the British in the length, breadth, and depth of their enormous meals.

Restaurants there were none, unless you could so name that redoubtable hostelry *La Tour d'Argent*, old then, older today. Now it serves *crêpes Suzette* and *canards pur-sang*, but in 1533 it was still dishing forth such favourites of the Middle Ages as dormouse pasty and a mixed pie of snake, porpoise, swan, and plum-stuffed crane.

It was that year that Fate and Pope Clement VII changed the table manners of Europe. The Holy Father, probably conscious less of the gastronomic importance of his act than of its political results, married off his niece Catherine de Medici to France's young Henry.

And Catherine took her cooks to France with her. They were probably the first great *chefs de cuisine* in that land, and galling though the fact may be to those Frenchmen who mix patriotism with their love of fine food, they were Italians every one.

Paris seemed harsh and boorish to the lonesome Florentines. They moped for the gay lightness of their own banquet-halls. There ladies and gentlemen were taught *The Fifty Courtesies of the Table* as soon as they were old enough to eat at all. Here in Paris many people still laughed jeeringly at "those Italian neatnesses called forks," and gulped down great chunks of strongly seasoned meats from their knife-ends or their greasy fingers.

Catherine's cooks shuddered, and conferred together in low voices. It was not long before they acted. Their innovation burst like a bomb over all the noble tables of Paris. Sherbets appeared! In every shape and colour, with flavours as clear and subtle as summer flowers, sherbets were set before the startled Frenchmen by the Queen's wily chefs.

Roughened tongues were made smooth, and hot throats cooled; palates, long calloused by the indiscriminate spicings of the dark centuries, slowly grew keen and sensitive.

The chefs chuckled. These Frenchmen might be able, in good time, to appreciate their Italian sauces and their tarts and soups. In good time!

By the beginning of the next century the French palate had indeed grown much more sophisticated, and some knowledge of culinary tricks was a necessary part of any worldling's education. Louis XIII, it is true, became his own cook less for pleasure than because of his inherited fear of being poisoned. His court, however, led by Richelieu's careful genius, developed a passionate interest in cookery.

It became smart to cook the main dish of a supper oneself. Kitchens, suddenly invaded by guests in elaborate costumes and dainty shoes, were the centre of attention. They bloomed with new pots, crest-emblazoned. A hundred impractical inventions of the amateur chefs for turning spits and whipping cream were discreetly ignored by harassed cooks, who worked as expertly as ever in this new shade.

Kitchen gardens, as well, grew very amusingly under the ecstatic gushings of court ladies and the silent care of gardeners, and a bouquet of lettuces and shallots was as chic as lilies.

The greatest men in all France became authors of strange poems on food and stranger recipes, which were greeted with peals of respectful laughter. Some of them, like Cardinal Richelieu's invention of a sauce made with eggs and oil which he called *maionnaise*, are as familiar a part of our diet today as almond milk and brawn were in 1600.

The next Louis, the fourteenth, and the fifteenth who was his great-grandson, were less timid than the king who feared poison. They loved good food as they loved war and fine buildings and beautiful women, with a boundless and intelligent zest.

Kitchens and kitchen gardens were just as fashionable under their energetic reigns, but it now became even more stylish to own a famous chef. Great men stooped to the most childish tricks to win a rival's cook or steward, and recipes were guarded like coronation jewels.

Diplomats and nobles were proud to give their revered family names to a new sauce or a bonbon, or share kudos with the chef who so honoured them. Soubise sauce, so subtly oniony, and Béchamel, that life-saver of *la haute cuisine,* are only two of the innumerable recipes that have come to us from the snobbish palates of the French eighteenth century.

Great chefs were its oracles, and wrote serious treatises on the arts of carving and serving, or the complexities of gastronomic etiquette. The Prince de Condé's chef, Vatel, who committed suicide when fish he had ordered for a dinner arrived too late to be served, gave some indication of his own seriousness as well as his art's, in the essay *L'Escuyer Tranchant.*

> "A carver," he dictates in one section, "should be scrupulous in his deportment; his carriage should be grave and dignified, his appearance cheerful; his eye serene, his head erect and well combed, abstaining as much as possible from sneezing, yawning, or twisting his mouth, speaking very little and directly, without being too near or too far from the table."

Oddly enough, Vatel's disciples earned their princely pay as much from those glamorous women kept by the diplomats as from the great men themselves. The pleasures of the table had become so important, by the time Madame du Barry and la Pompadour reigned over France, that no intelligent courtesan could afford to be without a fine chef. Dining eclipsed its old companion love-making, and many a beautiful *fille* was coveted more for her chef's skill with omelette than for her own artful thighs.

Waning passions, Louis the King's and Louis the fat silk-merchant's, were fanned by the invention of a thousand new recipes. It was thus, most probably, that started the extravagant fad for turkeys stuffed with truffles.

French interest in anything from the American Colonies ran high, and such dishes as Indian corn pudding and wild roasted turkey made any table smart. Prices for them ran into several figures —almost as expensive as truffles. It took a woman of unlimited income and capricious brain to combine the two whims of the moment, and serve a turkey stuffed with truffles to her admirers.

Immediately a rage for the crazy dish swept Paris. First the demi-monde and then the court devoured it, with only slight qualms at its exorbitant cost.

Then, in an epidemic frenzy, the middle classes, the little shopkeepers, the laundresses and coachmen were seized with a mad appetite for *dinde truffée*. Truffles became so scarce that they were escorted through the city with armed guards, and men ruined themselves in order to prove their social stability by serving one stuffed turkey.

Only the courtesans and the great lords could afford the dish. They soon tired of it. In a few months Paris had forgotten it, except in the bankruptcy courts.

Under Louis XVI, gastronomy continued its somewhat debauched course. Louis himself was a plain man, more interested in locks and musical timepieces than in the intricacies of sauce-making. His simplicity, though, may have had its own subtle influence on the reigning vogue of the court, for under his poor giddy queen the pastoral life was lived most artificially.

Marie Antoinette and all her ladies became, for several hours of every sunny day, milkmaids more exquisite than ever spaded dung in any truthful farmyard. Gowned in picturesque and very flattering costumes, they sat on ivory stools to milk their perfumed animals, and churned at little silver churns until their arms grew tired.

A dainty pat of butter made by a noble lady's own hands, with the print of a strawberry leaf upon its smooth fresh bottom, was a love token almost more desired than kisses, and deserved at least a folk-song in reply, or a country dance written for four partners.

Finally milk itself, so embarrassingly natural, was decided to be worthy of a true gourmet's attentions if it came from the hands of an aristocratic milkmaid. To add to the taste, so pure, so chastely sweet, the more promiscuous ladies gave special drinking-cups to their courtiers. Made of the finest porcelain from impressions taken at the height of their owners' loveliness, each cup mirrored the curves of a woman's breast, wanton, fragile, evanescent.

Napoleon broke like a bull into this china shop. But then the Revolution had already scattered the aristocrats, demoralized the servants, and wiped out the depraved etiquette of court life. The Little Corporal brought with him another world of pretentious newly-rich, sharp-witted and vulgar. Paris blazed with jewels and affectations, all awkwardly displayed.

Napoleon himself was a bad eater. He gobbled. He had little patience with the long silences and deliberate smackings of his gourmand friends, although he tried at times to imitate them.

Once, in a sorry effort to pretend that he really cared a tinker's dam about such things as eggs, he insisted that he could flip an omelette better than his lady ever could. It landed on the floor.

For days he was morose, hearing in his head the muffled snickers of Josephine and his agile courtiers. He really preferred scrambling treaties, anyway, and men, and boundary lines.

Two Birds Without a Branch

Apparently the chief purpose for stating intentions in an introduction is to have something later for contradiction and denial. Herewith I give you two recipes, for no reason at all unless it could be because I said that such a thing would never happen.

We knew a woman who sold real estate in a small beach colony. She had a face like a brick wall, and a desire, some sixty years old and still undaunted, to play ingenue rôles on Broadway. Her past was cautiously shaded.

We said we were going to live in France.

She said, "Where?"

We said, "Here, there—maybe Dijon——"

Suddenly her face was blasted. "Oh, Dijon!"

She put her hands up to her eyes and wept, and then cried fiercely: "The smell of it! The smell of Dijon gingerbread! When you are there smell it for me!"

So we did.

We smelled Dijon mustard, especially at the corner where Grey-Poupon flaunts little pots of it. We smelled Dijon cassis in the autumn, and stained our mouths with its metallic purple. But all year and everywhere we smelled the Dijon gingerbread, that *pain d'épice* which came perhaps from Asia with a tired Crusader.

Its flat strange odour, honey, cow dung, clove, something unnamable but unmistakable, blew over all the town. Into the theatre sometimes would swim a little cloud of it, or quickly through a café grey with smoke. In churches it went for one triumphant minute far above the incense.

At art school, where tiny Yencesse tried to convince the hungriest students that medal-making was a great career, and fed them secretly whether they agreed or not, altar smoke crept through from the cathedral on one side, and from the other the smell of *pain d'épice* baking in a little factory. It was a smell as thick as a flannel curtain.

This is the Dijon recipe, without, of course, the mysterious quality that makes each little gingerbread shop bake loaves quite different from any others:

Take two pounds of old black honey, the older and blacker the better, and heat it gently. When it has become a thin liquid, stir it very slowly and thoroughly into two pounds of the finest bread flour, of which about one-third is rye.

Put this hot paste away in a cold place. It must stay there for at least eight days, but in Dijon, where *pain d'épice* is best, it ripens in the cold for several months or even years!

Wait as long as you can, anyway. Then put it in a bowl and add six egg yolks, one level teaspoon of carbonate of soda, and three teaspoons of bicarbonate of soda.

Next comes the seasoning—and it is there, I think, that lies the magic. Try these the first time, before you begin your own experimenting: some pinches of anise, a teaspoon of dry mustard, and the zest of a large lemon.

Now beat it for a painfully long time. Put it in a buttered mould or pan and bake in a moderate oven for one hour—or less if you have divided this measure into more than one pan.

In Dijon little gingerbread orange slices are stuffed with marmalade and glazed, or great square loaves are sliced several times and spread with apricot jam before they are put together again. Or currants and candied fruits are baked in the loaves. Or they are left plain, to be sliced very thin and be spread with sweet butter for tea.

Whatever you do with your *pain d'épice*, you should put it away in waxed paper and an air-tight box. It will taste even better in two months or three.

The next recipe is very exciting, like finding a diamond on the garden path. For this recipe has never yet been printed nor even told, though a marshal of France begged for it, long ago.

How it comes to be here is a story in which duplicity plays a minute but important part. I prefer to forget it, and comfort myself with the surety of my friend's benign forgiveness.

I translate literally from his handwriting, a trifle shaky but still delicately ornate, in purple ink:

DIPLOMATE AU KIRSCH

A la manière de

PAPAZI

Confiseur-licencié ès . . . bec

For eight or ten people.

Cut eight small dry sponge biscuits into half-inch cubes. Into slightly smaller cubes cut a scant half-pound of fruits candied in syrup.

Soak the fruits in kirschwasser for thirty minutes. Drain them, and moisten the biscuit cubes with the same kirsch.

Whip three cups of cream which is sweet and very cold. When it is whipped, season it with powdered sugar and add a little vanilla flavour.

Put the whipped cream, the biscuits, and the candied fruits into a mould and mix them well. Cover the mould with a sheet of white paper and seal with its cover. (Be careful to butter the lip of the mould under the paper, so that salt will not make itself a part of the composition.)

Then put the mould for two hours into ice finely chopped and very salty—about two pounds of salt to ten of ice.

> The liquid Cream to Pour
> Over the Diplomate when
> It is Taken from the Mould
> Just Before Serving.

Into a double-boiler stir one full cup of milk, two egg yolks, one-fourth cup of powdered sugar, and one teaspoon of fine flour.

See that the mixture does not boil, and when it thickens take it from the stove. Then perfume it amply with kirsch.

Let it get very cold (either on the window-sill in winter or in summer in the ice chest), and pour it over the Diplomate and serve at once.

And be lifted, willy-nilly, to heavenly levels, for never was there a dessert more delicate, more fragrant, more sophisticated and naïve. In my mind I call it *L'Ingénue Libertine*, and already I regret having told its secret.

The Pale Yellow Glove

ONCE at least in the life of every human, whether he be brute or trembling daffodil, comes a moment of complete gastronomic satisfaction.

It is, I am sure, as much a matter of spirit as of body. Everything is right; nothing jars. There is a kind of harmony, with every sensation and emotion melted into one chord of well-being.

Oddly enough, it is hard for people to describe these moments. They have sunk beatifically into the past, or have been ignored or forgotten in the harsh rush of the present. Sometimes they are too keen to be bandied in conversation, too delicate to be pinioned by our insufficient mouthings.

Occasionally, in a moment of wide-flung inebriation or the taut introspection of search for things past, a person hits upon his peak of gastronomic emotion. He remembers it with shock, almost, and with a nostalgic clarity that calls tears to his inward-looking eyes.

If you can surprise him at such quick times, and make him talk, you are more than fortunate. It is as tricky a business as to watch a bird of paradise at play.

Two or three times I have been successful. Of course there were a few other times when I have almost felt so, but then I had asked. And if you ask people, they search their memories, and occasionally produce a sad shadow of the spontaneity you desire, a pale image of the vivid shaking recollection that should have sprung forth unaware.

I remember once I asked a beautiful flat-faced actress with golden hair and skin. She spoke vaguely and with a kind of embarrassment of two steaks that she had stolen from a rich woman's dog, and broiled over a driftwood fire, and shared on the Cape Cod beach with a hungry stonecutter.

Two or three people, when I've prodded them, have mumbled of apples: biting into them, feeling the cold juice flow into the mouth corners, hearing the snap of skin and pulp.

But the spontaneous revelations are rare. They must, from what I have discovered, be inspired by wine or high emotional pressure. They are thus doubly poignant.

(i) Miss Lyse was an English-teacher in a middle-sized town in Bavaria. She had been one ever since her militantly British mother had brought here there, some sixty years before. She would be one until she died, helped always and in spite of her dwindling powers of instruction by the impatiently thoughtful families whose parents and grandparents had recited the verb TO BE at her virginal knee.

It was easy to see that she had once been very lovely. Even now her small dark-eyed head rose above its lumpy old body like the dream of a swan, or a piece of Chinese crystal.

It was hard to see why she had not long since married some member of the aristocratic families with whom she lived; hard, that is, until you heard her describe—so lovingly, too—her genteel Tartar of a mother, who on her death-bed had made Lyse swear never, *never* to forget her English accent. And now, with this old maid who for more than half a century had spent all her days with the fine flower of Germany, her soft flat voice was as British as a currant bun; her intonation so carefully preserved marked her anywhere as a "Miss," never a *Fräulein,* and her German was half English, her English very German.

She was garrulous, with the embarrassingly naïve language of an aged person who has spent all her life explaining things simply to children who might have listened better had the explanations been complex.

She talked with a vivacity which had long since ceased to be affected, and was now as much a part of her as her jet brooch of the young Queen Victoria, or her lace fichu that had been admired (on another's shoulder) by Franz Joseph.

"Once, my dears," she told us on a chill October afternoon when even shawls laid along the window-ledges could not keep cold drafts from shushing into her high attic room, "once I stood so close to the great Sadi Carnot that to touch him I would have been able! Yes, then I was that near!

"That was the summer after we went to Garmisch, to the *Schloss* of my little pupils—you remember?"

She peered merrily at us, and we nodded recognition to a season dead some forty years before we were conceived. We poured another glass of sherry for her, the sherry we had brought to warm her bones while we were far from her and Bavaria.

(And here it is perhaps significant to say that all old pupils treated Miss Lyse thus, feeling a kind of guilty neglect if they did not often go to her stuffy pleasant garret with wine, a cold chicken, even a pat of sweet butter. I am sure that we kept her alive for years in this compulsive, desultory way——)

"Yes, that was *such* a nice summer! The trees in full bloom early were, and everybody said that *never* had there been so many forest flowers. I remember the *Graf* himself said that to me, one morning on the stairs!"

She coloured delicately, and raised her young dark eyes above the rim of her glass. "I used to wear flowers in my hair—it was black then—except at dinner, of course, when I was invited down to dine with the family if they needed an extra one at table.

"But there was one thing about that summer—when was it, in 'sixty-eight?" She looked sharply at our blank faces, as if she had a good mind to rap our knuckles for inattention, and then laughed. "What does it matter? It was several years ago, yes? A beautiful summer.

"My dear blessed mother was with me, in the village near the *Schloss*—I had not been long away from England, and she watched over me—and one day, one day we had a picnic, a real English tea in the forest! It was lovely!

"My mother, a sweet young Russian girl who taught also at the *Schloss*, and——"

Suddenly she put down her glass, giggled, and peeked naughtily at us between her knobby, loose-skinned fingers.

"Now you must never tell, never!" She looked stern for a second, and then giggled again. "It was very daring, but my dear mother was there and Tanya, and—three—young—gentlemen—from—the *Schloss*!

"*Yes*, my dears! We all went on the picnic, Tanya and the three young gentlemen (*so* handsome were they), and myself, and of course my dear good mamma to see that everything was proper.

"Well," and she settled herself back in her chair as we filled her glass again, "we went far into the woods, with a servant to carry the tea-basket. We came to a stream, such a small sweet brooklet was it, with flowers and watercress on its borders.

"My mother sat down, and whilst the servant built a little blaze yet, she got out her silver teapot, which had gone to India twelve times with her. It was a pretty teapot.

"We gathered watercress. One of the young gentlemen—what *was* his name, now?—got his gloves quite wet. They were pale yellow gloves, of the thinnest kid, and from München, too.

"Then my dear mamma boiled water from the little brook, the most sparkling water I have ever seen, and when it just began to bubble she poured it over the tea, and then we drank. And, my dears, I never, *never* have such tea tasted!"

Miss Lyse looked at us almost sombrely. We felt very young and serious as we watched her raise her glass slowly to her lips and then set it down again.

"No, it was tea like no tea before—or since. I have often boiled the water from brooklets, and poured it over the same brand of tea, *and* in my dear mother's silver teapot that to India twelve times went. But that tea, that summer afternoon near Garmisch, with dear mamma and Tanya and the three young gentlemen—and the little flowers, and I remember the poor yellow gloves——"

Miss Lyse was silent. She sipped slowly, and her eyes looked far back, like the picture of Albrecht Dürer's mother.

"Thank God in heaven," she concluded, emphatically, "that my poor departed mother watched over me, or I should not be where I am! That tea, so clear, so piquant like fine *Liebfraumilch*——"

(ii) Occasionally I hear from Al a dreamy, half-coherent reference to one day when he went to a small restaurant in Paris, and sat alone before an iced silver bowl of wood strawberries, spooning them up all coated with the fine effervescence of a bottle of champagne.

That must have been a good day, like the far September Wednesday in 1819 when John Keats wrote to his friend:

> "Talking of Pleasure, this moment I was writing with one hand, and with the other holding to my Mouth a Nectarine— good God how fine. It went down soft pulpy, slushy, oozy

—all its delicious embonpoint melted down my throat like a large beatified Strawberry. I shall certainly breed."

(iii) Sometimes it is hard to say, even from remembrance, just what magic chord has sounded for you with the right blending of time, space, and the physical sensation of eating. On a hot day it is easiest to think back to such things as silver-green mint juleps, or the smooth golden taste of cold papaya on a freighter near Guatemala, or crisp lettuce anywhere.

On a cold day such things as hot baked potatoes, all sprinkled over with fresh-ground pepper and sweet butter, or creamy tomato soup with a faint smell of cinnamon to it, or rare steaming beef, pink and succulent: these are the things that flow first into our remembrance on cold days.

There is one time, though, one souvenir of eating, that I can keep with impunity throughout all seasonal changes. Perhaps I remember it oftener in winter, but that does not affect its poignancy.

When I belonged to the Alpine Club of the Côte d'Or, I felt rather lost. The robust elderly members were more than courteous to me; the walks were energetic but agreeable; the carefully planned feasts at little village inns were masterpieces, even though each day's march was so routed that the most difficult part of it came after the many courses and as many wines of the dinner.

Still, I felt rather lonesome, "foreign," until one bitter February Sunday when we stood panting on a hill near Les Laumes-Alésia. The earth was hard as granite beneath me, and air drawn into my tired lungs felt like heavy fire before it thawed. I broke a twig clumsily between my mittened fingers.

"Here!" a voice said, roughly. I looked with surprise at the old general, who stood, shaggy and immense, beside me. He had never done more than bow to me, and listen now and then with a face of stony suffering to my accent, which always grew ten times as thick when he was near. What did he want now?

"Here! Try some of this, young lady!" And he held out a piece of chocolate, pale brown with cold. I smiled and took it, resolving to say as little as possible.

He cleared his throat grumpily and shifted his eyes to the far thunderous horizon.

In my mouth the chocolate broke at first like gravel into many separate, disagreeable bits. I began to wonder if I could swallow them. Then they grew soft, and melted voluptuously into a warm stream down my throat.

The little doctor came bustling up, his proudly displayed alpenstock tucked under one short arm.

"Here! Wait, wait!" he cried. "Never eat chocolate without bread, young lady! Very bad for the interior, very bad. My General, you are remiss!"

The soldier peered down at him like a horse looking at a cheeky little dog, and then rumbled, "Give us some, then, old fellow. Trade two pieces (and big ones, mind) for some of our chocolate?"

And in two minutes my mouth was full of fresh bread, and melting chocolate, and as we sat gingerly, the three of us, on the frozen hill, looking down into the valley where Vercingetorix had fought so splendidly, we peered shyly and silently at each other and smiled and chewed at one of the most satisfying things I have ever eaten. I thought vaguely of the metamorphosis of wine and bread——

The Brothers

ONCE there were two brothers. They were twins, but their nine closed months were all they had in common.

One brother, the elder by some minutes, was a big fellow, red-faced and hairy. He spent all his days afield and swiftly grew into a great hunter, and at night he made into savoury stews the day's killing. His father loved the stews and his elder son who made them.

The younger brother was his mother's love. In him she admired her own sly, clever ways. He stayed by her side and learned from her to make lentil pottage which he could sell each day, and profitably, to the workers.

One day the hunting was very bad, and the sun too hot. Then chill came suddenly into the darkening air, and the older brother, still far afield and very tired, turned empty-handed homeward. No fine stew tonight to cheer him and to warm his old man's innards! Afterwards no rest by the fire for the two of them! He sighed and longed to be home, full and warm.

The younger brother sat by a great pot of his steaming soup, with hard sour bread in a pile beside him. The day was almost over, with no more labourers to buy food from him. But he sat on, quiet and sure, waiting for what he knew must happen sometime, and perhaps today.

Suddenly his toes curled under him with scorn and fear, for he saw his elder brother. The great lazy spendthrift lout! He smiled and waited.

And you know what happened. Jacob was the little crafty fellow who sold lentil soup, and Esau was the hungry man who gave his birthright for a bowl of it. And Jacob's mother Rebekah was, like many women, a good cook and a good teacher of cookery for one purpose or another, but never for pleasure. She taught her dear son to be the father of all (almost all) *restaurateurs*.

Her other son she never understood, nor his father Isaac neither, for they would spend all day catching a deer, simply that they might cook it and eat it and then lie by the fire and talk about it. They may have been the first gastronomers.

Set-piece for a Fishing Party

1810 A.D.–1900 A.D.

France

THE twentieth century may yet be remembered as one of monstrous mass-feeding. Certainly the nineteenth will never be forgotten for its great contribution to gastronomy—the restaurants.

After the Revolution, Paris found itself practically kitchenless. Scullions had fled, or fought for their new estate; great chefs had scuttled to safety with their masters; most important, the money that had bought rare wines and strange exotic dishes was gone now from the hands that had known so well how to spend it.

Paris recovered quickly enough. Her citizens, uncomfortably Republican and somewhat more affluent than before, cast about restlessly for a new, a significant diversion.

It was not hard to find. Word was noised abroad that in the cellar of Number So-and-so, Rue Such-and-such, the ex-chef, Jean Durand, was cooking again.

What! Durand, the inventor of *petits pois aux noisettes grillées*, the great Durand who for twenty years had made famous the table of the ex-Marquise Sainte-Nitouche, ex-mistress of the even more ex-Duke Volte-face? But certainly not that Durand who once corrected Citizeness Marie Antoinette for adding mustard to a salad dressing before she had put in the salt? Impossible!

But—but can anyone go to Number So-and-so, Rue Such-and-such? Hah! Then I, Jacques Maillot, and I, Pierre Doudet, shall order the ex-chef of the ex-marquise to prepare a good dinner. It is expensive? Pouf! It is certainly worth the pleasure of eating what the damned aristos used to!

Thus Parisian restaurants blossomed from a few dark corners. Their trembling chefs, not long out of hiding, grew confident—and rich. They gathered round them enough of the old guard of pastry cooks, roasters, and *sommeliers* to keep things moving, and soon had more apprentices than they needed. Their furtive restaurants moved into fine quarters, and quickly became those boulevard palaces of fat gourmets, twinkling mirrors, pink plush, and belles, that Zola and Maupassant knew so well for us.

Fine food, once the privilege of the moneyed aristocracy, was now at the summons of any man with enough silver and manners to go to a good restaurant.

As the century rolled forward, and Jacques and Pierre flourished, the palaces grew more glittering, and their patrons more extravagant and gouty. But new blood, vulgar as it could be at times, brought freshness and vigour to the somewhat depleted art of eating. Vim and zest chased out the satiety which had become almost synonymous with pleasure under the several Louis. People ate enormously, with a lusty bourgeois delight born of strong constitutions and palates untouched by preciosity.

The fine art of eating was not wholly a thing of the stomach, however. Great minds considered it. As early as the 1820's, the learned Doctor Villermet presented a short but important paper to the Academy of Science. In it he proved conclusively that gourmands live longest and in the best health!

Nor is only their physical state influenced by gastronomy. Even the modern critic, in discusing that *bon vivant* Dumas, observes that "his marked intellectual superiority over his son may be readily attributed to his greater knowledge of dining." *Le Grand Diction-naire de Cuisine* helps prove it.

Indeed, the obsession for fine eating that swept over Europe, and especially France, during the nineteenth century, had a strange and wonderful influence on the literature of that world.

Grimod de la Reynière, who wrote *Le Manuel des Amphitryons* in 1808, and edited the great *Almanach des Gourmands*; Carême, who cooked for the princes of six countries and Baron Rothschild, and wrote books on everything from the maker of picturesque pastry to the history of ancient kitchens; Alexandre Dumas—all these skilled artists and many another lived then in the respect and admiration which were their due.

Strangely enough, the greatest of them was probably the least known, was in fact scoffed at by the Paris exquisites as a rough-mannered provincial. Brillat-Savarin lived quietly and very pleasantly, ate with a refined and prejudiced palate, thought for many years, and a few months before his death in 1828 published *La Physiologie du Goût*.

This work, a masterpiece of clarity and charm in any subject, is still without peer among books on eating. It is difficult to write about physical pleasures without being either coarse or over-delicate, vaguely sentimental or dry and scientific. *The Physiology of Taste* is none of these. It is as near perfection as we yet know it, and a constant wonder. The temptation to quote from its clear, pungent prose is hard to resist. Infinitely better, however, is the companionship of the book itself, for there is no superfluous word in it, no dull page.

While Brillat-Savarin finished his unobtrusive days in Paris and Belley, speculating with deliberate wisdom on the problems of transcendental gastronomy, Europe went mad over the art of dining.

Never have Continental restaurants been so crowded, unless perhaps it was during the First World War. The atmosphere differed, however, almost as much as the costumes.

In 1914-1918 women wore tight sheaths of glittering cloth over their slender bodies, and helped all the sad young men to be gay and gather rosebuds. In the nineteenth century women were fuller, softer, smoother. They dined opulently at all the best tables of every good restaurant in Paris, and knew to perfection the whims and dislikes of their fastidious gentlemen.

Foyot's, the *Café de Paris*, the *Brasserie Universelle*—there were a hundred temples of fine food, some chic for a moment, some apparently eternal in their devotion to *la gourmandise*.

Their chefs, seldom as coveted by princes as the great Carême, rejoiced nevertheless in as respectfully adoring a public as any royal offspring.

Their smallest triumphs were town gossip before the last bite was swallowed, and their most insignificant utterances were lapped up by such hungry brains as Dumas' and Maupassant's, to appear later in solemn or witty conversation.

It was toward the end of the First Empire that Brillat-Savarin and Carême, by persuasive argument, substituted the "made dish" for masses of roast meat, piled high on a platter and held clumsily erect by skewers. That modern gourmet, Paul Reboux (whose witty essay on gastronomy in a reputable encyclopædia is, tactlessly enough, flanked by a large and greyly horrible photograph of a gastric ulcer!), remarks that "these enormous, barbaric accumulations of food were yet another Bastille which the French Revolution overthrew." And for a few years, at least, they gave the Parisians almost as much to think about.

Meats, fruits, vegetables, wines, were combined and cooked and served in a thousand new ways. Flavours and aromas never dreamed of ran and rose from the exciting dishes. Gradually their appearance grew more rigidly ornate, and their construction more difficult. Finally the most complicated of these "made dishes" were classed by themselves, and *pièces montées* came into being.

Pièces montées were to Frenchmen of the last century what modern-art exhibits and automobile shows and fan dances are to John Doe today. Public contests were held, schools were founded to teach worthy chefs how to construct the sacred tricks, great artists drew designs, and solemn tomes were written on the art.

The Romans had pies which spilled out dancing dwarfs, or let fly up a flock of blackbirds and white doves. Later, in England, ponderous subtleties set all the banqueters guessing on full stomachs. It was in France, though, the brilliant vital France of the last century, that these inventions reached their peak of artistry and popularity.

Every good restaurant had its special department from which a *pièce montée* could be commanded for any kind of festivity, christening party or wake. If the prices were too high, there was the neighbourhood bakeshop, where even the apprentice could turn out a passable sugar dove rising from a nest of mocha and pistachio cream.

Of all the real artists of the set-piece, Carême was certainly the greatest. He had an uncanny ability to use pastry and sugar, and a mighty respect for them both. In one of his books he announces quite seriously:

"The Fine Arts are five in number: Painting, Music, Sculpture, Poetry, and Architecture—wherof the principal branch is confectionery."

As the vogue for set-pieces increased, he combined this reverential talent with all his others to produce amazing structures, dream-like, fantastic. His disciples exaggerated his strange juxtapositions and his mixtures of irony and beauty. Finally, as with every school of art headed by one man, cheap imitators crept after him with their coarsening touch, and by the end of the century set-pieces had become almost ridiculous, a synonym for the pretentious vulgarity of new-rich entertainment.

It is in Carême's own book on the subject, *Le Pâtissier Pittoresque,* or in the several other volumes of this period, that we must look to see *pièces montées* at their best. There countless engravings, as well as the restrained rhetoric of the prose, make very clear the incredible delicacy and variety of these strange dishes which cost thousands of francs and were seldom eaten.

One little engraving is very pleasant to remember. It shows a *pièce* which stands probably four or five feet high. A froth of green foliage forms its base—leaves of mashed potato as delicate as ever grew from pastry tube. From that a Doric column, garlanded with pale full-blown flowers of lobster meat, diminishes twice.

At the top, on a pedestal edged with little shells and shrimpy rosebuds, is a pool of the clearest blue-green sugar, crystallized. And from it, with only the ankles of his tail held in the crystal, curves a fresh plump fish, every scale gleaming, his eyes popping with satiric amusement, and a beautiful umbrella of spun sugar held over his head by one sturdy fin!

Above the engraving runs the legend, in that somewhat smudgy printing of the 1830's: *A Culinary Fantasy—the Cautious Carp.*

On Dining Alone

LUCULLUS, the Roman host whose dinners are still talked about for their elaborate menus and their fabulous cost, grew tired one day of dining with other men.

He ordered a meal for one person. When it was served to him, he was conscious of a certain slackness: the wine was perhaps a shade too cold, and the sauce for the carp, which certainly was less succulent than usual, lacked that tang for which his chef was justly famed.

Lucullus frowned and summoned the major-domo.

"Perhaps, perhaps," that official agreed, with a flood of respectful salutations. "We thought that there was no need to prepare a fine banquet for my lord alone——"

"It is precisely when I am alone," the great gourmet answered, icily, "that you require to pay special attention to the dinner. At such times, you must remember, Lucullus dines with Lucullus."

At such times few men realize that they are dining with themselves. In fact, they try to forget that rather frightening truth. They read the newspaper or turn on the radio if they are at home. More often they flee from themselves to friend-filled clubs, or to the noisiest nearest restaurant, where other lone humans eat crowded together in a hungry, ugly mob and take digestive pills between their hurried courses.

It is a pity. An occasional meal with himself is very good for Mr. Doe. It gives him time to look about him; quiet in which to savour his present mouthful; opportunity to broil his steak a new way or try again those dishes his wife hates.

He need not take it too seriously, however. Old Thomas Walker, The Original, whose preoccupation with the fine points of dining approached pomposity at times, declared himself thus on the problem:

96

"When dining alone is necessary, the mind should be disposed to cheerfulness by a previous interval of relaxation from whatever has seriously occupied the attention, and by directing it to some agreeable object."

The "interval of relaxation" might well be used for broiling a tender filet, although I doubt if Mr. Walker meant just that; and there could be no more "agreeable object" toward which to direct attention than a fine little bottle of red wine from the Côte d'Or. There with a leaf or two of salad and some crusty sour-dough bread, Lucullus has a meal fit even for Lucullus.

An Englishman, however, and an earl at that, once mapped out a slightly more complicated menu.

"A good soup," he said, "a small turbot, a neck of venison, ducklings with green peas or chicken with asparagus, and an apricot tart—it is a dinner for an emperor."

Perhaps he was right. Louis XIV of France, who always dined alone at one o'clock, ate several soups, three solid courses, and then a dessert.

He also ate only from a square table, and was served by nobles of his court, both facts probably influencing his digestion to a certain extent. (Many people enjoy good food only to the sound of soft music, or in a room with black walls. My mother cannot swallow if a cat is near her. Hunger, I observe, is not a part of these equations.)

I have known two people who understood, and probably without one thought about it, why Lucullus dined with Lucullus. One was an old man, the other a girl sixteen and usually inarticulate.

Biddy was tall and quiet, with magnificent brown eyes and the stiff awkwardness of a new-hatched butterfly. She lived in a kind of doze, seemingly placid, lethargic, docilely stubborn.

One day she took her week's allowance and moved tranquilly and relentlessly towards the tram, muttering of errands and birthdays and such. To her mother's puzzled questions she smiled reassurance, vague but firm.

Late that afternoon she came back.

She brought no birthday presents nor evidences of errands done, but one rather spotted paper bag, from which she drew a long brown cut of *apfelstrudel* for her mother. She was vaguer than usual, but seemed to be unharmed—and the *strudel* was delicious.

Later I saw Biddy. We were talking of restaurants. I saw her eyes flash suddenly when I mentioned Spring Street in Los Angeles, where, one man said, the best and worst food in seven states can be found in less than as many blocks.

"I hear you went to town last Saturday," I said, feeling like Sherlock Holmes and Tom the Peeper. "What did you do?"

Biddy looked quickly at me, and then smiled rather sheepishly.

"Spring Street, eh? Where did you go?"

"Well—I went to *Katie Levey's*. And why haven't you told me how good it is? And the people!"

"Lots of Austrian Jews, I suppose?"

"Naturally, in a kosher restaurant run by a Viennese! Of course," she added, carelessly, "Jews are the best indication of good food in a place."

I nodded recognition to one of her mother's favourite remarks, and asked, "But what did you do from eleven to three? You can't eat lunch for four hours."

Biddy answered me somewhat scornfully: "I ate breakfast, not lunch, and certainly I ate it for four hours: they understand things like that in a decent restaurant. I drank coffee, with lots of hot milk in it, and ate Viennese tarts and—and things."

"Things meaning salami and sweet pickles?"

"Mhm."

She looked dreamily past me. I said nothing, and finally she went on: "I sat by the cake counter and watched people in the mirror. They were so queer—so *pleasant* at eleven when everybody else in town was rushing around—and especially down there on Spring. And they spoke every language and dipped their tarts in their coffee-glasses.

"Yes," Biddy exclaimed, "my coffee was in a glass! It was wonderful!"

Her face was vivid, and in her dark eyes was a quiet awareness I had never seen before. She concluded, almost fiercely: "Four hours I sat there, watching them dip their bread in coffee-glasses, and thinking. And I'll do it again! It was—it was just what I needed."

Biddy breakfasted with Biddy, and saw in a mirror clearly, for the first of many times.

The other one who understood was an old man. I never knew who he was. Whenever we went to *Victor Hugo's* he was there, at a quiet corner table. He was dressed carefully in rather old-fashioned dinner clothes, with his feet in tiny twinkling pumps, like a doll's.

He ate little, and drank a half-bottle of wine with his meat. For dessert he went through a never-varying formula with the intensity and detachment of a high priest.

An avocado was brought to him, cradled in a napkin. He felt of it delicately, smelled it, usually nodded yes. It was cut in two with a silver knife. Then he himself detached the stone-skin from each half, placed one part of the fruit gently on a large plate before him, and sent the other back to the kitchen.

Powdered sugar was brought, and the old man pressed it into the hollow of the fruit. He spent some time over this, making it firm and even.

Next the *sommelier* appeared with a bear-shaped bottle of clear Russian *kümmel*. He poured a generous liqueur-glass of it, waited for the old man's sniff of approval, and went away.

Drop by drop the *kümmel* disappeared into the moon of white sugar, very slowly, very patiently. Very delicately it was stirred and pressed down and stirred again.

Finally the old man ate a small spoonful of the smooth green fruit-flesh, then another. Sometimes he stopped, sometimes he finished it. Then he drank a mouthful of coffee and left.

I have not yet tested his strange dish. I have never been able to construct its flavours for my mind's palate with any clearness. But very clear in my memory is the expression on the old man's face. He was happy as Biddy was happy with her coffee in a glass and her mirror. He was at peace, and aware—aware that Lucullus dined with Lucullus for a reason.

Sing of Dinner in a Dish

More than six per cent of the inmates of San Quentin give their previous occupation as cook (labourers form the largest group and cooks the second largest); but male cooks compose less than two-tenths of one per cent of the total U. S. population, according to the 1930 census.

I would like to know to what type of crime cooks are peculiarly given. I have heard it said by men who have been much up and down the world that cooks as a class are irascible men, with the instincts of dictators. It is an interesting speculation: does the profession attract men of a certain character, or are nerves and tempers shattered by the life they lead? Or does the emotional effect result from a physical deterioration of stomach and liver through too much tasting of their own cooking?

Just what, in brief, is the moral hazard involved in being a cook?

—*We Who Are About To Die*, DAVID LAMSON

"ALWAYS have a Chinese cook," said the woman who had followed her sailor seven times round the globe, and settled at last inside the Golden Gate. "Yes, always have a Chinese cook—and never go into the kitchen!"

Is this foul slander, or the cool tongue of wisdom? When on the bottom of a casserole doth grimed grease hiss, is ignorance bliss? Probably.

Surely I have eaten many a tart that felt the floor before it felt my plate, and more than a hundred bowls of soup whose temperature was tested, consciously or not, by a fat thumb. I have even pushed dead flies to one side of an omelette or ragoût, and eaten to the last bite undaunted. I have not really minded, inside of me, because what I ate was good, and I do not think that good food can come from a bad kitchen.

It can come from a cluttered kitchen piled with used dishes, redolent with the escaped smells of garlic, vanilla, and wine-vinegar, a kitchen steamy and full of rattle and clash.

Madame Rigagnier's is like that—a dark cabinet not nine feet square, its walls banked with copper pots and pans, and a pump for water outside the door. And from that little hole, which would make an American shudder with disgust, she turns out daily two of the finest meals I've yet eaten.

Or good food can come from a gigantic factory of fine dishes, such as Arnold Bennett describes so well in a book he wrote about grand hotels.

But good food can never come from a bad kitchen. A bad kitchen is what it is for two reasons: either nobody cares whether it produces decent victuals, or it is filthy. And if it is filthy, it is, says Webster, defiled with filth; foul; impure; obscene; unclean; squalid, and above all nasty.

I know one like that. It is the back side of a kosher restaurant. In the window are pans of *strudel* and *auf-lauf* and rice *kugel*, which look good. Furthermore, the prices are low and the tables are crowded—favourable signs, surely. Perhaps this is one of those rare little places that lurk in big towns like pearls in the sea.

We go in. There is a great clatter. Nobody notices us. All the tables are occupied, and we push toward the end of the long room. The last table is freed by two silent men, and a large waitress slaps at it with a cloth. She looks at us dully with monkey eyes, and hurries away.

We slide our legs under the slimy table-top. A pandemonium of cries and crashes swells in my ears whenever a waitress goes through the swinging doors beside me. I see Al, who faces it, peering with a strange expression, which he masks politely as I look at him.

My purse slips to the floor, and when I touch it again it is stuck all over one side with crumbs and nastiness.

I forget what we order. Whatever it is, we do not eat it. By now I too have peered through the swinging door, and I too have stiffened my face into politeness. We sit silently, watching with every pore, for this is a unique (Please God, unique!) experience, and we shall miss none of it by maiden squeamishness.

The kitchen is small and overcrowded and hot, as is Madame Rigagnier's—and our own. There the comparison ends.

The floor, slick and black, is uneven where dishtowels and utensils have been half-swallowed in its eternal ooze. Water from the grease-ridged sink runs over it in iridescent trickles, and crusts of bread and slippery wilted lettuce-scraps lie everywhere, never too trodden for the rats of dawn.

Up from the floor and in and down from the foul walls and ceiling seeps a smell more evil and obscene than Mr. Webster dreamed of. It is acrid and heavy, a slippery, dark grey smell, like the piled-up excrement of a million ducks.

Waitresses go in and out with the look of women who have been so nauseated for so long that it can never matter any more. Fortunately, we do not see the faces of the two cooks.

They are men, evidently, wearing old tennis shoes, trousers, oily grey underwear, and bandannas knotted around their heads.

They yell at each other and at the waitresses, and the waitresses yell frantically back at them, and nobody ever yells at the strange brown man who walks among them.

He carries trays of soiled dishes, sometimes on his head, and sometimes not, from the front of the restaurant to the kitchen. He might be a Filipino, but more probably he is a last Hawaiian or Tahitian. He looks like the pictures we see of those fading races of the world.

His body is good, with no bones holding it up, but not soft, either, and his hair is fine and purple above his dark face.

He moves like a wave, steadily and impersonally. Other people are shoved and pushed, but as he walks through the restaurant, balancing his body easily under the tray, he is never touched.

There is no sign that he sees or hears. His face is expressionless and his eyes are contracted and dull. He seldom moves them, and when they light on my face he does not see me, as I do not see one telephone pole among all the other poles from a train window.

He is full of drugs, or hypnotized; he is mad; he is transcendental, *taboo*.

We begin to feel uneasy, and go away, turning as we pass the street window for one more puzzled look at the false *apfelstrudel* lying there.

The air tastes like mead in our throats.

And the cleanest kitchen? That was at Beaune, in Burgundy, in the *Hospice* where the old and the poor and the fatherless have for centuries been fed by the sale of some of the finest wines of the Côte d'Or.

A black Virgin looks down upon the blue-curtained beds of the Convalescent Hall; exquisite faience jars hold medicines in the pharmacy; and in the kitchen the biggest, brightest copper kettles anywhere glow like moons on the dim walls.

That great room is warm and pungent in winter, and in summer cool and sweet as a well. It is spacious. Cupboards as big as pantries, and tables like ballroom floors, are easy in it. Ranges stretch for yards, with innumerable rounds for pots to rest on, and across the yawning hearths are spits sturdy for whole oxen and slender for the lark.

It smells good. It smells pure and kindly, like linen bleaching on a highland meadow. Herbs hang in bunches near the ceiling, and fume from a simmering pot or wooden chopping-bowl. Clean cloths dry by a stove, and hang, cheerily checkered, from shelf and window ledge. Above all, there is the smell of cleanliness. The stone floors, the walls and shelves and all the wood, the kettles and the pokers and the smallest pewter spoon, are clean with the devout scourings of not one century, but five.

That is indeed a good kitchen, in the *Hospice*. Simple food comes from it, gruel and stews for the very young, the weak, and the old, all good because of the kitchen.

It is a pleasant pastime to think of what might be a good kitchen for yourself. Just now it is very smart, too. Women's magazines flash with brilliant colour-photos of dream-like rooms where glass walls and metal sinks compete with electric dishwashers and mixers of cake for the fascinated reader's favour.

Washable chintz curtains wave in the controlled breeze. Ivy grows around the telephone table, where an easy-chair, a radio, and an alarmingly narrow cook-book shelf promise relaxation to the American *hausfrau*.

For myself, I should like a kitchen with some of these magic things, but none of the conscious design, the June-bride's-first-little-home look about it.

When I think of all the kitchens I have seen, there is not one I would willingly accept unchanged. Some are cool in summer, but too big, or snug for winter but inconveniently small. Almost all are cluttered with things that I would never need to use, or are too dark or too airless.

The kitchen in the Ducal Palace in Dijon was certainly sensible, built as it was like one great oven, with its whole roof the dwindling chimney for eight fires, its four sides and ample floor the interior of a stove capable of satisfying the hunger of even such great trencher-men as the old Burgundians.

For me, however, such stretched proportions would have to be carved down to a ridiculous smallness, and the picture of myself simmering alongside my five-pound roast of beef in a miniature ducal kitchen is almost insulting to the good mediæval architect who built for Philip the Hardy in the fourteenth century.

The first kitchen I ever had of my own was above a cake shop in the working-quarter of a small French city. It was perhaps five feet long, and certainly not more than three feet wide.

Its floor of uneven baked tiles was scoured to a mellow pinkness. There were two weak shelves, slanting toward the floor. A two-burner gas plate on a tottering wooden table was the stove. To stand at it I had to keep the door open into the other room. That was all right: the door had been stuck open for several decades.

I had four plates, four goblets, and some three or four or five pans and casseroles.

But I made very good things to eat in that kitchen, and I have always felt that this was partly so because one end of it, from side to side and from ceiling almost to floor, was a window.

It was a sparkling window of many-paned glass, a window cur-tained briefly with two silly little dabs of cheap net, a window split down the middle ready to fling open as wide as those windows can be flung, wider really than any others.

It looked over tree-tops into the square where gibbets and then a guillotine once stood, where wandering circus families set up their gas-flares for a night or two by the busy fountain and the *pissoir*, where people moved and talked incessantly above the high wail of a café phonograph playing ten thousand times the record of Josephine Baker's *"J'ai Deux Amours."*

All the noises flowed in and out the window of the tiny kitchen, gay and sombre and mysterious and always real, and I may be too sentimental in thinking that they helped me cook some good dishes —but I doubt it.

There is a Basque kitchen I once heard of that has very pleasant things about it, too. One wall of the stone-built room is packed with straw, all of it, solidly. Its surface is clipped to a neat smoothness. Then, the first cold night of autumn, the straw wall is lit from the bottom, and so cleverly has it been laid that the whole room blazes with a slow steady warmth until late spring comes. Ashes sift down all winter to the hot bed on the floor, where three-legged gipsy pots send out the heady odours of Basque stews; and no lamps are ever needed.

Of course this kitchen, obviously, is meant for long hard winters, and how intelligent and beautiful an arrangement it is! For me— no, it would not be practical. I should like to spend a time in it, though. The air would be strong, no doubt, but warm and hearty on a cold night.

The problem of an ideal kitchen grows more complex as I ponder on it. There are many small things I am sure about: no shelf-papers; no sharp edges or protruding hooks or wires; no ruffled curtains; and no cheap-coloured stove, mauve or green or opalescent like a modern toilet seat.

Instead of these things I would have smooth shelves of some material like ebony or structural glass, shelves open or protected by sliding transparent doors. I would have curved and rounded edges, even to the floor, for the sake of cleanliness, and because I hate the decayed colours of a bruise.

Instead of curtains I would have Venetian blinds, of four different colours for the seasons of the year. They would be, somehow, on the outside of the glass.

And the stove would be black, with copper and earthenware utensils to put on it. It would be a wood stove, or perhaps (of this I am doubtful, unless I am the charwoman and janitor as well as the cook) electrical with place for a charcoal grill.

There are other things, too, that would be very pleasant, like a little side-kitchen in which to make the ices and salads and tarts that should not be near the heat and high flavour of roasting meats, and racks let down from the ceiling for the pots and skillets to lie on, and a radio or an automatic phonograph to make dull tasks agreeable. I would want the sinks and the tabletops made to my own height, too, and not for some mythical short-legged cook.

All these, though, are relatively unimportant. There are only three things I need, to make my kitchen a pleasant one as long as it is clean.

First, I need space enough to get a good simple meal for six people. More of either would be wasteful as well as dangerously dull.

Then, I need a window or two, for clear air and a sight of things growing.

Most of all I need to be let alone. I need peace.

From there—from there, on the sill of my wide window, the plan is yours. It will include an herb-bed surely, and a brick courtyard for summer suppers. And an apple orchard perhaps? A far sea view?

Shell-shock and Richard the Third

1900 A.D. — —

Europe and America

WHEN humans are not especially hungry they love to play tricks with their palates. That was why Nicodemus, king of Babylon, chuckled and smacked his lips over his chef's dish of anchovies, which, it was disclosed, were really turnips disguised most artfully with oil and spice and poppy seeds.

For the same reason Petronius Arbiter's plump citizen could afford to boast:

> "Only command him, and my cook will make you a fish out of the pig's chitterlings, a wood-pigeon out of the lard, a turtle-dove out of the gammox, and a hen out of the shoulder!"

But all that is for play. It is different when men are hungry. Then in Alaskan snowfields they simmer old shoes for soup, and when they eat it they call it soup made from shoes, quite simply. Or, in Paris during the siege of the 1870's, scrambled rats and potted poodle-dog meat were delicacies candidly desired by the most fastidious of gourmets.

During the First World War, there were not even rats enough, in some parts of those countries which the more optimistic of modern historians call defeated. Their natives ate wood pulp in their cereals and chocolate, nut shells in their coffee, and Fuller's earth (when they were lucky) in their sugar. They were grateful, and when the war ended they were still very hungry, with distended stomachs and dulled palates.

All over Europe gastronomy lay in a kind of coma, shell-shocked.

The great chefs of *avant-guerre* were dead, or senile, or seemingly apathetic. The young apprentices, those boys who had learned so painstakingly how to glaze and stir and test in famous kitchens, lay in the earth now, or wandered restlessly.

By the 1920's, things had revived to some extent, especially in Paris. Hordes of refugees had flocked there, bringing strange tantalizing dishes from their own countries.

Americans, too, chased from their land by a political experiment which for a time reduced good native gastronomy to an equation of raw alcohol and five-cent candybars, marched like an innocent and enthusiastic army on Parisian restaurants.

Skullduggery was inevitable. Much bad food, much impure wine, was swallowed in honourable surroundings. Several of the old guard of mastercooks, recovered now from their apathy, retreated in disgust to England or Long Island. A few worked doggedly and with increasing affluence in Paris and Berlin and Vienna and Rome.

Gastronomy seemed normal again, as normal as the rest of the arts. Painting, it is true, was undergoing a series of -isms reminiscent of the whims of a pregnant woman. Architecture tiptoed gingerly toward steel-and-glass construction, and sculptors and writers used tin cans, matches, and dream sequences with symbolic seriousness.

This same symbolism increased in importance gastronomically. Academicians as well as dieticians pondered long on possible food combinations, both hygienic and esoteric.

Finally, as late as 1931, the peak of this new kind of eating was reached by an eminent figure, Signor Marinetti of the Italian Academy.

His proposals, based on the theory that the future will need birdmen, light and keen, rather than our present stodgy bodies, received much publicity. Most of it was decidedly jeering. And it is true that some of his ideas, such as one advising the use of concentrated foodpills in order to give men more time for the enjoyment of fine food, sound slightly silly. Many of them do not.

He wishes to take the first step in preparing for "an existence that will be more aerial and rapid" by abolishing flour pastes from diet. No more spaghetti, no more macaroni, no more of those viscous white masses that French children call *semoule* and Americans gulp down as breakfast food! That sounds practical, especially if one has ever watched little porkers being fattened with great troughs of steaming mush.

Further, the Italian prophet would abolish the very common delusion that weight and volume are factors in the appreciation of food. His preoccupation with this proves that many men, and some of them true lovers of fine eating, still measure their satisfaction by the tightness of their belts.

Marinetti also wishes to abolish traditional condiments. In their place he would revive such ancient excitants as perfumes to be blown into the air between courses. To anyone, however, who has tried to find the bouquet of a fine wine in the same room with highly-scented flowers or women, or has pretended to be able to taste a *pâté de foie gras* between puffs on a Turkish cigarette, this idea is somewhat ridiculous.

The next step in the forming of the future race is the abolition of routine, daily mediocre monotony. Marinetti is surely not the first who has pondered this, nor is Yuan Mei, the Chinese who wrote so beautifully of fine and simple foods. "Into no department of life," said he, "should indifference be allowed to creep—into none less than into the domain of cookery."

In modern families especially is this a very important problem. It is likely that more neurasthenics and downright homicidal maniacs have been formed by roast-on-Sunday, fish-on-Friday, than by any other social custom. And the same room for every meal, with the same pictures on the walls! Very dangerous.

Certain plates can be just as virulently monotonous. Baked potatoes, no matter how hot and flaky, become almost nauseating the seven-hundredth time they are served pinched open, with paprika and butter on the scar. They form a pattern with steak; then there are patterns of pork-and-applesauce, lamb-and-peas-with-mint-sauce, yams-and-sausage—all very good, all hideously familiar.

Here, according to Marinetti, is the solution: Show various dishes between courses (some to be eaten and some not), as did Robert May, who in his *Accomplisht Cook* laments in 1610 the fast-disappearing English custom of making dishes to arouse and startle the diners, as well as feed them. By doing this, say both men, you will excite curiosity, surprise, and the imagination.

And tint your potatoes blue or rose or green! How do you know that you will not like them? Put new names on old dishes. Be stimulating!

For instance, ask your artist friends to design some such plate as this one made for the academician by his futuristic *confrère* Prampolini:

Equator Plus North Pole

"Equatorial ring of hard-boiled egg yolks stuck here and there with bits of orange. In centre a white-of-egg cone crowned by truffles cut in the shape of airplanes."

That should at least rout dull monotony at a luncheon table!

Paul Reboux, whose view of modern gastronomy is equally sceptical but more humorous, has attacked the same problem of routine. In an aside on salads, he remarks:

"You need to have the soul of a rabbit to eat lettuce as it is usually served—green leaves slightly lubricated with oil and flavoured with vinegar. A salad is only a background; it needs embroidering. To give character to a lettuce salad, cut up slivers of orange rind as small as pine needles, and sprinkle them over the salad. If you want something still more entertaining for your guests, cut up a carrot into equally small slips. This will at once arouse the attention of any gourmet. Which is orange and which is carrot? he will wonder. How does the Orange come to have a taste of Carrot, and the Carrot a flavour of Orange? You will have given him a real gastronomic entertainment."

Another recipe which seems preoccupied with the routing of monotony from the table (and this time the king's, no less), gives a plan for a most amazing dish.

"Take a capon and a little pig," it instructs, "and smite them in the waist. Sew the hind part of one on the fore quarters of the other, and stuff, and roast, and serve them forth."

It was an unknown cook some six hundred years ago, his artistry marked down in *The Harleian Manuscript* 279 by a careful clerk, who seems to have been bothered even then by Marinetti's problem.

Does this mean that Richard the Third and Cæsar and Ahasuerus had their own *Equator Plus North Poles?*

The Social Status of a Vegetable

ALTHOUGH we had walked into the little Swiss village restaurant without warning, an almost too elaborate meal appeared for us in the warm empty room, hardly giving us time to finish our small glasses of thick piny bitters.

We were hungry. The climb had been steep, through bare vineyards and meadows yellow with late primroses. We ate the plate of sliced sausages, and then the tureen of thick potato soup, without much speaking. We hardly blinked at the platter of fried eggs—ten of them for only three people!—with dark pink ham curling all around like little clouds.

We reached for more bread, sighed, and pulled off coats. The wine was light and appetizing.

Mrs. Davidson's old face looked fresher now. She straightened her shoulders, and settled her hat with a slightly coquettish movement of gnarled arms. For a wonder, she had eaten without mention of her self-styled "bird-like" appetite, with no apology for the natural hunger which she usually felt to be coarse and carnal. (Or so at least we had gathered from her many bored, sad smiles at any admission on our parts that we did like to eat.)

Now, when   realized that she was at last on the point of recognizing the existence of such low lust in herself, I rushed to forestall her with instinctive perversity.

"That was good, " I said. "But I'm still hungry."

At once I was sorry, ashamed of myself. Mrs. Davidson looked cut into, and then settled her small handsome old face in its usual lines of refined disapproval. I had destroyed a rare human moment in her stiff life.

"So far, the meal, if you could really call such an impromptu thing a meal, has been quite passable," she admitted. "This inn, for such a small and unattractive village, seems respectable enough."

My nephew pulled the cork from another bottle, filled her glass, and quietly put more bread by her plate.

"I think its awfully decent of you to come here while we eat," he told her, his face smooth and innocent.

She looked flattered, and finished the bread without noticing it.

The waitress, fat and silent, staggered in under a tray, her knees bending slightly outwards with its weight. She put down a great plate of steaks, with potatoes heaped like swollen hay at each end. We looked feebly at it, feeling appetite sag out of us suddenly.

Another platter thumped down at the other side of the table, a platter mounded high with purple-red ringed with dark green.

"What—*what* is that beautiful food?" Mrs. Davidson demanded, and then quickly mended her enthusiasm, with her eyes still sparkling hungrily. "I mean, beautiful as far as food could be."

My own appetite revived a little as I answered: "That's a ring of spinach around chopped red cabbage, probably cooked with ham juice."

At the word spinach her face clouded, but when I mentioned cabbage a look of complete and horrified disgust settled like a cloud. She pushed back her chair.

"Cabbage!" Her tone was incredulous.

"Why not?" James asked, mildly. "Cabbage is the staff of life in many countries. You ought to know, Mrs. Davidson. Weren't you raised on a farm?"

Her mouth settled grimly.

"As *you* know," she remarked in an icy voice, with her face gradually looking very old and discontented again, "there are many kinds of farms. My home was *not* a collection of peasants. Nor did we eat such—such peasant things as this."

"But haven't you ever tasted cabbage, then, Mrs. Davidson?" I asked.

"Never!" she answered proudly, emphatically.

"This is delicious steak." It was a diplomatic interruption. I looked gratefully at James. He grinned almost imperceptibly, and went on, "Just let me slide a little sliver on your plate, Mrs. Davidson, and you try to nibble at it while we eat. It will do you good."

He cut off the better portion of a generous slice of beef and put it on her well-emptied plate. She looked pleased, as she always did when reference was made to her delicacy, and only shuddered perfunctorily when we served ourselves with the vegetable.

As the steak disappeared, I watched her long old ear-lobes pinken. I remembered what an endocrinologist had told me once, that after rare beef and wine, when the lobes turned red, was the time to ask favours or tell bad news. I led the conversation back to the table, and then plunged brusquely.

"Why do you really dislike cabbage, Mrs. Davidson?"

She looked surprised, and put down the last bite from her bowl of brandied plums.

"Why does anyone dislike it? Surely you don't believe that I think your eating it is anything more than a pose?" She smiled knowingly at my nephew and me. He laughed.

"But we *do* like it, really. In our homes we cook it, and eat it, too, not for health, not for pretence. We like it."

"Yes, I remember my husband used to say that same sort of thing. But he never got it! No fear! It was the night I finally accepted him that I understood why my family had never had it in the house."

We waited silently. James filled her glass again.

"We missed the last train, and couldn't find a cab, and of course Mr. Davidson, who thought he knew everything, wandered down the wrong street. And there, in that dark wet town, lost, cold, miserable ——"

"Oh, night of rapture, when I was yours!" James murmured.

"—cold, miserable, we were suddenly almost overcome by a ghastly odour!"

I repressed my instinctive desire to use the word "stink" and asked maliciously, "A perfume, or a smell?"

"A dreadful *odour*," she corrected me, with an acidulous smile at my coarseness. "It was so terrible that I was almost swooning. I pressed my muff against my face, and we stumbled on, gasping.

"When finally I could control myself enough to speak, I murmured, 'What was it? What was that gas?' My husband hurried me along, and I will say he did his best to apologize for what he had done—and well he should have!—by saying, 'It was cabbage, cooking.'

" 'Oh!' I cried. 'Oh, we're in the *slums*!'

"So you see what a terrible memory of it all I have kept. Is it any wonder that I shudder when I see it or have it near me? Those horrible slums! Its *odour!*"

We looked blankly at her. Then I asked, "But do you smell it now? Did it bother you on the table?"

Mrs. Davidson stared peevishly at me, and said to James, "Well, if you two have finished your food, I should like to go."

Then, as we walked down the stairs to the crooked narrow street, I thanked her for the pleasant meal. She almost smiled, and said, grudgingly, "It was, I admit, not bad—for the slums."

It is constantly surprising, this vegetable snobbism. It is almost universal.

My mother, who was raised in a country too crowded with Swedish immigrants, shudders at turnips, which they seem to have lived on. And yet there she ate, week in and week out, corn meal mush and molasses, a dish synonymous to many Americans with poor trash of the pariah-ridden South.

And my grandmother—I remember hearing her dismiss some unfortunate person as a vulgar climber by saying, quietly, "Oh, Mrs. Zubzub is the kind of woman who serves artichokes!"

Of course, to a child reared within smelling distance, almost, of the fog-green fields of those thistly flowers, such damnation was quite meaningless; but I suppose that to a Mid-Western woman of the last century it meant much.

Just a few years ago, the same class consciousness was apparent in a small college in Illinois, where students whispered and drew away from me after I had innocently introduced a box of avocados from my father's ranch into a dormitory "feast." From that unfortunate night, I was labelled a stuck-up snob.

The first time, though, that I ever felt surprise at the social position of a vegetable, was when I was a lower-classman in a boarding-school. Like most Western private schools, it was filled largely with out-of-state children whose families wintered in California, and the daughters of local newly-rich.

Pretension and snobbishness flourished among these oddly segregated adolescents, and nowhere could such stiff cautious conventionality be found as in their classrooms, their teas, their sternly pro-British hockey matches.

One girl, from Englewood in New Jersey or maybe Tuxedo Park, was the recognized leader of the Easterners, the "bloods." She was more dashing than the rest; she used with impressive imitation her mother's high whinnying gush of poise and good-breeding. She set the pace, and with a certain surety, too, for such an unsure age as sixteen. She was daring.

The reason I know she was daring, even so long ago, is that I can still hear her making a stupendous statement. That takes courage at any time, but when you are young, and bewildered behind your affectation of poise, and surrounded by other puzzled children who watch avidly for one wrong move, it is as impressive as a parade with trumpets.

We were waiting for the lunch bell. Probably we were grumbling about the food, which was unusually good for such an institution, but, like all food cooked *en masse*, dull. Our bodies clamoured for it, our tongues rebelled.

The girl from Englewood or Tuxedo Park spoke out, her hard voice clear, affectedly drawling to hide her own consciousness of daring. She must have known that what she said, even while aping her mother's social sureness, was very radical to the children round her, the children fed from kitchens of the *haute bourgeoisie* and in luxurious hotels. It was rather like announcing, at a small débutante ball in Georgia, "Of course, *I* prefer to dance with Negroes."

"I know it's terribly, terribly silly of me," she said, with all she could summon of maternally gracious veneer, "but of course I was brought up near Pennsylvania, and the customs there are so quaint, and I know you'll all be terribly, terribly shocked, but I *love*, I *adore* wieners and sauerkraut!"

Yes, it was surprising then and still is. All round are signs of it, everywhere, little trickles of snobbish judgment, always changing, ever present.

In France old Crainquebille sold leeks from a cart, leeks called "the asparagus of the poor." Now asparagus sells for the asking, almost, in California markets, and broccoli, that strong age-old green, leaps from its lowly pot to the *Ritz's* copper saucepan.

Who determines, and for what strange reasons, the social status of a vegetable?

César

For one reason or another it is thought advisable to change the names of real people when you write about them. I can do that sometimes, but not now. And of course there is no reason why I should. César is very real: he lives more surely than most men; and if he does read about himself in any book, which is doubtful, he will at the most be amused.

I cannot remember how we first met him. He was the butcher in a village of fishermen. We were foreigners, who stayed in the village several weeks. It is probably strange that we knew César so well, and he us.

The women of the village hated him and were afraid of him, but, "All I do is reach through my window at night," said César, "and there's a fine piece of woman waiting for me in the dark street. Any time, every night, I pluck them in."

The women hated him for two reasons. He had been very cruel to his termagant wife. She fled from him finally, and the two sons with her, after a fight between them and their father.

They were very strong men, all three, and when they were angry they swelled with muscle and spleen. César chased them out, all howling maledictions.

Later one of the sons crept back and stabbed at his father, but César broke the dagger between his fists and gave the pieces to his son's mistress, one night after he had plucked her through his window.

But it was sorrow for the poor wife, even if she was a foul-mouthed shrew, that made the village women hate César. That was the first reason. The second was that the men in the village loved César more than they did their women or their sons or even their boats.

They loved him for a thousand reasons and one reason. César was all that every man wants secretly to be: strong, brave; foul, cruel, reckless; desired by women and potent as a goat; tender and very sweet with children; feared by the priest, respected by the mayor; utterly selfish and as generous as a prince; gay. César was man. Man noble and monstrous again after so many centuries.

Once a week, two or three times a week, we'd walk down the one street, after noon dinner. All the boats beached on one side of us, all the doorsteps empty on the other, desertion would lie like dust in the air, with here and there a woman peering sourly from a dark room.

Madame Revenusso or Madame Médin, maybe, would call sullenly that César was looking for Monsieur Fischer.

Al's face would flash with joy, like a torch or a trumpet call. He'd hurry away. I'd go home alone, understanding some of the village women's jealous anger.

César's meat shop was behind the chapel, in a dirty alley. It was seldom peopled: women would buy no cuts from him, the devil, and even if they had wanted to, he was always saving the best for himself. Probably he ran the shop because it was an easy way to have good meat ready to hand.

Back of the store, there was one large room. It was dark, spotless, full of clean cold air from stone walls and floor, and almost bare. Under the lone window was César's big bed, very conveniently arranged for his carnal nocturnes. A wide ledge jutted from two walls, wide enough to sit on or lie on. There were one or two chairs on the scrubbed tiles of the floor, nuisances to stumble over in the room's darkness.

In the centre was the heart, the yolk, the altar, the great stone fireplace flat and high as a table, with an iron top for pots and a grill. And the whole ceiling of the room was its chimney, rising to a point and a far hole above the fire, like an ancient ducal kitchen.

It was there, to that big dark room, that the men would come, usually in the afternoon. I never saw them there, nor the room, neither, but I know they came to it as quickly as they could, very joyfully. César would say "Come!" and they would hurry.

On the stove there was always something steaming in a great black pot—a stew of tiny opaque whitebait, or tripe jugged in sour white wine, or succulent scraps whose origin César leeringly would not tell.

Piled on a chair, or on the floor near the stove, were steaks as thick as your fist, or four or five lamb's legs, or a kid ready to broil. On the stone ledge were two kegs of wine, or three, or bottles never counted.

The fire was hot, the steam rose toward the roof.

César stood taller and broader than any other man before his stove, stirring, basting, smelling. His voice was mightier.

"Drink!" he cried out. "Drink, eat!" And he roared with joy.

In the other houses women snapped at their children or perked their heads towards the chapel alley. When they heard songs and wild laughter, or more alarming silence, they sighed and looked black. If there'd only been bad strumpets there behind the butcher shop, they would have comprehended, but just men—it was unnatural.

If their husbands came home before dark, they would not eat fish soup and bread with the children. If they came too late for that, they leaped fiercely and silently on the sleeping women, or stood for a long time looking through the shutters at the sea, their faces very gentle and intent.

The women hated César.

The mornings after, they cackled maliciously when his shop stayed closed until noon, and when he finally opened its wide door, they looked sideways at his tired thick face.

"M'sieur César appears ill today," they would greet him, oilily.

"Ill? My God, no, dear Madame Dirtypot! Two quarts of purgative water is all I need—or three. And I'd advise the same for your husband—but in proportion, in proportion, my good Mrs. Soilskirt. I'd say a half-glass. More would tear his vitals clean off, with more loss to you than to him, eh, Madame Foulface?"

César's eyes, almost shut, gleamed wickedly, and he hoisted up his big sagging belly with lewd relish.

Then his face cleared. A young woman came towards him, with a warm little naked child on one arm. César called her.

"Célèstine! How goes it with your new rascal?"

He paid no attention to her stiff mouth and forehead, but looked lovingly at the tiny brown baby she had.

"Oh, he is a beauty, but a beauty, so strong and straight! Célèstine, you've done a fine job here. That's right, girl—smile. César is your good friend, really. And this child! He is a grand fellow, I tell you. Here, come to me, you little beautiful limb of the devil!"

César stood in the strong white sunlight, his two bottles of physic forgotten. The naked baby in his arms grinned up at him candidly while he murmured to it. He turned it across his arm, and ran his huge hand over its firm little bottom.

"My God!" he exclaimed, suddenly, "what delicious, truly what a delicious morsel that would be, broiled!"

With an outraged squawk Célèstine tore her baby from him and scuttled away. César yelled with laughter, belched mightily, and went toward his shop, his physic under his arms.

Whenever a strange creature came up in the nets, some sea beast's child or watery vegetable, the fishermen carried it to César.

He'd poke it, smell it, inevitably taste it. If he spat it out, they'd nod wisely. Poison! If he gulped it down alive, or cooked it up into a queer stew, they'd talk for days, admiringly. Brave man, to eat a mass of purple jelly with a little green-toothed mouth in its middle!

But do you remember, and their eyes would glisten with amazed delight, do you remember the time the crocodile died at the big zoo in the city, and César was called to skin it, and brought himself back a fine thick steak from it? Ah, do you remember?

The time came for us to go. We asked César to come to our house to eat a last supper.

I felt awkward, because I was a woman—but there was no other place for me to eat. César felt awkward for the same reason.

He came with a coat on, and a pink shirt, and silently handed me a massive filet of beef. I left the room with it, and heard him talking to Al, but when I came back he stopped.

The meal was strained at the beginning, but we had plenty of good wine, and the meat was the best I have ever tasted.

César put down his knife and fork.

"She likes it, she likes good food!" he said, wonderingly, to Al. "She cannot be a real woman!"

After that things were very pleasant. He took off his coat, and we ate and drank and talked, all a good deal.

"I hear you are married," César remarked. "It is a filthy lie, naturally?"

"But of course we are married," Al protested. "We have been married for several years."

César peered incredulously at us, and then laughed.

"Ridiculous! And why? Children, you are not married, I say—

because marriage is a rotten business, and you are not rotten." He spat neatly over his huge pink shoulder. "If you were married, Alfred, Alfred-the-Penguin, my Al, would not be a real man, happy. And he is. And you," he glared at me, "would not be sitting knowing good meat between your teeth. And you are.

"Therefore, my two peculiar little foreign children, you are not married! No, you are brother and sister, living in sinful glory!"

He laughed until the whole room shook, and tipped a full bottle of wine down his throat.

"I shall die soon," he said, "and when I die, every man in the village will laugh for many days. Do you know why? Because they'll have all my wine to drink, barrels and casks of it, to drink to my commands, and they'll all try to drink as I would, as I've taught them.

"Yes, they'll drink for me, to float my soul to Purgatory. And the biggest cask of wine will be my coffin. My friends know. They'll put me in it and bury me deep, and they and all the women, too, will weep."

He was silent for a minute, and then roared another laugh.

"And grapes will grow up from me," he cried, "and by God, what wine I'll make!"

Al and I looked and recognized there a ghost with us, another Man from whose dead heart had sprung a vine. Was he César, was César that dim great figure who heard of Pan's death and cried tears as big as ostrich eggs?

We parted merrily, with no farewells.

About a year later, a shabby post card came from the village on the Mediterranean coast. It was stiffly pencilled.

"My friends in Sinful Glory, plant a tree somewhere for César."

Since then we have planted many, almost all for him.

To End

We lived, once, above a little pastry shop which called itself "At the Sign of the Fin Gourmet." It sold probably the worst apricot tarts that ever sogged and stuck in throat.

"*N'est pas gourmand qui veut*," said Brillat-Savarin. The aphorism is, as I predicted at the first, inevitable. Truly a man is not a gourmand, much less a *fin gourmet*, by wishing to be so.

1941

Consider The Oyster

FOR DILLWYN PARRISH

*He was a bold man that first eat
an oyster.*

*—Polite Conversation
Jonathan Swift*

Love and Death Among the Molluscs

. . . Secret, and self-contained, and solitary as an oyster.
— *A Christmas Carol,* CHARLES DICKENS

AN OYSTER leads a dreadful but exciting life.

Indeed, his chance to live at all is slim, and if he should survive the arrows of his own outrageous fortune and in the two weeks of his carefree youth find a clean smooth place to fix on, the years afterwards are full of stress, passion, and danger.

He—but why make him a he, except for clarity? Almost any normal oyster never knows from one year to the next whether he is he or she, and may start at any moment, after the first year, to lay eggs where before he spent his sexual energies in being exceptionally masculine. If he is a she, her energies are equally feminine, so that in a single summer, if all goes well, and the temperature of the water is somewhere around or above seventy degrees, she may spawn several hundred million eggs, fifteen to one hundred million at a time, with commendable pride.

American oysters differ as much as American people, so that the Atlantic Coast inhabitants spend their childhood and adolescence floating free and unprotected with the tides, conceived far from their mothers and their fathers too by milt let loose in the water near the eggs, while the Western oysters lie within special brood-chambers of the maternal shell, inseminated and secure, until they are some two weeks old. The Easterners seem more daring.

A little oyster is born, then, in the water. At first, about five to ten hours after he and at least a few hundred thousand of his mother's eggs have been fertilized by his potent and unknown sire, he is merely a larva. He is small, but he is free-swimming . . . and he swims thus freely for about two weeks, wherever the tides and his peculiar whims may lead him. He is called a spat.

It is to be hoped, sentimentally at least, that the spat—*our* spat —enjoys himself. Those two weeks are his one taste of vagabondage, of devil-may-care free roaming. And even they are not quite free, for during all his youth he is busy growing a strong foot and a large supply of sticky cement-like stuff. If he thought, he might wonder why.

The two weeks up, he suddenly attaches himself to the first clean hard object he bumps into. His fifty million brothers who have not been eaten by fish may or may not bump into anything clean and hard, and those who do not, die. But our spat has been lucky, and in great good spirits he clamps himself firmly to his home, probably forever. He is by now about one-seventy-fifth of an inch long, whatever that may be . . . and he is an oyster.

Since he is an Easterner, a Chincoteague or a Lynnhaven maybe, he has found a pleasant, moderately salty bottom, where the tides wash regularly and there is no filth to pollute him and no sand to choke him.

There he rests, tied firmly by his left foot, which seems to have become a valve in the immutable way of all oyster feet. He devotes himself to drinking, and rapidly develops an envious capacity, so that in good weather, when the temperature stays near seventy-eight degrees, he can easily handle twenty-six or -seven quarts an hour. He manages better than most creatures to combine business with pleasure, and from this stream of water that passes through his gills he strains out all the delicious little diatoms and peridia that are his food.

His home—we are speaking now of domesticated oysters—is a wire bag full of old shells, or perhaps a cement-coated pole planted by a wily oyster-farmer. Or perhaps it is what the government describes winningly as "a particularly efficient collector," which is made from an egg-crate partition coated with a mixture of lime and cement.

Whatever the anchorage (and I hope, sentimentally again, that it is at least another shell, since because he is an Easterner our little spat can never know the esthetic pleasure of finding a bamboo stick in Japan, nor a hollow tile laid out especially for him in France or Portugal), whatever the anchorage, spat-dom is over and done with. The two fine free-swimming weeks are forever gone, maturity with all its cares has come, and an oyster, according to Richard Sheridan's *Critic*, may be crossed in love.

For about a year this oyster—*our* oyster—is a male, fertilizing a few hundred thousand eggs as best he can without ever knowing whether they swim by or not. Then one day, maternal longings surge between his two valves in his cold guts and gills and all his crinkly fringes. Necessity, that well-known mother, makes him one. He is a she.

From then on she, with occasional vacations of being masculine just to keep her hand in, bears her millions yearly. She is in the full bloom of womanhood when she is about seven.

She is a fine plump figure of an oyster, plumper still in the summer when the season and her instincts get the better of her. She has traveled some, thanks to cupidinous farmers who have subjected her to this tide and that, this bed and that, for their own mean ends. She has grown into a gray-white oval shape, with shades of green or ocher or black in her gills and a rudimentary brain in the forepart of her blind deaf body. She can feel shadows as well as the urgency of milt, and her delicate muscles know danger and pull shut her shells with firmness.

Danger is everywhere for her, and extermination lurks. (How do we know with what pains? How can we tell or not tell the sufferings of an oyster? There is a brain . . .) She is the prey of many enemies, and must lie immobile as a fungus while the starfish sucks her and the worm bores.

She has eight enemies, not counting man who is the greatest, since he protects her from the others only to eat her himself.

The first enemy is the starfish, which floats hungrily in all the Eastern tides and at last wraps arms about the oyster like a hideous lover and forces its shells apart steadily and then thrusts his stomach into it and digests it. The picture is ugly. The oyster is left bare as any empty shell, and the starfish floats on, hungry still. (Men try to catch it with things called star-mops.)

The second enemy, almost as dangerous, is a kind of snail called a screw-borer, or an oyster drill. It bores wee round holes in the shells, and apparently worries the poor mollusc enough to make men invent traps for it: wire bags baited with seed-oysters catch it, but none too efficiently, since it remains a menace.

Then there is a boring sponge. It makes tiny tunnels all through the shell like honeycomb, until an oyster becomes thin and weak from trying to stop up all the holes, and then is often smothered by the sponge from the outside, so that you know what Louisa May Alcott meant when she wrote, "Now I am beginning to live a little, and feel less like a sick oyster at low tide."

There are wafers, or leeches, and "Black Drums." And mussels too will smother oysters or starve them by coming to stay on their shells and eating all their food. Out on the Pacific Coast, slipper shells, which are somewhat fancily called *Crepidula fornicata*, will go the mussels one better. And even ducks, flying here and there as ducks must, land long enough to make themselves a disastrously good meal occasionally on an oyster-bed.

Life is hard, we say. An oyster's life is worse. She lives motionless, soundless, her own cold ugly shape her only dissipation, and if she escapes the menace of duck-slipper-mussel-Black-Drum-leech-sponge-borer-starfish, it is for man to eat, because of man's own hunger.

Men have enjoyed eating oysters since they were not much more than monkeys, according to the kitchen middens they have left behind them. And thus, in their own one-minded way, they have spent time and thought and money on the problems of how to protect oysters from the suckers and the borers and the starvers, until now it is comparatively easy to eat this two-valved mollusc anywhere, without thought of the dangers it has run in its few years. Its chilly, delicate gray body slips into a stew-pan or under a broiler or alive down a red throat, and it is done. Its life has been thoughtless but no less full of danger, and now that it is over we are perhaps the better for it.

A Supper to Sleep On

Oysters are very unsatisfactory food for labouring men, but will do for the sedentary, and for a supper to sleep on.

—The Philosophy of Eating, A. J. BELLOWS, 1870

THERE are several different kinds of stews. A stew can be a sweat or a welter in hot close atmosphere or, according to the English dictionaries, a swot. It can be a tank or pond for storing live fish. It can be a brothel.

It can be something cooked by long simmering in a closed vessel with little liquid in it. And there are probably several other things a stew can be, but even the American lexicographers seem ignorant of one of the best; have they never heard of an oyster stew?

Is it possible that they never knew, when they were children, the cozy pleasure of Sunday night supper in wintertime, when crackers and the biggest tureen of steaming buttery creamy oyster stew stood on the table, and were plenty?

Is it possible that when they grew somewhat older, those benighted men never went to Doylestown in Pennsylvania to get married or something, and thus never sat voluptuously at the Inn's dim oyster bar while their stew was flicked together before them in two or three little copper pans?

Is it possible that, sometime after the first joys of maturity and before they grew old enough to write dictionaries, those men never sat with a few friends and compared, solemnly and delightfully, their various methods of making oyster stews themselves?

It is possible, poor souls, and it is even probable, for how else could they print their sweeping statements about "long simmering in a closed vessel with little liquid" and not at least add "*except oyster stew*"?

Even a child knows as much if he has ever watched, a few times in his early winters, the simple making of his Sunday supper. He remembers the recipe too, partly because it is so simple and partly because no matter how long he lives afterwards, its recollection will add to what well-being he has or perhaps may once have had.

In spite of its simplicity, oyster stew has several formulae, or rather methods of putting together, since the ingredients are almost constant. Rich milk, butter, salt, pepper, and of course, oysters, make up every recipe I ever heard . . . except one . . . but the way these things are blended is the cause for long arguments and comparisons and even amicable differences among old friends.

Some insist that the oysters should be sizzled in the butter until they are curled, and then added to the hot milk. Others say they should be heated to boiling in their own juice, and that the boiling milk and the butter should be poured over them. Others say . . . But here is a sample of the variety of recipes which families and cookbooks have produced:

OYSTER STEW[1]

1 *quart oysters*	4 *tablespoons butter*
2 *cups oyster liquor*	*celery salt*
2 *cups heavy cream*	*pepper*

Bring one cup of the oyster liquor to a boil and when it has cooked for 5 minutes skim off the top, which will be foamy. Add the cream, butter, and seasoning to taste. Cook the oysters in the other cup of liquor until the edges curl (about 5 minutes), strain and add to the cream. Serve immediately.

The use of celery salt in this recipe is probably less a regional custom than a trick used by one enthusiastic family for so long that it can almost be called "New England" now. It is like the odd but excellent amount of paprika slapped into the next rule by the energetic Browns in their *Country Cook Book:*

[1] New England Cook Book, Culinary Arts Press, Reading, Pennsylvania, 1936. 15¢.

OYSTER STEW[2]

Rinse a stewpan and put it on the fire without drying, so the milk won't stick. Dump in one quart of milk and 1 dozen oysters with their liquor and plenty of salt. Cook very slowly, without boiling of course, and give an occasional light stir to see how the oysters are plumping out. Just before their edges begin to curl, dump in ⅛ pound of sweet butter and at least 2 tablespoons of paprika. More paprika won't hurt, but will give a richer hue to the stew, and make you wish you'd made twice as much. Swirl the paprika and melted butter around to make an attractive, mottled, topping and dish it out the second the edges begin to curl. If cooked any longer, the oysters will be hard.

The only stew I ever heard of made without either cream or milk, was from three gentle sisters. They spoke sadly at first, and then with that kind of quiet inner mirth that rises always in members of a family who have lived together for several decades, when they begin unexpectedly to remember things. These three sisters sat in the hot California light under a eucalyptus tree, and laughed at last in spite of all the things in between, as they recalled the way they always ate oyster stew when they were children in New Hampshire.

It was a strange stew, and could not have been as handsome as one made with cream, but it was even better, the sisters murmured with politeness but a kind of stubborn sensuality. It had a stronger, finer smell, they said . . . and it tasted purer, more completely *oyster*.

Their mother melted a good nubbin of fresh butter in a pan. In another pan she put the oysters, a dozen or so for everyone, with all their juices and about a cupful more of water for each dozen. She brought the water with the oysters in it just to the boil, so that the oysters began to think of curling without really getting at it, and then quickly skimmed them off and into a hot tureen. She brought the water to the boil again, and threw in pepper and salt. Then she poured the hot butter over the oysters, and the hot broth over all, and the three sisters and their other sisters and brothers and grandparents ate it steaming from the tureen, with butter crackers.

(And here is a recipe for butter crackers, probably much like the

[2] Brown's Country Cook Book, Farrar and Rinehart, New York, 1937.

ones eaten, those Sunday nights long ago, by the three gentle sisters. It is from *Common Sense in the Household*,[3] and is as far from packaged U-No-Snaps and all our cellophaned conformity as 1870 is from blitzkriegs:

BUTTER CRACKERS

1 *quart of flour*	1 *saltspoonful salt*
3 *tablespoonfuls butter*	2 *cups sweet milk*
½ *teaspoon soda, dissolved in*	
hot water	

Rub the butter into the flour, or, what is better, cut it up with a knife or chopper, as you do in pastry; add the salt, milk, soda, mixing well. Work into a ball, lay upon a floured board, and beat with the rolling-pin half an hour, turning and shifting the mass often. Roll into an even sheet, a quarter of an inch thick, or less, prick deeply with a fork, and bake hard in a moderate oven. Hang them up in a muslin bag in the kitchen for two days to dry.

(This is something you will probably never taste in your life, unless you are stubborn or have a crazy cook, but it is nice to know that there still live people who have eaten something other than the light dead things we call oyster crackers with their stews.)

Probably the best stew I ever ate was at the Doylestown Inn. It may have been so good because I was escaped from a long ride, cold enough to make my eyeballs hurt. Maybe it was because I was pleased by the narrow dark room and the Dutch farmers sitting quietly at the bar and the smell of the place, clean and masculine. I was happy to be there for those reasons and because I had long waited for the day, eager from tales I had heard. So the stew tasted better than any I had ever eaten, because of all that and because it was so good anyway.

It was made in three copper saucepans, as I remember, by a thin young-old man who said nonchalantly that oyster stews in Dublin were pretty good too, but couldn't touch his, of course. He strolled up and down the narrow gangplank behind the counter, and talked and put a platter of crackers and a hideous glass shaker of dark sherry in front of me, and all the time kept his eyes on the three pans, shaking them and pouring as he went.

---

[3] By Marion Harland, Scribner Armstrong and Company, New York, 1873.

In the smallest he put some butter from a big cool pat, and let it froth up once and then rest at the back of the stove. In the next he put oysters, fresh from their shells which he tossed into a bin under the counter. In the third, which was deeper and more a real saucepan than a kind of skillet, like the others, he put about a pint of milk and let it heat until it shivered on top. He kept his eye sharply on all three, so that the butter and the oysters and the milk never got beyond him.

As soon as the butter had frothed and settled he poured it quickly over the oysters and started skimming them around and around in the pan, like an old woman making an omelette at Mont Saint-Michel. In about one minute, not three or even five as so many recipes will say, he whiffed them past his questioning nose and then into the hot milk, which was just on the point of steaming. He put in red pepper and salt in a flash, and before I realized it the oyster stew I had so long talked about and waited for was under my own nose, and the young-old man stood watching me.

I sat for a minute, letting my eyeballs come into focus again and smelling the fine straightforward smell of the stew, and he got impatient and flicked a few drops of sherry into my plate, hinting that I get down to business. I did. It was as good as he had said, the best in the world, and as all the other people had told me . . . mildly potent, quietly sustaining, warm as love and welcomer in winter.

Like most people, though, who have ever tasted oyster stew in their first years, I still think the kind we used to make on Sunday nights when I was little was the kind I might make myself if I wanted one again . . . which I often do.

Now I am older, and I know that good stews can be made as we made them then, but with tinned Willapoint oysters and store butter and bought milk. In spite of this knowledge, less my choice than a compromise with progress, I like to think of those first stews as the perfect ones, the dream stews.

The oysters were Chincoteagues . . . or would be if I were little again and in my dream at the same time . . . Chincoteagues alive and fluttering their gills minutely as they felt the air about them. They were dropped, clean and fat, into the heating milk . . . and the milk was not pasteurized and flat, nor was it homogenized and thick and "good for you," but it was whole milk from a cow half-Jersey and half-Guernsey. Just before the milk with the oysters in it began to steam, a few chunks of sweet saltless butter were put on the top, and salt and pepper, so that as the stew was poured into the hot tureen (a sturdy oval pot of white bone-china with a fat gold band around it) the butter and the condiments poured too, and mixed themselves evenly with the milk.

By then the oysters had grown even plumper, and were heated through but still tender. It was a fine stew, and we ate hot buttered toast with it. The toast is perhaps easier to duplicate now, but my memory of both is fine and reassuring, and "will do . . . for a supper to sleep on."

R is for Oyster

C. Pearl Swallow
He died of a bad oyster.

That is carved on a tombstone in a graveyard in Maine—Paris Hill, I think the place is called. The man's name was good for such an end, but probably the end was not.

If Mr. Swallow really died of a bad oyster he was a most miserable man for some hours, certainly. The bad oyster itself was rotten to his taste, so that he knew as soon as he had eaten it that he was wrong. Perhaps he worried a little about it, and then forgot and ate other things to rub the coppery taste from his tongue. He may, even in Maine, have washed it down with drink.

In two or five or six hours, though, he remembered. He felt faint, and cold fingers whuddered over his skin, so that he reeled and shivered. Then he was sick, violently and often. He could barely lift his head, for the weakness and the dreadful cramps in his belly. His bowels surged, so that he felt they would drain his very heart out of him. And, God, he was thirsty, thirsty. . . . I'm dying, he thought, and even in his woe he regretted it, and did not believe it. But he died.

Perhaps he died of a bad oyster. Oysters can be bad, all right, if they are stale and full of bacteria that make for putrefaction. Mushrooms can be deadly, too. But mushrooms and oysters are alike in that they take the blame, because of superstition and something innately mysterious about their way of life, for countless pains that never are their fault.

It is true that people have died from eating mushrooms, because there are at least two deadly ones and innocently or not, men have been fed them. It is true, too, that some men have eaten rotten oysters and died, hideously, racked with vomiting.

But quite often, I feel sure, mushrooms and oysters too are blamed for sickness that could equally be caused by many things like piggishness or nerves or even other poisons.

What man knowingly would eat a bad oyster, anyway? A bad oyster looks old and disagreeable in its shell, and it smells somewhat of copper and somewhat of rotten eggs. Of course, it might be hidden in a pie or a patty or under a coating of rich spiced sauce in a restaurant. But even so, a man's tongue would warn him that something was very wrong, I think, unless he was half under the table he sat at.

(In this, the oyster is kinder than the mushroom, which can taste most delicious when it is most deadly. And that is seldom, I insist.)

And in case a man's tongue warns him that he has at last swallowed that gastronomical rarity, a bad 'un, he should leave the board at once and do what men have always known how to do, even the dainty ones, and get rid of it.

There would be no mistaking it, once on the tongue. When people say, "I must have eaten a bad oyster yesterday . . . I've felt a bit dauncy ever since!" you can be sure that they have eaten a great many other things, and have perhaps drunk over-well, but that they certainly have not swallowed what is so easy to blame. If so, they would have known the unpleasant truth immediately, because it would taste so thoroughly nasty . . . and of course within six hours or less they would have been sick as hell, or even dead.

Probably more people eat oysters now than ever before, because it is easier than ever to ship them from their beds and bottoms to the dining-tables of this nation and any other nation whose people still have time for such things.

The old-fashioned habit of sniffing each oyster more or less delicately before swallowing it is as nearly extinct as its contemporary trick of gulping, with an all but visible holding of the nose, which was considered genteel . . . and so much safer.

Restaurants, even air-cooled perforce in the midst of hot sand, like Palm Springs, or as far from the sea as Oskaloosa in Iowa, can serve oysters without fear these days. Tycoons with inlets in Maryland have their highfalutin molluscs flown for supper that night to a penthouse in Fort Worth, or to a simple log-cabin Away from It All in the Michigan woods, and know that Space and Time and even the development of putrescent bacteria stand still for dollars. Bindlestiffs on a rare bender in Los Angeles (Ell-ay, you say) gulp down three swollen "on the half's" with a rot-gut whiskey chaser in any of a dozen joints on Main Street, and are more than moderately sure that if they die that night, it won't be from the oysters.

Men's ideas, though, continue to run in the old channels about oysters as well as God and war and women. Even when they know better they insist that months with R in them are all right, but that oysters in June or July or May or August will kill you or make you wish they had. This is wrong, of course, except that all oysters, like all men, are somewhat weaker after they have done their best at reproducing.

Several decades ago, a jolly man wrote:

> *"Let's sing a song of glory to Themistocles O'Shea*
> *Who ate a dozen oysters on the second*
> *Day of May . . ."*

And even the government tells us R's are silly. "A clean fat oyster may be eaten with impunity at any time of the year," the officials say in folder after folder.

Doctors tell us so. "Hell, if it smells good, it's okay," they say, with modifications dictated by their practices and their positions in the Association.

Men who write pamphlets called *Hypochlorite process of oyster purification, report on experimental purification of polluted oysters, on commercial scale, by floating them in sea water treated with hyperchloride of calcium. (Public Health Reprint 652.)* . . 5 . . T27 . 6/a: 652 say so, as do earnest Japanese who deliver papers before the Kokusai Yorei Kabushiki Kaisha called *Kaki no banasi,* which means *Talks on Oysters,* with surprisingly un-Oriental bluntness.

They all say that oysters are all right any time as long as they are healthy . . . all, that is, except the oyster-farmers.

The farmers' actions are understandable, after all. Their main interest is in growing as many good crops as they can, and it stands to reason that if a healthy female, round with some twenty million eggs, is taken from the water before she has a chance to birth them, the farmers lose.

May and June and July, and of course August, are the months when the waters are warmest almost everywhere along the coasts, and it is remarkably convenient that oysters can only breed their spawn when the temperature is around seventy degrees and in months with no R's in them. How easy it has been to build a catchy gastronomic rule on the farmers' interest in better crops!

People who have broken the rule and been able to buy oysters in the forbidden months say that they are most delicious then, full and flavorsome. They should be served colder than in winter, and eaten at the far end of a stifling day, in an almost empty chop-house, with a thin cold Alsatian wine to float them down . . . and with them disappear the taste of carbon dioxide and sweaty clerks from the streets outside, so that even July in a big city seems for a time to be a most beautiful month, and C. Pearl Swallow's ghost well-laid.

The Well-dressed Oyster

Any man may be in good spirits and good temper when he's well dressed. There ain't much credit in that.
—Martin Chuzzlewit, CHARLES DICKENS

THERE are three kinds of oyster-eaters: those loose-minded sports who will eat anything, hot, cold, thin; thick, dead or alive, as long as it is *oyster*; those who will eat them raw and only raw; and those who with equal severity will eat them cooked and no way other.

The first group may perhaps have the most fun, although there is a white fire about the others' bigotry that can never warm the broad-minded.

There is a great deal to be said in favor of the second group, for almost every oyster-eater who does not belong whole-heartedly to the third and last division, would die before denying that a perfect oyster, healthy, of fine flavor, plucked from its chill bed and brought to the plate unwatered and unseasoned, is more delicious than any of its modifications. On the other hand, a flaccid, moping, debauched mollusc, tired from too much love and loose-nerved from general world conditions, can be a shameful thing served raw upon its shell.

It is then that the third group, the fanatical believers in the power of heat and sauces to hide a multitude of real or imagined evils, comes triumphantly into its own. Any oyster, even a tinned steamed Japanese bastard from the coast of Oregon can be in good spirits and good temper when he's well dressed, they say. And they are right.

That is unfortunate, if you distrust the saw that what you don't know can't hurt you, for in that case any cooked oyster is suspect, and good old-fashioned ptomaine leers behind every casserole and chafing dish.

It is fortunate, in that the inventing of disguises has brought forth a wealth of subtle ingenious recipes, rather as fast-days in the Middle Ages forced the Church's greatest minds to invent ways to make eggs and cheese taste like roast veal. Some of the recipes for cooking oysters are simple, and no less good, and some of them are as insanely elaborate as the jaded bilious gourmets who gave birth to them.

One of the best and easiest dishes that can be made, if you like it, is baked oysters, and this is as good a recipe as any, whether you call it baked or scalloped or *en casserole* or what:

BAKED OYSTERS

Into a shallow baking dish, well buttered, spread a light layer of bread or cracker crumbs. Then put in a layer of oysters, and season well with salt and fresh-ground pepper and bits of sweet butter. Then put more crumbs and alternate in this fashion until the dish is almost full, and put crumbs and butter on top. Pour enough oyster juice to moisten things, and bake in a quick oven until brown but not bubbling.

Variations can be played *ad infinitum* on this theme, even by beginners and harried hurriers, and sliced onions, tomato sauce, herbs, mustard, cream all find a fairly safe resting-place in it.

Probably the next simplest way to cook an oyster, and the one most commonly accepted in restaurants, is to fry him. It is too bad, since the method can be good, that so many chefs dip their oysters in a thick and often infamous batter, which at once plunged into the equally obscene grease, forms an envelope of such slippery toughness that the oyster within it lies helpless and steaming in a foul blanket, tasteless and yet powerfully indigestible.

Firm chilled oysters rolled quickly in crumbs and dipped into good fat for almost no time at all, and then served quickly on hot plates with an honest tartar sauce or lemon slices, can be one of the best dishes anywhere, and it is perhaps a proof that optimism is inherently human and that after several hideous experiences with restaurant-fried oysters, I still say it.

A good tartar sauce can be bought in a bottle, like several other things, but a better one can be made from this recipe, which is easy if you have an herb garden, and impossible, but still fun to think about, if you do not:

TARTAR SAUCE[1]

1 *cup mayonnaise*
1 *teaspoon chopped Chives*
1 *teaspoon Tarragon*
1 *teaspoon Chervil*
1 *chopped gherkin*

1 *teaspoon capers*
dash cayenne
1 *chopped olive*
prepared mustard to taste
(optional)
wine vinegar to taste

Mix all ingredients except vinegar, then put that in slowly until the proper tartness is obtained. Approximately 1 tablespoon will be necessary.

As soon as oysters leave the relatively safe confines of butter-and-seasoning, the sky, illimitable, is the limit, and man's inventive genius plays one wild trick after another. In spite of all the zany recipes, however, many are good, if somewhat too elaborate, and the oyster usually emerges from them in spite of all its trappings.

It is pleasant, now and then, to make a good mushroom and cream sauce, mix oysters in it, and put the whole in ramekins, with crumbs on top, for a hot minute or two.

Or, hardly fancier, this Louisiana recipe for a gumbo (without okra, oddly enough for such a local dish) is easy to make and very good, and the saffron in it makes you think of *bouillabaisse* in Marseille, or of *risotto* under the glass arcade at Biffi's in Milano:

OYSTER GUMBO

⅔ *cup finely diced onion*
2 *tablespoons butter or good olive oil*
4 *tablespoons flour*
2 *bay leaves*
1 *teaspoon salt*
5 *drops Evangeline (or tabasco) sauce*

2 *dozen oysters*
1½ *cups water*
3 *tablespoons finely cut parsley*
1½ *to 3 teaspoons powdered saffron, according to taste*

Sauté the onion in butter in a heavy pan or casserole until limp but not brown. Blend in flour and bay, salt, and tabasco.

Drain the oysters, saving the liquor, and add liquor and water

[1] Herbs for the Kitchen, Irma Goodrich Mazza. Little, Brown and Company, Boston, 1940.

gradually to the mixture, stirring well. Cook about fifteen minutes, stirring now and then.

Add the oysters, parsley, and saffron, and stir well. Serve as soon as steaming, in a bowl with a dish of fluffy hot rice beside it. Ladle onto the rice on generous dinner-plates.

Or, in natural progression toward the baroque and away from simple things, this recipe from *Fit for a King*[2] is good, in spite of its little dibbles and dashes of this and that . . . and it is given by Roy Alciatore, the slender-faced son of the house of Antoine, in New Orleans, which should make it triply worthy (and also explain how so many sauces could be assembled for one little dish):

OYSTERS À LA FOCH

Spread a piece of toast lightly with sausage meat and cook under a salamander. Fry ½ dozen oysters and place on toast. With ¾ Espagnal and ¼ tomato make a sauce to which you will add a spoonful of Hollandaise sauce, a dash of Lea and Perrins sauce and a dash of sherry wine. Mix well together and pour over the oysters on toast. Serve.

Far removed as this recipe may seem from the ordinary kitchen's possibilities, it still has not that fabulous quality of the rule quoted by everyone from Richelieu's chef to Crosby Gaige, in which you put one thing inside another until you have something more or less the size of an elephant, then roast the whole, and finally throw away all but the innermost thing. For instance, you start with an oyster. You put it inside a large olive. Then you put the olive inside an ortolan (a wee bird called "the garden bunting," in case you are among the under-privileged), and the ortolan inside a lark, and so on and so on. In the end, you have a roasted oyster. Or perhaps a social revolution.

Probably the most rabble-rousing recipe I ever heard, if the rabble could have listened, was one told me under the table, so to speak, by a cadaverous old man who had reigned at various times in the kitchens of all the crowned heads and banker-princes of *fin-de-Hapsbourg* Europe. He was a Russian, as far as could be known, and when I met him he was running a little box near Toulon in

[2] Merle Armitage, Longmans, Green and Company, New York, 1939.

France, the kind frequented by Turkish and Egyptian millionaires who gave him three days' warning and came in twelve Rolls-Royces, and he was living solely on American gin and bicarbonate of soda.

He felt toward gastronomy as some men feel toward beautiful terrible women, and his conversation was for the most part a series of diatribes and scurrilous anecdotes about dishes he had made, much as most lecherous old men's leering reminiscences would be about girls they had done the same thing to.

His recipe for "Oysters à la Bazeine," as far as it can be cleared of his multi-lingual obscenities, is as follows, and is obviously not recommended to the bride of three weeks who just loves to stir up pretty dishes in her kitchenette:

OYSTERS À LA BAZEINE

OR

Honi Soit Qui Mal Y Pense

Have on hand adequate supplies of sauce Béchamel, sauce Soubise, *and* velouté. (*Recipes can be found in Escoffier's* Guide Culinaire, *in Dumas'* Grand Dictionnaire de Cuisine, *or even in André Simon's* French Cook Book.)

Prepare a roux *of chopped chives, butter, and rice-flour, and set it aside.*

Slice truffles paper-thin, and cut into the shapes of dolphins, crabs, and other sea-monsters. Set them aside.

Poach brook trout, preferably alive, in a court-bouillon *made with a good dry champagne instead of ordinary wine and water. Set them aside.*

Make a marinade, *using fine instead of wine-vinegar, and in it marinate small cubes of Parma ham for several hours, or until a faint iridescence appears. Drain, and set aside.*

Prepare croutes *by browning thick slices of fine white bread in Strasbourg goose-fat, and do not set aside.*

Instead, place them quickly on heated plates. Spread each tranche *with Béchamel and then the* roux. *Set a trout carefully upon it, and coat with Soubise. Over this sprinkle the cubes of Parma ham, and then a thin layer of velouté. Decorate lavishly with the truffle-silhouettes, and serve at once under bells with a modest but well-bred Sainte-Croix du Château Pinardino '08.*

Or fry oysters and serve with ale.

Take 300 Clean Oysters

Oysters are the usual opening to a winter breakfast . . .
indeed they are almost indispensable.

—Almanach des Gourmands, 1803

For hundreds of years men have ascribed all kinds of potent qualities to oysters, aphrodisiac and more purely practical. For one, they are supposed to be good for you.

Restaurants and bars and even governments bring out various attractive kinds of propaganda, and tell in a thousand ways why you should eat the molluscs which in spite of publicity have been a favorite food for thousands and thousands of years.

Oysters are healthful and nourishing, full of all the chemical elements such as oxygen, hydrogen, nitrogen, and on and on, which occur regularly in your own body and are necessary to it. They keep you fit, do oysters, with vitamins and such, for energy and what is lightly called "fuel value." They prevent goiter. They build up your teeth. They keep your children's legs straight, and when Junior reaches puberty they make his skin clear and beautiful as a soap-opera announcer's dream. They add years to your life . . .

And . . .

They contain more phosphorus than any other food!

Phosphorus is a brain food, the most important one, according to popular belief for centuries and publicity men for oyster companies and even a few reputable scientists. It has been called that for a long time: Cicero ate oysters to nourish his eloquence, and the ancients used them with a startlingly cold-blooded combination of gastronomy and pure hygiene.

Long before the fifteenth century of our era, people ate them and

144

other fish to aid their intellects. Somewhere after 1461, indeed, Louis XI made it obligatory, at least for the group of great men he gathered to him in his fabulous reign, to swallow a certain amount of such easy phosphorus each day.

The king's physicians ruled him as thoroughly as he ruled the Scots and Italians and Portuguese in his councils, and since Louis ate oysters by prescription, so did all influential France, less from choice than from political wisdom. And the professors of the Sorbonne, the real wisemen of France, could not even pretend that politics entered into their diet.

Professors, Louis reasoned, should be as intelligent as possible, since they represented him, "le roi terrible," and therefore he saw that they did not disappoint him. Once a year, willy-nilly, they were served a dinner at the king's orders, and at that dinner they were bound to eat, and eat prodigiously, of oysters. It was to make them bright, and once accomplished, keep them so!

A little later, in the times of Voltaire and Pope and Swift, oysters were considered less as a food than as an *apéritif*, so that it was quite usual to serve ten or twelve dozen to each guest as a "starter" for a banquet. An old recipe begins: "Take 300 clean oysters and throw into a pot filled with nice butter . . ." One man, old Marshal Turgot, who knew almost too much about famines, was able in fatter days to eat a hundred oysters before breakfast just to whet his appetite.

And when the infamous Whistling Oyster of Drury Lane started his daily pipings on the pub-bar (which kept up for a suspiciously long time when you consider the seasonal existence of such shellfish), and drew enormous hungry crowds of delighted listeners, oyster-eating became a necessity not only to the snobs but to the common people, not to mention the *bourgeoisie*.

Since then, really, almost any Western man with a few cents in his pocket and a little time on his hands can swallow a certain amount of phosphorus, and it is still good as long as the oysters are fresh and clean, whether it goes to nourish his brain, his belly, or his most private parts.

A Lusty Bit of Nourishment

Cook, white, must understand oysters. Apply aft. 1 P.M.
Iliffe, 847 E. Allegheny.

—Adv. in *Philadelphia Inquirer*, March 1941

THE flavor of an oyster depends upon several things. First, if it is fresh and sweet and healthy it will taste good, quite simply . . . good, that is, if the taster like oyster.

Then, it will taste like a Chincoteague or a blue point or a mild oyster from the Louisiana bayous or perhaps a metallic tiny Olympia from the Western coast. Or it may have a clear harsh flavor, straight from a stall in a wintry French town, a stall piled herring-bone style with Portugaises and Garennes, green as death to the uninitiated and twice as toothsome. Or it may taste firm and yet fat, like the English oysters from around Plymouth.

Then an oyster will taste like what the taster expects, which of course depends entirely on the taster. Myself, since I was seventeen I have expected all oysters to be delicious, and with few exceptions they have been. In the same way, some people wait, if they manage to swallow these shell-fish at all, to gag more or less violently. And they gag.

Oysters can be eaten for themselves, as on the half shell or even in cooked dishes; they can be eaten primarily for the sauce that coats them, as in Oysters à la Rockefeller and all their offspring; and they can be eaten as a flavoring . . . oyster stuffing, for example.

Oyster stuffing, for turkeys naturally, is as American as corn-on-the-cob or steamed coot, as far as Americans know or care. To many families it is a necessary part of Christmas dinner, so that its omission would at once connotate a sure sign of internal disintegration, as if Ma came to church in her corset-cover or Uncle Jim brought his light-o'-love to the children's picnic.

146

It would mean financial failure too, to leave out those oysters which not so long ago were brought carefully a thousand miles for the fortunate moneybags in Iowa and Missouri who could boast of them in their holiday stuffings. Not every man could buy them, God knows, even if he wanted to, and a Middle Westerner was even prouder than a man from Down East to have these shell-fish on his feast-day.

Perhaps it is because they were somewhat lacking in their first freshness by the time they reached Peoria; perhaps it was because the people of this land so far from seashores were abashed by shells: whatever the reason, oysters in the Middle West were always cooked . . . and still are, mostly. And in spite of evidence, turkey stuffing seems primarily a part of that cookery. In it, oysters are used for their flavor, quite simply.

There are many recipes, from New England cookbooks as well as those spotted brown pamphlets issued yearly by the Ladies' Aids and Guild Societies of small towns beyond the Mississippi. All of them agree that it is almost impossible to put too many oysters in a turkey dressing if you are going to put in any at all.

The method of using them differs, of course, so that one rule will say, "Mince ½ dozen thoroughly and sprinkle throughout the crumbs," and another will command more generously, "Fill cavity of bird with large plump blue points." A fair medium, however, is the following recipe from Mrs. William Vaughn Moody's *Cook Book*:[1]

DRESSING FOR TURKEY OR OTHER FOWL WITH OYSTERS

1½ qts. of fine counts	1 qt. of oyster juice
1 qt. of lightly fried crumbs	salt, pepper, celery salt, and paprika

Wing the oysters. Add the bread crumbs, oyster juice, and seasoning.

I would add, with the Browns in their *Country Cook Book*, that "Perhaps Oyster stuffing is one of the best, but the crumbs, which are mixed with the oysters and oyster liquor, should be literally soaked in melted butter, as should all crumbs that go into a turkey."

---

[1] Charles Scribner's Sons, New York, 1931.

For myself, I also like a cup or more of finely chopped celery stirred in with the crumbs, rather than Mrs. Moody's celery salt.

There is a recipe in the book Merle Armitage and his wife cooked up called *Fit for a King* which is less conventional, but very good for those who don't want any nonsense about hiding the oysters. It is called, simply enough,

OYSTER STUFFING

Toast some thin slices of bread until brown and butter them. Lay 2 slices flat inside the turkey and over them put a good layer of raw oysters seasoned with salt and pepper, lemon juice, and a few pieces of butter. Over this lay two more slices of toast and then a layer of oysters as before. The resulting flavor is delicious.

Between these two recipes there are ten thousand variations, probably, but the general idea of using oysters as a flavoring is no new one to us, any more than it has been for some several thousand years to the Chinese.

They probably are the longest users of these molluscs in such fashion. It has been going on for centuries, like so many other quaint Oriental customs, so that the oldest cookbooks give practically the same recipes used today in Hongkong and the kitchens of bewildered blonde brides in other outposts-of-Empire.

There are two kinds of oysters used in Chinese cooking for their flavor. There is *ho tsee*, the dried oyster, and then there is *ho yeou*, which is so much like our old-fashioned oyster catsup that I wonder if it was not brought back to us by one of those doughty old sea captains whose spirits still search for the Northwest Passage far past Java Head.

Marion Harland's 1873 edition of *Common Sense in the Household* gives a recipe that is probably as good as any outside a Chinese grocery, although other more modern cookbooks are less bound by tee-totalitarianism than she, and more willing to forego vinegar altogether and put in a full quart of sherry for each quart of shellfish. Here is Mrs. Harland's recipe:

OYSTER CATSUP

1 *quart oysters*	1 *tablespoon salt*
1 *teacupful cider vinegar*	1 *teaspoon cayenne pepper, and*
1 *teacupful sherry*	*same of mace*

Chop the oysters and boil in their own liquor with a teacupful vine-gar, skimming the scum as it rises. (It is here that such devil-may-care moderns as the Browns in their *Country Cook Book* say, "To each pint of oysters add a pint of sherry, let come to a boil . . .") *Boil three minutes, strain through a hair-cloth, return the liquor to the fire, add the wine, pepper, salt, and mace. Boil fifteen minutes, and when cold, bottle for use, sealing the corks.*

Mr. Henry Low, who is an authority on Chinese food, says of a *ho yeou* which might as well be Mrs. Harland's, for all the difference we could know, "Very delicious to serve with cold boiled chicken." In spite of the somewhat Charlie Chan-ish swing to this sentence, the opinion is a good one.

So is his inclusion, in *Cook at Home in Chinese*,[2] of at least one recipe using dried oysters, which can be bought at almost any Oriental grocery store in this country and are very much like the smoked oysters people give you now at cocktail parties, excellent little shriveled things on toothpicks which make your mouth taste hideous unless you drink a lot, which may also make your mouth taste hideous. Probably our smoked oysters could be used as well as *ho tsee*, but I doubt if they should be soaked. Or perhaps I am mistaken.

Anyway, here is Mr. Low's recipe for

DRIED OYSTERS WITH VEGETABLES
(Ho Tsee Soong)

½ lb. dried oysters (ho tsee)
1 cup chopped bamboo shoots (jook tsun)
1 cup chopped Chinese cabbage (bok choy)
1 cup peeled chopped water chestnuts (ma tai)
½ cup chopped raw lean pork
1 clove crushed garlic
1 piece crushed green ginger

2 tablespoons oyster sauce (ho yeou)
½ teaspoon sugar
½ cup water
a pinch of salt
a dash of pepper
½ head shredded Boston lettuce
1 teaspoon gourmet powder (mei jing)
2 teaspoons cornstarch

Soak oysters five hours and cut off hard parts. Chop fine. Mix together all chopped ingredients, add ginger, garlic, gourmet powder,

[2] The Macmillan Company, New York, 1938.

salt, pepper and sugar. Put in a hot, well-greased skillet and cook four minutes. Add oyster sauce and water and cook four minutes more. Add cornstarch, which has been made into a smooth paste. Stir, and cook one minute. Arrange lettuce leaves on platter and pour cooked mixture over them.

It is not such a far cry as it seems from the exotic blendings of this Ho Tsee Soong to the pungency of Oysters à la Rockefeller. Both dishes depend almost more upon the herbs that make up their body than they do upon the oysters that are the *raison d'être*, and whether they are "dry and putrid" in a dark kitchen in Chungking or San Francisco, or fresh in New Orleans, the herbs must be prepared with finicky attention.

There are too many legends, really, about Oysters Rockefeller for any one to dare say what he thinks is the true one. It is equally foolish to say what is the true recipe since every gourmet who has ever dined in that nostalgically agreeable room of Antoine's on St. Louis Street figures, after the third or fourth sampling if not the first, that he has at last discovered the secret.

It is true that Mr. Alciatore, like his father and grandfather, has managed to keep his Rockefellers consistently delicious. That is perhaps the reason they are so justly famous, rather than any special secret formula. Other restaurants serve their own versions, which may be a little cheaper or even a little more expensive, and may look almost like Antoine's. But they are undependable, so that sometimes the rock-salt they rest on is half an inch thick and sometimes an inch; sometimes the covering, that little soft green blanket over each oyster, is dark, and sometimes it is lightly mottled, with logical differences in the flavor of the dish itself.

(This simple, apparently difficult secret for success has also been copied by the bar-men in the Roosevelt Hotel in New Orleans, too: unchanging excellence. According to their publicity, they are the only makers of the Original Ramos Gin Fizz, that subtle smooth-like drink which has nourished reporters and politicians and other humans through many a long food-less summer near the simmering bayous.

(Once, for reasons of research, I drank two Ramos fizzes away from the hallowed Roosevelt. They were truly bad. I went back to the hotel, and watched eagerly while the old bar-man put little dashes of this and that together and then handed it all to the strong young stevedore who was chief shaker. I decided that infinite care, unhurried patience, and a never-varying formula were more the secret than any magic element such as dried nectar-crumbs or drops from a Ramos philter.

(I proved this theory, at least to my pleasure, when with infinite care and a certain amount of unhurried patience I too made a Ramos, after a recipe I found which was printed in 1900 for Solari's Grocery. It was easy to assemble, once I located some orange-flower water . . . and it was, Heaven protect me for this blasphemy!, as good as any ever shook up at the Roosevelt.)

Oysters Rockefeller, then, surrounded as they are by pomp and legend, are not impossible to copy. Their miracle is that *chez Antoine*, where the last two Alciatores have served them ever since 1889, they have always been delicious. Probably it is safe to say that they have not varied one jot or tittle in all these years, so that Mr. Roy could feel quite safe in sitting down to the millionth order, complete with photographers and head-waiter-with-wine-basket, to dip into the first succulent shell with only a faint sign of suspicion on his small intelligent face.

The postcards resulting from this occasion are given to every person who eats Oyster à la Rockefeller at Antoine's, and on each one, like the number of your duck in the old days at the Tour d'Argent in Paris (Where else?), is stamped the number of your plate of these famous morsels. It is an endearing bit of *chi-chi*, which is barely marred by the italics under the picture: *The recipe is a sacred family secret.*

That is rather more than *chi-chi*, although equally endearing in its solemnity. It is what could be called an exaggeration of the truth, since, although the Alciatores may use ¾ of a teaspoon of this or that rather than ½, there are many private cooks who have a recipe which is as good, Louisiana gourmets say, as Antoine's own.

This is it, reprinted from *A Book of Famous Old New Orleans Recipes Used in the South for More Than Two Hundred Years:*[3]

---

[3] For sale at Solari's and other New Orleans stores.

OYSTERS ROCKEFELLER

Procure oysters on the half shell, wash them and drain them, and put them back on the shells. Place ice cream salt to the thickness of about one half inch on a platter and preheat, placing the oysters that are on the half shells on the hot salt and run them in the broiler for five minutes. Then cover with the following sauce and bread crumbs and bake in the hot oven until brown. Serve hot.

SAUCE FOR OYSTERS ROCKEFELLER

1 *cup oyster water*	1 *oz. herbsaint*
1 *cup plain water*	1 *cup best butter*
¼ *bunch shallots*	¼ *bunch spinach*
1 *small sprig thyme*	1 *tablespoon Worcestershire*
½ *cup ground bread crumbs*	*sauce*
toasted and sifted	2 *small stalks green celery*

Grind all the vegetables in the chopper. Put the water and the oyster liquor together, and let boil vigorously for about five minutes then add the ground vegetables and cook about twenty minutes or until it's to the consistency of a thick sauce.

Stir in the butter until melted and remove from fire, add the herbsaint, pour sauce over oysters on the shells, sprinkle with bread crumbs return to hot oven for five minutes and serve piping hot on the platter in which you cooked them.

(Herbsaint is a cordial made in the deep South from various herbs but mostly anise, so that it tastes very much like that clear *Anis Mono* that used to be served in Spanish pubs, or even like Pernod. Some people say that Antoine's spurns it in Oysters Rockefeller, but I wouldn't know. Myself, I think not.)

It is more than likely that if Mr. Alciatore, to say nothing of his Head Chef Camille Averna, should see this recipe he would toss his head slightly, or perhaps even sneer. However, sacred family secret or no, I still believe that any good cook with skill and, above all, unfailing patience can make Oysters à la Rockefeller that are as like Antoine's as one angel can be like another.

The question is, Who wants to? Perhaps you are an habitué or perhaps you have been to Antoine's once or twice. The inescapable charm of that simple, almost austere room, with mirrors for walls; with the blue gas lamps flickering through all the evening while the electric lights snap on and off for the blazings of *crêpes Suzette* and *cafés brûlots au diable*; with its high cashier's seat at the back and its deft impersonal waiters who let the pantry doors swing wide open now and then to show the ordered shimmer of the wine-glass cupboard: all that makes a family secret much more precious than any recipe, and one that means untellable pleasure to untold amateur gourmets.

Whether they are men like "The Grand Duke Alexis, brother of the Czar of Russia," or Sinclair Lewis, or "Mr. Nobody from Nowhere," they find at Antoine's something remembered, something perhaps never known but recognized, so that dining there is full of ease and mellowness. *Huitres en Coquilles à la Rockefeller* appear magically, prepared with loving patience for each eager diner as if he were the first and only *gastronome*, and their tedious preparation is something that can best be left to Camille Averna's direction.

It should never matter that other people, armed with determination and an almost perfect copy of the Alciatores' recipe, could probably do just as well. Better go once to the little place on St. Louis Street in New Orleans, and eat them as they should be eaten, than struggle doggedly a thousand times with hot salt-beds and spinach-grindings in Connecticut or California. Oysters à la Rockefeller any place but *chez* Antoine are not quite as delicious, not quite as *kosher* nor as *comme il faut*.

There are, of course, at least ten other precious recipes for every thousand humans who have ever cooked an oyster. There are fairly complicated ones, like the following rule contributed to the first number of the magazine *Gourmet* by the Hotel Pierre of New York and its Head Chef Georges Gonneau:

FRENCH CREAMED OYSTERS

Put one cup of butter into the top of a lighted chafing-dish; add one tablespoon English mustard, ¼ teaspoon anchovy paste; salt, pepper, and a dash of cayenne pepper to taste; stir until mixture is thoroughly blended. Add three cups finely chopped celery and stir almost constantly until celery is nearly cooked. Pour in 1 quart rich, fresh cream slowly, stirring constantly until mixture comes to a boil. Add four dozen oysters, cleaned and free from beard, and cook two minutes. Finally, add ¼ cup good sherry wine. Serve on freshly made toast on hot plates, and garnish with quartered lemon and crisp young watercress. Dust each serving with paprika, mixed with a little nutmeg.

This recipe, an excellent way to exercise man's basic fascination for chafing dishes and vice versa, is naturally much simpler than some, even though sautéed ham and mushrooms be added, or truffles; and on the other hand it is a great deal more elaborate than such a one as Marion Harland gave in 1870 and many years before.

She wrote with a passion which was always ladylike in spite of its perhaps ungenteel *gourmandise*, as her period dictated, but she was never squeamish, and her "receipts" are to a large number of *aficionados* as beautifully rounded as the Songs of Solomon. Witness what she said, so long ago and only yesterday, about

ROAST OYSTERS

There is no pleasanter frolic for an Autumn evening, in the regions where oysters are plentiful, than an impromptu "roast" in the kitchen. There the oysters are hastily thrown into the fire by the peck. You may consider that your fastidious taste is marvelously respected if they are washed first. A bushel basket is set to receive the empty shells, and the click of the oyster-knives forms a constant accompaniment to the music of laughing voices. Nor are roast oysters amiss upon your own quiet supper-table, when the "good man" comes in on a wet night, tired and hungry, and wants "something heartening." Wash and wipe the shell-oysters, and lay them in the oven, if it is quick; upon the top of the stove, if it is not. When they are open, they are done. Pile in a large dish, and send to table. Remove the upper shells by a dexterous wrench of the knife, season the oyster on the lower, with pepper-sauce and butter, or pepper, salt, and vinegar in lieu of the sauce, and you have the very aroma of this pearl of bivalves, pure and undefiled.

Or (she adds, rather in anti-climax), you may open while raw, leaving the oysters upon the lower shells; lay in a large baking-pan, and roast in their own liquor, adding pepper, salt, and butter before serving.

Probably the "pepper sauce" used by Mrs. Harland's frolicking family was made more or less after this old New England recipe:

ROAST OYSTER SAUCE

2 tablespoons butter   4 drops tabasco sauce
juice of 1 lemon   juice of ½ onion

Melt the butter, stir in the other ingredients and pour over oysters.
Serve hot.

The Harland recipe is not much different from one given in *Plats
du Jour*[4] by Paul Reboux, but its style is as much like his as his own
flippant punning words are like the silence that comes now from his
once garrulous land of wit and gaiety:

GRILLED OYSTERS

*. . . Surely, this recipe would not have the approval of the S.P.C.A.
But it is probable that oysters possess a sensitivity analogous to that
of the French tax-payer, so that they are incapable of very characteristic reactions. That, then, is why there is little reason for
weeping tenderly at the idea that these molluscs must be placed on
the grill.*

*As they submit to the same end that overtook Saint Lawrence,
the oysters open. It is exactly like the purse of the government pen-
sioner as Income Tax Day rolls around: one does the only possible
thing in the presence of bad luck.*

*Take advantage of their being open to pop in a little melted butter,
some pepper, and some bread crumbs. Then close them up again: at
this moment they will be too weak to resist you. Let them cook a
little. And serve them very hot.*

Some people like this very much.

All oysters cooked in sauce, whether their own or manufactured,
are necessarily of a certain complexity. They may be as simple as
Marion Harland's or Reboux's; they may be coated with the intricacies of *roux* and white-wine sauces. They may even be surrounded
by the strange legends of Antoine's, so that their consumption becomes more a rite than the simple manifestation of a hunger.

According to the little black-and-gold booklet published for
Antoine's centennial, Oysters à la Rockefeller contain "such rich

---

[4] Flammarion, Paris, 1936.

ingredients that the name of the Multi-Millionaire was borrowed to indicate their value." Some gourmets say that any oyster worthy of its species should not be toyed with and adulterated by such skullduggeries as this sauce of herbs and strange liqueurs. Others, more lenient, say that Southern oysters like Mr. Alciatore's need some such refinement, being as they are languid and soft-tasting to the tongue.

They are, you might say, more like the Southern ladies than the brisk New Englanders. They are delicate and listless . . . and ice is scarce, or used to be . . . and the weather's no good for saving; best cover the bayou-molluscs with a fine New Orleans sauce, or at least a dash or two of red Evangeline. . . .

But further north, men choose their oysters without sauce. They like them cold, straightforward, simple, capable of spirit but un-adorned, like a Low Church service maybe or a Boston romance.

And oysters of the North Atlantic Coast are worthy of this more or less unquestioning trust. They are firm and flavorful, and eaten chilled from their own lower shell with a bit of lemon juice squeezed over them they are among men's true delights.

There are, oddly enough, almost as many ways to eat such a simple dish as there are men to eat it.

First, several millennia ago, men cracked the shells and sucked out the tender gray bodies with their attendant juices and their inevitable sharp splinters. Then, when knives came, they pried open the two shells and cupped the lower one in their hands, careful not to spill its colorless elixir. And always, even from the beginning, there have been variations on these two simple processes; there has been invented a series of behavior-rules as complex as the recipes to prevent sea-sickness or how to arrange three tulips in a low jade-green bowl for the local garden show.

If a man cared, and knew all the rules, he would be really fright-ened to go into a decent oyster-bar and submit his knowledge to the cold eyes of the counter-man and all the local addicts. He would be so haunted by what was correct in that certain neighborhood and how to hold the shell and whether lemon juice should be used and so on that he would probably go instead to a corner drug store and order a double chocolate banana-split.

Fortunately, though, almost everybody who goes into an oyster-bar or even eats in a restaurant is so pleased with the oysters themselves that he eats them in his own fashion without giving a toot or a tinkle about what other people think.

In America, on the East Coast, oysters are usually served on a plate of shaved ice, with small round white crackers in a bowl or vase. Quite often a commendable battery of bottled sauces such as tabasco and horse-radish accompanies the order, and in many restaurants a little cup of red sauce with a tomato base is put in the middle of the plate of ice-and-oysters. Either this little cup of sauce or one of the bottles contains gastronomic heat in one form or another.

In New Orleans' oyster-bars, and all over the Western World in what used to be called "places of the people . . . common places," the procedure is simpler, almost as simple as the English pub-custom of shoving you your oysters, a toothpick to pluck them with, and a shaker of weak vinegar if you're toff enough to want it. Down South there is a long marble or hard wood counter between the customer and the oyster-man, sloping toward the latter. He stands there, opening the shells with a skill undreamed of by an ordinary man and yet always with a few cuts showing on his fingers, putting the open oysters carefully, automatically, on a slab of ice in front of him, while a cat waits with implacable patience at his ankles for a bit of oyster-beard or a caress. He throws the top shells behind him into a barrel, and probably they go into a road or a wall somewhere, later, with cement to bind them.

A man comes into the bare place, which has hard lights, and sawdust on the floor. He mutters "One" or "Two" to the oyster-man, and pulls a handful of square soda-crackers from the tipped glass jar at the end of the counter. If he wants to, he spoons out a cupful of tomato sauce from a big crock.

By then his one or two dozen oysters wait in a line for him upon the cold counter, their shells tipped carefully so that the liquor will lie still in them and not flow down the sloping marble and into the bins of unopened shells underneath. He picks up an oyster on a pointed thin little fork, and holds the shell under his chin while he guides it toward his mouth, having dunked it or not in the garish sauce, and then he swallows it.

If he likes raw oysters he enjoys this ceremony very much. Many do not, and may they long rest happy, if envious. Now, having wasted too many years in shuddering at oysters, I like them. I *thoroughly* like them, so that I am willing to forego comfort and at times even safety to savor their strange cold succulence.

I was quite willing, once at the Old Port in Marseille before things changed, to risk their brassy greenness at a quay-side stand. Once I knowingly ate a "bad one" in the Pompeiian Room at the Bern-Palace rather than cry them shame. And now, after more than a few years of prejudiced acquaintance, I can still say that oysters please me.

Those years, which have not been quite empty of perception, have made me form a few ideas of my own, since it is impossible to enjoy without thought, in spite of what the sensualists say.

I am still very ignorant, but I know that I used to like *Portugaises vertes* and oysters from Garennes, in the times that seem so far from me now . . . as far as the well-fed French people who once plucked the shells with me from their willow baskets on the Rue de la Gare, when the old man sliced open the rough long shells with his knife there or in front of Crespin's in Dijon in the winter, and the little oyster-stalls stood bravely near the stations in all the province-towns of France. The greenness and the tepid brassiness of those shell-fish were at first a shock, and I also thought I should suspect their unhygienic deaths . . . but none ever hurt me, and my palate always benefited as well as my spirit.

In America I think I like best the oysters from Long Island Sound, although I have eaten Chincoteagues and some others from the Delaware Bay that were very good. Farther south, in spite of my innate enthusiasm, I have had to admit that the oysters grow less interesting served in the shell, and almost cry out for such delicious decadences as horse-radish or even cooking, which would be sacrilege in Boston or Bordeaux.

On the Mexican Gulf they are definitely better cooked, although skilled gourmets have insisted otherwise to me, and one man from Corpus Christi once put his gun on the table while he stated quietly that anybody who said Texas blue points weren't the best anywhere was more than one kind of insulting liar. I still prefer cooked oysters in the South, since for me one of the pleasures of eating a raw oyster is the crispness of its flesh (*crisp* is not quite right, and *flesh* is not right, but in the same way you might say that *oyster* is not right for what I mean) . . . and crispness seems not to exist in the warm waters there.

And on the West Coast, I like the metallic tiny bites of the Olympias, and patriotism or no patriotism, find the Japanese-spawned Willapoints from Oregon tasteless and too bulky to be eaten from the shell. One thing, to my mind, should accompany all such oysters served this way as inevitably as soda-crackers go with soup in a drug store or Gilbert with Sullivan or Happy New Year with Merry Christmas: buttered brown bread and lemon.

In the Good Old Days, those good old days so dull to hear about and so delightful to talk of, thin slices of real pumpernickel-ish brown bread (No machine-sliced beige-colored sponge, for God's sake!) and honest-to-Betsy lumps of juicy lemon used to come automatically with every half-dozen of oysters, whether you sat in the circle at the Café de Paris or stood with one foot in the sawdust down near the third-class restaurant of the Nurnberger-Bahnhof. They picked up the sometimes tired flavor of the oysters, and I soon discovered that a few drops of lemon juice on the buttered bread tasted much better than on the shell-fish themselves.

I have thought seriously about this, while incendiary bombs fell and people I knew were maimed and hungry, and I believe that all American oyster-bars and every self-respecting restaurant in this good land which presumes to serve raw oysters in their shells or even naked in a cup, should at once make it compulsory to serve also a little plate of thin-sliced nicely buttered good dark bread, preferably the heavy fine-grained kind and buttered with sweet butter I should say, and a few quarters of lemon.

I think the oyster-men and the owners of restaurants would find this little persnicket a paying one, and that even if they charged a few cents extra for the lemon or the butter or even the bread, like Lipp's and some of the old places in Europe, they would sell enough more oysters to repay them many times.

And for the person who likes oysters, such a delicate, charming, nostalgic gesture would seem so delicate, so nostalgically charming, so reminiscent of a thousand good mouthfuls here and there in the past . . . in other words, so *sensible* . . . that it would make even nostalgia less a perversion than a lusty bit of nourishment.

Pearls Are Not Good to Eat

Pearls are calcareous concretions of peculiar lustre, produced by
certain molluscs, and valued as objects of personal adornment.
*   —Encyclopædia Britannica*

THERE are several things to do with oysters beside eat them, although many people believe firmly in that as the most sensible course.

Oysters themselves (that is, the living creatures within their shells) can harbor little crabs called, plainly enough, oyster-crabs. They are about the size of a six-year-old girl's thumb-nail, and look exactly like a normal crab seen through the wrong end of an opera-glass, square and ruddy and well fringed with legs and such. They are one of the most delicious delicate by-products in the world, on land or sea.

It is perhaps only a gastronomical coincidence that they seem to be most numerous when whitebait are in season, but the combination so often met with in New York and other Eastern cities about Christmas-time is perfect: tiny crisp fried oyster-crabs and little almost formless fish about an inch long, piled on plates big enough for humans but still looking like something prepared for a banquet at the court of Lilliput. They are served with lemon and parsley, either fresh or fried, and watercress is good with them too. So is champagne. So, really, is beer, light and cold.

There may be other things than crabs about the oysters themselves that can be used by humans, but I do not know them. Of course there are various catsups and spices that are made, all over the world but especially in China, but they cannot properly be called other than food. And once the oyster is dismissed and the shell is considered, gastronomy takes second place.

160

Oyster shell will probably never be called good to eat, unless by certain worms and by hens, who are, perhaps fortunately, mute on the subject of *la gourmandise*. They have been nibbling on shells for centuries without too much protest, and the more eggs they lay the more they love to peck into their little boxes of nice sharp oyster shell. Calcium and lime are to them, apparently, as instinctive a necessity as the fine dreams to a confirmed opium smoker, so that in spite of themselves they must have the wherewithal. In the case of the hens the problem is a simple one, and farmers and their wives in no matter what far country can buy crushed shell for their barnyards.

It is only near the sea coasts, though, that oyster shells are used for roads and ditch-linings and such rougher businesses, and there certainly you would not find a gastronomic connection . . . unless for remembering, with far-fetched romanticism, that every shell once held its tasty lodger, which must have been swallowed somewhere, by someone, before the road could be paved.

In Louisiana, in the winter between rains, the edges of the high causeways over the bayous and paddies are white and sharp-looking with tons of pounded shells. They hold back the mud like mortar, and past them the flat dead rice fields look soft and treacherous. If the wheel of your car slips off the road there is a high squealing crunch, and all the birds eating rice grains near the flocks of little cows fly up for a second, and then settle again around the ruminating beasts.

The best known of all an oyster's parasites (if anything as crisp and delicate and tiny as a crab could be called such) and all its by-products of chicken-scratch and paving-crumbs and even catsups, is something that for centuries has meant love and bloody battle to mankind: the pearl.

In India and China and even in the chill courts of Scottish kings, pearls have been set in metal and hung from pins and chains as long as such things existed. And they have never been thought cheap.

They grow slowly, secretly, gleaming "worm-coffins" built in what may be pain around the bodies that have crept inside the shells. Sometimes it is indeed a kind of tapeworm, a larva that bores deep into the oyster's soft flesh, carrying as it goes some particles of the creature's injured mantle. These particles take with them their power to start the secretion of the same mother-of-pearl that lines the shell, rather as yeast carried from one sour-dough pot to another fresh one will start its business all over again. And ultimately the unwelcome worm is encased in its rare coffin, and within the two shells lies a pearl.

(Some quibblers think, and who can say how well or wrongly, that water-mites on ducks cause pearls, and the Encylopædia Britannica says that "many different exciting causes" may lead to their formation. But, worms or lice or other excitations, pearls still enchant mankind.)

They can be flat on one side, never quite free within the shell, and then they are called *"boutons."* They can be hollow, warty blisters, *"coq de perle,"* or they can be irregular and *"baroque."* They are all valuable. To be of the first water, though, they must be perfectly spherical, or symmetrically pear-shaped, like a tear without its imagined point, and skin and orient must satisfy: that is, their texture must be delicate and flawless, of an almost translucent white, and their sheen must be subdued and yet iridescent. It is surprising, really, that there are so many correct ones in the world: pink, quickly fading, from the West Indies; the rare black ones from Mexico; white ones everywhere.

As far as can be known, pearls grow best in stunted, irregular shells, and almost everywhere in the world where there is at least a short period of warmth, since it is then that the secretion takes place every year. Any time after their fourth year they are worth finding.

In India and the southern seas, where most pearls are found, the divers bring up perhaps a thousand shells for every one with a jewel in it, and consider the hunting good. In rivers, from Japan to Ireland to our own state of Iowa, such ratios are unknown, and only the fact that pearls are actually there, somewhere, makes the fishers keep on their tedious work.

The job is not an easy one, and pearl-divers are short-lived. Sometimes their lungs burst. Sometimes they are killed by sharks, who live almost always near the oyster-beds, so that the divers must go armed with knives or ironwood spikes. Things have not changed much anywhere since Marco Polo wrote of the pearl grounds off the Malabar, on the south shores of Coromandel.

In the fisheries, he says, the merchants always arranged for "certain enchanters belonging to a class of Brahmans" to sit in the boats accompanying the divers, and to utter spells, so that the numerous fierce sharks which roamed the waters thereabouts should not attack. And at night these wizards discontinued their spells and magical cantations so that the sharks might patrol the places and thus in their own way act as police against other robbers.

Marco Polo could see the same enchanters in the pearl boats off India now, and probably hear the same spells, for sharks still live hardly less dangerously than the divers they attack, and pearls are still worth men's lives.

In Japan and China it is girls who do the diving, but they risk little, for the pearls they seek are not forty feet deep and uncharted, but only a few feet down and put there cannily by men who have been growing such rare jewels like sea-radishes for hundreds of years.

The girls wear queer rumpled turbans, and flop into the water at regular intervals, several at a time, like drunken birds. Ninety per cent of their shells have pearls in them, and if from disease and general bad luck only five per cent of the whole fishing is marketable, the merchants feel fat and happy. For cultured pearls are so beautiful that they can only be told from "natural" ones by X-ray, and in spite of their elaborate care, they are still a profitable crop.

In China, until recently at least, there has been an ancient market in Soochow where pearls in the shape of the Buddha could be bought, or even tiny fish or rings or lewder symbols. They were made carefully by men who put the matrices carefully into the shells in May or June: images of wood or tin or lead. Then the oysters were fattened for three years or so in tubs of sea-water well spiked with human dung, and when the time was ripe the beautiful images were sold to the religious and the curious, and the oysters were enjoyed in the kitchen. (Probably, since the Chinese are a thorough race, the shells were used in building walls, and thus full value received from the unprotesting bivalve.)

Pearls have been cultivated all over the world, even in Sweden, but probably the Japanese have been most persistently successful, so that the following recipe must be carried out somewhere in the coastal waters of Nippon, just as most such rules should be followed in kitchens or pantries.

TO MAKE A PEARL

1 *healthy spat*
1 *mature oyster*
1 *bead*
1 *wire cage*
  ligatures

scrubbing brushes, etc.
unnameable wound-astringent
  provided by Japanese gov-
  ernment
1 *diving-girl*

Introduce the spat, which should be at least 1/75 of an inch long, to the smooth surface of the cage. Submerge him in quiet clean water, where the cage will protect him from starfish, and frequent inspections and scrubbings will keep his rapidly growing shell free from boring-worms and such pests.

In three years prepare him for the major operation of putting the bead on his mantle (epithelium). Once the bead is in place, draw the mantle over it and ligature the tissues to form a wee sac. Put the sac into the second oyster, remove the ligature, treat the wound with the unnameable astringent, and after the oyster has been caged, put him into the sea.

Supervise things closely for seven years, with the help of your diving-girl. Any time after that you may open your oyster, and you have about one chance in twenty of owning a marketable pearl, and a smaller but equally exciting chance of having cooked up something really valuable.

It may be felt by some people that a simpler process would be to eat oysters until a pearl appeared. That is even longer, however, and in many years of oyster-eating and oyster-talking, the only person I have ever met who found one is myself.

It was at Galatoire's, in New Orleans, and for a few seconds after I almost cracked my tooth on the jewel, I sat in a reeling dream of riches and royalties, while the fine noisy odorous room grew dim around me. All the tweedy debutantes with their dark hair lying on their shoulders, and the thin Jews eating *pompano en papillotte* quietly while their friends drank, and the military men in civilian clothes and the high-class courtesans in uniform, and the politicians and reporters watching everyone in the mirrors between delicious mouthfuls: all that danced about me in an odor of fish and wine and general gastronomic sanctity. My head was filled with phrases: pearl of great price, pearls before swine, of Orient pearl a double row, Cleopatra's "pearl dissolved in royal wine," pearls on snow. . . .

Finally I worked my excitement into audible form and the pearl toward the front of my mouth, but by the time everyone around me knew what had happened and I had spat it fairly genteelly into my hand, I knew without looking at it what I would see.

It was a small, brownish, rough thing, rather like an abnormally dingy piece of gravel, and I put it by my plate to take home, and forgot it when I finally left the restaurant. It *was* exciting for a few minutes, even though I agreed thoroughly with the Chinese proverb that "Pearls and Precious Stones are not good to eat or drink."

Those Were Happy Days

*An old gentleman t'other day in discourse with a friend of his
(reflecting upon some adventures they had in youth together),
cry'd out, Oh Jack, those were happy days!*

—*The Spectator*, RICHARD STEELE

THERE are stories that in their telling spread about them a feeling
of the Golden Age, so that when you listen you forget all but the
warmth and incredible excitement of those other farther times;
oysters can be as fine as Ozymandias king of kings in them, and as
unforgettable.

I shall remember always the mysterious beautiful sensation of well-
being I felt, when I was small, to hear my mother talk of the suppers
she used to eat at boarding school. They were called "midnight
feasts," and were kept secret, supposedly, from the teachers, in the
best tradition of the 1890's. They consisted of oyster loaf. There
may have been other things. Maybe the most daring young ladies
even drank ginger beer, although I am afraid it was more likely a
sweet raspberry shrub or some such unfortunate potation. Maybe
there were cigarettes, and pickles, and bonbons. But it is the oyster
loaf that I remember.

I know I shall never taste one like it, except in my dreams,
nor will my mother . . . if she ever really did so. But I can see it,
and smell it, and I even know which parts to bite and which to let
melt against the roof of my mouth, exquisitely hot and comforting,
although my mother surely never told me.

It was made in a bread loaf from the best baker in the village,
and the loaf was hollowed out and filled with rich cooked oysters,
and then, according to my mother's vague and yet vivid account,

the top of the loaf was fastened on again, and the whole was baked crisp and brown in the oven. Then it was wrapped tightly in a fine white napkin, and hidden under a chambermaid's cape while she ran from the baker's to the seminary and up the back stairs to the appointed bedroom.

The girls, six or seven of them because an oyster loaf was really very large, sat in their best flowered wrappers on the floor, while one of them kept watch at the keyhole and saw that no light flickered from her candle or the shaded lamp.

The maid slipped into the whispering, giggling huddle, and put down her warm bundle, and although she had been well paid was always willing to take a pocketful of the rich cookies the young ladies' mothers sent them every week from home. Then she left, and the oyster loaf was unwrapped.

Now, today, it may sound untidy and foolish and a fine prelude to biliousness, but then there was something exciting and good about such schoolgirl gourmandise, so that when my mother told me of it, I thought with the old gentleman in *The Spectator* that those were indeed happy days, happier than I could ever know myself.

After I grew up I always looked, under *oysters* in any cookbooks I happened to be using, to see what was said about oyster loaves. It was not that I planned to make one: I simply remembered, once again, my mother's casual reminiscence. Usually the recipe was more or less like this one, from André Simon's *French Cook Book:*[1]

PAIN D'HUITRES
(Oyster Loaf)

Put into a bowl 2½ ounces of finely sifted bread crumbs, work into them 2 ounces of butter, season with seasoning salt; add 3 yolks, the liquid obtained from two dozen sauce oysters, and the oysters themselves, bearded and cut into dice.

Line a well-buttered charlotte mold with fish forcemeat about an inch thick; put the oyster mixture into the hollow, cover it with more of the forcemeat, and poach very gently for about 45 minutes.

Of course this is an exceedingly tony version, which Monsieur Simon admits he got from an Englishman, of what can be a pretty crude and terrible kind of stodgy meat loaf made of inferior oysters,

[1] Little, Brown and Company, Boston, 1938.

which is sold sometimes in bad restaurants along the Atlantic Coast. I have seen it, but have fortunately been talked out of tasting it, even for research purposes. Monsieur Simon's recipe is a good one . . . but still it has no connection with the one my mother talked of.

I have found one or two that were more or less as they ought to be, but still my mind's palate, educated to the smooth hot perfection of that "midnight feast," has known that they were poor things really. Even Mrs. Simon Kander, who usually tempers the cold practicability of her *Settlement Cook Book*[2] with her innate Jewish warmth, disappointed me with a dull recipe for "oysters in Crust Cases."

Finally, a few years ago, I found in the *Sunset's All-Western Cook Book*[3] a whole column called, praise be, "*Oyster Loaf.*" It gave three or four ways to make what it implied, with pardonable insularity, was a dish particularly appreciated by San Franciscans, and at least one of its rules sounded, at long last, much as I have always hoped my mother's schoolgirl feast should be.

Sunset recommends, among other things, filling a hollowed-out loaf with an oyster-and-bread stuffing such as you put in a turkey, and then baking it, slicing it, and serving it with a cream or cheese sauce.

It says you can fill hollowed-out French or finger rolls with creamed oysters, which you then bake and serve very hot.

It gives some more recipes.

But the one that makes me like the whole thing with an almost affectionate nostalgic liking is this:

OYSTER LOAF

Cut off the top of a crusty loaf of bread, and hollow out the center. Brush with butter, and put into a hot oven to heat through and toast slightly. While this is going on, coat medium-sized oysters with egg and crumbs, and fry them brown in deep or shallow fat. Fill the loaf with the oysters, pour melted butter over them, put on the lid which also has been toasted, and it is ready to eat . . . or to wrap thickly in wax paper and take on a picnic. A small loaf to serve two people is most convenient for serving.

---

[2] Milwaukee, 1931.
[3] Genevieve A. Callahan, Lane Publishing Company, San Francisco, 1935.

For me at least, that recipe is at last the one I have been looking for. I can change it as I will, and even pour a little thick cream over the loaf, or dust it with cayenne, but basically it is right with my childhood dream . . . and quite probably it is much better than the one the young ladies ate in their stuffy lamp-lit rendezvous so many years ago.

And yet . . . yet those will always be, in my mental gastronomy, on my spiritual taste-buds, the most delicious oysters I never ate.

Oh, Mother, those were happy days!

Soup of the Evening, Beautiful Soup

All ought to be made to taste the soup . . .
—Grimm's Fairy Tales

THIS is not that, and that certainly is not this, and at the same time an oyster stew is not stewed, and although they are made of the same things and even cooked almost the same way, an oyster soup should never be called a stew, nor a stew soup. It is perfectly clear, if you respect oysters and the words about them, and are annoyed by home economics articles, complete with soup recipes, which begin, "Dress up your oyster stew . . ."

An oyster stew is made quickly, about as fast as the hand can follow the mind or the mind the eye. Oyster soup takes longer, can cost much or little, and pleases some people even more than it bores others.

The great difference between it and the stew, probably, is that the soup has a thickening in it of flour or crumbs or egg, or, as one precise chef says, "*Rice! Never* flour or cornstarch!" It is richer, and yet oddly enough is often served before a large meal, whereas oyster stew is considered by even the heaviest gourmands as a meal in itself.

An inexpensive soup which tastes more like oysters than its recipe would lead you to suspect, especially if you have been reading older rules that call nonchalantly for quarts and pails, is the following, found in a newspaper:

CREAM OF OYSTER SOUP

¼ cup butter
2 tablespoons flour
1 quart milk
½ pint oysters (!)

1 teaspoon salt
¼ teaspoon celery salt
dash pepper

Melt butter in top of double boiler, remove from heat, and blend in flour. Add milk and stir constantly over direct heat until mixture boils and thickens slightly. Add seasonings and place over boiling water; cover. Remove any bits of shell from oysters. Chop oysters, using chopping bowl; add with liquor to hot mixture, heat thoroughly, approximately ten minutes, and serve piping hot with crisp crackers or buttered toast rings and strips. Serves six.

This recipe, especially when boxed on a newspaper page with its accompanying photograph, smudged but still modern in the Let-Us-Keep-Our-Kitchens-Gay manner, is almost actively abhorrent. It represents, with its efficiency, its lack of imagination, its very practicability, everything that Brillat-Savarin, in his forthright manner, would have belched at gastronomically.

And yet it can be a good soup. Basically it is well constructed, and, most valuable, it allows for certain extremely personal deviations: a pinch of fresh marjoram buds by Mrs. Zanzibar Woodbury, herbologist extraordinary of the East Dingle-Dell Garden Club; a dash of dry sherry by Y. Erpington Grubb, *bon-vivant*-emeritus of the English department of Stokes-on-the-Hudson College for Young Gentlemen; a rousing grind of fresh pepper by Charles (Chub) Bye, late of the Left Bank and later still of assorted Southern and Far Western "artists' colonies." The lady and the professor and the chubby yearner have reason; any addition, or all, to this sterile recipe can do small harm, and at best make it yet plainer that basically it is good enough to stand well-nigh incredible assaults, even to using tinned oysters.

Other rules for soup are less amenable. One which sounds almost like the newspaper recipe, and comes from the *New England Cook Book*, could no more be made with Number 2 cans of steamed Willapoints than Flying Fortresses with match-boxes . . . and as for imaginative additions, a flick of paprika is probably as far as even the most sacrilegious gourmet should let himself go:

OYSTER SOUP

1 *quart oysters*	2 *tablespoons flour*
3 *cups milk*	1½ *teaspoon salt*
1 *cup cream*	¼ *teaspoon pepper*
3 *tablespoons butter*	1 *tablespoon grated onion*

Melt the butter and stir in the flour and blend well. Slowly add the milk, stirring all the time, then the cream and seasonings, and grated onion. Keep hot over a low flame. Bring the oysters to a boil in their own liquor. Cook about five minutes or until the edges curl. Strain. Add oysters to the milk stock, heat about five minutes without boiling. Serve immediately.

Some books, less blunt in their manner than the austere New England pamphlet, call their soups bisques, and in general such a change of wording indicates either richer ingredients or a more finicky rule of procedure, with perhaps a few words of kitchen French thrown casually in with the English. Equally in general, such recipes are excellent.

One of them, given in Merle Armitage's *Fit for a King,* is a good model for all such rules:

OYSTER BISQUE

Make a roux of butter and flour. Add a large onion finely chopped and brown the mixture. Then add a quart of boiling water, 4 dozen oysters and their liquor, a generous square of butter, bay leaf, thyme, and salt and pepper. Boil this soup for twenty minutes, then remove two dozen of the oysters and chop them finely. Then pass the soup and the rest of the oysters through a sieve, mashing the oysters. Now add the chopped oysters and 4 sprigs of parsley. Serve steaming.

Mrs. William Vaughan Moody, who can always be trusted to cope with any of the finer problems of American gastronomy, also calls her soup bisque, and adds, as is her wont, a good gout of whipped cream which almost, but not quite, makes her recipe "ladies' luncheon":

OYSTER BISQUE[1]

1 qt. of oysters	½ cup of cracker crumbs
1 pint of cream	onion
1 pint of milk	salt, pepper, paprika
1 cup of whipped cream	mace

Put the oysters over to heat in a dish by themselves.

Put the pint of milk and the pint of cream in a double boiler, with a sprig of mace, and half a sweet onion. Remove the onion and mace when their first flavor is imparted.

When the oysters, and the milk and cream are hot, strain out the oysters, and put the liquor into the hot milk. Throw the oysters into cold water. Skim off any froth that rises to the top of the mixture in the double boiler. Add pepper and salt to taste, ½ cup of cracker crumbs, and 1 tablespoon of sweet butter. Let all cook together for a few minutes until the soup is well blended.

Strain the water off the oysters. Dry them on a clean piece of cheesecloth. Put them into the soup and serve at once, with a tablespoon of whipped cream on each cup.

Mrs. Moody's literary style, or rather aroma, is almost as delicate as her genteel methods for making a soup taste like onion without having any onion showing in the final dish, and there are some irreverent souls who will follow her excellent rule even to putting the bisque in the cups and the whipped cream on the bisque, and then destroy her delicacy with a hearty tap of cayenne pepper over each rich melting mound. Such behavior is audacious, but in spite of evidence to the contrary, it is hard to believe that Mrs. Moody herself would not approve of it.

The recipe (or, as she called it, the receipt) set forth by Marion Harland in her *Common Sense in the Household* is, surprisingly enough, the most elaborate. Of course, in the 1870's in eastern America there was a plenitude of what that good woman winningly called "girls," along with most other housewives of our land, and even "second girls" were common in houses that today boast nothing more efficient than a vacuum cleaner and an electric dish-washer. Mrs. Harland, although much more sensible than most of her colleagues, still gauged recipes and their construction in terms of hours spent

---

[1] Mrs. William Vaughn Moody's Cook Book published by Charles Scribner's Sons.

by Irish scullery-maids rather than minutes dashed off by wives just home from the office. For that reason, as well as others, her rules are as quaint as Elizabethan diaries by now, and yet are practical, if carried out with a grain or two of that common sense she so heartily recommends:

OYSTER SOUP (NO. 2)

2 *quarts of oysters*	1 *qt. milk*
2 *eggs*	1 *teacupful of water*

Strain the liquor from the oysters into a saucepan, pour in with it the water. Season with cayenne pepper and a little salt, a teaspoonful of mingled nutmeg, mace, and cloves. When the liquor is almost boiling, add half the oysters chopped finely and boil five minutes quite briskly. Strain the soup and return to saucepan with the milk. Have ready some forcemeat balls, not larger than marbles, made of the yolks of the eggs boiled hard and rubbed to a smooth paste with a little butter, then mixed with six raw oysters chopped very finely, a little salt, and a raw egg well beaten, to bind the ingredients together. Flour your hands well and roll the forcemeat into pellets, laying them upon a cold plate, so as not to touch one another, until needed. Then put the reserved whole oysters into the hot soup, and when it begins to boil again, drop in the forcemeat marbles. Boil until the oysters "ruffle," by which time the balls will also be done.

Serve with sliced lemon and crackers. A liberal tablespoonful of butter stirred in gently at the last is an improvement.

Everyone, from Mrs. Harland to the anonymous ascetic New Englanders and back again to various extollers of the elegant bisque, agrees that Oyster Soup is something made with cream and thickening . . . and oysters, whole or chopped, fresh (God willing) or even tinned.

But there is a way to make a soup from oysters that demands only oysters. Oysters there *must* be, and for the rest, you make or even pour from a tin the best beef consommé you can get, and heat it and put in the cold washed shell-fish. Then you put an unbroken egg yolk tenderly into each soup-plate, and pour the consommé with its multitude of oysters over it, in a gentle way so that the yolk will cook a little and stay whole. That is all. It is quick, and easy, and it is good, too.

Love Was the Pearl

Then love was the pearl of his oyster,
And Venus rose red out of wine.

—*Dolores,* C. A. SWINBURNE

THE love-life of an oyster is a curious one, dependent on the vagaries of temperature and the tides. If its world is warm, if the water around it is about seventy degrees, it is able to send out a little potent flood of milt and thus excite a female to her monstrous spawning, now five million eggs, now fifty. And if the tide is right, the milt will meet the eggs, and spats will result.

Spatting and spawning, spawning and spatting . . .

The love-life of a man has also been called curious, and part of it has long depended on the mysterious powers of this bi-valved mollusc which most of the dictionaries say is usually eaten alive.

Women have been known to be influenced, and whether to the good or nay is not for me to say, by the schemed use of these shell-fish, and there is one man named Mussolini who lives near Biloxi, in Mississippi, who swears that he has cured seven frigid virgins by the judicious feeding of long brownish buck-oysters from near-by bayous.

It is men, though, in astounding numbers, who will swear, in correctly modulated voices, a hundred equally strange facts. Women of the East, they will tell you if you are acceptable for such confessions, are built crossways, so that love-making is even more exotic than erotic with them. They know it for a fact. And there is an equally astounding number of men, and some of them have actually graduated from Yale, and even Princeton, who know positively that oysters are an aphrodisiac . . . one of the best. They can tell of countless chaps whose powers have been increased nigh unto the billy-goat's, simply from eating raw cold oysters.

There are many reasons why an oyster is supposed to have this desirable quality, embarrassing if true . . . and although the term is literally incorrect, most of them are old wives' tales.

Most of them are physiological, too, and have to do with an oyster's odor, its consistency, and probably its strangeness. All of them, apparently, are fond but false hopes, and no more to be relied on than that a horse-hair dropped into a trough in the full of the moon will swim about and hiss, an honest-to-God snake.

There was a thin little man once, at Harvard probably. He was not quite a virgin, being about twenty-two years old, and for some reason he managed to date himself, one wintry Saturday night, with a very very terrible very very divine girl of the upper classes known by young men of the same classes as La Belle Dame sans Culottes.

The thin little man, hardly more than a lad as his Grandfather used to say, felt full of tremblings and awed withdrawals, and consulted with several of his more obviously virile friends. Oysters, they said firmly. Oysters are the answer.

So about noon on the dated Saturday the chapkin dropped in at the Grand Central Oyster Bar. It was December, and the oysters, raw and chilled, were not only delicious but correctly in season for any and all correct young men. Ours bolstered himself with some ale, all by himself but still thinking of it (since English B4 with good old pipe-smoking Cyril Dinwiddie) as a noggin rather than a glass, and ate one dozen more than he really wanted.

About two o'clock he was horrified to see that it was not three, and roamed thinly into the cold streets, his mind trying with a dawning hopelessness to call up some of the more torrid reminiscences of his approaching date . . . reminiscences of his roommates, that is.

He took a taxi to the Plaza Grill, looked with what jauntiness he could summon at the raddled brokers eating delicious things like scrambled eggs and hot baked potatoes, and ordered another dozen oysters. He wished it was about six o'clock . . . by then there would at least be one or two lovely actresses to peek at, and he would be within an hour of . . . of . . .

He ordered another dozen.

A little later he walked over to Sixth Avenue and headed boggily toward the RKO Gateway. He had always liked oyster-bars. He had always thought they were fun, removed as they were for the most part from the shrill chitterings of debutantes. But now, as it grew dark and people scuttled for busses all about him, he began to think that a sweet little debutante sipping her tea-and-Martinis at "21" would be heaven. He could pay the bill when she was finished with her childlike pleasures, take her to her mother's safely respectable elevator . . . and go home.

But tonight he was meeting the Belle of the Balls . . . and alone . . .

He turned into the Gateway, and in a small hopeless voice ordered two dozen blue points.

When the bar-man peered at him he snapped, in a masculine way he hoped, "That's what I said, isn't it?" For a minute he felt almost warmed by his own unsuspected fire, and then as he started diligently to swallow his prescription he was nearly overcome by a dreadful weariness, so that if he had not represented the Alma Mater he surmised he did, he would have stretched out quietly on the soft-looking white tile floor and given himself to safe dreams.

Instead, he pulled in his stomach as far as he could, and sipped seemingly at his ale, and gradually ate two dozen more of the same.

About six-thirty that night, this thin little man, looking much older than twenty-two for the first time in his life, walked slowly and uncertainly up the steps of the Harvard or whatever Club. Visions of rosy flesh and honey-colored thighs were quite wiped out, at last, by the chill certainty that Old Chick and Old Bill and Old Rot-Gut had betrayed him. Yes, he was betrayed . . . thank God.

Bed, he thought solemnly. Bed is what I need . . . and *alone.* I'm still a man, he thought with his last remaining spark of masculinity . . . I'm still a man, in *spite* of the blasted shell-fish . . .

And he stuck out his chest and almost fell flat on his peaked oyster-colored face.

"Here, *here,* sir," the porter clucked, feeling somewhat wearily that another chance to prove himself a real father stared him in the face. "Not *here,* sir. You just come with me."

And he tucked his arm winningly, seductively, with practiced skill, into the thin little man's, and together they wove toward a comfortable couch.

My Country, 'Tis of Thee

"The oyster cocktail is a cocktail, no? As is the Martini?
Then they are together on the menu . . . and besides, it is
already printed. Why change it?"

—MEXICAN MAITRE D'HOTEL

INTERNATIONAL confusion in restaurants can be terrible or it can be
utterly-mad-and-amusing, depending entirely upon the gastronomic
humor of the diners. I have seen three Englishmen eating Algerian
couscous and drinking great swigs of a particularly rich Tokay Aszu
in a little Spanish café in Switzerland, and because of their good will
enjoying it, in spite of its basically horrible melange of flavors, as
much as the refugees around them who ate hare cooked in olive
oil from their own town of Madrid and squirted thin *vino rojo* into
their faces from the common long-nosed carafe.

Usually it is most fortunate, if you are eating something Russian,
to drink what a Russian would like to drink with it . . . or its
nearest equivalent. Vodka is fine with caviar, but if you have no
vodka (and do have the other, which seems highly improbable these
days) a glass of dry gin is far from heretical.

In the same way a pint of old-and-mild goes with a cut off the
joint at Simpson's, but if you are safely distant from staunch London's Strand and its present preoccupation with things other than the
pleasures of the table, you can do yourself passably well with a
glass of good local beer and a slice of roast beef, even in a Connecticut hamburger-joint or a fabulous California "drive-in."

Oysters, being almost universal, can be and have been eaten with
perhaps a wider variety of beverages than almost any other dish I
can think of . . . and less disastrously. They lend themselves to the

178

whims of every cool and temperate climate, so that one man can drink wine with them, another beer, and another fermented buttermilk, and no man will be wrong.

Patriotism is always present, of course, so that it is almost as difficult for a Frenchman to watch you drink anything but wine with your slate-blue, black-gilled Portugaises as it is for him to imagine cooking them. There is a strong feeling in almost every Gallic heart that heating an oyster makes it infamous, such that even such a reputable gourmet as Paul Reboux must preface any recipe for cooking them with cajolery. "I understand," he says at the beginning of "Baked Oysters" in his *Plats du Jour*, "that you haven't much sympathy for hot oysters. But . . . perhaps you could bring yourself to try the recipe that follows?"

The Portugaise and the rarer European (*Ostrea edulis*) should be eaten in one way, and one only, a Frenchman thinks . . . and therefore he feels with some firmness that all other oysters in the world should be so treated. It should be opened at street temperature in a cool month, never iced, and plucked from its rough irregular shell at once, so that its black gills still vibrate and cringe with the shock of the air upon them. It should be swallowed, not too fast, and then its fine salt juices, more like the smell of rock pools at low tide than any other food in the world, should be drunk at one gulp from the shell. Then, of course, a bite or two of buttered brown bread must follow, better to stimulate the *papilles* . . . and then, of course, of course, a fine mouthful of a white wine.

The safest wine, probably, to order with these winter pleasures is a good Chablis. It travels well, and if it is poured at the same temperature as the oysters it can be good whether it comes in a bottle from the Valmur vineyard's best vintage or in a carafe with the questionable name "Chablis Village."

On the other hand, I have had Pouilly-Fuissé, various kinds of champagnes *nature*, a pink Peau d'Onion, and both bottled and open wines of Anjou with oysters in France, and whether they were correctly drunk or not, I was. Nobody knew it except my own exhilarated senses and my pleased mind, all of which must enter into any true gastronomic experience.

In England ales are the rule with the fat round oysters of the coastal beds, and any pub can recommend its own brew when the season's on. And of course sherry is safe.

It is partly because wines are dear that Britishers stick so firmly to their ales, but a small amount of good stiff patriotism, I suspect, makes most of them insist that anything else kills the flavor of their famous shell-fish. Myself, I have drunk good and fairly inexpensive *steinwein* from Wurzburg in a small restaurant in Liverpool, and had other people enjoying their own oysters with a glass of Guinness whisper about me as I ate mine. Needless to say, I have also drunk Guinness with the best of them, and thought, at least temporarily, that the British were right—about their oysters anyway.

Here at home we can, and do, drink what we want, and not always with such fortunate results as the more custom-bound Europeans get from their rigid rules and recipes. In London, once, I knew a Yankee who threw a small pub into shocked worried silence by drinking three whiskeys and then eating a plate of cold raw Whitestaples. Everyone watched him as if at any moment he might fall into a fit or turn bottle-green, and when he left, the bar-maid asked a constable to see him to his hotel, convinced as she was that that hard liquor would turn the oysters in him to some poisonous kind of rubber.

Unfortunately that is almost true, and it is foolish thus to cook the poor fish before they can say scat or realize that they've been swallowed. Another reason, perhaps even more important esthetically, is that anything as strong as whiskey or gin or brandy will sear, in a way, the delicate surface of a human's palate, so that if he drinks before he swallows his oysters, the theory is that he might as well eat soft tar or egg-white for all the pleasure his taste-buds can give him.

It is still the custom here, though, to have a cocktail or so before a meal, or in an oyster-bar to have a couple of quickies while the shells are being opened. We continue to drink, and we continue to eat millions of oysters every year . . . and we continue, perversely, to enjoy them probably as much as the Frenchman with his white wine and the Britisher with his ale.

We can, and often do, drink good white wine from California, or light beers, because we are perhaps the least insular gourmands of any in the world. But most often we do what we like best, regardless of custom, and pour ourselves a good stiff drink as prelude to that most sensitive of foods, the oyster. And live to tell it.

As Luscious as Locusts

The best in this kind are but shadows . . .

—A Midsummer Night's Dream,

WILLIAM SHAKESPEARE

THERE is a little book called *Eloge de la Gourmandise,* one of those thin witty pompous books that have appeared for decades in the Paris bookshops, in which Jean-Louis Vaudoyer speaks of a woman he once watched eat something especially delicious.

She savored her enjoyment with a carefully sensual slowness, and then she sighed, as it came to its inevitable end, "Ah . . . what a pity that I do not have little taste-buds clear to the bottom of my stomach!"

Such a remark could not seem anything but gross to an ascetic man, partly because a woman said it and partly because all such frank gastronomic pleasures are inexplicable to him. The joys of the table are not within his ken, and therefore he suspects, with some possible rightness, their devotees.

And yet to a man who has once eaten something and taken thought about it . . . not merely digested it and remembered that, but eaten, digested, and then *thought* . . . such a blatantly sensual remark as that made by Vaudoyer's friend is not only comprehensible but highly intelligent.

Almost every man keeps in his own mind a few such intense moments, when his senses combine with his vocabulary to make him say some such spontaneous and even shocking thing about a taste or a whole dish. And after, when he remembers, he thinks, "That was the best melon, or pheasant, or sausage, I ever ate in my life." He means it.

Often the place and the time help make a certain food what it becomes, even more than the food itself. Vaudoyer does not say when, or why, his companion made her epic comment on *la gourmandise,* but it is easy to imagine her a beautiful, gently rounded woman with dark eyes and dainty wrists, who ate with delicate avidity at a ripe peach after a summer afternoon full of love. It is easy, and pleasant too . . .

In the same way you can remember hearing an old fisherman in a little bar in southern Delaware say to the room with real solemnity, "Them was the best God-damned swimpses I ever et," and you wonder about him and his life and his shrimp-nets and what the day was like when he ate his own catch.

There is a man in California who used to know George Sterling and Jack London and such foggy minor gods, and who now, inevitably, has become to the young coastal yearners almost as mythical as his dead friends. He holds what might be called soirées, and malicious critics suspect, not too silently, that his famous booming laugh and his broad quips at these parties which a few years ago would still be called Bohemian, contain almost as much corn as they do bourbon. Nevertheless he is no worse than any valiant shadow, and when he is alone, free for a few minutes from the midge-like clouds of admiring college people who usually surround him, his voice grows quiet and his face sags and he talks to himself out loud of other days.

"Hang Town Fry," he'll say, tenderly and practically at the drop of a hat. "Hang Town Fry!"

Then, when he doesn't say any more, you realize that he is at last serious, if not sober, and you ask him, "What about it?"

"What about Hang Town Fry? You don't know? And you call yourself a San Franciscan? Why, it's the best food that ever sat before misbegotten man, and early in the morning with a hard day ahead, or before that when you're wondering why you did it, or at night for a nice supper with your girl . . . Why, Hang Town Fry . . . I remember once . . ."

Then, for a few minutes or seconds before the part he has been playing so long submerges his real thinking self, and smudges all the outlines into those of a campus character, you see what this big deaf lost man must have been, one night down near the Ferry Building when he ate Hang . . . Town . . . Fry. . . .

This is the way it was made, if his beer-joint had a decent Chinese cook as they all did in those times. Why it was the best thing in the world to him you can never know, but the recipe is good, and his private sensual delights need not affect your own more immediate pleasure, some night with a friend or two and a chafing dish, for instance:

HANG TOWN FRY

(from the *Sunset Cook Book*)

Drain and pat dry 2 dozen medium-sized California Eastern [!] oysters, season them with salt and pepper and roll first in flour, then in beaten egg, and then in fine white bread-crumbs. Put them into a hot frying-pan with melted butter, and fry to a golden brown on one side; before turning them over pour over all 4 or 5 whole eggs beaten light. Let cook a minute, then turn over and brown on other side to color them just as desired. The resulting dish will look like an egg pancake with oysters mixed in. Serve two or three links of tiny browned breakfast sausages and shoestring potatoes with Hang Town Fry.

Another man, Bob Davis, who writes with coherent enthusiasm of "a few intrepid souls who have time to cook and who approach the task with pride," tells briefly but clearly in Armitage's *Fit for a King* about a bayman's home on the marshes of Massapequa, on Long Island, where one chill fall afternoon he went duck hunting with someone.

"The housewife asked us if we liked onions . . . 'Yes' . . . and if we liked oysters . . . 'Yes' . . . and at once disappeared into the kitchen. In fifteen minutes we had our gum boots under the table and both our elbows on top. Bad manners, but good cooking. I secured the recipe. Here it is:"

(And Mr. Davis' recipe seems given in the same voluptuous generous way that makes such men as he say, "That . . . now *that* was the best thing I ever ate in my life . . .")

OYSTERS AND ONIONS

Slice enough small white onions to cover half an inch in depth the bottom of a skillet; pour half a pint of oyster juice over all and let simmer until onions become transparent. Add pepper and salt and a tablespoonful of butter; cook until butter melts. Spread over onion base a solid blanket of blue point oysters . . . about forty . . . and cook with lid off for five minutes. Place lid on and cook until oysters begin to scallop. Serve on toast with pancake turner, so as not to disarrange the layer. . . . No duck hunter who pretends to be half a man can face the crack of gray dawn better equipped.

That is one man's decision, of course. I know of another, who faced the gray dawn once in a Chesapeake Bay inlet as big as a buttonhole, where he hid from a howling wind when he and another little boy got storm-bound in their boat.

They rocked quietly all night, while the air moaned above them, and in the morning they saw that they were floating above oysterbeds as perfect as something in a dream.

They pulled off their clothes and swam down through the stilled water, and brought up oysters bigger than their hands, and sat there in the cool fresh grayness of the dawn, cracking open the shells and sucking down the firm fish within. When each little boy had emptied his shells, he dove down for more, and all the hidden fears of the hard night vanished as they ate, and dove, and ate, naked as they were born in the growing light.

The end of the story was that a bullet plunked into their little cabin wall, because they were stealing oysters from one of the most famous privately owned beds of the most delicious strain of the whole Atlantic Coast. The guard frightened them, and then pitied them and let them go, and they headed into the bay full of the best breakfast they were ever to eat in their lives, wiser but not sadder little boys.

1942

How To Cook A Wolf

FOR LAWRENCE PAUL

There's a whining at the threshold,
There's a scratching at the floor.
To Work! To Work! In Heaven's name!
The wolf is at the door!
—C. P. S. Gilman

How to Cook a Wolf was first published in 1942, when wartime shortages were at their worst. It was revised by the author in 1951, by the addition of copious marginal notes and footnotes and a special section of additional recipes. These have now been incorporated in their proper places in the text, and are enclosed in brackets, as is, for an example, the Introduction to the Revised Edition which follows.

THE PUBLISHERS

Introduction to the Revised Edition

[It is hard to know whether war or peace makes the greater changes in our vocabularies, both of the tongue and of the spirit.

Certain it is, however, that in less than ten years this book about living as decently as possible with the ration cards and blackouts and like miseries of World War II has assumed some of the characteristics of quaintness. It has become, in short, in so short a time, a kind of period piece. In its own way it is as curious, as odd, as any fat old gold-ribbed volume called, a hundred years ago instead of nine or ten, *Ladies' Indispensable Assistant and Companion, One of the Best Systems of Cookery Ever Published for Sister, Mother, and Wife.* . . .

Of course, it is difficult, in spite of the obvious changes in our physical problems since *How to Cook a Wolf* was first published in 1942, to say truthfully and exactly when we are at war.

Now we are free of ration cards (It was shocking, the other day, to hear that after almost twelve years gas rationing had come to an end in England. What a long time! Too long . . .): no more blue and red tokens, no more flimsy stamps to tear out or not tear out.

We can buy as much porterhouse and bourbon and powdered sugar as our purses will allow, given the rise of almost one hundred percent in the cost of such gastronomical amenities.

We need not worry, temporarily at least, about basic cupboards for blackouts . . . while at the same time we try not to think, even

187

superficially, about what and when and how and where to nourish survivors of the next kind of bomb.

Thus stated, the case for Peace is feeble.

One less chilling aspect of the case for War II is that while it was still a shooting affair it taught us survivors a great deal about daily living which is valuable to us now that it is, ethically at least, a question of cold weapons and hot words. (In one week from the writing of this cautious statement, or one hour from the final printing of it, double ridicule can be its lot. Are weapons ever cold?)

There are very few men and women, I suspect, who cooked and marketed their way through the past war without losing forever some of the nonchalant extravagance of the Twenties. They will feel, until their final days on earth, a kind of culinary caution: butter, no matter how unlimited, is a precious substance not lightly to be wasted; meats, too, and eggs, and all the far-brought spices of the world, take on a new significance, having once been so rare. And that is good, for there can be no more shameful carelessness than with the food we eat for life itself. When we exist without thought or thanksgiving we are not men, but beasts.

War is a beastly business, it is true, but one proof that we are human is our ability to learn, even from it, how better to exist. If this book, written in one wartime, still goes on helping to solve that unavoidable problem, it is worth reading again, I think, no matter what its quaint superficiality, its sometimes unintentionally grim humor.

That is why I have added to it, copiously. Not everything new in it is purely practical, of course. But even the wolf, temporarily appeased, cannot live on bread alone.

(And *that* is why I have added even more, I have sneaked other recipes into the book. Some are hopelessly extravagant (16 eggs!) and some are useful and some are funny, and one is actually for bread that even a wolf would live on.

These "extra" recipes are culinary rules to be followed with not a thought of the budget, not even half an ear cocked toward that sniffing at the door. I know, because I *know*, that one good whiff from any of these dishes will send the beast cringing away, in a kind of extrasensory and ultra-moral embarrassment.)]

M. F. K. F.

How to Be Sage Without Hemlock

How often when they find a sage
As sweet as Socrates or Plato
They hand him hemlock for his wage
Or bake him like a sweet potato!
> —*Taking the Longer View*, DON MARQUIS

IN spite of all the talk and study about our next years, and all the silent ponderings about what lies within them for our sons [Why only sons? Since I wrote this I have acquired two daughters, and they too shape the pattern's pieces, and the texture of my belief!] it seems plain to us that many things are wrong in the present ones which can be, *must* be, changed. Our texture of belief has great holes in it. Our pattern lacks pieces.

One of the most obvious fallacies is that of what we should eat. Wise men forever have known that a nation lives on what its body assimilates, as well as on what its mind acquires as knowledge. Now, when the hideous necessity of the war machine takes steel and cotton and humanity, our own private personal secret mechanism must be stronger, for selfish comfort as well as for the good of the ideals we believe we believe in.

One of the stupidest things in an earnest but stupid school of culinary thought is that each of the three daily meals should be "balanced." [This still goes on in big-magazine advertising, but there seems less and less insistence on it in real life: baby-doctors and

189

even gynecologists admit that most human bodies choose their own satisfactions, dietetically and otherwise.]

In the first place, not all people need or want three meals each day. Many of them feel better with two, or one and one-half, or five.

Next, and most important perhaps, "balance" is something that depends entirely on the individual. One man, because of his chemical set-up, may need many proteins. Another, more nervous perhaps [or even more phlegmatic], may find meats and eggs and cheeses an active poison, and have to live with what grace he can on salads and cooked squash.

Of course, where countless humans are herded together, as in military camps or schools or prisons, it is necessary to strike what is ironically called the happy medium. In this case what kills the least number with the most ease is the chosen way.

And, in most cases now, the happy medium, gastronomically, is known as the balanced diet.

A balanced diet in almost any well-meaning institution is a plan for meals which means that at each of the three daily feedings the patient is given a set amount of carbohydrates and protein and starch, and a certain amount of International Units, and a certain number of vitamins in correct ratio to the equally certain amount of minerals, and so on and so forth.

What it boils down to [an unhappy if accidental play on words: the trouble with almost all cooking is the boiling down thereof, and the resultant dearth of gastronomical guts] is that for breakfast you have fruit or a fruit juice, hot or cold cereal, eggs and cured pork in any of about four ways, bread or toast, and coffee (or tea, or milk). For the noon meal you eat soup, potato, meat, two vegetables or one and a "salad," a pudding or cake of some sort, and tea or coffee or milk. And for supper, to continue the drearily familiar song, you probably eat soup again, eggs again, a vegetable again, and stewed fruit . . . and tea, coffee, or milk.

Of course, this sad rigmarole varies a little in every institution, but it can be considered either a proof of democracy or a shocking human blindness, that intrinsically it is the same at the Arizona Biltmore and your county hospital. [Of course, oysters or caviar before the soup (*consommé double*); beef filet grilled with *pâte de foies gras*, instead of eggs; a cloud-light pile of zucchini Florentine instead of the respectable peas-and-carrots of Old Watanooga . . . and *compote de fruits* instead of stewed prunes . . . and it is *still* a meal of ghastly good balance!]

One of the saving graces of the less-monied people of the world has always been, theoretically, that they were forced to eat more unadulterated, less dishonest food than the rich-bitches. It begins to look as if that were a lie. In our furious efforts to prove that all men are created equal we encourage our radios, our movies, above all our weekly and monthly magazines, to set up a fantastic ideal in the minds of family cooks, so that everywhere earnest eager women are whipping themselves and their budgets to the bone to provide three "balanced" meals a day for their men and children.

It is true, without argument of any kind, that as a people we know much more about correct human nutrition than we did even a few years ago. But we are somewhat confused by all the exciting names [riboflavin, monosodium glutamate, arsofinibarborundum . . . all fine things, when used with a modicum of non-hysteria . . .] and more so by the solemn exhortations of the "food editors" of all the slick magazines we read to improve ourselves.

We want, and not only because we are told to but because we sense instinctively that it is right, to give Mortimer III the vitamins and minerals he should absorb in order to be a fine sturdy little Mortimer indeed. But what a rat race it is: formulas, schedules, piles of dishes, little dabs of this and that three times every monotonously regular day! And Mortimer III rebels sometimes ("Poached egg *again*? I had one *yesterday*!") and sometimes so does his stomach, because how can you know that tomato juice and toast play hob together in certain insides?

This bugbear of meal-balancing is hard not only on the wills and wishes of the great American family, but is pure hell on the pocketbook. There are countless efficient-looking pages in "home magazines" each month, marked into twenty-eight or so squares with a suggested menu for each meal of the week, and then one supposedly tempting dish to prepare every day. The lead usually cries, "Let's economize, Mothers! Here is how you can do it for only 39¢ per person! Try it, and help Uncle Sam!" [Not today, you can't! Not if you follow the balanced-meal plan, you can't! Not even if you buy it wholesale and cook it for fifteen people at a time, you can't! I know. I tried it. I went to auctions for unwanted potatoes, for dented cans. . . . All I got was more red in my budget book and more gray in my hair.]

And then you start reading the familiar old routine: BREAKFAST, fruit juice, hot or cold cereal, scrambled eggs with bacon, buttered toast, coffee or tea or milk; NOON-DAY MEAL, tomato soup, beef patties, mashed potatoes, lima beans, Waldorf sal . . . but why go on? It is familiar enough.

It is disheartening, too. Now, of all times in our history, we should be using our minds as well as our hearts in order to survive . . . to live gracefully if we live at all. And people who fought to know better keep telling us to go on as our mothers did, when it should be obvious to the zaniest of us that something was wrong with that plan, gastronomically if not otherwise. [It may not have seemed wrong *then*. Now we have polio, let us admit. But fifty years ago babies died of Summer Complaint. We progress.]

No. We must change. If the people set aside to instruct us cannot help, we must do it ourselves. We must do our own balancing, according to what we have learned and also, for a change, according to what we have *thought*.

Given that Mortimer should eat fruit, vegetables, a starch, and perhaps meat or another protein every day. (Almost any good dietician will tell you that a normal "rounded" food plan includes all the necessary vitamins without recourse to pills and elixirs.) Given also that Mortimer is in average physical fitness. (Otherwise he and you should be guided by a doctor, who might tell you to stop all fruit, or even milk, for a time. . . .)

Then, instead of combining a lot of dull and sometimes actively hostile foods into one routine meal after another, three times a day and every day, year after year, in the earnest hope that you are being a good provider, try this simple plan: *Balance the day, not each meal in the day.* [This is a very solemn footnote, and if I could I would, a hundred and eight years from now and with serene confidence, make another footnote to this footnote. It is true, and true things are worth repeating, perhaps *ad nauseam* because all truth smacks of smugness, but never to the point of ridiculosity.]

Try it. It is easy, and simple, and fun, and—perhaps most important—people like it.

At first older ones who have been conditioned through many unthinking years will wonder where the four or five dull sections of each dinner have gone to, and will raise their heads like well-trained monkeys after the meat course, asking automatically but without much real enthusiasm what kind of pudding there will be *tonight*.

The best answer to that is to have such good food, and such generous casseroles and bowls and platters of it, that there cannot be even a conditioned appetite for more, after the real sensuous human one is satisfied.

Your plan, say, for Mortimer as well as for the others who depend on you for nourishment, includes one meal of starches, one of vegetables or fruits, and one of meat. There are amplifications and refinements to each, naturally [There are indeed many: some human beings bog down with too much meat or too much starch, for instance. Such peculiarities must of course be noted by a loving provider.] but in the main they can be thus simplified.

Breakfast, then, can be toast. It can be piles of toast, generously buttered, and a bowl of honey or jam, and milk for Mortimer and coffee for you. You can be lavish because the meal is so inexpensive. You can have fun, because there is no trotting around with fried eggs and mussy dishes and grease in the pan and a lingeringly unpleasant smell in the air.

Or, on cold mornings, you can have all you want of hot cereal . . . not a pale pabulum made of emasculated wheat, but some brown nutty savorous porridge. Try it with maple syrup and melted butter instead of milk and sugar, once in a while. Or put some raisins or chopped dates in it. It is a sturdy dish, and better than any conventional mélange of tomato juice and toast and this and that and the other, both outside and within you.

If you want Mortimer to drink a fruit juice [I continue to be atonished at the number of people who automatically down a glass of fresh fruit juice, especially before the unavoidable kick of morning coffee. I believe firmly that the combination is pure poison, according to the chemical balance of the one man who, along with several million others, considers it his meat.] you can almost certainly arrange to have it given to him in the middle of the morning or afternoon, when it will not war with the starches in his own middle, and will give him an unadulterated and uncluttered lift.

For lunch, make an enormous salad, in the summer, or a casserole of vegetables, or a heartening and ample soup [. . . with hot tea for the oldsters, and milk at will for everyone . . . and plenty of good buttered toast]. That is all you need, if there is enough of it.

And for dinner, if you want to stick solemnly to your "balanced day," have a cheese soufflé and a light salad, or, if you are in funds, a broiled rare steak and a beautiful platter of sliced herb-besprinkled ripe tomatoes.

That, with some red wine or ale if you like it [and a loaf of honest bread, with or without butter, and toasted or not] and good coffee afterwards, is a meal that may startle your company at first with its simplicity but will satisfy their hunger and their sense of fitness and of balance, all at once. [An unnecessary peptic goad, but a very nice one now and then, is a good soft stinky cheese, a Camembert or Liederkranz, with what is left of the bread, the wine, the hunger.]

And later, when they begin to think of the automatic extravagance of most of our menus, and above all of the ghastly stupid monotony of them, they too will cast off many of their habits, and begin like you to eat the way they *want* to, instead of the way their parents and grandparents taught them. They will be richer, and healthier, and perhaps, best of all, their palates will awaken to new pleasures, or remember old ones. All those things are devoutly to be wished for, now especially.

How to Catch the Wolf

A creative economy is the fuel of magnificence.

—*Aristocracy*, RALPH WALDO EMERSON

ONCE during the last war ["The last war" means something different now. I was thirty-ish when I wrote this, thinking of 1917 and thereabouts. Now I am infinitely and eons more than forty-ish, and my mind says "next" sooner than "last". . . .] when rationing of sugar and butter had been in effect just long enough to throw all the earnest young housewives into a proper tizzy, my grandmother sat knitting and listening to a small excited group of them discuss with proper pride their various ways of making cake economically. Each felt that her own discovery was the best, of course, and insisted that brown sugar or molasses-with-soda was much better than white, or that if you used enough spices you could substitute bacon fat for butter, or that eggs were quite unnecessary.

Finally my grandmother folded her knitting and then her hands, which was unusual for her because she believed that no real lady's fingers should ever be idle.

"Your conversation is very entertaining, indeed," she said with somewhat more than her ordinary dryness. [People tell me that Grandmother could not possibly have been as unpleasant as I always picture her. Only a psychiatrist would know . . .] "It interests me especially, my dears, because after listening to it this afternoon I see that ever since I was married, well over fifty years ago, I have been living on a war budget without realizing it! I never knew before that using common sense in the kitchen was stylish only in emergencies."

My grandmother's observation need not have been so sardonically phrased (from what I have heard about her she felt it a sign of weakness to be anything but firmly disagreeable most of the time),

195

but probably it was true then . . . and it is even more appropriate now. [As well as *now*, eight years later and in so-called Peace Time!]

Every slick magazine in the country is filled with full-page advertisements suggesting that all Americans "try the new thrill of thriftier meat-cuts," and home economics editors in the women's journals are almost incoherent over the exciting discovery that dollars can and should buy more. Vitamins are written and talked about with eager—if at times somewhat confused—enthusiasm, and the old saw that Europe could live on what we throw away rears its inane head in every editorial column. [The word *inane* seems crude and bloodless here, applied to such painful truth. All over the world great piles of wasted potatoes and coffee and tender piglets and dried milk make that truth more shameful, in our economy as well as our hearts.]

In other words, not all women are as sensible as my grandmother . . . until they have to be. Then, I believe, after the first spate of eager bewilderment they can be fully as practical as she, and certainly a lot less grim about it.

It is true that, when the wolf first proves he is actually there, you feel a definite sense of panic. "To work! To work! In heaven's name!"

You talk with your friends. They are either as bewildered as you, or full of what sound like ghastly schemes for living with three other congenial couples and buying all their food from the city dump.

You talk with an older woman, and usually she writes you a long list of recipes full of eggs and cream, both of which give your husband hay fever even if you could afford them, which looks more and more doubtful.

You read magazine articles filled with complicated charts and casual references to thiamin, riboflavin, non-organic nutritional essentials, and International Units. You try to be serious about them all, and with a dictionary and a pencil you fill in at least the first week on a monthly chart, putting little circles, triangles, and arrows for minerals and vitamins and such, until you see practically the same chart in a rival magazine and realize that it has switched the symbols on you. [I don't think we get as excited about such schemes as we used to. Perhaps that is a bad sign: pills and injections can't do *everything!*]

Out of the murk of misinformation and enthusiasm that bedims even the advertisements in the first months of war (one double-page spread used the words *thrifty* and *thriftier* seventeen times, with an almost breathless sense of discovery!), and the monotony of the articles about what fun it is to buy cheap food and less of it, a better knowledge of each dollar's purchasing power is bound to come.

Women who never thought one way or another about such things before, are going to find that fuel and light, even if they have enough money to pay for them, may be scarce and impossible to hoard, and after the first sense of irritation will learn to cook well and intelligently and economically with very little gas or electricity. [Present-day pottery and kitchenware, available in peacetime, are a wonderful investment for wartime economy. Used intelligently, it makes something as simple as boiling an egg cost half as much as it would in a thin, badly designed, utensil, even though a three-minute egg still takes about as long today as it did in 1722.] Magazines give a great many good hints about such thriftiness, usually, and so do other people like my grandmother, and so, in the end, does your own good sense.

It is all a question of weeding out what you yourself like best to do, so that you can live most agreeably in a world full of an increasing number of disagreeable surprises. [Some of them are merely funny, like the carefully sealed cans filled with milk-solids, nitrous-oxide gas, and suchlike, which spit out a "dessert topping" vaguely reminiscent of whipped cream when held correctly downwards, and a fine social catastrophe when sprayed, heedlessly upright, about the room.]

How to Distribute Your Virtue

Economy is a distributive virtue, and consists not in saving, but in selection.

—*Letters to a Noble Lord*, EDMUND BURKE, 1796

ALMOST all people, whether they are potential or actual grandparents, have practiced certain forms of economy in their day, even if they are not like my own grandmother who practiced it her whole life. Sometimes their systems have a strange sound indeed, after the thin days are past and they can look back with a perspective which is impossible while the wolf seems actually at the door.

I think especially of one man, moderately famous now as a deliverer of weighty papers before weightier minds (the kind of papers, and minds, that are filled with abstruse puns in nine languages, at least five of which are dead). [The best talker I ever heard once said to me, "Never ruin a good story by sticking to the truth." That may be why this one, essentially as it appears here, has been read in somewhat more embroidered versions, stitched both by me and by my various loyal friends. The famous-deliverer-of-weighty-papers himself, wiser if no better nourished than so long ago, prefers *this* version.] When he was working on his doctorate in a small French university, he discovered the rather macabre delights of a poverty which could have been depressing to an older tireder man but was gleeful and exciting to him.

He stopped shaving, because he never had any hot water, or sharp razors, or soap, and finally not even a mirror. The result was a fine Old Testament beaver, full of genius.

198

He bought food at the market on Mondays and Thursdays, after his credit ran out at a succession of lower-than-lowest-grade boarding houses, and cooked on a one-burner gas plate which was, for some reason, in the outside privy of his mean lodgings.

He began by making himself fairly neat, well-ordered little meals. But washing dishes with no water was a problem, so he found himself using fewer and fewer plates. He was tempted to throw them all away and simply fish things out of the stew-pot with his fingers, but he sensed that man must keep a few barriers between himself and savagery, and compromised on one large soup dish and one spoon.

For several weeks he ate thus in solitary manliness, so pleased with himself and the free good life he was living that he never noticed how ugly and smelly and surly his room and his landlady were. [Good honest stew is better the second day, and better yet the third. But on the fourth, unless the weather be cool and right. . . .]

Finally, however, inertia and a desire perhaps for complete functionalism overcame him, and he found that rather than ask or hunt for water for his one dish and his one spoon he was eating whatever was in or on them and then spending several minutes licking them clean, very slowly and meticulously, so that they shone and twinkled as much as the cheapest ware can manage to.

He says now, when pressed, that he sat for several minutes on the edge of his bed, and then in a quiet and rather sad way broke the plate so freshly polished, bent the shining spoon into a hoop, went to the corner *coiffeur* and had his beard hacked off, and borrowed enough money to become a boarder again at a moderately bad restaurant. (He also adds with some glee that he was sick as a pup after the first incredibly elaborate meal, after months of monotonous good health with his own spartan stew.) [I know a man who killed another with kindness and too much rich food upon a long-starved stomach. It was clearly accidental manslaughter, not murder, for he had never seen his victim before then, nor heard of him.]

There may be a lesson in this. It sounds rather like it. At least it proves that when he is living with himself a man can do things that in front of other people might seem ugly, or undignified, if he needs to in order to live at all. [I cannot swallow a raw egg in front of anyone in the world, no matter how much I want it. Or so I *think*.]

There are many other ways to save money, some of them written in cookbooks for people to study, and some of them only hidden in the minds of those who might have been hungrier without them. It is good, now when war and its trillion grim surprises haunt all our minds, to talk with other older humans about what they have done in their days to fool the wolf.

One will tell you about hayboxes. Hayboxes are very simple. They are simply strong wooden boxes, one inside another with hay packed between, and if possible a stout covering of linoleum or oilcloth on the outside. You bring whatever food you want to a sturdy boil, put it tightly covered on a layer of hay in the inside box, pack hay all around it, and cover the box securely. [First catch your hay, to paraphrase an old gastronomical adage about hares! Who *has* hay, these days?] Then you count twice as long as your stew or porridge or vegetables would have taken to cook normally, open the haybox, and the food is done. It is primitive, and it is a good thing to know if fuel is a problem for you.

A more modern answer, and a fine one if you can afford the initial expense, is the kind of pressure cooker which looks like a Dutch oven with a whistle on top. It does almost miraculous things: string beans are cooked in three minutes, a Swiss steak is tender and juicy and full of flavor in but a few more, and on and on. It reduces cooking time to an almost boring minimum . . . which of course is worth it if you are skimping on gas or working in a munitions factory with neither time nor inclination for the pleasures of the kitchen.

Another amateur economist will tell you of countless ways to make little seem like more. Most of them sound foul, after a few minutes of such reminiscences, but in practice they are trustworthy, if not admirable esthetically. For instance, you can make scrambled eggs "go a lot further" by putting bread crumbs in them when they are a little more than half done, and as a matter of fact if you use decent crumbs [say, of homemade bread or of an honorable pumpernickel] the eggs have a very good flavor indeed, and a nice texture. Or in a soufflé, add one cup of puffed cereal to the three separated eggs, and you will have food for four people [. . . at least three of whom, I feel impelled to add, you dislike intensely and hope never to see again].

Another trick is to cut the consumption of sugar in half when you are making jams and preserves by mixing one cup of sugar with every two cups of fruit and the correct amount of water, and then adding one-half a teaspoonful of bicarbonate of soda. I have never done this, but ardent housewives who lived through the last war in both England and America swear that it works, and of course the wear and tear on sugar cards is cut down considerably. [Another way, of course, is by now almost universal: pectin. I hate it. I swear I can always detect it, by the ugly solid dull grainy look of anything that contains it. I would rather eat one spoonful of jelly made with fruit and sugar than a dozen jars of the other stuff. Or perhaps vice versa.]

As for butter and other shortenings, I have always felt that I should prefer too little of the best to plenty of an inferior kind. However, there are many families who are used to a great deal of pastries and fried foods, and who find it difficult to forego them. There are several reputable substitutes, not only for butter, but for butter substitutes! [It is said that scientists are evolving a new and excellent salad- and cooking-oil made from grapefruit skins.]

If you use oil or lard for deep frying, never let it smoke much, but use when it is bluish and not moving on the surface. If you eat much bacon, save the fat, and pour it always into a metal container and then pour water over it. The burned food particles will sink into the water, and the fat will rise as it cools and be clean and easy to lift into another cup or bowl. Such fat should be kept in a cool and dark place, as should olive oil if you are lucky enough to own any, but never in an icebox.

As for your icebox. (It is easiest to take it for granted that you still have one, and that it works, and that it is not an annex for the local Red Cross and filled to bulging with blood plasma.) [This is one of the doggedly cold reminders that this current war is, or so everyone tells me, cold. . . .] As for your icebox, then, there are several ways to use it with the most intelligence.

Of course, keeping it clean eliminates waste from spoiled food, and defrosting it regularly makes it use surprisingly less fuel, if it is an automatic one. Never put meat or other foods in it in their store-wrappings; they use extra cold and are less good. Almost the same is true of butter, which should be taken from its box but left in its thin paper protection or else put into a covered dish. Vegetables should always be washed if they are to be stored in the box, and lettuce and other salads should have the white cores cut out. Little green onions and such sturdy herbs as parsley can be kept fresh and pungent for a long time if they are washed and drained and put into tightly covered jars, and it is a nice feeling to know that they are there, ready for use, whenever you want them (which will be oftener than you realize, once you have caught the habit).

If you cook rice or such pastes as spaghetti and macaroni very often, you can keep them from boiling over and at the same time lay the foundation for a decent soup by putting in about a teaspoonful of butter or suet or oil. [Quote now that the war is over hah hah unquote, I would add about three times that much fat to the pot.] After you have drained what you are cooking, save the water and cook it again with a little onion, some meat stock if you have it, or a couple of bouillon cubes, and you have a nutritious broth that would shame nobody.

When you cook such things as rice, or potatoes or spaghetti or any of the starches, cook enough for two meals instead of one. It costs about the same, in heat consumption, and you have the food ready to heat in various ways and serve again, a few days later. [Ah, rice pudding, rich with raisins! Ah, spaghetti baked with honey and shaved almonds in a buttery dish! Ah, potatoes any way at all but perhaps especially mixed with egg and cheese and fried! Ah.] (The same is true of almost everything; most vegetables, for instance, are delicious chilled in salads, especially if you have put them aside without buttering them.)

More or less, this simple but surprisingly little-practiced rule is true in using an oven: try to fill every inch of space in it. Even if you do not want baked apples for supper, put a pan of them with whatever is baking at from 250 to 400 degrees. They will be all the better for going slowly, but as long as their skins do not scorch they can cook fast. They make a good meal in themselves, with cream if you have any, or milk heated with some cinnamon and nutmeg in it, and buttered toast and tea.

Another thing to do while the oven is going is to put in a pan of thinly sliced bread which is too stale to use any more. It makes good Melba toast, if you watch it so that it does not get too brown. If you want to you can soak it first in water or watery milk with a little sugar in it, or even a little salt and pepper, to make zwieback that is very good indeed with soup or tea. [These petty tricks seem somewhat more so when gas flows through the pipes and firewood is available and electricity actually turns on with a button. But in each one of them there is a basic thoughtfulness, a searching for the kernel in the nut, the bite in honest bread, the slow savor in a baked wished-for apple. It is this thoughtfulness that we must hold to, in peace or war, if we may continue to eat to live.]

Or you can roast some walnuts in their shells, and eat them while they are still pretty hot, with fresh cold apples and a glass of port if possible, for one of the desserts most conducive in this world to good conversation.

While these various shortcuts to economy are simmering and fuming in their borrowed heat, you can be roasting a large joint of beef, which will seem expensive beyond reason when you pay for it but which will last a long time if your family is of normal size and appetite. Potatoes can be baked around its pan, about an hour before it is done, and if their skins are oiled and they are pricked when they are taken from the oven they will not grow soggy and may even be used after they are cold, if they are good potatoes, for a casserole or a salad.

Or you can cook what the home economists love to call a "one-dish meal," a "co-ordinated dinner," or, less genteelly, a casserole. This, if it is intelligently planned and seasoned, can be delicious (and will leave fine fundaments for another meal tomorrow, unless it is already at work using up yesterday's).

For instance, make a Baked Ham Slice. [This, I notice eight years later, is clearly documented on page 266. My main comment on it is monotonous: I like it. My main change would be to use cider or white wine for the cup of water. And any kitchen-idiot would know enough to core the apples.] Get a little more meat than you plan to use at dinner, because it is fine the next day diced in a macaroni-and-cheese casserole, or in an omelet or any way you want it.

A green salad is good with this, and either a light beer or a rather sharp white wine. And for dessert, if you want one, nothing can be a better complement to the tang of ham and apples than hot gingerbread, the dark kind that springs practically full-born from a paper carton and the gracious shadow of Mary Ball Washington [it says on the advertisement], or can be made a little better and a little less expensively from a trusted recipe of my mother's, called Edith's Gingerbread. The recipe is given on page 315. [A quick but thoughtful look forward confirms my belief that this is the best recipe for gingerbread ever devised. Farewell, gracious packaged shadow of Mary Ball Washington!]

A little sherry poured over the bread while it is hot makes it even better, if you plan to eat it all at once, with sweet butter too if possible. If not, a simple wine sauce or a hard sauce is good.

If there is any gingerbread left, it is almost better cold than hot. When it gets stale (although I have never known any to last that long), it is delicious split open and toasted, for tea. [Tea? Who drinks tea anymore? It used to be something "people" did: the gentle ritual, the delicate ceremony. For me it meant a discreet adolescent gobbling of cakes and cookies, nigh unto my thirtieth year, while older wiser creatures sipped alongside. Now? Now I could not face a saffron-bun or a plum-heavy . . . and tea makes me drunk.]

And what ham is left, if you don't like macaroni and cheese, you can dice and put in a buttered casserole the next day with cooked noodles, and a small can of mushrooms, browned in shortening. Season it with salt and fresh-ground pepper, and heat thoroughly (small ramekins take less heat than a big casserole). This makes another "one-dish meal," with a salad, cheese, and coffee.

While the oven is cooking the ham, you can be baking some clean sweet potatoes or yams in their skins, and either a pan of apples or another cake, or anything else that takes a moderately slow oven. Then, in a couple of days, you can make some such hearty dessert as Sweet Potato Pudding.

Or mash and season the peeled yams, put in a buttered shallow pan, and cover with little sausages which have been brought to the boil in plain water. Put in a hot oven until the sausages are thoroughly cooked and brown, at least twenty minutes.

A surprisingly good cake, which I loved so much in the last war that I dreamed about it at night, and which I have tried on this war's children with practically the same results, can be whipped together and put in the oven with the ham and whatever else you are storing up for the week ahead. It is called War Cake, for want of a pleasanter name, and is a rather crude moist dark loaf which keeps well and costs little. [I seem to have said at least twice in this book that I dreamed about War Cake at night. On rereading page 312 I am inclined to suggest a touch of indigestion and change "dream" to "nightmare." The trouble is that I know the recipe to be excellent.]

Sliced thin with a glass of milk, it is a pleasant lunch. Or it can be sliced and toasted, basted with sherry, and served hot with wine sauce for a good dessert, once it seems somewhat past its prime. [Wonderful example of understatement! I really mean: "When the cake is curled, stiff, and apparently unusable."]

The absorbing and profitable pastime of seeing how many things you can cook at once in an oven is almost as good applied to the top of the stove, especially if you have a steam-cooker or even a roomy Dutch oven. Then you can cook several vegetables at once, or less economically but still with a certain amount of good sense cook each one separately, one after another, using the same pot and the same steam, so that at the end you have several things ready for re-heating through the week, and a fine heady broth that will do wonders with any dish that calls for stock or even plain water.

It is best to keep it in an old gin bottle in the icebox, alongside the other old gin bottle filled with juices left from canned fruit. You can add what's left of the morning tomato juice. You can squeeze in the last few drops of the lemon you drink in hot water before breakfast, if you still do that. You can put canned vegetable juices in. You can steep parsley stems in hot water and pour their juice into the bottle. In other words, never throw away any vegetable or its leaves or its juices unless they are bad; else count yourself a fool. [That's right!]

If you keep your old gin bottle cold and reasonably on the move it need never spoil nor be anything but a present help in time of trouble, and a veritable treasure jug for vitamins and minerals that otherwise would have gone down the drain. [That's *so* right!]

Sometimes try a glassful, no matter from what vegetables, fresh-cooked or canned, you may have salvaged it, diluted if you wish with tomato juice or a little lemon and seasoning. It will make you feel astonishingly energetic—almost human, really [. . . a condition devoutly to be aimed for, given our basic state].

All vegetables, whether they are steam-cooked or not, should be done as quickly as possible, and in as little water. In this way at least fifty per cent of the minerals are collected in the water. They should be drained at once, and either prepared for serving or allowed to cool for the icebox and another day. If they are to be used later, they should be underdone rather than tender, since the reheating will cook them again; and of course they should not be seasoned and buttered until they are ready to be used, except for the herbs you may have cooked with them. [I know a little more now and would seldom cook herbs with vegetables I planned to use another day. I would add them *that* day.]

Vegetables cooked for salads should always be on the crisp side, like those trays of zucchini and slender green beans and cauliflowerlets in every *trattoria* in Venice, in the days when the Italians could eat correctly. You used to choose the things you wanted: there were tiny potatoes in their skins, remember, and artichokes boiled in olive oil, as big as your thumb, and much tenderer . . . and then the waiter would throw them all into an ugly white bowl and splash a little oil and vinegar over them, and you would have a salad as fresh and tonic to your several senses as La Primavera. It can still be done, although never in the same typhoidic and enraptured air. You can still find little fresh vegetables, and still know how to cook them until they are not quite done, and chill them, and eat them in a bowl. [Why do we not do this oftener, much time as it will take? I am tired of "tossed green salads," no matter what their subtleties of flavor. I want a salad of a dozen tiny vegetables: rosy potatoes in their tender skins, asparagus tips, pod-peas, beans two inches long and slender as thick hairs. . . . I want them cooked, each alone, to fresh perfection. I want them dressed, all together, in a discreet veil of oil and condiments. Why not? What, in peacetime, is to prevent it? Are we too busy being peaceful for such play?]

You can still live with grace and wisdom, thanks partly to the many people who write about how to do it and perhaps talk overmuch about riboflavin and economy, and partly to your own innate sense of what you must do with the resources you have, to keep the wolf from snuffing too hungrily through the keyhole.

How to Boil Water

"Here, Miss," I says, "what d'ye call this?" "Soup, Sir," she says.
"Soup? Soup? Well, blast me then!" I says, polite-like. "Is this
what I've been sailin' on for the past fifty years?"
—The Peppery Sayings of an Old Salt,

HENRY TREWELYAN, 1869

THERE was a semi-apocryphal figure, in my childhood, who could not even boil water. I forget who she was: a Southern girl, I think, who went to finishing school in Virginia with my mother.

"Oh," my mother used to say, snorting a little and tossing her head half scornfully and half with a kind of wistful envy, "oh, she couldn't even boil water!" Then my mother would add, ". . . before she was married!"

For a long time I believed that the first pangs of connubial bliss brought with them a new wisdom, a kind of mystic knowledge that slipped with the wedding ring over all the fingers of the bride, so that at last and suddenly and completely she knew how to boil water.

Now, I believe otherwise. Now, I believe that few women, Southern or not, even virgins or not, ever realize the spacious limits of putting water in a pot and boiling it. When is water boiling? When, indeed, is water water?

Water is water, Webster says, when it is a colorless, inodorous, transparent fluid, consisting of two volumes of hydrogen to one of oxygen. It can also be rain, or the sea, or a diamond's luster. The water I mean, though . . . the water the Southern maiden couldn't boil . . . is the clear good water that flows from a tap, or if you are lucky from a spring or well. It is the best for cooking wolves.

207

And when is water boiling? It can be said, with few people to argue the point, that water boils when it has been heated to two hundred and twelve degrees Fahrenheit. Myself, I would say that when it bubbles with large energetic bubbles, and looks ready to hop from the kettle, and makes a rocky rather than a murmuring noise, and sends off a deal of steam, it is boiling. [A friend of mine who grew up alongside a samovar has only one way to describe water proper for tea: "A *mad* boil." In the same forceful way she never says rolls or toast must be hot, or very hot. They must be "hot-hot-*hot!*" This is pronounced as much as possible like a one-syllable sound of intense excitement, about no matter how dull a bun.]

At this point, full of sound and fury, it is ready to be used, given, of course, that it has been prepared in a clean vessel for some purpose other than the purely scientific one of discovering when it would boil. Most people, whether or not they are married and therefore prescient, as I so long ago thought they would be about water at least, do not know that there is one moment at which it is *au point,* and then all the rest of the time it is overdone, most as surely as is a broiled sirloin steak or a *crêpe suzette.*

The quaint old fiction of the kettle simmering all day on the hearth, waiting to be turned into a delicious cup of tea, is actively disturbing to anyone who cares very much whether his tea will be made from lively water instead of a liquid which in spite of its apparent resemblance to Webster's definition is flat, exhausted, tasteless—in other words, with the hell cooked out of it. [Altitude changes the sound, as well as the speed, of boiling water. There seems to be more noise, high up.]

It is safe to say that when the water boils, as it surely will, given enough heat under it, it is ready. Then, at that moment and no other, pour it into the teapot or over or around or into whatever it is meant for, whatever calls for it. If it cannot be used then, turn off the heat and start over again when you yourself are ready; it will harm you less to wait than it will the water to boil too long.

And now, irrespective of your virginity or lack of it, you may consider yourself able to boil water. Nobody will ever shake her head about you, as my mother still does occasionally about the Southern girl; or if heads are shaken now and then, at least you will know that it is not because your tea is made with an overdone mélange of hydrogen and oxygen.

I I

The natural progression from boiling water to boiling water with something in it can hardly be avoided, and in most cases is heartily to be wished for. As a steady diet, plain water is inclined to make thin fare, and even saints, of which there are an unexpected number these days, will gladly agree that a few herbs and perhaps a carrot or two and maybe a bit of meager bone on feast days can mightily improve the somewhat monotonous flavor of the hot liquid.

Soup, in other words, is good. [As a matter of fact, soup is even better, in my gastronomy, than it was nine years ago. This is due partly to my increased knowledge of its ever-changing structure, and partly to my own increased age. A good hot broth is more welcome now, and will be more so in yet another decade . . . or two or three!]

It is probably the oldest cooked food on the earth, after roasted meat (in spite of the great Mâitre Escoffier's dictum that "the nutritious liquids known under the name of Soups are of comparatively recent origin and as now served do not date any farther back than the early years of the nineteenth century").

How it was discovered is best left unpondered except by radio script-writers and people who try to interest children in the Stone Age. Its inevitable progress from a pot with a watery bone in it to potage à la Reine and Crème Vichysoisse is for anyone to read in forty thousand cookbooks, most of them bad. [By now there must be fifty thousand, most of them still bad, or at least dull. It is safe to wager that in the past eight years not more than eight really important cookbooks have been published in America . . . and that, of those, not more than one is *essential*. (At first I wrote: "Not *one*.")]

"Certain fundamental rules must be carefully assimilated before one can learn all the requirements for making a truly excellent soup stock," one gastronomist writes, and then goes on to give a good if elaborate ritual. Probably the best of these is Sheila Hibben's, in her *Kitchen Manual*; the result is as clear, rich, and comforting as her own prose, and worthy to be well studied by anyone who wants at least a nodding acquaintance with *la haute cuisine*. It is probably unfortunate that such classical procedures as hers and Mrs.

Moody's and Escoffier's for making the basic stock will become increasingly good escape-reading material in direct ratio to the possibility of following them in our small kitchens and hurried hours.

Another drawback to this, and probably the most important one for people who are pondering how best to cook the wolf that sniffs through the keyhole every night about twelve-thirty [My own wolf, by now almost a member of the family, presently sniffs loudest about four in the morning. The change in his hours is variously ascribed to modern-day tension, daylight saving, and glandular change (mine, not his). He still sounds hungry.] is that by the time you have taken a day off and assembled the necessary ingredients and used enough fuel to braise them, simmer them, boil them, and clarify them properly, you have spent a fair portion of the week's food budget. The result is good, but Man should not live on consommé alone, and if you make the stock as you are told to, there will be very little money left for anything else.

A great deal of misinformation has been quoted for several centuries about the delicious soup that sits for years at the back of every good French stove. It is supposed to be like old-fashioned yeast, always renewing itself and yet always stemming from the original "starter," so that a chicken bone thrown in last Easter may long since have disappeared but will still lend its aromatic aura to the present brew.

I do not like this fiction, and prefer not to believe it. I think soup-pots should be made fresh now and then, like people's minds at the New Year. They should be emptied and scrubbed and started over again, with clean water, a few peppercorns, whatever little scraps are left from yesterday, and then today's bones and lettuce leaves and cold toast and such. Set at the back of the stove and left to simmer, with an occasional stir from the cook, they can make a fine clear stock for sauces as well as a heartening broth.

And . . .

In the country, or wherever there is a big kitchen with constant heat in the stove, they are economical. Otherwise they are foolish and outmoded, and will make fuel bills rise and apartments smell.

People who work whether in offices or Red Cross rooms, must glean what nostalgic comfort they can from merely reading Escoffier and Hibben and the others, and resign themselves (without too much difficulty, I hope!) to some such potage as the following, which costs little, takes even less time to make, and has infinite variations, according to the state of the vegetable bin.

CHINESE CONSOMMÉ

2 cups beef or chicken con-
somme (1 can) or vegeta-
ble juice saved from cooking
2 cups (1 can) tomato juice
1 stalk celery sliced very thin
½ cup dry white wine (or juice
of ½ lemon)

1 green onion and stalk, sliced
very thin and/or a few very
thin slices of whatever
vegetable lurks in the bin,
such as squash, cucumber,
radish, etc.
1 tablespoon butter or olive oil

Heat the consommé and tomato juice. Put everything else into a hot tureen or casserole, pour the soup over, and serve at once. The nearly transparent rounds and crescents of the raw vegetables float on the top, and with the wine give a delicate flavor that seldom needs other seasoning.

This consommé, in spite of the fact that it need not even have meat broth in it, is very stimulating, as well as beautiful to look at, and could never be dismissed as thin, the way Abraham Lincoln did a "homeopathic soup that was made by boiling the shadow of a pigeon that had been starved to death." It is an appetizing first course; with buttered toast and perhaps baked apples and cream to follow it makes a simple pleasant supper.

Another good consommé which takes little time is a variant of the onion soup of blessed memory you used to drink early in the morning at Les Halles, after you'd watched the last of the big wagons piled with baby carrots and round satiny onions unload and trundle off again. (Was it you, or was it someone else you remember meeting once in a dream . . . a long peaceful dream, but beautiful and exciting too.)

[I have found only one onion soup I could not like, a rich cloying thickened purée, brown but not brown enough, served for the diehards like me at second-rate balls in French Switzerland. They were indeed routs, given for the benefit of everything from laryngitic yodelers to needy edelweiss-hounds, always in beautiful dusty old abandoned casinos, always with good champagne and "jazz-hot" bands down from Paris. I was an habituée. But I couldn't stand the pre-dawn soup. . . .

All other soup recipes called *onion* are, so far, all right. Ambrose Heath has some reliable beauties in his little classic named, bluntly, *Good Soups*. His best is probably No. 1, which he ends with the wonderful cook-to-cook statement: "It is the soup of soups." He also gives Mrs. Glasse's recipe (1767), and quotes my favorite, which I have never been able, for fair reasons or foul, to essay. He refers to it somewhat ambiguously as *peculiar*. I can state more openly that it has haunted me since I first read it in Paul Reboux's *Nouvelle Cuisine* many years ago; that it contains, beside the requisite onions, dry champagne, half a ripe Camembert, several beaten eggs, and 30 well-skinned walnuts; that in my edition of the fantastic collection of recipes it ends, "Eat between 3 and 4 A.M. for optimism."

On second thought, and after due consideration of M. Reboux's suggestions, I think the safe sane eminently *basic* recipe which follows should stand alone. May the printers forgive me . . . !]

PARISIAN ONION SOUP

2 *cans* (1 *quart*) *beef or con-*
   sommé
2 *or* 3 *sweet onions, sliced very*
   thin
3 *tablespoons butter or good oil*

1 *heaping tablespoon flour*
rye bread, sliced thin and
   toasted
grated snappy cheese (Par-
   mesan type)

Brown the onions in the fat, sprinkle with flour, and stir while it simmers for ten minutes. Add the soup, preferably heated, and let boil slowly until the onion is very tender. Spread the cheese thickly on the toast, and melt under a quick broiler. (This is better than putting the toast and cheese on the soup and then melting, since the toast stays crisper.) Pour the soup into a hot tureen, cover with the toast, and serve at once.

This is what might be called a "light but hearty" soup, and with a good salad and fruit and coffee would please any hungry family. [All cookbooks are interesting, at least to me, but I think some of the most readable of them have been written about soups (Ambrose Heath's, Mrs. Mabon's), just as often the best section of a comprehensive book like Escoffier's may concern the same infinitely variable subject.]

There are many others, which are even more a complete meal in themselves, and which like all such dishes can be changed according to the will and pocketbook of the chef. Here is a basic recipe for chowders, which can be stretched this way or that and made country-simple or town-elegant.

CHOWDER

½ *pound lean bacon or salt pork,*
  cut in small cubes
2 *large onions, chopped fine*
½ *green pepper chopped fine*
  (optional)
3 *cups water*
3 *large potatoes, cut in small*
  cubes
  salt and pepper as desired

½ *cup rich cream (optional)*
1 *small can chopped pimientos*
  (optional)
1 *can whole-kernel corn or* 1
  can chopped clams or 1 *can*
  tomato-pulp or whatever
  else you can think of

Fry the bacon until crisp. Add the onions and green pepper and brown well. Add the water, and bring to a boil. Put in the potatoes and let cook slowly until tender. Add the rest of the ingredients, heat thoroughly, and serve. [If this is too thick, fish stock or more water or more cream can be added. My father likes to stand a spoon in this, but I myself prefer it somewhat wetter.]

There are some proud boosters of regional cookery who say that a chowder made with anything but crumbled soda crackers is heinous and insulting. They can but ignore the potatoes, then, and substitute their chosen thickener, and feel happy.

There is another well-worn controversy among chowder-lovers as to which is correct, the kind made with milk or the kind made with tomato and water. Long ago it may have been dependent on transportation and climate and so forth, so that in the winter when the cow was still fresh there was milk, and in the summer when the tomatoes were plump and heavy they were used. . . .

Who knows? Furthermore, who cares? You should eat according to your own tastes, as much as possible, and, if you want to make a chowder with milk *and* tomato, and crackers *and* potatoes, do it, if the result pleases you (which sounds somewhat doubtful, but possible).

Once the Vicomte de Mauduit remarked to somebody, or perhaps somebody remarked to the Vicomte de Mauduit, that eating is an art worthy to rank with the other methods by which man chooses to escape from reality. Stripped of its slightly pontifical rhythm, this statement sounds quite true. And one of its strange proofs, in some ways, is the present vogue for Vichysoisse.

This bland unctuous broth, served in a hundred modish restaurants from New York to San Francisco, seems in some mysterious way to soothe the throbbing minds of today's children even as it calmed the outraged stomachs of yesterday's aristocratic grandfathers, who absorbed it willy-nilly by prescription at Vichy and Baden-Baden, instead of ordering it eagerly at the Ruban Bleu or Jack's.

There seems to be something about its robust delicacy, its frigid smoothness, its slightly vulgar but so dainty sprinkling of chives on the white surface, that makes even young-ancient metropolites with sinus trouble or other occupational diseases forget the age they live in, and sit back refreshed and quiet for a minute or two.

It is too bad that this current piece of gastronomical voodoo is so expensive and complicated to make—at least, like Mrs. Hibben's classical consommé, *correctly*. The cream must have exactly 24% fat content: sometimes the mixture should be at 196° Fahrenheit, sometimes at 212° Fahrenheit. One-sixteenth of a teaspoonful of ground mace must be added at just the correct moment.

However, there are compromises which can be admitted, whether you approve of them or not. Here is a recipe, a combination really of Escoffier's Soupe à la Bonne Femme and one I found in a calendar published by the gas company in the Canton of Vaud in Switzerland. It is excellent hot, but to make it into a mighty passable Vichysoisse it should have some cream [sour, or very thick] beaten into it and be put into the coldest part of the icebox for at least twenty-four hours.

CREAM OF POTATO SOUP

4 medium potatoes, peeled and sliced thin
2 mild onions, sliced thin
2 tablespoons flour
4 tablespoons butter (no compromise here)

salt and pepper
1 cup potato water
3 cups rich scalded milk
1 tablespoon chopped parsley
1 tablespoon chopped chives if possible

Stew the onions gently in one-half the butter for fifteen minutes. Add the potatoes and cover with a small amount of water, about two cups. Cook gently until tender. Drain, saving one cup of the water, and put the vegetables through a strainer. [A fine strainer.

I notice increasingly that most average cooks, of which or whom I am one, grow careless about sieves and strainers. They usually compromise, after a few years in the kitchen, with one general-utility implement which will cope more or less with their normal duties. Tut, tut, tut! (Shall go to the hardware store tomorrow . . . no, today!)]

Make a roux of the remaining butter and the flour, add the potato water and the seasoning, and stir in the scalded milk. Combine this mixture with the strained vegetables and heat thoroughly, beating with an egg beater for several minutes. Add the chopped herbs and serve at once. (Or chill and serve next day as Vichysoisse.)

There is another kind of soup, certainly not bland but with a freakish appeal to it [I do not know why I said freakish. This soup, which is more widely served each summer in America, is as respectable as any Yankee chowder.] which should be served as icy-cold as Vichysoisse and might well act as an alternative to those weary brittle souls who live through the summer months in any city, thanks mainly to what their grandmothers probably called "cold potato cream." It is simple to make, and inexpensive, and unlike Vichysoisse is fairly elastic, depending in the main on how fortunate you are in growing or buying herbs.

This recipe stems partly from Paul Reboux and partly from a Spanish chef on an Italian freighter which once ran between Marseilles and Portland, Oregon.

GASPACHO

[Within the past few years I have found myself involved in a discussion, esoteric as well as practical, about the correct way to make a Gaspacho. I still stay loyal to this recipe, while accentuating the fact that it, like rules for all good native soups, can vary with each man who makes it.]

1 generous mixed handful of chives, chervil, parsley, basil, marjoram . . . any or all, but fresh	1 small glass olive oil (or really flavorful nut oil or substitute)
1 garlic clove	juice of 1 lemon
1 sweet pepper, pimiento or Bell	1 mild onion, sliced paper-thin
2 peeled and seeded tomatoes	1 cup diced cucumber
	salt and pepper
	½ cup bread-crumbs

Chop the herbs and mash thoroughly with the garlic, pimiento, and
tomatoes, adding the oil very slowly, and the lemon juice. Add about
3 glasses of cold water [I still say this is the correct *liquid. But often*
I use good meat or fish stock.] or as much as you wish. Put in the
onion and the cucumber, season, sprinkle with bread-crumbs, and
ice for at least four hours before serving.

This Gaspacho can be altered to fit what comes from the garden,
but it should always have oil and garlic and lemon juice and herbs
rubbed heavily together [this is the important trick: a kind of thick
marinade, really, of the macerated herbs, oil, acid . . .] and onion
and some other vegetable floating around in it; and it should be
very cold indeed. Then it is a perfect summer soup, tantalizing,
fresh, and faintly perverse as are all primitive dishes eaten by too-
worldly people.

It is good for lunch, or for supper. [In hot Spain ice cubes float in
it. Most Americans shy away from this strangeness, I find.] It is
especially good if you have a barbecue, and want some legitimate
and not too alcoholic way to keep your guests busy while you turn
the steak: put a big tureen of it on the table, and let them serve
themselves into cups, and eat toasted crusts with it if they want to.
Then when you declare the entrée done, whether it be filet or
ground-round patties, you will find appetites sharp and wits fairly
clear, and a satisfying patina of conversation glimmering in the air.
[I always see to it that I have made too much Gaspacho. It ripens
well, when kept chilled, and it is a soul-satisfying thing to drink,
chilled, midway in a torrid morning. It is also one of the world's best
breakfasts for unfortunates who are badly hung over.]

[Another fine summer soup is made by the following recipe. It
is one of my growing number of Things I Do Not Mention Gastronomically. If I tell the smiling people who sip at it that it is made
of mashed shrimps and especially *buttermilk*, they wince, gag,
hurry away. So I say nothing, and serve it from invisible hogsheads
to unconscious but happy hordes.

COLD BUTTERMILK SOUP

1½ pounds shrimps, cooked and
    chopped
½ medium cucumber, finely
    diced
1 tablespoon minced fresh dill

1 tablespoon prepared mustard
1 teaspoon salt
1 teaspoon sugar
1 quart buttermilk

*Mix together shrimps, cucumber and seasonings; stir in buttermilk
and chill thoroughly. Yield: 6 portions.]*

III

Probably the most satisfying soup in the world for people who
are hungry, as well as for those who are tired or worried or cross
or in debt or in a moderate amount of pain or in love or in robust
health or in any kind of business huggermuggery, is minestrone.

Minestrone, according to some devotees, must of necessity be
based on a bean broth. Others say that minestrone started with a
purée of dried soaked cooked beans is not minestrone at all, but
minestra. Still others say that: 1. It must be seasoned with vegetables which have been glazed with a generous handful of diced
ham or bacon. 2. It must never be breathed upon by meat in any
form. The same question exists about adding or not adding small
cooked pasta like broken spaghetti at the last minute. There are
probably other differences, for like all basically pure and honest
dishes it has as many interpretations as it has makes.

Always, though, it is a thick unsophisticated soup, heart-warming
and soul-staying, full of aromatic vegetables and well bound at the
last with good cheese. "A plate of this pottage," Mrs. Mazza once
wrote, "topped with grated Romano, served with crisp garlicked
sour-dough bread, a salad and a glass of wine, and *I have dined.*"

This soup is an economical one, partly because it is even better
the second or third day than it was the first, and what may have
seemed a rather long cooking time really averages but a few minutes
for each serving. Onions, garlic, potatoes, and young cabbage are
almost always in the markets or your own vegetable bins, and any
other vegetables in season may be added with impunity. Fresh ones
are best, undoubtedly, but frozen ones can be kept, a little from each
package, for the weekly or bimonthly minestrone, and even canned

ones are better than none, if you really want to arm your moral and physical guts with this somewhat finicky but all-satisfying soup.

A BASIC MINESTRONE

½ pound bacon or salt pork or
    fat ham
 1 small onion, chopped
 1 stalk chopped celery
 1 handful chopped parsley

2 cups tomatoes, peeled
1 teaspoon fresh   ⎫ op-
   basilico   ⎪ tional
1 teaspoon oregano ⎬ but
1 teaspoon sweet basil ⎭ nice

Soften onion in heated meat-fat, add celery, parsley and herbs, and stir for 10 minutes, to make a glaze, adding a little water if necessary to keep from sticking.

   Add the tomato, stirring constantly and taking care not to burn.

   Stir in 2 or 3 quarts of water. Add a little mace if you like it. (This soup is fun, because it's so malleable!)

   Put at least the first five of the following vegetables through the fine grinder of the vegetable chopper [Or cut them not too finely, let them simmer until tender, and then mash them well with a potato masher before you add any pasta. I like this method better than the one I gave before.] and add them to the soup:

2 large onions
1 potato, skin and all
1 (or 2) cloves garlic
½ small cabbage (Savoy preferably)
3 carrots

6 stalks celery
some spinach . . . say, a big
   handful
some green beans . . . the
   same
(You see what I mean?)

Bring the whole thing slowly to a boil, and then let simmer until the vegetables are very tender. Add some pasta twenty minutes before serving if you like it (not until the next day if you plan to use the minestrone more than once). Churn the soup ferociously, and serve over thin toasted bread or not, but always with a good ample bowl of grated dry cheese to sprinkle upon each serving, as the pleased human who eats it may desire.

For the rest of the meal, Mrs. Mazza and I are as one. There is no point doing much else, the night you make minestrone, because nobody will eat anything else anyway. Save your tarts for a leaner hungrier night.

I V

There are many variations of any recipe for a soup which includes chopped vegetables. They depend on the ingenuity of the cook and the size of the purse . . . not to mention a few other things like climate and war, and even political leanings. (I know several earnest thoughtful women who would rather see their children peaked than brew something with the foreign name minestrone, because in this year of 1942 the United States is at war with Italy. There is a fundamental if tiring truth about all this, and you and I can only hope that right will conquer over might before too long.) [In the 1950's some people feel helplessly antagonistic to *borscht!* Fortunately, I do not.]

If by any chance you cannot or do not like or do not want to like minestrone as such, I suggest that you try this wholesome variant, which itself can be changed somewhat to suit your garden but obviously is best when its ingredients are cheapest at home or in the market:

GREEN GARDEN SOUP

2 *tablespoons butter or good oil*	1 *handful parsley*
1 *bunch watercress*	2 *cans (4 cups) chicken or beef*
½ *head lettuce*	*broth*
3 *small onions and tops*	1 *egg yolk*
2 *or* 3 *cabbage leaves*	½ *cup thick cream (also if pos-*
4 *celery-stalk tops*	*sible)*
1 *sprig thyme or marjoram if*	*seasoning*
possible	

Chop or grind [I think every kitchen should have a good mortar-and-pestle. My own is wooden, but I would like a stone one some-day.] the vegetables (clean, of course). Heat them gently for about 10 minutes with the oil, and add broth. Cover and simmer slowly until very tender, about 45 minutes. Beat egg yolk and cream together, and add after the soup is in the tureen. Sprinkle with freshly ground black pepper.

[A much more elegant version of this trustworthy Green Garden Soup is the following one, which depends not only on certain un-changing ingredients (mainly sorrel) but on the almost Chinese urgency of its timing.

It was first made for me by a handsome woman in San Francisco who had once been prima ballerina in second-rate cities all around the Mediterranean . . . a wearing life which apparently made child's play of her cooking and serving eight-course finicky dinners.

I have concocted her soup often since I met her, but never with her unflustered gracefulness. For her I call this *Potage Else*, rather than her more unconsciously (and modestly) pontifical *Potage Bonne Femme "Esquin."*

POTAGE ELSE

3 tablespoons butter
3 sprigs parsley
3 leaves lettuce
1 medium onion
1 pint sorrel
  nutmeg, salt, pepper

2 tablespoons flour
2 quarts rich veal stock, boiling
4 egg yolks
1 cup cream
  chervil, if possible

Melt butter in large saucepan. Finely chop parsley, lettuce, onion, sorrel, and add with pinch of nutmeg and salt and pepper to pan. Cover closely and let wilt over slow heat for 10 minutes. Add flour and mix well. Gradually add 2 quarts of boiling stock. Add a little minced chervil, if available. Let the whole boil ten minutes. Beat the eggs, mix thoroughly with the cream, and add this liaison *slowly to the soup, stirring constantly.* Do not allow to boil again. *Serve at once.*]

[One delicious soup I have gradually evolved is made of about one quart of garden lettuces, scallions, parsley, herbs, all chopped fine and then ground to paste in the mortar. Slowly I add seasoning and one quart of rich milk, and then chill it very well . . . for a summer lunch.]

On the other hand, if you say phooie to the whole school of minestrone and feel that chopped vegetables have their rightful place only on the trays of toothless infants and gaffers, your best procedure is one of experimentation.

First install a solid and well-known can-opener in a sensible place in your kitchen: above or to one side of the sink, for instance. (Of course I mention the kind that works like an old-fashioned sidewinder victrola, since any other, to my mind, is a potential source of bad temper, a dirty floor, and finally blood poisoning.) [Most of them now, to the mutual benefit of the manufacturer and the cook, fasten to the wall with a gadget which enables you to put up an ice crusher (fine in summer), a knife-sharpener (wonderful any time at all), and so on. They are a good investment.]

After your fairly expensive opener has been firmly screwed into place, prepare to collect dividends from it as long as your arm can crank it and you can find things in cans to buy. Fill one shelf, if you can afford it, with tinned soups to start with: nationally advertised names are always reputable, and usually there is a local cannery in your district that makes unheard-of but surprisingly delicious (and cheap) mushroom bisque or clam broth or tomato purée, according to the region you live in.

Once the cupboard is stocked with things you like and a few you are not sure about, start combining. [Or *adding!* Slices of ripe avocado on black bean soup, for instance, or fried cucumber slices in thin pea soup.] Put this and that together in a pan, stir them, heat them, and serve them as they are: tomato juice and clam juice, for instance.

Or add a dash of sherry at the last to cream of mushroom and tomato soup, or a flick of cinnamon or nutmeg over the top. Cream of pea and tomato soup are good with a little fresh-chopped basil. Chicken consommé and tomato juice are fine together, and even finer with a little lemon juice and a sprinkling of grated cheese at the last minute. A gout of sweet or sour cream is good in almost any clear soup, added at the last and stirred once or twice to make a swirl in the plate.

Or start at the beginning instead of the end, and stir a handful of chopped green onion into a little butter until wilted, and then pour tomato juice and beef bouillon into the pan, heat through, and serve with croutons made of little bread cubes fried in bacon until they are crisp and quite brown. These can be made in fairly large quantities and heated in the oven when they are needed, with a paper towel under them to collect the unnecessary fat.

It has been reported by fairly trustworthy travelers that natives along the Orinoco River in South America made a special kind of mudball for their soup, and think it a tasty tidbit indeed. Our present hemispheric policy of hands-across-borders forbids our murmuring anything but *¡Que deliciosa!* Here, in place of the clay-tinged delights of down yonder, we can make little balls of chopped raw beef mixed with fine herbs, roll them in flour to hold them together, and drop them into boiling beef and tomato consommé for five or ten minutes before serving.

Or we can buy a can of the excellent fishballs which are made in this country now instead of in Sweden, and put them, juice and all, into hot potato soup, with a goodly handful of chopped parsley to keep it all from looking too pale.

Or mix one egg and a scant cup of bread crumbs and about two tablespoonfuls of grated cheese together. Add a little nutmeg, just to be reckless, and some salt and pepper. Have any kind of consommé you like boiling on the stove and then pour the mixture into it, beating like sixty-five all the time. Cover for about five minutes, beat again, and you have a shortcut Potage Mille Fanti, and very good too . . . probably. [Something average cooks do not do enough is use a liaison: an egg yolk or more, stirred in a little cream or stock and added just before serving to almost any kind of soup, to make it smoother, thicker, and more flavorful.]

Or put cooked rice or a little instant tapioca or a handful of the smallest kind of vermicelli into any thin soup you may have. (If you feel as I do about such pastes, and especially tapioca, you can pretend almost too easily as you eat it that you are back in a second-rate Swiss pension, watching three English women of advanced spinsterhood measure out their digestive tonic and trying not to listen to the Austrian honeymooners one table behind you. Even nostalgia is a doubtful pleasure when evoked by limp globules of starch in the bouillon.)

Perhaps it would be better to call the whole thing off, that you should sink so low. Perhaps, rather than reach the point where you would willingly put tapioca in the soup, you should open the door, let the wolf prance in, and sigh, like the Southern lady, that you can't even boil water! [Unless . . . unless you can, thanks to a mad purchase or a generous uncle, make Consommé Talleyrand: Grate 4 large unpeeled truffles into a generous tureen. Add scant cup very dry sherry, 1 pinch cayenne. Cover and let stand 1 hour. Pour over it 3 pints hot rich consommé in which have been boiled 2 tablespoons tapioca. This is delicious.]

How to Greet the Spring

Young leaves everywhere;
The mountain cuckoo singing;
My first Bonito!

—*Japanese hokku*

FOR centuries people have believed that fish should be eaten (1) because it is a brain food and (2) because it is easily digested and (3) because it is bloodless and therefore suitable for religious fasts. Aside from these reasons, it has always been true that, in times of peace at least, fish is usually plentiful and more than usually good.

Now, however, with all the waters of the earth troubled and suspect, fish as a food has become a rarity. Even the gulls are starving, and the fishermen are fighting or in prison camps, and the people who once "had a kipper to their tea" . . . it is only to be wished for that they have found other adequate if less delectable substitutes. [From what I have heard, the exotics in English fish stalls, everything from whale to toheroa, were one of the heaviest crosses British cooks had to bear, during the long war (and "peace") years.]

In spite of the fact that many sea villages have lived for centuries on fish and bread and wine, there are wise biochemists who believe that fish as a food is harmful to the human system. This is truer of highly civilized cuisines than of the simple food in villages, but it is true everywhere that fish, like poultry, is a flesh that deteriorates rapidly unless it is kept very cold or mummified by smoking. At least one of these processes makes it harder to digest, just as baking the sensitive body of a hen's egg makes it tougher than leather in the human stomach.

War, then, which will fill all our refrigerated freight-carriers with

223

other more vital cargoes, will make sea-fish as rare as dolphins' eggs, in the Middle West, and lake-fish something that children can read about in history books along the coasts.

The best way to have fish for supper, in most places, will be to go out along the river or in your dinghy at the tide's change, if you can get past sentries and avoid the mines, and catch some mudcats or a few bass on your own hook. The next best thing will be to eat some canned tuna or salmon, if you can still find a store that carries it . . . for the Italian fleet at San Francisco's Fisherman's Wharf is tied up now, and the canneries along the coast are waiting for other men to take the place of all the Japanese who used to work so neatly, slashing off heads and pressing out guts and packing the bodies in straight lines.

"The better the fish the simpler should be its preparation," Sheila Hibben says, and if you can find a fresh fish to cook, her wise word is the first to remember. [I have developed a real respect for frozen fish, both in filets and, as currently with trout, entire.] If the fish is good at all, its flavor will emerge much more honestly if it be simply broiled rather than covered with an intricate and expensive sauce. The grill should always be hot, so that the fish will not stick and break when it is moved, and of course should be hottest for the smallest fish, so that with thick slices it will not burn the outside before the interior is done.

A fish, which is usually prepared by the merchant, should be washed, dried, and then oiled, before it is seasoned for the grill. The same is true if it is to be broiled in a shallow casserole. There should be plenty of melted butter, preferably heated with lime or lemon juice in it; and that, in most cases, is the perfect sauce, without even the distraction of a few minced herbs. [I usually rub soy sauce on fish before I oil it, unless it is very fresh and delicate indeed and especially if it is frozen. This adds a good taste to the final sauce. I buy soy sauce by the quart, but it might as well be the gallon, from a Korean-American called Paul.]

One of the great troubles about most fried fish in America (that is, *honest* fried fish, and not the sickening batter-coated monstrosity often sold in even reputable restaurants), is that it is overdone. Fish, like eggs, should be cooked quickly and lightly, and served at once in its own odorous heat.

The kind of fat you use for frying depends on your habits and your purse. Perhaps you believe that unsalted butter is the only proper medium, and that it should be poured away as soon as the fish is brown and more should be melted and poured over the dish. Perhaps you believe that a little bacon fat is a mighty fine thing, even for fresh trout, and that it's good not only on the fish but on some toast to eat alongside. The two schools of thought might be called *Haute Cuisine* and Campfire. There is no arguing with either, as long as the dish is fresh and the fat is honest. [I used to stand in line for catfish sent down from the Sacramento River, and the New Orleans girl named Bea who was helping me cook then would dip them lightly in white cornmeal which was quite heavily seasoned with *cayenne pepper*, before she fried them in good bacon grease. This may be a common trick, but I do not know of it. It works miracles.]

Any reputable cookbook holds many good recipes for preparing various kinds of fish, and such books as Mrs. Hibben's *Kitchen Manual* and Escoffier's American edition of the *Fine Art of Cookery* contain admirable discussions of the subject. [And I consider Brillat-Savarin's discussion of "The Art of Frying," in *The Physiology of Taste*, necessary to any literate cook's background.] And if you get tired of the whole thing, you can slice almost any fine-grained fish in thin pieces, cover them with lemon or lime juice, and find them cooked in four hours without aid of stove or fire. They make a good hors d'œuvre, drained and coated lightly with a peppery mayonnaise.

In spite of some hidebound gastronomic judges who believe that any fish from a tin is fit only for alley cats, modern canned tuna and salmon and shrimps are a sensible addition to your menus, if you can get them. Indeed, you are probably safe to use any tinned fish you find, given, of course, that the tin itself is intact. [Cans grow surer all the time. One that looks puffed, and sends out a wheeze or whiff when pierced, should be discarded without cavil. Black insides are most often highly suspect too. And I rely mostly upon my Curious Nose. But in general modern canning is almost as dependable as those other two omnipresent realities, Death and Taxes.]

There are countless economical ways to prepare canned fish, and most of them take so little time that they are especially sensible for you if you work in a factory or an office.

Remember that the odor and flavor of the packed fish will be stronger than that of a fresh kind, and season your dish accordingly higher. Canned fish is already cooked, so need be heated only long enough to cook the other ingredients and blend the various flavors. It breaks easily, so should be added last to any sauce that needs stirring. The liquid that comes in the can is good, used in the same dish if possible. If it is an oil (which is increasingly unlikely), it is good in French dressing, for a change.

A nice Spanish recipe, which is easy and quick to make, is good with potatoes which have been peeled, diced, boiled quickly, and shaken with a handful of minced herbs and some butter.

SALMON (OR TUNA) PANCAKE

2 eggs	1 tablespoon minced parsley
1 cup canned salmon	2 tablespoons melted butter or oil

Beat eggs, shred salmon, mix lightly, and add parsley. Form into a thick pancake, making solider with dried crumbs if necessary, and fry golden brown in the butter.

A recipe rather like this is from Hawaii, by way of China probably. It is a whole meal, and a good one too, with light beer or white wine to keep it company and perhaps a lime-and-pineapple ice afterward, if it is summer and you feel festive.

HAWAIIAN SHRIMPS

3 tablespoons fat	1 small minced onion
2 cups tinned or fresh shrimps	3 tablespoons soy sauce
½ cup minced celery	3 cups cooked rice
½ cup chopped green pepper	3 eggs
½ cup chopped tinned or fresh mushrooms	3 tablespoons water

Lightly brown onion in fat. Add celery, pepper, mushrooms, and cook 2 minutes.

Add shrimps, and turn lightly for 2 minutes. Then add the rice and soy (or Worcestershire) sauce [If you use Worcestershire, make it one tablespoon, of course. Soy sauce is salty, not peppery, as is the other.] and turn until hot, or about 2 minutes.

Stir the water and eggs together, and pour into the mixture. Stir all together quickly, and serve at once.

Another delicious shrimp dish, which is called a curry, although it has small resemblance to the real thing, is delicious with a plain green salad to follow, and then coffee.

SHRIMP AND EGG CURRY

2 teaspoons curry powder (according to taste)
⅔ cup light cream
2 cans condensed cream of mushroom soup
1½ cups shrimp (cooked, canned, or frozen)

4 hard-cooked eggs, sliced
hot fluffy rice
curry accompaniments: coconut, chutney, candied ginger, etc.

Blend the curry powder and cream. Add to the soup, and mix well. Add the shrimp and eggs, and heat over hot water, stirring as little as possible. Serve with hot rice and the accompaniments of any curry. This is well-adapted to chafing-dish cookery and is good for buffet suppers.

Condensed mushroom soup, while far from perfection, is a very present help in time of culinary trouble, and has made many a Queen Anne dish out of a Mary Anne base. The following recipe is typical of many such, and can be varied according to the herbs and ideas you possess:

BAKED TUNA (OR SALMON) WITH MUSHROOM SAUCE

1 large can of fish
salt and pepper
1 sweet onion, sliced in thin rings
1 green pepper, cut in thin strips

1 can of condensed cream of mushroom soup
½ can of water
2 teaspoons minced parsley
grated cheese (optional)

Butter a baking dish generously, and make layers in it of the flaked fish, onion, pepper, and parsley. Dilute the soup with the water, and pour over all. Put grated cheese on top if desired. Bake about 20 minutes in a moderately hot oven (400).

Of course, any such dish can be made in small casseroles, which take less time to bake. [Or in generous shells. I find most natural shells too small . . . like most sherry glasses . . . like most Gibson glasses . . . especially like most champagne glasses.] Canned mushrooms can be added, or sliced pimiento, or leftover peas . . . on and on.

It is a pity, in spite of biochemists who believe that we are better off without fish inside us, that war has interfered with our contrary tastes. The thought of all the bewildered sturgeons and barracudas dodging depth bombs is a sad one, as is the end of that wistful little Japanese who wrote so tenderly of the first succulent taste of bonito in the spring.

How Not to Boil an Egg

Hard-boiled, unbroken egg, what can you care
For the unfolded passion of the Rose?

—H. P. PUTNAM

PROBABLY one of the most private things in the world is an egg until it is broken.

Until then, you would think its secrets are its own, hidden behind the impassive beautiful curvings of its shell, white or brown or speckled. It emerges full-formed, almost painlessly [The *egg* may not be bothered, but nine years and two daughters after writing this I wonder somewhat more about the *hen*. I wrote, perhaps, too glibly.] from the hen. It lies without thought in the straw, and unless there is a thunderstorm or a sharp rise in temperature it stays fresh enough to please the human palate for several days.

In spite of the complete impersonality of its shell, however, some things about an egg can be guessed. People who know how can decide several rather surprising facts about it by holding it before a strong light, and even a zany will tell you that if it is none too fresh it will stand up and perhaps bob a little in a bowl of water.

The best thing to do with aged eggs is not to buy them, since they are fit for nothing, and a poor economy. If you find yourself the owner of a few, change your merchant with no more ado.

Hens, as long as they can find enough to eat, go right along at their chosen profession whether the country is at war or not, but unfortunately the product of all their industry is so delicate and perishable that when most of the fast trucks of the land are being used to shift soldiers here and there, the price of eggs goes much too high for comfort, whether or not the supply is good [. . . and so does the cost as well as the procurability of their feed].

229

During the last war housewives used to buy several dozen eggs when they were cheapest, and cover them in a crock with a singularly unpleasant stuff called water glass.

I can remember going down to the cellar and fishing around in the stone jar for two eggs for a cake the cook was making: the jellied chemical made a sucking noise as I spooned out the thickly coated hideous stuff, and I felt squeamish and afraid, alone there in the cool dark room. I decided then, and I still hold to it, that I would rather eat a good fresh egg only occasionally than have a whole cellarful of those dishonest old ones, which in spite of being "almost as good as new" would not make omelets, even, but had to be used in cakes and cookies.

Of course, the finest way to know that the egg you plan to eat is a fresh one is to own the hen that makes it. This scheme has many drawbacks, and I for one, as a person who has never felt any bond of sympathy between myself and chicken[1] (their heads are too small, somehow, for their stupid, scratching, omnivorous bodies), have always been content to let someone else tend to the hen-house, even if I had to buy the product at much more than it would cost me to own one myself.

Eggs are a good investment now and then, expensive or not, and unless you are told otherwise by your doctor, or hate them in any form, they should be eaten in place of meat occasionally. The old-fashioned idea that they are "invalid food," something light and inconsequential, is fairly well proved foolish by the fact that two eggs are fully as nutritious as a juicy beefsteak . . . and ten times as hard to digest unless they are cooked with great wisdom.

Probably the wisest way to treat an egg is not to cook it at all. An accomplished barfly will prove to you that a Prairie Oyster [. . . as set forth on page 239] is one of the quickest pickups known to man, and whether you are hungover or merely tired, a raw egg beaten with a little milk or sherry can make you feel much more able to cope with yourself, and shortly too. [My children react happily to an egg yolk spread on dark bread and then well sprinkled with brown sugar, for a potent snack.]

A biochemist once told me that every minute an egg is cooked

---

[1] I think this should have an S on it: alive rather than prone upon a plate. I could happily forego that too, even when cooked with the divine touch . . . or mushrooms.

makes it take three hours longer to digest. The thought of a stomach pumping and grinding and laboring for some nine hours over an average three-minute egg is a wearisome one, if true, and makes memories of picnics and their accompanying deviled eggs seem actively haunting.

The simplest way to eat an egg, if you refuse to swallow it raw, even in its fanciest high-tasting disguises, is to boil it. Rather it is *not* to boil it, for no more erroneous phrase ever existed than "to boil an egg."

There are several ways *not* to boil an egg so that it will be tender, thoroughly cooked, and yet almost as easily digested as if it were raw.

One fairly good one is to drop the egg gently into simmering water, first running cold water over it so that it will not crack, and then let it stand there in the gentle heat for whatever time you wish. It will cook just as fast as if the water were hopping about in great bubbles, and it will be a better-treated egg, once opened.

Another way, which I think is the best one, is to cover the egg with cold water in a little pan. Heat it briskly, and as soon as it begins to bubble, the egg is done. It will be tenderer than when started in hot water, which of course makes the part nearest the shell cook immediately, instead of heating the whole thing gently.

I have never yet seen an egg crack when started in cool water, but some people automatically make a pin-hole in every egg they boil, to prevent possible leaks, lesions, and losses.

(If you still want hard-boiled eggs, after pondering the number of hours, or days, it would take to digest them according to the biochemist, start them in cold water, turn the heat off as soon as it begins to bubble, and let them stand in it until it is cold. They will be tender, and comparatively free from nightmares.) [This is not as good a system as it is cracked up to be, to make a timid little pun. More often than not, I have found since I so optimistically wrote of it, the eggs do not peel properly. Half of the white comes off with the shell. Ho hum.]

If you think eggs boiled in their shells are fit food for the nursery, and refuse to admit any potential blessing in one delicately prepared, neatly spooned from its shell into a cup, sagely seasoned with salt and fresh-ground black pepper and a sizeable dollop of butter, all to be eaten with hot toast, then it is definitely not your dish.

Instead, try heating a shallow skillet or fire-proof dish, skirling a lump of butter [preferably waiting in the bottom, to absorb good melting heat from the egg . . .] or bacon grease or decent oil [This must have been a wartime aberration. Just lately I fired a cook who fried eggs in my best olive oil. The eggs, the oil, the whole house, and finally the cook took on an unbearable *slipperiness*.] in it until it looks very hot, and breaking a fresh egg or two into it. Then . . . and this is the trick . . . turn off the heat at once, cover the pan tightly, and wait for about three minutes. The result will be tender and firm, and very good indeed with toast and coffee, or with a salad and white wine for supper.

This method, of course, is a compromise. It is not a fried egg, strictly speaking, and yet it is as near to making a *good* fried egg as I have ever got.

I can make amazingly *bad* fried eggs, and in spite of what people tell me about this method and that, I continue to make amazingly bad fried eggs: tough, with edges like some kind of dirty starched lace, and a taste part sulphur and part singed newspaper. The best way to find a trustworthy method, I think, is to ask almost anyone but me. Or look in a cookbook. Or experiment.

There are as many different theories about making an omelet as there are people who like them, but in general, there are two main schools: the French, which uses eggs hardly stirred together, and the puffy or soufflé, which beats the white and yellow parts of the eggs separately, and then mixes them.

Then, of course, there is the Italian *frittata* school, which mixes all kinds of cooked cooled vegetables with eggs and merges them into a sort of pie; and a very good school that is.

Moreover, there is the Oriental school, best exemplified by what is usually called *foo yeung* in chop-suey parlors and is a kind of pancake of egg and bean-sprouts and and and.

To cap the whole thing, there is the school which has its own dependable and usually very simple method of putting eggs in a pan and having them come out as intended. Brillat-Savarin called them *œufs brouillis* and I call them scrambled eggs.

The best definition of a perfect French omelet is given, perhaps unwittingly, in Escoffier's American translation of his *Guide Culinaire*: "Scrambled eggs enclosed in a coating of coagulated egg." This phrase in itself is none too appetizing, it seems to me, but it must do for want of a better man to say it. [This is said much more simply in its own language: *une omelette baveuse*.]

A French omelet worthy of the man, if not the definition, can be made, the second time at least if the first time it turns into a stiff ugly curd, by following these directions:

BASIC FRENCH OMELET

6 *eggs*   *salt and pepper*
3 *tablespoons butter (good oil*
    if absolutely necessary)

Be sure that the frying pan (8 or 10 inches) is smooth on the inside. Heat the butter in it until it gives off a nutty smell but does not brown. ("This will not only lend an exquisite taste," Escoffier says, "but the degree of heat reached in order to produce the aroma will be found to ensure the perfect setting of the eggs.") Roll the pan to cover the sides with butter.

Beat eggs lightly with a fork, add seasoning, and pour into pan. As soon as the edges are set, run a spatula under the center so that all the uncooked part will run under the cooked. [By now I know, fatalistically, that if I am using a pan I know, and if I have properly rolled the precise amount of sweet butter around that pan, and if the stars, winds, and general emotional climates are in both conjunction and harmony, I can make a perfect omelet without ever touching a spatula to it. Such occasions are historical, as well as accidental.] Do this once or twice, never leaving it to its own devices. When it is daintily browned on the bottom and creamy on top, fold it in the middle (or roll if you are a master), slide it onto a dish, and serve speedily.

Chopped herbs, cheese, mushrooms, and almost anything else may be added at your discretion, either at the first in the stirred eggs or when it is ready to fold. [Delicate creamed fowl or fish, generous in proportion to the size of each omelet, can be folded in, or new peas or asparagus tips, lightly cooked in butter.]

The second school of omelets is roughly defined as belonging to those addicts who believe eggs should be separated and then beaten hard, and then brought together again. Probably the main trick to remember in this technique is that the resulting foamy delicate mass should be cooked slowly instead of fast. [I don't know why I said this. It is true about scrambled eggs, surely, but a good omelet (soufflé) should be baked in a quick oven for 15 to 20 minutes, or so I now firmly believe.] If this is done, it will "stand up firm and proud, instead of collapsing like a tired horse," says Mrs. Mazza. And she is right.

BASIC SOUFFLÉ OMELET

6 eggs	5 tablespoons hot water
3 tablespoons butter (or decent oil for want of better)	salt and pepper

Separate eggs and beat whites until very stiff and yolks until creamy. Add the hot water and seasoning to the yolks, mix well, and fold in the whites. Heat a smooth skillet, add the butter, and roll it around the sides until it bubbles. Pour in the egg mixture, and leave over a very low fire until it is brown on the bottom. Place under the broiler to brown lightly on top. Test as for a cake with a toothpick, which should come out dry and clean when the omelet is done.

This omelet can be cut in two parts and any number of sauces of filling put between the layers and on top: Spanish sauce, chicken livers, left-over creamed sweetbreads, mushrooms in sherry . . . on and on.

Or try pouring a little rum over it and sprinkling it with powdered sugar, for a fine dessert. Or spreading it with chutney or any good preserve and grilling it again very quickly for a strange savory tail-piece to a meal. [Jeanne Bonamour in Dijon used to make cheese soufflés the way a good bartender mixes dry Gibsons, secure in a trance of habit and supreme self-confidence. She was careful to use moist fresh Swiss cheese and very fresh eggs (6), butter (4 T), and milk (1 c.). She mixed the milk and some flour in a small casserole . . . but her recipe is in any reputable collection of plain French cookery.]

An Italian *frittata*, which like all omelets is a fine dish for lunch or supper in any language, is a kind of pie or pancake filled with vegetables. It is made with olive oil instead of butter (if possible). Whatever odorous mulch of herbs and legumes that you make should be cooled and then added to the eggs.

FRITTATA OF ZUCCHINI (*For example*)

3 tablespoons olive oil (*or rep-*
  utable substitute)
1 onion or three green onions
1 clove garlic
5 small zucchini

1 large fresh tomato or 1 cup
  solid-pack canned tomatoes
salt and pepper
1 teaspoon herbs . . . parsley,
  sweet marjoram, or thyme

9 eggs

*Heat oil in skillet and cook minced onion and garlic slowly in it
10 minutes. Add zucchini cut into thin slices. Add peeled and cut-up
tomato, seasoning, and herbs. Cover, and cook until the vegetable
is tender. Take from stove and cool.*

*Beat eggs lightly, season, and mix with cooled vegetables. Pour
back into skillet, cover tightly and cook over a slow fire until the
edges of the* frittata *pull away from the pan. If the middle puffs up,
prick it with a long sharp knife [. . . or better yet, pull away from
sides once or twice with large spoon, to let the soft middle flow
outward].*

*When it is solid, brown lightly under a slow broiler flame in a
preheated oven, cut in slices like a pie, and serve at once.*

This *frittata* is a good dish. It can be made with almost
anything: string beans, peas, spinach, artichokes. Cheese can
be sprinkled over it. [As an older and easily wiser *frittata* cook
I almost always, these richer days, add a scant cup of good dry
grated Parmesan cheese to the eggs when I mix them. Often I add
rich cream, too. How easy it is to stray from austerity!] Different
kinds of herbs like sweet basil, summer savory, on and on, can
change its whole character. And with a glass of wine and some
honest-to-God bread it is a meal. At the end of it you know that Fate
cannot harm you, for you have dined.

Foo yeung is really another cut off the same loaf. The main difference between it and a *frittata* is that in the Oriental version the
vegetables are diced and cooked only until they are crisply heated
so that the whole texture is one of surprises, a mixture of sharp and
soft, crisp and mellow, as all good Chinese dishes should be. This
recipe can of course use gourmet powder (*mei jing*) [So many
editors have shuddered away from my opinions on what we pompously call something like monoglutium sodomate that I'll only repeat here that it is a fine thing now and then, *but not all the time*

and in candy and coffee and on fresh green peas.] diced roasted pork (*foo yuk*), diced peeled water chestnuts (*ma tai*), diced bamboo shoots (*jook tsun*), and a dozen other delicious things which are sold in Chinese stores. It can also be made without one of them and still taste as fresh and strange as any genuine Chinese omelet.

BASIC FOO YEUNG

4 *eggs*	½ *cup celery*
3 *tablespoons good fat*	½ *cup green pepper*
½ *cup onion*	½ *cup mushroom*

Brown chopped onion lightly in fat. Stir chopped or minced vegetables lightly into eggs. Let get firm and brown in pan, stirring up center once in a while. Cut into sections and serve quickly.

There are almost as many variations to this recipe as there are Chinese characters. Add shrimps. Add cooked rice. Add diced chicken. Add fried almonds [. . . or minced cooked porkhambeefvealfish]. Try mixing all the ingredients together and then frying in little cakes in the hot fat. It depends on whether you come from Canton, Changsha, or West Hollywood.

In between what I think are the most delicious eggs in the world and these other almost equally palatable concoctions with their exotic names—*frittata, soufflé aux fines herbes, gai foo yeung*—are a thousand dishes made from the fruit of the hen's expert if unconscious labor, and mixed according to your whim. Almost every good cook in the world has at least one ritual, usually histrionic, and more power to him! Here are three, fully guaranteed (although one of them is far from economical, and recommended only on state occasions, if the wolf seems definitely at the door).

EGGS IN HELL
[*Uova in Purgatorio, Œufs d'en Bas, etc.*]

4 *tablespoons olive oil (substitute will do, dad blast it)*	1 *teaspoon minced mixed herbs (basil, thyme)*
1 *clove garlic*	1 *teaspoon minced parsley*
1 *onion*	*salt and pepper*
2 *cups tomato sauce (Italian kind is best, but even catsup will do if you cut down on spices)*	8 *eggs*
	slices of French bread, thin, toasted

Heat oil in a saucepan that has a tight cover. Split garlic length-wise, run a toothpick through each half, and brown slowly in oil . . . Add the onion, minced, and cook until golden. Then add the tomato sauce and the seasonings and herbs. Cook about fifteen minutes, stirring often, and then take out the garlic.

Into this sauce break the eggs. Spoon the sauce over them, cover closely, and cook very slowly until eggs are done, or about fifteen minutes. (If the skillet is a heavy one, you can turn off the heat and cook in fifteen minutes with what is stored in the metal.)

When done, put the eggs carefully on the slices of dry toast, and cover with sauce. (Grated Parmesan cheese is good on this, if you can get any.)

There are too many variations of this recipe, even in my own mind, to be able to write. One I remember that we used to make, never earlier than two and never later than four in the morning, in a strange modernistic electric kitchen on the wine terraces between Lausanne and Montreux. We put cream and Worcestershire sauce into little casseroles, and heated them into bubbling. Then we broke eggs into them, turned off the current, and waited until they looked done, while we stood around drinking champagne with circles under our eyes and Viennese music in our heads. Then we ate the eggs with spoons, and went to bed.

A fair substitute for those far-away delightful shadows is what one young-painter-in-Mexico invented, called Eggs Obstaculos with nary a double-entendre in any language:

EGGS OBSTACULOS

2 tablespoons butter or oil	*8 eggs*
¾ cup hot tomato sauce (salsa piquante) *or ¾ cup tomato sauce and 8 drops tabasco sauce*	*1 cup beer* *hot toast*

Heat oil and sauce in a shallow dish, rolling it well around the edges. When bubbling, break eggs into it. Heat slowly until the eggs are done, pour the beer over, and serve at once, with hot toast.

This recipe, like most good ones, has many variations, and unlike most of them, it is inexpensive if you have the ingredients at all.

It leads, by a somewhat crooked path, to what I think is the best way to cook eggs (unless you count hard-boiling them, cracking them on your own head, and eating them with salt and pepper and a glass of cold beer some hot summer day).

Scrambled eggs have been made, and massacred, for as long as people knew about pots and pans, no doubt. Very few know the rudiments held in this recipe now. I say it complacently, for I have tried it at least a hundred times, on people as various as a three-year-old Irishman and a poet laureate. (I have also tried to tell four cooks how to make it. Three of them were professionals and one was willing. All failed, I must add with somewhat less complacency.) [I am even less complacent than I was, having coped, like all honest cooks, with the uncountable quirks of eggs, and their unsuspected degrees of freshness and senescence. But I still feel that this recipe is superb, if you like very delicate creamy things now and then.]

SCRAMBLED EGGS
(*This dish is not very economical, but it is nourishing and pleasant enough for an occasional splurge.*)

8 *good fresh eggs* ½ *pint rich cream . . . or more*

[*. . . yes, good fresh eggs and rich cream . . . and yet I have produced something very good indeed with tired corner-store eggs and diluted condensed milk, given the time, which is, I am told, the essence.*]

salt and freshly ground pepper | grated cheese, herbs, whatnot, if desired

Break eggs gently into cold iron skillet. Pour cream in, and stir quietly until the whole is blended, but no more. Never beat or whip. Heat very slowly, stirring from the middle bottom in large curds, as seldom as possible. Never let bubble. Add seasoning at the last stir or two.

This takes perhaps a half hour. It cannot be hurried.

Serve on toast, when it is barely firm. If herbs or cheese or mushrooms (or chicken livers and so forth) are added it should be when the eggs are half done.

It is a poor figure of a man who will say that eggs are fit only to be eaten at breakfast, served as they can be in these and countless other fashions. He himself may be as innocent as a new-laid egg, and unconscious of the manifold disguises, not to mention the artful invitations and devices, that can tempt him and the egg too. Let him ponder then, and if, wisely or not, he choose from all the possible forms an egg fresh-broken from the shell, cupped with a bit of lemon juice and pepper and any other seasoning to hand, and called an Oyster,[1] we can but hope that he has drunk well the night before and slept the sleep of the satisfied if not the just.

---

[1] [The combination of one fresh raw unbeaten egg, one douse of Worcestershire sauce, one souse of whiskey or brandy, and one optional dibble of Tabasco-or-Evangeline-or-*salsa-piquante* (in that order of hell-fire progression); it represents to many a jaded rounder the next morning's Last Resort. Not so to me. I often make one for myself before I must do something I dislike: go to the dentist, say. . . . I have been madly in love with mine, in a mild way, since I was nineteen, but I still need a Prairie Oyster to be able to stand going into his office.]

How to Keep Alive

Appetite, a universal wolf.

—SHAKESPEARE

THERE are times when helpful hints about turning off the gas when not in use are foolish, because the gas has been turned off permanently, or until you can pay the bill. And you don't care about knowing the trick of keeping bread fresh by putting a cut apple in the box because you don't have any bread and certainly not an apple, cut or uncut. And there is no point in planning to save the juice from canned vegetables because they, and therefore their juices, do not exist.

In other words, the wolf has one paw wedged firmly into what looks like a widening crack in the door. Let us take it for granted that the situation, while uncomfortable, is definitely impermanent, and can be coped with.

The first thing to do, if you have absolutely no money, is to borrow some. Fifty cents will be enough, and should last you from three days to a week, depending on how luxurious are your tastes. [How grimly ridiculous *that* sounds, these days!] (Doctor Horace Fletcher, who believed that chewing food until it disappeared would help prevent senility, decayed teeth, stomach ache, and several other equally tiresome phenomena, lived for years on eleven cents a day. And I know a man who spent two years at college on less than that, except that he cheated occasionally.)

As soon as you have procured fifty cents, find some kind soul who will let you use a stove, a food-grinder [any reasonable variation of what is now called a "food mill" is useful, for puréeing cooked vegetables and so on . . . unless that safe *chewed* texture is as unpleasant to you as to me. . . .] and a big kettle . . . the first for about three

240

hours and the last for as long as you have any food. If you must pay for the stove, it will probably cost about ten cents for the current or gas. That cuts you down to forty cents.

You can either make a week's supply without meat, or about four days' with meat. Say you choose to be Lucullan: then buy about fifteen cents' worth of ground beef from a reputable butcher. (Be sure that it is beef and not what is none too euphoniously referred to as Hamburger.) This much meat will have few nourishing qualities, but it will make a good taste and its fat will stimulate you and help keep you warm. [Anywhere along here is all right for my heartfelt comment that this sounds both silly and disagreeable, but that basically it is a workable suggestion, given reasonable good sense and a certain amount of desperation, both of them dictated by the actual State of War . . . against either wolf or fellow man.]

Buy about ten cents' worth of ground whole-grain cereal. Almost any large grocery carries it in bulk. It is brownish in color, coarsely mealy in texture, and has a pleasant smell of nuts and starch.

Spend the rest of your money on vegetables. Buy them if you can at a big market which most probably has a counter of slightly wilted or withered things a day old maybe. Otherwise buy the big coarse ugly ones in any store. If you know the merchant and he likes you, he will feel passionately interested in your well-being and will help you economize as if you were his own child, with mutual amusement.

Get one bunch of carrots, two onions, some celery, and either a small head of cabbage or the coarse outer leaves from some heads that should be trimmed a bit anyway. It does not matter if they be slightly battered: you will wash them and grind them into an odorous but unrecognizable sludge.

The other vegetables depend on how much money you have left and what the season or your will may be. Squashes, like zucchini, are good, and of course tomatoes. Beans are fine. There can hardly be too much celery, if you like it. A clove of garlic is highly to be recommended . . . *if* you like it. Turnips are too strong, and beets of course would make the whole thing into a ghoulish, ghastly and completely horrendous mess of pink and cerise [. . . and finally gray]. Potatoes are useless; the cereal takes care of any need for starch, and bulk as well.

Assemble what vegetables you have. Grind them all into the pot.

Break up the meat into the pot. Cover the thing with what seems too much water. Bring to a boil, let simmer about an hour, and stir in the ground grain-cereal. Mix thoroughly, and cook very slowly another two hours, or longer if possible. Let cool, and keep in a cold place (the cellar in summer if you have no icebox handy or borrowable).

You can eat it cold and not suffer much, if your needs are purely animal and unfinanced, but if you can heat what you want two or three times a day it will probably taste much better. (A little of it sliced and fried like scrapple is absolutely delicious, but of course that takes it into the luxury class, what with the fat you'd need, and the fire.)

It is obvious to even the most optimistic that this sludge, which should be like stiff cold mush, and a rather unpleasant murky brown-gray in color, is strictly for hunger. [One way to make it prettier, gastronomically, is to brown the meat in a handful of flour, to a handsome walnut shade. Another is to use a douse of dear old Kitchen Bouquet, toward the end but while you can still stir it thoroughly into the aptly named Sludge.] It is functional, really: a streamlined answer to the pressing problem of how to exist the best possible way for the least amount of money. I know, from some experience, that it can be done on this formula, which holds enough vitamins and minerals and so on and so forth to keep a professional strong-man or a dancer or even a college professor in good health and equable spirits.

The main trouble with it, as with any enforced and completely simple diet, is its monotony. It must be considered, then, as a means to an end, like ethyl gasoline, which can never give much esthetic satisfaction to its purchaser or the automobile it is meant for but is almost certain to make that automobile run smoothly.

"When food is not appetizing it lies in the stomach like lead," an American gastronomist named Henry Finck decided in 1913. The idea was not original with him but it is a good one, and makes it plainer than ever that this Down-with-the-Wolf formula could very easily lie like lead unless you really needed it.

Then, if you had to choose between it and hunger, with its inevitable aftermath of fatigue and bad teeth and dull hair and wrinkles, you would eat it three times a day as long as the emergency lasted and perhaps even derive a certain esthetic satisfaction from your own good sense, if not from the food itself.

Other systems for living on little have been evolved, of course, and for a time at least have proved fairly successful. One mother of five growing children fed them and their father and herself, during what is still referred to as The Depression, on something like five dollars a month for five months. She went so far as to write a book about it, illustrated with a family photograph of what looked like slightly overweight but average people. [The fat look of some starving people is even more familiar now than in 1942, unhappily.]

I have occasionally thought of her and her system, and have wanted, in a faintly masochistic mood, to see what five years rather than five months of farinaceous vegetables and cheap spaghettis and breads would do to the teeth and innards of her brood. According to most nutritionists, the picture would not be so pretty. [One boy I know, who was adolescent during the thinnest months of Occupation in Burgundy, is now too tall and very listless. And a girl, adolescent now and a happy baby then, is much more bitterly ill-tempered and voracious than her age would justify.]

The man I know who lived for two years on about seven cents a day (this was in the early thirties at the University of California) was and still is a bonny figure indeed, tall, lean, and wholesome . . . physically at least. (Spiritually he is a disciple of Henry Miller, which in some people's eyes is a form of disease.) Perhaps an empty stomach is not a good literary adviser, to misquote Einstein's observation about hunger and politics. [I think the parenthetical and unsolicited cultural comment should close here and not above. It still stands, according to some critics.]

His formula was simple, but as I said before, he cheated now and then.

He would buy whole ground wheat at a feed-and-grain store, cook it slowly in a big kettle with a lot of water until it was tender, and eat it three times a day with a weekly gallon of milk which he got from a cut-rate dairy. Almost every day he stole a piece of fruit from a Chinese pushcart near his room. (After he graduated he sent the owner a ten-dollar bill, and got four dollars back, with an agreeable note inviting him to a New Year's party in Chinatown in San Francisco. He went.)

Every three weeks or so he had a job as waiter at fraternity-house banquets and other such collegiate orgies. He always took a basket and a rope, and let down into the alley sometime during the evening a surprising collection of rolls, butter, olives, pie, and even chicken or meat. After one or two sad experiences with alley cats, who found his basket before he got to it, he knew how to close it firmly against any marauders but himself, and would hurry back to his room with it as soon as the waiters were dismissed.

He confessed much later that the food never tasted good and that it was always a relief to get back to boiled wheat and milk again but that for two years he wolfed down those frowsy stolen scraps as if they were his one link with *la gourmandise*.

He was fortunate that his chosen way to keep alive agreed with his guts, if not completely with his gourmet instincts. The woman who fed her family cooked starch for five months was perhaps equally lucky; at least she kept them alive, which is supposed to mean heaven for true mothers. Myself, I shall choose my own peculiar brew of vegetables and meat and cereal if need be, for like the student and the mother and every other human, I feel that my own system is the best . . . until a better one occurs to me. [It has not yet done so. I believe more firmly than ever in fresh raw milk, freshly ground whole grains of cereal, and vegetables grown in organically cultured soil. If I must eat meats I want them carved from beasts nurtured on the plants from that same kind of soil. As for fish . . . they can choose their own way of life in my gastronomy, unless we interrupt it with split atoms.]

And to all of us I shall say, with wise Aesop, "You have put your head inside a wolf's mouth and taken it out again in safety. That ought to be reward enough for you."

How to Rise Up Like New Bread

"Lord Jesus Christ, have mercy and save me! Let me lie down like a stone, O God, and rise up like new bread," Platon prayed, and turning over, he fell asleep at once.

—*War and Peace*, TOLSTOY

FOR years you have had to be a voice crying in the wilderness [now comparatively crowded, thank God] to dare say anything against the mockery of our staff of life, and now, when war and perhaps a growing sensibility have made us think more of vitamins and their relation to poor teeth and jumpy nerves and such, we still condone the stupid bread in this country. [True, in spite of the optimistic note just above.]

Newspapers tell us, with government permission, that wheat costing some five cents a pound is "refined" until it is not only tasteless but almost worthless nutritionally, and that the wheat germ which is thus removed is then sold for at least a dollar and a half and at the end put back into the bread, so that in loaves it can be sold for a little more than the ordinary price and called "Super-Vitaminized" or "Energized" or some such thing.

The English Food Ministry has been trying ever since the second World War began to make its subjects buy whole-cereal breads rather than the emasculated pale stuff sold by every self-respecting bakery. Apparently class snobbism has conquered once more over good sense, for no matter what proof the Ministry gives that white bread will cause bad teeth, poor eyes, weak back, fatigue, the Britishers go on eating what has for decades meant refinement and

245

"good taste," socially if not gastronomically. [In Switzerland, at least when I lived there, every bakery must make a daily batch of "federal formula bread," according to its total output. It always embarrassed Francois, my houseman, to have me buy the dark nutty moist stuff instead of gentler paler loaves.]

Here we are perhaps less stubborn, since we are made up of a lot of different nationalities mainly brought from the lower classes, and in almost any decent-sized village of our country there is a baker from Hungary or Poland or France who can and does still make his round odorous healthful loaves.

In every big city there is a good handful of restaurants, mostly kosher, which put flat baskets of various breads on every table, and the breads are so good, so dark and crusty and full of flavor, that the waiters have to hop to keep them filled, whether the diners be Jew or wandering Gentile.

And in spite of this, and what seems an inborn and growing hunger for decent bread, we continue everywhere to buy the packaged monstrosities that lie, all sliced and tasteless, on the bread-counters of the nation, and then spend money and more money on pills containing the vitamins that have been removed at great cost from the wheat. [Today, with a bakers' strike on, the only bread at my store came from a small Franco-Italian factory. It lay piled in fine unsliced unwrapped odorous loaves, and all the housewives looked blankly at it and asked, almost in tears, "But where's the *sandwich* bread?]

It is a crying shame, for fair.

Lately, perhaps because of the very propaganda that seems so contradictory, it has been easier to buy bread with a little taste to it, once you have conquered your distrust of the thick neat slices and the transparent wrappings. You have even been able to get sour-dough bread once a week in some groceries: a frail wisp of the old nose-tickling loaf, but at least an effort in the right direction.

It is hard, often, not to be impatient at our slowness. Sometimes, when you go past a little factory in the "foreign" section of a town, and smell the honest exciting smell of real bread baking, you remember a part of your childhood, and feel a child's helplessness before the fact of a whole nation's cautious acceptance of its own simplicity. It is difficult for us, after years of trying to be highfalutin and refined, to admit that plush drapes in the parlor and pale white bread are not our dish at all.

Perhaps this war will make it simpler for us to go back to some of the old ways we knew before we came over to this land and made the Big Money. Perhaps, even, we will remember how to make good bread again.

It does not cost much. [It costs more than ordinary chain-store stuff. But it is a sound investment, at least now and then.] It is pleasant: one of those almost hypnotic businesses, like a dance from some ancient ceremony. It leaves you filled with peace, and the house filled with one of the world's sweetest smells. But it takes a lot of time. If you can find that, the rest is easy. And if you cannot rightly find it, make it, for probably there is no chiropractic treatment, no Yoga exercise, no hour of meditation in a music-throbbing chapel, that will leave you emptier of bad thoughts than this homely ceremony of making bread.

You should have four bread pans, which can be bought usually at a junk-man's if one of your female relatives does not have them stuck away in some cupboard under the back stairs. [I had four of my maternal grandmother's: a good friend quietly liberated two, and an enemy the rest. I still have Grandmother's black cast-iron "gem-tins," and *I plan to keep them.* I haven't made a popover for years, but when I do I'll need those "tins" and no others.] You might even buy the glass ones, which are very good, although less romantic. You will need a big bowl, too.

Given these props, then, and an oven that will hold the four pans, you can safely embark on what may, for the first time at least, be a harrowingly entertaining experience, but will probably lead to many calmer, peace-bringing times.

WHITE BREAD

4 *cups* (1 *quart*) *milk*
¼ *cup sugar*
4 *teaspoons salt*
2 *tablespoons shortening*

1 *cake compressed yeast, or* 1
package dry granular yeast
¼ *cup lukewarm water*
12 *cups sifted all-purpose flour*
(*approximately*)

From there on, when you first assemble the ingredients, the dance begins. It is one that should be rehearsed a few times, probably, but

I know that it can be done with astonishing if somewhat frenzied smoothness the first time.

First scald the milk. Then add the sugar, salt, and shortening, and let the whole cool until it is lukewarm. Then add the yeast, which has been softened in the tepid water.

Start stirring in the flour, mixing it slowly and thoroughly. When the dough is stiff enough to be handled easily, turn it out onto a lightly floured board or table-top, and knead it until it is smooth and satiny.

Kneading bread means pressing it rhythmically with the heel and fingers of each hand, in a gentle rocking movement, turning the dough over on itself with each push, folding it lightly, pushing, pressing. It is a calming, musical rhythm. In eight or ten minutes, when the dough looks and feels as smooth as silk, you can stop.

Then shape the kneaded dough into a smooth ball, and place it in a bowl which has been lightly greased. [Fresh unsalted butter or virgin peanut oil I like best, whenever I indicate grease or fat. But according to the uses of the bread, anything good can be used, from bacon drippings to goose-schmaltz.] Brush the surface fleetingly with melted fat, cover with a lid or a heavy cloth, and let rise in a warm place until it has doubled in bulk. Overnight is easiest. If you press the dough gently with your finger and a hole stays there, it is light enough.

Punch with your folded fist into the soft white mound, down as far as you can go. Then fold the edges into the hole you have made, turn the ball smooth side up, and cover and let it rise again.

When it is light enough to hold the impression of your finger, punch into it again. Then divide the dough into four even parts with a sharp knife, and round each part lightly into a smooth ball. Cover them well, and let stay tranquil for about fifteen minutes.

Mold each one, then, into a loaf, by flattening it, and folding and stretching and rolling and stretching and folding until it will fit lightly into a greased pan, with the last seam on the bottom and a firm smooth top where it should be. [A temporarily retired lieutenant-colonel with jitters calmed himself by baking for his friends, and evolved a flattish tough wonderful loaf we all called Old Testament, made of stone-ground flours. He put about three of them onto a big cookie sheet. They were truly Biblical, and made clearer the significance of "breaking bread."]

Brush the tops with melted fat, and let rise in a warm place until they have doubled in bulk. And then bake in a moderately hot oven (400 to 425°) for forty to forty-five minutes.

When the loaves are golden, slip them from their pans onto racks of any kind, to cool.

You can stand and look at them, even the first time, with an almost mystical pride and feeling of self-pleasure. You will know, as you smell them and remember the strange cool solidity of the dough puffing up around your wrist when you hit it, what people have known for centuries about the sanctity of bread. You will understand why certain simple men, in old centuries, used to apologize to the family loaf if by accident they dropped it from the table.

There is another recipe for a good bread, which will interest you perhaps enough to try, once you have proved at least your armchair wings with the first one:

HOT LOAF

1 *pint milk*	1 *cake yeast*
1 *boiled potato*	1 *teaspoon salt*
1½ *tablespoons lard*	*flour*
1 *tablespoon sugar*	

Mash the potato and beat until light. After the milk is brought to a boil, add the potato, lard and sugar and salt. When the mixture is lukewarm, add the yeast which has been dissolved in a little of the potato water.

Sift in enough flour to make the dough soft and workable. Then knead well, place in a large bowl, and set in a warm room to rise overnight.

Next morning turn the dough out onto a floured board and knead 2 or 3 minutes. Form into a round loaf, and place in a greased lard bucket. Let rise for two hours, and bake in a moderate oven until a fine golden crust is formed.

This rather quaint rule is from an old Virginian cookbook, and I for one am quite ignorant of what a lard bucket looks like. It reminds me of what a Frenchman once told me, though, about the bread that was baked in his home when he was little. It was always put into clean clay flowerpots, he said! It has a fresh sweet flavor that no other bread could ever have . . . and "Try it," he said. "You will see! You can make tiny loaves for each person, and the clean washed clay will change your bread as you never thought man-made thing could dare to!" [I almost lost a dear friend with this trick: apparently she was too sparing with the butter on the clay, or the clay was not wet enough to begin with. . . . The loaves stuck. She has since forgiven me and brings me fresh warm bread wrapped, as it should be, in a clean tattered linen napkin.]

And here is the recipe for:

ADDIE'S QUICK BUCKET-BREAD

1 *cake fresh yeast*	1½ *tablespoons salt*
1 *cup lukewarm water*	3 *tablespoons sugar*
3 *tablespoons shortening*	10 *to* 12 *cups all-purpose flour*
1 *quart whole rich milk*	*grease, butter*

Dissolve the yeast in the water. Melt the shortening in the milk, but do not let it boil. Combine the two liquid mixtures in a big bowl. Into another big bowl or kettle sift the blended salt, sugar, and flour. Pour the liquid gradually into the flour, mixing well, and when feasible knead until smooth. Put the dough into a heavily greased pan, cover with a clean napkin or towel, and let stand in a warm place until double in size. Knead lightly, and let rise once more (about 3½ hours altogether). Make into loaves (Addie slashes her dough into pieces with a sharp knife and then slaps it into shape as if it were a Bad Boy . . . but any good recipe gives as logical, if less lusty, a procedure), put into well-greased pans, and bake at 350° for about 1 hour. Brush butter on the tops when once they start to brown, and again when the loaves are removed from their pans.

This bread is fine in regular pans, but Addie uses two- (or one- or three-) pound coffee-tins. A ball of dough at the bottom of one will make a loaf about four times as high, a delightful slightly buttery light odorous thing, fine for toast, sandwiches, eggs poached or pseudo-Benedict or or or. . . .Children love its roundness.

And aside from the quaint practicability of the pans the recipe is valuable, I think, because it makes excellent bread in a much shorter time than most cooks will grant is possible.]

But whether it be flowerpots or modern glass or old Southern lard bucket, or even coffee-tins, there are always containers for the bread to rise and bake in. Why is that? Why can you not make the kind of round loaf, perhaps with a cross slashed on the top of it, that you used to see through a cellar door when you walked home from the theater late at night in France? The white-faced baker's boy, with flour in his eyebrows and his pores and probably his lungs, slid it surely, intensely, on a long shovel into the blaze of the open oven. It was naked, like a firm-hipped woman, without benefit of metal girdlings. It came out, in an hour or so, ready for next morning's breakfast, round and brownly even and filled with an honorable savor. It was good bread, and you can make it.

You can forget the soggy sterile slices that pop up dourly in three million automatic toasters every morning. [Why do I say three, either then or now? I own one myself, which makes it at least three million and one, and I hate everything about it, except a rare slice of bread which seems in conjunction with the workings of the robot within, and springs up rightly golden, rightly crisp.] and instead cut for yourself, if you will, a slice of bread that you have seen mysteriously rise and redouble and fall and fold under your hands. It will smell better, and taste better, than you remembered anything could possibly taste or smell, and it will make you feel, for a time at least, newborn into a better world than this one often seems.

How to Be Cheerful Though Starving

Obsession by economic issues is as local and transitory as it is repulsive and disturbing.

—The Acquisitive Society, RICHARD HENRY TAWNEY

WHEN you are really hungry, a meal eaten by yourself is not so much an event as the automatic carrying out of a physical function: you must do it to live. [I now disagree completely with this, and could and probably will write a whole book proving my present point, that solitary dining, no matter what the degree of hunger, can be good.] But when you share it with another human or two, or even a respected animal, it becomes dignified. Suddenly it takes on part of the ancient religious solemnity of the Breaking of Bread, the Sharing of Salt. No matter what your hunger nor how fiercely your fingers itch for the warmness of the food, the fact that you are not alone makes flavors clearer and a certain philosophic slowness possible.

And it is well to eat slowly: the food seems to be more plentiful, probably because it lasts longer.

There are many ways to make a little seem like more. They have been followed and changed and re-invented for ten thousand years, with small loss of dignity to mankind. Indeed, sometimes their very following is a thing of admiration, because of the people who are poor and who refuse to be obsessed by that fact until it becomes "repulsive and disturbing."

Of course, it takes a certain amount of native wit to cope gracefully with the problem of having the wolf camp with apparent permanency on your doorstep. That can be a wearing thing, and even the pretense of ignoring his presence has a kind of dangerous monotony about it.

For the average wolf-dodger, good health is probably one of the most important foils. Nothing seems particularly grim if your head is clear and your teeth are clean [Toothpaste now contains chlorophyl. Animals still chew grass.] and your bowels function properly.

Another thing that makes daily, hourly thought about wherewithals endurable is to be able to share it with someone else. That does not mean, and I say it emphatically, sharing the fuss and bother and fretting. It means being companionable with another human who understands, perhaps without any talking at all, what problems of basic nourishment confront you. [This still obtains, as my legal friends say. It is the condition most devoutly to be wished for. However, the years have taught me compromises, as they have all thinking creatures.] Once such a relationship is established, your black thoughts vanish, and how to make a pot of stew last three more meals seems less a nightmare than a form of sensual entertainment.

There was one person, though, who was a part of my education and who refuted all my tentative rules for fortunate wolf-dodging, and did it with such grace that I often think of her half-doubtingly, as if she were a dream.

Her name was Sue. She was delicate bodily . . . not ill, but never well the way most people are well. She flitted like a night moth through all her days, bemazed by the ardors of sunlight but conducting herself with wary sureness, so that she seldom banged against shut doors or hit her thin bones on sharp table corners.

She was, as far as anyone knew, completely alone. It was impossible to think of her in any more passionate contact with other humans than the occasional suppers she gave for them. The fact that once she must have been young did not change her present remoteness: you could not see her any warmer at seventeen than at seventy.

But her withdrawn impersonal attitude did not make her any less delicately robust. She loved to eat, and she apparently loved, now and then, to eat with other people. Her suppers were legendary. Of course, it depended on who was telling about them: sometimes they were merely strange, or even laughable, and sometimes they sounded like something from a Southern California Twelfthnight, with strange games and witch-like feastings.

Sue lived in a little weatherbeaten house on a big weatherbeaten cliff. At first when you entered it, the house seemed almost empty, but soon you realized that like all dwellings of old lonely people, it was stuffed with a thousand relics of the fuller years. There were incredibly dingy and lump-filled cushions that Whistler had sat on, and a Phyfe chair that had one stormy night been kicked into kindling wood by Oscar Wilde. It was held together with rubber bands, and naturally was not to be used as a chair, but rather as a casually treated but important altar.

When you went to her house, you ate by one candle, no matter whether you were two or eight at table. Of course this seemed intensely romantic to young Americans, but it was because she could afford neither more candles nor electricity.

The walls, covered with third-rate etchings by first-rate men, and a few first-rate ones by the almost unknown Sue, emerged gradually from the dingy darkness. There was an underlying smell, delicate as early death, of age and decay.

The main smell, though, was a good one. It never had the forthright energy of braised meat (although I remember one time, when I may have looked a little peaked, that Sue went against her custom and put a tiny morsel of cooked liver on my plate, and said, "Now, I want you to try to eat *all* of this!" It was no bigger than a dollar, and I made it into at least twelve bites, in a kind of awe).

There was always the exciting, mysterious perfume of bruised herbs, plucked fresh and cool from the tangle of weeds around the shack. Sue put them into a salad.

Then there was usually sage, which she used like a Turk or Armenian in practically everything that went into her pot. She gathered it in the hills, and dried it in bunches above her stove, and in spite of gastronomical scouts who wail now that California sage all has a taste of turpentine, hers never did. She knew only about a hundred kinds, she confessed quietly; someone had told her that the hills behind the village held at least fifty more.

Sue had only a few plates, and no knives. You ate everything from one large Spode soup plate, when you went there, but it never seemed mussy. And knives were unnecessary, because there was nothing to cut.

As I remember now, her whole cuisine was Oriental. There were the little bowls of chopped fresh and cooked leaves. There were the fresh and dried herbs, which she had gathered from the fields. There was the common bowl of rice (or potatoes which Sue had probably stolen the night before from some patch up the canyon). There was tea, always. There was, occasionally, a fresh egg, which also was stolen, no doubt, and which Sue always put in the teapot to heat through and then broke over the biggest dish of food.

I have never eaten such strange things as there in her dark smelly room, with the waves roaring at the foot of the cliff and Whistler's maroon-taffeta pillow bruising its soft way into the small of my back. People said that Sue robbed garbage pails at night. She did not, of course. But she did flit about, picking leaves from other gardens than her own and wandering like the Lolly Willowes of Laguna along the cliff-tops and the beaches looking in the night light for sea-spinach and pink ice-plant. [For long now the cliffs have been covered with villas, and the wild herbs have vanished. I still taste and smell them in my memory, and feel the close-packed cold beads of the ice-plant's leaves and petals.]

The salads and stews she made from these little shy weeds were indeed peculiar, but she blended and cooked them so skillfully that they never lost their fresh salt crispness. She put them together with thought and gratitude, and never seemed to realize that her cuisine was one of intense romantic strangeness to everyone but herself. I doubt if she spent more than fifty dollars a year on what she and her entranced guests ate, but from the gracious abstracted way she gave you a soup dish full of sliced cactus leaves and lemon-berries and dried crumbled kelp, it might as well have been stuffed ortolans. Moreover, it was good.

I doubt very much if anybody but Sue could make it good. Few other humans know the secret of herbs as she did . . . or if they know them, can use them so nonchalantly.

But anyone in the world, with intelligence and spirit and the knowledge that it must be done, can live with her inspired oblivion to the ugliness of poverty. It is not that she wandered at night hunting for leaves and berries; it is that she cared enough to invite her friends to share them with her, and could serve them, to herself alone or to a dozen guests, with the sureness that she was right.

Sue had neither health nor companionship to comfort her and

warm her, but she nourished herself and many other people for many years, with the quiet assumption [this is very important] that man's need for food is not a grim obsession, repulsive, disturbing, but a dignified and even enjoyable function. Her nourishment was of more than the flesh, not because of its strangeness, but because of her own calm. [And this, too, is very important.]

How to Carve the Wolf

Meat puddings should be served between the months of September and April; during the months without an "R" in them meat pies should replace them.

—LE VICOMTE DE MAUDUIT

[It is unflattering but fortunate that nobody has ever asked me the difference between a meat pie and a meat pudding. Do I really know?]

FOR several years before France fell, Paris newspapers as different at *Le Temps* and *L'Intransigeant* ran irate and direful letters from old-fashioned chefs predicting that sure as shooting something awful would happen to the whole country unless the young people forgot their new fad for sports and grilled steak-with-watercress and went back intelligently to the rich *cuisine des sauces* of their fathers.

Not only was this shocking appetite driving the chefs themselves to the poorhouse, but it was un-French. It bespoke a crass lack of national spirit, a betrayal of all that was best in the Gallic culture, to order a Chateaubriand (*saignant*) in a decent restaurant, when one could as easily command a little pigeon simmered artfully with red wine and truffles and this and that and mushrooms maybe . . . and many spices . . . and one or two kinds of fat . . . and probably a little basting of marc or brandy at the last.

What the chefs would say now, if they could, can never be known. The young girls and men who ate grilled steak in their sport clothes at the Café de Paris are as much a secret as the Café de Paris itself. Ghosts of the great restaurants and their cooks may cry that lack of spirit and finesse betrayed the old as well as the unborn; ghosts of the young may answer that richness and subtlety were

257

but a kind of phosphorescence on the decayed culture that Carême and Vatel and all the other masters left to them.

Ghosts are not worried by wolves. The psychological effects of grilled or be-sauced beef on a nation's temperament cannot matter much to clay, or so we prefer to think. [When I am cook for the carnivorous, my true salute to them is a beef filet, of about four pounds. I turn it for at least three hours in a garlicky marinade, half olive oil, half soy sauce. I roast it on a rack for one-half hour in a very hot oven. I slice it one-inch thick, slip generous wedges of maitre-d'hotel butter between each slice, pour a good cup of red wine over the whole, and serve it in its various hot juices. Even ghosts . . .] But to the living, who must eat to stay so, beef in any form is a problem indeed.

There are several more or less logical reasons why meat grows scarce in wartime: soldiers need it, there are fewer cattle, zub zub zub. It is unfortunate that so many human beings depend on eating some form of animal flesh every day for strength. Many of them do it because their bodies, weakened or diseased, demand it. Others simply have the habit. Habit or necessity, it becomes a truly worrisome expense in wartime, so that money spent for meat must be used to buy as much nourishment as possible, even at the risk of a certain monotony.

The old idea that if you boil even a useless piece of meat long enough you will extract all its juices, which then form a fine stimulating nutritive broth, is looked on with suspicion by most modern food-experts [. . . including Brillat-Savarin, who died in 1825, only a few years ago]. They say that by the time you drink the juices, they are so dead that they are useless to any human organism. Instead, the experts advise, the quickest and easiest way to absorb all the minerals and vitamins present in a piece of meat it to chop it finely and eat it raw.

This brutal simplification should make the ghosts of the Paris chefs wail even louder, and itch to write another letter to *L'Intransigeant*. But I remember several times in their city, living then, when I was tired and wanted a quick pickup (or when I had eaten one too many of their artful sauces), that they made Bœuf Tartare for me. Of course, they elaborated it as much as possible, and each time it was a little different, like a good Indian curry, but this is the basis:

BŒUF TARTARE

¼ pound beef per person (or
    more)
  1 egg per person
    lemon juice

olive oil
parsley, chives, basil, any
    herbs
salt, pepper

Remove all fat from meat and grind rather coarse. Form lightly into mounds or pats, one for each person. Make a little dent on the top.

Break the eggs carefully, saving the whites for another purpose, and put a yolk in a half-shell in the dent on each pat.

Chop the herbs separately and put into little bowls. Serve the olive oil in a cruet. Garnish the meat with lemon-quarters. Other things like little pickled onions and chopped dill pickles and so forth may be added to the tray.

To eat, put the egg-yolk into the dent, cover the whole with whatever herbs desired, add olive oil and lemon juice and seasoning, and mix lightly.

This somewhat barbaric dish is best with crisp bread and a glass of fairly plain red wine. It is quickly digested and leaves a pleasant feeling on the palate, if you can swallow it at all, which some people would rather starve than do [. . . or if you can keep it from the eager exhibitionism of the waiter, who pants to turn it into a gastronomical proof that gray can be made with even a few too many colors (or flavors) mixed together].

The distinction between raw and rare is a subtle one, only to be settled in the individual mind. Many a person who could not even think of eating Bœuf Tartare without gagging (unfortunately, because it can be made of inexpensive and often highly nutritive cuts of beef), would willingly assault a thick bloody lukewarm "cut off the joint" and feel himself secure in the tradition of Simpson's and the Plaza and Dave Chasen's . . . and Henry the Eighth's own dining hall, as far as that goes.

There is no doubt about it, a handsome roast *is* handsome, and probably the most satisfying meat to the average Anglo-Saxon hunger. It grows increasingly scarce and relatively priceless.

Nevertheless, it is a wise extravagance now and then if it can be had at all, since for the average family it will make several meals, and only the first cooking uses much fuel. (There will be cold roast beef with salad, and then sandwiches, and then perhaps Bœuf Moreno or some such concoction, and then maybe hash [A hash can be very fine indeed. The worst thing that can happen to it is a grinder; everything that is choppable in it should be *chopped*.] or even a curry, or croquettes if you can afford a "frying kettle" and approve of these synthetic pyramids . . . on and on . . . or maybe it disappears practically at once! In this case you had better not buy it again for a long time, unless your rich godfather dies.

There are two definite ways to start to roast beef, or any meat. For the last few years the government experts have urged that women put the meat into an oven 300 degrees, at which temperature it remains for an average of 20 minutes per pound. The loss by shrinkage is practically erased, and the flavor of the meat, it is said, is much better. The meat browns gradually, until by the time it is done, it is as beautiful as it should be.

The older school disagrees thoroughly with this system, and at least has custom on its side, if not economy. It holds that the first twenty-five minutes of a roast's final death are the most important. They should be spent at a temperature of about 500 degrees, so that the whole surface is seared and all the juices are sealed into the meat. After that, the oven heat is reduced to about 300 degrees, as in the other process. [The proof of the roasting is the taste therefrom, and certainly the new system tastes best to me, in the face of my recognized masters.]

Aside from the first temperature, the way to roast a good cut of beef, preferably one with about two ribs in it, is the same. The meat is wiped carefully with a damp cloth or a cut lemon, and then rubbed with salt and pepper and fresh herbs in a little oil if you like them. It is good fat-side-up on the rack of an open pan (never a closed roaster, since that belies its name by steaming the meat), and basted frequently with pure fat until done. [I now use a patented V-shaped gadget, a kind of adjustable rack, for almost every kind of meat. And I almost never baste a roast any more. Instead I roll it well in seasoned fat or olive oil, for an hour or so, and of course put it in the rack with the fattest side up.]

It is important that the basting liquid contain no water, nor indeed anything but good butter or beef-fat or oil, since anything else will open the seared pores and let the imprisoned juices flow away. Sheila Hibben, who writes with stern good sense about such matters, admits that in the case of a large roast a little water may be put under the rack, so that the bastings will not stick to the pan and be wasted.

Of course, the best gravy is one quite innocent of flour, in spite of what your grandmother would say. It is made by swirling a little boiling stock or water into the rich odorous pan as soon as the roast is removed. It is boiled for a scant five minutes, skimmed lightly, thickened with a little fresh butter, and strained into a hot sauceboat.

Long ago in Burgundy, when we ate the Sunday roast of beef or lamb, Madame Bonamour always put a big spoonful of this hot juice into the salad just before she stirred it. We liked it, especially if the bowl held escarole and what we rather indelicately called *pisse-en-lit*.

A rolled roast seems more economical at first sight, because you do not buy the rib bones. But you must remember that bones are conductors of heat and make meat cook about six minutes faster to the pound, thus cutting down on the fuel bill for the rib-roast. Moreover, if you are going to splurge on anything as elegant as a roast, you might as well get the best, for nothing gives a better flavor to already fine meat than cooking it on the bones it grew on.

What used to be called the cheaper cuts of meat, such as the rump, can be cooked in a number of ways, but always following the main rules given in any good cookbook for pot-roasting or braising. One trouble with them is that they are seldom treated with due respect, but are seared in any kind of fat and then allowed to stew in some water until they are moderately tender, and more than a little stringy. They should be seasoned and watched with even greater care than a roast, since they have perhaps less dignity to start with.

Economically they are not very wise, since they take a long time to cook, and demand attention. They can be delicious, of course (What meat-eater would not approve of Escoffier's Bœuf à la Mode?), but they are less adaptable than roast the second or third day, and thus become more of a luxury than what you may still like to call a necessity.

Probably the most popular kind of beef, after a ruddy roast, is broiled or grilled steak. This, to be at its best, should be what you yourself prefer: T-bone, porterhouse, tenderloin, and so on. You will undoubtedly have your own way of preparing it. You will, in your dreams at least . . . for such cuts of meat are far beyond the reach of wolf-dodgers.

You can buy a cheap cut, of course, like a round-bone steak, and have the butcher run it through a fantastic little electric machine called a Tender-Lux or some such thing. Then it comes out looking all nibbled, and supposedly tasting like the finest T-bone. [Now there are popular little flat pats of lean beef, frozen, which people keep assuring me are delicious "minute steaks." I have tried several times to agree . . . it would be so convenient if I could! . . . but I continue to find them stringy and innocuous and one more depressing proof of our gradual mediocrization, in the process of which we are forced to eat so many down-right poor foods that we leap with sincere delight for the mediocre.]

Or you can make a mixture of equal parts of oil and vinegar, and rub it very hard into a tough steak, and then let it stand for two hours, with the fond conviction that the meat will be tenderer, which it probably will. [I use a mixture of oil and soy sauce now, on almost any cut of meat and many kinds of fish. This strange trick comes from a Japanese cook; he always coated fish with the sauce before putting it in the icebox, and it never smelled *fishy*. And it kept much longer and better, if need be. And best of all, it never tasted of soy sauce!]

Or you can save your meat money for quite a while, and buy a good tenderloin and broil it as you and only you know how, and eat it like a man.

Of these courses the last is probably the most satisfying, esthetically if not dietetically, unless you are among those miserable ones who must have meat in some form every day because you always *have* had meat in some form every day. In that case, this little catalog of tricks on wolf-catching is not for you, and neither good sense nor the dictates of earthly war can still your carnivorous hunger.

Cheap is a word said in these times with a gallant laugh and a devil-may-care toss of the head, but it continues to modify the parts of a beef's body, like the chuck or the rump, which cannot possibly be sold at a higher price for broiling.

One way to use cheap meat is to buy that butt of gibes and snobbism, ground round steak. "Ground beef" is cheaper yet, but not a good investment because it contains so much fat and shrinks so in cooking that it is neither good for you nor economical.

The first thing to know about ground round steak is that it should not be that at all. Round steak is a fairly good cut of meat which can be bought in one piece and braised like a pot roast and prepared in various lengthy but delicious manners. It is foolish to grind it, since other parts of the meat can be ground into an ever better-tasting mess for less money.

Butchers, usually, are very pleasant people, in spite of having at some time in their lives deliberately chosen to be butchers. They will assist your efforts to economize with amazing benevolence, and will agree with you that a piece of "lean end" or flank, stripped of its cartilage and fat and put once through the grinder, is as good meat an anybody could ask for.

Get the bones, if any, for your dog or your soup kettle, and the fat to chop later and fry crisp and dark brown for cabbage or even an omelet. Or make:

CRACKLING BREAD

1 cup cracklings, diced	¾ cup wheat flour
1 measure cornmeal pancake-flour	½ teaspoon soda
or	¼ teaspoon salt
1½ cups cornmeal	1 cup sour milk

Cracklings are the pieces of meat remaining after the lard has been rendered from the fat (Pork in the South). Make the prepared batter or mix and sift together the dry ingredients, add the milk. Stir in the cracklings. Form into oblong cakes and place in a greased baking dish. Bake in hot oven (400°) about 30 minutes.

This is an old-fashioned recipe, except for the modern dodge of using a reputable prepared cornmeal mixture if you want to. It is a cheap and pleasant way to use something that otherwise would be wasted, and to give at least a savor of richness and solidity to a supper that might, without it, consist of plain cornpone and a glass of milk. [A delicious supper, cracklins or no.]

To return to your momentous purchase of some ground beef: with the meat in your hand, as it were, go home and unwrap it and cook it, or if you plan to keep it for a time in the icebox, be sure to bring it back to room-heat for a good two hours before using it. Then form it lightly into cakes, one for each person and rather on the large side if you are hungry, since one big one is much better than two or three little ones. [Unless you like meat very well done. I have trouble getting it any other way, unless I cook it myself.]

Heat a heavy skillet very hot, so that a drop of water dances and vanishes on its surface, which seems to look more stretched than you thought iron could look.

Put in the pats of beef. There will be a great smoke and smell, so windows should be open if possible. In about two minutes turn the cakes over with a spatula, and probably with your fingers masked in a pot-holder. There will be more smell. Keep the heat high for two more minutes or until the meat is thoroughly brown, and then slap on a tightly fitting lid and turn off whatever fuel you use. If you like your meat rare, you must act quickly from now on, but however you like it, the heat in the skillet will be sufficient. [It is more sensible to have the herbs ready before you start the pan-broiling of the meat. Now, especially for barbecues (this is fine for thick steaks, too), I put the herbs, wine, and a generous pat of butter in a bowl at least an hour before I'll want them, and then pour the mixture into the empty fuming skillet and, without covering it, let it blend for not more than a minute, just long enough to melt the butter, before I put it on the steak.]

Chop chives (or a little green onion split from end to end), parsley, basil, any other herbs you like and want, either fresh or dried . . . about two tablespoonfuls for each cake of beef. Have one-fourth of a cup red wine or tomato juice or vegetable stock for each one, and if the latter two are used add a little Worcestershire sauce. [Now and then very strong fresh coffee, one-fourth cup per serving, is delicious.]

Remove the cakes of meat to hot plates or a hot shallow casserole before they are quite done to your taste, since they will continue to cook. Then throw in the herbs and the liquid. There will be another great sizzle and fume. Put the cover on quickly, to catch all the first fine savor. In about fifty seconds, stir the mixture thoroughly to catch all the meat-essence in the pan, add a little butter, and put the mixture with a spoon over the cakes of meat. Serve at once, with hot French bread and a crisp green salad, and red wine or ale if you can and will.

Herb butter, a little blob on each cake just before serving, is perfect for this. [Here I obviously meant: "perfect for grilled beef cakes *instead* of the herb and wine sauce."] It is simply unsalted butter creamed with a little lemon juice and whatever finely chopped herbs you like. The mixture is packed into a jar, covered, and kept indefinitely in the icebox. If you are knowing about such things, you can have a different kind for every herb you know, and use them according to your hungers. [For instance, put 1 teaspoonful of basil butter in each small hollowed tomato, and grill for 5 minutes . . . delicious with lamb chops.]

They make almost any kind of meat or fish taste better than it meant to. They are not necessary, but they are *nice*, in the right sense of the word, so that eating meat becomes not a physical function, like breathing or defecating, but an agreeable and almost intellectual satisfaction of the senses.

I I

Of course, there are many other ways to eat the flesh of animals than in its simplest states, raw or roasted or broiled or braised. According to some people, including the mournful ghosts of those masters who once ruled Paris kitchens and wrote letters to the *Times,* they are the only ways, since barbarians alone can stomach the sweet bloody savor of rare meat.

There are a thousand ways to cook it, all of them set forth in cookbooks of varied merit. The trouble with most of them is that they take too long and call for too many disguises which in themselves may seem inexpensive but added together make a surprising cost for the whole dish.

A stew, for instance: it is supposed to be the simplest of dishes, and probably in the fargone days it was, when you threw a piece of meat and some water into a pot, and let them boil together until they had blended into one edible thing. Now, a stew means something richer, and can be a fine tantalizing dish indeed, full of braised meat and many vegetables and all bound together by a gravy heady with herbs and wine. We are proud to have raised it from its lowly place, and in so doing we have cheated ourselves of its first frugal goodness, for once having tasted the new kind, our palates are chilled by the starkness of the old.

Nonetheless, if you have the time and the fuel, make a stew for your soul's sake. It is a satisfying procedure, and can do no harm to man or beast. There is a different recipe for everyone who has ever thought of making one, but in general the rules are simple:

Braise the meat, which has been cut into small pieces, in fat.

Season with whatever herbs you like [This means peppercorns, bay leaves, perhaps cloves stuck in an onion. The fresh herbs I would add only a few minutes before serving: basil or rosemary or marjoram, for instance, and parsley.], cover amply with stock or vegetable juice or water or wine, and simmer until almost done. Half-cook [. . . preferably braising first] any kinds of vegetables you like, except beets which of course make a filthy color. Thicken the juice around the meat. Add the vegetables. Let the whole thing rest for a few hours . . . a day is better [. . . not better, *best*] and then bring to the boil and serve, preferably in soup plates. The variations on this theme are as obvious as they are entertaining.

One good way to cook meat slowly without feeling completely extravagant is to arrange several other things which require the same temperature in the oven and can be cooked at the same time. A roast takes up most of the space in any modern oven I have ever seen, but there are other meats to bake in shallow pans or casseroles. A good one is:

BAKED HAM SLICE

1 *one-inch slice of ham (or thicker if you can afford it!)*
1 *handful parsley*
2 *teaspoons hot mustard*
1 *tart apple for each person*

1 *sweet potato for each person*
1 *cup brown sugar*
1 *cup hot water [or cider, or white wine]*

Pare the fat from the ham and mince with the chopped parsley and mustard. Spread thickly on the meat.

Slice the unpeeled apples ½ inch thick. Peel and slice the potatoes lengthwise ½ inch thick.

Place the ham in the center of a pan, with the apples and then the potatoes in a ring around it. Add the hot water, and sprinkle with the brown sugar.

Bake in a 325-350° oven, basting often, until the potatoes are tender. [This bakes faster if put in a shallow casserole and covered for the first half-hour.]

Another good way to cook ham, if you can afford it at all and want something that simmers along nicely with an ovenful of other things, is to get two slices and put them into a pan with chutney or any left-over preserves between the two, like a sandwich. Spread prepared mustard on the top, sprinkle some brown sugar over all, pour a little water or white wine or even stale beer into the dish, and cook for about an hour, basting frequently.

[Baked Ham in Cream is a richer dish, but very good indeed, now and then. There should be a generous, indeed a *Hungarian*, hand with the paprika, and the browning thickening cream in the flat dish should be spooned often over the slices of meat, gradually to form a pink-brown sauce, which sometimes curdles but with no danger to the whole.

This is a good thing to know about, with an air of luxury to it.

BAKED HAM IN CREAM

Have loaf-boiled ham cut in ½-inch slices. Cut each in two, place together like sandwiches. Place in baking pan with a little brown sugar and plenty of paprika. Baste often with cream. Bake in moderate oven for 25 minutes. Serve with pickled pears, figs, or prunes.

[Fine with casserole of noodles, butter, crumbs, and mushrooms sautéed.]

A flank steak is supposedly a cheap cut of meat, and the following recipe, while rather fussy to begin with, uses both the meat and the moderate heat of an oven which we'll hope is well filled with other things. There are of course many changes to be rung on this:

MOCK DUCK

1 *flank steak, cut very thin*	*seasoning for dressing: sage,*
2 *cups bread crumbs*	*pepper, etc.*
1 *egg*	3 *tablespoons oil or fat*
	water or stock or wine

Make a highly seasoned dressing according to your favorite rule. Mix the egg into it.

Roll it into the steak, and tie tightly. Brown the roll in the hot fat, put into a pan, and cover with whatever liquid you like: tomato juice, red wine and water, vegetable stock . . . baste frequently. Cook until tender: the time will vary after one hour according to the thickness of the roll. Remove the string before serving.

This is good with fresh green beans or a plain salad, and brown rice. The gravy can be thickened or not, as desired; personally, I find that a little butter is enough change in it.

[One of the best things I can make, for a winter dinner, is the Prune Roast whose recipe I give below. I am told by other cooks that it is not wholly dependable: sometimes the prunes cook to bits; sometimes the sauce is too thin or too thick. I have never found this to be true, but I do know that no recipe in the world is independent of the tides, the moon, the physical and emotional temperatures surrounding its performance. Having taken all these into consideration, the only other questionables in the problem are the meat and the prunes, and my one remark about them is that they should be of good but not luxurious quality. This roast, served on a generous platter and carved at the table into thick slices, with ample sauce and a bowl of buttered noodles and a crisp bowl of salad greens, with good bread and wine, and cheese to follow, makes a delicious dinner to come upon. It is pungent and hearty, and the world seems more real.

PRUNE ROAST

4 to 5 pounds rump roast	½ cup cider vinegar
2 teaspoons salt	½ cup water
pepper	1 cup light brown sugar
2 cups washed, dried prunes	¼ teaspoon ground cloves
2 cups boiling water	1 teaspoon ground cinnamon

Heat a heavy, deep pan on top of range. Add roast, turning so it will brown on all sides. Sprinkle with salt and pepper. Add prunes and water, cover, and simmer until tender (about 3 hours). Remove meat from liquid to hot platter. Stir in vinegar, water, sugar, cloves, and cinnamon; cook rapidly until a thick sauce is formed. Pour sauce over and around meat, serve immediately. Serves 8 to 10.]

Almost all cookbooks, especially the endearing paper-bound volumes edited around the turn of this century by farflung Ladies' Guilds and other churchly societies, contain many such recipes. They should be read with one canny eye on the cooking time, since fuel is an increasing expense and time itself is not a thing to be thrown about lightly.

Another point about which to be wary in the usually dependable recipes given in most such collections is the seasoning; it is, to put it mildly, a challenge to your inventive palate, since it either says, "Salt, pepper," or "Salt." Apparently any other condiments were considered foreign and perhaps even sacrilegious by members of the Saint James' Sewing Circle in 1902. Otherwise, recipes in such books are dependable, if you like such things.

III

One way to horrify at least eight out of ten Anglo-Saxons is to suggest their eating anything but the actual red fibrous meat of a beast. A heart or a kidney or even a sweetbread is anathema. It is too bad, since there are so many nutritious and entertaining ways to prepare the various livers and lights. They can become gastronomic pleasures instead of dogged voodoo, so that when you eat a stuffed baked bull's heart, or a grilled lamb's brain or a "mountain oyster," you need not choke them down with the nauseated resolve to be braver or wiser or more potent, but with plain delight. [I believe this more firmly than ever, but am years wearier in my fight. Now, when I want to eat what English butchers call "offal," I wait until everyone has gone to the Mid-South Peoria Muezzins' Jamboree and Ham-bake, and then make myself a dainty dish.]

I must admit that my own first introduction to *tête de veau* was a difficult one for a naive American girl. The main trouble, perhaps, was that it was not a veal's head at all, but half a veal's head. There was the half-tongue, lolling stiffly from the neat half-mouth. There was the one eye, closed in a savory wink. There was the lone ear, lopped loose and faintly pink over the odd wrinkles of the demi-forehead. And there, by the single pallid nostril, were three stiff white hairs.

At first I thought the world was too much with me, and wondered how gracefully I could leave it. Then what I am sure was my good angel made me stay, and eat, and finally ask for more, for *tête de veau,* when it is intelligently prepared, can be a fine exciting dish.

["I don't go much out," as a German-American friend of mine says, but even so I have lived about three-fourths of my life in the United States and I have *never* been served anything even faintly suggestive of the undisguisable anatomy of a boiled calf's head, in this my homeland. The nearest I have ever come to it was, when I was little, delicious cold shaky slices of Head Cheese for summer lunch, and even that was genteelly called "cold shape" by my English aunt who had the courage to make it for Southern Californians . . . until I grew up enough to make it myself. I give her basic recipe, to be flavored to differing tastes, and then my own version of the classic rules of Tête de Veau: Escoffier, for instance, dictates using a "white court-bouillon," but I like a less subtly delicate broth to cook the meat in . . . I like it cooked in halves, *à l'anglaise*, but served with a vinaigrette sauce instead of the proper "boat of parsley sauce" . . . and so on.

AUNT GWEN'S COLD SHAPE (!)

1 *calf head, quartered*
  salt, pepper, bay, herbs as de-
    sired

½ *cup lemon juice*
  or
1 *cup dry white wine*

Remove most of fat, and the brains (save for another dish), ears, eyes, and snout (a kindly butcher will do this for the finicky). Soak for ½ hour in cold water, wash off, cover with cold water, and sim-mer until the meat starts to fall from the bones. Drain in large colander over another kettle, saving all the cooking liquor. Dice the meat ("in pretty pieces," Aunt Gwen directed), add the stock amply to cover, and mix gently with seasoning to taste. Simmer for ¾ hour, add the lemon juice or wine, and pour into a mold. Cover with a cloth, weight well, and chill. Serve in slices. (Aunt Gwen used bread-pans for the molds, clean bricks for the weights . . . and there were always cucumber-chips on the platter.)

TÊTE DE VEAU

1 *calf head*
2 *or 3 quarts water*
1 *carrot*
1 *onion*

1 *small head celery or 3 large*
  stalks
1 *lemon in quarters*
  salt, pepper, 2 bay leaves, 6
    cloves

Have head cut in half. Soak for 1 hour in cold water. Boil water and rest of ingredients for 10 minutes. Drain halves, add to liquid, and simmer, well covered, for about 1½ hours or until the cheeks are tender. (The tongue and brain can be removed, the former to be cooked with the head, the latter added to the bouillon for the final quarter-hour of simmering. They should be nicely trimmed, sliced, and served with the halves.) Drain, and serve at once surrounded by parsley, with a sauce-boat of vinaigrette made of 1 part vinegar, 1 part of the cooking liquor, and 2 parts oil, with the required seasonings. Or . . . drain, rub carefully with a cloth soaked in lemon juice to keep the flesh from darkening, and chill well. Serve surrounded by small green onions, capers, parsley, and sliced cucumbers, with a sauce-boat of vinaigrette to taste.]

Why is it worse, in the end, to see an animal's head cooked and prepared for our pleasure than a thigh or a tail or a rib? If we are going to live on other inhabitants of this world we must not bind ourselves with illogical prejudices, but savor to the fullest the beasts we have killed.

People who feel that a lamb's cheek is gross and vulgar when a chop is not are like the medieval philosophers who argued about such hairsplitting problems as how many angels could dance on the point of a pin. If you have these prejudices, ask yourself if they are not built on what you may have been taught when you were young and unthinking, and then if you can, teach yourself to enjoy some of the parts of an animal that are not commonly prepared.

Sweetbreads of course are in somewhat snobbish repute, and are indeed worthy of their reputation. Unfortunately they are expensive.

The same is true of liver, which is supposed to be one of the best things in the world to eat if you are anemic. It should be beef or calf liver, since pork liver is fat and heavy to the taste, and according to some authorities actively impure.

There are many fine recipes for preparing liver, but it should always be cooked swiftly so as not to be toughened. It is good the next day, cooked with other left-overs with some sherry added to the sauce, and brown rice to eat with it. (It is also delicious cold, with a glass of beer and some fresh-ground pepper, and a few sprigs of parsley, if you're of the same turn of mind as I am.)

Tongue is of course more acceptable socially than some of the other functional parts of a beast's anatomy. Its main trouble as an economical thing to prepare is that it takes a long time to cook. It is a deceptively mild meat, and needs some characterful sauce well laced with condiments or wine to stand by it.

Brains are, to my mind, unfortunately coupled with scrambled eggs on most menus. The combination is an unpleasant one, because of the similar textures of the two things. Instead, I think brains should be cooked so that they are crisp, and should be served with crisp things, to offset the custard-like quality of their interiors. The following recipe from Barcelona is a good example, and is delicious with fresh peas, hot toast, and fruit:

CALVES' BRAINS

1 *pair calves' brains*	*parsley, 5 or 6 sprigs*
¼ *cup good vinegar, or 1 lemon*	*salt and pepper*
3 *tablespoons butter or good oil*	

Blanch brains in boiling water. Remove outer skin, taking care not to break inner tissue. Place in cold water for 1 hour. Drain, sprinkle with vinegar or lemon juice, and let stand ½ hour.

Drain and salt the brains and fry until golden brown in the hot fat. Place on a hot serving plate and fry the parsley. Add the remaining vinegar or lemon juice to the pan, heat well, and pour over the brains. Garnish with the crisp parsley, and freshly ground pepper. [If you like deep-frying, there are fine tricks to play with various crisp "fritters" made of brains or sweetbreads.]

Another vital part of a beef is the heart, which is not well enough known as a meat unusually rich in vitamins and minerals too. A large heart should be stuffed with a regular poultry-dressing, aromatic with fresh or dried herbs, and basted often with fat of rich stock in a slow oven until it is tender. The process is rather long, but is well worth it if you can fit other things into the oven at the same time.

Smaller hearts can be split, braised, and simmered in the oven or a heavy skillet with strips of bacon, until they are tender. Then put them under the broiler long enough to brown.

Small veal or lamb hearts can be sliced thin, braised quickly in hot fat, and then simmered in stock with cubed vegetables and herbs for a fine savory stew to eat with rice. A little sherry and sour cream stirred in just before serving make the flavors even more satisfying.

Another way to use a large heart, which will take much less time than would baking it whole, is to grind it. Mix it with a ground onion, celery if you like it, a couple of eggs, whatever stock or tomato juice you have in the icebox, and some bread crumbs if it seems too moist. Season it with fresh pepper, a little dill, some sweet marjoram . . . any herbs you like. Pack it into a breadpan or make it into a loaf, and bake it an hour or until done in a moderate oven, basting frequently. [I would now say: "*At least* two hours." Long slow cooking makes it especially good and firm, for slicing for a cold buffet or for sandwiches.]

Kidneys are in better repute than some of the other innards, mainly because English arbiters of our gastronomic likes and dislikes eat them broiled, and right they are. There is nothing much better than a sizzling skewerful of little lamb kidneys, bacon, mushrooms, and maybe a few dwarf-size tomatoes, all dipped in butter and twilled for five minutes or so in a hot broiler: nothing much better, that is, if you like it. Some people do not. They *loathe* kidneys, with a loathing that is impregnable to temptation. There is nothing to do about it, apparently, but remember not to serve them to those unfortunate souls.

One good basic recipe, which can be varied indefinitely and is good warmed over or made in a chafing dish or on an outdoor barbecue, is:

KIDNEYS IN SHERRY

2 *tablespoons butter or good oil*	½ *cup sherry*
1 *sweet onion, minced*	*watercress*
1 *pair veal kidneys*	*toast, rice or whatever*
seasoning	

Wash kidneys and cut into little pieces. Brown the onion in the fat and add the meat. Add seasoning (salt, pepper, fresh-chopped parsley or basil or whatever herb you like). Add the sherry and simmer five minutes. Serve very hot, with the watercress as a garnish.

This recipe I got from Spain, but it is the same everywhere. Different herbs are used, or lemon juice instead of sherry, or sour cream [one cup thick sour cream, just after the sherry: very good with kasha or wild rice, very Smetanaish] is put in at the last, or a little brandy is poured in. Mushrooms are browned with the onion in the fat. Capers and shaved almonds are tossed in just before serving; the mixture is put into hollowed tomatoes and grilled.

In other words, you can do what you like, remembering always that kidneys have a strong pungent taste which needs to be curbed by the even stronger flavors of herbs and liquors.

A very quick dish which is inexpensive, and good with a salad and cheese and coffee for supper, is:

SAUSAGE PIE (OR SARDINE PIE)

½ *pound sausage [or bacon] (or*   1 *teaspoon grated onion*
  ½ *can sardines)*   *or chopped green onion*
  tomato sauce
  biscuit-mix

Spread sausage [or bacon or fish] thin in pie-pan or shallow casserole. Let heat in quick oven and pour off almost all fat. (Leave oil on sardines.)

Make one-half usual baking powder biscuit, mixing with tomato sauce [. . . or meat stock. It is a question of flavors. One good combination with bacon strips is milk in the biscuit-mix, plus a generous half-cup of grated cheese.] instead of milk or water. Add the onion and any chopped herbs you like. Pour over the sausage, and bake in hot oven until firm and brown [. . . about 20 minutes].

Shrimps are good in this pie too; indeed, it came from Portugal, where they used to grow on bushes, practically.

Left-over meats are always fun to cope with, and one of the nicest ways, which for some reason always surprises people, is in Canelloni. Canelloni are simply small unsweetened pancakes like delicate *enchiladas,* which are filled with what the recipe discreetly calls "any plausible mixture": meat, fish, herbs, egg yolks, on and on.

They are rolled and laid in a shallow dish, on spinach purée if you like. Then they are sprinkled with grated cheese and browned quickly. [A nice thing about them is that the pancakes can be made several hours in advance (they should be thin, like French *crêpes*). So can the "mixture." They should be combined at the last. If something in a sauce is used for the filling, like creamed chicken, some of the sauce should be put over the whole.]

There are always curries, of course, which are really not curries at all, but simply left-over meat served in a gravy flavored with curry powder. [This is a horrible definition, and only the next sentence saves me from gastronomical guilt.] They can be very good or ghastly, according to the cook. The following recipe is uninspired, but dependable.

AN ENGLISH CURRY

1 onion, sliced
3 to 4 tablespoons fat or 2 slices
   bacon
1½ tablespoons hot curry
   powder

¼ cup vinegar
¼ cup water
1 cup tomato sauce
left-over meat and gravy

Fry onion golden brown in fat or with chopped bacon. Mix the curry, water, and vinegar, and add to the onion. [Mix briskly over hot flame; this develops the curry powder's flavor.] Add the tomato sauce, and cook 5 minutes. Cut the meat into small pieces, add it to the sauce with any of its gravy, and cook until heated through. This is better for standing a few hours [Not much better. A real curry is, but this hasty makeshift must sink or swim, to quote myself a bit further down, on the basic goodness of its immediate contents.], and should be served with rice and a syrupy preserve (figs, peaches).

Another good way to use meat, aside from the time-honored and never to be scorned Third-Day Hash, which like curry sinks or swims with the cook who compounds it, is this:

TURKISH HASH

2 tablespoons butter or fat
1 chopped onion
½ cup uncooked brown rice
1 cup water or stock
1½ cups cooked diced meat
1 bud garlic

1 cup tomatoes, cooked or
   fresh
1 tablespoon horseradish (optional)
salt, pepper, any desired
   herbs

Cook the butter, onion, and rice in a heavy skillet until brown, turning often. Add the rest of the ingredients, mix thoroughly, and cover the skillet tightly. As soon as it steams, turn the fire very low, and cook for about 20 minutes or until done.

Lin Yutang, more than once, has written that it is a shock to him to see how much an average American family spends on meat. He says that we could cut our bills in half, and that is quite a lot, by cooking as the Chinese people do and using more vegetables.

It is all a question, according to him, of marrying the tastes of the meat and the green things in the kitchen, instead of letting them meet each other for the first time "when served on the table in their respective confirmed bachelorhood and unspoiled virginity."

In spite of inventions and conceits, however, and the dogged appliance of good common sense, meat continues to be the most expensive part of the modern diet.

Each person must evolve his own system of eating as much as possible of what he wants and needs. For myself, if I were rationed to two ounces of meat a day, as many of our brothers are (to mention only the more fortunate ones) [true today, only more so] I should prefer to save it for a week perhaps, and make a nice stew of it, or fix it in some way so that for one meal at least I would feel myself safe and fat again in the time of plenty.

Other people would not agree with me. But for all of us, no matter what our tastes, life would be simpler and the wolf would howl less loudly if we could adjust our minds to admit, even if we never quite believed it, that a tender sizzling rare grilled tenderloin was a luxury instead of a necessity.

How to Make a Pigeon Cry

Here's a pigeon so finely roasted, it cries, Come, eat me!
—Polite Conversation, JONATHAN SWIFT

FOR centuries men have eaten the flesh of other creatures not only to nourish their own bodies but to give more strength to their weary spirits. A bull's heart, for example, might well bring bravery; oysters, it has been whispered, shed a new potency not only in the brain but in certain other less intellectual regions. And pigeons, those gentle flitting creatures, with the soft voices and their miraculous wings in flight, have always meant peace, and refreshment to sad humans.

Perhaps it is an old wives' tale; perhaps it is a part of our appetites more easily explained by *The Golden Bough* than by a cook or doctor: whatever the reason, a roasted pigeon is and long has been the most heartening dish to set before a man bowed down with grief or loneliness. In the same way it can reassure a timid lover, or comfort a woman weak from childbirth.

It is not easy to find pigeons, these days. Most of the ones you know about in the city are working for the government. In the country there are few farmers, any more, that have kept their dovecotes clean and populous . . . and fewer hired men who will kill the pretty birds properly by smothering them. By far the easiest way to make a pigeon cry "Come, eat me!" is to buy it, all cleaned and trussed, from a merchant.

It is usually expensive, in a mild way. [How can extravagance be mild? And what is mild about a minimal $1.25 per bird? But I still say it is worth it, now and then.] But if you like the idea at all, it is worth saving your meat-money for a few days, and making a party of it; eating a roasted pigeon is one of the few things that can be done all by yourself and in sordid surroundings with complete impunity and a positive reaction of well-being. [And for two, four, or six people who know each other well enough to eat with their fingers, there is no pleasanter supper than hot or cold roasted pigeons, with kasha or wild rice and undressed watercress and good bread . . . and, of course, plenty of good red wine.]

[It seems impossible that there is, apparently, no recipe for Kasha in this book so trustingly dedicated to my fellow philosophers in Operation Wolf. Kasha is a fine thing. In spite of unhappy political as well as gastronomical overtones just now, I must say that Russians are strong people because of it (. . . and cabbage and black bread and sour cream and floods of hothot*hot* tea). It can be bought most easily, at least in Western America, from "health food stores." Package directions should be followed carefully, for unfortunately some of the stuff is pre-cooked now, and turns into a horrid mush if you go on with the old routine of slow steaming. Properly prepared, kasha makes a wonderful aromatic nutty accompaniment to meat or fowl, and alone it is delicious, with an extra pat of butter, and combined with mushrooms it is heavenly, and and and. . . .

KASHA

2 cups kasha (whole or cracked groats)
1 or 2 fresh eggs
4 or more cups hot water or stock

butter or fat, about ⅗ tablespoon
salt, pepper

Put kasha into heavy skillet and mix egg into it until each grain is coated. Stir often over very low fire, until the grains are glazed and nut-like. Add liquid slowly, put fat in center, and cover closely, to cook until fluffy and tender (about ¾ hour). Season and add more butter if wished. Serve.]

I have eaten a great many pigeons here and there, and I know that the best was one I cooked in a cheap Dutch oven on a one-burner gas-plate in a miserable lodging. The wolf was at the door, and no mistake; until I filled the room with the smell of hot butter and red wine, his pungent breath seeped through the keyhole in an almost visible cloud.

Supper took about half an hour to prepare (I could have done it more quickly, but there was no reason for it), and long before I was ready to put the little brown fuming bird on my one Quimper plate, and pour out my second glass of wine, I heard a sad sigh and then the diminishing click of his claws as he retreated down the hall and out into the foggy night. I had routed him, because of the impertinent recklessness of roasting a little pigeon and savoring it intelligently and voluptuously too.

This is the way I cooked that innocent brown bird, and the way, with small variations, I have often treated other ones since then:

ROAST PIGEON

1 pigeon
1 lemon
2 slices fat bacon (or 2 table-
    spoons butter or oil)
parsley

red wine (or cider, beer,
    orange juice, tomato juice,
    stock . . .), about a cupful
water
salt, pepper

Melt the fat. [If bacon is used, cook it until crisp, and then remove it until time to serve it alongside, over, or even under the little bird.] See that the bird is well plucked, and rub her thoroughly with a cut lemon and the seasoning. Push the parsley into the belly. Braise well in the hot fat.

Add the liquid, put on the lid quickly, and cook slowly for about 20 minutes, basting two or three times. If you are going to eat the bird cold, put into a covered dish so that it will not dry out. [And if hot, make a pretty slice of toast for each bird, butter it well (or spread it with a bit of good pâté de foies for Party!), and place the bird upon it. Swirl about one cup of dry good wine and 2 tablespoon-fuls butter in the pan, for 4 birds, and spoon this over each one immediately, and serve.]

The accompaniments to this little bird (I ate it hot) were what was left of the red wine, which was a Moulin à Vent at twenty-six cents a quart, a rather dry piece of bread which was perfect for sopping all the juice from the plate, and three long satiny heads of Belgian endive. Celery hearts would have been just as good, I think, or *almost* as good.

Another heartening thing to eat, made from a wild creature, has always been associated with good-fellowship and even a bit of jolly poaching, if not with the reconciliation of man and his fate. Rabbit, or hare, or *lièvre*; it makes a strong and yet delicate dish no matter how it is prepared, if you remember one or two subtle tricks to play upon it first.

Always soak the hare for an hour or so in salty water, which has lemon juice or about a quarter-cup of vinegar in it. Then dry it well before cooking. A small piece of fat pork, either salted or fresh, will make the flavor of the meat much richer if they are cooked together. A tender hare [or domestic rabbit, for that matter] can well be prepared for frying like a chicken, but it is a dry meat and is usually better with a sauce around it. Almost all such recipes begin with soaking and then braising the meat, and letting it simmer slowly in a juice which can be as your wishes dictate. The following has always pleased me:

RABBIT IN CASSEROLE

1 *large or 2 smaller rabbits*	*salt, pepper, speck of clove,*
hot water	*etc.*
salt	1 *cup stock or water*
lemon juice (or vinegar)	1 *cup red wine*
3 *slices fat bacon*	1 *handful chopped fresh herbs*
4 *tablespoons butter*	*(parsley, sage, etc.)*
4 *tablespoons olive or other oil*	1 *cup tomato juice*
½ *cup flour*	

Cut up rabbit and soak for an hour or more in the hot salty water and lemon juice. Cut the bacon into small pieces and fry in the butter and oil.

Dry the meat, and shake well in a paper bag with the flour and condiments. Fry in the hot fat, turning often until each piece is very brown.

Add the stock, wine and herbs, and cover closely. Cook slowly about one hour or until tender.

Remove the meat to a hot casserole. Add the tomato juice to the skillet and stir thoroughly until the sauce is thick and bubbling. Pour over the rabbit and serve.

This recipe can of course be varied according to what supplies you have and how much time and money you want to spend on its preparation. Another good one which takes longer and is worth it, is a kind of composite of *civet de lièvre*, hasenpfeffer, and

JUGGED HARE

1 large or 2 small rabbits
water
vinegar or wine
1 onion, sliced

salt, pepper, cloves, bay leaves
butter
oil
1 cup sour cream

Cut up the rabbit and lay in a jar. Cover with equal parts of water and either vinegar or wine; add the onion and spices. Allow this to soak two days, turning the meat at least once.

Remove the meat, and brown thoroughly in a mixture of oil and butter, turning it often. When it is well browned, cover gradually with the pickling sauce, as much as you want. Let it simmer for about half an hour, or until tender. Before serving stir the sour cream into it.

This dish, like any other honorable stew, is best served with noodles or rice or French bread to help with its dark-brown delectable juices, and a salad of green leaves from the garden. [Classic accompaniments are Brussels sprouts, puréed chestnuts, watercress, fried bread spread with tart jelly, variations of *sauce espagnole,* sliced lemons, fried hominy, fresh dill somewhere or other, dumplings, stewed prunes or pears, grilled mushrooms . . . !] If red wine is a part of it, the same honest, rather crude wine is meant to drink along with it (since, *bien entendu,* you would not use a wine anywhere in cooking that was disagreeable to drink by itself). If the sauce has been helped by plain stock, a rather heavy ale is good, since it relates itself well to the rich aromatic flavors of the dish.

It may seem that such birds as partridges are far from the cupboards of good wolf-cookers, but now and then a friend sends you one, or there is a little stock of them at the market begging to be bought.

The following recipe, given to me by a Nivernais farm woman who to her own constant surprise was a famous lecturer on Greek at a French university, can be used for any poultry or small game which may seem dry or a little tough, although it is meant for partridge or pheasant. I have cooked an ancient chicken and an equally experienced rabbit according to its formula.

PARTRIDGE OR PHEASANT WITH SAUERKRAUT

salt and pepper
2 small or 1 large bird (or 1 rabbit)
bacon slices
3 tablespoons butter or good oil

1 ½ pounds sauerkraut
1 cup peeled and sliced apples
1 cup dry white wine (or half and half with water or vegetable stock)
1 tablespoon flour

Rub birds with cut lemon, and salt and pepper them. Wrap with the bacon and tie securely with twine. Heat the fat and brown the birds.

Wash the drained sauerkraut (unless it is very mild, when just drain it). Place a layer of it with the apple slices in the bottom of a casserole and imbed the birds. Cover with the rest of the kraut and apple, add the liquid, and cover closely. Let simmer very slowly for about 2 hours.

Put the birds on a hot plate, and thicken the kraut with the flour. Make nests in it, and replace the birds in them, ready to serve.

[An even better dish, I feel since I have become the willing victim of an annual donation of frozen pheasant, is the recipe I give herewith. I am sorry to say that I have never handled freshly killed game in this country, but I have coped, for want of a better procedure, with an infinitude of withered, almost sexless, apparently ageless birds in their repulsive peaky feathers and their gaseous envelopes filled with invisible but still potent "dry ice." I have done horrendous things with them, and then admitted my own courage and downed my own successes. (Once I roasted ducks and pheasants in the same big pan . . . it was a marvellous thing, which I have never before confessed to.) This present recipe is an excellent rule for enjoying a bird of questionable dates (birth, death, all that), and as far as I know it would be somewhat better with one of *proper* timing.

NORMANDY PHEASANT

Brown pheasant in butter. Quarter, peel, mince, and slightly toss in hot butter 6 medium-sized apples and 3 small minced onions. Place pheasant on mixture in terrine, sprinkle with about ½ cup fresh cream, cover, and cook in moderate oven about ½ hour.]

Most of the ways for cooking poultry and game with economy seem to end inevitably as one form or another of the primeval stew. There are several reasons, most of which are followed almost intuitively by people who want to eat the best possible food for the least amount of money and time.

Roasting, for instance, except in the case of very small birds like pigeons, takes two hours or so of almost constant attention with a basting spoon, whereas a stew, after the meat is first braised, can be left to its own devices for about the same length of time. (You should make sure that the fire is under control and the casserole reasonably filled with liquid before you leave it.)

A roasted bird or little beast, while one of the most delicious things to eat that man has invented, emerges from the oven with no accompaniment except its own few unconsumed essences, and more often than not it has shrunk some into the bargain. A stew, on the other hand, seems to make a much bigger meal, because other things are usually cooked with it and have absorbed some of its flavor, and at the same time it is making a generous amount of fine odorous sauce which can be eaten with the meat and also with rice or potatoes or the humble and almighty crust of bread.

As for frying poultry, who could deny the delights of young pullets put to this test, if they are properly treated? Indeed, to believe the menus everywhere in America, fried chicken is neck and neck with grilled steak as the dish most people will order when they "eat out."

On the other hand (the wolf's side of the question!), it is an expensive job to fry enough young chicken in good fat for a family, and accompany it with the rich gravy, the mashed potatoes, the buttered peas, the hot biscuits and honey, and finally the pie or ice cream, that since our country first stood on its own legs have meant Company or Sunday Dinner.

A frying chicken, if he escapes being broiled, should weigh about three pounds. If he keeps on growing and in turns escapes being roasted at about five pounds, he is ready (albeit unwilling) "to grace the fricassée pot with aplomb and elegance," Mrs. Mazza says, "still young, still tender, but mature and at his zenith of plumpness." And when you consider the various exciting sauces which can smother his neat sections, once he is browned in honest fat, you wonder at ever believing that the only good way to prepare him was fried in a skillet.

One thing to remember about cooking any fowl, whether wild or domesticated, is that a good scrub with a cut lemon, never water, will make it tenderer and will seal in its flavors. Another thing is that a mixture of butter and oil or fat is the best one for braising it: it seems to make an evener and more delicious brown.

If you have bought or been given a chicken (it is very nice indeed, these days, to have generous friends who live in the country and send you unexpected lagniappes!), cut it up, scrub it with lemon, and season it. Try a little cinnamon and allspice with the omnipresent salt and pepper. After it is brown, put in a generous handful of chopped herbs (parsley, rosemary, basil, thyme, whatever you and your whims can pluck or purchase), and a minced clove of garlic. Add a cup or so of tomato, either fresh or canned, and some dry white wine. Stir the whole thing, cover, and let simmer until tender.

In Italy such a savory dish used to be called *pollo in umido*. [One Yankee standby I have never been able to savor with more than a clinical interest is stewed hen with dumplings and gravy. I have probably eaten it at its best, and I am sure I have eaten it at its worst, and I still find it a pale thing.] It varied a little in every district or village—in every kitchen, really—but always it was served with the sauce in a separate dish, to be eaten with the spaghetti or the polenta.

You can see, probably, how good it would be. It is one of those "naturals" which take their own dignified place in any meal, whether it is served in midsummer on a breathless balcony, or in the windy months beside a fire. Whatever its milieu, it is eminently satisfying, and at the same time a great deal easier on your pocketbook than the same amount of chicken Maryland, even though you add wine and mushrooms and perhaps a crazy dash of pickled capers or nasturtium seeds.

You can eat it tomorrow, too . . . and fool the wolf . . . and if it is necessary, comfort yourself by reading this strange quotation from Wesker's *Secrets of Nature*, which was published in 1660:

Take the goose, pull off the feathers, make a fire about her, not too close for smoke to choke her, or burn her too soon, not too far off so she may escape. Put small cups of water with salt and honey . . .

also dishes of apple sauce. Baste goose with butter. She will drink water to relieve thirst, eat apples to cleanse and empty her of dung. Keep her head and heart wet with a sponge. When she gets giddy from running and begins to stumble, she is roasted enough. Take her up, set her before the guests: she will cry as you cut off any part and will be almost eaten before she is dead. . . . It is mighty pleasant to behold.

How to Pray for Peace

Pray for peace and grace and spiritual food,
For wisdom and guidance, for all these are good,
But don't forget the potatoes.

—*Prayer and Potatoes,* J. T. PETTEE

IT IS easy to think of potatoes, and fortunately for men who have not much money it is easy to think of them with a certain safety. Potatoes are one of the last things to disappear, in times of war, which is probably why they should not be forgotten in times of peace.

They can be bought, until things change even more radically than the pessimists predict, in sacks at almost any market. There are various names for them, and nice ones too: Idaho Russet, White Rose, Late Beauty of Hebron. They are a vegetable, white inside and shirted in a fine silky brown coat which is like a thin layer of cork, but much more delicious when washed and cooked with the rest.

Potatoes, like most other vegetables and animals, soon die when their skins are removed, so that it is better to boil or bake them entire, and then remove the delicate coat if you prefer to eat them peeled.

If your tastebuds are truly civilized, however, one of the best meals in the world is a pot of medium-sized unpeeled potatoes, boiled briskly in hot water until they are done, and then drained and "shook" over the flame for a minute until the brown coverings split. Either throw in a handful of chopped fresh herbs like parsley and marjoram and chives (or green onions), and some butter, and shake it all around [A celestial variation is to add to fresh green peas,

286

cooked rapidly in a little chicken broth or water and then drained and tossed generously in sweet butter, half their amount of small new potatoes, cooked and of course unpeeled, and half *their* amount of little braised white onions.] or pour the vegetables straightway into a hot bowl and eat them the way the Swiss do, with a good nubbin of cheese and a good gout of sweet butter and coarse salt and pepper for each biteful. This, with a glass of milk or some white wine and fruit, is a fit supper for Lucullus.

If your oven is going at about 300 to 350°, wash a few even-sized potatoes, dry them, and rub them with a little oil or butter. You can split them if you are in a hurry, buttering their cut sides, of course. As soon as they are tender [. . . or better yet, I now know, when you first put them in the oven] pierce them with a fork to keep them from growing soggy, and then eat them, if you are hungry, with plenty of butter and salt and fresh-ground pepper, not forgetting the delicate nut-like brown skin.

Or hollow them gently, stir the white part briskly with an egg and some seasoning, and put it back in the shells, with a little cheese or a couple of baby sausages on top to brown under the broiler. (These last potatoes can be made several hours before they are to be broiled, and are especially good in winter.)

[It is too bad that so many people have either not yet acquired a healthy acquaintanceship with good potato soup, or have had it shocked out of them by early exposure to a pasty and unreasonable facsimile. Most people I know fall into one of these categories, until I give them, for a winter lunch or a Sunday-night supper or some such loose-jointed feast, a steaming tureen of soup based, just as loose-jointedly, on the following rule:

QUICK POTATO SOUP

(Referred to sardonically by my father as Poor Man's Potage . . .)

¼ *pound good butter*	2 *quarts whole milk*
4 *large potatoes*	*salt, pepper, minced parsley*
4 *large onions*	*if agreeable*

Melt the butter in large kettle, or in fireproof casserole in which the soup can be served. Grate the clean potatoes into it. (I like to leave them unpeeled, but the soup is not so pretty unless chopped fresh herbs, added at the last, change its natural whiteness enough to

*hide the bits of brown skin . . .) Grate the peeled onions into it . . .
or slice them very thin. Heat the mixture to bubble-point, stirring
well. Then reduce the heat, and cover closely for about ten minutes
or until the vegetables are tender but not mushy, shaking the pot
now and then to prevent sticking. Add more butter (or chicken-fat)
if it seems wise. Heat the milk to boiling point but not beyond, add
slowly to the pot, season, and serve. Variations of this recipe are
obvious. One of my father's favorites is the last-minute addition of
a cup or so of cooked minced clams. A half-pound of grated fresh
mushrooms, added to the vegetables just before pouring in the hot
milk, is fine. And so on and so on.]*

These are such simple procedures, and other ways of cooking
starchy foods are so simple too, that it is almost shocking how badly
they are usually done. Rice, for instance, which is one of the most
primitive foods in the world, if you consider the number of unedu-
cated people who eat it: more often than not it is stodgy, sticky, and
unappetizing, or else rinsed until it is as tasteless as library paste,
and probably less nourishing.

There are two ways to boil rice correctly. [How arbitrary can you
be? I should have said: "*I think* there are. . . .!" I still think so, but
am open to persuasion now, being older and hopefully wiser.] One
way is to pour one well-rinsed cup of it slowly into a lot of rapidly
boiling salted water (at least three quarts), and let it race around
until a grain of it smashes between the fingers.

If it boils quickly it will never stick. A small dab of butter [or even
better, a dollop of good oil . . .] will keep the pot from boiling
over, and not harm the flavor. When the rice is almost done, it
should be drained into a colander (the water should be saved if your
family eats a lot of soups), and then rinsed thoroughly with cold
water. Then it should be heated again by a quick immersion in
boiling water before serving, or it can be steamed to the proper
temperature. [I still prefer the steaming, but if I could I would re-
write this whole procedure. I suggest that anyone who acknowledges
the value of good cookery in a life deliberately full of love, happiness,
and health (that is, anyone who *cares* about human dignity!) read
several other books and from them and this one and most of all from
himself produce his own decision.]

The other accepted method is sometimes called Chinese and
sometimes Indian, but it is a good one if you can do it. I think

the secret is to have a thick pot, with a good lid, and a stove that will turn almost completely off without blowing out.

CHINESE RICE

1 *cup rice*   1½ *cups water*

Wash rice thoroughly in several changes of water, until there is no cloudiness. Put the rice in a pot, add the water, and bring to a boil. Boil five minutes with the lid off. Turn the flame lower and let the water boil away. Then turn the flame to its lowest point, put on the lid, and heat 20 minutes without stirring. A crust should form at the bottom, but it should not burn.

The last sentence in this recipe is a warning, but do not let it disturb you if you like rice and want to eat it when it is at its best; I have never yet cooked it this way without having it stick to the pot, but by dint of great care I have never burned it. And each time I've done it it has seemed simpler. [If the crust has not changed color, I put some stock or milk on it and make anything from a soup to a pudding from the fine soft grains that gradually detach themselves into the liquid . . . certainly a most pleasant way to clean the pot!]

Rice, whether cooked this way or that, is an ideal accompaniment to almost any dish that has a savorous sauce with it. It is a godsend for making left-overs into gastronomical adventures, and can stand to be left in the icebox and then reheated more than once. As a dessert it can be used with eggs and milk and raisins, as what child of the *fin de siècle* does not know? Or it is good, if your tastes are simple, cold with a little brown sugar and milk, for supper or an ice-box snack . . . a quick return to the nursery, which can be soothing indeed.

Brown rice is better for you than polished rice; it has more of the rich nutritive coat left on it. It takes a little longer to cook than other kinds. White rice, especially if you can still find the short chubby Chinese variety, has a lightness about it and is dry and fluffy when it is correctly prepared. [A new "instant-cook" rice is everywhere. I use rice so simply that it must be very good, but cooks who make myriad rings-molds-doodads tell me this is perfection. I continue to remember the water I once poured off a pound of it, after a few minutes of washing: it was turgid with added chemicals.]

Another way to cook rice, which seems more intelligent than boiling it when you think of the dread pasty monotony of most rice as it is served in our country, is to cook it in oil and then with other things, instead of in plain water. It can be called a *risotto*, or a *sopa de arroz*, or a *pilaf*, but what it is is rice browned gently in oil or butter, with any herbs you like, and then cooked without stirring in a heavy pan with wine or stock until it is tender. Meat can be added, or mushrooms, and saffron in the old days in Milano, or pepper sausage, and almonds and raisins in Singapore, before the causeway was blown up.

It is important, [not *too* important, I have decided with the inevitable and perhaps cynical laissez-faire of Time] with any of these *risotti*, to rub the rice clean in a towel first, and then not to stir things after the liquid has been added. Always have more juice than you think you will need, and add it a cup at a time as it disappears, so that at the end the mixture is dry and fluffy, without visible sauce.

Almost any quick mixtures which are made with a modicum of gastronomic intelligence and a generous hand with the sauce are good served with rice, which can be left-over and reheated, or even taken from a can. [Cooked rice from a can? Was I dreaming? Should I ask my grocer? Where have I *been*?! Mea culpa.] Noodles and spaghetti have the same blessed resistance to ill treatment, and after several days unheeded in the icebox, can be steamed and shaped into more-than-acceptable companions to good meals.

One very simple casserole, which is delicious with baked ham, is made of lightly boiled noodles tossed with plenty of salt and pepper and one can of mushroom pieces which have been well browned in butter or good oil. You can put a few crumbs on the top if you like them [. . . or a crumbled handful of angel-hairs, finer than vermicelli, toasted nut-brown in a dry pan].

Any of these starches . . . *pastasciutti*, rices, potatoes . . . can be good alone, heated [Here I plainly mean "warmed over," the second or even third time. The tricks are to cook more than is needed for one meal, and to cook *lightly* and not to a starchy mush. Such left-overs are excellent fried, the way the Chinese treat rice.] and then stirred in a double boiler with butter, paprika, a little garlic if you like it, and a generous sprinkling of whatever chopped fresh herbs you have at hand. The garlic should be taken out of the butter before the rest is added.

Spaghetti, one of the most misunderstood simple foods in the world, can be one of the best when it is properly treated. It should in the first place be good, and fresh, and made with honest semolina flour so that it is hard and horny when uncooked, and firm, clean, smooth when it comes from the pot.

It should be cooked in a large quantity of salty boiling water, and stirred often. After about twenty minutes it should be tested several times by pressing a piece between your thumb and finger, so that it will not be too done and soft and soggy. When it is *almost* tender, run a little cold water into the pot to stop the cooking, and then drain it thoroughly so as not to spoil whatever sauce is coupled with it.

The next most important thing is to serve it while it is hot and at its peak of texture. If you like it as I do, in its simplest form, have a hot casserole with a generous amount of fresh melted butter in it. Pour in the spaghetti, which is of course in its original long strands, swirl it around a few times, and rush it to the table. There, on hot plates, let your guests eat it loaded as they will with more butter, salt and fresh pepper, and grated dry cheese of the Parmesan type. Salad or fruit and a plenitude of thin red wine makes this a perfect meal.

If you like a sauce with your spaghetti or any of the fifty children such as vermicelli, orzi, pennini, you can concoct just about such a brew as your fancy calls for—remembering always that mushrooms and tomato sauce and what herbs you can find should be a kindly part of it.

It is good to remember never to use flour in such a sauce, nor a canned tomato soup, but always let the canned or fresh tomato thicken by itself. Another important thing is to have the sauce ready before you cook the paste, and in the same way to have your guests ready to eat it before you serve the dish, since once cooked and mingled it cannot wait. The sauce, of course, can be prepared many hours before you want it, but if by any chance you must serve the paste long after it is cooked, drain it and wash it thoroughly before it is quite done, and then heat it quickly in boiling water before serving it.

Always have a well-heated and generous platter ready for the paste and the sauce, which should either be mixed lightly together just before serving or shaped into a filled mound which can be tossed and spooned together as it is given to each person. Grated cheese should be served separately.

One of the best sauces for spaghetti is, or was, a favorite one in Naples, and it is so simple and satisfying that even confirmed meat-eaters forget their conditioned hungers when they have it. (It is agreeably economical, too.)

NAPOLITANA SAUCE FOR SPAGHETTI

5 tablespoons olive oil (or decent substitute, if any)	½ green pepper
2 cloves garlic	2 cups tomato sauce (2 small cans)
1 sweet onion	salt, pepper
1 carrot	3 tablespoons herbs

Mince the garlic, onion, carrot, and pepper into the oil. Cook, stirring gently, for 10 minutes. Add the tomato sauce and the seasoning and herbs, such as chopped marjoram and thyme and parsley. Cook slowly for about 20 minutes, stirring often. Serve with hot paste and grated cheese.

Probably the nearest thing to polenta our country can lay claim to is Southern spoon bread, which is a dainty and more expensive and at the same time more limited dish than its Italian ancestor. It is very good indeed, as any authentic Carolina cook, past, present, or future, will be glad to prove to you. It can be served, delicate and steaming, with chicken or whatever casserole you may have. It can even act as backbone for a dishful of left-over gravy or sauce, to which you have probably added a few canned mushrooms and some fresh herbs and sherry. [I often use olives in such brews, the black pitted medium or small size, halved or quartered. It is best to toss them and the mushrooms thoroughly in a little oil or butter, then add the herbs, then the left-over sauce, and finally the sherry. Everybody stays unquestioning and pleased, especially olive-loathers, of whom there are many.]

SOUTHERN SPOON BREAD

2 cups cornmeal
1 ½ cups sweet milk
2 cups boiling water
1 teaspoon salt

3 large tablespoons butter,
melted
3 eggs

Sift the meal three times and mix until it is smooth into the boiling water. Add the melted butter and salt, and thin with the milk.

Separate the eggs, and beat until light, folding first the yolks and then the whites into the batter. Pour into a buttered baking dish, bake about 30 minutes in a moderate oven (350°), and serve in its dish.

Polenta, in contrast to this somewhat ephemeral and ladylike dish, is a sturdy, forthright, almost truculent mixture, the kind that has survived centuries of loving obedience from hungry simple peoples. It is really cornmeal mush, nothing more. But it is dressed for the fair, in its most exciting clothes, and it can be the mainstay of a poor family's nourishment or the central dish of a buffet supper for twenty jaded literary critics with equal nonchalance. [One of the most painful things about X's annotating X is a sentence like this. ". . . with equal nonchalance" should follow the phrase "and it can." It is apparently more obvious to X now than it was in 1942. X blushes.]

It should be prepared just before it is to be served, and the plates should be hot, for like all starches it chills quickly and loses some of its good nut-like taste as it does so. It can be cooked for about one hour in a thick iron pot, and stirred often with a wooden paddle. It will form a crust inside the pot, which should not be disturbed nor permitted to burn. Or it can cook about three hours in a double boiler without stirring. The first method is plainly quicker, but needs more attention. If the polenta becomes too thick, add more water.

The sauce for it, which can be practically anything you like as long as it is dark and aromatic with herbs and filled with succulent morsels of mushrooms and olives and whatever else you want, can have beef in it or chicken or even shellfish, according to your pocketbook. Or it can stand on its own feet, as I have often proved, without any assistance from flesh, fowl, or fish. Make it the day before you use it, if you want to.

The main thing to remember, probably, is that polenta is not ordinary cornmeal, but a much coarser "grind" which can be bought in any Italian grocery store, or in most large markets.

POLENTA

3 cups cold water
3 cups boiling water
2 cups polenta meal
2 teaspoons salt

(1 cup diced Monterey or mild goat cheese; optional but good)
grated Parmesan-type cheese

Stir the meal gradually with the cold water to form a smooth mixture. Slowly add it to the boiling salted water, stirring constantly to prevent lumps. If in a double boiler, cook without further stirring for three hours. If in a heavy iron pot, stir gently now and then for an hour with a wooden paddle, taking care not to disturb the crust that will form against the pot.

The polenta should be about the consistency of spoon bread when done. If too thick, add more hot water.

Stir in the cubed cheese at the last if desired. Then shape into a mound and cover with grated cheese, to be served separately with whatever sauce is desired. Or make into a ring around the sauce on one plate.

A BEEF SAUCE FOR POLENTA

¼ cup olive or other good oil
1 large onion, chopped
1 clove garlic, minced
1 cup chopped celery
1 carrot, sliced thin
1 large can solid-pack tomatoes
1 bay-leaf

1 whole clove
2 peppercorns
salt and herbs to taste
½ cup dried mushrooms
1 cup hot water
2½ pounds beef cut into 1-inch cubes

[I think this is too much beef, and in too large pieces. I would settle for half the quantity, cut or chopped into much smaller morsels. And I have decided that a twig of fresh or dried rosemary is a happy herb to add and then fish out at the last. And I like green pepper, in slivers or squares.]

Sauté the onion, garlic, carrot, and celery in the oil until they are relaxed and beginning to be brown. Add the tomatoes, spices, and herbs (thyme, marjoram, basil).

Soak the mushrooms in hot water until tender. Cut into small pieces, strain the water, and add it all to the sauce. Cover, and let simmer for 3 to 4 hours.

Brown the beef in a little fat or oil. Add a little boiling water or stock and let simmer until tender. Add to the sauce about 1 hour before serving, so that the two may marry their flavors.

Serve in a large bowl, to be poured [ladled is a better word here] over the sliced polenta on each plate.

A sauce made with chicken is less strongly seasoned. One with hare is better if a good dry wine is used instead of water, as indeed any can be, according to your tastes and prejudices. [If made with cooked shrimps, they should be added about ten minutes before time to serve the whole. Little clams, oysters, or shrimps, either raw and shucked or raw and frozen (and, of course, shucked!), should be simmered in butter until they curl and then added just before serving. And so on . . . a combination of common sense and courage is indicated!]

Polenta is one of those ageless culinary lords, like bread. It has sprung from the hunger of mankind, and without apparent effort has always carried with it a feeling of strength and dignity and well-being.

It costs little to prepare, if there is little to spend, or it can be extravagantly, opulently odorous with wines and such. It can be made doggedly, with one ear cocked for the old wolf's sniffing under the door, or it can be turned out as a well-nourished gesture to other simpler days. But no matter what conceits it may be decked with, its fundamental simplicity survives, to comfort our souls as well as our bellies, the way a good solid fugue does, or a warm morning in spring.

How to Be Content with a Vegetable Love

If he's content with a vegetable love which would certainly not suit me,

Why, what a most particularly pure young man this pure, young man must be!

—*Patience*, W. S. GILBERT

PURITY may have something to do with a vegetable love, but is almost certain to have nothing to do with a love of vegetables, since *petits pois à la Française* have been known to appeal to the lowest as well as the loftiest emotions of at least one hardened sinner.

[There is, of course, an excellent recipe for this naive and delicate dish in Escoffier and many another cookbook. And like many another cook I seldom pay any attention to it. Instead I fit the ways to the means: I use uniformly mediocre frozen peas in preference to unpredictably uneven market peas, if I cannot pick my own from a now vanished garden. If I have good garden shallots or onions I use them. If I have my own lettuces I am happiest, but I have often settled, with silent resignation, for a small tight head of taste-less "Alaska" (which is insultingly called Los Angeles Lettuce in salad-happy San Francisco!). I use salted butter, for want of the sweet. And so on and so on. My *petits pois* more-or-less *à la Fran-çaise* always please me . . . as long as I manage not to have the telephone ring at the moment they should be done, and let them turn pale or puckered.

296

PETITS POIS A LA FRANÇAISE

½ cup water
1 head lettuce
6 green onions
  handful of parsley

2 pounds peas
¼ pound good butter
  salt, fresh pepper

Put water in heavy casserole or pot; shred lettuce coarsely into it;
add onions split and cut in 2-inch pieces, using tops; chop parsley
and add. Put peas on this bed, and put chunk of butter on top. Cover
tightly and bring slowly to boil, shaking now and then. Lower heat,
let cook for about five minutes, and serve at once, mixing all well
together and seasoning to taste. There should be almost no liquid.
More butter can be added at the last if it seems desirable.]

What can be said about vegetables as a form of gastronomical
entertainment is best said simply, since once past the basic behavior,
all such recipes depend on you and what you need.

Almost all vegetables are good, although there is some doubt still
about parsnips (which I share). [I am no longer doubtful. I *know*.
And rutabaga has joined the exclusive group.]

All of them whether tender or hard, thick-skinned or thin, die
when they are peeled . . . even as you and I. Therefore it is better
to cook them always in their skins, at least until they are partly
done, and then prepare them as you had planned.

With the exception of cabbage, and very strong tough and
probably inedible turnips, vegetables should be cooked in as little
water as possible. [I now know that I can cook quartered cabbage in a
cup of water, and shredded cabbage in no water at all but instead
a pat of butter or a little good fat or oil. As for the turnips I describe
so bluntly . . . why bother?] Steam cookers are good, or the new
pressure cookers which are so economical if you can afford to buy
them at all.

When what is left of the steam and water is not to be used as
a sauce, with a little butter stirred into it, it should be poured
into a bottle and kept in the icebox. Any such juices you have can
be mixed together, and then shaken before they are used.

And used they will be: in clear soups, as stock in sauces, as a
quick pickup when you are tired, (ice-cold with a little lemon
juice or an equal part of tomato juice). The natural salts from

all the different vegetables will make a pungent palatable stock, usually, without any salt or pepper.

The same is true of any juices from canned vegetables: they should *never* be thrown away, but drained with due respect for their value into the stock-bottle, along with the rest of the essences.

Canned vegetables are usually good, and often have more of the all-necessary vitamins and minerals in them than do the same vegetables cooked at home. This is mostly true because they are cooked within the can, and therefore lose none of their attributes. Also, the wily packers, anxious to build up the weight of each tin, use as much water as they dare, which by the time it gets to you is beautifully rich and full of flavor.

Frozen vegetables are very good. The directions on the package should be followed carefully, except that usually even less time is needed than they say, to cook the peas or beans or corn to perfection.

For that matter *no* vegetable should be cooked as long as you think. Of course this depends a little on altitude and fuel and pot, but in general it is true that vegetables are almost always overcooked.

Some people use salt in the water, but for myself I prefer to add whatever seasoning I want just at the last. The vegetables seem tenderer, and the flavor of sweet butter and freshly ground pepper is more characterful.

This is not the case, naturally, with fresh herbs: they should be put in right at the beginning, tied in a bundle if you want to remove them before serving. [My taste has changed. Some herbs, but not all, should be cooked at length. Rosemary, for instance, can stew for a long time in a chicken pot or a saucepan. So can thyme or bay. But marjoram, parsley, anise . . . I put them in at the last. It is apparently a question of current favor as well as flavor!] The possibilities of their flavors, blended or alone, are limitless: the basils, the marjorams, thyme, the sages, mint, anise . . . what delights they conjure, if you want them to!

It is possible, and also practical, to buy vegetables once or twice a week at a big market, and prepare them all at once. [This is indeed a practical idea, but I do not approve of it in theory. The gastronomical values of most vegetables do dwindle with time.] It is a rather long but restful job, to wash and cut and chop and then cook what you will want for the next few days, and there is something more than satisfying in the beautiful crisp piles on your drain-board.

You should undercook everything, and then when it is cool put it in the icebox, in covered dishes, if it has a strong flavor like cauliflower. You will feel good, looking into the box and seeing several meals practically ready to eat. You can think of simple things for one dish, like hot buttered crumbs poured over the cauliflower, or a can of bean-sprouts mixed with some chopped pepper and the green beans.

Or you can plan a grand hash at the end of the week, of every vegetable that is left, tossed in a skillet with some chopped bacon and tomatoes. Or a *frittata*, made with eggs. Or a delicately heartening salad, made in a bowl the way you used to see it in Venice, the cooked and the raw entwined in an exciting marriage. [One of the most happily ubiquitous of cooked vegetables is the new potato, preferably pink-skinned and tiny. In salads it is wonderful. Hot, combined with peas or green beans or broiled mushrooms or or or, it is heavenly. Alone, in a mist of sweet butter, it is divine. And there is no right word in my lexicon for new potatoes very cold, in their skins of course, with a bowl of thick sour cream alongside to dunk them in.]

There are many ways to love a vegetable. The most sensible way is to love it well-treated. Then you can eat it with the comfortable knowledge that you will be a better man for it, in your spirit and your body too, and will never have to worry about your own love being vegetable.

How to Make a Great Show

By economy and good management, by a sparing use of ready money, and by paying scarcely anybody, people can manage, for a time at least, to make a great show with very little means.
—*Vanity Fair,* THACKERAY

IN spite of the present flurry of interest in gastronomical and household economy, brought on by the first realization of war here at home, not even the most excited magazine advises quite such a philosophy as was practiced by Thackeray's Becky. Her attitude was cynical, and probably too empty of that slight touch of sentiment which almost every woman enjoys in her relations with the world. For without sentiment, how else could you explain some of the incredible suggestions for economy offered in the backs of cookbooks for the last hundred years, even unto 1925?

I am sure that a strong but secret desire to impress your mother-in-law, or perhaps your husband or growing daughter, with your brave martyrdom and gallantry, is all that would make you follow most of the "helpful hints," or what are called in one astonishing English book, "Wrinkles for the Cook."

Does the fuel problem seem grim and thin? Here are some suggestions which sound touched with a kind of sordid whimsy until you to try them. Then they really work, and make you feel noble and brave at the same time.

Get one package of fireclay from a fuel-man, and mix it into a stiff paste with water. Make it into balls about the size of oranges (or a little smaller if you are thinking of California navels). Dry them in the oven: you are having baked potatoes and a pot-roast anyway that night. Leave them overnight in the cooling oven if you can, and when they seem dry put them into the fire.

That is all. They get red-hot, and give off a lot of heat, and if you treat them gently with the poker and when you are cleaning the hearth, they will last "for ages," as the book rather naively puts it. Also, somewhat naively, they are called Hot Spots!

Or if you don't want to muck around in wet fireclay, put an empty tin can or two in the center of your burning fire . . . if you still have any tin cans. It will last three or four days, and will send off a surprising lot of heat that apparently was going up the chimney before.

And you can make one burner of a gas stove heat about four pots if you put a twelve-inch square of sheet-iron over it and *if* you have an old-fashioned stove. (This "hint" smacks definitely of 1897, when it was published.) A modern stove with its burners prettily embedded in large spaces of white enamel would be ruined beyond hope, probably, after any such attempt at economy.

A thousand other suggestions for saving money are as plainly dated, in most of the books. How many women now care about knowing how to clean horsehair cushions, or what to do with moulting feather beds . . . or even how to "treat an Art-Work Brass Bed"? (Except as a conversational gambit at a cocktail party.)

In almost every list, which is usually at the back of the volume, just before the index, and is called everything from "Large Helps in Little Hints" to "Experientia Docet," there is at least one tip about how to cure hiccups. This seems strange, or perhaps it is merely a tactless admission that some of the recipes preceding it are none too digestible.

"In Case of Fire" is another old faithful, and it advises everything for putting out the blaze, from throwing one pound of sulphur up the chimney to making complicated liquids which must be stored in a cool dark cellar . . . to putting on plenty of water.

Beauty, as it should be, is another problem that is fairly well covered in the hints. To Whiten the Arms, A Lotion to Remove Freckles, A Remedy for Tender Feet or Fingertips . . . how they all bring back a faint but heady memory of the great belles, and heavy velvet swags, and pink candle-shades and cigars-with-the-port!

But when the belles grew less so, and their hair a little thin at the sides of the pompadours, did they really rub their scalps with onion juice several times a week? Did they (*could* they?) put gasoline liberally on their heads daily and coconut oil three times a week, if their gilded tresses finally began to fall in earnest?

Or did they retire to their boudoirs, read a hint entitled, starkly, Nervous Breakdown, and proceed to develop all its carefully detailed phenomena?

Some of the recipes for family necessities given in these collections are really useful, however, like the one called A Pleasant Tooth Wash, which was discovered several months ago by a woman with five children who gargled, swished, and spat their way through countless quarts of expensive antiseptic solutions with Gargantuan abandon.

It is a formula suggested by a book printed during the first World War, when alcohol in England was almost as dear and as difficult to find as it will soon be in America in the second, and it is an agreeable and cheap and generally adequate substitute for the various bottled washes we have been educated to consider an intrinsic part of our daily toilets.

MOUTH WASH

2 *ounces borax*	1 *teaspoon tincture of myrrh*
1 *quart hot water*	1 *teaspoon spirits of camphor*

Dissolve the borax in very hot water. When it has cooled, add the other ingredients and bottle. (A little pink coloring can be added if your children demand it.)

There are many tooth powders which can be made at the cost of a few cents, and which after the first shock are as good as the commercial ones, if not quite so suave and sweet. Once when I was hard-up (to make a definite understatement), I used a mixture of equal parts of baking soda and common salt, mixed in a mason jar with a few drops of peppermint to take off the curse, or most of it. [It was horrible. I still remember it with revulsion, and if I had to depend on it again would prefer to use a willow twig, or let my teeth crumble.]

And then there is a recipe in one of the older cookbooks which says to mix equal parts of castile soap, powdered orris root, and precipitated chalk. I am unable to see castile soap in anything but uneven and sharp-edged bilious cakes, in my mind's eye, and on mature consideration would have none of this prescription, since I think it could be almost as disagreeable as it sounds.

And soap: it probably will be harder to get in wartime than you yet realize. English women, the papers whisper, are putting special strainers in their kitchen drains to catch all the grease . . . an ugly picture but perhaps not much less so than one conjured by this recipe:

MONKEY SOAP

Mix together equal parts of soft soap, bath brick, and whiting. Make into convenient cakes. Dry slowly.

If you want to be clean and still keep at least part of the skin where it should be on your body, the following recipe is perhaps more merciful:

TO MAKE SOAP

5 *pounds melted grease (fats not fit for food)*	1 *teaspoon salt*
1 *one-pound can lye*	2 *tablespoons sugar*
1 *quart cold water*	½ *cup cold water*
3 *teaspoons borax*	¼ *cup ammonia*

Dissolve the lye in cold water and let cool. Then add the fat slowly, stirring constantly. Mix the other ingredients together and add to the first mixture. Stir the whole until thick and light in color. Pour into a pan lined with cloth, and mark into pieces before the soap becomes hard. When it is hard, break apart and pile so that it will dry thoroughly.

There are many variants of this basic rule, which is purely functional and looks ugly and smells worse. It is better than nothing, however—*much better*, if you agree that cleanliness runs a close second to godliness. [To a friend in England, a beautiful and quite ungodly woman but very clean, I send regularly a package containing about five kinds of plain good soap: powdered, flaked, unperfumed in cakes. She loves it more than orchids.]

There is one recipe, again from an English book, which has puzzled me for a long time and which need only be read by some master of the straight face to sound like the most involved suggestion. It talks about one thing, but even my dazed mind feels that it wishes to talk about another and at the same time spare the delicate feelings of true ladies born-and-bred.

TO CURE BRUISED WITHERS

Ladies who ride astride on horseback may be glad to know of the following remedy. . . . Lay on the sore or bruised part a damp sod of earth, about two inches thick, mold side next to the horse. It should be about two inches larger than the affected part. Fasten on under the night sheet and roller. Leave it on all night.

You can use tea leaves (to skip with discreet haste to another field) in an alarming number of ways after they have fulfilled their natural function of making tea. They are fine for keeping down the dust on Aubusson carpets, the books say . . . or any kind of carpets at all. They make it easier to clean out a fireplace without getting ash all over everything. They are also good to clean the insides of water bottles, the books say again, but it is hard to understand why the insides of water bottles should be dirty with anything but water anyway. [I evidently did not know much about water in 1942! I have since discovered that nothing can make worse stains, and that the best way to keep bottles sparkling is to use something like Ke-Nu in them. Probably feeding two babies had added to my knowledge!]

You can also steep them and tint lace with them, thank God.

And to sum up the whole atmosphere of economy as preached, if not always practiced, in the section of cookbooks of another generation than this one (again we can give praise!), here is a hint which can be found in at least five volumes, the first edited in 1840-something, and the last published by the Ladies of the Saint Matthias Guild of a Far West church in 19—yes, 19, not 18—25. It reads, in each version, almost exactly like this, and should be a lesson to us all:

TO STUFF PINCUSHIONS

Coffee grounds, well steeped and dried, make an excellent stuffing. They are economical and keep the needles and pins from wasteful rust, and will not pack down.

Pax Vobiscum.

How to Have a Sleek Pelt

I love little pussy!
Her coat is so warm!
And if I don't hurt her
She'll do me no harm.

—JOHN SEBASTIAN DOE

THIS optimistic jingle has probably done more to exasperate embryonic poets than any other in the English language. Not only is it sanctimonious and sticky; it has an impossible rhyme. The last word should be *horm*, unless you speak in German dialect; and what is *horm*? Horm might be a new kind of sandwich spread, or a revitalizing tonic, but it is certainly not what Pussy will do to you. Pussy will and can do a lot of other things to you, though. (Pussy is an insipid name, associated in my mind for some thirty years with the glazed pink-and-white blue-eyed mug of the unhealthily plump little girl whose picture illustrated the nursery jingle. It will be more agreeable, I think, to assume that you have a cat named Blackberry, and a dog named P'ing Cho Fung by the Kennel Association and Butch by you.)

Blackberry and Butch, then, can cause you a lot of extra worry, now that men have decided to live by the sword again, temporarily.

They and other furry creatures are among the first to suffer, like the meek. The thought of all the fine shining cows crying in agony to be milked along the roads of France and Belgium, while the hungry people fled past them, is an ugly one. And at the beginning of this war, it was a sorrowful idea in England that pets should not drink and eat the precious food, nor breathe the invaluable cellar air that their human masters might use. In Honolulu, on another

305

island, the same thoughtless instinct rose in the first days of war, and the civilians were urged not to waste food on pets.

There is one eccentric and wealthy old lady in Cornwall, the kind who is often the victim in mystery stories, who was stoned in 1940 because she had refused to kill her cat and her terrier. Moreover, she had turned her cellars and her air-raid shelter into a haven for every pet she could rescue from the panicky village. That seemed terrible to the people, to feed and protect brute-beasts while little children were bombed and might be hungry too. The old lady was most unpopular, in 1940.

But in 1941 she was not. By then the rats and mice were scampering prolifically and plumply through many another village than hers, and contrary to centuries of habit, people beamed instead of groaned when they saw an *enceinte* alley cat, or heard a terrier ratting in the barn. All the eccentric old ladies and the others who from sentiment or cool-headedness had refused to do away with their Butches and Blackberries were enhaloed, and it was confessed, as it soon must be in any beleaguered place, that there are worse things than sharing what food there is with old friends, even supposedly soulless ones.

It is of course harder and more expensive to feed animals in wartime. It takes more thought and planning, just as with humans.

Dogs are more of a problem than cats, since they are believed to be carnivorous and have small scope to exercise that nature, fortunately for us. (One of the handsomest I ever saw, though, with a pelt like a Russian opera-singer's winter overcoat, was a vegetarian from birth . . . and a police dog at that!) They must be fed with more expense, if not more care, than the ordinary house-cat . . . who if she's worth her salt will do a bit of mousing, war or no war, and can fend for herself with the inspiration of a good saucer of milk now and then, and a comforting bite from the kitchen left-overs. [Most cats and many dogs appreciate dainty tidbits, and I always share my scraps with my current feline companion. She and I nibble at the same food, from different dishes and physical levels, and feel companionable. It is another good argument for the spiritual value of left-overs, with their accumulated savor.]

Dogs, like men, can grow lean in wartime with no great danger and perhaps some good, and like men they will show by their outsides how their simpler diet agrees with them. If their eyes are dull, and their fur is lifeless and thin, and their nails are cracked, and they seem easy prey to drifting disease clouds, then they are malnourished just as surely as any sad wretch kept alive in a concentration camp on thin soup and bread.

There are countless little books and pamphlets, most of them published by pet-food packers, to tell you how to feed your dog correctly. In spite of their eagerness to prove that Rex-O or Pussy-Purr-More is the only correct food, most of them agree that a fairly ideal diet for a dog should consist roughly of ⅓ meat, ⅓ vegetable, and ⅓ starch. This, with variations according to the individual, is basically man's diet too!

In time of war, when eating becomes less of a gastronomic exercise and more a part of a determined will-to-live, you can nourish yourself and Butch on the same schedule, and do harm to neither of you. The sludge I write about in the chapter on how to keep alive is, in my experience, the finest all-in-one diet for any normal dog or cat alive.

It can be made more coarsely, chopped instead of ground, for big animals whose guts are longer and stronger than a terrier's or a Peke's. It should always be broken up nicely in the dish (it gets very solid when cool), but should never be made soupy with additional liquid. If possible it should be warmed a little in cold weather. And one meal of it a day will keep any type of dog I have known in such top form that veterinarians will blink with jealousy.

Another thing to give Butch, and Blackberry too, is an occasional nibble of fresh yeast. It seems to make their coats even finer, and their mouths sweeter. They can have a quarter- or a half-cake at a time, maybe once or twice a week. You can see that it is no great addition to the budget, and it is well worth it.

Most of the reputable canned foods are all right, especially if they are given only occasionally as a treat (which is also easier on the pocketbook). They can be mixed with sludge, to go farther.

A raw egg, now and then, for your pets is a good investment, too. [My own offspring down an occasional raw yolk from its half-shell, and I am convinced that their sleek pelts are the sleeker for it . . . and their palates the happier!] It should be stirred into milk or sludge, since it is rather slithery to lap up, I imagine.

If you give canned milk, always dilute it, preferably with tomato juice or the juices you have saved for your own use from canned or cooked vegetables. Needless to say, your animals need vitamins and minerals just as you do, and what you have you should share with them as long as you assume the responsibility of keeping them alive at all.

Myself, I have always said (and practiced) [This still stands, as does the whole chapter.] that I would never give a dog or a cat what I would not eat myself. Sometimes it has been hard to discard a whole can of some new recommended food, which when I opened it sent out such a stink of old meat and spurious seasoning that I knew I could never swallow the trial bite of it.

In reverse, though, it is fairly safe to say that what neither Blackberry nor Butch will touch is no fit food for you. For instance, canned luncheon meat, which resembles dog food in many ways, except that it is more expensive: if neither animal enjoys a bite of it, you can count on its being too salty or too impossibly pink and healthy with a mass of preservatives which will parch your tongue and burn your innards.

Once, in a madcap mood indeed, I bought a generous tin of sliced smoked salmon from Poland. I made a beautiful platter of it for an hors d'œuvre, and then, feeling magnanimous, put one slice on a plate for Bazeine, the current Blackberry.

He sniffed it, backed away as if it had snapped at him, and with a reproachful glare at me disappeared for two days. Which is almost what happened with the humans a little later, since I couldn't bring myself to throw away fifteen francs, and served the salmon in spite of Bazeine's blunt hint.

The next morning I made a little pile of all the beautiful paper-thin bright orange slices, and carried them mournfully down through the vineyard to the compost pit. They looked gay and still delectable, there on top of all the vegetable trimmings and dead flowers.

Months later, when I was cleaning away the leaves of a magnificent melon that grew from a seed in the pit and covered it for a whole summer, I saw the smoked salmon again.

It sat just where I had placed it, on top of all the dead vegetation. The sun had not faded its gay color, and snow and wind and rain had not warped its oily squareness. Birds had ignored it, or flown away in fright perhaps, and even the wise ants had left it inviolate.

Finally the pit was covered with earth, and soon lush wild flowers grew where it had been. But I have a feeling sometimes that if I ever get back to that meadow below the vineyard in Switzerland, the strange frightful square of bright orange salmon will have worked its way up through the ground and the roots and be lying there, a deathless taunt to my gastronomic snobbism and the time I refused to take a cat's advice. [For one of the few times in the past thirty-odd years I am pleased with something I have written. I think this is a good chapter.]

How to Comfort Sorrow

I'll make her a pudding, and a pudding she'll like, too. . . .
Many a one has been comforted in their sorrow by seeing a
good dish come upon the table.

                                              —*Cranford*, MRS. GASKELL

THERE are those of us, and perhaps it is a good sign, who hold that puddings are fit food for babes and dodderers and such misfortunates with few teeth and less esthetic taste. Others, and who is to say whether they are right or not, would agree with Cranford's quaint character that a pudding can be a fine heartwarming thing indeed, in times of sorrow.

In times of war, however, puddings can be pesky nuisances. If you are cooking for people who feel that because they ate some such sweet desserts once a day when they were young, they must perforce eat them once a day when they are middle-aged and working like everything to save democracy, you will be hard put to it to make their prejudices fit your food bill. Eggs and cream and cinnamon, not to mention fuel needed for long slow bakings, have suddenly become rare and precious things to be used cunningly for a whole meal or a weekly treat, not as the routine and unctuous final fillip to a pre-war dinner.

In England now, many of the gruesome gastronomical pixies of the last unpleasantness have come into the open again, and you can buy powdered War-Egg-O ("Housewives . . . stir in a bit of water and treat your family *tonight* to a tempting custard sauce!") and even something called Nooeg, which is guaranteed to contain no egg at all, but will please your friends with its rich delightful smoothness ("upon tinned fruits").

310

These doubtful triumphs of science over human hunger are perhaps less dreadful to the English than to us, for in spite of our national appetite for pink gelatine puddings, we have never been as thoroughly under the yoke of Bird's Custard Sauce as our allies. [This situation no longer obtains. We not only buy incredible quantities of packaged American puddings, but we can now, oh, happy people, get *Bird's* in our "better" groceries!] Let us hope, without malice, that Nooeg stays on the right side of the Atlantic.

For those who must have some "shapeless nothing in a dish," war or no war, at the end of every night-time meal, the easiest and cheapest (and most pitying) answer is the boxed ready-prepared gelatine dessert. It is well advertised and even well thought of in some circles. Therefore, let us dismiss both it and its admirers from our thoughts.

Probably one of the best ends to a supper is nothing at all. If the food has been simple, plentiful, and well prepared; if there has been time to eat it quietly, with a friend or two; if the wine or beer or water has been good: then, more often than not, most people will choose to leave it so, with perhaps a little cup of coffee for their souls' sake.

Another fine thing for the soul, after a meal in the evening, is one of those herbal teas which French people used to call *tisanes*. [Serving a *tisane* before bedtime may sound affected, but very few people are anything but pleased by one, if also somewhat startled.] They are simply hot water poured over a few dried leaves of mint or verbena or lime flowers or camomile. They can be drunk with or without sugar, and a twist of lemon can be added. They smooth out wrinkles in your mind miraculously, and make you sleep, with sweet dreams, too.

So thoroughly do even the most sophisticated of gastronomists believe in the magic of *tisanes*, that the following recipe was given only a few years ago with complete seriousness by the Vicomte de Mauduit:

INFUSION OF LADIES' SLIPPER ROOT

Last thing at night drink an infusion made of ladies' slipper root. Then under your pillow case place a mixed bouquet of this root and skullcap, which you have previously dried in the oven. This is a permanent *cure for sleeplessness.*

If you have supped well, for instance, on ham baked with apples and sweet potatoes and a green salad, you will probably agree that the best possible ending to such a savorous meal is a bowl of walnuts which have been roasting in their shells in the hot oven while you ate. Coffee is fine with them, but a glass of port is even better . . . or ordinary red wine.

Coffee, by the way, is one thing which cannot be made skimpily. If you are going to economize with it, do so by using it less often, but never by trying to make it with less coffee and cooking it longer. Almost any good grocery store sells a very inexpensive, moderately well-roasted brand of coffee in the grain, which you can have ground to your taste in half-pound lots, so that it is used before it grows too stale. (Or if you are lucky you can grind it yourself as you need it, on your nice old-fashioned coffee mill or your nice new-fashioned electric grinder.) This bulk coffee costs about half the price of tinned brands, and is good.

If you use Sanka or Kaffee Hag, you can do it with a clear conscience and a certain malicious pleasure in the number of people you fool, if you make it with a generous hand: two tablespoonfuls to the cup.

And any coffee, emasculated or not, is better than perfect if it is made with chicory. It can be bought in this country, in spite of what many stubborn repatriated gourmets say, in convenient little brown tablets. It is cheap and easy to use, and not only improves the flavor of no matter what brand of coffee, but with a certain amount of judicious experimenting can be made to make a pound go much further than it is meant to by the merchants. [There is a good "Italian over-roast" brand of canned coffee now generally obtainable. I am sorry to say that the little chicory tablets seem to have disappeared, and that they are a gastronomical loss which I am apparently alone in feeling!]

Coffee, when it is brewed intelligently, is a perfect accompaniment to any dessert, whether it be a Soufflé au Grand Marnier or a bowl of frost-whipped Winesap apples, crisp and juicy. It is good, too, with a piece of fruity cake, and here is a recipe for one which is foolproof to concoct, and guaranteed to make the wolf take at least two steps back, instead of one step nearer.

It is a remnant of the last war, and although I remember liking it so much that I dreamed about it at night [Unimportant note: I mentioned this with some embarrassment on page 205. Now I dream of caviar. And if I should live so long, will it be of gruel and milksops?] like all the other children who ate it, I can't remember that it was ever called anything more appetizing than

WAR CAKE

½ cup shortening (bacon grease can be used, because of the spices which hide its taste)
1 teaspoon cinnamon
1 teaspoon other spices . . . cloves, mace, ginger, etc.
1 cup chopped raisins or other dried fruits . . . prunes, figs, etc.

1 cup sugar, brown or white
1 cup water
2 cups flour, white or whole wheat
¼ teaspoon soda
2 teaspoons baking powder

Sift the flour, soda and baking powder. Put all the other ingredients in a pan, and bring to a boil. Cook five minutes. Cool thoroughly. Add the sifted dry ingredients and mix well. Bake 45 minutes or until done in a greased loaf-pan in a 325-350° oven.

War cake can be made in muffin-tins, and baked more quickly, but in a loaf it stays fresh longer. It is very good with a glass of milk, I remember. (I am sure that I could live happily forever without tasting it again. There are many things like that: you recall with astonishment and a kind of admiration some of the things eaten with sensual delight at eight or eighteen, that would be a gastronomical *auto da fé* for you at twenty-eight, or fifty. But that does not mean that you were wrong so long ago. War Cake says nothing to me now, but I know that it is an honest cake, and one loved by hungry children. And I'm not ashamed of having loved it . . . merely a little puzzled, and thankful that I am no longer eight.)

Another good cake, to eat plain with coffee, or frosted with a covering of cream cheese and powdered sugar and a little rum if possible, is

TOMATO SOUP CAKE

3 tablespoons butter or shortening
1 cup sugar
1 teaspoon soda
1 can tomato soup
2 cups flour

1 teaspoon cinnamon
1 teaspoon nutmeg, ginger,
  cloves mixed
1½ cups raisins, nuts, chopped
  figs, what you will

Cream butter, add the sugar, and blend thoroughly. Add the soda
to the soup, stirring well, and add this alternately to the first mixture
with the flour and spices sifted together. Stir well, and bake in a pan
or loaf-tin at 325°.

This is a pleasant cake, which keeps well and puzzles people who
ask what kind it is. It can be made in a moderate oven while you
are cooking other things, which is always sensible and makes you
feel rather noble, in itself a small but valuable pleasure.

Another excellent way to use any space left from cooking meat
or a casserole or anything that wants a moderate heat, is, as I have
already argued, to make baked apples. They are good hot or cold,
stuffed with raisins or with brown sugar. [Or mincemeat or left-over
jam. Canelloni (p. 274) are also a fine dessert made with jam.]
They can make a whole supper, with plenty of hot buttered toast,
or they can be the rather heavy but savory and wholesome dessert
of a dinner, served with sour cream or my grandmother's recipe for
Cinnamon Milk.

BAKED APPLES

apples . . . almost any kind, although Deliciouses are delicious
brown sugar (1 tablespoon for
  each apple)

cinnamon, nutmeg
raisins, dates, left-over jam
butter (optional)
water

Core the apples, and put in a baking dish. Fill each hole with the
fruit or jam, and put a dab of butter on top if you want to. Mix
the sugar with enough water to fill the dish almost to the top, and
bake slowly until the apples are tender.

CINNAMON MILK
(For Baked Apples or Apple Dumplings)

1 pint milk   1 tablespoon butter (optional)
1 teaspoon cinnamon or mixed
    spices

[Age makes me less ascetic, and the butter is no longer optional! And now I use creamy milk and add either 3 tablespoonfuls of brown sugar or about half that amount of good molasses. Other people like it better too!]

Heat milk in double boiler. Add spices (and butter). Pour into heated jug and serve like cream.

An easy and inexpensive hot dessert, if your oven is going anyway, is a shallow buttered casserole with a handful of gingersnaps [. . . or vanilla wafers or old sponge cake . . . and of course the fruit is well *drained*] in the bottom and a can of peaches on them. Put a little butter in each peach, sprinkle some nutmeg here and there, and if you feel lavish pour a little sherry into the dish. Broil, and serve with or without cream, which is better sour than sweet for most such tried temptations. [A more interesting variation is canned nectarine-halves in a shallow buttered dish, filled with left-over preserves, a little lump of butter nutmeg if desired. I grill them for 5 minutes, and for company or fun pour a little dark rum over them and let it burn off at the table. No cream, of course.]

The recipe for my mother's gingerbread must be almost identical with the excellent one which comes out of a box. It is cheaper to make, if you have the time and the oven is going anyway. It sends out a fine friendly smell through the house and is so good that it usually disappears while it is still hot, which is too bad because it is so good cold.

EDITH'S GINGERBREAD
[. . . which I mentioned on page 204, I believe.]

¼ cup shortening   cloves and salt
¼ cup sugar   ¾ cup boiling water
½ cup molasses   ¼ teaspoon soda
½ teaspoon soda   1¼ cups flour
  1 teaspoon cinnamon   1 teaspoon baking powder
  1 teaspoon ginger   1 beaten egg

Cream the shortening and sugar. Sift the spices and flour and baking powder together. Beat the ½ teaspoon soda into the molasses until it is light and fluffy, and add to the shortening and sugar. Add the ¼ teaspoon soda to the boiling water, and then add it alternately with the sifted dry ingredients. Fold in the beaten egg when all is well mixed, pour into a greased and floured pan, and bake about 20 minutes, at 325°. This mixture will seem much too thin to make a cake, but do not increase the quantity of flour, as many doubting cooks have tried to do.

Either of the following simple sauces is good with it, although myself I think unsalted butter, preferably pressed into little pats with a cow on one side and a daisy on the other, is the most fitting partner.

A WINE SAUCE

[Another excellent sauce is made of equal parts of brown sugar, butter, and sherry, beaten together while it slowly melts, and kept hot, but never bubbling.]

¼ cup butter	*1 cup sherry*
¾ cup powdered sugar	*nutmeg*
½ cup hot water	

Cream the butter, add the sugar gradually, and cream well. Add the nutmeg. Stir in the hot water and add the wine.

A HARD SAUCE

¼ cup butter (or vegetable shortening, I hate to admit)	*2 tablespoons lemon juice*
	salt
½ cup powdered sugar	*(rum if you like it)*

Beat until very fluffy. (Add ¼ cup chopped nuts if desired.) [Or shredded coconut or chopped candied fruits. I like it best without additions.] Chill in a bowl and serve with hot gingerbread or any other hot cake.

It is hard to know whether a gingerbread should rightly be called a pudding when it is eaten hot with a sauce over it. (I remember pale squares of warm cakey tastelessness, covered limply with a film of lemon-tinted sauce, which were called Cottage Pudding at boarding school.) The following rule, although it sounds rather like a cake, makes a pleasant hot dessert which is definitely a pudding. It is called Date Delight, through no fault of mine.

DATE DELIGHT

¼ cup butter or shortening
⅔ cup sugar
2 eggs
3 cups soft crumbs
2 cups chopped dates
1 .teaspoon ginger

⅔ cup milk
¼ cup flour
½ teaspoon salt
2 teaspoons baking powder
⅛ teaspoon soda
½ teaspoon cinnamon

Cream shortening, eggs, sugar, until fluffy. Add ⅓ crumbs, dates, and then the rest of the crumbs and milk alternately. Add the sifted dry ingredients. Beat briskly one minute, and bake in a greased pan 1 hour at 325°. Serve warm with hard sauce flavored with rum.

This, you can see, is a heavy dish, and more expensive than many. It should be made the main point of a meal, with perhaps soup and a light green salad first. It is a winter thing, and men usually like it more than women do.

Another hearty dessert, which can be made of sweet potatoes or yams left from day before yesterday's supper, is

SWEET POTATO PUDDING

6 sweet potatoes
6 tablespoons butter (or vegetable shortening)
6 tablespoons brown sugar

grated rind and juice from 1
   lemon or 1 orange
2 bananas (optional)
cinnamon

Peel the cooked or baked potatoes and mash smooth. Add the melted butter and brown sugar, the lemon rind and juice, and beat thoroughly. Pour into a buttered casserole (lined, if you wish, with sliced bananas) [. . . or any other fruit: pineapple, peaches, apples]. Put more brown sugar and a little butter and cinnamon, if possible, over the top, and bake ½ hour at 325-350°.

Left-over rice is another thing that can be used almost as many ways as there are people to eat it. Some of them think it a crying shame to do more than put some brown sugar and rich milk over it, and let it speak for itself. Others, more complicated in their actions, like some such recipe as the following, which I got from a Swiss woman:

RICE AND SPICE

2 eggs
2 cups milk
¾ cup raisins
1¼ cups cooked rice
½ cup brown sugar

½ teaspoon cinnamon
¼ teaspoon each nutmeg, ginger, salt
1 tablespoon powdered sugar

Separate the whites and yolks of the eggs. Add to the yolks 2 table-spoons of the milk, and place the rest of it in a double boiler. Wash the raisins, put them in the milk, and cook about 15 minutes or until they are soft. Add the rice, cook five minutes more, then stir in the yolks, sugar, salt, and spices. Cook for 2 to 3 minutes, stirring well. Pour into the serving dish. Beat the whites, add the powdered sugar, spread on the pudding, and brown delicately in the oven. Serve very cold.

This recipe is a dainty one, and will surprise people who remember rice pudding from their childhood with some unwillingness. There are many others like it, finicky to make perhaps but inexpensive and pleasant if you like them at all. [I still remember a basically similar pudding, but almost as crisp as a cake, made by a Turkish friend when I was only vaguely past childhood. It was of cooked vermicelli baked slowly in an oiled shallow pan, with more oil and much more honey basted over it until it could absorb no more. Perhaps there was a spice in it. It made my teeth ache.]

[A much daintier dish than Rice and Spice is Riz à l'Impératrice . . . or so I can read and have too often been assured, by friend and relatives raised, perforce and/or willy-nilly, in luxury hotels from Buda-Pesth to Colorado Springs. It is a dessert of the *fin de siècle*, a costly trifle to be played with before the hot-house peach, the Bock y Panatela . . . and people of about my age who raced the corridors of the Ritzes and the Trois Couronnes three or four decades ago can eat it with a poignant nostalgia unknown to me, the California kid, the crude *auslander*. It seems like a balm, a tonic, to their weary palates. And it is, in spite of its bland intricacy, a very gentle dish . . . somewhat like a notorious actress who is still naive . . .

(This recipe I give in a sketchy way, a fleeting cock-snoot at the wolf still sniffing hungrily. It is obvious that a good creamy rice-pudding, tricked out with apricot jam and currant jelly and well chilled, could nobly serve the purpose of the elaborate classicism I now outline:)

RIZ À L'IMPÉRATRICE

Wash, parboil, and then drain 1 pound of the finest rice. Slowly bake it with a vanilla bean, 1 quart of boiled rich milk, 2 cups fine white sugar, ¼ pound fresh butter. Keep covered and do not stir. When still hot add gently the beaten yolks of 16 eggs (ah, that happy wolf . . . !). When cool add 1 cup minced candied fruits and 1 cup apricot jam, 1 pint thick English custard, and 1 pint whipped cream heavily flavored with Alsatian kirsch. Put a thick layer of red currant jelly in the bottom of a Bavarian-cream mold, pour the above cream upon it, and let chill thoroughly. To serve, turn out so that the jelly runs down over the firm sides. (This last is what sets off the cautious fireworks of reminiscence in my stomach-weary contemporaries who lived on such fatuous delicacies rather than my own grandmother's "plain boiled rice with cream and sugar.")]

"The proof of the pudding is in the eating," it says in *Don Quixote*. I believe it, myself, and would as soon have a hollowed ring of cold cooked cereal, Roman Meal, or Wheatena of hallowed memory, with the hollow filled with grated maple sugar and a fat pot of cream waiting, as I would Cherries Jubilee. But then, in spite of Cervantes and a host of awesome authorities, I would rather have some ripe grapes or a little properly selected cheese than any of their artful messes. Or nothing . . . wolf or no wolf.

How to Be a Wise Man

> *A wise man always eats well.*
>
> *—Chinese proverb*

EVERY now and then a sensitive intelligent thoughtful person feels very mournful about this country and, deciding with Brillat-Savarin that "The destiny of nations depends upon what and how they eat," he begins to question.

Why, he asks, are we so ungastronomic as a nation?

Why do we permit and even condone the feeble packaged bread that our men try to keep strong on? [And women . . . and, worst of all, *children!*]

Why do we let our millers rob the wheat of all its goodness, and then buy the wheat germ for one thousand times its value from our druggists so that our children may be strong and healthy?

Why do we go on eating cakes and puddings after good meals, because we always did when we were children?

Why do we talk longingly of the honest beef stew our Aunt Matilda used to make while we spend a dollar or two eating third-rate steamed chicken dipped in batter and fried in a shameful pot of synthetic grease in some roadside hashery?

It is because we are sentimental, probably, and loyal to what we want to remain sweet memories of our younger years. It is because we are proud, and vain, and unwilling to admit our own weaknesses. And most of all it is because we, and almost all American Anglo-Saxon children of the second generation, have been taught when we were young not to mention food or enjoy it publicly.

If we have liked a meringue, or an artful little curl of pastry on a kidney pie, or a toasted walnut placed as only a child would like it right in the middle of a chocolate blanc-mange, we have not been allowed to cry out with pleasure but instead have been pressed down, frowned at, weighted with a heavy adult reasoning that such display was unseemly, and vulgar, and almost "foreign."

320

Once when young Walter Scott, who later wrote so many exciting books, was exceptionally hungry and said happily, "Oh, what a fine soup! Is it not a *fine* soup, dear Papa?," his father immediately poured a pint of cold water into what was already a pretty thin broth, if the usual family menu was any sample. Mr. Scott did it, he said, to drown the devil.

For too many nice ordinary little Americans the devil has been drowned, so that all their lives afterwards they eat what is set before them, without thought, without comment, and, worst of all, without interest. The result is that our cuisine is often expensively repetitive: we eat what and how and when our parents ate, without thought of natural hungers.

It is not enough to make a child hungry; if he is moderately healthy he will have all the requisites of a normal pig or puppy or plant-aphis, and will eat when he is allowed to, without thought. The important thing, to make him not a pig or puppy, nor even a delicate green insect, is to let him eat from the beginning with thought.

Let him choose his foods, not for what he likes as such, but for what goes with something else, in taste and in texture and in general gastronomic excitement. It is not wicked sensuality, as Walter Scott's father would have thought, for a little boy to prefer buttered toast with spinach for supper and a cinnamon bun with milk for lunch. It is the beginning of a sensitive and thoughtful system of deliberate choice, which as he grows will grow too, so that increasingly he will be able to choose for himself and to weigh values, not only sensual but spiritual.

He will remember, some time when he is a man, that once he decided not to eat a chocolate bar, but to let the taste of a stolen apple ride an hour or two longer on his appreciative tongue. And whatever decision he must make as a man will probably be the solider for that apple he ate so long since.

The ability to choose what food you must eat, and knowingly, will make you able to choose other less transitory things with courage and finesse. A child should be encouraged, not discouraged as so many are, to look at what he eats, and think about it: the juxtapositions of color and flavor and texture . . . and indirectly the reasons why he is eating it and the results it will have on him, if he is an introspective widgin. (If not, the fact that what he eats is not only good but pretty will do him no harm.)

If, with the wolf at the door, there is not very much to eat, the child should know it, but not oppressively. Rather, he should be encouraged to savor every possible bite with one eye on its agreeable nourishment and the other on its fleeting but valuable esthetic meaning, so that twenty years later, maybe, he can think with comfortable delight of the little brown toasted piece of bread he ate with you once in 1942, just before that apartment was closed, and you went away to camp.

It was a nice piece of toast, with butter on it. You sat in the sun under the pantry window, and the little boy gave you a bite, and for both of you the smell of nasturtiums warming in the April air would be mixed forever with the savor between your teeth of melted butter and toasted bread, and the knowledge that although there might not be any more, you had shared that piece with full consciousness on both sides, instead of a shy awkward pretense of not being hungry.

[I feel, even more strongly than I did in 1942, that one of the most important things about a child's gastronomical present, in relation to his future, gastronomical and otherwise, is a good *respect* for food. In horrifies me to see contemporary mothers numbly cooking and then throwing away uneaten lamb chops, beans, toast; mussed but unsavored puddings; deliberately spilled or bedabbled milk. I think children should be given small portions of food, according to their natures, and allowed to cope with them at their own speeds, but *finish* them, before more is trotted out in the currently fashionable pediatric pattern. . . . They learn their capacities. They learn good manners. Above all, they learn to respect the food so many other children cry for.]

All men are hungry. They always have been. They must eat, and when they deny themselves the pleasures of carrying out that need, they are cutting off part of their possible fullness, their natural realization of life, whether they are poor or rich.

It is a sinful waste of human thought and energy and deep delight, to teach little children to pretend that they should not care or mention what they eat. How sad for them when they are men! Then they may have to fight, or love, or make other children, and they won't know how to do it fully, with satisfaction, completely, because when they were babies they wanted to say, "*Oh*, what a fine soup!" and instead only dared murmur, "More, please, Papa!"

How to Lure the Wolf

*She wrenched from her brow a diamond and eyed it with
contempt, took from her pocket a sausage and contemplated it
with respect and affection.*

—*Peg Woffington,* CHARLES READE

LET US sing the praises, willy-nilly, of the wolf in human form or
otherwise who can with straight face and unwrinkled muzzle woo a
tousled kitchen maid. His muzzle, wrinkled or smooth, must be
insensate, thus to ignore her locks all heavy with the perfumes of
the frying pan. His so-called face, straight or wolfishly crooked, must
either be without eyes or unduly charitable, thus to forego at least
one cruel glance at her shiny nose and her gnawed lips and the
chapped remnants of her last-week's manicure.

In other words, any normal wolf would be a fool to take a tousled
kitchen maid at her own face value, since the very fact that she is
tousled should prove to him her sluttish nature.

If you want to lure a wolf, no matter what his form, there are
certain tricks known heretofore among a chosen few, which can at
last be released to the general class of kitchen maids (the plural of
which was long held to be *kitchen midden* by one otherwise erudite
scholar. He may have been the same one, although it seems somewhat improbable, who wrote an essay in his younger days about the
pleasures of picking dewberries in the Maine woods in the summertime. It was not until his form-master was removed from the
classroom in a state of near hysteria that this future semanticist
learned that dewberries are what rabbits make as well as what they
nibble).

One way to look your prettiest in the kitchen, and make the wolf think that even if his hot breath whuffs through the keyhole and ruffles your very curls you are nigh adamant, is to put up a little mirror.

Myself, I have a right nice mahogany frame which once held a prim silhouette, with a band of spotted dingy gold inside it. The mirror within is wavy and cheap, and the whole thing hangs on a wall that shakes and sends it all crooked every time anyone bangs a door in the house, and I have to lean over the vegetable bin and squint like sixty to see anything at all, but probably I give myself a reassuring look or tweak or pat by way of that mirror at least five times a day, and feel the better for it.

Sometimes I look into it confidently, hot and steamy from stirring a sauce, but feeling quite attractive, when somebody pulls at the front-door bell, and I stop short and say, "Hey!" There is not much to do about it then. I have struck bottom. But usually I look into it when the bell peals, and I can see either that things are under control beautifically or that a certain amount of smoothing, poking, and composing will do some good.

And even if nobody else notices, the fact that I have seen my own disorder and recognized it makes a great psychological difference. I have always felt that if the Prince of Wales or Charles Boyer came to the door, I would much rather know about the smudge on my nose than not. [Today I am not so sure.]

Sometimes, especially in small apartments, dinner guests arrive at one door before you can snake through another to dull the finish on your nose and get back before the peas turn black. So a little shelf under the mirror ought to be very nice indeed. On it you could put a compact, and a lipstick perhaps. Neither should have a strong perfume, since any fabricated odor mixed with the heady and if possible agreeable smells of the meal-in-progress would be more than unpleasant.

Some women keep a bottle of hand lotion in the cupboard. (Horrible thought for blackouts, when they may reach for the salad-oil or the vinegar!) If you use such a lotion anyway at other times this is probably all right. You must be careful, though, never to put it religiously and righteously on your hands, as the advertisements tell you to, and then pull apart the leaves for a salad or peel tomatoes or some such thing: the result will be nauseous.

Instead, you may quite economically do what I have done for a great many years, and use whatever sweet-smelling oil or fat or grease is wandering around begging for a taker. If you unwrap a quarter-pound of butter, rub the paper on your hands before you throw it away. If you are making salad dressing, catch the last drop of oil from the bottle on your fingers. If you mix ground meat with tomato juice and egg and crumbs for some kind of loaf, rub the film of fat into your hands instead of washing it off at once; it will soon vanish, and you will have smoother fingers and more firmly beautiful nails.

Rubber gloves are supposed to be a good idea, and indeed rare and strange wonders are worked in spite of them in surgeries, where living rather than dead flesh is carved to make more life. In kitchens I think it is perhaps better to be unprotected: few chefs have hands as valuable as a good doctor's, or as well trained, and the common tasks need not be so difficult as to do harm to hypersensitive fingers. [I know more now. I even know a fine chef who is diabetic, and must wear gloves on his very dry hands because of the insulin he absorbs, and the way his skin would disappear if he did not . . . or so he explains it.]

It is true that onions or garlic often leave a wretched haunting stink, and one not yet associated in the common male mind with glamor. The answer to that is to slice any of the bulbs (onions, scallions, garlic, leeks, chives) under running water. Then, as soon as the job is done, wash the knife and your hands thoroughly in cold and still running water, and *then*, if you are a fussbudget, rub a cut lemon on them. And then again, if by chance your skin is the kind that holds such undignified odors, simply stop slicing onions and all their ilk.

Washing dishes, according to advertisements and a large percentage of the radio dramas, has ruined many an otherwise lovely woman's chance for happiness. Her hands, rough, chapped, utterly repellent, have driven Mr. Right away. Then, if she has been wise, or perhaps even had a neighbor who tipped her off in time, she has given herself a ten-day test and washed in ordinary soap with her left hand and in super-oxygenized Drift-O with her right hand, in a miraculous test of legerdemain.

In seven or eight days she has seen the difference: her roughened, reddened left hand has shamed her. In another week, or even less, that hand, all white and silken, sparkles with a great big glorious solitaire, and burns with the hidden ecstasy of Mr. Right's first and perhaps last kiss. All is well, and from that day forward she washes dishes with just oodles of soapsy sudsy bubble-squubble Drift-O.

Or, Mr. Right or no Mr. Right, she never uses soap at all. It is surprising how clean dishes can be, and how effortless the task can be, and how small the soap bill can be, given a small stream of moderately hot water and a stiff brush. With a certain amount of practice your hands, even the one holding the plate or cup, need never be in the water . . . and if you scrape the plates first, which of course you would do, the sink stays clean, the drains stay fresh, and your brush, which you get free from the Fuller man, lasts for a boringly long time.

You hold the plate under the running water, turn it with one hand and scrub it with the other, and put it in a rack on the drain-board. When you have collected a few, you dry them—before they are cold.

This scheme sounds rather dreamy, put down in cold print, but it works well, much to the disgust of better and older dishwashers than I could ever be.

Or do I mean that? They may be *older* . . . but I would be willing to bet fifty thousand Chincoteagues that never in my life have I put a dish with a slippery bottom into a china cupboard, and that not one of them could say the same. Of course there is no proof of my wager, except my own conscience. That, on the subject of clean dishes at least, is clear as an autumn sky. I have taxed the soul of many an experienced housekeeper because I have refused to make a great pan of suds and douse glasses and dishes in it . . . and with utter smugness I still feel that I use no more water, and certainly a lot less soap, and that I bother the skin of my hands not at all, by my slipshod easy method of scraping dishes and then scrubbing them under a little hot water. [I continue to get letters of disgusted protest about this system. I continue not only to believe in it but to practice it, and I begin to suspect that I probably have consistently cleaner dishes than any other "general housekeeper" I have ever met. Such bland self-satisfaction merits, and generously *gets* a dressing down.]

Naturally this method presupposes at least a limited supply of that. In case of shortage or broken water lines or some such wartime inconvenience, other means would be found by any ingenious woman. Probably the easiest, and one perhaps enforced whether or no, would be to stop eating at all.

In case you are fortunate enough to have a kitchen with a stove in it and something to cook on it when you read this, you may also have a dish that calls for, say, one onion browned in two tablespoon-fuls of fat. You may also have pretty brown or gold or black hair hanging in loose curls about your face, or even skinned up into a modish if unbecoming nob on top of your head [. . . or, nowadays, snipped as short as Peter Pan's].

In any case you should tie a washable scarf about what hairs you have when you fry onions or broil a steak or whip together a mixed-grill for your monthly treat. You will be much more alluring after-wards, even unto the next day, for fumes from fine dishes have a marked tendency to linger in the mind's covering as well as the mind.

Indeed, it can be said that fumes linger, period. They lurk in cupboards. They drift subtly through closed doors, no matter what cunning draft you may enforce, at risk of double pneumonia, through the kitchenette. They hang in the curtains, and fall out at you two nights later like overripe shreds of dead ghost.

There is not much to do about it; you either like fried onion or hot cabbage salad enough to endure them, or you eat lettuce or green peas instead.

Or you compromise by covering one fume with another. [Jeanne Bonamour believed firmly that a couple of cloves of garlic boiled with cabbage or cauliflower would hold down the distasteful fumes. What she did was double them! But her cauliflower was the best I ever ate.]

You can do it, according to the Stark Realism school, by lighting a crumbled piece of newspaper and dashing through the rooms with it. You can, much more effectively [. . . and tidily . . .] pour a drop or two of oil of eucalyptus or pine on a hot shovel and wave it around. If you want to feel like a character from one of the James brothers' looser romantic moments you can float a few drops of oil of lavender in a silver bowl filled with hot water.

And if you are somebody I do not know and furthermore do not care if I ever meet, you can burn a little cone of incense. [Various kinds of liquid candles like Air-Wick have come into our lives since this was written. They evaporate much as any candle burns, and they are based, or so I surmise, on extracts of live chlorophyl. I like them, as a last but reliable resort. Better are strong plants of philodendron, preferably grown around porous slabs of moistened bark. In the face of possible horror from hidebound nannies, I say they are wonderful in nurseries, to wash and sweeten the sometimes overburdened air.]

Or you can broil the meat, fry the onions, stew the garlic in the red wine . . . and ask me to supper. I'll not care, really, even if your nose is a little shiny, so long as you are self-possessed and sure that wolf or no wolf, your mind is your own and your heart is another's and therefore in the right place.

How to Drink to the Wolf

They eat, they drink, and in communion sweet
Quaff immortality and joy.

—JOHN MILTON

ONE infallible way to know that a country is at war is to read of the increased activity of the militant prohibitionists. Another fairly good way is to read statistics about the rise in pub-crawling, or as some people call it, alcoholic consumption. Which comes first, the chicken or the egg . . . the blue-nose or the red-nose?

Whichever, there can be no doubt that war's fever breeds drought as well as thirst, and that for countless centuries some men have frowned and scolded and some men have drunk deeper as Mars squeezed them.

Less than a month after our country entered this last war, Washington prohibitionists were praying and proving that Pearl Harbor, not to mention France's Fall, was directly traceable to the bottle. At the same time other men in Washington (not to mention Pearl Harbor and perhaps even Fallen France's safe cellars) were wetting their throats and drinking to what they hoped was their own and the nation's health.

If you happen to be unencumbered by childhood's scruples and maturity's sage ponderings, you will have gone to a great many cocktail parties in your time and will have decided, along with almost every other thing human left alive, that they are anathema. They are expensive. They are dull. They are good for a time, like a dry Martini, and like that all-demanding drink they can lift you high and then drop you hideously into a slough of boredom, morbidity, and indigestion.

When you reach this point of perception, and admit once for all

329

that such routs shall see no more of you, there is but one step more. Then you will decide that from now on you'll drink as you please, and with whom, and where, and how . . . and what.

Given a number of present-day ways to be poor (and whether you earn an immediately impressive salary or not, you will feel poor for several days or hours before each new check is cashed, in wartime), there is one sure way to feel poorer. That is to form the specious habit of stopping at the local grog-shop, the Greek's around the corner, Ye Cozie Nooke Cocktail Lounge. Even if cocktails keep their pre-war prices, the liquor is bound to fluctuate in quality, and it is easy as scat to pile up astonishing bills in one or two pre-dinner drop-ins, and even more horrendous hangovers.

The first thing to do, of course, is to stop going there. The next thing is to find a reputable substitute, since even a young man cannot too easily quit such solace as is offered by the dim jukey confines of the neighborhood gin-mill.

One of the best antidotes, if anything so pleasant could be termed so damningly, is to decide the person you like best to drink with and see if you can arrange to have a pre-dinner nip with her or him . . . alone. *Alone* does not necessarily connote *salaciously, lasciviously,* or even amorously, since if you like a person well enough to drink alone with him, he will be the kind who will have worked all day and be as glad as you to sit back and absorb a little quick relaxation from a glass and then eat, quaffing immortality and joy. He will if possible be your husband or your own true love, and you will find in this sudden quiet and peacefulness something that has sometimes seemed much too far from you both, lately. [I consider myself more fortunate than most women in that I know several good drinking companions of my own sex. They are for the most part well past sixty, a significant fact in the study of Alcohol in Modern Society, I imagine. . . . The best of them, eighty-two last Christmas, has taught me much of both self-control and sensual pleasure from her enjoyment of a weekly glass of dry champagne.]

If you (and occasionally Z and A, but never everyone in between) are used to hard liquor, you would do well to stick to it, for a time at least. In comparison with bar-prices, it costs very little to buy an ordinary but reputable gin by the gallon jug. [There are few such jugs, but in spite of local laws most good liquor stores will still give discounts on case-lots of fifths or quarts.] Dry vermouth from California or New York or South America are equally reputable and not at all ordinary. These two mixed knowingly with a little ice make a mighty passable Martini by any standards, and are doubly titillating drunk for a change in the airy sanctum of your own or a good friend's room.

Whiskey drinkers, whose name (to coin a phrase again) is legion, will drink Scotch, or bourbon, or rye, *or* blended spirits. They rarely admit being able to swallow more than one of the varieties. If you are in this general group, either swear off or choose a brew you can afford, and then save enough money until you can buy a case of it. (All this, granted that you are a moderate drinker-for-pleasure, and not a thirsty unhappy soul who must empty every bottle willy-nilly to drown some worm in the brain.)

Liquor by the case is generally about ten per cent less expensive than by the bottle, and generally it disappears at least ten per cent faster, so you must gauge your own purse and proclivities. If you can accept a case loose in the pantry with equanimity, use it sparingly but well, on yourself and your favorite friends.

Have a good drink before dinner, in comparative peace. Try drinking about one part whiskey to two of plain water, without ice. Old-time drinkers swear that is the only way to treat a good liquor, and after the first shock, when your palate expected a cold watered mouthful, you will probably agree. It is a better drink, and it will make a surprising difference not only in your digestion but your budget. Both will be stronger for the lack of ice and synthetic bubbles.

If you are even more haunted by the wolf at the door and still like your toddy, cut yourself down with some brutality to the starkness of sherry [. . . or a good vermouth]. At first it will seem pale, innocuous, a child's tipple. After a week you will look forward to it, and if you are sensible and fortunate enough to have fallen on a decent if much-maligned California bottle, you will tot up your budget with some relief.

Sherry by the bottle, naturally, costs more than sherry by the gallon. Sherry by the gallon, in the Eastern states at least, is often shameful. Try to find a good merchant . . . Italians usually have a nice feeling for the fortified wines . . . and if you can trust him at all you can trust him not to give you a jug half full of chemicals. Then decant it yourself; you can buy a ten-cent funnel and use the washed vermouth bottles from your occasional Martinis. A gallon will last a long time and should cost up or down around a dollar, in spite of what the self-styled connoisseurs will say. [I cannot believe this was true, even an eon of nine years ago! Surely I meant "quart," not "gallon" . . . and I still do.]

An agreeable drink with a surprising lift to it is the following:

HALF-AND-HALF COCKTAIL

½ *cup dry vermouth* *ice*
½ *cup dry sherry* *dash of angostura bitters if*
½ *lemon* *desired*

Pour vermouth and sherry into shaker over cracked ice. Add lemon juice and bitters. Stir well, pour into glasses and top with the rest of the lemon rind.

Little salty crackers or a bowl of freshly toasted nuts are good with sherry, or with Half-and-Half. These drinks can be served in the old Martini glasses, and afterwards you can have a china pitcher or a carafe of wine on the table.

If your sherry merchant is honest about the sherry he will probably be honest about other wines as well, and you should with impunity be able to fill a gallon jug for little more than a dollar with good characterful red or white wine, not notable but not infamous. [This is possible only if you know the vintner and can go to his cellar, jug in hand. But there are several reputable blended table wines available now, for about three dollars a gallon. They made an occasional ceremonial bottle of fine wine taste even finer.] It should be the kind that makes good food taste better, and leave a nice clean budding on your tongue, and makes the next morning seem fortunate rather than a catastrophe.

It is surprising how many confirmed likkadrinkas blossom and unwind and emerge from their professionally hard shells on such a liquid accompaniment to a good supper. Some insist later that it is the shock to their system . . . the sudden shift from grain to grape . . . that has caused the change. Most of them, any subtle host can see, are secretly or unconsciously relieved not to have to lap up their usual quota of pre-meal highballs or cocktails.

A pleasant aperitif, as well as a good chaser for a short quick whiskey, as well again for a fine supper drink, is beer . . . if you like it. Beer in big cities can be sent out for in a bucket to the corner pub, even from Park Avenue, but probably even on Park Avenues, in New York or elsewhere, it is better in bottles.

It should be bought by the case, because it is cheaper that way and easier to have delivered. You should save the tops. (I cannot think just why, but I am sure that something is done with them. The beer-man would know.) And of course you should save the bottles, instead of doing several other obvious things with them.

The present war will probably affect such fantastic problems as the one involving the transportation of lager from Milwaukee to Sunset Beach, California, and in the main it may be a good thing.

There are a thousand small honest breweries in this country which because they have been too poor and localized to compete with the big boys have been forced to close, or else operate under famous names while they turned out yeast, or hops, or some other important but unnamed ingredient of the main company's beer. Now, with trains full of soldiers and supplies rather than pale ale, perhaps people far from the great breweries will turn again to their local beer factories and discover, as their fathers did thirty years ago, that a beer carried quietly three miles is better than one shot across three thousand on a fast freight. [I am sorry that this did not happen. War seemingly made it easier and cheaper than ever to drink Milwaukee beer in Sunset Beach.]

Beer is a good drink. ("Teetotalers seem to die the same as others," A. P. Herbert wrote once between sessions in the House of Commons. "So what's the use of knocking off the beer?") Wine is a good drink, if you can get it, and now as never before in this country you can get it with confidence that it will be honest and full-bodied and all the other things that even grudging tasters say about a decent drink of it.

Hard liquors like gin and whiskey are more difficult to get, especially if you are thinking of economy, but they can still be found (circa 1942). [As I remember, the worst result of a War II block was a flood of Argentine gin. Sensitive Martini-boys and Gibson-girls still shudder. . . . They took to tequila and vodka, but only in desperation and fortunately for only a few weeks.] If you cannot afford them (and will admit it, which is rare), you might try to find an honest but unscrupulous druggist and buy a quart of good alcohol. Then, armed with this recipe, which stems via a Junior Leaguer from Ohio through Tiflis in what was once known as Georgia (Europe), you can make a mighty powerful drink which will treat you honestly and please you meanwhile.

A VODKA

[*This is still a good recipe, and worthy of individual study and experimentation. My uncle Walter, the most accomplished early-morning drinker I have ever known, says it is superlative in tomato juice.*]

1 *quart water*	½ *orange rind, shaved*
1 *teaspoon glycerin or sugar*	1 *quart alcohol*
1 *lemon rind, shaved*	

Simmer first four ingredients very gently about 20 minutes. Remove from stove. Add alcohol and cover instantly with a tight lid. Let cool and strain.

To make a very acceptable liqueur add more fruit shavings and a spoonful or so of honey.

A Mr. Furnas, who writes more wisely and less pompously than most men about other men, bread and destiny in a book called *Man, Bread and Destiny*, discusses at some length the various prescriptions throughout the ages for love potions. He mentions all the known ones, like Spanish fly and pork-chops-with-pepper, and a great many less prevalent charms. Finally he decides, and almost with a sigh of relief, that probably the best excitant in the world is sweet music and a moderate amount of alcohol! [Just lately I heard a modern lover state his vision of pure bliss, unconscious of his parody of Omar Khayyam: "A horn of gin, a good cigar, and *you*, Babe."]

When he writes so sensibly, it is hard not to say, along with the Governor of South Carolina who was talking to the Governor of North Carolina, that it's a long time between drinks, especially when there is sweet music and your love and good liquor. Then you can raise a glass to the wolf with impunity and a courage that is real, no matter how alcoholic, and know that even if you regret it tomorrow, you have been a man without qualms either amorous or budgetary tonight. [I believe, even more strongly now than then, that the important thing about drinking is that it be done for *pleasure*. Then, and then only, the sad fear of alcoholism never rises from its slough to haunt us, and neither our manners nor our digestions can be criticized.]

How Not to Be an Earthworm

[This whole chapter has the faintly phosphorescent humor of decay about it. It is as outmoded as a treatise on how to treat javelin-wounds, now that we know even earthworms are not inviolate.]

> *Streamlined to the ultimate for functional performance the earthworm blindly eats his way, riddling and honeycombing the ground to a depth of ten feet or more as he swallows.*
>
> —*Anatomy Underfoot*, J.-J. CONDE

OTHER wars have made men live like rats, or wolves, or lice, but until this one, except perhaps for the rehearsal in Spain, we have never lived like earthworms.

Now we bend our minds, with the surprised intensity of any nonplused [In the face of continued disapproval I think this should have two esses, just as I think the word busses is proper in the plural for both a vehicle and a kiss. Buses, indeed! I am *not* nonplused.] creatures, to existing as gracefully as possible without many of the things we have always accepted as our due: light, free air, fresh foods, prepared according to our tastes. It can be done, of course, since we are humans as well as rats, wolves, lice and earthworms.

You may have heard of one woman in England who withdrew to her tidy little bomb-shelter in the garden when the first siren sounded, and emerged, rather dreamily, some two weeks later. She'd been quite comfy, she told her worried neighbors, but she did hope the blinkin' raids would not always last quite so long.

There is more than a modicum of British deadpan humor in this wry story, as you will agree if you have ever stood, even for a few minutes, in one of the dreadful little strongboxes we are meant to hide in when bombs fall. No matter how much effort architects and decorators spend on making them habitable, they are shameful

335

places, cramped and stuffy and ugly. They are a means to an end, which is to survive, but they have only that virtue.

Blacked-out rooms are another thing. Usually they are places we recognize, with familiar chairs and pictures. They are not cells or holes to hide in, but chambers with their lights blinded from the outside, where we can continue in an almost normal way our nightly life of supper, and reading, and playing the phonograph or rummy and always the game of Being Casual.

Blackouts happen at night, of course, and so, usually does dinner. For that reason it is wise, if possible, to have the kitchen one of the rooms most adequately equipped to operate normally under the various restrictions of your neighborhood and your own common sense, when the siren sounds.

In a small house you can make this one room into a very pleasant place for the whole family . . . unless you are unfortunate enough to have what used to be called a "kitchenette," which means that it is impossibly small, even for its original function. In that case, you should try to black out both it and the next room, never forgetting that there are a few other functions as necessary, if not as pleasant, as eating, and that an easily accessible toilet is more important than any stove.

Since this country went to war, a great deal has been done to prepare us for emergencies (a polite word for bombings, invasions, and many other ugly things). Much has been good, and intelligent, and it is too easy and perhaps very wrong to criticize some of the less good and intelligent moves. It is hard not to wonder, however, how some of the sensible women who are planning such things as emergency rations can be so blandly impractical, especially when most of them are graduate home economists and dieticians.

There are many lists being prepared by various organizations, mapping out twenty-four-hour emergency rations for school children, hospitals, and so forth. Here is a sample [I refer to this later as "nauseating," but no one word is strong enough to suggest my scorn of it, esthetically as well as biochemically. It is a shocking example of gastronomical panic, and if it were heeded would soon reduce us to malnourished as well as spiritually weakened creatures, past much harm from bursting atoms.] which is of course made up of foods which can be stored indefinitely, and which have been calculated down to the last soda cracker for five hundred people:

BREAKFAST

Tomato juice
Peanut butter
Soda crackers or Melba toast
Hot milk chocolate

DINNER

Spaghetti with tomato purée
Corned beef
Peas and carrots
Soda crackers
Penny chocolate bars

SUPPER OR LUNCHEON

Tomato soup with canned milk
Soda crackers
Fruit cup
Graham crackers

These three meals, to be prepared for such a large number of people, most of whom are supposed to be children, would be heated on "a barbecue or make-shift inside camp cooking equipment," the folder says!

Aside from the obvious fact that few people eat three hot meals a day, even in peacetime ("Warm foods are not the only 'warming foods.' . . . Get out of the habit of cooking a hot meal every day," the British Ministry of Food urges in one of its regular newspaper bulletins.), it is foolish to think of the number of plates and cups and utensils which would have to be washed to provide for these impractical and nauseating feasts.

Have the earnest ladies of the Parent-Teachers Advisory Board forgotten that water may be as much of a problem as fuel, if things are so upset that five hundred people are hiding together in the basement of a schoolhouse? The old economy of paper cups and plates exists no longer, and the idea of washing at least twenty-five hundred different vessels into a passably sterile state is an uncomfortable one.

There are other problems than the main one of serving this

pathetic attempt at a "balanced diet" to five hundred ill-assorted and bewildered people. The dieticians must begin, always with the hope that it will never be needed, to borrow knowledge from the women in England, who after the countless nights of this war have gradually evolved their own rules.

In the meantime, you feel, as almost all people do without even realizing it, that you would rather be at home than anywhere else, if enemy planes are scouting somewhere in the air. As long as it can be done without too much danger, that is just where you should be, and aside from the inescapable unpleasantness of your reasons for being there, it can be downright entertaining to spend your evenings in your blacked-out rooms.

There is something innately desirable about a room shut off completely from the eyes of other humans. [I continue to agree with something Colette once wrote about the primitive satisfaction of a low dark place to eat in. This is a fine conversational gambit . . . who can resist discoursing on *his* ideas of the perfect dining room, whether he be dyspeptic, ascetic, or simply hungry?] It makes you feel protected, probably the way a kitten feels when it hides in a coat-sleeve, or a child under the blankets. Unfortunately, like the coat-sleeve or the blankets, it can be very stuffy, as the English have discovered. Intelligent designers are thinking and writing about that, and such magazines as the January, 1942, *Architectural Forum* are very helpful.

Given a moderately well-ventilated kitchen, which is large enough in itself or is next to another blacked-out room, you can live there with people you like and find life decent indeed.

The people in England have found that electricity usually stays on longer than gas in an actual bombing, so most well-equipped private shelters have little electric grills in them, or at least toasters and hot-plates. Now would be a good time to get out the old chafing dish, if you have not already done it. (The next thing is to hope that you can buy alcohol for it, but sufficient unto the day is the evil of that particular shortage.) [Ordinary rubbing compounds will do, in spite of their weird smells and the ugly incrustations they make upon the copper.]

In spite of your optimistic refusal to believe that anything could happen to *your* gas main or *your* power lines, it is a wise thing, if you know that you are to be blacked out that night, to cook as much food as you can during the day. Make things that can be reheated or served cold.

Another good reason for cooking while it is light is that few kitchens are as well ventilated as they should be at the best of times, so that at night with the windows closed and several people in the room, the air should not be overheated and filled with steams and fumes of food. This is especially true if you are reduced to cooking with an open flame or with coal oil: the air quickly becomes poor.

It is better, for the same reason, to cook things that do not have too strong a smell. Cabbage, for instance, is unwise. Kidneys, unless they are prepared beforehand, are too strong in the air. (They are easy, though, to fix in a chafing dish, smell or no smell.)

In the old days, before Stuka and blitz became a part of even childish chitchat, every practical guide to cookery urged you to keep a well-filled emergency shelf in your kitchen or pantry. Emergency is another word that has changed its inner shape; when Marion Harland and Fanny Farmer used it they meant unexpected guests. You may, too, in an ironical way, but you hope to God they are the kind who will never come.

It is often a delicate point, now, to decide when common sense ends and hoarding begins. Preparing a small stock of practical boxed and canned goods for a blackout shelf, in direct relation to the size of your family, is quite another thing from buying large quantities of bottled shrimps and canape wafers and meat pastes, or even unjustified amounts of more sensible foods.

Probably the best way to stock your shelf is to buy two cans of vegetables and so forth when you need only one, if your local rationing allows it. Make a list of what you would like to have, and gradually accumulate it, if you can afford to.

Even if you cannot afford to, try to put aside at least an Iron ration of a few cans of tomato juice, a box of cube sugar (to eat for warmth and quick energy), a little tea, a sealed box of whole-wheat wafers, some tinned beef.

When you buy in cans, remember that many of the prepared "luncheon loaves" are extremely salty. It is impractical to give your family such food in blackouts, especially if the toilet is far away or non-existent and the drinking water is limited.

A useful thing to have on your shelf is a supply of gingersnaps or vanilla wafers. [Much as I hate to admit it, weary English housewives have convinced me that packaged puddings are heaven-sent for such cookery: they have enough sugar in them to bolster energy, and even made with water they are palatable, at least to hungry and uneasy children and the gaffers.] These innocuous (or obnoxious, if you feel that way about them) cookies are useful at turning a can of fruit into a somewhat more nourishing and much more attractive dish, if you can put them all together and broil them for a few minutes, with the fruit on top. A little butter and brown sugar and even a dash of sherry will help.

Vanilla wafers may bring tears of anguish to the eyes of some self-respecting gourmets, but canned beef-gravy will make them sob aloud. And yet . . . may I be forgiven for admitting it . . . or may I? . . . canned beef-gravy is a "natural" for you if you have someone in your family who feels faint and weak unless he smells at least synthetic meat once a day. You can make many a good tricked dish, with a few mushrooms, some left-over rice, and a dash of wine, if you have one of those frightening, efficient cans of "rich brown *meat* gravy" on hand. It is spurious, maybe. It is chicanery. But it is economical and useful psychologically, especially if you are three miles from a market and the siren blows just as you are pumping up your bike-tire.

Another useful thing of doubtful origin for your blackout shelf is a moderate supply of cheeses in glass. The damnable things are fakes; they admit it on the labels . . . *simulated* Romano, Cheddar *type*, and so on. They are flatulently proud of being pasteurized. But they perform a special function, I think, in making people feel hungry. [I deplore the stupid over-use of monosodium glutamate, but in various "flavoring salts," called anything from Tang-oh to Mete-dee-lite, it does manage to lend a valuable if fleeting desirability to basically dull dishes.]

Cheese has always been a food that both sophisticated and simple humans love. And even if some doctors may not feel that it is wise to eat it, in a time of peril and unspoken fear it is an anesthetic and can make your guests, your own self, feel slightly stimulated by its unmistakable flavor and more than a little reassured to know that it still exists. Put a little bit on crackers, or on crisp toast if your oven is still working. Try it on a tired factory worker some day, or a nervous neighbor, with a glass of milk if possible or a cup of tea, and watch the unfolding of a lot of spiritual tendrils that were drawn up into a tight heedless tangle. [The lunch of draymen and farmers-at-market in French Switzerland is one of the best in the world: a slab of bread, a cut of slightly grainy mountain-cheese, a glass of thin white wine . . . I have seen it work miracles of restoration.]

If you are used to drinking, and can, it is pleasant to have whiskey or a good stable wine in your cupboard. A glass in your hand makes the ominous sky seem very high above you.

If by chance you want to be out in the streets, benefit by many a Londoner's experience and carry a little flask, since welcoming pubs are few and far between, and none too eager to open their doors even to old friends when unidentified planes are reported within sound of the listening posts.

(Do you remember that bar in Berne, during the Munich business, the night before what we all thought would be M-Day? There was a total blackout, and you went down a long hall through patent-leather curtains and then sat with a lot of other silent people in the dim room, while the tropical birds in the glass walls, which were really cages that imprisoned you caught in another and still another cage, flitted and screamed silently behind the glass. Everybody sat with a waiting look. It would have been better to stay away, probably.)

It is practical for blackouts, as well as for general "common sense in the kitchen" to cook more than you need for one meal. There are many simple recipes which can be made into a whole meal if you have some boiled rice handy, or some left-over green peas, or a bowl of cold cooked meat or spaghetti or almost anything you can think of (except maybe fried oysters!).

If you and your household are in a state of active emergency, you will survive, probably, without heat or light or anything but what you can scrape from the shelves. This picture is not one you care to dwell on, but it is a possibility. If it comes to that, no book on earth can help you, but only your inborn sense of caution and balance and protection: the same thing cats feel sometimes, or birds or elephants. Everything resolves itself into a feeling that you will survive if you are meant to survive, and every cell in your body believes that.

If you are not in a state of active emergency, but merely living as so many people have lived for many months now, taking sirens in your stride and ration cards with a small cautious grin, you will be able to make very good meals indeed for the people who live with you. As long as the gas or the electric current supply you, your stove will function and your kitchen will be warm and savory. Use as many fresh things as you can, always, and then trust to luck and your blackout cupboard and what you have decided, inside yourself, about the dignity of man.

How to Practice True Economy

Mere parsimony is not economy. . . . Expense, and great expense, may be an essential part of true economy.

—*Letters to a Noble Lord,* EDMUND BURKE, 1796

THERE is supposed to be something intrinsically satisfying about writing the last chapter of a book, even if it is written before the end. There should be something doubly so about writing of half-forgotten luxuries and half-remembered delicate impossible dishes at the end of a book of resolutely practical recipes for foxing the wolf and keeping him either at his proper distance, or well-jointed in a stew-pan. It should be like waking from a dream of your loved one, and finding perfume on your lips.

Such impossible delights are necessary, now and then, to your soul, and your body, too. You can cope with economy for only so long. ("So long" is one of those ambiguous phrases. It means "so long as you do not feel sick at the sight of a pocketbook.")

When you think you can stand no more of the wolf's snuffing under the door and keening softly on cold nights, throw discretion into the laundry bag, put candles on the table, and for your own good if not the pleasure of an admiring audience make one or another of the recipes in this chapter. And buy yourself a bottle of wine, or make a few cocktails, or have a long open-hearted discussion of cheeses with the man on the corner who is an alien but still loyal if bewildered.

It is plain that a great many of the things in the following recipes are impossible to find, now. That immediately puts the whole chapter in the same class as Samarkand and Xanadu and the *terrasse* of the

343

Café de la Paix. It is perhaps just as well; for a time there are other things than anchovies that must be far from actuality.

Sit back in your chair, then. Drop a few years from your troubled mind. Let the cupboard of your thoughts fill itself with a hundred ghosts that long ago, in 1939, used to be easy to buy and easy to forget. [This therapy, unconscious or deliberate, is known to any prisoner of war or woe, and some the the world's most delectable cookbooks have been written, at least conversationally and now and then actually, in concentration camps and cell-blocks.] Permit your disciplined inner self to relax, and think of caviar, and thick cream, and fat little pullets trotting through an oak grove rich with truffles, "musky, fiery, savory, mysterious." Close your eyes to the headlines and your ears to sirens and the threatenings of high explosives, and read instead the sweet nostalgic measures of these recipes, impossible yet fond.

SHRIMP PÂTÉ

4 *pounds fresh shelled cooked shrimp or 6 cans dry-pack shrimp*	3 *tablespoons lemon juice*
	½ *cup mayonnaise*
	salt, pepper, dry mustard,
1 *onion, minced very fine*	*whatever other spice you*
½ *cup melted butter*	*want*

[Now I use a full cup of melted butter, and more if the paste seems dry.]

Mash the clean shrimp very fine in a big bowl with a potato masher, and add the onion as you do it. When you can mash no more, pour in the melted butter, mixing it thoroughly. Add the lemon juice and mayonnaise, and continue to pound it. It will be a stiff paste. Season it highly: if you plan to use it within two days use fresh herbs at your discretion, but if you will be keeping it in the icebox use powdered condiments.

Pack the mixture into a mold, and press it down well. Chill it for at least twelve hours in an icebox. When you are ready to serve, turn it out and slice it thin with a sharp hot knife. [I used to eat potted shrimps by the scoopful, in a small swank restaurant in London. They were shelled, whole and tiny, held firmly together in a little fat jar by an aromatic butter. I should think San Francisco's "bay shrimps" would be almost as good for such a forthright accessory to the pleasures of the table . . . but the shrimps must indeed be tiny, no longer than a bee, no thicker than a violet's stem.]

Or leave it in the presentable mold, preferably an oblong one, and serve it slice by slice as the *maîtres d'hôtel* used to do in little places like the Roy Gourmet and big little places like Lipp's and enormous little places like the Ritz, or the Casino at Evian in summer. There are still a few restaurants in the world that can think about *pâtés de maison*, and one of the best of their heady, almost phosphorescent, pastes is made essentially after this recipe—with perhaps a bristol mortar instead of a plain bowl and potato masher, and a good dash of smooth ancient brandy to lace it all together, just before it is packed into the mold.

Such a paste can be kept for weeks or months, or perhaps even for years, if it contains enough spices and alcohol, is correctly sealed into its mold with coagulated fat, and is kept reasonably cold. Given these three prime benefits, it can be produced when you will, like a mad maiden aunt, or a first edition (in Russian, naturally) of *Crime and Punishment*.

Eggs with anchovies. Ah me, to put it mildly! The recipe comes from an American woman who, for various reasons both sociological and esthetic, lived in Switzerland before this war. Although she was almost a stranger to me, I admired her house and many of the meals she served there, high above the lake with the vineyards pressing as close as their Swiss discretion dared against the terrace and the kitchen and the wide windows. She was I . . . and her recipe was good.

EGGS WITH ANCHOVIES

8 *large fresh eggs*
2 *tins or 1 cup filet of anchovies*
3 *cups rich thick cream*
1 *cup broiled mushrooms (can be tinned) in pieces*

2 *tablespoons chopped parsley*
½ *cup grated Parmesan cheese*
fresh-ground pepper

Mash the filets of anchovies in the bottom of a shallow baking dish (save oil for a salad-dressing). Mix the cream with them, and put the dish in a hot oven.

Stir two or three times after it has started to bubble, turning in the golden crust. Add the mushrooms and the parsley.

When reduced about one-third, turn off the oven. Remove the dish, and break the eggs carefully into it. Put the cheese over them, and the pepper. Then put back into the lowest part of the oven, and when the gentle heat has made the eggs firm but not hard, usually in about fifteen minutes, remove and serve.

This recipe makes enough for three or four people, and is best with thin toast and a salad of little romaine hearts tossed lightly in seasoned walnut oil and lime juice. A recent Dazaley [This is spelled Dézaley. And, of course, the alcoholic pattern of another's feast would not be as Swiss as I made mine in 1942. Each to his own nostalgia! In the 1950's . . . would it start this way: an oily Dutch gin with the smoked salmon...?] at cellar temperature should be served amply with it, and with the coffee, strong and plentiful and preferably in café-glasses, you would undoubtedly have a *marc du Valais*, rather yellow and well able to jar your guests slightly where they sit.

The first sip would be polite. The second would be dogged. The rest would be good robust happiness, especially after the bland delicacy of the supper. The summer fireworks would start across the lake at Evian, and the baker boy who worked at night in Vevey would come hurtling down the road on his bicycle, yelling like a hilarious banshee as he took the curves of the Corniche. The marc would make a warmth in you that might well last for several colder years.

Bœuf Moreno, like Eggs with Anchovies, or any other good recipe, needs no nostalgic introduction except the one you will always give it in your mind, after the first time you eat it. It is, like so many of the classics [. . . as well as in the undying perfection of the Laws of Moses] a hideous combination dietetically, and well worth trying.

BŒUF MORENO

2 *tablespoons butter*
2 *tablespoons flour*
¾ *cup stock*
4 *tablespoons mixed parsley and chopped green onion or chives*
½ *cup mushrooms or pitted olives*
2 *tablespoons butter*

2 *tablespoons chopped green pepper or pimiento*
1 *pound left-over steak or roast beef, 2 inches thick, cut in thin strips*
½ *cup sour cream [I have now increased this to one cup.]*
3 *tablespoons brandy or whiskey*
hot rice or toast

Make a roux of the butter, flour, and stock. Add the onion and parsley, and simmer in a double broiler 20 minutes. Season.

Heat the peppers and mushrooms in 2 Tablespoons butter in the bottom of a shallow casserole. Add the thin slices of beef and heat thoroughly.

Add the cream slowly to the roux, and stir in the brandy. Pour over the meat in the casserole. Serve at once, with hot fluffy rice or thin buttered toast.

A casserole which always makes me think of valentines, for no good reason, is made with young chicken and cream and is a fine way to ask "Will you be my love?"

POULET À LA MODE DE BEAUNE

1 *tender chicken of about three pounds, cut in pieces*
½ *lemon*
  mixture of butter and olive oil [or chicken-fat from an earlier feast . . . and what is left makes a fine thing, once chilled, to eat upon good bread or toast.]

salt *and fresh pepper and a little nutmeg*
1 *pint rich cream*
1 *dozen large mushrooms*
3 *tablespoons butter*
½ *cup fine brandy or marc*

Scrub the pieces of chicken thoroughly with the cut lemon. Dry, season, and fry thoroughly to a golden brown in the mixture of butter and oil.

Place the pieces in a casserole, and cover with the heated cream. Let cook in a moderate oven until tender.

Put butter in each mushroom cap, which has been washed quickly but not peeled, and cover the contents of the casserole with them. Broil quickly until done, about five minutes. Then quickly stir the mushrooms and the brandy into the casserole, and serve at once.

This is a rich and heady dish, as you can see. It needs a very cold and somewhat heavy white wine, like a Haut Sauternes. Or champagne will do nicely!

A refreshing delicate dessert that yet does not taste too sensible is indeed a rarity. Ices after heaviness are good, as the Italian cooks who first brought them to the French well knew, but they can seem overly thin. Fruit is the same, almost too natural and shocking after the high perverted flavors of some such masterpiece as Bœuf Moreno.

But since a pudding or a soufflé would be unthinkable, why not serve thick slices of fresh pineapple soaked for several hours in an Alsatian *kirschwasser*, and then topped with a sherbet made with lime juice?

I ate this once in the richly muted dining room of a beautiful woman, and drank a dry champagne with it, and even if there had not been caviar in a big bowl long before, and little orchids like moths flying from a pink ruffled shell on the table, it would have been one of the perfect things of my gastronomic life.

The following recipe is very old, as age goes here. It was made often in Williamsburg, before there was any need of restoration, and undoubtedly pleased many a high-living Father of Our Country, both great and small.

COLONIAL DESSERT

2 *cups thick cream*   1 *cup brown sugar*
4 *egg yolks*

Boil the cream one minute. Pour over the well-beaten egg yolks. Heat in a double boiler 8 minutes, beating constantly. Pour into a shallow dish from which it will be served, and chill overnight.

Two hours before serving cover with a half-inch layer of brown sugar, and brown very quickly under a hot broiler. Chill again, and serve with thin crisp cookies such as langues de chat.

A salad made of fruits, you could call the following eccentric dish. Paul Reboux, that antic gourmet, evolved it in his inimitable *cuisine au cerveau*, and called it, in the days when such things were slightly less impossible than now,

FRUITS AUX SEPT LIQUEURS

Put into an ample bowl the following: slices of orange, tangerines, and bananas; pitted cherries; wood strawberries and peeled grapes; sliced peeled peaches and plums and ripe pears. Sprinkle them with sugar and a little lime juice.

Pour over them the following liquid, which has been made of a wineglassful each of the following but no other liqueurs, all mixed thoroughly together: brandy, kirsch, cointreau, benedictine, maraschino, and a touch of kümmel.

Stir the salad lightly, and put on ice for two hours. Just before serving, pour half a bottle of demi-sec *champagne over it.*

Yes, it is crazy, to sit savoring such impossibilities, while headlines yell at you and the wolf whuffs through the keyhole. Yet now and then it cannot harm you, thus to enjoy a short respite from reality. And if by chance you can indeed find some anchovies, or a thick slice of rare beef and some brandy, or a bowl of pink curled shrimps, you are doubly blessed, to possess in this troubled life both the capacity and the wherewithal to forget it for a time.

Conclusion

[THIS BOOK came to its own conclusion several years ago, and upon rereading it I myself have reached a few more. But both the book and I agree, on one point made much further back than 1942, that since we must eat to live, we might as well do it with both grace and gusto.

Those few of us who actually live to eat are less repulsive than boring, and at this date I honestly know of only two such lost souls, gross puffy creatures, both of them, who are exhibited like any other monstrous curiosity by their well-fed but still balanced acquaintances.

On the other hand, I cannot count the good people I know who, to my mind, would be even better if they bent their spirits to the study of their own hungers. There are too many of us, otherwise in proper focus, who feel an impatience for the demands of our bodies, and who try throughout our whole lives, none too success-fully, to deafen ourselves to the voices of our various hungers. Some stuff the wax of religious solace in our ears. Others practice a Spartan if somewhat pretentious disinterest in the pleasures of the flesh, or pretend that if we do not *admit our* sensual delight in a ripe nectarine we are not guilty . . . of even that tiny lust!

I believe that one of the most dignified ways we are capable of, to assert and then reassert our dignity in the face of poverty and war's fears and pains, is to nourish ourselves with all possible skill, delicacy, and ever-increasing enjoyment. And with our gastronomical growth will come, inevitably, knowledge and perception of a hundred other things, but mainly of ourselves. Then Fate, even tangled as it is with cold wars as well as hot, cannot harm us.]

1943

The Gastronomical Me

> To be happy you must have taken
> the measure of your powers, tasted the
> fruits of your passion, and learned
> your place in the world.
> —Santayana

Foreword

PEOPLE ask me: Why do you write about food, and eating and drinking? Why don't you write about the struggle for power and security, and about love, the way others do?

They ask it accusingly, as if I were somehow gross, unfaithful to the honor of my craft.

The easiest answer is to say that, like most other humans, I am hungry. But there is more than that. It seems to me that our three basic needs, for food and security and love, are so mixed and mingled and entwined that we cannot straightly think of one without the others. So it happens that when I write of hunger, I am really writing about love and the hunger for it, and warmth and the love of it and the hunger for it . . . and then the warmth and richness and fine reality of hunger satisfied . . . and it is all one.

I tell about myself, and how I ate bread on a lasting hillside, or drank red wine in a room now blown to bits, and it happens without my willing it that I am telling too about the people with me then, and their other deeper needs for love and happiness.

There is food in the bowl, and more often than not, because of what honesty I have, there is nourishment in the heart, to feed the wilder, more insistent hungers. We must eat. If, in the face of that dread fact, we can find other nourishment, and tolerance and compassion for it, we'll be no less full of human dignity.

There is a communion of more than our bodies when bread is broken and wine drunk. And that is my answer, when people ask me: Why do you write about hunger, and not wars or love?

M. F. K. F.

The Measure of My Powers

1912

THE first thing I remember tasting and then wanting to taste again is the grayish-pink fuzz my grandmother skimmed from a spitting kettle of strawberry jam. I suppose I was about four.

Women in those days made much more of a ritual of their household duties than they do now. Sometimes it was indistinguishable from a dogged if unconscious martyrdom. There were times for This, and other equally definite times for That. There was one set week a year for "the sewing woman." Of course, there was Spring Cleaning. And there were other periods, almost like festivals in that they disrupted normal life, which were observed no matter what the weather, finances, or health of the family.

Many of them seem odd or even foolish to me now, but probably the whole staid rhythm lent a kind of rich excitement to the housebound flight of time.

With us, for the first years of my life, there was a series, every summer, of short but violently active cannings. Crates and baskets and lug-boxes of fruits bought in their prime and at their cheapest would lie waiting with opulent fragrance on the screened porch, and a whole battery of enameled pots and ladles and wide-mouthed funnels would appear from some dark cupboard.

All I knew then about the actual procedure was that we had delightful picnic meals while Grandmother and Mother and the cook worked with a kind of drugged concentration in our big dark kitchen, and were tired and cross and at the same time oddly triumphant in their race against summer heat and the processes of rot.

Now I know that strawberries came first, mostly for jam. Sour red cherries for pies and darker ones for preserves were a little later,

354

and then came the apricots. They were for jam if they were very ripe, and the solid ones were simply "put up." That, in my grandmother's language, meant cooking with little sugar, to eat for breakfast or dessert in the winter which she still thought of in terms of northern Iowa.

She was a grim woman, as if she had decided long ago that she could thus most safely get to Heaven. I have a feeling that my Father might have liked to help with the cannings, just as I longed to. But Grandmother, with that almost joyfully stern bowing to duty typical of religious women, made it clear that helping in the kitchen was a bitter heavy business forbidden certainly to men, and generally to children. Sometimes she let me pull stems off the cherries, and one year when I was almost nine I stirred the pots a little now and then, silent and making myself as small as possible.

But there was no nonsense anyway, no foolish chitchat. Mother was still young and often gay, and the cook too . . . and with Grandmother directing operations they all worked in a harried muteness . . . stir, sweat, hurry. It was a pity. Such a beautifully smelly task should be fun, I thought.

In spite of any Late Victorian asceticism, though, the hot kitchen sent out tantalizing clouds, and the fruit on the porch lay rotting in its crates, or readied for the pots and the wooden spoons, in fair glowing piles upon the juice-stained tables. Grandmother, saving always, stood like a sacrificial priestess in the steam, "skimming" into a thick white saucer, and I, sometimes permitted and more often not, put my finger into the cooling froth and licked it. Warm and sweet and odorous. I loved it, then.

A Thing Shared

1918

Now you can drive from Los Angeles to my Great-Aunt Maggie's ranch on the other side of the mountains in a couple of hours or so, but the first time I went there it took most of a day.

Now the roads are worthy of even the All-Year-Round Club's boasts, but twenty-five years ago, in the September before people thought peace had come again, you could hardly call them roads at all. Down near the city they were oiled, all right, but as you went farther into the hills toward the wild desert around Palmdale, they turned into rough dirt. Finally they were two wheel-marks skittering every which way through the Joshua trees.

It was very exciting: the first time my little round brown sister Anne and I had ever been away from home. Father drove us up from home with Mother in the Ford, so that she could help some cousins can fruit.

We carried beer for the parents (it exploded in the heat), and water for the car and Anne and me. We had four blowouts, but that was lucky, Father said as he patched the tires philosophically in the hot sun; he'd expected twice as many on such a long hard trip.

The ranch was wonderful, with wartime crews of old men and loud-voiced boys picking the peaches and early pears all day, and singing and rowing at night in the bunkhouses. We couldn't go near them or near the pen in the middle of a green alfalfa field where a new prize bull, black as thunder, pawed at the pale sand.

We spent most of our time in a stream under the cottonwoods, or with Old Mary the cook, watching her make butter in a great

356

churn between her mountainous knees. She slapped it into pats, and put them down in the stream where it ran hurriedly through the darkness of the butter-house.

She put stone jars of cream there, too, and wire baskets of eggs and lettuces, and when she drew them up, like netted fish, she would shake the cold water onto us and laugh almost as much as we did.

Then Father had to go back to work. It was decided that Mother would stay at the ranch and help put up more fruit, and Anne and I would go home with him. That was as exciting as leaving it had been, to be alone with Father for the first time.

He says now that he was scared daft at the thought of it, even though our grandmother was at home as always to watch over us. He says he actually shook as he drove away from the ranch, with us like two suddenly strange small monsters on the hot seat beside him.

Probably he made small talk. I don't remember. And he didn't drink any beer, sensing that it would be improper before two un-chaperoned young ladies.

We were out of the desert and into deep winding canyons before the sun went down. The road was a little smoother, following streambeds under the live-oaks that grow in all the gentle creases of the dry tawny hills of that part of California. We came to a shack where there was water for sale, and a table under the dark wide trees.

Father told me to take Anne down the dry streambed a little way. That made me feel delightfully grown-up. When we came back we held our hands under the water faucet and dried them on our panties, which Mother would never have let us do.

Then we sat on a rough bench at the table, the three of us in the deep green twilight, and had one of the nicest suppers I have ever eaten.

The strange thing about it is that all three of us have told other people that same thing, without ever talking of it among ourselves until lately. Father says that all his nervousness went away, and he saw us for the first time as two little brown humans who were fun. Anne and I both felt a subtle excitement at being alone for the first time with the only man in the world we loved.

(We loved Mother too, completely, but we were finding out, as Father was too, that it is good for parents and for children to be alone now and then with one another . . . the man alone or the woman, to sound new notes in the mysterious music of parenthood and childhood.)

That night I not only saw my Father for the first time as a person. I saw the golden hills and the live-oaks as clearly as I have ever seen them since; and I saw the dimples in my little sister's fat hands in a way that still moves me because of that first time; and I saw food as something beautiful to be shared with people instead of as a thrice-daily necessity.

I forget what we ate, except for the end of the meal. It was a big round peach pie, still warm from Old Mary's oven and the ride over the desert. It was deep, with lots of juice, and bursting with ripe peaches picked that noon. Royal Albertas, Father said they were. The crust was the most perfect I have ever tasted, except perhaps once upstairs at Simpson's in London, on a hot plum tart.

And there was a quart Mason jar, the old-fashioned bluish kind like Mexican glass, full of cream. It was still cold, probably because we all knew the stream it had lain in, Old Mary's stream.

Father cut the pie in three pieces and put them on white soup plates in front of us, and then spooned out the thick cream. We ate with spoons too, blissful after the forks we were learning to use with Mother.

And we ate the whole pie, and all the cream . . . we can't remember if we gave any to the shadowy old man who sold water . . . and then drove on sleepily toward Los Angeles, and none of us said anything about it for many years, but it was one of the best meals we ever ate.

Perhaps that is because it was the first conscious one, for me at least; but the fact that we remember it with such queer clarity must mean that it had other reasons for being important. I suppose that happens at least once to every human. I hope so.

Now the hills are cut through with super-highways, and I can't say whether we sat that night in Mint Canyon or Bouquet, and the three of us are in some ways even more than twenty-five years older than we were then. And still the warm round peach pie and the cool yellow cream we ate together that August night live in our hearts' palates, succulent, secret, delicious.

The Measure of My Powers

1919

I KNOW a beautiful honey-colored actress who is a gourmande, in a pleasant way. She loves to cook rich hot lavish meals. She does it well, too.

She is slender, fragile, with a mute otherwordly pathos in her large azure eyes, and she likes to invite a lot of oddly assorted and usually famous people to a long table crowded with flowers, glasses, dishes of nuts, bowls of Armenian jelly and Russian relishes and Indian chutney, and beer and wine and even water, and then bring in a huge bowl of oxtail stew with dumplings. She has spent days making it, with special spices she found in Bombay or Soho or Honolulu, and she sits watching happily while it disappears. Then she disappears herself, and in a few minutes staggers to the table with a baked Alaska as big as a washtub, a thing of beauty, and a joy for about fifteen minutes.

But this star-eyed slender gourmande has a daughter about eight or nine, and the daughter *hates* her mother's sensuous dishes. In fact, she grows spindly on them. The only way to put meat on her bones is to send her to stay for a week or two with her grandmother, where she eats store ice cream for lunch, mashed potatoes for supper, hot white pap for breakfast.

"*My* daughter!" the actress cries in despair and horror. I tell her there is still hope, with the passage of time. But she, perhaps because of her beauty, pretends Time is not.

The truth is, I think, that small children have very sensitive palates. A little pepper is to them what a highly spiced curry is to us. They can stand sweetness best, perhaps, but anything sour or spiced is actually painful to them.

359

The ability of an adult to enjoy a subtle goulash or a red-hot enchilada or even a well-hung bird is due partly to his dulled taste buds, calloused by other such delightful ordeals and the constant stupefaction of alcohol and cigaret smoke. Young humans, not yet tough, can taste bland delight in dishes that would sicken older men.

On the other hand, it is wrong to think that children with any spirit and intelligence welcome complete monotony. I know that, because I remember most clearly a cook we had when I was about nine, named Ora.

My grandmother, who oddly seems to have been connected with whatever infantine gastronomy I knew, spent the last thirty years of her life dying of some obscure internal ailment until a paralytic stroke finished her in four days. She was a vigorous woman, tight with repressed emotions, and probably had a "nervous stomach." She spent a lot of time at sanatoria, often genuinely ill, and when she was with us we had to follow her dietary rules, probably to our benefit: no fried things or pastries, no oils, no seasonings.

Grandmother, a handsome dignified old lady, had been told by her doctors to belch whenever she felt like it, which she did . . . long voluptuous Gargantuan belches, anywhere and any time at all, which unless you knew Grandmother would have led you to believe that our table was one of fabulous delights. And once, for a few weeks, it was. That was during Ora's sojourn in our kitchen.

Ora was a spare gray-haired woman, who kept herself to herself in a firm containment. She took her afternoons and Sundays off without incident or comment, and kept her small hot room as neat as her person. The rest of the time she spent in a kind of ecstasy in the kitchen.

She loved to cook, the way some people love to pray, or dance, or fight. She preferred to be let alone, even for the ordering of food, and made it clear that the meals were her business. They were among the best I have ever eaten . . . all the things we had always accepted as food, but presented in ways that baffled and delighted us.

Grandmother hated her. I don't know any real reasons, of course, after such a long time, but I think it was because Ora was not like the friendly stupid hired girls she thought were proper for middle-class kitchens. And then Ora did things to "plain good food" that made it exciting and new and delightful, which in my poor grandmother's stern asceticism meant that Ora was wrong.

"Eat what's set before you, and be thankful for it," Grandmother said often; or in other words, "Take what God has created and eat it humbly and without sinful pleasure."

Most of the things Ora brought to the table Grandmother professed to be unable to touch. Her belches grew uncompromisingly louder, and she lived on rice water and tomatoes stewed with white bread.

"The girl is ruining you," she would say to Mother when Monday's hash appeared in some new delicious camouflage. But the bills were no larger, Mother must confess.

"The children will be bilious before another week," Grandmother would remark dourly. But we were healthier than ever.

"Their table manners are getting worse," Grandmother observed between belches. And that was true, if you believed as she and unhappy millions of Anglo-Saxons have been taught to believe, that food should be consumed without comment of any kind but above all without sign of praise or enjoyment.

My little sister Anne and I had come in Ora's few weeks with us to watch every plate she served, and to speculate with excitement on what it would taste like. "Oh, *Mother*," we would exclaim in a kind of anguish of delight. "There are little stars, all made of pie crust! They have seeds on them! Oh, how beautiful! How good!"

Mother grew embarrassed, and finally stern; after all, she had been raised by Grandmother. She talked to us privately, and told us how unseemly it was for little children to make comments about food, especially when the cook could hear them. "You've never behaved this way before," she said, thereby admitting the lack of any reason to, until then.

We contented ourselves with silent glances of mutual bliss and, I really think, an increased consciousness of the possibilities of the table.

I was very young, but I can remember observing, privately of course, that meat hashed with a knife is better than meat mauled in a food-chopper; that freshly minced herbs make almost any good thing better; that chopped celery tastes different from celery in the stalk, just as carrots in thin curls and toast in crescents are infinitely more appetizing than in thick chunks and squares.

There were other less obvious things I decided, about using condiments besides salt and pepper, about the danger of monotony . . .

things like that. But it is plain that most of my observations were connected in some way with Ora's knife.

She did almost everything with it, cut, and carved, and minced, and chopped, and even used it to turn things in the oven, as if it were part of her hand. It was a long one, with a bright curved point. She brought it with her to our house, and called it her French knife. That was one more thing Grandmother disliked about her; it was a wicked affectation to have a "French" knife, and take it everywhere as if it were alive, and spend all the spare time polishing and sharpening it.

We had an old woman named Mrs. Kemp come to the house every Saturday morning, to wash Grandmother's beautiful white hair and sometimes ours, and she and Grandmother must have talked together about Ora. Mrs. Kemp announced that she would no longer come through the kitchen to keep her appointments. She didn't like "that girl," she said. Ora scared her, always sitting so haughty sharpening that wicked knife.

So Mrs. Kemp came in the front door, and Anne and I kept our tongues politely silent and our mouths open like little starved birds at every meal, and Grandmother belched rebelliously, and I don't remember what Mother and Father did, except eat of course.

Then, one Sunday, Ora didn't come back with her usual remote severity from her day off. Mother was going to have a baby fairly soon, and Grandmother said, "You see? That girl is way above herself! She simply doesn't want to be in the house with a nurse!"

Grandmother was pleased as Punch, and that night for supper we probably had her favorite dish, steamed soda crackers with hot milk.

The next day, though, we found that Ora, instead of leaving her mother after a quiet pleasant Sunday in which the two elderly women had gone to church and then rested, had cut her into several neat pieces with the French knife.

Then she ripped a tent thoroughly to ribbons. I don't know how the tent came in . . . maybe she and her mother were resting in it. Anyway, it was a good thing to rip.

Then Ora cut her wrists and her own throat, expertly. The police told Father there wasn't a scratch or a nick in the knife.

Mrs. Kemp, and probably Grandmother too, felt righteous. "I just *felt* something," Mrs. Kemp would say, for a long time after Ora left.

I don't know about Father and Mother, but Anne and I were depressed. The way of dying was of only passing interest to us at our ages, but our inevitable return to ordinary sensible plain food was something to regret. We were helpless then, but we both learned from mad Ora, and now we know what to do about it, because of her.

The Measure of My Powers

1919–1927

THE first thing I cooked was pure poison. I made it for Mother, after my little brother David was born, and within twenty minutes of the first swallow she was covered with great itching red welts. The doctor came, soda compresses were laid on, sedatives and mild physic were scattered about, and all subsided safely . . . except my feeling of deep shock and hurt professional pride. As the nurse, Miss Faulck, pointed out, I should have been content to let well enough alone.

The pudding was safe enough: a little round white shuddering milky thing I had made that morning under the stern eye of Miss Faulck and whoever it was that succeeded mad Ora in the kitchen. It had "set" correctly. It was made according to the directions for Invalid Cookery in Mother's best recipe book, and I had cleaned my fingernails until tears filled my eyes before I touched so much as the box of cornstarch.

Then, in the middle of the afternoon, when the pudding slid with a chill plop into the saucer, I knew that I could not stand to present it, my first culinary triumph, in its naked state. It was obscenely pure, obscenely colorless.

A kind of loyalty to Ora rose in me, and without telling Miss Faulck I ran into the back yard and picked ten soft ripe blackberries. I blew off the alley-dust, and placed them gently in a perfect circle around the little pudding. Its cool perfection leaped into sudden prettiness, like Miss America when the winning ribbon is hung across her high-breasted symmetry.

And even a little while later, when Mother lay covered with compresses and Miss Faulck pursed her lips and David howled for a meal he couldn't have because he might drink hive-juice, Mother

364

smiled at my shocked anxious confusion, and said, "Don't worry, sweet . . . it was the loveliest pudding I have ever seen."

I agreed with her in spite of the despair.

I can't remember ever learning anything, that is, I don't hear Mother's voice saying to me, "Now this is a teaspoon, and this is the way you sift flour, and warm eggs won't make mayonnaise . . ." But evidently I loved to cook, and she taught me several things without making them into lessons, because in the next few years I knew how to make white sauce, and cup cakes with grated orange rind in them. (Father was always very complimentary about them, and Anne and I loved to save ours until the rest of the family had left the table, and then cover them with cream and sugar and eat them with a spoon.)

I could make jelly rolls, too, which seems odd now; I don't think I've even tasted one since I was about ten, much less had any interest in putting one together.

I loved to read cookbooks (unlike my feeling for jelly roll that passion has grown stronger with the years), and inevitably I soon started to improve on what I had read. Once I made poor Anne share my proud misery with something I called Hindu Eggs. I was sure I had read about it in Fanny Farmer; all you did was add curry powder to a white sauce and pour it over sliced hardboiled eggs.

When Mother said she and Father would be away one night, and I might get supper alone, I hid the gleam in my eye when she told me to put the sauce and the eggs in a casserole, and be sure to drink milk, and open a jar of plums or something for dessert.

"Yes, Mother, I know I can do it," I said smoothly, and the word *Hindu* danced sensuously in my mind, safely unsaid until Mother was out of the house.

The casserole was handsome, too, when Anne and I sat down to it in exciting solitude at the big table. Anne admired me, there was no doubt of it . . . and I admired myself. The rich brown sauce bubbled and sent out puffs of purely Oriental splendor. I sat in Father's place, and served each of us generously.

The first bite, and perhaps the next two or three, were all right; we were hungry, and in a hurry to feel the first warmth in our little bellies. Then Anne put down her fork. She beat me to it, so I continued to hold mine, determined like any honest cook to support my product.

"It's too hot, it burns," my little sister said, and gulped at her milk. "Blow on it," I instructed. "Mother's not here."

We blew, and I ate three more bites to Anne's dutiful one. The heat seemed to increase. My influence over Anne must have been persuasive as well as autocratic in those far days, because she ate most of what was on her plate before the tears started rolling down her round brown cheeks.

I ate all mine, proudly, but inside I was cold with the new knowledge that I had been stupid. I had thought I remembered a recipe when I didn't, and I had used curry without knowing anything about it, and when the sauce looked boringly white I had proceeded to make it richly darker with probably five tablespoonfuls of the exotic powder.

I ate all I could, for fear Father would see how much we threw into the garbage pail, and then after my sweet forgiving little sister helped me straighten the kitchen we went upstairs and, with the desperate intuition of burned animals, sat on the edge of the bathtub for a long time with our mouths full of mineral oil. She never said anything more about it, either; and the next morning there were only a few blisters, just inside our lips.

When I was eleven we all moved to the country. We had a cow, and chickens, and partly because of that and partly because Grandmother had died we began to eat more richly.

We had chocolate puddings with chopped nuts and heavy cream. The thought of them makes me dizzy now, but we loved them. And lots of butter: I was good at churning, and learned very well how to sterilize the wooden churn and make the butter and then roll it into fine balls and press it into molds. I liked that. And we could have mayonnaise, rich yellow with eggs and oil, instead of the boiled dressing Grandmother's despotic bowels and stern palate called for.

Mother, in an orgy of baking brought on probably by all the beautiful eggs and butter lying around, spent every Saturday morning making cakes. They were piled high with icings. They were filled with crushed almonds, chopped currants, and an outrageous number of calories. They were beautiful. Saturday afternoons they sat cooling, along with Mother and the kitchen after the hectic morning, and by Sunday night they were already a pleasant if somewhat bilious memory.

After about a year of this luscious routine, Mother retired more or less permanently to the front part of the house, perhaps with half an eye on the bathroom scales, but before she gave up cooking, I learned a lot about cakes from her. The fact that I have never made one since then—at least, the kind with many layers and fillings and icings and all that—has little to do with the gratitude I have often felt for knowing how to measure and sift and be patient and not be daunted by disappointment.

Mother, like all artists, was one-sided. She only cooked what she herself liked. She knew very little about meats, so I gradually learned all that myself. She hated gravies, and any sauces but "white sauce" (probably a hangover from Grandmother's training), so I made some hideous mistakes with them. And there was always an element of surprise, if not actual danger, in my meals; the Hindu eggs had larned me but not curbed my helpless love of anything rare or racy.

But in spite of all that, I was the one who got dinner on the cook's off-night. I improved, there is no doubt about it, and it was taken for granted that I would step into the kitchen at the drop of a hat.

Perhaps Anne would have liked a chance at having all the family's attention for those few hours. If so she never got it. The stove, the bins, the cupboards, I had learned forever, make an inviolable throne room. From them I ruled; temporarily I controlled. I felt powerful, and I loved that feeling.

I am more modest now, but I still think that one of the pleasantest of all emotions is to know that I, I with my brain and my hands, have nourished my beloved few, that I have concocted a stew or a story, a rarity or a plain dish, to sustain them truly against the hungers of the world.

The First Oyster

1924

THE intramural complexities of the faculty at Miss Huntingdon's School for Girls have become much clearer to me since I left there, but even at sixteen I knew that Mrs. Cheever's social position was both uncomfortable and lonely.

She had her own office, which was certainly more than any snobbish Latin teacher could boast. She was listed as part of the school's administration in the discreet buff and sepia catalog; I cannot remember now just what her title was, except that it implied with high-sounding ambiguity that she was the housekeeper without, of course, using that vulgar word itself.

She was a college graduate, even though it was from some domestic-science school instead of Smith or Mount Holyoke.

She was, above all, a lady.

She was almost a super-lady, mainly because it was so obvious that the rest of the faculty, administration as well as teachers, considered her a cook. When she stepped occasionally after dinner into the library, where I as an honor Sophomore was privileged to carry demitasses to the Seniors and the teachers on alternate Wednesday nights, I could see that she was snubbed almost as thoroughly as her well-fed colleagues snubbed the school nurse, one notch below the housekeeper on the social scale but also a colleague as far as the catalog went.

No malicious, inverted, discontented boarding-school teacher on God's earth, however, could snub the poor nurse as much as Mrs. Cheever could. Her coarsely genteel face under its Queen Mary coiffure expressed with shocking clarity the loathing she felt for that gentle ninny who dealt out pills and sticking plasters, and all the loneliness and bitter social insecurity of her own position showed in the way Mrs. Cheever stood proudly alone in the crowded library, smiling with delicacy and frightful pleasure at the nurse, whose hand

368

trembled clumsily as she sipped at her little coffee cup and tried to look like a college graduate.

The two women studiously spoke to no one, mainly because no one spoke to them. Perhaps once or twice, long since, the nurse may have said a timid nothing to the housekeeper, but Mrs. Cheever would have bitten out her own tongue before loosening it in charity toward a sister outcast.

Once it almost looked as if she would have a friend on the faculty, when a new gym teacher came. So often athletic people were not exactly . . . that is, they seldom had M.A.'s, even if they seemed really quite lady-like at times. And Mrs. Cheever felt sure that the new colleague would be as scornful as she was herself of all the pretentious schoolma'ams, with their airs and graces.

But after the first week, during which the little gym teacher stood shyly by the housekeeper for coffee, or nibbled in her room on the pink grapes and small frosted cakes that Mrs. Cheever sent her, the other women discovered that not only was she from Barnard . . . *summa cum laude, parbleu!* . . . but that she had the most adorable little cracked voice, almost like a boy's. It was perfect with her hair, so short and boyish too, and by the end of the second week three of the teachers were writing passionate notes to her, and Mrs. Cheever once more stood magnificently alone on her occasional visits to the library after dinner.

Perhaps loneliness made her own food bitter to her, because Mrs. Cheever was an obvious dyspeptic. The rest of us, however: Miss Huntingdon herself, remote and saint-like; Miss Blake, her shadow, devoted, be-wigged, a skin-and-bone edition of Krafft-Ebing; all the white women of the school, fat, thin, frantic or calm, and all the Filipino servants, pretty little men-dolls as mercurial as monkeys, and as lewd; all the girls, who felt like victims but were really the *raison d'être* of this strange collection within the high walls . . . Mrs. Cheever fed us four times a day with probably the best institutional food in America.

She ran her kitchens with such skill that in spite of ordinary domestic troubles like flooded basements and soured cream, and even an occasional extraordinary thing like the double murder and hara-kiri committed by the head-boy one Good Friday, our meals were never late and never bad.

There were about seventy boarders and twenty-five women, and for morning-recess lunch a pack of day-girls, and most of us ate with the delicacy and appreciation of half-starved animals. It must have been sickening to Mrs. Cheever to see us literally wolfing her well-planned, well-cooked, well-served dishes. For in spite of doing things wholesale, which some gastronomers say is impossible with any finesse, the things we ate at Miss Huntingdon's were savory and interesting.

Mrs. Cheever, for instance, would get a consignment of strange honey from the Torrey pine trees, honey which only a few people in the world were supposed to have eaten. I remember it now with some excitement, as a grainy greenish stuff like some I once ate near Adelboden in the Bernese Alps, but then it was to most of us just something sweet and rather queer to put on hot biscuits. Tinned orange marmalade would have done as well.

At Thanksgiving she would let the Filipinos cover the breakfast tables with dozens of odd, beautiful little beasts they had made from vegetables and fruits and nuts, so that the dining room became for a while amazingly funny to us, and we were allowed to make almost as much noise as we wanted while we ate forbidden things like broiled sausage and played with the crazy toys. The boys would try not to laugh too, and even Mrs. Cheever would incline her queenly topknot less scornfully than usual when spoken to.

Saturday noons we could eat sandwiches and cocoa or pink punch on the hockey field, and have ice cream from the soda fountain in the village if we told Mrs. Cheever between eight and nine that morning. I sometimes went without it, or got another girl to order for me, simply because I could not bear to go into the little office and have the housekeeper look at me. She made me feel completely unattractive, which is even worse at sixteen than later.

She would sit stiffly at her desk, waiting for orders with an expression of such cold impersonal nausea on her face that I could hardly believe the gossip that she had made a fat sum weekly by charging us almost double what the drug store got for its cartons of ice cream and its incredibly sweet sauces.

She would make precise notations on a sheet of paper while we mumbled our orders, and sometimes even suggested in her flat clear voice that salted pecans might be better than strawberry syrup on chocolate-icecream-with-butter-scotch-sauce. Her expression of remote anguish never changed, even when she reminded us, with her eyes resting coldly on a bulging behind or a spotty chin, that we were limited to one pint apiece.

It was for festivals like Easter and Old Girls' Day, though, that she really exercised her talents. Now I can see that she must have filled many hours of snubbed isolation in plans for our pleasure, but then I only knew that parties at Miss Huntingdon's School for Girls were really fun, mostly because the food was so good. Mrs. Cheever, callously ignored by the girls except for a few minutes each Saturday morning, and smiled at condescendingly by her unwilling colleagues with university degrees, turned out rare bats into what could truly be called small gastronomic triumphs . . . and the more so because they were what they were within high walls.

Old Girls' Day, for instance, meant to all but the Seniors, who had to be nice to the returning alumnae, that we spent a long gray warm June day on the sand and the rocks, and that we could wear our full pleated gym-bloomers and *no stockings*, and take pictures of each other with our Brownies, and, best of all, that at half past noon a procession of house-boys would come down the cliffs from the school with our lunch for us in big baskets.

There would be various things, of course, like pickles and napkins and knives and probably sandwiches and fruit, although how Mrs. Cheever managed it with the school full of hungry shrieking postgraduates is more than I can guess. Perhaps she even sent down devilled eggs to make it a real picnic.

I don't remember, because all that we thought about then, or could recall now if we ever dared to think at all of those days, were the hot crisp fried halves of young chickens, stiff and tempting. We could have all we wanted, even three or four, and we could eat with our fingers, and yell, and gobble. It was wonderful.

There must have been chaperones, but they seemed not to exist down there in the warmth and the silly freedom, and when a stately figure stood for an instant on the cliff top, wrapped fussily in an afternoon gown for the Old Girls, and looked down at us with her face set in a sour chill smile, we waved our greasy drumsticks hilariously up at her, and cried,

> *Miss-is Chee-ver*
> *Miss-is Chee-ver*
> *Miss-is Chee-ver*
> *Rah-ah-ah-ah,*

almost as if she were a whole basketball game between the Golds and the Purples. For one moment, at least, in the year, we were grateful to her for our deliciously full mouths.

She did her conscientious best to be sensible in her menus, and fed us better garden things and fresher cream and milk than most of us have eaten since, but there must have been a dreadful impatience in her for such pap, so that occasionally she would give us the Torrey pine-honey for breakfast, or have the Chinese cook put chives over the Friday fish instead of a cream sauce.

Once, for the Christmas Party, she served Eastern oysters, fresh oysters, oysters still in their shells.

Nothing could have been more exotic in the early twenties in Southern California. The climate was still considered tropical, so that shellfish imported alive from the East were part of an oil-magnate's dream, or perhaps something to be served once or twice a year at Victor Hugo's, in a private room with pink candleshades and a canary. And of course any local molluscs were automatically deemed inedible, at least by *nice* people.

The people, that Christmas Party night, were indeed nice. We wore our formals: skirts not less than eight nor more than fifteen inches from the floor, dresses of light but not bright colors and of materials semi-transparent or opaque, neck-lines not more than three inches below the collar bone and sleeves long or elbow-length. We all passed the requirements of the catalog, but with such delectable additions as long chiffon scarves twined about our necks in the best Nita-Naldi-bronchitic manner, or great artificial flowers pinned with holiday abandon on our left shoulders. Two or three of the Seniors had fox furs slung nonchalantly about them, with the puffy tails dangling down over their firmly flattened young breasts in a most fashionable way.

There may even have been a certain amount of timid make-up in honor of Kris Kringle and the approaching libertinage of Christmas vacation, real or devoutly to be hoped for, but fortunately the dining room was lighted that night by candles only.

Mrs. Cheever had outdone herself, although all we thought then was that the old barn had never looked so pretty. The oblong tables, usually in ranks like dominoes in their box, were pushed into a great horseshoe, with a little table for Miss Huntingdon and Miss Blake and the minister and the president of the trustees in the middle, and a sparkling Christmas tree, and . . . yes! . . . a space for dancing! And there were candles, and the smells of pine branches and hot wax, and place cards all along the outer edge of the horseshoe so that the Freshmen would not sit in one clot and the other groups in theirs.

We marched once around the beautiful room in the flickering odorous candlelight, singing, "God Rest You Merry, Gentlemen" or some such thing to the scrapings of the assistant violin instructor and two other musicians, who in spite of their trousers had been accurately judged unable to arouse unseemly longings in our cloistered hearts.

Then we stood by the chairs marked with our names, and waited for the music to stop and Miss Huntingdon and the minister to ask the blessings in their fluty voices. It was all very exciting.

When I saw that I was to sit between a Senior and a Junior, with not a Freshman in sight, I felt almost uplifted with Christmas joy. It must mean that I was Somebody, to be thus honored, that perhaps I would even be elected to the Altar Guild next semester. . . .

I knew enough not to speak first, but could not help looking sideways at the enormous proud nose of Olmsted, who sat at my left. She was president of the Seniors, and moved about the school in a loose-limbed dreamy way that seemed to me seraphic. Inez, the Junior, was less impressive, but still had her own string of horses in Santa Barbara and could curse with great concentration, so many words that I only recognized *damn* and one or two others. Usually she had no use for me, but tonight she smiled, and the candlelight made her beady eyes look almost friendly.

The grace done with, we pulled our chairs in under the unaccustomed silkiness of our party-dress bottoms with less noise than usual, and the orchestra flung itself into a march. The pantry doors opened, and the dapper little house-boys pranced in, their smooth faces pulled straight and their eyes snapping with excitement.

They put a plate in front of each of us. We all looked mazily at what we saw, and waited with mixed feelings until Miss Huntingdon had picked up her fork (where, I wonder now, did Mrs. Cheever even find one hundred oyster forks in a California boarding school?), before we even thought of eating. I heard Inez mutter under her breath, several more words I did not recognize except as such, and then Olmsted said casually, "How charming! Blue Points!"

There was a quiet buzz . . . we were being extremely well-bred, all of us, for the party . . . and I know now that I was not the only Westerner who was scared shaky at the immediate prospect of eating her first raw oyster, and was putting it off for as long as possible.

I remembered hearing Mother say that it was vulgar as well as extremely unpleasant to do anything with an oyster but swallow it as quickly as possible, without *thinking*, but that the after-taste was rather nice. Of course it was different with tinned oysters in turkey dressing: they could be chewed with impunity, both social and hygienic, for some reason or other. But raw, they must be swallowed whole, and rapidly.

And alive.

With the unreasoning and terrible persnicketiness of a sixteen-year-old I knew that I would be sick if I had to swallow anything in the world alive, but especially a live oyster.

Olmstead picked up one deftly on the prongs of her little fork, tucked it under her enormous nose, and gulped, "Delicious," she murmured.

"Jesus," Inez said softly. "Well, here goes. The honor of the old school. Oi!" And she swallowed noisily. A look of smug surprise crept into her face, and she said in my ear, "Try one, Baby-face. It ain't the heat, it's the humidity. Try one. Slip and go easy." She cackled suddenly, watching me with sly bright eyes.

"Yes, do," Olmsted said.

I laughed lightly, tinklingly, like Helen in *Helen and Warren*, said, "Oh, I *love* Blue Points!", and got one with surprising neatness into my mouth.

At that moment the orchestra began to play, with sexless abandon, a popular number called, I think, "Horses." It sounded funny in Miss Huntingdon's dining room. Olmstead laughed, and said to me, "Come on, Kennedy. Let's start the ball rolling, shall we?"

The fact that she, the most wonderful girl in the whole school, and the most intelligent, and the most revered, should ask me to dance when she knew very well that I was only a Sophomore, was so overwhelming that it made even the dream-like reality that she had called me Kennedy, instead of Mary Frances, seem unimportant.

The oyster was still in my mouth. I smiled with care, and stood up, reeling at the thought of dancing the first dance of the evening with the senior-class president.

The oyster seemed larger. I knew that I must down it, and was equally sure that I could not. Then, as Olmsted put her thin hand on my shoulder blades, I swallowed once, and felt light and attractive and daring, to know what I had done. We danced stiffly around the room, and as soon as a few other pairs of timid girls came into the cleared space by the tree, headed toward Miss Huntingdon's table.

Miss Huntingdon herself spoke to me by name, and Miss Blake laughed silently so that her black wig bobbled, and cracked her knuckles as she always did when she was having a good time, and the minister and Olmsted made a little joke about Silent Sophomores and Solemn Seniors, and I did not make a sound, and nobody seemed to think it strange. I was dumb with pleasure at my own importance . . . practically the Belle of the Ball I was! . . . and with a dawning gastronomic hunger. Oysters, my delicate taste buds were telling me, oysters are *simply marvelous!* More, more!

I floated on, figuratively at least, in Olmsted's arms. The dance ended with a squeaky but cheerful flourish, and the girls went back to their seats almost as flushed as if they were returning from the arms of the most passionate West Point cadets in white gloves and coats.

The plates had been changed. I felt flattened, dismayed, as only children can about such things.

Olmsted said, "You're a funny kid, Kennedy. Oh, green olives!" when I mumbled how wonderful it had been to dance with her, and Inez murmured in my ear, "Dance with me next, will you, Baby-face? There are a couple of things boys can do I can't, but I can dance with you a damn sight better than that bitch Olmstead."

I nodded gently, and smiled a tight smile at her, and thought that she was the most horrible creature I had ever known. Perhaps I might kill her some day. I was going to be sick.

I pushed back my chair.

"Hey, Baby-face!" The music started with a crash, and Inez put her arms surely about me, and led me with expert grace around and around the Christmas tree, while all the candles fluttered in time with my stomach.

"Why don't you talk?" she asked once. "You have the cutest little ears I ever saw, Baby-face . . . like a pony I had, when I was in Colorado. How do you like the way I dance with you?"

Her arm tightened against my back. She was getting a crush on me, I thought, and here it was only Christmas and I was only a Sophomore! What would it be by April, the big month for them? I felt somewhat flattered, because Inez was a Junior and had those horses in Santa Barbara, but I hated her. My stomach felt better.

Miss Huntingdon was watching me again, while she held her water glass in her white thin fingers as if it had wine in it, or the Holy Communion. She leaned over and said something to Miss Blake, who laughed silently like a gargoyle and cracked her knuckles with delight, not at what Miss Huntingdon was saying but that she was saying anything at all. Perhaps they were talking about me, saying that I was nice and dependable and would be a good Senior president in two more years, or that I had the cutest ears. . . .

"Relax, kid," Inez murmured. "Just pretend . . ."

The pantry door swung shut on a quick flash of gray chiffon and pearls, almost at my elbow, and before I knew it myself I was out of Inez' skillful arms and after it. I had to escape from her; and the delightful taste of oyster in my mouth, my new-born gourmandise, sent me toward an unknown rather than a known sensuality.

The thick door shut out almost all the sound from the flickering, noisy dining room. The coolness of the pantry was shocking, and Mrs. Cheever was even more so. She stood, queenly indeed in her beautiful gray evening dress and her pearls and her snowy hair done in the same lumpy rhythm as Mary of England's, and her face was all soft and formless with weeping.

Tears trickled like colorless blood from her eyes, which had always been so stony and now looked at me without seeing me at all. Her mouth, puckered from years of dyspepsia and disapproval, was loose and tender suddenly, and she sniffed with vulgar abandon.

She stood with one arm laid gently over the scarlet shoulders of the fat old nurse, who was dressed fantastically in the ancient costume of Saint Nicholas. It became her well, for her formless body was as generous as his, and her ninny-simple face, pink-cheeked and sweet, was kind like his and neither male nor female. The ratty white wig sat almost tidily on her head, which looked as if it hardly missed its neat black-ribboned nurse's cap, and beside her on the pantry serving table lay the beard, silky and monstrous, ready to be pulled snug against her chins when it was time to give us all our presents under the Christmas tree.

She looked through me without knowing that I stood staring at her like a paralyzed rabbit. I was terrified, of her the costumed nurse and of Mrs. Cheever so hideously weeping and of all old women.

Mrs. Cheever did not see me either. For the first time I did not feel unattractive in her presence, but rather completely unnecessary. She put out one hand, and for a fearful moment I thought perhaps she was going to kiss me: her face was so tender. Then I saw that she was putting oysters carefully on a big platter that sat before the nurse, and that as she watched the old biddy eat them, tears kept running bloodlessly down her soft ravaged cheeks, while she spoke not a word.

I backed toward the door, hot as fire with shock and the dread confusion of adolescence, and said breathlessly, "Oh, excuse me, Mrs. Cheever! But I . . . that is, *all* the Sophomores . . . on behalf of the Sophomore Class I want to thank you for this beautiful, this *simply marvelous* party! Oysters . . . and . . . and everything . . . It's all *so* nice!"

But Mrs. Cheever did not hear me. She stood with one hand still on the wide red shoulders of the nurse, and with the other she put the oysters left from the Christmas Party on a platter. Her eyes were smeared so that they no longer looked hard and hateful, and as she watched the old woman eat steadily, voluptuously, of the fat cold molluscs, she looked so tender that I turned anxiously toward the sureness and stability of such small passions as lay in the dining room.

The pantry door closed behind me. The orchestra was whipping through "Tales from the Vienna Woods," with the assistant violin instructor doubling on the artificial mocking bird. A flock of little Filipino boys skimmed like monkeys into the candlelight, with great trays of cranberry sauce and salted nuts and white curled celery held above their heads, and I could tell by their faces that whatever they had seen in the pantry was already tucked far back behind their eyes, perhaps forever.

If I could still taste my first oyster, if my tongue still felt fresh and excited, it was perhaps too bad. Although things are different now, I hoped then, suddenly and violently, that I would never see one again.

The Measure of My Powers

1927

THAT year I graduated from boarding school, and my parents, occupied by three younger children and perhaps an unusual flurry of deaths-and-taxes . . . I don't remember . . . did not really know what to do with me.

My mother had gone gracefully through finishing school, a long well-chaperoned stay in Europe, and even more than the required number of hearts. Then, in the correct time, she had married . . . a starved-looking country-newspaper editor instead of one of the plump-cheeked rising young thises-and-thats she might have chosen from, but still it was marriage. My many cousins, on her side of the family at least, followed much the same pattern, and after school made debuts and married.

It was different with the "other side": my father's mother, as well as his father, had graduated from college. It took her eight years to do it, because she went a year and then had a baby for a year until four sons and a Bachelor of Arts were behind her. All her boys went through college, too, and my father's nieces were going as a matter of course.

But at home there was an almost invisible feeling of resentment between my parents about it. If Father would mention casually, and I am sure innocently, that So-and-so's wife was a college graduate, Mother would be huffy.

She would be huffy in such a subtle delicate way that I don't think Father noticed it very often: her right foot would tap in the small rapid tapping that only my mother can do, impossible to imitate, and she would take pains to show that she was better educated,

378

farther traveled, more widely read than So-and-so's wife . . . all of it true, usually. In fact, she made it quite clear, to me at least, that So-and-so's wife was a "so-and-so" too, and that college educations might be fine for women who could get no other advantages, *but* . . .

The odd thing was that Mother never seemed to realize that the "advantages" she referred to with such bland satisfaction were as lacking in my life as in any other benighted female's who wanted to go to a university: I had never traveled more than a twelve-hour trip home from school for vacations; I lived in the country outside a very small California town; I had almost no friends there, because I had been away a long time and grown very shy and rather snobbish; I was as sexless as a ninety-year-old nun, in spite of a few timid dreams that Ronald Colman would see me someplace and say, "That's the girl I must have in my next picture!"

And there I was suddenly, big, moody, full of undirected energies of a thousand kinds. Father and Mother, panicky, decided to put me in one of the large universities in Los Angeles, where I would "be near home" until . . . until some miracle happened, I suppose.

But to be near home was the one thing I could not tolerate just then. I fought against it as instinctively as a person on the operating table fights against ether. The time had come for me to leave, and leave I must, strong always with the surety that I could return to my dear family.

I lived through two months or so of learning to play bridge because I was told I'd be a complete social failure if I didn't, and of sorority rushing parties at which other girls whispered to me that if I ate the lettuce under my so-called salad I would be blackballed. Then, probably because I was so obviously miserable, my father and mother reversed all their protective tactics, gave me a large letter of credit, and with carefully hidden anguish put me on the train for a semester in Illinois with my cousin . . . one of the many times they have thus astonished me, and perhaps themselves.

I went as far as Chicago with my Uncle Evans, Mother's brother. He was a quietly worldly man, professorial at times but always enjoyably so, who knew more about the pleasures of the table than anyone I had yet been with.

Before Prohibition he had loved to drink beer and good whiskey, and May wine in the spring, enough to sing and sometimes weep a little, for he was very sentimental. But as soon as alcohol was illegal, he stopped drinking it; he was a teacher of law, and too honest to preach what he did not practice. He was rare.

Personally I regret his honesty, because I think he would have been a fine man to drink with, and by the time I knew how to, and the country could, it was too late. He had been killed by a drunken driver.

But, the summer I was nineteen and went away to a new land, I started out with him, and learned for the first time that a menu is not something to be looked at with hasty and often completely phony nonchalance.

I must have been a trial, or at least a bore, on that trip. I was horribly self-conscious; I wanted everybody to look at me and think me the most fascinating creature in the world, and yet I died a small hideous death if I saw even one person throw a casual glance at me. In the dining car, which was an unusually good one rather the way the Broadway Limited was to be later, with an agreeable smooth dash to it, I would glance hastily at the menu and then murmur the name of something familiar, like lamb chops.

"But you know what lamb chops taste like," my uncle would say casually. "Why not have something exciting? Why not order . . . uh . . . how about Eastern scallops? Yes," he would go on before I could do more than gulp awkwardly, "we will have scallops tonight, Captain, and I think an avocado cocktail with plenty of fresh lime juice . . ." and so forth.

My uncle was so quiet about it that he made me feel free and happy, and those dinners with him are the only things I remember about the long hot filthy trip.

Then, when we got to Chicago, his son met us. Bernard was by far the brainiest member of our generation in the family, on Mother's side, and I was much in awe of him. He may even have been of me, for other reasons of course, but he never showed it. The minute I saw his solemn young face under its big brow I forgot all the ease that being with my uncle had brought me, and when we went into a station restaurant for dinner and my uncle asked me what I would like to eat, I mumbled stiffly, "Oh, anything . . . anything, thank you."

(That was an excellent restaurant: a rather small room with paneled walls and comfortable chairs and old but expert waiters. It was in the Union Station, I think. I went back years later, and found it had a good wine list and a good chef. It was like coming full circle, to find satisfaction there where I first started to search for it.)

"Anything," I said, and then I looked at my uncle, and saw through all my *gaucherie*, my really painful wish to be sophisticated and polished before him and his brilliant son, that he was looking back at me with a cold speculative somewhat disgusted look in his brown eyes.

It was as if he were saying, "You stupid uncouth young ninny, how dare you say such a thoughtless thing, when I bother to bring you to a good place to eat, when I bother to spend my time and my son's time on you, when I have been so patient with you for the last five days?"

I don't know how long all that took, but I knew that it was a very important time in my life. I looked at my menu, really looked with all my brain, for the first time.

"Just a minute, please," I said, very calmly. I stayed quite cool, like a surgeon when he begins an operation, or maybe a chess player opening a tournament. Finally I said to Uncle Evans, without batting an eye, "I'd like iced consommé, please, and then sweetbreads *sous cloche* and a watercress salad . . . and I'll order the rest later."

I remember that he sat back in his chair a little, and I knew that he was proud of me and very fond of me. I was too.

And never since then have I let myself say, or even think, "Oh, anything," about a meal, even if I had to eat it alone, with death in the house or in my heart.

The Measure of My Powers

1927–1928

THE winter of 1927-28 was one of conscious gourmandise for me, or perhaps gluttony would be the word.

The small college my cousin Nan and I went to was riddled with tradition and poverty. The Underground Railway still tunnelled under the fine old houses and the stately avenues of tall elm trees, and rats ran healthily in their own tunnels through the walls of the big brick dormitory where we lived. I remember that the wing with my room in it was leaning away from the main building, so that I had six-inch blocks under one side of my bed, my desk, and my fairly modern (that is, post-Civil War) bureau.

The meals were bad. We ate them ravenously, because classes were almost a two-mile walk from the Hall, and by the time we had sprinted home for lunch we were hungry indeed. By the time we had walked back and then to the Hall again for dinner we were frankly starved, and would joyfully have wolfed down boiled sawdust.

The only actual thing I can remember about any meals but breakfast is that once I walked by mistake through the back lot of the Hall, and passed a pile taller than I was of empty gallon cans labeled Parsnips.

Breakfasts, every Sunday morning, consisted of all we could hold of really delicious hot cinnamon rolls. We had to eat them by a certain time . . . undoubtedly a dodge to get us up for church. Nan and her roommate Rachel and I used to dress in our church clothes, eat cinnamon rolls until we were almost sick, and then go back to bed. By mid-afternoon we were indigestibly awake, and the day usually ended in homesick mopes, misunderstandings, and headaches.

It all seems incredibly stupid now, but was natural then.

Quite often Rachel and Nan and I would invent some excuse . . . a birthday or a check from home or an examination passed . . . and would go to The Coffee and Waffle Shop, where we could have four waffles and unlimited coffee or a five-course meal for forty cents. Then we would go to the theatre and eat candy; there were still small companies playing *Smilin' Through* and *Seventh Heaven* then, or traveling magicians. And after the show we'd have another waffle, or two or three cups of hot chocolate.

On dates, which were limited because we were Freshmen, we drank chocolate or coffee and almost always ate chili beans. We would sit out in the cars, no matter how cold it was, and drink and eat. Then we would go back to the dance or the Hall. Everybody did that, and I suppose everybody smelled of chili powder and onions, so we never noticed it.

Now and then visiting relatives or kind family friends would invite us either to The Colonial Inn or to their homes. The food was always divine; that was the word we used, and we really meant it, after days of meals at the Hall. There were fine cooks in that part of Illinois, most of them colored, and I regret that I knew so little then about the way they handled chickens and hams and preserves and pickles.

Always for dessert there was pie *and* ice cream, on separate plates but to be eaten in alternating bites. Sometimes there were two kinds of pie, pumpkin and mince, with homemade eggnog ice cream, rich enough to make your teeth curl.

Most of the people who went to the college were poor. There were a few boys with raccoon coats and flasks, but all we really knew about the drinking that had the nation worried was what we read in *College Humor*.

The dates I liked best were with a twenty-year-old Irish edition of Jimmy Durante named Cleary, who divided his passion between football and James Branch Cabell, with practically none left over for me.

I used to sit with surprising docility through country high-school football games he was refereeing, so cold that when I stood up my ankles would bend without my knowing it, and whereas now I think I would really die under such conditions without at least a few drags at the schnapps bottle, then I felt quite happy with a little lukewarm coffee after our side had lost. Cleary was said to drink a little . . . any man full of forward passes and Cabellian double-talk needs to

... but I never saw liquor while I was feeling my first freedom, with him or the other people I dated in Illinois. That is probably surprising.

So is the fact that Nan and Rachel and I never finished the first year there at that college, and that we all left without burst appendixes, ulcers, or any such minor banes as adiposity, dyspepsia, or spots.

I shudder wholeheartedly and without either affectation or regret at what and how we ate, nine tenths of the time we were there, and remember several things with great pleasure: Mr. Cleary, of course; the dishes of pickled peaches like translucent stained glass, at the Inn when we were taken there for Sunday dinner; best of all, probably, the suppers Nan and Rachel and I would eat in their room.

Now I think we ate them the way puppies chew grasstops. They probably saved our lives.

We would buy ginger ale, rolls, cream cheese, anchovy paste, bottled "French" dressing, and at least six heads of the most beautiful expensive lettuce we could find in that little town where only snobs ate anything but cabbage, turnips, and parsnips for the winter months.

We would lock the door, and mix the cheese and anchovy together and open the ginger ale. Then we would toast ourselves solemnly in our toothbrush mugs, loosen the belts on our woolen bathrobes, and tear into that crisp cool delightful lettuce like three starved rabbits.

Now and then one or another of us would get up, go to a window and open it, bare her little breasts to the cold sweep of air, and intone dramatically, "Pneu-mo-*o-o-onia!*" Then we would all burst into completely helpless giggles, until we had laughed enough to hold a little more lettuce. Yes, that was the best part of the year.

Sea Change

1929–1931

In 1929 the stock market crashed, and I got married for the first time and traveled into a foreign land across an ocean. All those things affected me, and the voyage perhaps most.

Everyone knows, from books or experience, that living out of sight of any shore does rich and powerfully strange things to humans. Captains and stewards know it, and come after a few trips to watch all passengers with a veiled wariness.

On land, the tuggings of the moons can somewhat safely be ignored by men, and left to the more pliant senses of women and seeds and an occasional warlock. But at sea even males are victims of the rise and fall, the twice-daily surge of the waters they float on, and willy-nilly the planetary rhythm stirs them and all the other voyagers.

They do things calmly that would be inconceivable with earth beneath them: they fall into bed and even into love with a poignant desperate relish and a complete disregard for the land-bound proprieties; they weep after one small beer, not knowing why; they sometimes jump overboard the night before making port. And always they eat and drink with a kind of concentration which, according to their natures, can be gluttonous, inspired, or merely beneficent.

Sometimes, if people make only one short voyage, or are unusually dull, they are not conscious of sea change, except as a feeling of puzzlement that comes over them when they are remembering something that happened, or almost happened, on board ship. Then for a few seconds, they will look like children listening to an old dream.

Often, though, and with as little volition, people will become ship addicts, and perjure themselves with trumpery excuses for their trips. I have watched many of them, men and women too, drifting in their drugged ways about the corridors of peacetime liners, their faces full of a contentment never to be found elsewhere.

(I know only one person who ever crossed the ocean without feeling it, either spiritually or physically. His name is Spittin Stringer, because he spits so much, and he went from Oklahoma to France and back again, in 1918, without ever getting off dry land. He remembers several places I remember too, and several French words, but he says firmly, "We must of went different ways. I don't rightly recollect no water, never.")

The sea change in me was slow, and it continues still. The first trip, I was a bride of some eleven nights, and I can blame on the ocean only two of the many physical changes in me: my smallest fingers and toes went numb a few hours after we sailed, and stayed so for several days after we landed, which still happens always; and I developed a place on the sole of my left foot about as big as a penny, which has to be scratched firmly about five times a week, a few minutes after I have gone to bed, whether I am on land or sea. The other changes were less obvious, and many of them I do not know, or have forgotten.

For a while, several years later, I mistrusted myself alone at sea. I found myself doing, or perhaps only considering doing, many things I did not quite approve of. I think that may be true of most women voyaging alone; I have seen them misbehave, subtly or coarsely, not wanting to, as if for a few days more than the decks beneath them had grown unstable. Then, as land approached and they felt nearer to something they loved, or at least recognized, their eyes cleared, as if they were throwing off an opiate, coming into focus again.

Yes, I have been conscious of that, and mistrusted it, so that I usually acted so stiffly virginal as to frighten even myself when for many reasons I had to go alone to America or back to France or Switzerland. I think that by now I am old enough, though, to know why such things happen, or at least how to cope with the ramifications and complexities of loneliness, which is by now my intimate and, I believe, my friend.

The first time I was with my husband I was shy, and surrounded with that special and inviolable naïveté of a new bride, so that Al and I walked about, and ate, and talked, almost without contact with the rest of the ship. That seemed natural to us.

I remember now that there were two young Jewish medical students going to Glasgow who eyed us often at meals. They looked nice, but it never occurred to me to speak to them or even smile, and I am sure that such an idea would have shocked them, because of the connubial glow that enfolded me.

Al bandied a few words of Princetonian Greek with a priest returning to Athens, and now and then we bought Martinis for a seedy English major who was going back to mythical clubs in London after an equally mythical and important lecture tour. He was unpleasant, in a vague way, and after he asked me to lead him, one night when we were dancing, I dismissed him with faint repugnance and no regret from my dream-filled life.

Al and I, partly because it fitted our budgets and mostly because it was the exciting, adventurous, smart thing to do, were traveling in what was called Student Third, on the *Berengaria*. I would quite frankly hate it now, but then it was part of the whole perfect scheme of things—even the one time I felt squeamish, from sloshing around in a wooden tub full of hot sea water right over the screws.

It seemed strange to find "Victoria and Albert" painted in the bottom of the throne-like toilets, when I knew British royalty could not be represented on the stage.

And in spite of my rosy daze I knew that the food was bad . . . heavy and graceless. People in the low stuffy dining hall ate hungrily of it, even when it was called Yorkshire Pudding with blasphemous misrepresentation. But I plucked happily at the baskets of grapes and beribboned goodies that bulged out the walls of our minute cabin, and sniffed at the wilting flowers from well-meaning relatives, and beamed at the blue September water that washed past our single porthole.

Occasionally I pinched my little fingers, but they were still asleep . . . like me.

11

The next time I went on the ocean I was alone. It was two years later, and my family felt that it was time for me to be in California again for a few weeks.

My mother, who believed in the "niceness" of the Cunard Line almost as firmly as she approved of the Forsyte Saga, sent me a passage to New York from Cherbourg on one of the lesser liners, which at that time were trying to appeal to the democratic spirit by abolishing classes and selling only Cabin and Tourist tickets. I was Tourist.

The month was May, and we took almost twelve days instead of nine. There were about eighty passengers instead of a thousand, too, and down in the bowels, where my cabin was, no attempt was made to ventilate after the portholes were firmly closed for the duration. It was miserable, and I thought of my first trip, so gay and airy, and of my husband whom I still loved dearly.

If I stayed below I felt stuffy (I was still too young to admit I felt damnably sick), so I walked miles every day, clutching at ropes put up along the deck and talking into the wind with a man named Thames Williamson who had written a couple of good books and felt as mournful as I at the slow but irrevocable approach of the American shore-line.

I can remember nothing about the food except that it was inferior to the *Berengaria's,* and that I ate almost none of it in spite of the fact that my cabin, this time, was as empty of hothouses grapes as it was of my dear Al.

The sub-assistant purser, a small pale youth, had seen that I was assigned to his little table, the first meal out, and I was too naïve and shy to change things. But my total and obvious disinterest in him or any other male, and my exaggerated primness at finding myself alone in the middle of the ocean, soon reduced him to a state of dyspeptic boredoom. Once he asked me to join him and the other officers for a drink, where I don't know, but my thank-you-no was so firm that he hardly dared mumble good-evenings to me for the rest of the trip.

I was desperately lonely, but I didn't know what to do about it. Besides the purser and Mr. Williamson there were some harried but attractive university people named Stewart, the only other people in Tourist Class, I think. He was returning from a sabbatical. They had two little children with flower-faces. I talked shyly a few times with Mrs. Stewart, but when I dared go alone to the grim smoking room, ostentatiously carrying a book, and they smiled at me, I hurried away to bed.

Once their little girl, who was about four, looked at me as I plodded along the sloping deck in the morning, and asked, "Why don't you just get a pan and womm-up, the way my mother does? It's much easier." I knew it would be, but I felt that if I unloosened enough to be sick, the way my body wanted to be, and scared and lonely, the way my heart felt, I'd never be able to stand the rest of the summer! I'd never be able to get off the boat in New York.

As it was I arrived, impregnably friendless, some fifteen pounds thinner and looking very chic. There were two groups of relatives who had never met before, Al's and mine, waiting protectively for me. They stood around the dock for six hours, with increasing politeness, while I proved to a suspicious customs man that the trunkful of old stained woolen underwear Al had saved from Cody, Wyoming, for skiiing and then decided to save a few more years for something else did not have diamonds in the seams.

Now and then one or another of my unrelated relatives would say, "Well, there's nothing like a sea trip!"

Finally, when the customs man was either worn out or convinced, my cousin Weare Holbrook, who had given up writing the Great American Novel to be a professional humorist on the *Herald Tribune* and who at that time wore a beautiful red beard, took all of us except the inspector to a Schrafft's, where we ate strawberry shortcake.

And I dared at last be violently and thoroughly seasick all the way to Chicago. . . .

III

Near the end of that summer I went back to France, convinced to my own bitter satisfaction that I did not agree with my family about at least one thing: my mother's theory, generously supported with tickets and traveling allowances, that it does wives and husbands good to take long vacations from each other.

I was willing then, as now, to admit that not all wives were like me, but I have never profited from being away from men I have truly loved, for more than a few days. I think that when two people are able to weave that kind of invisible thread of understanding and sympathy between each other, that delicate web, they should not risk tearing it. It is too rare, and it lasts too short a time at best. . . .

I took my sister Norah with me. She was about thirteen, I think . . . a quiet thoughtful child, potentially beautiful but too tall and clumsy then, and somewhat given to exchanges of quotations from Ruskin with her pure-minded schoolmaster.

My parents did not know what to do with her; she was far ahead of her class in public school, and too dreamily sensitive to be put into any distant and probably hockey-mad private school. So, in one of their more inspired inconsistencies, my Father and Mother stopped calling me unstable, scratterbrained, and profligate long enough to tuck a letter of credit, several trunk checks, and Norah's hand in mine, and wish us Godspeed for another year or so. Fortunately Norah liked me almost as much as I did her.

That was before trains were air-conditioned, of course, but we had a compartment. We dressed just long enough to change stations in Chicago, and the rest of that August trip we spent lying on our berths, covered only with perspiration and a light coat of cinders, drinking ice-cold milk, and eating fruit a few minutes faster than it could rot in two large baskets that had been sent us.

As we got nearer New York, I fought a constant sense of uncertainty; there had always been cousins or parents or Al, before, to see that trains and boats left correctly with me even more correctly on them, and suddenly I was alone with a large child and tickets and baggage. . . .

A few hours out of New York I added to my secret panic by getting a steel splinter in one eye. That meant leaving Norah in a hotel bedroom while I went to an emergency hospital.

The doctor was an old Frenchman, from Dijon, where Al and I had been living! I had a quiet cry on his sere but willing shoulder, and after convincing him that when the boat sailed that night I'd be on it, even as blind as most of the other passengers but for a different reason, he took out the splinter, filled my eye full of opiates and me full of brandy, and gave me several addresses to Dijonnais I already knew.

The day passed agreeably. I could have handled several more judiciously spaced brandies with enthusiasm, but Prohibition still existed, and even if I had known how to go alone to New York speakeasies I would not have left Norah. So we shopped at De Pinna's and ate iced melon in a tea-room, and I frightened only a few people by having one eye that gushed steadily.

That night our cousin Bernard, the bright one in the family who has always seen me at my worst, in railroad stations and such, took us to dinner at a place in Brooklyn hung with life preservers and fish nets. The view, which twinkled foggily through my flow of tears, was lovely, and we ate a rather elaborate *prix-fixe* meal containing either steak or chicken, I am sure. I decided then, once and for all, that I would never again willingly try to eat in the same room with a dance orchestra, and except for one night in Paris at the Ritz, several years later, I don't think it has happened.

Our ship was a completely characterless and classless matron, English of course, since my mother had bought the tickets. Our cabin, thanks to the depression, was almost empty of "steamer baskets," but to our snobbish horror we found that what had been labeled Sofa on the deck plan was already well occupied by a woman, and that hanging in front of the porthole was her canary in a cage. The agent who had promised us the cabin to ourselves was in California; the ship was already shuddering in the river: we responded chillingly to the other passenger's sleepy goodnight and went to bed.

She turned out to be a small polite Englishwoman, and I cannot remember ever seeing her wash her teeth or dress or undress. She was always neatly in bed, or gone . . . and her canary was even more circumspect; I don't believe that he made either a sound or a dropping during the whole voyage.

Norah solved any nautical problems she might have had by sleeping almost continually until we got to Cherbourg.

I was consumed by a need to get there, get home, get back to Dijon and the arms of my love, and what sea change I felt took the form of refusing a few invitations to the bar and always speaking in French to Norah when she made her few sleepwalking appearances at table.

I thought the French was to get her used to it, but probably it was a childish wish to hide from the people around me . . . a kind of refusal to identify my real self with this interminable voyage home. It embarrassed nobody; Norah was too drowsy to pay any attention to me, and the other people at our table were thick quiet Flemish farmers.

I don't know what they were doing at that time of year in the middle of the Atlantic. I never saw them except at meals, and they never saw me at all. They ate several kinds of cheese at every meal, but especially at breakfast . . . which is absolutely the only thing I can remember about food, that trip. I have since learned to enjoy a breakfast of cheese and beer very much myself, especially if I have drunk too much the night before. (I know a Swiss surgeon who always eats freely of cheese if he has drunk much wine at a meal. He calls it a prophylactic [!] and says that it makes sure that in case of an emergency his hand and his eye are steady. It is, apparently, as if the concentrated and fermented curd acts as a sponge for alcohol. I wonder.)

And then the little yellow bird sighted Land's End through the porthole and burst into song, and his mistress began to chatter to us in a high laughing voice. Norah opened her eyes, so brown and deep. And there on the pilot boat outside Cherbourg was Al, fantastically handsome in the peasant boots and black corduroy suit he loved, with his hair too long. "Is he a poet?" lady passengers whispered to Norah on the boat train. And I ate and ate of the good bread, and laughed and put my head on his shoulder right in the restaurant car, knowing he was.

The Measure of My Powers

1929–1930

PARIS was everything that I had dreamed, the late September when we first went there. It should always be seen, the first time, with the eyes of childhood or of love. I was almost twenty-one, but much younger than girls are now, I think. And I was wrapped in a passionate mist.

Al and I stayed on the Quai Voltaire. That was before the trees were cut down, and in the morning I would stand on our balcony and watch him walk slowly along by the book stalls, and wave to him if he looked up at me. Then I would get into bed again.

The hot chocolate and the rich *croissants* were the most delicious things, there in bed with the Seine flowing past me and pigeons wheeling around the gray Palace mansards, that I had ever eaten. They were really the first thing I had tasted since we were married . . . tasted to remember. They were a part of the warmth and excitement of that hotel room, with Paris waiting.

But Paris was too full of people we knew.

Al's friends, most of them on the "long vac" from English universities, were full of *Lady Chatterley's Lover* and the addresses of quaint little restaurants where everybody spoke in very clipped, often newly acquired British accents and drank sparkling Burgundy.

My friends, most of them middle-aged women living in Paris on allowances from their American husbands "because of the exchange," were expensive, generous, foolish souls who needed several champagne cocktails at the Ritz Bar after their daily shopping, and were improving their French by reading a page a week of Maurois' *Ariel*. Al and I got out as soon as we politely could, or a little sooner, not downcast, because we knew we would come back.

On the way to Dijon we had lunch in the courtyard of the old post-hotel in Avallon. We were motoring down with two large soft Chicago women who were heading for Italy, mainly, it seemed, because they "simply couldn't sit *five minutes* in a restaurant in Rome" without being subtly assaulted by lovesick Army officers. "Italians *appreciate* mature women," they said, their chaste bosoms heaving with a kind of innocent yearning lechery I have often noticed in American females of their class.

I remember that once on the road, when the chauffeur got out to look at a wheel, his coat flapped open as he bent over. Both of our companions squeaked at what they saw, and hustled out of the car. They asked a question in dreadful Italian, and whipped back the lapels of their own traveling suits. And then the fat shifty-looking driver and the two elegant middle-aged women stood in the dust, their eyes fixed on one another's magic enameled Fascist Party pins, so carefully hidden until now, and the three of them solemnly saluted, chins out, just like Mussolini in the newsreels.

Al and I were oddly embarrassed, and did not look at each other.

The hotel in Avallon, because of its ancient location on the Paris-Lyons post-road, had inevitably been taken over by a noted chef, with all the accompanying *chi-chi*. I went back there several times in the next few years, because it was convenient and the redecorated bedrooms were comfortable. The kitchen wall into the courtyard had been replaced by an enormous window, I remember, and the swanky motorists who stopped there for lunch and the modern water closets could watch the great cook and his minions moving like pale fish behind the glass.

The food was not bad but not very good, when you knew what it might have been under such a once-famous man. But that September noon in 1929, when Al and I ate in the courtyard with the two kind silly women and felt ourselves getting nearer and nearer to Dijon, one important thing happened.

We were hungry, and everything tasted good, but I forget now what we ate, except for a kind of soufflé of potatoes, It was hot, light, with a brown crust, and probably chives and grated parmesan cheese were somewhere in it. But the great thing about it was that it was served alone, in a course all by itself.

I felt a secret justification swell in me, a pride such as I've seldom known since, because all my life, it seemed, I had been wondering rebelliously about potatoes. I didn't care much for them, except for one furtive and largely unsatisfied period of yearning for mashed potatoes with catsup on them when I was about eleven. I almost resented them, in fact . . . or rather, the monotonous disinterest with which they were always treated. I felt that they *could* be good, if they were cooked respectfully.

At home we had them at least once a day, with meat. You didn't say Meat, you said Meat-and-potatoes. They were mashed, baked, boiled, and when Grandmother was away, fixed in a casserole with cream sauce and called, somewhat optimistically, O'Brien. It was shameful, I always felt, and stupid too, to reduce a potentially important food to such a menial position . . . and to take time every day to cook it, doggedly, with perfunctory compulsion.

If I ever had my way, I thought, I would make such delicious things of potatoes that they would be a whole meal, and never would I think of them as the last part of the word Meat-and-. And now, here in the sunny courtyard of the first really French restaurant I had ever been in, I saw my theory proved. It was a fine moment.

We stayed at the Cloche in Dijon for a few days, mainly because it was the biggest and best-known place in town. We knew too little yet to appreciate its famous cellars, and found the meals fairly dull in the big grim dining room. Later we learned that once a year, in November for the Foire Gastronomique, it recaptured for those days all its old glitter. Then it was full of gourmets from every corner of France, and famous chefs twirled saucepans in its kitchens, and wine buyers drank Chambertins and Cortons and Romanée-Contis by the *cave*-ful.

But for us it was not the place to be, and while Al was blissfully submerging himself in the warm safe bath of University life, filling out scholarly questionnaires and choosing his own library corner for writing (which he soon exchanged for a quiet table at the Café de Paris), I hopped in and out of fiacres looking for a flat to live in.

The streets were narrow and crooked, in the district around the Faculté, and at that time of year rich with a fruity odor of cellars, dog dirt, and the countless public urinals needed in a wine town. In all the little squares yellowing chestnut leaves fell slowly down, and fountains spouted. I felt very happy when I started out, with a discreetly small dictionary in one hand and the University list of approved boarding houses in the other. The horse wore a straw hat with red crocheted gloves for his ears sticking out of the crown, and there were cafés everywhere, so that even if I took only one quick dismayed glance at the next place on the list, my driver had time for a drink and remained cheerful.

When I remember now how tired I got, and how discouraged, I think I should have joined him at least once out of every four or five times.

The house we were to live in for the next two years, and where a part of me will always be, was the first one I saw. It was near the Faculté . . . it was perfect. But I didn't know that until I had seen a few of the others on the list.

It was a real Burgundian townhouse, in two parts, one on the street and the other at the back, beyond a deep narrow courtyard. A covered stairway zigzagged up one side of the court, connecting the two halves floor by floor, and the rooms I looked at were on the top, in the back part. There was a narrow deep room with a big bed and an *armoire* in it, and another even narrower room with a couch and a desk and shelves. There was a little closet off the stairs, with running cold water in a tiny washbowl and a one-burner gas plate. There was a big window in each room, looking down into the hard gray little court, and there was steam heat. The bedroom was papered in mustard and black stripes, about eight inches wide, with a wide band of American beauty roses around the ceiling; the smaller one was in several shades of purple and lavender, with brown accents . . . a more feminine décor, the landlady pointed out.

In the little closet were all the necessities . . . a potty, a kidney-shaped pan on legs . . . but down in the court there was also a real toilet, with a pitcher of water and a neat pile of newspapers beside it. You pulled a handle which flapped back the bottom of the toilet, and you could look right down into the gurgling waters of the ancient Dijon sewer. (I learned that later, of course.)

There was also a bathroom, on the ground floor, and the landlady assured me that for seven francs, or six if we used our own soap, a bath could be drawn at only a few hours' notice.

The entrance to the whole place was a normal-sized door cut in the great double door that once had let carriages into the courtyard, under the front half of the house, and on one side was the bathroom and on the other, in what probably had once been the door-keeper's room, was the dining room. There, the landlady told me, we would eat well, three times a day, with her husband, her stepson, one or two carefully selected students, and herself.

I bowed myself into my fiacre, not knowing what a jewel I thus nonchalantly toyed with.

Three or four hours later, after looking at a dozen places without water, without heat, certainly without bath, but all with a dank smell which I had not caught in the house on Petit-Potet, I hurried back as fast as the weary hack would pull me. It was the opening of a new session at the Faculté . . . Dijon was probably teeming with students all more sensible than I . . . I was a fool. Central heating, a real toilet, a nice smell. . . .

It was growing dark when I pulled myself for the last time out of the fiacre. I banged on the little door in the big door, and someone shrieked harshly to come in. Madame Biarnet darted from the kitchen, which lay just beyond the dining room, under the first rise of the staircase. She had on a filthy apron, and I could hear someone rattling pans and chopping and beating.

Madame pushed her hennaed hair back from her forehead, assured me that I had the air well fatigued, and said that the rooms were still free. I almost cried. I gave her all the money I had, even without getting Al's opinion first, and said haltingly that we would arrive the next noon.

"We?" she said, with a sharp mocking voice that I was to know very well, and grow fond of.

"Yes . . . my husband . . . I am married."

She laughed loudly. "All right, all right, bring your friend along," she said, but there was nothing mean about her voice.

" 'Voir, 'tite 'zelle," she called hurriedly and disappeared into the kitchen as I closed the door and climbed wearily into the fiacre. But before we could start, she came shrieking out onto the narrow sidewalk, with a scrawled piece of wrapping paper in her hand, a receipt for what I had paid her.

I turned back to smile at her as we drove off. She was standing with one foot over the high doorsill, hands rolled in her apron, watching me with a mixture of affection and innate scorn which I soon learned she felt for all creatures, but mostly humans.

11

The next night, after we had moved and arranged about having Al's trunks of books sent from the station, I looked up the word anniversary in my dictionary and told Madame that it was our first one. "Impossible," she shouted, glaring at me, and then roaring with laughter when I said, "Month, not year." We would like to go to a nice restaurant to celebrate, I said.

She ripped a piece of paper off a package on the wine-stained tablecloth, scrawled on it with a pencil stub she always seemed to have somewhere about her, and said, "Here . . . you know where the Ducal Palace is? The Place d'Armes? You will see a sign there, the Three Pheasants. Give this to Monsieur Ribaudot."

And she laughed again, as if I were amusing in an imbecilic way. I didn't mind.

We changed our clothes in the unfamiliar rooms. The lights were on wires with weighted pulleys, so that by sliding them up or down you could adjust their distance from the ceiling, and there was a kind of chain running through the socket of each one, which regulated the power of the light. There were fluted glass shades like pie-pans, with squares of brown and purple sateen over them, weighted at each corner with a glass bead. The shadows in the unfamiliar corners, and on our faces, were dreadful in those mauve and mustard chambers.

But we felt beautiful. We put on our best clothes, and tiptoed down the wide stone stairs and past the lighted dining room, with a great key in Al's pocket and our hearts pounding . . . our first meal alone together in a restaurant in France.

First we went up the Rue Chabot-Charny to the Café de Paris, by the theatre. It was Al's first love, and a faithful one. He worked there almost every day we lived in Dijon, and grew to know its waiters, the prostitutes who had their morning cards-and-coffee there, its regular patrons and the rolling population of stock-actors and singers who were playing at the theatre across the street. It was warm in winter, and cool and fresh as any provincial café could be in the summer. I liked it as soon as I walked shyly into it, that first night.

We were very ignorant about French apéritifs, so Al read from a sign above the cash desk when the waiter came, and said, "The

Cocktail Montana, please." The waiter looked delighted, and dashed to the bar. After quite a while he brought a large tumbler, rimmed with white sugar, and filled with a golden-pink liquid. There were two straws stuck artfully on the frosted glass, one on Al's side and one on mine.

Al was a little embarrassed that he had not ordered clearly for both of us, but as it turned out, anything else would have been a disaster: the Cocktail Montana whipped up by the Café de Paris was one of the biggest, strongest, loudest drinks I ever drank.

We learned later that a traveling cowboy, stranded from a small Yankee circus, offered to teach its priceless secret to the café owner for free beer, promising him that Americans for miles around would flock to buy it . . . at nine francs a throw, instead of the one franc fifty ordinary drinks cost there. Of course, there were no Americans to flock; the few who stopped in Dijon sipped reverently of rare wines at the Three Pheasants or the Cloche, and would have shuddered with esthetic and academic horror at such a concoction as we took turns drinking that night.

We enjoyed it immensely (we even had it once or twice again in the next two years, in a kind of sentimental loyalty), and walked on toward the Ducal Palace feeling happier than before.

We saw the big gold letters, Aux Trois Faisans, above a dim little café. It looked far from promising, but we went in, and showed Madame Biarnet's scribbled note to the man behind the bar. He laughed, looked curiously at us, and took Al by the arm, as if we were deaf and dumb. He led us solicitously out into the great semi-circular *place,* and through an arch with two bay trees in tubs on either side. We were in a bare beautiful courtyard. A round light burned over a doorway.

The man laughed again, gave us each a silent little push toward the light, and disappeared. We never saw him after, but I remember how pleased he seemed to be, to leave his own café for a minute and direct such obviously bemazed innocents upstairs to Ribaudot's. Probably it had never occurred to him, a good Burgundian, that anyone in the world did not know exactly how to come from any part of it straight to the famous door.

The first meal we had was a shy stupid one, but even if we had never gone back and never learned gradually how to order food and wine, it would still be among the important ones of my life.

We were really very timid. The noisy dark staircase; the big glass case with dead fish and lobsters and mushrooms and grapes piled on the ice; the toilet with its swinging door and men laughing and buttoning their trousers and picking their teeth; the long hall past the kitchens and small dining rooms and Ribaudot's office; then the dining room . . . I grew to know them as well as I know my own house now, but then they were unlike any restaurant we had ever been in. Always before we had stepped almost from the street to a table, and taken it for granted that somewhere, discreetly hidden and silenced, were kitchens and offices and storage rooms. Here it was reversed, so that by the time we came to the little square dining room, the *raison d'être* of all this light and bustle and steam and planning, its quiet plainness was almost an anticlimax.

There were either nine or eleven tables in it, to hold four people, and one round one in the corner for six or eight. There were a couple of large misty oil paintings, the kind that nobody needs to look at, of Autumn or perhaps Spring landscapes. And there were three large mirrors.

The one at the end of the room, facing the door, had a couple of little signs on it, one recommending some kind of cocktail which we never ordered and never saw anyone else drink either, and the other giving the price by carafe and half-carafe of the red and white *vin du maison*. As far as I know, we were the only people who ever ordered that: Ribaudot was so famous for his Burgundian cellar that everyone who came there knew just what fabulous wine to command, even if it meant saving for weeks beforehand. We did not yet know enough.

We went into the room shyly, and by luck got the fourth table, in a corner at the far end, and the services of a small bright-eyed man with his thinning hair waxed into a rococo curlicue on his forehead.

His name was Charles, we found later, and we knew him for a long time, and learned a great deal from him. That first night he was more than kind to us, but it was obvious that there was little he could do except see that we were fed without feeling too ignorant. His tact was great, and touching. He put the big menus in our hands and pointed out two plans for us, one at twenty-two francs and the other, the *diner de luxe au prix fixe*, at twenty-five.

We took the latter, of course, although the other was fantastic enough . . . a series of blurred legendary words: *pâté truffé Charles le Téméraire, poulet en cocette aux Trois Faisans, civet à la mode bourguignonne* . . . and in eight or nine courses. . . .

We were lost, naturally, but not particularly worried. The room was so intimate and yet so reassuringly impersonal, and the people were so delightfully absorbed in themselves and their plates, and the waiter was so nice.

He came back. Now I know him well enough to be sure that he liked us and did not want to embarrass us, so instead of presenting us with the incredible wine book, he said, "I think that Monsieur will enjoy trying, for tonight, a carafe of our own red. It is simple, but very interesting. And may I suggest a half-carafe of the white for an appetizer? Monsieur will agree with me that it is not bad at all with the first courses. . . ."

That was the only time Charles ever did that, but I have always blessed him for it. One of the great wines, which I have watched other people order there through snobbism or timidity when they knew as little as we did, would have been utterly wasted on us. Charles started us out right, and through the months watched us with his certain deft guidance learn to know what wine we wanted, and why.

That first night, as I think back on it, was amazing. The only reason we survived it was our youth . . . and perhaps the old saw that what you don't know won't hurt you. We drank, besides the astounding Cocktail Montana, almost two litres of wine, and then coffee, and then a little sweet liqueur whose name we had learned, something like Grand Marnier or Cointreau. And we ate the biggest, as well as the most exciting, meal that either of us had ever had.

As I remember, it was not difficult to keep on, to feel a steady avid curiosity. Everything that was brought to the table was so new, so wonderfully cooked, that what might have been with sated palates a gluttonous orgy was, for our fresh ignorance, a constant refreshment. I know that never since have I eaten so much. Even the thought of a *prix-fixe* meal, in France or anywhere, makes me shudder now. But that night the kind ghosts of Lucullus and Brillat-Savarin as well as Rabelais and a hundred others stepped in to ease our adventurous bellies, and soothe our tongues. We were immune, safe in a charmed gastronomical circle.

We learned fast, and never again risked such surfeit . . . but that night it was all right.

I don't know now what we ate, but it was the sort of rich winy spiced cuisine that is typical of Burgundy, with many dark sauces and gamy meats and ending, I can guess, with a soufflé of kirsch and *glacé* fruits, or some such airy trifle.

We ate slowly and happily, watched over by little Charles, and the wine kept things from being gross and heavy inside us.

When we finally went home, to unlock the little door for the first time and go up the zigzag stairs to our own room, we wove a bit perhaps. But we felt as if we had seen the far shores of another world. We were drunk with the land breeze that blew from it, and the sure knowledge that it lay waiting for us.

III

The dining room at the Biarnets' was just large enough for the round table, six or eight chairs, and a shallow kind of cupboard with a deerhead over it and two empty shell-cases marked *Souvenir de Verdun* on the top. It was an ugly little room, spotted and stuffy, with a cluster of mustard and spice pots on the dirty checked table-cloth. But it was pleasant while Madame was in it. Her wonderful honest vulgarity made us alive too, and after a meal, when she finally stopped pestering the cook and stretched her tired piano-teacher hands out across the cloth, her talk was good.

She was always late for meals; her pupils were for the most part young or stupid, and she was too much interested in even the dullest of them to send them off at the strike of the hour. Instead, she pounded out do-re-mis on the big piano under our rooms so long and so violently that from pure exhaustion the children grasped their rhythmic monotony before she let them go home. Then she came running down to the dining room, the lines deep in her red face.

She was usually two courses behind us, but caught up with our comparatively ponderous eating almost before we could wipe our lips or drink a little wine, which on her instruction Monsieur Biarnet kept well watered in our tumblers. She ate like a mad woman, crumbs falling from her mouth, her cheeks bulging, her eyes glistening and darting about the plates and cups and her hands tearing at chunks of meat and crusts of bread. Occasionally she stopped long enough to put a tiny bite between the wet delicate lips of her little terrier Tango, who sat silently on her knees through every meal.

Under and around and over the food came her voice, high and deliberately coarse, to mock her prissy husband's Parisian affectations. She told jokes at which her own lusty laughter sounded in the hot air before ours did, or proved that Beethoven and Bach were really Frenchmen kidnapped at birth by the Boches. She became excited about the last war, or the lying-in of a step-daughter by one of her three other marriages, or the rising prices, and talked in a frantic stream of words that verged on hysteria and kept us tense and pleasurably horrified.

We were hypnotized, Al and I and any other transient diners whose extra francs were so irresistible. Madame glanced at our faces as if we were her puppets, her idiotic but profitable puppets. Her eyes, amicably scornful, appraised us, felt the stuff of our clothes, weighed the gold in our rings, and all the time she saw to it that we ate better than any other *pensionnaires* in town, even if she did make more money out of us than any other landlady.

Her reputation was a strange one, and everyone in Dijon knew her as the shrewdest bargainer, the toughest customer who ever set foot in the markets. One of her husbands had been a pawn-broker . . . but gossip said that she taught him everything he ever knew. She was supposed to be wealthy, of course, and I think she was.

She drove herself cruelly, and looked younger than many women half her age, except for the hardness in her finely modeled mouth when it was still. She supervised the cooking, gave music lessons, played in the pit for visiting musical shows, and if the leading man pleased her slept with him . . . gossip again . . . and did all the marketing.

I was to learn, a couple of years later, that collecting enough food for even two people in a town the size of Dijon meant spending two or three days a week scuttling, heavily laden, from the big market to the *charcuterie* around the block, to the *primeur's*, to the milk-shop. And Madame's system was even more complicated by her passion for economizing.

Storekeepers automatically lowered their prices when they saw her coming, but even so she would poke sneeringly at the best bananas, say, and then demand to be shown what was in reserve. Up would come the trapdoor to the cellar, and down Madame would climb, with the poor little fruit man after her. She would tap and sniff knowingly at the bunches hanging in the coolness, and then, on her hands and knees, pull off the greenish midgets that grow along the step at the bottom of the great clusters.

They were worthless: the man had to admit he gave them to his children to play house with. Into the black string bag they went, for a magnanimous twenty centimes or so . . . and in a few days we would have them fixed somehow with cream (at half-price because it was souring) and kirsch (bought cheaply because it was not properly stamped and Madame already knew too much about the wine merchant's private life). They would be delicious.

And while she was in the cellar she would pick up a handful of bruised oranges, a coconut with a crack in it, perhaps even some sprouting potatoes.

The little fruit man shook his head in an admiring daze, when she finally dashed out of the shop.

She sometimes wore several diamond rings left to her by her late husbands, and when she was playing at the music hall she had her hair freshly tinted and waved. The rest of the time, in the daily hysterical routine, her appearance meant nothing to her if it involved spending money. She had an old but respectable fur coat, but scuttled around town in two or three or four heavy sweaters rather than wear it out, and when even they did not hold off the dank Dijon cold, she simply added more layers of underwear.

"Eugénie," her husband said one day, in his precise pettish voice, rolling his eyes waggishly, "it is hardly seemly that a woman of your age go around looking as if she were about to produce twins."

Jo, his gentle effeminate son, flushed at the ugly reference to human reproduction. He was used to enduring in stiff silence his stepmother's vulgarities, but could usually trust his father to behave like a member of the upper classes to which they both so earnestly aspired.

Madame looked quickly at them. Two men, her eyes seemed to say, but neither one a man. . . .

She screamed with laughter. "Twins! No fear, Paul! The Dijonnais would never blame *you* for twins. If anything but a little gas should raise my belly, there would be more horns in this room than those on the deer's head!"

Her eyes were screwed into little points, very bright and blue under the tangled hair. She was cruel, but we had to laugh too, and even Monsieur Biarnet grinned and stroked his little moustache.

He accepted his advancing years grudgingly, and floated from one unmentioned birthday to the next on an expensive flood of "virility" tonics. Of course, the labels said Rheumatism, Grippe, Gout, but we saw around him an aura of alarm: Eugénie stayed so *young*. . . . In spite of his Royalist leanings and his patent embarrassment at her robust vulgarity, he knew she had more life in her eyelashes than he in his whole timid snobbish body. He took refuge in wincing at her Burgundian accent, and raising his dainty son to be a gentleman.

Madame had a hard time keeping cooks in the house. They found it impossible to work with her, impossible to work at all. She was quite unable to trust anyone else's intelligence, and very frank in commenting on the lack of it, always in her highest, most fish-wifish shriek. Her meals were a series of dashes to the kitchen to see if the latest slavey had basted the meat or put the coffee on to filter.

She could keep her eyes on the bottle that way, too. All her cooks drank, sooner or later, in soggy desperation. Madame took it philosophically; instead of hiding the supply of wine, she filled up the bottles with water as they grew empty, and told us about it loudly at the table, as one more proof of human imbecility.

"Poor fools," she said, her strong flushed face reflective and almost tender. "I myself . . . what would I be if I'd spent my life in other people's swill? The only cook I ever had that didn't take to the bottle ate so much good food that her feet finally bent under when she walked. I'd rather have them stagger than stuff."

Madame herself drank only in Lent, for some deeply hidden reason. Then she grew uproarious and affectionate and finally tearful on hot spiced *Moulin à Vent*, in which she sopped fried pastries called *Friandises de Carême*. They immediately became very limp and noisy to eat, and she loved them: a way to make long soughings which irritated her husband and satisfied her bitter insistence that we are all beasts.

She let the little dog Tango chew soft bits from the dripping crullers in her big fine hands, and they both grew more loving, until finally poor Biarnet flounced from the room, *L'Action Française* tucked under his arm.

Madame loved boarders; they amused her, and brought in regular money which became with her magnificent scrimpings a fat profit every month. When Al and I came we were the only ones, but in the next few months, before she had rented the house with us in it to the Rigagniers, there were probably twenty people who came and went, most of them foreigners.

Monsieur Biarnet, who resented having paying strangers at his table, but had little to say about it in the face of his wife's pecuniary delight in them, only put his foot down, and then lightly, about Germans. He loathed them. They made him choke. He would starve himself rather than be polite to them, he said.

Madame shrugged. "We all must eat. Who knows? Someday they may come to Dijon as bosses, and then we'll be glad we were decent to them."

So there were a few who ate with us now and then. They never stayed long. Paul Biarnet really won, because he was so loathsomely, so suavely polite, so overpoweringly the tight-lipped French courtier, that the poor baby-Boches soon found other places to eat. Madame grinned affectionately and rather proudly, and soon refilled the empty chairs with pretty Rumanian girls, or large heavy Czechs.

She liked to have at least one safely attractive female at the table; it kept Paul's small pretentious mind off his various aches and grouses, and made it easier for her to continue her own robust and often ribald life. I did very well . . . I was young and amusing, and at the same time safely and obviously in love with my husband. Monsieur Biarnet made himself truly charming to me, and even Jo, now and then, would flutter from his sexless dream world long enough to make a timid joke with me. It was good for my French, and pleased Madame. Life would have been hell if it hadn't.

We used to sit there at the table, after the noon dinner or on Sundays, and talk about the private lives of ghosts and archbishops and such. Occasionally, the cook would hiccup.

"You hear that?" Madame would interrupt herself. Then she would shout toward the kitchen, *"Imbécile!!"*

We would go on talking, cracking little wizened delicious nuts that had been picked up off the cellar floor of some helplessly hypnotized merchant. We would be pleasantly full of good food, well cooked, and seasoned with a kind of avaricious genius that could have made boiled shoe taste like milk-fed lamb *à la mode printanière*.

Maybe it *was* boiled shoe . . . but by the time Madame got through with it, it was nourishing and full of heavenly flavor, and so were all the other courses that she wrung daily, in a kind of maniacal game, from the third-rate shops of Dijon and her own ingenuity.

She would look at us, as we sat there cozily in the odorous little room, and while she told us the strange story of one of her pupils who ran off with a priest, her mind was figuring what each of us had paid her for the good meal, and how much profit she had made.

"Imbécile!" she would scream ferociously at another helpless hiccup from the kitchen. And when we finally left, she would dart to the sink, and we would hear her say, gently, "Girl, you're tired. Here's enough cash for a seat at the movie. Finish the dishes and then go there and rest your feet. And don't bring home any soldiers."

Then Madame would laugh loudly and, if it were Sunday, go to her little salon and play parts of a great many things by Chopin . . . all tenderness and involuted passion.

To Feed Such Hunger

1930

AFTER Christmas the foreign students changed, at the University in Dijon. The hungry Poles with too-bright eyes, who lived through the warmer months on international fellowships and pride in un-listed attics, went back to Warsaw. The few pretty American girls who bothered to come to such a stuffy little town stopped baffling Frenchmen by their bold naïveté, and left the tea shops and the cafés for Evanston, Illinois. The cool long-limbed Swedes smelled snow, and hurried back to their own ski slopes.

Now, instead of a dozen accents in the halls of the Faculté, you heard only one, and it was German. There were Lithuanians and Danes and Czechs, but German was the tongue.

The girls all looked much alike, thick and solemn. They walked silently about the streets, reading guidebooks, in flat broad shoes and a kind of uniform of badly tailored gray-brown suits.

The men, most of them, were young and pink-cheeked and oddly eager. They sat lonesomely in the cafés, and seldom spoke to one another, as if they had been told not to. The Dijonnais students, who were still fighting the war of '71, when the Boches had besieged the town, were politely rude to them, and they seemed to be scattered like timid sheep, longing for a leader. It was only at the University that they dared band together, and almost before the first class of the new semester, they elected a Prussian the president, as if to prove that there at least they were united and strong.

I had not much to do with the student body as such; my own life with Al was too absorbing and complete. But I couldn't help feeling surprised to learn that Klorr was our new leader.

He was quite unlike any of the other young Germans, who seemed to dislike and almost fear him, in spite of their votes. He was as

408

tall as they, probably, but there was something about the set of his bones that made him seem slight and weak. He wore his brownish hair rather long and slicked back against his head, not in a fair brush; and he dressed in bags and tweed jacket like an Englishman, not in a stiff short coat that showed his hips, and narrow trousers, as his compatriots did.

He had a thin sneering face, too, all of a color with his pale slick hair, and it stuck forward on his neck, instead of being solid between his shoulders.

He was, I think, the most rat-like human I have ever seen, and at the same time he was tall, well set-up, intelligent looking . . . a contradictory person. I dismissed him from my thoughts, as someone I would not care to know, and most surely never would.

I noticed him, though, because he and a girl distracted me several times in class before I knew who she was. I was surprised to see him with her. She was one of the big pallid ones, and I'd have thought him the type who would marry her finally but spend his "student days" with someone small, light, exciting.

The two of them always seemed to be sitting right in front of me in classes, and always very close together, so that her thigh pressed hard against his and her large face almost touched him. They would whisper all through the lectures. It annoyed me. I found it hard enough to keep my mind on the professorial drone about the preposition "à" without having to sort it out from their moist Germanic hissings.

Usually they were reading parts of letters to each other, and usually Klorr sneered coldly at the girl, who seemed to be defending what they read.

Then at the end of the class they would go silently out of the room, she carrying all his books as well as her own. Often she carried his thick topcoat, too.

I found myself interested enough in them to tell Al about them. They seemed such a strange pair to be so intimate, and I was very naïve then about the many visages of love.

One night at supper Madame Biarnet tore through her meal faster than ever, pushed her plate away and the dog Tango off her lap as if she had come to a great decision, and in her slowest, richest Burgundian accent asked us to make up our minds. At once, she said. There and then.

Her voice rose like a general's. Her long nose whitened. Her beautiful hard shrewd eyes, deep in wrinkles but young, looked at us with infinite enjoyment of the comedy she was playing.

"The time has arrived," she said harshly, and we wondered in a kind of stupor what joke she would tell, how soon she would burst into a great gust of laughter and release us from her teasing. We were used to her by now, but constantly fascinated, like a magician's petted nervous rabbits.

Monsieur Biarnet stirred fussily, and popped a vigor pill under his little waxed gray moustache. "Eugénie," he murmured. "Enough. Don't shout so, please! My nerves tonight . . ."

She slapped, absently, fondly, at his shoulder. "Make up your minds! You Americans are all dreamers! Are you going to stay or go?"

"Go where? Why? Do you want us to go, Madame?" We were stammering, just as she planned us to, and we must have looked quite flabbergasted at the thought that we might want to leave our snug small home at the top of the house.

She shrieked, delighted with her game, and then wiped her eyes with her napkin and said softly, almost affectionately, "Calm yourselves! It's about renting the rooms. We'll have a new guest tomorrow, and if you plan to stay she shall have the third floor room on the street, next to Jo's. And if you . . ."

"But of course we plan to stay . . . as long as you want us."

"That's the ticket, then," she said in pure gutter-French, with a malicious grin at her husband.

And as always, as if to prove to himself or someone that he at least was a man of the world, the *upper* world, he murmured in his most affected way, "Charming! Charming children!"

Madame whispered to us before noon dinner the next day that the new boarder was in the dining room. She was Czech, a ravishing beauty, daughter of a high official, someone completely sympathetic and destined to be my undying confidante.

Of course, it was Klorr's friend. Her name was Maritza Nankova, and she spoke when spoken to, in French somewhat better than mine was then. She was very shy for many days, but I could tell that she was lonely and envied me for being gay and happy and in love. I was almost completely uninterested in her.

She spent much of her time alone in her room when she was not at the Faculté. Now and then we would hear her solid shoes climbing the stairs late at night, and I would feel a little ashamed of my own fullness, and think I should go pay her a visit, talk with her about her country and her family and clothes . . . things girls are supposed to talk about together.

A few weeks after she came, there was a minor drama going on in the Biarnet ménage. We could only guess about it. Madame's voice was more hysterically high than ever, and her nose whiter in her red face; and quite often her husband and Jo did not eat at home, or sat icily silent through a meal. Finally one day Maritza was not there for lunch, and as if she had pulled a cork out of the situation when she went through the little door into the street, all three Biarnets started talking at once to us. We felt flattered, of course, and somewhat dazed. Even Jo waved his delicate hands excitedly, and shook back his silky hair with dainty fire.

Madame, they all told us, had been asked by La Nankova to make a place at the table for her friend Klorr. "No, no, and again no," the two men thundered in their small ways.

"But he will pay well," Madame said. "Even filthy Boches must eat."

"Not here. Not with us. The food would choke us," they answered.

"But," she said, "La Nankova says he is very powerful, and important already in Germany . . . and what if someday he comes here the way they came in '71? *Then*," she went on triumphantly before they could interrupt, "then we will be glad to have a friend in him."

The enormity, the basically female realism of it, floored us all for a minute.

Then Monsieur, with a flattering little bow to me, and a slight twist of his moustache with two fingers to prove himself not only masculine but always the *boulevardier*, said, "It is bad enough, Eugénie, my dear, to have to see that well-behaved but clod-like peasant virgin twice a day, sitting in the same room with you and Madame Fischer. The addition of a yearning Prussian swain is more than I could bear."

Madame laughed delightedly. "Virgin, yes," she agreed shrilly. "Swain, definitely not. Klorr is much more interested in finding a good meal than exploring Maritza's possibilities. She has the appeal of a potato."

Jo flushed. "Papa is right," he said, and I thought that at last he had expressed himself, even so circumspectly, on a sexual matter. But he went on, "Mademoiselle Nankova is dull enough. No Boches, please, Belle-mère."

Madame looked gently at him. He usually called her Madame. It was as if anything more intimate to this coarsely vital woman who had taken his dead mother's place would betray him and his father too, and he was endlessly cruel to her, the way a young person can be.

She laughed again, then, and banged on the table. "I give up," she cried. "You are all against me . . . yes, you two smug American lovers too. No Boche. If we starve, we starve together. But," and she looked maliciously at her husband, "when Paul is away on business this Klorr can eat here. My stomach is not so delicate as some, and Klorr may not be bad-looking, even if he is a German."

So she won, after all. We celebrated the ambiguous victory with a little glass of marc all 'round. It was the nicest lunch Al and I had eaten with them, because we felt that we were no longer well-mannered paid-up boarders, but confidants of the family. We wished Maritza would stay away oftener, or always.

The cold winter dragged into Lent. Klorr came a few times to the dining room, always when Monsieur was away, and if Jo was caught there he ate almost nothing and excused himself. The German sensed it, I think. He was very charming to Madame, and was an entertaining talker, except for his lisp. He had a way of leaning across the table after a meal, rolling bread crumbs between his white knobby fingers, with his small strange eyes fixed almost hypnotically on his listener's.

He paid little attention to me, and none at all to Maritza, but seemed much attracted to Jo when he was there, and to Al. Al met him a few times in cafes, and told me Klorr talked mostly of the coming renaissance in Germany. Klorr said it would be based on a Uranic form of life.

I looked up the word Uranism. I *think* it was Uranism. It seemed to agree with what I had seen of Klorr, at least in his attitude toward Maritza. She never spoke at the table when he was there unless he addressed her by name, and then she flushed and seemed almost to tremble. It was a strange kind of love affair, I thought.

I grew more curious about her, and determined, tomorrow or

tomorrow, to see more of her, go chat with her in her room. She never looked either happy or unhappy, except now and then after a meal, when she and the Madame would go into a kind of orgy of ghost stories.

Then Maritza's face would flush under her white skin, and her large dull eyes would be full of light and almost beautiful. She would talk rapidly in her up-and-down Czech accent, and laugh and clasp her big strong hands in front of her.

Madame loved it, and sometimes matched her, tale for tale, and sometimes let her go on alone, with her strange village stories of ghouls and charms and lost cats miraculously found, and of what it meant to sneeze three times . . . that sort of thing. Maritza's eyes would stare into the steamy air, and sometimes they almost frightened me with their mute superstitious mysticism. There was the same thing about them that I have never been able to accept in some Wagnerian music, a kind of religious lewdness, maybe.

One night Al and I came through the silent streets quite late, midnight or so. We had gone to a movie and then sat drinking *café-crème* and listening to the exhausted music at the Miroir, hating to go out into the raw cold Dijon air.

We saw that Maritza's two windows were brightly lighted, with the curtains not drawn. It was strange; always before, ever since she came, they had been dark when we unlocked the little door. We both spoke of it, and then went on tiptoe up the stairs, forgetting her for ourselves.

Much later, I opened our windows. There, across the deep silent courtyard, her inner window still shone, beside Jo's dark one. The curtains were not pulled.

It upset me a little. I stood watching for a minute, but I could see nothing. I got back into bed. I would surely go see her tomorrow, I thought . . . maybe ask her to have tea with me.

I was asleep when the knock came on the door. We both sat up sharply, like startled children; it was the first time anyone had ever come to our door at night. Al clambered out, and ran on his bare brown feet to open it, with his heart probably pounding like mine, from sleep and bewilderment.

It was Jo. He stood there in a mauve woolen bathrobe, carefully not looking toward me in the bed, and asked softly, "Is Madame here? I beg her pardon a thousand times, and Monsieur Fischer's . . . but if Madame would perhaps come." He was stammering, speaking very softly with his eyes cast down.

"What's wrong?" Al asked bluntly, taking him by the arm. I don't know what he thought had happened.

"It's Mademoiselle la Nankova. She still has the light on in her room, and I can hear her. But I don't know whether she is laughing or crying. It is very soft. But it is late. I'm worried. I thought Madame Fischer, as a woman . . ."

"I'll come, Monsieur Jo," I said, and he bowed without looking at me. We heard his light steps down and up the zigzag stairs, and then the firm closing of his door on the landing across the courtyard.

Al looked upset. "Why not ask Madame Biarnet?" he said. "I don't like your being called this way. It's cold tonight. It's . . . it's an imposition."

"You're jealous," I said, while I put his warm bathrobe over my pajamas. "You'd like to go yourself."

"That pudding!" he said, and we both had to laugh, even while I hurried, and his eyes blinked at me with curiosity in them as well as sleep and crossness and love.

The light was on over the top zigzag of the wide stone staircase. I went quickly, wondering what was wrong with the girl. She seemed such a dull lump. Probably she was homesick, or had cramps . . . I knocked on her door, and while I listened I could hear a little rustling in Jo's room; he was listening too, close there behind the safety of his wall. There was no sound at all in Maritza's room. I knocked again. Finally a chair was pushed back, and I heard what I thought were her firm steps across the room.

But when the lock turned and the door opened, deliberately, it was Klorr who stood there, with a white napkin held to his mouth.

I don't know what I thought: I was not embarrassed for either of us, and for some reason not surprised. We stood looking at each other, and I could see that his eyes were not pale at all, as I had thought, but very dark above the napkin. He kept patting his lips. In the room behind him I could hear Maritza breathing in long soft moaning breaths, monotonously.

I started to say why I had come, but he interrupted me in a smooth courtly flow . . . I was so kind to worry . . . just about to call me . . . our little Czech friend seemed upset . . . he had stopped for a few minutes in passing . . . undoubtedly a small indisposition that I, a sister creature, would comprehend . . . a thousand thanks, goodnight, goodnight. And he was off down the stairs, silent and unruffled as a rat, with the napkin in his hand.

I went reluctantly inside. The room was bright with light from an enormous bulb that hung, unshaded, over the middle of the big bed. I went quickly to the curtains, and covered all the windows, like a fussy old nursemaid or like a mother protecting her daughter's modesty, for Maritza was lying there in that light, naked except for a few crumbs and grapeskins on her belly.

When I had with my instinctive gesture made things more seemly, I looked full at her.

The bed was covered with a big white sheet, as if it were a smooth table, and she motionless in the middle, lying with her arms at her sides. I was surprised at how beautiful her body was, so white and clean, with high firm breasts and a clear triangle of golden hair, like an autumn leaf. There were no pillows on the bed, so that her head tilted back and I could see pulses beating hard in her throat. Her eyes were closed, and she kept on breathing in those low soft moans.

I leaned over her. "It's Madame Fischer, Maritza."

She did not answer or open her eyes, but at the sound of my voice she started to tremble, in long small shudders that went all over her, the way a dead snake does. I spoke again, and when I picked up one heavy arm it fell softly back. Still, I felt she knew everything that was going on.

I was not exactly puzzled . . . in fact, I seemed at the time to take the whole thing as a matter of course, almost . . . but for a minute I stood there, wondering what to do. Maritza's face was very hot, but the rest of her was cold, and shaking now with the long shuddering ripples, so I covered her with a coat from her *armoire*, after I had pushed the grapeskins and crumbs off her.

They were only on her belly. There were several crumbs down in her navel, and I blew at them, without thinking it funny at all. I put them all in my hand, and then onto a plate on the little table, before I realized how strange it was.

It was set up by the fireplace, with a linen tablecloth, and placed precisely on it were a plate of beautiful grapes with dark pink skins, an empty champagne bottle and a fine glass, and a little round cake with a piece out of it. It looked like the kind of table a butler arranges in the second act of an old-fashioned bedroom comedy, except that there was only one glass, one plate, one fork.

I knew Klorr had been supping there, while Maritza lay naked on the bed and moaned for him. And I knew that he had put the empty grapeskins on her unprotesting flesh without ever touching her.

My hands felt foul from them. I went to the *armoire*, to look for some alcohol or toilet water to rub on them, but I could see none in the neat bareness of the shelves.

I ran silently as I could to our rooms. Al was lying in bed, reading, and when he asked me mildly what was going on, I suddenly felt a strange kind of antagonism toward him, toward all men. It was as if Maritza had been ashamed in some way that only women could know about. It was as if I must protect her, because we were both females, fighting all the males.

"Nothing . . . it's all right," I said crossly. "She's got the jitters."

"Oh," Al said, and went on with his book.

I ran down the stairs with a bottle of eau de Cologne. I thought I would rub Maritza with it. I closed her door, and pulled the coat gently off her.

"It's Madame Fischer," I said, because her eyes were still closed.

I rubbed in long slow motions up her arms, and up her legs from her ankles, the way I remembered being massaged in a Swedish bath when I was younger. Gradually she stopped making the moan with every breath, and the unnatural shudders almost ceased. Her face was cooler, too.

"You are better, now, Maritza," I kept saying as I rubbed the toilet water into her fine white skin. "You are all right now."

It was like quieting an animal, and had the same rhythm about it, so that I don't know how long it was before I saw that the door had opened silently, and Klorr stood there watching me.

Maritza's eyes were still shut, but she felt something in my hands, although I did not feel it myself, and she began the long hard shuddering again.

Klorr was staring at me with jet-bead eyes, and hate seemed to crackle out of him in little flashes, like electricity in a cat's fur. I glared back at him. I must have looked fierce, because as I got up slowly and approached him, he backed away and out into the hall by Jo's door. He had the napkin in his hand, and he held it out to me. I closed the door into the girl's room.

"What do you want?" I asked, speaking very distinctly. I could hear my own voice, and impersonally I admired my accent. I am in a rage, a real rage, I thought, and rage is very good for the French accent.

Klorr smiled weakly at me, and wiped his lips again.

"I was just passing by," he said for the second time that night. "I . . . how is our little Czech friend? I appreciate your unusual interest in her. How is she, if I may be so bold as to enquire? Tell me, dear Madame . . . what is wrong with her?"

His smile was stronger now, and he was speaking smoothly, with his eyes staring scornfully, sneeringly at me.

Then I drew myself up. It sounds funny even to write about now, or think about, but I actually did draw myself up, until I seemed much taller than he. And very distinctly, in the most carefully enunciated and completely pompous French that has ever been spoken outside a national theatre, I said, "What is wrong with her? Mademoiselle Nankova, Monsieur Klorr, is suffering from an extreme sexual overexcitement!"

Those were my words, which sprang unsought for into my furious brain. Yes . . . they rolled out magnificently . . . *une sur-ex-ci-ta-tion se-xu-el-le* . . . syllable by mighty syllable, even to the final "le," like a quotation from Racine.

Klorr looked away. He bowed stiffly, and then as if he could not stand it any longer he threw the napkin at me and ran again down the stairs, as silent as a rat.

When I went back into the room, Maritza was curled up like a child in the middle of the bed, crying peacefully into her hands. She was rosy and warm, and I put the coat over her and turned out the light and went home. I felt terribly tired.

Al was asleep. He never asked me anything about it, and I never told him.

The next day Maritza was the same as always, shy and dull as if she did not know me, and in about a week she left, without saying goodbye to any of us. Madame said that she and Klorr, by a very odd coincidence, were going to be in Venice together for the Easter celebrations.

"Love is hair-raising," Madame said. "Imagine that great lump in a gondola."

"I for one am thankful," Monsieur said, rolling his eyes first toward the good God in heaven and then toward me. "Now we can resume our old chats, without having to wait for La Nankova to keep up with us, and without having to escape her questionable Prussian acquaintance. It will be excellent for practice, for perfecting the accent."

Jo looked at me, and before he lowered his soft eyes in their deep curling lashes, he smiled in an abashed way at me, and murmured, "But Madame's accent is already excellent at times, Papa."

And I burst out laughing, and could tell nobody why. Whenever I say those words in my mind, I must laugh now, in spite of the feminine shame I feel to think of that table laid in the bright room, and the strange ways of satisfying hunger.

The Measure of My Powers

1930–1931

WHEN the Rigagniers rented the house on the Rue du Petit-Potet from the Biarnets, they took us along with the stuffed deer's head and empty *Souvenirs de Verdun*. We stayed on in our little mustard-and-purple rooms, crammed by now with our own bookish castings, and we ate in the same stuffy spotted dining room. Our new friends were as extravagantly lavish as the others had been penny-pinching, and we tasted some of the headiest dishes of our lives there.

We were the first boarders the family had ever had, and I am sure that we ate and drank much more every month than we paid for. There was nothing to do about it; the family was on the brink of complete financial ruin, after twenty years of living on Madame's enormous but now vanished *dot*, and even if we had tried to eat one less slice of brandy-cake, one bowl less of hot creamy soup, the Rigagniers would have gone on, bilious and gay, buying fine legs of lamb and casks of wine and baskets of the most expensive vegetables.

Madame herself did the cooking, helped by a series of numb orphan slaveys, and even in the better days, when she had commanded her own small staff of servants, I think she probably kept one foot in the kitchen. She was the daughter of the finest *confiseur-patissier* in Alsace, a spoiled stuffed daughter who when her husband's penchant for provincial backstage beauties drained the last francs from her fabulous *dot* dropped all her elegant . . .

It is strange . . . or perhaps it is natural . . . that I cannot go on as I had planned.

I meant to write about what I learned, my gastronomic progression there with the Rigagniers . . . and even if I'd willed it otherwise there would have been some of that progression, close as I was to people who knew flavors as their American counterparts knew baseball batting averages, whether they were twelve like Doudouce or seventy-five like Papazi.

But now when I think of the hot quarrelsome laughing meals: the Sunday dinners in the formal *salle à manger* and the enormous suppers so soon afterwards, when Papazi produced his weekly triumph of a tart as big as a cartwheel, with all the apple slices lying back to belly to back in whorls and swoops; the countless birthdays and name-days and saint-days with their champagne and their truffled geese; the ordinary week-day suppers, "light" after the heavy meal at noon, when soufflés sighed voluptuously at the first prick, and cold meats and salads and chilled fruits in wine and cream waited for us . . . no, when I think of all that, it is the people I see. My mind is filled with wonderment at them as they were then, and with dread and a deep wish that they are now past hunger. They were so unthinking, so generous, so stupid.

Papazi and Mamazi, the grandparents, lived in another house, a lovely place with chestnut trees in the courtyard and thin-legged gold chairs in the darkened drawing room, but their hearts were still in Alsace in the fine rich days of wealth, when Papazi was known everywhere for his chocolates and his wedding cakes. Now he hobnobbed like an exiled king with the better of the Dijon *confiseurs*, and listened to Beethoven concerts on his TSF, and every week or so baffled his grandchildren with a deft masterpiece for Sunday supper or for fun. He was a merry old man, in spite of his pomposities.

Mamazi was a small bewigged woman, still weeping for her son lost in the first war, and meekly waspish. She shook like an idling ocean liner from all the digitalis she took, and died a little while after I saw her last.

The two old people would come every Sunday to dinner, which was a long delicious almost overpowering meal, and then would stay for supper, which was also such a long delicious almost overpowering meal that Al and I finally took to sneaking away, as soon as we had partially recovered from the first one, and going to Crespin's for a few oysters, or to any place at all for a salad and a piece of bread.

Sometimes M. Rigagnier would see us, on his way home after an afternoon of café-gambling or other more active gambols, and then there would be red-eyed Monday questions from Madame. It was impossible to tell her that we simply could not eat for a few hours; she did not know people like that.

She herself was one of the most unreservedly sensual people I know of. She was not at all attractive physically. She neglected her person, mainly because she gave every ounce of her time and energy to feeding us. So she was bedraggled and shiny and often smelled. And, what is even more distasteful, she was needlessly ailing. Such a state is repulsive to me. She had really violent monthly headaches which were, even to my ill-trained eye, pure bilious attacks. For three or four days she would stagger from stove to table and back again, cooking and then eating with the same concentrated fervor as always, while her eyes were almost mad with pressure, and her face was gray.

She connected these *crises de nerfs névralgiques*, as she always called them, in some way with her unhappiness in marriage, and spent a good part of her time convincing her one daughter that taking the veil was much preferable. In spite of my exasperation with her, as I saw her eating with such steady gourmandise at her own rich soups and tarts and stuffings, I knew she suffered like hell and I longed to help her.

She was still a terrible snob, in spite of the cruel way her life had changed from its first spoiled lavish opulence, and would sweep and market all morning and then put on her one good black dress and go to a concert, where she sat in the stiff position taught her in school in Germany and listened to music which her poor tired ears could never hear. She saw to it that somehow her children went to the correct piano teachers and the best schools, not because she wanted them to be well educated but because she was proud in the face of her own steady social decline, and knew that she was better than any of the plump matrons who now occupied the position she had once taken as her right.

She was a stupid woman, and an aggravating one, and although I did not like her physically I grew to be deeply fond of her and even admiring of her. For years we wrote long and affectionate letters, and on the few times I returned to Dijon we fell into each other's arms . . . and then within a few minutes I would be upset and secretly angry at her dullness, her insane pretenses, and all her courage and her loyal blind love would be forgotten until I was away from her again.

When we were living with her, she often said that she would like to teach me what she knew about cooking. In many ways I was a fool not to accept her offer. But I knew that she would drive me crazy, shatter all my carefully educated reserve and self-control, so that I might scream at her or hit her with a spoon. Instead, I said that my university work took all of my time, and without her knowing it I learned much more from her, perhaps, than she could ever have told me. I learned about omelets and salads and roasts of meat, as well as sauces both natural and concocted and a few human foibles, both despicable and fine.

We used to talk a lot about marriage. I was interested in hers, because after almost twenty years it was so obviously a bad one. She admitted that herself, and in the insidious way of good women she managed beautifully to make the three children hate their father for her battered sake. She had been married, thanks to her dowry, to a promising young automobile inventor, and then spent the rest of her life watching him laugh and wink his way through all the money and a hundred careless jobs, until at last he was a garage mechanic and she was a penniless slave; and still she believed passionately that the provincial French system of marriage was the only successful one. I on the other hand argued as fervently for the American way of encouraging young people physically attracted to one another to marry in spite of a complete lack of parental and financial blessings.

Madame and I got divorces in the same year, and exchanged somewhat woe-begone letters on the subject. Hers were full of a kind of courage I shall probably never have, and were written by a mind perhaps ten or eleven years old.

After the divorce she left Dijon, where she had struggled so miserably against poverty and the town's pity, and went with Papazi and the two younger children nearer their dear Alsace. Then she was evacuated. . . .

Monsieur Rigagnier was a coarse kind-hearted man, who in this country would belong to the American Legion and any local clubs that had good times. In Dijon he lived mostly in the cafés, playing cards and talking about the happy war-days, when he'd been a captain and had a mistress who later became a famous movie star. He'd also won a few decorations, but they were not important to him compared with *la belle Arlette* or whatever her name was.

He drank a lot, especially if he knew that Madame had one of her headaches or there were an unusual lot of bills to be paid. He was always polite, and even gay, with us, but sometimes he used to snarl at the children. Papazi he feared and respected, and borrowed money from, as if the old man had supported him for so long that it was only logical to continue. Papazi was equally polite, and as soon as Dédé was twenty-one paid for a divorce. He despised his son-in-law.

The children did too, in that insidious way of young things . . . never openly mocking, but always a little too meek, too indomitably servile.

Dédé was the oldest, a surly oafish boy, with thick outlines and small eyes like his father's. He openly hated the way his mother had to work, and was the only one of the family who ever seemed to resent our presence. His table manners were dreadful, and I resented him even more than he did me, probably.

He studied with a kind of dogged hopelessness for Saint-Cyr, and finally got in, the last name on the list. His mother wrote of his marriage . . . much beneath him, she managed to imply. And when France fell he was a captain in the *Pompiers de Paris*, and had a "pretty eight-room apartment near his garrison where Amélie awaits the first-born son," Madame wrote in her fine over-crossed lines of purple ink. So much for Dédé. He was a boor, in spite of his fine palate.

Plume was another thing entirely. He was the most like an elf of any person I have known, and also like a monkey, with the same bright inhuman gaze. He was about fourteen when we knew him. He refused to go to school, so in turn Papazi bribed every reputable candy-maker in Dijon to take him as an apprentice. He made all the workers laugh so hard they ruined the bonbons and the tarts, and the bosses shivered in their beds with worry over his next trick. Would Plume decorate the wedding cake of a maiden trying to hide her Semite origins with a Star of David made of rosebuds? Would he put oil instead of Cointreau in the little chocolate bottles for the Bishop's Christmas party?

Plume, in spite of Papazi's renown, was forced to conclude that he would like to be a piano-tuner, a watchmaker, a lawyer, and a dancing master. Nothing perturbed him, and he flitted like a gentle grinning little satyr through the offices and factories and streets of Dijon.

We used to see him sometimes coming out of the most expensive brothels, always with the same mischievous detachment in his small face, and some of the prostitutes told Al that he was a great favorite among them, so tender and courteous and charming. He was that way at home too, and we all loved him.

After we left he got a job with the automobile factory where his father had once been well known, and suddenly, perhaps because of the divorce, his fey attitude clarified and he became almost a wizard with engines. He went to Algiers. His mother wrote happily about him. He was invalided home once while I was in France, and I saw him for a minute, shaking with fever. He bent over my hand. I still felt as if he were fourteen, not in his twenties, and could hardly keep from smiling. I felt his kiss on my skin for a long time.

Then, in the first criminal hysteria of mobilization in France, he was snatched from the auto works where by now he was a prized technician, and put to digging trenches. Within a few days he died of pneumonia.

"When you watch the dirt being shoveled onto your son's coffin," his mother wrote to me in her precise flowing hand, "you have an almost uncontrollable desire to throw back your head and howl like a wounded beast."

And Doudouce? Her name was France, because she was born on the first Armistice Day. She was a serious little girl, short and round, with worry in her eyes, and her mother's sensual mouth. Even when we knew her, starting her 'teens, she worked heavily and earnestly at her lessons. She was already resolved never to marry, never to subject herself to the monthly headaches and the daily labor that she saw in her mother, and she had decided for herself that being a teacher was better than being a nun. We used to try to make her seem more like a little girl, but it was not until after we left, after the divorce, that Plume taught her gayety. Doudouce kept on with her studying, but she danced too.

She passed her examinations. Then, to her mother's proud bewilderment, she went all alone to Paris, studied medicine, and became a roentgenologist. She was there when the city fell, and I wonder now whether Papazi's fanatical hatred of the Boches has upheld her, or whether the latent sensuality in her small round body has taught her that headaches are not always made by men, even German men.

I think often of her, and of Plume so quickly out of it, and of my poor stupid friend their mother, and the pouting Dédé. I remember with a kind of anguish the prodigal bounty of their table, and their child-like inability to conceive of anything but richness and warmth and sensory perfection for themselves and their friends. They were less able than ordinary people to withstand the rigors of physical hunger.

I think of them as I used to see them, the three children bending over the steaming stove, their eyes intent and beautiful, their ears listening reverently to Papazi as he waved a spoon and told them the history of the *sauce Soubise* or the carp dumplings he concocted, while Madame sat for a few stolen moments at the dining-room table, account books spread before her straining eyes but a little plate of *truffes au chocolat* beside her one free hand, or a small glass of *anisette* . . . I long impotently to feed those kind simple-minded friends of mine, if they still live.

Perhaps Papazi was luckiest. "You will be saddened, my dear," Madame wrote a few months before war started, "that our beloved Papazi is no more. His end was one you will appreciate, as the good God's special reward to such a devout and faithful servant of Epicurus.

"Lately my poor father has forgotten his many financial misfortunes, and our table has been worthy indeed of the greatest *confiseur-pâtissier* of Alsace, past, present, and future. Wednesday noon, in honor of Plume's new position at the factory, Papazi prepared with his own hands and very little help from me a repast such as we have not seen for years. We began, as a compliment to me, with my own recipe for *Potage Richelieu* (Bring 200 grammes of the finest butter to the bubble, add . . . but I shall write it on another sheet of paper, my dear . . .), and then had snails which Plume and Doudouce and I gathered ten days ago in the woods, just as in the old days . . . do you remember the many times we starved them in the courtyard, and you helped us wash the shells with Papazi's little brushes? . . . and after a small but delicious soufflé of Gruyère to refresh our palates, we ate a tongue with *sauce Philippe*, which recipe I shall also enclose in case you do not remember it.

"I do not wish to weary you, my very dear friend. Suffice it to say that at the end there was to be a *Diplomate au Kirsch d'Alsace*, made just as always with the marinated fruits. With that, having opened almost the last of our best bottles for the first part of the repast, I planned to serve coffee in the Algerian way to please Plume, rather than champagne as we used to do it in Dijon.

"But just before we reached that course, our dear Papazi . . . this is painful, as you will understand . . . our dear Papazi, who had been gay and young all day, suddenly stood up, emptied his glass, and then sat down again with a strange smile on his face. His stomach gave out a loud rumble, and he was gone from us."

Noble and Enough

1929–1931

WE lived for almost three years in Dijon, which the Burgundians called without any quibble and with only half-hearted contradictions "the gastronomic capital of the world." We were lucky to know people there of almost every class, and to be within ourselves eager, interested, and above all husky-gutted. Most of our orgies were voluntary, but even so I doubt if more jaded livers than ours could have stood the thousand bilious blows we dealt them.

We went as often as we could afford it to all the restaurants in town, and along the Côte d'Or and even up into the Morvan, to the Lac de Settons, to Avallon . . . and down past Bresse. We ate terrines of *pâté* ten years old under their tight crusts of mildewed butter. We tied napkins under our chins and splashed in great odorous bowls of *Ecrevisses à la nage*. We addled our palates with snipes hung so long they fell from their hooks, to be roasted then on cushions of toast softened with the paste of their rotted innards and fine brandy. In village kitchens we ate hot leek-soup with white wine and snippets of salt pork in it.

And in Dijon we went to Ribaudot's when we were flush, or perhaps the Chateaubriant, which we never grew to like much, except in the summer when we could eat dust and iced fruits on the sidewalk. At the end of Liberty Street was the Buffet de la Gare. It had a good old reputation, and was nice in the winter because of the enormous iron stove as well as the ancient waiters and the bowls of flowers from Nice that conductors on the PLM expresses would throw off every day, probably in memory of good food they had eaten there. The Buffet was especially proud of its *Tournedos Ros-*

427

sini, which my husband liked very much, with its suave combination of fresh beef and almost putrescent *pâté de foie gras.*

Back up the main street, across from the Chateaubriant, was the Grande Taverne, which tried hard to bring a snappy big-business Parisian atmosphere to Dijon, and failed completely. Its electric lights were all masked in slabs of cheap frosted glass cut on the diagonal ... *l'art moderne,* the proprietor said proudly ... and signs on the mirrors recommended regional specialties with a kind of condescending fervor. But the Dijonnais who had been reading *Le Temps* and *L'Intran* under its lights since gas was first installed continued to go there ... and the chef would always push aside his "Burgundian delicacies" long enough to make me a rum omelet, with three harsh scars of burnt sugar across its plump top where he laid the poker on to make an F for me.

Then there was Crespin's, the simplest and one of the best places in the world. It was on one of the oldest streets, between the markets and the church I liked the best, and in the winters an old oyster-man stood outside always by his fish, stamping his feet like a horse and blowing on his huge bloody mottled hands. He was the best one I have ever seen for opening those devilish twisted shells, but still there was always a fresh cut somewhere on his grotesque stubs of fingers.

He had baskets of dark brown woven twigs, with the oysters lying impotently on seaweed within ... Portugaises, Marennes, Vertes of different qualities, so fresh that their delicate flanges drew back at your breath upon them. Inside the little restaurant you could eat them with lemon and brown buttered bread, as in Paris, or with a plain crust of the white bread of Dijon.

Then there were snails, the best in the world, green and spitting in their little delicate coffins, each in its own hollow on the metal plates. After you pulled out the snail, and blew upon it cautiously and ate it, you tipped up the shell for every drop inside, and then with bread you polished the hollow it had lain in, not to miss any of the herby butter.

Crespin's always had *tripes à la mode de Caen,* too, in little casseroles in which it could keep indefinitely, and salad and a piece or two of cheese. And that was all ... another proof of my firm belief that if a restaurant will be honest about a few things, it can outlive any rival with a long pretentious menu.

There was another place almost as simple, down on the Place d'Armes near Ribaudot's, but plain in the same self-contained deliberate way. It was called the Pré aux Clercs, and my husband liked to go there because it made very good grilled rare steaks with watercress, which at that time were beginning to be in great vogue in the big cities among the younger generation . . . *"les sportifs"* . . . but were dismissed with impatient disgust by older gourmands raised in the intricate traditions of fine sauces and culinary disguise.

And of course there were places like the stand out in the park that made wonderful sandwiches of crisp rolls with loops and dollops of sweet home-cured ham in them . . . and the houses along the canal that sold hot minnows, cooked whole and piled unblinking in a bowl . . . and little cafés that because their proprietors liked hot cheese cakes made hot cheese cakes once a week.

And everywhere, in every village pub or great temple of gastronomy, there were the proper wines, whether they came out of a spigot into a thick tumbler or slipped from a cradled cobwebbed bottle into the bottoms of glasses that rang thinly in the faintest stir of air. We grew to know, but always humbly, what wines of Burgundy and which years were regal, and how to suit the vintage to the hour. (Much of what I learned then I've forgotten. I feel it is a pity, but perhaps like any fish I shall remember how to swim if I am thrown back in the water before it is too late.)

Much of the time we were learning and tasting all these things, we were living with the Biarnets or the Rigagniers, so that some of our tutelage was of course involuntary. With them most of it, thank God, was good as well.

Of course I, as the wife of an almost-faculty-member, had to go to tea with my almost-colleagues much too often; I was young and felt earnestly that afternoons spent in the upstairs *salon* of Michelin's eating almost unlimited pastries would help my husband's career. And once we had to go to a formal luncheon at the Rector's.

He was to French pedagogues what a combination of Nicholas Murray Butler and Robert Hutchins might be in this country, and Al and I were invited mainly because a visiting New England scholar had to be entertained. Like most ambassadors sent for one reason or another from America, he did not speak the language of the country he was to win to whatever cause he represented, and since I had gradually erased the firm impression among the faculty wives that all Yankee women either got tight in public on strange cocktails or spat in the drawing room, I was seated next to him.

He was a nice man, head of the English Department in a famous university. He had the same apparently instinctive naïveté of Wendell Willkie, which of course always wins people, especially when it is accompanied by slightly rumpled hair and a wide grin.

The luncheon was the most impressive private meal I have ever gone to. (Thank God, I add. I sometimes feel that I am almost miraculously fortunate, to have lived this long and never sat through one of the "state banquets" I have read about.) The Rector was noted for his table, but this time his chef had been helped by Ribaudot, and several of the *restaurateur's* best men were in the dining room with the butler and regular footman.

There were ranks of wine glasses, and the butler murmured the name and year of each wine as he poured it. Each one was beautiful.

All the ladies, including the hostess, wore hats, and some of them gloves rolled up around their wrists, and I felt slightly hysterical and almost like something out of Count Boni de Castellane's visits to Newport in the 1880's.

One of the courses was whole *écrevisses* in a rich sauce, served of course with the correct silver pliers, claw-crackers, gouges, and forceps.

The guest of honor was being very diplomatic, bending his white top-knot first to the hostess and then to me, but when he saw the hard big coral fish lying in their Lucullan baths, he leaned against my shoulder and most unacademically he muttered, "Help, for God's sake, sister! What do I do now?"

I knew, because I had struggled before with the same somewhat overrated delicacy, and I had no patience with manmade tools in such emergencies. It would have been tactless for me to remind him that he could watch his hostess, so I winked at him and said, "Watch me."

I picked up a shrimp between my left thumb and forefinger, cracked both its claws with the silver crackers, ate what meat I could with the little fork, and then dunked the rest out of the sauce with a crust of bread. The visiting scholar sighed happily, and set to.

And that is the way everybody at the long oppressively polite table ate the rest of the course, and from then on things went fairly amicably and faculty feuds were forgotten or ignored, and at the end Madame la Recteur embraced me and made a date for tea.

(The whole incident sounds a little too charmingly barbaric . . . "these delightful American savages" . . . but I still do not believe that a host should serve anything that cannot be eaten with ease and finesse by all his guests who are reasonably able-bodied. In the case of *écrevisses* it is different of course when they are served with the claws cracked and the tails split. But in France it was felt, I think, that such sissy preparation ruined much of the flavor . . . and I have yet to see the most adept gourmet succeed in eating even one such crustacean with the prescribed tools. Cuffs rolled back, napkin under chin, an inevitable splash or two and more than that number of loud sucking noises: that is the routine at Prunier's, at the Rector's and at the Café de l'Escargot d'Or down on the edge of any lake in shrimp season.)

Of course, there was the Foire Gastronomique every autumn, in Dijon: we went to the long tents and drank quite a lot of *vin mousseux*, but we were not important enough to be invited to any of the official banquets and could only read the fantastic menus in the paper. Prices went up for the visitors, most of whom were wine dealers, and gossip said that all the restaurants put an extra lot of seasonings in their sauces so that even mediocre wines would taste superlative. We liked Dijon better in its normal state of mass-gourmandise.

Probably the most orgiastic eating we did while we lived there was with the Club Alpin. Monsieur Biarnet proposed us for membership soon after he had decided for himself, over the dinner table in his stuffy little dining room, that we were amusing and moderately civilized. It was supposed to be an honor, as well as making it possible for the club to get better rates on its feasts by having a larger number of members, and certainly it was a fine although somewhat wearing experience for us.

We heard good French from the lawyers and retired army officers and fuddy-duddy architects like our friend Biarnet who belonged, for one reason or another but mostly gastronomic. We saw castles and convents and wine *caves* that were seldom bared to public eyes. We walked and crawled and slithered and puffed over all that corner of France, in the cold March rains, the winy gold-leafed days of autumn, April's first tantalizing softness.

We all had to wear properly stiff heavy boots, and on almost every one of the bi-monthly promenades we managed to find a small safe grotto or gully to explore, so that the Alpine part of our club's name would not be too much of a joke, even in the heart of smooth-rolling Burgundy. Our rooms in Dijon were in one of the most perfect and beautiful fourteenth-century townhouses in Europe, and we often listened solemnly to lectures there about the places we would visit in the future.

The real reason, though, for submitting to these often boring duties was that every time we spent half a day plugging doggedly across muddy fields and shivering in bat-filled slimy ruins, we spent an equal amount of time sitting warmly, winily, in the best local restaurant, eating specialties of the village or the region more ardently than ever peak was scaled or Gothic arch gazed on.

The schedule was always the same: a brisk walk from the station and the little train that had brought us from Dijon, four or five hours of eating and drinking, and then the long promenade, the climbing, the viewing of monuments and fallen temples. Al and I were probably the youngest in the club by some thirty years, but more than once pure bravado was all that kept us from tumbling right into the nearest ditch in a digestive coma. The colonels and counsellors slapped their aged chests enthusiastically as the air struck them after the long hours in the restaurants, and they surged like a flock of young colts out into the country. We trotted mazily after them, two thin little American shadows convinced for a time at least that they were cousins of Gargantua.

The meals went on for hours, in spite of the length of the walk planned for later, and as a matter of pure research, based of course on our interest in folkways as well as culture, we arranged to taste not only the most noted dishes of the cook of the house, but also the Widow LeBlanc's way of pickling venison, and Monsieur le Curé's favorite recipe for little whole trout marinated in white wine and served chilled with green sour grapes.

The chef and his family would come in to enjoy our enjoyment, and then Widow LeBlanc and the Curé and the Curé's cook, and all of us would compare, with well-selected examples, the best local and district wines for each course. We always paid due homage to the ordinaries first, and then gradually lifted ourselves toward the heights of local pride, the crowned bottles known to every connoisseur alive, but never treated more respectfully than in their own birthplaces.

Sometimes the mayor or the lord of the château, knowing the Club Alpin of Dijon for what it really was, would send with his compliments a few bottles of such wines as I can only dream of now, wines unlabeled, never tired by travels, inviolate from the prying palates of commercial tasters. Then the gabble would die down, and Monsieur le Curé would bend his head over his goblet as if he were praying, and finally one or two of the old warhorses would murmur reverently, with his eyes focused far inwards, "*Epatant . . . é-pa-tant!*"

The club secretary always tried to arrange our sorties so that after we had studied a regional cuisine with the thoroughness it deserved, and had made solemn notes both physical and spiritual on the vintages that flourished there, or there, or there, we could devote ourselves with equally undivided zeal to the promenade itself.

More often than not, though, we would quite by accident find that along with the château in a little village some two hours' walk past dinner, there was also a tiny pastry shop where a certain ancient dame made sour-cream *fantaisies* the like of none other in all France.

"My God," Monsieur Vaillant, the retired advocate, would cry, halfway through our tour of a private country house where one of Maintenon's exiled lovers had spent twenty leisurely years painting Chinese pagodas on the wainscoting. "My God and double-*zut!* This is infamous! Here we are within ten minutes' delightful promenade from one of the great, the *great* pastry-makers of all time! She is modest, yes. She is content with a small fame. She made her *fantaisies* for my dear mother's First Communion. They came in a wooden trunk, packed in layers of silk-paper and dead leaves to survive the trip.

"Stop the tour!" Monsieur Vaillant would snort, his face flushed with inspiration, and a dawning appetite in his rheumy old eyes. And he would send a boy ahead, to warn the old witch to start up her fire and bestir her bones.

And then after we had looked dutifully at the rest of the wall-paintings, and some of the more erudite had identified classical symbolism in the obscure little scenes, and some of the more lecherous had identified with equal pleasure a few neo-classical positions among the slant-eyed nymphs and mandarins, we would head for the pastry shop. Even Al and I would forget our surfeit, whipped by the clean air and Monsieur Vaillant's jubilant memoirs into a fresh hunger.

Sure enough, the toothless village heroine's sour-cream *fantaisies*, light, delicate, fried in pure butter to a color clearer than gold, paler than Josephine Baker but as vital, would be the most delicious pastry in all of France, and Monsieur Vaillant the proudest member of our club.

We'd drink hot wine . . . "Nothing better against these November winds," we agreed with Vaillant valiantly . . . and then climb up perhaps only three of the four hills planned on by the optimistic secretary, before we caught the stuffy train back to Dijon. We'd smoke and talk and doze, in that intimacy peculiar to a third-class French "local" on Sunday night, and never once did we regret in any way, digestive or moral, the day's licentious prodigality of tastes and sensuous pleasures.

Once a year, on Ascension Day, the club left all such energetic ideas of rising above the earth-level strictly to the church, and held its annual banquet without benefit of sortie, promenade, or appreciation of any well-preserved ruins other than the fellow members.

The only year I went to the Ascension Day banquet we dined for six hours at the Hôtel de la Poste in Beaune. That was long before the old place had its face lifted, and we ate in the dark odorous room where generations of coachmen and carriage drivers and chauffeurs had nourished themselves as well as their masters did "up front."

There was a long table for us, and an even longer one for the wines. Piles of the year's last grapes made the air tingle with a kind of decadent promise, but there were no flowers to interrupt our senses.

We toasted many things, and at first the guests and some of the old judges and officers busied themselves being important. But gradually, over the measured progress of the courses and the impressive changing beauty of the wines, snobberies and even politics dwindled in our hearts, and the wit and the laughing awareness that is France made all of us alive.

The Measure of My Powers

1931

When I went back to Dijon, after the summer spent with my family, it was plain that the time had come for Al and me to live by ourselves. For two years we had eaten all our meals with good, interesting, even affectionate people, and lived in their house. We had learned much from them and accepted a thousand courtesies. Now, suddenly, they were intolerable, they and their sad quarrels and their gay generosities, they and their fine feathery omelets and their shared meats and vintages. We loved them, and we fled them like the black pox.

Even after so long in an army town, I still could not always tell a "*gros numéro*" from a reputable house, and managed to interrupt several business transactions and even exchange a few embarrassed salutations with unbuttoned University friends before I found the little apartment we were to live in.

It was in a "low quarter," everyone assured us with horror. The tram ran past it, and it looked down on a little square that once had held the guillotine and now, under the shade of thick plantains, housed two or three *pissoirs* and an occasional wandering sideshow, with small shops all around.

Indeed, the quarter was so low that several Dijonnais who had been friendly with us stopped seeing us altogether. What had been an amusing social pastime in the fairly dull town life, coming to tea with us in the Rue du Petit-Potet safely surrounded as we were there by mayors and bishops and the smell of thirteenth-century cellars, became an impossibility when it meant walking through streets that were obviously inhabited by nothing but artisans and laborers. We

435

basked in the new freedom, and absorbed sounds and vapors never met in a politer life.

Our apartment was two floors above a pastry shop, Au Fin Gourmet, and was very clean and airy, with a nice smell. The smell was what made me decide to take it, after days of backing confusedly out of brothels and looking at rooms dark and noisome and as lewdly suggestive as the old crones who showed them to me.

We signed several official certificates, bending over peach tarts and a row of soggy *babas* to reach the ink bottle. The proprietor looked at our signatures, and asked, "Married?"

"Yes," Al said, raising one eyebrow almost invisibly in a way that meant, in those days at least, that in spite of his politely innocent manner his words carried a tremendous reprimand or correction or general social commentary. "Yes. You see we have the same name, and I have marked us as Monsieur and Madame."

"Well," the man said, "it is less than nothing to me, you understand. But the police must be satisfied." He looked amicably at us, wiped his hands again on his sugary apron, and marked out Madame and my profession as student. In place of it he wrote, "Monsieur Fisher, and woman."

His wife, a snappish-looking small woman with pink eyebrows and tight mouth, gave us our keys and warned us again that the chambers were now in perfect condition and were expected to remain that way, and we went up the stairs to our own private home for the first time in our lives.

There was a big room with a shiny but uneven tiled floor and two wide windows looking down on the dusty little square. The bed, half-in-half-out a little alcove, did not keep everything from looking spacious and pleasant, especially when we pushed the round table into the corner and put books on the fake mantelpiece under the wavy old mirror. There was a kind of cupboard, which Madame the owner had called "*la chambre noire*"; we got some candles for it, and turned one of our trunk tops into a washstand, and it was very matter-of-fact in spite of its melodramatic name.

Outside our front door, on the landing, was a little faucet, where we got water for washing and cooking. It was a chore to carry it, and even more of one to empty the pail from the Black Chamber and the dish water and what I washed vegetables in, but it was something so new that I did not much mind it. There was a fountain in the square, of course, and I soon learned to take my lettuces and such down there and let the spout run over them, like the other women in the quarter.

The kitchen was astonishing to me, because I had never lived in a place like New York, where people cook on stoves hidden in their bureau drawers, I've heard. It was perhaps five feet long, perhaps three wide, and I had to keep the door open into the other room when I stood at the two burner gas-plate. There was a little tin oven, the kind to be set on top of a stove, and a kind of box with two shelves in it, for storage and instead of a table.

And there was the window, one whole wall, which opened wide and looked down into the green odorous square, and out over the twisted chimney pots to the skies of the Côte d'Or. It was a wonderful window, one of the best I can remember, and what I saw and thought and felt as I stood in it with my hands on the food for us, those months, will always be a good part of me.

Of course, we celebrated, the first night in the new place, and dined well and late at Ribaudot's, so that in the morning it was fun to lie in our niched bed and listen to the new noises.

They made a pattern we soon knew: the workers in their hard shoes, then the luckier ones with bicycles, and all the bells ringing; the shop-shutters being unhooked and folded back by sleepy apprentices; a great beating of pillows and mattresses, so that now and then brown feathers floated past our windows; and always the clanging of the little trams going up into the center of things.

That first morning there was something more, something we were to hear every Wednesday and Saturday, a kind of whispering pattering rush of women's feet, all pointed one way. I should have listened harder and learned.

When we finally got up, and went to the little café on the corner for our first breakfast, we saw that the soft rushing came from hundreds of women, all hurrying silently, all dressed in black and carrying black strings or pushing little carts and empty baby buggies. And while we were sitting there in the sun, two easy-going foreigners, some of the women started coming back against the stream, and I knew that they came from the big market, *les Halles*.

Their bags and carts were heavy now, so that the hands that held and pushed them were puffed and red. I saw the crooked curls of green beans and squashes, the bruised outer leaves of lettuces, stiff yellow chicken-legs . . . and I saw that the women were tired but full of a kind of peace, too. I had no black-string bag, no old perambulator. But I had a husband who enjoyed the dark necessity of eating, as I did myself. And I had a little stove. . . .

I stood up. It was almost noon, and too late now to go to the market. I planned innocently to pick up enough food at local stores to last until the next regular day, and headed for a store I'd often passed, where pans hung in rows in the window, and on the sidewalk clay casseroles and pots lay piled.

The first week I tried to feed us was almost too difficult. I learned a hundred things, all the hard way: how to keep butter without ice, how to have good salads every day when they could only be bought twice a week and there was no place to keep them cool (no place to keep them at all, really), how to buy milk and eggs and cheeses and when and where. I learned that *les Halles* were literally the only place to get fresh vegetables and that two heads of cauliflower and a kilo of potatoes and some endives weighed about forty pounds after I'd spent half an hour walking to market and an hour there and missed three crowded trams home again.

I learned that you bought meat and hard cheese and such by the kilo, but that butter and grated cheese, no matter how much you wanted, always were measured in grams. I learned that the stall-keepers in the market were tough loud-mouthed people who loved to mock you and collect a little crowd, and that they were very friendly and kind too, if you did not mind their teasing.

I learned always to take my own supply of old newspapers for wrapping things, and my own bowls and cans for cream and milk and such. I learned, with the tiredest feet of my life, that feeding people in a town like Dijon meant walking endless cobbled miles from one little shop to another . . . butter here, sausage there, bananas someplace again, and rice and sugar and coffee in still another place.

It was the longest, most discouraging, most exciting and satisfying week I could remember, and I look back on it now with an envy that is no less real for being nostalgic. I don't think I could or would ever do it again; I'm too old. But then, in the town I loved and with the man I loved, it was fine.

We ate well, too. It was the first real day-to-day meal-after-meal cooking I'd ever done, and was only a little less complicated than performing an appendectomy on a life-raft, but after I got used to hauling water and putting together three courses on a table the size of a bandana and lighting the portable oven without blowing myself clear into the living room instead of only halfway, it was fun.

We bought four plates and four forks, instead of two, so that we could entertain! Several of the people we knew found it impossible to condone our new address even with the words "whimsical" and "utterly mad," and very conveniently arranged to meet us in restaurants when they wanted to see us. The faithful ones who picked their way through the crowded streets and up our immaculately clean tenement steps were few, and they were welcome.

I wanted to invite the Rigagniers, but even if we could have asked them to bring their own plates and forks, I did not think the little stove would be able to cook anything they would honestly or even politely call a meal. And by then I was already beginning to have theories about what and how I would serve in my home.

I was beginning to believe, timidly I admit, that no matter how much I respected my friends' gastronomic prejudices, I had at least an equal right to indulge my own in my own kitchen. (I am no longer timid, but not always adamant, when it is a question of religion or old age or illness.)

I was beginning to believe that it is foolish and perhaps pretentious and often boring, as well as damnably expensive, to make a meal of six or eight courses just because the guests who are to eat it have always been used to that many. Let them try eating two or three things, I said, so plentiful and so interesting and so well cooked that they will be satisfied. And if they aren't satisfied, let them stay away from our table, and our leisurely comfortable friendship at that table.

I talked like that, and it worried Al a little, because he had been raised in a minister's family and taught that the most courteous way to treat guests was to make them feel as if they were in their own homes. I, to his well-controlled embarrassment, was beginning to feel quite sure that one of the best things I could do for nine tenths of the people I knew was to give them something that would make them forget Home and all it stood for, for a few blessed moments at least.

I still believe this, and have found that it makes cooking for people exciting and amusing for me, and often astonishingly stimulating for them. My meals shake them from their routines, not only of meat-potatoes-gravy, but of thought, of behavior. Occasionally I am fond enough of a person to realize that any such spiritual upset brought about by my serving an exotic or eccentric dish would do more harm than good, and I bow. It is usually women past middle age who thus confound me, and I have to be very fond of them indeed. They are few fortunately, and in spite of my solicitude I still think sometimes I am betraying them and myself too.

Perhaps it is not too late for them, I think; perhaps next time they come I will blast their safe tidy little lives with a big tureen of hot borscht and some garlic-toast and salad, instead of the "fruit cocktail," fish, meat, vegetable, salad, dessert, and coffee they tuck daintily away seven times a week and expect me to provide for them.

Perhaps they *should* feel this safe sand blow away so that their heads are uncovered for a time, so that they will have to taste not only the solid honesty of my red borscht, but the new flavor of the changing world. But when they come, they are so polite, so dazed, so genteelly dead already. . . .

The people who came oftenest to our room above the Fin Gourmet were Norah, on her free Thursday afternoons away from the convent, and the American student Lawrence, who was like our brother. They were both simple people, and reassuring. For Norah I would get a pitcher of milk and a pot of honey. I'd put them with the pat of sweet butter on the table, and a big square block of the plain kind of Dijon gingerbread that was called *pavé de santé*. There would be late grapes and pears in a big bowl.

Norah and I would sit by the open window, listening to the street sounds and playing Bach and Debussy and Josephine Baker on the tinny portable phonograph. The food was full of enchantment to my sister, after her gray meals in the convent, and she ate with the slow voluptuous concentration of a *dévouée*.

Lawrence was as satisfactory. He came for real meals, of course, and always brought a bottle of red wine, cheap but good. There would be candles on the table, because the one light-bulb in the room was far in the opposite corner, by the bed.

We would have a big salad always, and something I had made in one of the clay casseroles. I invented with gusto, and after the first days of experimenting with stoves, pots, and the markets, I turned out some fine odorous dishes that were a far cry, thank God, from the Hindu eggs that tortured my little sister Anne, the first time I ever let my imagination conquer over the printed recipe.

Our long stay with the Rigagniers, where Lawrence still lived, had given all of us a lust for simplicity after Madame's heady sauces. As I remember, the thing we all liked best, with the salad and Lawrence's wine, was a casserole of cauliflower, and bread and fruit afterwards. I made it so often that it became as natural as sneezing to me, and I was put off the track completely when I got back to America and found how different it was . . . the manner of doing it, the flavor, everything.

There in Dijon, the cauliflowers were small and very succulent, grown in that ancient soil. I separated the flowerlets and dropped them in boiling water for just a few minutes. Then I drained them and put them in a wide shallow casserole, and covered them with heavy cream and a thick sprinkling of freshly grated Gruyère, the nice rubbery kind that didn't come from Switzerland at all, but from the Jura. It was called *râpé* in the market, and was grated while you watched, in a soft cloudy pile, onto your piece of paper.

I put some fresh pepper over the top, and in a way I can't remember now the little tin oven heated the whole thing and melted the cheese and browned it. As soon as that had happened we ate it.

The cream and cheese had come together into a perfect sauce, and the little flowers were tender and fresh. We cleaned our plates with bits of crisp bread crust and drank the wine, and Al and Lawrence planned to write books about Aristotle and Robinson Jeffers and probably themselves, and I planned a few things, too.

And as I say, once back in California, after so many of those casseroles, I found I could never make one. The vegetable was watery, and there was no cream thick enough or unpasteurized and fresh. The cheese was dry and oily, not soft and light. I had to make a sauce with flour in it. I could concoct a good dish, still . . . but it was never so *innocent*, so simple . . . and then where was the crisp bread, where the honest wine? And where were our young uncomplicated hungers, too?

Quite often Jean Matruchot would come at noon.

He never went anywhere at night, and of course at the Lycée and the University where he taught there were a hundred stories about his licentious nocturnals. The truth was, I think, that the state of his poor popping eyes, which made it almost impossible for him to read large print in daylight, turned nights into a complete blackness which his pride would never let him confess. He was a misanthrope, and like most such men had fifty friends who would have been glad of a chance to walk with him along the dim crooked streets; but instead, he sat alone in his hideously furnished "bachelor suite" and went about only in daylight.

He ate his meals in the pensionnaires' room at Ribaudot's, and when he came to us for lunch he was like a man breathing after being almost too long without air.

"No rich dark-brown gaudy sauces," he would mutter, bending over his plate and sniffing what he could hardly see. "No ancient meats mummified with spices, exhumed and made to walk again like zombies! My God, no dead birds, rotting from their bones, and hiding under a crust five men have spent their lives learning how to put together so my guts will fall apart!"

"Madame," Jean would say, rising gallantly and spilling all the red wine in our glasses, which he did not see, and putting his napkin carefully on top of the salad, which was two feet away and therefore invisible to him, "chère Madame, a true victim of gastronomy, a fugitive from the world-famed Three Pheasants, a starved soul released temporarily from the purgatory of la Cuisine Bourguignonne, salutes you!"

Jean would bow, I would thank him, Al and I would whisk the more obvious damage from the table, and we would sit back to a somewhat heavy but enjoyable noon dinner.

Jean liked potatoes, so there would be a casserole of them fixed in the cauliflower routine, and quite often a watercress salad and steaks broiled somehow on the top of the stove. Then we would eat some good cheese . . . the Brie from the shop across the square was wonderful in that autumn weather, with the hot days, and the chilly nights to keep it from ripening too fast . . . and drink some more wine.

He had been an interpreter for the Americans in the last war, and on his good days he would tell us fantastic stories about the peaceful occupation of Beaune and all the homesick generals who called him Johnny. On his middling days he would tease me masterfully, like a fat Voltaire, for my class translations of "Gilpin's Ride." And on his bad days he would mutter such cynicisms as we had never heard, in French as rich and ripe as the cheese he loved, about the world and his honest hatred of it.

He was a strange passionately cold man, the kind who wants to be disliked and has true friends like us to refute all his intellectual desires. I think often of him, and of the hunger he showed for our food, and of the half-blind way his eyes would watch our faces, as if behind all the smug youthful foolishness he saw something he was looking for.

He was very different from Miss Lyse. She came often to eat with us, too, and I don't think she ever looked once at us. If she did, we were simply a part of all the sixty or so years of people who had fed her. She was charming to us; she sang for her supper, as life had taught her to, and she ate with the same ferocious voracity of any little bird while she kept us entertained.

She was about eighty then, I think, with a small pyramid of a body, and a fine proud little head with dark eyes and an ivory skin inherited from her Portuguese father. She had lived in Dijon since she was a girl, teaching English to the upper families. She still knew some conversation, all of it in simple words for the children she was used to talking to, but it was plain the French was more comfortable for her. She spoke it with a rank British accent, which she had promised her Devonshire mother never to abandon, and in spite of all the decades she had spent in the nurseries and drawing rooms of Burgundy, she sounded like a schoolgirl on a month's holiday from London, except for her volubility.

For years now, since her tyrannical dam breathed one last command and folded her hands in the death-grip over her cut jet locket, Miss Lyse had been cadging meals. She did it charmingly, amusingly.

She knew everybody, and all of the provincial gossip. She went to all the weddings of her former pupils, and then the christenings and the weddings of their children . . . and when the season was slack, and they remembered, they sent baskets of wine and cakes and butter to her attic room, as if in apology for the lack of festivals.

She was a character, everyone in Dijon said. She had followed the Bishop up the bloody steps of Saint Jacques, during the great troubles between Church and State, and had been stoned for it. Sadi Carnot had lain dying in her arms, assassinated. She had been a child in India where her father was ambassador and she knew how to charm snakes. That was the way the Dijonnais felt about her.

Myself, I was more than interested; there was something so indomitable about the set of her head and the fine flash of her old, old eyes. But it was her hunger that held me.

I don't know how she ate so much at one time. It was the result of years of practice, surely, years of not knowing just when another good meal would come her way. She was like a squirrel, with hidden pouches for the future. Norah and Lawrence and Jean Matruchot were as spindly ghosts compared with her, and meals big enough for six of us melted to a few crumbs almost before I had the time to serve them. Her manners were good, and she talked constantly in her funny mixture of nursery-English and London-French, and yet the lunch would be liquidated in the time Al and I usually spent on a salad or a tart.

I tried sometimes to see if I could stump her; I would make a bowl of two whole kilos of Belgian endive, cut into chunks and mixed with marinated green beans and sweet red peppers and chives. There would be a big casserole of fish and mushrooms and such in cream. I'd buy rich tarts at Michelin's.

Halfway through the meal Al and I would lie back in our chairs, listening and watching in a kind of daze. Miss Lyse was like something in a Disney film . . . nibble bite chew nibble nibble . . . through everything on the table, until it would not have surprised us at all to have her start conversationally, daintily, with a flick of her bright dark eyes and a quirk of her white head, on the plates themselves and then the books, right down the mantelpiece, Shakespeare, Confucius, *Claudine à l'Ecole* . . . *les Croix de Bois, The Methodist Faun* . . . nibble nibble crunch.

"That was so delicious, my dear," she would say at the end, wiping her mouth nicely and getting up with a brisk bob. "You are most kind to an old lady. And now I must thank you and be off. The Countess Malinet de Rinche is in from the country and I am having tea with her. This was *such* a nice little lunch together! Shall we say for the same day next week? Then I can tell you all about the dear Countess! Her sons! *Mon Dieu!*"

And Miss Lyse would give me a dry sweet-smelling peck on both cheeks and be out of the door before we could even get to our feet.

Would she really have tea with the unknown Countess What's-her-name, whose sons were less interesting than dead sea-fruit to us? Would she eat again until we next saw her? Did she really have *sous* enough for bread? We never knew.

It worried me, and I resolved to buy nine caramel tarts, instead of six, for the "little lunch" we knew she would not forget to take with us in exactly a week. . . .

I had one letter from her after the invasion. It was vigorous and amusing, although by then she must have been almost a hundred years old. She had been evacuated to a wretched little village near Clermont-Ferrand, and she had organized all the children into a band, to be ready to greet the Tommies in their own tongue when they came marching in. She said nothing about herself . . . but I have a belief that as long as there was life in that proud-headed little body, she would find crumbs.

The Measure of My Powers

1931–1932

ONE night about ten o'clock, perhaps a week after Al was awarded his doctorate at the Faculté, we stopped on our way home from a dinner party and stood looking at each other for a minute in the cold street.

Then, without a word, we headed for the station. We bought two tickets for Strasbourg on the midnight train, *that* midnight, not the one a week away when we had planned to go.

Most of our things were ready to be shipped. We arranged with the station master to have them brought from our apartment in a day or two. Then we ran down the back streets to our flat, routed out the saw-faced cake-maker who lived just below us in his libellously named shop, Au Fin Gourmet, and arranged in five minutes all such questions of refunds, taxes, rental papers as he would have preferred to spend five hours on. We threw what wasn't already packed into suitcases.

We left the door open on our dear little apartment without one backward glance of regret or even gratitude, and when we were finally sitting in the Buffet de la Gare, drinking a last coffee with a porter who had become our friend in the past years, we breathed again.

We were fleeing. We were refugees from the far-famed Burgundian cuisine. We were sneaking away from a round of dinner parties that, we both felt calmly sure, would kill us before another week was over.

Ever since Al's masterly and amusing public oral defense of his thesis, which drew almost as big a crowd in the Faculté amphitheatre as had the last visit from a footloose Balkan regent, we had

446

been deluged with invitations. Most of them were from lawyers, viscounts, and even professors who, in spite of the obvious cordiality of the Faculté Dean and the Rector toward us, had peered suspiciously at us over the tops of their newspapers and waited until now to bestow the accolade of their social recognition.

For almost two and a half years they had watched us, and observed to their cynical amazement that we were breaking every precedent established by former American students: we stayed; we didn't get drunk; Al actually worked hard enough to be awarded a degree, and I actually let other men alone, in spite of wearing the same color lipstick as the upper-bracket broads. And now we were guaranteed safe. Al had earned a right to wear a little round bonnet edged with rabbit fur and I, fortunate among all women, could now look forward to being the wife of a full professor some day, instead of an instructor.

"They really seem charming," people whispered about us in the discreetest drawing rooms of Dijon. "Lunch? A small dinner?"

Suddenly we were like catnip, after all those blessed months of being stinkweed. The closed doors swung open, and we found ourselves drowning in a sea of Burgundy's proudest vintages, Rheims' sparkle, Cognac's fire. Snails, *pâtés, quenelles de brochet;* always a great chilled fish *in toto* on a platter; venison and pheasants in a dozen rich brown odorous baths; intricate ices and well-laced beaten creams . . . and all of them served to the weighty tune of polite conversation, part condescending and part awed: it was too much for us.

The unsuspected strain of getting ready for the doctorate and then this well-meant deluge of hospitable curiosity made us feel that "we must press lettuce leaves upon our brows," or die.

And that is why we were hiding in the Buffet, that cold November night. We suddenly felt rested, knowing the train was almost there for us. We would send telegrams . . . I would write letters. . . .

Our friend the porter piled us into the compartment. We shook hands. The train shivered for a minute, and then started slowly to pull northward.

We heard a shout outside.

The porter was running along beside our window, and with him was Paul de Torcy, little hunchbacked Paul who adored Al, Paul who was rich and spent all his money publishing volumes of dreadfully poor poems for bankrupt provincial welshers. Paul loved Al more than any of them, and showed him his most private room, hung with black velvet and with . . . yes, it is true . . . with a skull on the carved oak desk. Paul wore a flowing tie. Paul hated me. Paul's drunken father had thrown him down the château steps when he was little.

And there he was running desperately along the platform, his great head with its sunken temples rolled back against his hump. How had he learned that we were fleeing? What suspicions hissed behind his wild pleading eyes?

He was weeping, glaring up at Al. And without wanting to, God knows, we began to laugh, there in the hastening train, in our own safety and warmth. We stood in the window looking down at Paul and *laughing*, because his eyes, so enormous and hopeless, looked like the eyes of a planked turbot we had been served so few hours before at dinner.

The turbot lay regally on its linen couch, bedecked with citrons and fresh herbs. Paul, more alive, ran crazily along the gray platform, unadorned. But their eyes, their great deep glassy eyes, were the same eyes, wild and full of a mute adoration and a terrible humility.

We kept on laughing, in a kind of sickness. And as the porter grabbed Paul's arm to stop his running, Al raised his fingers in a queer gesture that was half kiss, half salute.

11

It was early morning when we got to Strasbourg. By then we were numb with weariness. We went across the big square in front of the station to a hotel, and it wasn't until almost eighteen hours later that we woke up enough to realize that we were in the biggest bed either of us had ever seen. It must have been ten feet across, and it was clean and very comfortable. We felt fine.

Our watches had stopped, and when we telephoned to the clerk we found that it was long after midnight. He sent us up some cold sausages and rolls and beer, good Walsheim beer. We ate every crumb, and licked the foam from the stein-rims, and then slept again for several hours. When we awoke the second time we felt even finer. Al had his precious doctorate, and we were in love, and Strasbourg lay before us.

We bathed and dressed, and went out into the icy streets. There were already ranks of little fir trees in the Place Kléber, and gingerbread stands readied for Christmas, as there had been the year before when we went through on our way to Nürnberg. And we remembered our way to the great rosy-faced cathedral, and to the Kamarzellhaus that crouched beside it.

The Kamarzellhaus was almost objectionably quaint, but downstairs there was a cozy little taproom, and upstairs in the small restaurant the food was always better than good when we went there.

The first time, on our way to Germany, we had sat downstairs while our meal was being made. There were big soft leather chairs, and on the dark table was a bowl of the first potato chips I ever saw in Europe, not the uniformly thin uniformly golden ones that come out of waxed bags here at home, but light and dark, thick and paper-thin, fried in real butter and then salted casually with the *gros sal* served in the country with the *pot-au-feu*.

They were so good that I ate them with the kind of slow sensuous concentration that pregnant women are supposed to feel for chocolate-cake-at-three-in-the-morning. I suppose I should be ashamed to admit that I drank two or three glasses of red port in the same strange private orgy of enjoyment. It seems impossible, but the fact remains that it was one of the keenest gastronomic moments of my life.

And of course by the time the waiter called us upstairs, Al's carefully chosen dinner was more than wasted on me. I felt very sorry about that. He forgave me, and we went back, that next time in Strasbourg, and ate it over again.

There were several other restaurants of some note in the town, but there was the same kind of confusion in them that we felt everywhere; they were neither French nor German, and certainly there was no proof that the autonomy so fiercely wished for by many of the Alsatians could succeed in their kitchens. Almost every little pub advertised its own *choucroute garnie*, of course, and sometimes it was good indeed, and sometimes it was a sad and soggy mess, a dingy pile of sauerkraut no longer sour, gray aged potatoes, and *wursten* wrinkled as autumn leaves but less delectable.

There was one tavern run by the Walsheimbier concern, where Al and Norah and I used to go on Sunday afternoons after our long cold walks along the Rhine and into the little woods.

Norah was in a convent in the town then, after Christmas. It was plain she was a North-type woman, even in her fourteenth winter:

she bloomed like a beautiful young pine tree in the cold air of Strasbourg, and there was a kind of leashed vitality about her that I have never seen so plainly since. She had to be back inside the convent gate by six, so we would end our walks as soon as the sun began to set, at three-thirty or even three, and head by bus or tram-car, the quickest way, toward the Walsheim tavern.

It was very German, noisy warm *good* German, filled with large families who had spent their Sundays much as we had and were hungry in the same tingling robust way. We would sit with other people, usually, who smiled and greeted us and then went on with their own lives, and we would order large beers and whichever of the two specialties we had decided on during the walk: Walsheimplatten, which were plates covered with a dozen or so small but sturdy open-faced sandwiches, or bread-and-cheese.

Cheese there meant one kind, the soft ripe Münster, like Limburger or our Liederkranz or a strong Brie. It was always served with a pile of chopped onion and one of caraway seeds, and the whole combination was what my father would describe as "fruity."

I have often wondered what olfactory effect Norah had on the nice little girls in her dormitory, most of whom had spent Sunday either on their knees or in the chaste company of visiting cousins. We had things so well timed that just as the Sister at the gate put her key in the lock Norah, like a large happy uniformed bat straight from the mouth of a purely Protestant hell, would shoot past and into the convent, trailing an almost visible cloud of beer and cheese and good humor behind her. She would turn once and wink at us, and then murmur, "*Merci, ma soeur*," and bow her head in its neat convent hat with a kind of regal docility as she disappeared until the next Sunday.

Perhaps it was wrong to take such a young girl into a public tavern with us, and let her drink beer, but it did not seem so. Physically she was bigger and stronger than either Al or I . . . and in other ways I like to think that the walks and then the honest smells and tastes and sounds of the pub left something good in her heart, as they did in mine.

The other place in town where Al and I went most often was called Philippe's. It was a big extravagant *brasserie* exactly like the best ones in Paris, and it was supposed to be financed and directed by the French government, as part of the propaganda to keep Alsace away from the Germans. Certainly it was run with an almost frantic lavishness. The service was perfect, and everything from a glass of beer to a ten-course dinner with the finest wines was not only the best but the cheapest, probably, in all that part of France.

We went there most often with a man named Franz, who was ostensibly the manager of the government tobacco factory in Strasbourg, but was really a secret agent. He told us that Philippe's cost the taxpayers thousands of francs a day, and I could see how. I have never eaten better oysters than there. They came by plane every morning from the coast. And *moules marinières* . . . the memory of them makes me sigh. And of course *pâtés* of Strasbourg, in aspics, in crusts, in mousses. . . . And the wines in carafe were the finest I have ever tasted. Franz said the government went so far as to buy bottled vintages and then empty them into the cheap open pitchers, to make the Alsatians learn to know something besides beer and the Rhine wines imported at low prices by the Germans.

Yes, we went often to Philippe's, by ourselves or with Franz and his strange little protégé, the Annamite prince, whose political education was also a part of Franz's peculiar duties, as well as an obviously amorous pleasure. There was something exciting about the whole place, and very wrong, like a beautiful young woman with a cancer.

III

Al and I lived for two or three months in the top of a house out by the Orangeries, but it did not work.

We had a queer little kitchen which every morning had an icicle on the one water faucet, and a dingy little living room with one round window in it about the size of a Thanksgiving pie, and then at the other end of a long hall a small bedroom. There was no way of bathing, so that in spite of bi-weekly treks to the municipal bath-house I felt an inevitable dirtiness creep over me.

There was a little black tiled stove in the living room which held about a pint of coke at a time and had to be stoked at least once every half-hour to stay even lukewarm.

We were almost three miles from markets. Al was good about bringing things home, and when I was too cold to cope with trams I would walk up to the café at the corner and telephone for groceries. But still it was discouraging to have to put on my fur coat and gloves to cook a meal in the little kitchen, where steam would stiffen into ice as soon as it hit the sloping uninsulated ceiling.

I tried to write . . . I think then I had decided, with mistaken smugness, that I could turn out a much better shilling-shocker than many already in print . . . but my hands and head were too cold.

I used to go across into the Orangerie when I felt too cold to sit still, and watch what animals had thick enough fur to wander outside their cages. I'd stand and stand, waiting for some sign of life from the rumpled creatures on the other side of the bars, but even the guinea pigs were too stiff to carry out their usual haphazard copulations. The storks, symbol of Alsace, would stare bleakly at me and occasionally drop a languid feather into the frozen filth, and I would turn back to my home, stumbling a little in my haste to get there before the fire went out again.

Some time every early morning, a pair of very old beggars hobbled cursing and singing past the house. I began to wait for them. Several times I looked at them, while I stood shuddering in the bedroom window. The man had a peg-leg, and the woman, as far as I could ever see in the moonlight on the snow, no face at all. They were always drunk, and sometimes they would stop and caress each other and sometimes the old man would knock his partner down a dozen times before they disappeared toward the end of the street.

I stopped watching them, but I began to know when they were coming long before I heard the tap-tap of his leg on the ice, and finally I knew, in spite of all my good sense, that one night he would come in through the locked gate, through the door, up the stairs, through our own solid door, into the room, tap-tap-tap. . . .

Then Al decided to make a tamale pie. I had never tasted one, which was his excuse, but he may have felt about it rather as I had about the potato chips at the Kamarzellhaus. He spent days preparing it, and buying the proper casserole, the best Greek olives, a chili powder sent down from a grocery in Paris, cornmeal found finally at an obscure "health food store."

At last everything was assembled. He stayed home from the University, where he was doing some work, and thanks to his enthusiasm and probably his actual physical presence, the apartment was almost warm. I was glad I had not spoken of my foolish fears. We made a little salad of bland Belgian endive, a good complement to the spices of Al's masterpiece, and drank a firm-bodied red wine, and the tamale pie was very good indeed.

It was probably one of the best that has ever been made, anywhere in the world where anyone would bother to make one, and I hope it was the only one I shall ever eat.

Of course it was not the concoction itself that broke my spiritual back. I know that well. But a little while after I finished eating it (I should say well within the four-hour period of a more or less normal digestion), I began to cry. It was the first time Al had even seen a tear in either of my eyes. Now there were thousands. They fell down my cheeks without a sound or a sigh from me, and my nose did not even turn red. I simply sat wordless, held in a kind of stupefaction, too limp to put a handkerchief to my drenched cheeks. I was humiliated, but without the energy to hide myself.

Al watched me for a time, and asked like any normal male, "What have I done?" Then, for he was practical as well as erudite, he stoked the fire, put a glass of brandy within reach of my numb hand, and left for the University.

I sat in the gradually chilling room, thinking of my whole past the way a drowning man is supposed to, and it seemed part of the present, part of the gray cold and the beggar woman without a face and the moulting birds frozen to their own filth in the Orangerie. I know now I was in the throes of some small glandular crisis, a sublimated bilious attack, a flick from the whip of melancholia, but then it was terrifying . . . nameless. . . .

When it was time for Al to come home I drank the brandy, which stopped the steady flowing of my large soft tears, and made myself as pretty as I could. I felt desperately ashamed, and full of bewilderment.

We went to Philippe's for supper, and everything was fine until we started homeward. Then tears began to slip down my face again, and all my bones turned sick and limp. I could only roll my eyes dazedly at my poor husband, and shake my head.

He was wonderful. He took me to the warmest hotel-room in all the town, full of firelight and plump white pillows and red-damask featherbeds with ruffles. He ran a bath for me in a huge white tub with bronze spigots shaped like spitting swanheads. And while I made myself feel really clean for the first time in weeks, he went all the way back to our apartment on the tram and got some night-clothes for us.

And the next day we moved to the Pension Elisa, without any words of question or reproach, then or ever.

The Elisa was much too expensive, and we stayed there in a cozy careless hibernation for the many weeks before we went south. It was near the University, and I saw much more of Al.

For a time I was languid, like a convalescent, and at night listened willy-nilly for the tapping of the beggar's wooden leg. In daylight I lay on a chaise-longue behind the white linen billows of curtain in our alcove and listened to the homesick Polish consul in the next room play on his concertina, and watched the bridge across the canal. I got to know many Strausbourgeois, and just when, each day, to look for the school children, the fat furred rich women with their match-ing dachshunds on studded leashes, the pale clerks, the mincing prostitutes.

Gradually I began to work again. It was very poor stuff I wrote, but healthy. I went to the Cathedral a lot, and the museums, and felt warm all the time, and Al and I had fun together, in the taverns and the streets and in the dark dining room of the Elisa, where we ate even darker meals of roasted wild-boar meat and such. There were always purées, as I remember, as if the fifty-odd *pensionnaires* had no teeth: peas, lentils, potatoes, chestnuts, rubbed to a suave paste and decorated unfailingly with gouts of a sauce which never varied its fairly potent flavor nor its rich blackish shade.

Soon I forgot the awful way tears had rolled from my eyes, as if I were not human. By now all I can say about that evil day, really, is that I am content with utter illogicality to dislike the thought of eating a tamale pie again.

Sea Change

1932

THE next time we put to sea, in 1932, was not so much later, about a year . . . but I was more than a year older. I don't know why; I simply matured in a spurt, so that suddenly I knew a lot about myself and what I wanted and what I had to do. It made me soberer, and I was much less shy.

It was hard to leave Europe. But I knew that even if we stayed, our young days there were gone. The first insouciant spell was broken, and not by the act of buying tickets, as Al seemed to believe. Nor could it ever be recaptured; that would be monstrous, like a man turned child again but still caught in his worn big body.

We ate lunch before the boat sailed at a restaurant on the Old Port in Marseille. Al and I had often been there before, and Norah, who was unusually acute about flavors, almost like a French child, was excited at the prospect of one final orgy of real *bouillabaisse*. We almost didn't get it, though.

It was the first time I had ever been turned away from a restaurant, and it left me strangely shaken; we walked in the door and a waiter came hurrying toward us through the crowded room and before we knew it we were out on the street again . . . shoo, shoo, as if we were impudent chickens on a lawn.

Then the proprietor rushed out. He recognized Al and me. He screamed at the officious waiter. We all laughed and laughed . . . the waiter had seen my accordion, which Al carried under his arm because we couldn't find a safe parking place for it before the boat sailed, and had thought we were hungry street-singers planning to cadge a meal.

We bowed and grinned and blushed, and there Norah and Al and I were, sitting at the best table on the balcony, looking down on the Old Port in the full spring sunlight, drinking several different kinds of the proprietor's private stock of wines and trying not to wonder how we could bear to leave this land.

The *bouillabaisse* sent up its own potent saffrony steam. We mopped and dunked at its juices, and sucked a hundred strange dead creatures from their shells. We toasted many things, and often, but ourselves most of all.

And then it was time to go. I played the proprietor and several waiters my best tune, still feeling, through the good wine and food, a sense of shock that I or anyone else in the world could be turned away from a door. We all had a final drink, in a *marc du Midi* that would jar Jupiter, and then we left France.

The ship was a small Italian freighter, carrying about fifteen passengers. She was called the *Feltre*, I think, and was lightly loaded with wines and oils for sale, a small famous sailing boat being taken to America to race, and an enormous quantity of food for the crew, since Mussolini would not allow any but Italian products to be eaten by his men on the three months' voyage.

(The ship's cargo was also suspected, by the Marseille police, of including two desperate men who had killed bank clerks and taken a sum of money that increased from twenty-five hundred to a quarter of a million francs while the holds were searched and the captain fumed. Finally, after everything including my poor accordion had been undone, unbuttoned, and unlocked, the police went crankily away, and we could creep past all the docks . . . the smallest, silentest start on a sea voyage I have ever made.)

We stopped at several Spanish ports, big ones like Barcelona or simply a pier thrust weakly into the water, covered with square gleaming tins of olive oil. Once there was a great slick of oil to meet us, and the crew cursed the idle Spanish stevedores who stood smiling and smoking and refused to load any of the tins. They were splitting in the sun, so that the greenish oil dripped from every crack in the pier.

It was sabotage, the captain told us: things were in a bad way in Spain . . . the Communists, of course . . . there would be revolution soon.

We wallowed for two days in the slick swell. A few dozen cans were found whose solder had not melted, and we loaded them and left, with the fine rich smell of the lost oil following us for hours over the water.

In Malaga we sat under a tree by a café and drank dutifully of the thick brown wine, and then after a decent interval switched gladly to watered *Anis Mono* . . . a savage combination, but I think it offended no one.

I decided I wanted to live near Malaga. On deck, drinking weak Italian beer, we watched the tawny hills slip by, and it was like California between Balboa and San Diego, and I loved it.

Then, days later, when we moved slowly past the Canaries, I decided, almost, that I wanted to live there. What would it be like to live on an island, such a small intensely islandic island? No. . . .

It would be something like living for so many somnolent weeks on a small ship, as we did. There would be unrecognized emotions, and perhaps sudden flarings of strong action, and tears and then quiet again among the inhabitants. It takes detachment to live in a place where the physical boundaries are visible in every direction. And for me there is too little of life to spend most of it forcing myself into detachment from it.

The captain was a young fat man with impersonal eyes which should have been full of light. I felt that he resented and disliked passengers and his life as a kind of wet nurse to them, and I could not blame him. But even without us, I don't believe he was a sea captain, the way a Dutchman or a Swede or perhaps even an Italian can be. He seemed as far from his ship as from us, which gave me an uncomfortable sense of insecurity.

He was perhaps less cool with other people; there were at least two bursts of jealous tears somewhere in the Caribbean, I remember, because he talked in his cabin with the two strong-chinned American girls returning from a year in Florence instead of with young Mrs. Feinmann, who had run away with an Italian and was being brought back to her forgiving husband by her mother. ("Isn't it just like something on the radio?" both women asked me with romantic and proud relish a few hours out of Marseille, when they told me for the first of perhaps forty times about the flight, the pursuit, the capture.)

Al and Norah and I, because of our natures, kept sea changes to ourselves, and lived in a small proud world. Our cabins on the upper of the two tiny decks opened into a kind of salon, and we ate there with a family of four Swiss people as quiet as we.

My little fingers and toes went to sleep, of course, and for a few days outside of Gibraltar I was more frightened than I had been in all the months Norah was my charge; the two of us, for the only times in our lives, had cruel earaches, so that we moved and spoke as if we were made of glass. There was no nurse on board, which is against international law, I believe. The captain had medicines in his cabin, but I felt something ridiculous in our going there, two tall fair women, asking that fat impersonal man for pills.

"Drink a lot of water and keep warm," I said firmly to Norah, my mind trembling around words like mastoid, and my head pierced with hot wires.

And in about four days we suddenly were free again. I wonder about that . . . whether it was a germ . . . certainly we did not dream it, nor I the repressed panic I felt about Norah and all the water between her and help.

The other changes were less violent, less tangible.

I don't know about Al; he looked at the water, and talked with the man who sailed the racing boat for an American millionaire, and with a big Italian wrestler from San Francisco. He made notes on tiny papers in his almost invisible writing. He was very good to look at, when we got down into the real warmth and he could wear white cotton clothes. But inside . . . I don't know at all.

It is almost the same with Norah. She read a lot of French novels I had brought for myself (and I in turn read *Monte Cristo* in eight volumes and religious tracts borrowed from the Swiss). One time I heard her talking in her cabin, and I went to see why. She was standing in the middle of the little white room, looking at the beetles that roamed the walls and ceiling as they did everywhere, and saying, "I won't stand it another minute. I simply refuse to stand it!"

She was crying, and stiff with anger at the black bugs. I felt very sorry for her, but I said, "You are twelve days from Gibraltar and about twenty from the next port, Norah," and went back to my own cabin.

She was all right by lunchtime, but for two or three days she had a quiet almost exhausted look about her. It is hard to recognize inevitabilities with grace, and probably she will never quite recover from the shock of hearing me say what she was trying not to admit. She was very young for such a thing.

And I was by myself most of the time, knitting and reading and cautiously poking into my own mind. I had found out several things about my relationship to my family, and to other men than Al, and while the ship rolled slowly forward across all the waves, I discussed them, usually alone but sometimes with him.

I don't think he really heard me, knowing perhaps that I was talking to myself. And perhaps he too was talking silently. That seemed natural, there on the quiet little ship. Nothing was real except what happened in my mind. (Would that be true on an island, too?) The outside things were shadowy, the pleasant daily rhythm of meals and greetings and gossip, and even earache and the occasional obtruding passions of other voyagers.

There was of course another kind of life going on, among the crew, but they seldom came near us. They were quiet for Italians, and not gay. Our cabin boy was a pale blond boy named Luigi, who shook with embarrassment when we spoke to him, and had a very strong smell. I cannot remember the waiter, except that he was nice. When it got too hot to eat the veal and pork we had every noon, he worried, especially about Norah, and brought small strange salads to her. That was against orders, because by then there was just enough lettuce left for the Captain's Dinner, some four weeks away.

The cheeses and the bread were delicious, and there was always wine on the table. Sometimes it tasted strange after the red and white Burgundies we had grown to know. It was more like the wines of the Midi, not the ones that were exported for gourmets, but the local kinds, fuller, coarser, heavier. I liked it. The waiter would bring me a little ice, and I would drink it with everything: the heady slices of salami, the cheeses, the fruit.

When we began to touch at ports in Central America we had wonderful papayas, cold and smooth as butter, and green-skinned oranges as big as melons, and bananas. There were avocados too, good with the fine crusty bread. And the dark yellow wines, the bluish red ones, were just what I wanted with these things, simple and straightforward in all the lush heat of the coastal waters.

We were really hard-up, and what money we had was carefully apportioned: one beer a day, one vermouth before dinner, tips at San Pedro, "incidentals." Al did not favor the wines. His mind's palate still echoed to the firm notes of a Chambertin '19, and he could ill adjust himself to lesser vintages. So Norah and I gave him our beers, not suffering much from such watery losses.

Once, on her birthday, we drank champagne. It was sweet and warm, and little gnats swarmed over the glasses in the steaming dark. Outside we could hear natives splashing in the stockade built in the bay to keep out sharks. The ship was silent. The captain lifted his glass shyly to us, and we all sighed, wishing that we could like one another.

I was even stupider then than I sometimes admitted; now it seems plain to me that poor Al did not stay aboard because bad pork surged in his bowels. He had a deep and violent and really fearful hatred of insects . . . bugs . . . things that sucked and bit. Probably he lay wanly in his bunk because of them, of knowing that where we would go the earth teemed with them, and every tree was heavy with them. Probably . . . I hate now to think of my dull misunderstanding . . . probably he was sickened to think of my coming back from those dreamy trips ashore, covered with invisible pests. But he said nothing, and I went with Norah and the others into the jungle villages.

Once I looked at a man in one of them, and stood fixed, a moth on a pin; he was very brown, in old tattered pants like a movie beachcomber's, and he had blue eyes and six fine strong toes on each foot. I do not know how I saw two such startling facts at once, but I did.

And when I stopped looking at him, I turned mazedly to speak to Norah, and could not because an old woman so leprous that only the bare white bones of her hand rested on Norah's arm, stood clutching at her. I turned hot with horror, and then shrugged . . . it was all part of the dream, and rushing for antiseptics and scaring people and shocking them would do no good. I gave the old woman some money, and as she moved off into the shadows, like a rotten apple rolling, I said nothing. What use?

I put my hand just where the leper's had lain, and we too went into the shadows.

Once, I remember, we sat for hours in a cool bar with a dirt floor, drinking milk from coconuts which the boss pulled up from a deep covered well in the center of the room. He would get down on his knees as he saw us tipping the shells back further, and haul up the nuts in a kind of seine, cold and dripping. He could poke the eyes out with his thumb. We drank in a kind of frenzy. The milk was like balm after the coarse wines and the sea air. We felt a little sick for a few hours, but it was good to sit there so quietly with the earth under our feet.

Another time everybody on ship went to a palmy courtyard for a dinner. It was inside a hotel, a small dirty place without any doors, where the toilet was a hole in one corner of a room with several hammocks in it and several sleeping men in the hammocks.

We walked through a few little streets where every house was open, with a handsome Sears-Roebuck bed under a lithograph of the Sacred Heart, like the whores' rooms in Cristobal, and then hammocks swung for the real family life.

We started to eat, in a patio filled with vines and parrots and our long table, before the light left. A tiny gray-bearded man in white cotton trousers and a pink silk polo-shirt served us, helped by two children only a little taller than he.

We ate and ate. I can't remember much of it except avocados in several different manners. There was meat, though, probably found at great cost and, for me at least, impossible either to chew or swallow. There were dozens of little dishes of sweet cooked fruits and flat tidbits which could have been bats' ears or sliced melon-rind. The man, his large eyes devoutly veiled, slid them in front of us, hour after hour.

Occasionally came a dish of chicken boiled with peppers and choco-late . . . something like that, as loud as a trumpet call in all the sweetness.

We sat eating, big pale strangers, and the patio grew dark. By the time we had drunk coffee and finished our beer and paid, the night was black. Under a streetlight three prisoners stumbled past us. Their irons rang against the occasional pavements, and sucked at the mudholes. And outside the village, before we came to the dock, fireflies taunted us in the forest, like mischievous candles, the biggest in the world.

The Captain's Dinner was strange, too. We were off the coast of Lower California. The water was so calm that we could hear flying fish slap against it. We ate at a long table out on deck, under an awning between us and the enormous stars.

The captain looked well in his white uniform, and smiled almost warmly at us all, probably thanking God that most of us would leave him in a few days. The waiters were excited, the way the Filipino boys used to be at boarding-school when there was a Christmas party, and the table looked like something from a Renaissance painting.

There were galantines and aspics down the center, with ripe grapes brought from Italy and stranger fruits from all the ports we'd touched, and crowning everything two stuffed pheasants in their dulled but still dashing feathers. There were wine glasses on stems, and little printed menus, proof that this masterpiece of a meal was known about in Rome, long since.

We ate and drank and heard our own suddenly friendly voices over the dark waters, and forgot that Mrs. Feinmann was in her cabin because the captain wouldn't put the Italian wrestler in irons for "making a pass at her," and that Thoreau's grand-niece was very pale from the hemorrhage that had engulfed her earlier in the day. The waiters glided deftly, perhaps dreaming that they served at Biffi's instead of on this fifth-rate freighter, and we drank Asti Spumanti, undated but delightful.

And finally, while we clapped, the chef stood before us, bowing in the light from the narrow stairs. He wore his high bonnet and whites, and a long-tailed morning coat, and looked like a drawing by Ludwig Bemelmans, with oblique sadness in his pasty outlines.

There was a silence after our applause. He turned nervously toward the light, and breathed not at all. We heard shufflings and bumps. Then, up through the twisting white closeness of the stairway, borne on the backs and arms of three awe-struck kitchen boys, rose something almost too strange to talk about.

The chef stood back, bowing, discreetly wiping the sweat from his white face. The captain applauded. We all clapped, and even cheered. The three boys set the thing on a special table.

It was a replica, about as long as a man's coffin, of the cathedral at Milano. It was made in white and pink sugar. There was a light inside, of course, and it glowed there on the deck of the little ship, trembling in every flying buttress with the Mexican ground swell, pure and ridiculous; and something about it shamed me.

It was a little dusty. It had undoubtedly been mended, after mighty storms, in the dim galleys of a hundred ships, better but never worse than this. It was like a flag flying for the chef, a bulwark all in spun sugar against the breath of corruption. It was his masterpiece, made years ago in some famous kitchen, and he showed it to us now with dignity . . .

Sea Change

1935

ABOUT three and a half years later, I think, in 1935 or 1936, I went back to France with Chexbres and his mother. The whole thing seems so remote now that I cannot say what was sea change and what had already happened on land. I know that I had been in love with Chexbres for three years or so.

I was keeping quiet about it; I liked him, and I liked his first wife who had recently married again, and I was profoundly attached to Al. Even while I hurried to New York for such an odd jaunt, with Al's apparently hearty approval, I was making plans for the next years with him, the rest of my life with him.

I was full of resolutions never to be caught in the whirlpool of being a "faculty wife," and was planning to adopt several children, raise goats, not feed more than twenty hungry students a week with my exciting stews and broths; that is to say, I was a typical young faculty wife. A few more years, and I'd have been wearing brown-satin afternoon dresses and wearily eating marshmallow salads at committee luncheons with the best of them.

Instead, I stepped aboard the *Hansa*, one ice-heavy February midnight.

The *Hansa* was a tidy, plump little ship. There was something comfortable about her, and at the same time subtly coarse and vulgar, like a motherly barmaid married to a duke in an English novel.

Several things happened to me aboard her that I have often wanted to write about, but I never have and perhaps never will because I feel very strongly about prejudicing people. These things were about Germans, not the kind good Germans who cared for us, but evil men and women. Before the war I did not want to rouse distrust, and have the good judged by the evil ones . . . and in wartime there is enough hatred, both real and imaginary, without my adding to it.

There was indeed too much ugliness on that pretty little ship. It was all a part of what is happening now in the world, and has always happened, and always will happen while men stunt their souls.

Fortunately it did not touch many people then. Chexbres' mother did not know about it, nor would she have recognized it if it had reared and hissed at her, so excited was she to be once more pointed toward the Paris of fifty years before, when she studied in Chaplin's *atelier* and her homesick father, wordless and bewildered, fished with the other old men along the quais.

Yet, it is better, I think, to forget the bad things on that ship. There were many good ones, and funny too . . . like the concert-grand piano in the Ladies' Salon, painted a rich creamy pink (with mother-of-pearl keys), so that it looked like a monstrous raspberry in the pistachio mousse décor. Or like my attitude toward life during the first two days of the voyage, when I spent much of the time beating my breast and being Good, Noble, and High-minded.

Then came a small storm. I found myself standing alone in the cold moonlight, with spray everywhere and my black cape whipping, and my face probably looking a little sick but covering, I am sure, wild and unspeakable thoughts. Suddenly I seemed so ridiculous, so melodramatically Mid-Victorian about my Hopeless Passion, that I blushed with embarrassment, straightened my hair, and went down to the bar.

Chexbres was there, of course. We celebrated, with the first of ten thousand completely enjoyable drinks: I, my release from my own private soap-opera, and he, my God-sent recovery from what was to him an inexplicable case of frigid and sour-pussed ill humor. Everything was all right after that, for as many more years as he was on the earth, and I lived secure and blessed for those years too, through many terrors.

Sometimes at night, after the Grand Concert or the Dancing had finished and Chexbres' mother had gone to bed, we sat in the bar, watching and drinking and talking. But the men there did not drink well, or at least not according to our tastes. They liked Turkish Blood, which was English ale and red vintage Burgundy mixed together . . . an insulting thing to do to good wine, I felt. They drank champagne, too, but doggedly and often laced with brandy or even whisky.

The favorite cocktail was called an Ohio. It was drunk at any time of the day or night, from double-sized champagne glasses which must have held ten or twelve ounces of the mixture, and were rimmed heavily with sugar.

I knew the formula, from watching the barman make so many, but I forget everything now except that it was coarse, stupid, and fantastic, like the men who drank it. There were two or three cherries in each glass, and several kinds of alcohol: brandy, gin, cordials. Champagne was used as a filler.

I never tasted one, but the barman, who spent what spare time he had in practicing elaborate scroll-writing under the top of the bar, told me they were very sweet. He said I wouldn't like them.

I didn't like the way they made people act, certainly, and after one nightcap in the bar I was always glad to go to my cabin.

It was clean and cosy, with light shining on the cherry-satin feather-puff and the gleaming sheets, and I could lock the door against evil, which for the first time had touched me, there on that little ship in my twenty-seventh year. At first I thought it was part of the sea change, to see what one man did, and how the purser quailed before a name famous in the Reich, and how my maid wept, knowing why I must lock my door. Now I think it was all part of the sickness and terror of the *Hansa*'s homeland.

There was always a little silver tray in my cabin at night: thin sandwiches of rare beef, a pepper mill, a tiny bottle of cold champagne. (Chexbres said his sandwiches were bigger, and his tipple was stout . . . and for his mother there was hot chocolate in a thermos, with little cakes which in spite of her disinterest in them were always gone by morning.)

I would bathe elaborately, calmly, and then lie safe under the feathers, moving with the water all around me, flat so that when the ship rolled I could feel my guts shift delicately against my spine. I would sip, and nibble, and read somnolently of other more tepid dramas than my own, mystery stories as mild as pap beside what was happening on that ship. . . .

The days, which began for me with a twelve-o'clock beer in the bar with Chexbres, were like a gluttonous dream. I was not hungry, really, nor was anyone else on the *Hansa*, as far as I could see, but the passengers ate systematically, steadily, thoughtfully, through all the waking hours. I myself was interested in this German way of keeping them occupied, and I went to most of the ship's meals except breakfast. But I felt that most of the other people were eating almost as if the whipped cream and pressed ducks and *pâtés de foie gras* would be stored somewhere in their spiritual stomachs, to stay them soon, too soon, in a dreadful time of hunger.

There was a small restaurant, a pleasant room with wide windows and birds in cages, where we lunched. Each day the meal was copied from a different country, always in a heavy German accent, of course. The strangest was probably the one called Mexican, which started with what might be called enchiladas, and then went philosophically back to stuffed Munich goose. The Swedish and even the Italian were really good, in an incredibly heavy-handed way.

It was like playing a game, to order the North German Lloyd equivalents of every national apéritif and wine and punch and beer. The aquavit was fine, the only possible introduction to the almost endless meal that followed. And the vodka was fine too, when we ate almost enough caviar at the Russian lunch.

Most of the thirty or so passengers in the little room, though, drank three Ohios before each meal. They were real swells, and they always came in to their tables a few seconds after the enormous glasses full of cherries and liquors had been lined up in a row before each place. They stood up and lifted their glasses to the picture of Hitler at one end of the room with the first drink. By the end of the third, their monocles were falling out, but it didn't matter.

I know it seems strange now that Chexbres and his mother and I sat there in our own private enjoyment, under such a picture with such fat starving souls. So it was, though.

And the last night, or perhaps the one before, we went to a Forest Feast or some such thing. The picture was still there, but almost hidden by real pine boughs everywhere, with cabin boys hidden behind them whistling like birds, and a delightful smell in the air. The meal was long and amazing, with things like *truites au bleu* and wild boar . . . wild things that did not taste as if they had made countless trips in tanks and freezing units. Whenever the hidden but occasionally giggling boys had to rest their whistles, a phonograph played "Tales from the Vienna Woods" and such.

And at the end of this solemn banquet, so elaborately planned and carefully performed, we were given wooden pistols and baskets of little white cotton balls. It was so funny, so weighty and well-meaning, that Chexbres' mother laughed like a girl and popped one bullet straight at a small dour professor who always ate alone, never speaking or smiling. He stood up, bowed, and left the room.

It was a good idea; the party was over, and Chexbres, and his mother, still smiling delightedly at herself, and I in a dress I had never dared wear when I chaperoned dances at Al's college, drank quite a lot of champagne, all by ourselves in the room with the pink piano.

I I

Coming back to America, a few months later, the ship was almost the same as the *Hansa*.

There was a pink piano. There was a Forest Festival, with hidden birds and toy guns and extravagant rich dishes. The captain was small and fat instead of lean and dourly tall, and was quite candid about liking to get drunk in the bar every night. There was evil, too.

Chexbres' mother was tired from so many weeks of trying to recapture what she remembered from fifty years before, and I think even she heard at last the undervoice of decadence and hysteria that was there among the Germans. Chexbres was like a cat, always watching, sharpening his claws.

By this time I felt no fear, nor even much disgust. I watched a beautiful girl fall into pieces in the seven days. I heard her cry out for love of me, and saw ten famous brewers on a Good Will tour to Milwaukee pour champagne between her breasts, and the next day take out their monocles and pose with steins for newsreels, with the Statue of Liberty for a background. I read English thrillers under my cherry-satin feather-puff, and drank quietly and perhaps more thoroughly than ever before with Chexbres, and ate of the familiar crazy "lunches" in a copy of the other restaurant on the *Hansa*.

But for the first time at sea my little fingers were hardly numb, except at the tips. I knew why. It was because I was so occupied with sorting my thoughts and making my plans that even the tides had not been able to affect me. I was almost *in absentia*, like a woman concentrating on bearing a child.

The world I had thought to go back to was gone. I knew it, and wondered how I could make Al know too, and help build another one.

Sea Change

1936

THE next ship was a delightful one, a little Dutch passenger-freighter. Al and I boarded her at San Pedro, in 1936.

She stopped at fewer Central American ports than the *Feltre* had, but at the English end of the voyage we spent days in Liverpool and Southampton and London, and in Glasgow, where the stevedores seemed almost toothless, and ate like wolves at gray doughy meat-pastries wrapped in old newspaper. In Liverpool we sat in a bar-parlor by a fire, and I ate winkles off a pin.

The captain was a fine man. All his family for centuries had either taught or sailed, and he was a combination, so that he loved to give little lectures, always over a glass of Katz-gin and to an audience of one, about stars and ships and winds. He was a very brave man, too, and only a while ago I read of how he had taken a crippled ship into port, after a bombing. I hope to know his like again, or better yet, know him.

His ship was like a well-loved animal or woman, sensitive and intelligently grateful, the realest ship I ever knew.

There were several young Merchant Marine officers on board, getting their training. They ate in a different mess, and we seldom saw them. They were shy, polite, with pink cheeks, and looked longingly at me and two English girls from under their pale lashes. The captain was firm with all three sets of us, passengers, crew, trainees: no mixing.

Al went a few times to the chief engineer's cabin; we exchanged paper-bound thrillers with him. And occasionally we had a drink before dinner with him, the captain, the swarthy first mate, and the timid young doctor, who ate at a table together in our dining room.

469

There was one passenger, a sweet-faced old lady, who was something of a tosspot in her genteel way. She was newly widowed, a typical relic of that type of prosperous American business man who "protects" his little wife to the point of imbecility. Now, at sixty-seven or more, she was feeling the first titillations of freedom, which she naturally interpreted as grief.

She believed she was making a sad pilgrimage on the last ship she and her dear husband had sailed in, to keep his image fresh in what was left of her mind after fifty years with him, but as a matter of fact she blossomed like a weak but pretty old apple tree between San Pedro and the mouth of the Thames. She was spoiled and foolish and boring, but there was something truly heartening in her . . . one more proof that it takes a lot to kill the human spirit.

She loved to drink, on doctors' orders of course, and would sit for hours absorbing whiskey-and-soda and Al's talk. He was wonderful with her; he would start with palmistry, and without her knowing it end with *Das Kapital*.

The only thing she could not forgive either the captain or us was that we refused to play bridge with her. We compromised with cribbage, rummy, and cocktail parties, at which the few passengers who could or would drink anything sat in a stiff circle, their chairs buttoned to the oilcloth floor, while the old lady stood in the center like the dauntless DAR she was, and the whiskey in her glass tipped to the roll of the ship but never spilled. She was happy, convinced that her social poise and bravery in the face of personal grief was bringing some light into our lives. She was generous, and we drank well and ate the special canapés the chef always fixed for such chaste orgies.

They were, for the most part, hot meat croquettes, which someone had told him should be nibbled daintily from toothpicks at the cocktail hour. His were three or four inches long, and so heavy that the little wooden sticks bent like paper under them. They were hot as hell, and the outer crispness covered what was almost a soup inside . . . but we ate them somehow, knowing that Kris watched every bite we took, to report it to the proud chef.

Kris was the steward. He took care of our drinks, our wants on deck and in the big room with the piano, and our behavior. He was the crankiest man I have ever met. He was dreadfully bent with arthritis, so that until we grew used to him it was active pain for us as well as him to order a bottle of beer and have him shuffle along the deck with it.

He loathed the sea, and everytime he got to Rotterdam he signed off, said goodbye to the captain, and took his earnings. Then he got soaking drunk, and signed on again, wherever the captain was. The two men had been together since the captain's first voyage, when Kris was already snarling, stiffening, almost middle-aged. The captain told us he had been thinking for several years that every voyage would be the last for Kris . . . the sea was bad for his pain.

For two weeks or so I was scared of him, as I always am of bad-tempered people. Then I got used to him, and finally I found myself liking him.

I think he felt a little the same way: first I was an annoyance, then I was simply neutral, and by the time we smelled Ireland he began to have a grumpy respect for me, so that he would pour my beer without a cuff, knowing I liked it that way, or gruffly mutter to me to watch off portside if I wanted to see a pretty ship in half an hour or so.

In the mornings he was in the greatest pain, and it was agony to watch him stand by his tray at eleven, handing hot soup to the passengers, with his fingers like twisted, knotty rope. When the days grew hot we had a sickly purplish kind of ice in the mid-mornings, too thin for sherbet but almost too stiff to drink. It was in water glasses, and it was sweet and oily. I don't know whether it was Dutch, or merely an inspiration of the chef's, like the dainty cocktail canapés. I never said anything about it, but whenever we had it Kris would bring me a glass especially full, and look at me from his small old eyes, almost grinning. I would thank him, and then grin too. It was his way of teasing me, to let me know he liked me.

I used to stay on deck, in my chair, very late at night when it was hot. Sometimes I would see him, far forward, prowling restlessly in bare feet. We never spoke . . . but the next day the captain would ask me carefully how I had slept, and I knew Kris had talked to him, just as he did if ever the English girls exchanged even a faint smile with any of the training men.

I don't remember much about the food, except that it was very different from the almost lavish cuisine of the other freighter we knew, the Italian one. It was dull, good, heavy food, but there were many vegetables and salads all the way to England. The coffee was fine, and this time we could afford to drink Dutch beer when we wanted it, and quite a lot of delicate Rhine wine.

The baker had a fight with the chef soon after we left port, and the barber took over all the pastry making . . . or so we heard. We had cake twice a day, in many different shapes but always the same. It was almost like cold omelet, as if it were made of hundreds of egg yolks stirred with a lot of sugar and a little flour and then baked. It was usually in thin solid pieces, like small bricks, elaborately topped with glacéed fruits and always served with flavored whipped cream.

We often had a thick green soup, in the colder seas, filled with cabbage and potatoes and leeks and always with slices of link-sausage floating in it.

And there was one unattractive but delicious thing, a kind of sludge of different vegetables flavored with ham, which the waiter called Udgie-pudgie. I finally saw on a menu that it was Hodge-podge. The captain said the crew loved it, and it was indeed good, in a simple crude way that might offend or bore sophisticated palates.

There were about twenty passengers. Aside from the awakening old widow, and the two giggling English girls who spent most of the time trying to get past Kris to the training quarters, I remember little about them. Three or four, or maybe more, were taking the long quiet voyage after serious illnesses, so that when they came to the dining room at all they were barricaded behind bottles of tonic, peptic powders, and laxatives.

One was an old schoolteacher, returning to Scotland on her pension. She was seasick constantly, and came on deck only once in all the five weeks, like a gaunt gray-faced bean-pole, with the elaborate and youthful clothes she had spent all her money on slapping wryly against her poor weak shanks.

The young doctor worried about her, and timidly asked me to see if when I was in her cabin she would not forget her queasiness long enough to swallow a little gruel or tea. She would struggle into a ridiculous shell-pink satin negligee puffy with cheap maribou . . . she had always wanted one, she told me, and *wouldn't* it just impress her relatives in Glasgow! . . . and we would talk and drink broth secretly reinforced with brandy and vitamins by the worried doctor.

And then she would dash weakly for the bathroom, and I would try not to listen, and feel very queasy myself in sympathy.

It was useless. I told the doctor and the captain that perhaps the trip to Scotland, which she had saved and planned for during almost fifty years, was really the end of her life, and that now she was actually on her way she was trying to die rather than arrive there. They looked at me doubtfully, worriedly. The sea does strange things, they said.

When we got to Glasgow she was still alive. She looked like an ancient molting flamingo, standing on the dock with all her dour cousins. They hired a taxi, and as it drove off she looked back longingly at the little Dutch ship, and us waving. . . .

Define This Word

1936

THAT early spring I met a young servant in northern Burgundy who was almost fanatical about food, like a medieval woman possessed by the devil. Her obsession engulfed even my appreciation of the dishes she served, until I grew uncomfortable.

It was the off season at the old mill which a Parisian chef had bought and turned into one of France's most famous restaurants, and my mad waitress was the only servant. In spite of that she was neatly uniformed, and showed no surprise at my unannounced arrival and my hot dusty walking clothes.

She smiled discreetly at me, said, "Oh, but certainly!" when I asked if I could lunch there, and led me without more words to a dark bedroom bulging with First Empire furniture, and a new white bathroom.

When I went into the dining room it was empty of humans . . . a cheerful ugly room still showing traces of the *petit-bourgeois* parlor it had been. There were aspidistras on the mantel; several small white tables were laid with those imitation "peasant-ware" plates that one sees in Paris china stores, and very good crystal glasses; a cat folded under some ferns by the window ledge hardly looked at me; and the air was softly hurried with the sound of high waters from the stream outside.

I waited for the maid to come back. I knew I should eat well and slowly, and suddenly the idea of dry sherry, unknown in all the village *bistros* of the last few days, stung my throat smoothly. I tried not to think of it; it would be impossible to realize. Dubonnet would do. But not as well. I longed for sherry.

The little maid came into the silent room. I looked at her stocky young body, and her butter-colored hair, and noticed her odd pale voluptuous mouth before I said, "Mademoiselle, I shall drink an *apéritif*. Have you by any chance—"

"Let me suggest," she interrupted firmly, "our special dry sherry. It is chosen in Spain for Monsieur Paul."

And before I could agree she was gone, discreet and smooth.

She's a funny one, I thought, and waited in a pleasant warm tiredness for the wine.

It was good. I smiled approval at her, and she lowered her eyes, and then looked searchingly at me again. I realized suddenly that in this land of trained nonchalant waiters I was to be served by a small waitress who took her duties seriously. I felt much amused, and matched her solemn searching gaze.

"Today, Madame, you may eat shoulder of lamb in the English style, with baked potatoes, green beans, and a sweet."

My heart sank. I felt dismal, and hot and weary, and still grateful for the sherry.

But she was almost grinning at me, her lips curved triumphantly, and her eyes less palely blue.

"Oh, in *that* case a trout, of course—a *truite au bleu* as only Monsieur Paul can prepare it!"

She glanced hurriedly at my face, and hastened on. "With the trout, one or two young potatoes—oh, very delicately boiled," she added before I could protest, "very light."

I felt better. I agreed. "Perhaps a leaf or two of salad after the fish," I suggested. She almost snapped at me. "Of course, of course! And naturally our *hors d'oeuvres* to commence." She started away.

"No!" I called, feeling that I must assert myself now or be forever lost. "No!"

She turned back, and spoke to me very gently. "But Madame has never tasted our *hors d'oeuvres*. I am sure that Madame will be pleased. They are our specialty, made by Monsieur Paul himself. I am sure," and she looked reproachfully at me, her mouth tender and sad, "I am sure that Madame would be very much pleased."

I smiled weakly at her, and she left. A little cloud of hurt gentleness seemed to hang in the air where she had last stood.

I comforted myself with sherry, feeling increasing irritation with my own feeble self. Hell! I loathed *hors d'oeuvres*! I conjured disgusting visions of square glass plates of oily fish, of soggy vegetables glued together with cheap mayonnaise, or rank radishes and taste-less butter. No, Monsieur Paul or not, sad young pale-faced waitress or not, I hated *hors d'oeuvres*.

I glanced victoriously across the room at the cat, whose eyes seemed closed.

I I

Several minutes passed. I was really very hungry.

The door banged open, and my girl came in again, less discreet this time. She hurried toward me.

"Madame, the wine! Before Monsieur Paul can go on—" Her eyes watched my face, which I perversely kept rather glum.

"I think," I said ponderously, daring her to interrupt me, "I think that today, since I am in Burgundy and about to eat a trout," and here I hoped she noticed that I did not mention *hors d'oeuvres*, "I think I shall drink a bottle of Chablis 1929—*not* Chablis Village 1929."

For a second her whole face blazed with joy, and then subsided into a trained mask. I knew that I had chosen well, had somehow satisfied her in a secret and incomprehensible way. She nodded politely and scuttled off, only for another second glancing impa-tiently at me as I called after her, "Well cooled, please, but not iced."

I'm a fool, I thought, to order a whole bottle. I'm a fool, here all alone and with more miles to walk before I reach Avallon and my fresh clothes and a bed. Then I smiled at myself and leaned back in my solid wide-seated chair, looking obliquely at the prints of Gibson girls, English tavern scenes, and hideous countrysides that hung on the papered walls. The room was warm; I could hear my companion cat purring under the ferns.

The girl rushed in, with flat baking dishes piled up her arms on napkins, like the plates of a Japanese juggler. She slid them off neatly in two rows on to the table, where they lay steaming up at me, darkly and infinitely appetizing.

"*Mon Dieu!* All for me?" I peered at her. She nodded, her discretion quite gone now and a look of ecstatic worry on her pale face and eyes and lips.

There were at least eight dishes. I felt almost embarrassed, and sat for a minute looking weakly at the fork and spoon in my hand.

"Perhaps Madame would care to start with the pickled herring? It is not like any other. Monsieur Paul prepares it himself, in his own vinegar and wines. It is very good."

I dug out two or three brown filets from the dish, and tasted. They were truly unlike any others, truly the best I had ever eaten, mild, pungent, meaty as fresh nuts.

I realized the maid had stopped breathing, and looked up at her. She was watching me, or rather a gastronomic X-ray of the herring inside me, with a hypnotized glaze in her eyes.

"Madame is pleased?" she whispered softly.

I said I was. She sighed, and pushed a sizzling plate of broiled endive toward me, and disappeared.

I had put a few dull green lentils on my plate, lentils scattered with minced fresh herbs and probably marinated in tarragon vinegar and walnut oil, when she came into the dining room again with the bottle of Chablis in a wine basket.

"Madame should be eating the little baked onions while they are hot," she remarked over her shoulder as she held the bottle in a napkin and uncorked it. I obeyed meekly, and while I watched her I ate several more than I had meant to. They were delicious, simmered first in strong meat broth, I think, and then drained and broiled with olive oil and new-ground pepper.

I was fascinated by her method of uncorking a vintage wine. Instead of the Burgundian procedure of infinite and often exaggerated precautions against touching or tipping or jarring the bottle, she handled it quite nonchalantly, and seemed to be careful only to keep her hands from the cool bottle itself, holding it sometimes by the basket and sometimes in a napkin. The cork was very tight, and I thought for a minute that she would break it. So did she; her face grew tense, and did not loosen until she had slowly worked out the cork and wiped the lip. Then she poured an inch of wine in a glass, turned her back to me like a priest taking Communion, and drank it down. Finally some was poured for me, and she stood with the bottle in her hand and her full lips drooping until I nodded a satisfied yes. Then she pushed another of the plates toward me, and almost rushed from the room.

I ate slowly, knowing that I should not be as hungry as I ought to be for the trout, but knowing too that I had never tasted such delicate savory morsels. Some were hot, some cold. The wine was light and cool. The room, warm and agreeably empty under the rushing sound of the stream, became smaller as I grew used to it.

My girl hurried in again, with another row of plates up one arm, and a large bucket dragging at the other. She slid the plates deftly on to the table, and drew a deep breath as she let the bucket down against the table leg.

"Your trout, Madame," she said excitedly. I looked down at the gleam of the fish curving through its limited water. "But first a good slice of Monsieur Paul's *pâté*. Oh yes, oh yes, you will be very sorry if you miss this. It is rich, but appetizing, and not at all too heavy. Just this one morsel!"

And willy-nilly I accepted the large gouge she dug from a terrine. I prayed for ten normal appetites and thought with amused nostalgia of my usual lunch of cold milk and fruit as I broke off a crust of bread and patted it smooth with the paste. Then I forgot everything but the exciting faint decadent flavor in my mouth.

I beamed up at the girl. She nodded, but from habit asked if I was satisfied. I beamed again, and asked, simply to please her, "Is there not a faint hint of *marc*, or perhaps cognac?"

"*Marc*, Madame!" And she awarded me the proud look of a teacher whose pupil has showed unexpected intelligence. "Monsieur Paul, after he has taken equal parts of goose breast and the finest pork, and broken a certain number of egg yolks into them, and ground them *very*, very fine, cooks all with seasoning for some three hours. *But*," she pushed her face nearer, and looked with ferocious gloating at the *pâté* inside me, her eyes like X-rays, "he never stops stirring it! Figure to yourself the work of it—stir, stir, never stopping!

"Then he grinds in a suspicion of nutmeg, and then adds, very thoroughly, a glass of *marc* for each hundred grams of *pâté*. And is Madame not pleased?"

Again I agreed, rather timidly, that Madame was much pleased, that Madame had never, indeed, tasted such an unctuous and exciting *pâté*. The girl wet her lips delicately, and then started as if she had been pin-struck.

"But the trout! My God, the trout!" She grabbed the bucket, and her voice grew higher and more rushed.

"Here is the trout, Madame. You are to eat it *au bleu*, and you should never do so if you had not seen it alive. For if the trout were dead when it was plunged into the *court bouillon* it would not turn blue. So, naturally, it must be living."

I knew all this, more or less, but I was fascinated by her absorption in the momentary problem. I felt quite ignorant, and asked her with sincerity, "What about the trout? Do you take out its guts before or after?"

"Oh, the trout!" She sounded scornful. "Any trout is glad, truly glad, to be prepared by Monsieur Paul. His little gills are pinched, with one flash of the knife he is empty, and then he curls in agony in the *bouillon* and all is over. And it is the curl you must judge, Madame. A false *truite au bleu* cannot curl."

She panted triumph at me, and hurried out with the bucket.

III

She *is* a funny one, I thought, and for not more than two or three minutes I drank wine and mused over her. Then she darted in, with the trout correctly blue and agonizingly curled on a platter, and on her crooked arm a plate of tiny boiled potatoes and a bowl.

When I had been served and had cut off her anxious breathings with an assurance that the fish was the best I had ever tasted, she peered again at me and at the sauce in the bowl. I obediently put some of it on the potatoes: no fool I, to ruin *truite au bleu* with a hot concoction! There was more silence.

"Ah!" she sighed at last. "I knew Madame would feel thus! Is it not the most beautiful sauce in the world with the flesh of a trout?"

I nodded incredulous agreement.

"Would you like to know how it is done?"

I remembered all the legends of chefs who guarded favorite recipes with their very lives, and murmured yes.

She wore the exalted look of a believer describing a miracle at Lourdes as she told me, in a rush, how Monsieur Paul threw chopped chives into hot sweet butter and then poured the butter off, how he added another nut of butter and a tablespoonful of thick cream for each person, stirred the mixture for a few minutes over a slow fire, and then rushed it to the table.

"So simple?" I asked softly, watching her lighted eyes and the tender lustful lines of her strange mouth.

"So simple, Madame! But," she shrugged, "you know, with a master—"

I was relieved to see her go; such avid interest in my eating wore on me. I felt released when the door closed behind her, free for a minute or so from her victimization. What would she have done, I wondered, if I had been ignorant or unconscious of any fine flavors?

She was right, though, about Monsieur Paul. Only a master could live in this isolated mill and preserve his gastronomic dignity through loneliness and the sure financial loss of unused butter and addled eggs. Of course, there was the stream for his fish, and I knew his *pâtés* would grow even more edible with age; but how could he manage to have a thing like roasted lamb ready for any chance patron? Was the consuming interest of his one maid enough fuel for his flame?

I tasted the last sweet nugget of trout, the one nearest the blued tail, and poked somnolently at the minute white billiard balls that had been eyes. Fate could not harm me, I remembered winily, for I had indeed dined today, and dined well. Now for a leaf of crisp salad, and I'd be on my way.

The girl slid into the room. She asked me again, in a respectful but gossipy manner, how I had liked this and that and the other things, and then talked on as she mixed dressing for the endive.

"And now," she announced, after I had eaten one green sprig and dutifully pronounced it excellent, "now Madame is going to taste Monsieur Paul's special terrine, one that is not even on the summer menu, when a hundred covers are laid here daily and we have a head-waiter and a wine waiter, and cabinet ministers telegraph for tables! Madame will be pleased."

And heedless of my low moans of the walk still before me, of my appreciation and my unhappily human and limited capacity, she cut a thick heady slice from the terrine of meat and stood over me while I ate it, telling me with almost hysterical pleasure of the wild ducks, the spices, the wines that went into it. Even surfeit could not make me deny that it was a rare dish. I ate it all, knowing my luck, and wishing only that I had red wine to drink with it.

I was beginning, though, to feel almost frightened, realizing myself an accidental victim of these stranded gourmets, Monsieur Paul and his handmaiden. I began to feel that they were using me for a safety valve, much as a thwarted woman relieves herself with tantrums or a fit of weeping. I was serving a purpose, and perhaps a noble one, but I resented it in a way approaching panic.

I protested only to myself when one of Monsieur Paul's special cheeses was cut for me, and ate it doggedly, like a slave. When the girl said that Monsieur Paul himself was preparing a special filter of coffee for me, I smiled servile acceptance; wine and the weight of food and my own character could not force me to argue with maniacs. When, before the coffee came, Monsieur Paul presented me, through his idolater, with the most beautiful apple tart I had ever seen, I allowed it to be cut and served to me. Not a wince or a murmur showed the waitress my distressed fearfulness. With a stuffed careful smile on my face, and a clear nightmare in my head of trussed wanderers prepared for his altar by this hermit-priest of gastronomy, I listened to the girl's passionate plea for fresh pastry dough.

"You cannot, you *cannot,* Madame, serve old pastry!" She seemed ready to beat her breast as she leaned across the table. "Look at that delicate crust! You may feel that you have eaten too much." (I nodded idiotic agreement.) "But this pastry is like feathers—it is like snow. It is in fact good for you, a digestive! And why?" She glared sternly at me. "Because Monsieur Paul did not even open the flour bin until he saw you coming! He could not, he *could* not have baked you one of his special apple tarts with old dough!"

She laughed, tossing her head and curling her mouth voluptuously.

I V

Somehow I managed to refuse a second slice, but I trembled under her surmise that I was ready for my special filter.

The wine and the fortitude had fled me, and I drank the hot coffee as a suffering man gulps ether, deeply and gratefully.

I remember, then, chatting with surprising glibness, and sending to Monsieur Paul flowery compliments, all of them sincere and well won, and I remember feeling only amusement when a vast glass of *marc* appeared before me and then gradually disappeared, like the light in the warm room full of water-sounds. I felt surprise to be alive still, and suddenly very grateful to the wild-lipped waitress, as if her presence had sustained me through duress. We discussed food and wine. I wondered bemusedly why I had been frightened.

The *marc* was gone. I went into the crowded bedroom for my jacket. She met me in the darkening hall when I came out, and I paid my bill, a large one. I started to thank her, but she took my hand, drew me into the dining room, and without words poured more spirits into my glass. I drank to Monsieur Paul while she watched me intently, her pale eyes bulging in the dimness and her lips pressed inward as if she too tasted the hot, aged *marc*.

The cat rose from his ferny bed, and walked contemptuously out of the room.

Suddenly the girl began to laugh, in a soft shy breathless way, and came close to me.

"Permit me!" she said, and I thought she was going to kiss me. But instead she pinned a tiny bunch of snowdrops and dark bruised cyclamens against my stiff jacket, very quickly and deftly, and then ran from the room with her head down.

I waited for a minute. No sounds came from anywhere in the old mill, but the endless rushing of the full stream seemed to strengthen, like the timid blare of an orchestra under a falling curtain.

She's a *funny* one, I thought. I touched the cool blossoms on my coat and went out, like a ghost from ruins, across the courtyard toward the dim road to Avallon.

The Measure of My Powers

1936–1939

Un pâquis, the French dictionary says, is a grazing ground or pasture. But when we bought our home in Switzerland, and found that it had been called Le Pâquis for several centuries by all the country people near it, we knew that it meant much more than "pasture" to them. The word had a tenderness to it, like the diminutive given to a child or a pretty girl, like the difference between *lambkin* and *lamb.*

One reason our Pâquis had this special meaning was that it was almost the only piece of land in all the abrupt terraced steeps of the wine coast between Lausanne and Vevey that did not have grapes on it.

Instead, it was a sloping green meadow, held high in the air above the Lac Léman by stone walls. A brook ran through it under pollarded willows, and old trees of pears and plums and apples bent away from the pushings of the lake winds. The ancient soil was covered with a dazzling coat always, low and filled with violets and primulas and crocuses in the spring, waist-high with such flowers in summer as I have only seen like shadows in real gardens.

They would be delicate in the beginning of the year . . . blue hepaticas along the icy brook, and all the tender yellow things. And then as the summer came and the time for harvesting, the colors grew more intense, more violent, until finally the wild asters bloomed, *les vendangeuses,* the flowers that meant all the village girls must go into the vineyards again to cut the grapes.

Three times every summer the man across the road reaped our hay, while we could not bear to look . . . and then in a week or so the flowers were back again, pushing and growing and covering all the short grass with a new loveliness, while the fruits ripened and the little brook ran busily.

There was a fountain, too, near the road by the stone house. It had been there for longer than even the Federal maps showed, and people walking up the long pull from lake level knew it as well as they knew their mothers, and stopped always to drink and rest their backs from the pointed woven baskets they wore. Even after we came, and planted more trees and added rooms to the house, they continued to stop at the fountain, and that made us feel better than almost anything else.

And all those things . . . the fresh spouting water, the little brook under the willows, the old rich bending trees, the grass so full of life there on the terraced wine-slopes laced by a thousand tiny vine-yards . . . they were why when the peasants said Le Pâquis they meant The Dear Little Meadow, or The Sweet Cool Resting Place, or something like that but more so.

II

We started a garden before the ground thawed, while the Italian masons burned their fingers on the cold stones for the new part of the house. We had to make all the beds in small terraces; hard work in the beginning, but wonderful to work in later, when the paths were set and the little patches lay almost waist-high waiting to be cared for. As soon as we could we planted, while we kept on building walls and cultivating the rich loam, and by the time my father and mother came to see us, at our apartment down on the Market Square in Vevey because the house was not yet ready, the peas were ripe, and the evenings were softly warm.

We would go up the hills from town after the workingmen had left, and spread our supper cloth on a table under the terrace apple tree, among all the last rubble of the building. As fast as Father and Chexbres could pick the peas, Mother and I would shell them, and then on a little fire of shavings I'd cook them perhaps four or five minutes in a heavy casserole, swirling them in butter and their own steam. We'd eat them with little cold pullets cooked for us in Vevey, and good bread and the thin white wine of the coast that lay about us.

The evening breeze would freshen across the long sweep of the lake, and as the Savoy Alps blackened above the water, and it turned to flat pewter over the edge of the terrace, the first summer lights of Evian far down toward Geneva winked red at us. It was always hard to leave. We'd put our things silently into the baskets, and then drive with the top of the car lowered along the narrow walled roads of the Corniche, until we came to a village where we could sit again on a terrace and drink bitter coffee in the darkness.

Chexbres was a fine gardener; he read books and liked to experiment with new ways of doing things, but besides all that he had the feeling of growth and fertility and the seasons in his bones and his flesh. I learned all the time from him, and we worked together two summers in Le Pâquis.

The peasants of our village, and all the vineyardists, thought we were crazy not to leave such work for hired gardeners, gardeners who *knew*. They used to lean over the walls watching us, occasionally calling suggestions, and it embarrassed us when oftener than not we did things as they had never before been done there in that district, and got much better results for less effort in less space. That seemed almost like cheating, when we were newcomers and foreigners too . . . but why should we put in fifty tomato plants with elaborate stakes, as our neighbors told us to do, when we could get as much fruit from ten plants put in the way we thought best? Chexbres studied the winds, the soil, the way the rains came, and he knew more about how to grow things than the peasants could have learned in a thousand years, in spite of their cruel toiling. He felt truly apologetic about it.

Our garden grew and grew, and we went almost every day up the hill to the sanatorium for poor children with the back of our little green Fiat filled with fresh things to eat.

I canned often, too. We had three cellars, and I filled one of them with beautiful gleaming jars for the winter. It was simple enough to do it in little bits instead of in great harried rushes as my grandmother used to, and when I went down into the coolness and saw all the things sitting there so richly quiet on the shelves, I had a special feeling of contentment. It was a reassurance of safety against hunger, very primitive and satisfying.

I canned tomatoes and beans and vegetable juices, and many kinds of pickles and catsups more for the fun than because we wanted them, and plums and peaches and all the fruits. I made a few jams, for company, and several big jars of brandied things. I was lucky; nothing spoiled, everything was good.

When we left, before the war came, it was hard to give up all the bottles of liqueurs and *eaux-de-vie*, not yet ripe enough to taste, harder than anything except the bottles in the wine cellar, some still resting from their trips from Burgundy, and all our own wine made from the little yellow grapes of our vineyard for the two years past. . . .

In spite of the full shelves in the cellar, though, and our trips up the hill for the children and the baskets we took to friends in Vevey whenever we could stop gardening long enough to go down there, things grew too fast for us. It was the oldest soil either of us had ever touched, and it seemed almost bursting with life, just as it was alive with insects and little creatures and a hundred kinds of worms waiting to eat what grew in it. We ran a kind of race with it, exciting and exhausting.

One time Chexbres put down his hoe and said loudly, "By God, I'll not be dictated to! I'll show you who's boss!" He was talking to the earth, and like a dutiful wife I followed him up past the violently fertile terraces to the house, and listened while he telephoned to the Casino at Evian and reserved a table in the main dining room and ordered an astonishing meal and the wines for it.

I despaired somewhat in dressing: my nails were rough and stained, and I was too thin and much too brown for the dress I wanted to wear, and high heels felt strange on my feet.

But by the time we had driven over the Haute Corniche to Lausanne, right into the setting sun, and had sat at a little deck table on the way to Evian, wrapped in the kind of sleepy silence that those lake-boats always had for us, I felt more beautiful than possible, and knew that Chexbres in his white dinner coat and his white topknot was that way too. The maître d'hôtel and the barman and the sommelier agreed, when we got to the Casino, and it was a decadent delightful night.

But when we drove into Le Pâquis in the first shy sunlight, we shed our city clothes and bathed and put on dungarees again, and hurried down into the garden. We had been away too long.

We grew beautiful salads, a dozen different kinds, and several herbs. There were shallots and onion and garlic, and I braided them into long silky ropes, and hung them over the rafters in the attic. In one of the cellars we stored cabbages and apples and tomatoes and other things on slatted shelves, or in bins. And all the time we ate what we were growing.

The local cuisine was heavy, a wintery diet influenced by the many German-Swiss who lived near by. I talked more with the Italian-Swiss, and learned ways of cooking vegetables in their own juices, with sweet butter or thick olive oil to encourage them a little: tomatoes and onions and sweet peppers and eggplants, and all the summer things. And Chexbres could fry tomatoes the way his family cook Madie did, in Delaware, so that the slices were dark brown and crisp all through, and yet delicate and tender. Sometimes we made corn oysters. We'd sit right by the stove, and lift the shaggy little cakes from the hot butter to our plates, and float them down with beer chilled in the fountain.

(The corn we brought from America, and except for young cow-corn eaten by a few hardy peasants near Zurich, it was the only such thing for humans in all Switzerland, I think. The passing country people watched it curiously, and so did we, because it behaved as if it knew itself to be in alien lands, helpless before strange winds and stranger weather, and sent out a dozen crazy tassels for every ear, to be sure of survival. The next year it was less hysterical, and several neighbors planted it from our seed, and ate it from our recipes.)

III

The part of the house we added to the little stone building was, I suppose, quite impractical for anyone but us. It disturbed and shocked the architect and all the contractors for floor and plumbing and such, because it was designed so that we, the owners of the place, could be its cooks and servants. That was not becoming to our station. We got what we wanted, though, and the kitchen and pantry were part of the living room . . . up and down a few steps, around a corner or two . . . so that music and talk and fine smells moved at liberty from one part to another.

It was fun to invite Swiss people there for meals; they were baffled and titillated. Once in the winter, I remember, some oddly mixed expatriates and French-Swiss friends came from Montreux. They knew us only in restaurants and as dancing partners and such until then, because we were too content alone at Le Pâquis to invite many others there, and they were frankly curious about the house and the way we lived, so different from anything they knew.

Because it was winter and the dormant garden gave us leisure, Chexbres and I had made everything ready long before they came. After conventional canapés . . . for the conventional people we knew our guests to be, so that they would not be alarmed at the start . . . we planned to let them serve themselves in the kitchen from a large pot of really masterful stew, and a big salad, and a basket of crisp rolls made up in the village that afternoon. Then there was to be a chilled bowl of pears baked in a way I'd evolved, with honey and kirsch, and served with sour cream.

In the kitchen there was only the casserole on top of the stove, while the salad chilled in the cellar with the dessert, and the rolls waited warmly in a napkined basket out of sight. Plates and silver tools looked like part of a pattern on the old dresser. The ventilator whirred almost silently, and in the wide deep windows my ferns moved a little. There were pictures on the walls, and cookbooks mixed with pewter plates on the open shelves, and it was indeed a deceptive place to be called a kitchen in the average vocabulary.

When the people came they exclaimed as everyone did at the first sight of the big living room, with the windows looking over the terrace and the far lake into another land. Then, almost frightened by the distance of their vision, they came down near the fireplace, and comforted themselves with its warmth and the reassurance of the drinks waiting for them on the long oak table.

In many polite ways they began to ask about the house: was it true we had no servants living with us, and only part-time help from the village? But how . . . but what . . . ?

They began to look alarmed, thinking of the long cold drive from Montreux to this strange place without a dining room, without a cook and a maid or two. And when they wandered up the stairs into what they could only guess to be a kind of stage-kitchen, and they saw no signs and smelled no smells of supper, their faces were long and dismal under all the politeness.

Chexbres and I let them suffer until we thought the alcoholic intake was fairly well adjusted to their twelve or fifteen rather jaded bodies. Then, with the smug skill of two magicians, we flicked away the empty glasses and the tired canapés, and slid the salad and the rolls into place on the old dresser. He gave the *ragoût* a few odorous stirs while I saw that little tables in the living room were clear of ashtrays and such . . . and the puzzled hungry people, almost tittering with relief and excitement, flocked like children into the kitchen for their suppers.

They ate and ate, and talked as they had not dared talk for too many years, and laughed a great deal.

There was an old Swiss judge, important as God to himself and his small community, who drank a special little toast to his fat wife, and said without any importance at all in his suddenly human voice, "Anneli, my dear, I had forgotten I could have such an agreeable evening with you in the room." She lifted her glass to his with great dignity, knowing what he meant after so many years of provincial respectability.

Monsieur Kugner, who owned the kind of small luxurious hotel in Montreux that always had at least two Eastern princes in it, and a handful of the kind of pre-war munitions magnates who traveled with personal chefs as well as valets and chauffeurs and secretaries, tucked his napkin under his chin and murmured, "*Ça, alors! Formidable!*"

Several times during the evening he took Chexbres or me aside, and asked who our cook was. He refused, quite candidly and politely, to believe that I had made the stew, just as he refused to accept my recipe for it; he was convinced that in our pride we were hiding a famous chef somewhere in the cellars. It was a little embarrassing, but funny, to think of our being able to afford a hidden cook at all, and then to be accused of guarding him so jealously that we even faked recipes for him.

The stew itself was good, but the reason it seemed so *formidable* to poor Kugner was because for most of the years of his life he had been eating in luxury hotels. He was so sated by their uniform excellence, and by the obsequious waiters, the silver-covered dishes, the smooth linen, that when he could eat an honest stew from an old soup plate with a spoon, he thought it was ambrosial.

He thought, "Why not hire the chef who made this, and let him serve it to me whenever I command it? There is undoubtedly some special secret about it, because I who have not been really hungry for forty years am now going to that ridiculous sham-kitchen for a third plateful. Therefore I could charge a great deal . . . have it made on order for my favored guests. . . ."

If Monsieur Kugner had not felt so well, in the warmth and talk and pleasantness that evening, he would have been more than haughty at our stubborn selfish way of lying to him! As it was, he laughed and even sang a little, very pink at first above his pointed beard and then forgetting his dignity entirely to buzz out five long verses of a Romanche ballad he assured us was unprintable. When someone suggested writing an open letter to one American who was too ill to come, he slapped the table as he had probably not done since he was an apprentice at the Paris Ritz, and was the first to sign the long piece of paper I mailed the next morning to our bedridden compatriot (who, Chexbres and I knew all the time, was indeed in bed, but not alone and certainly not in need of hot bottles, liniments, or our sympathies to keep him warm).

"Dear Mr. Courtney," Kugner wrote, in the English we had decided would be most cheering to a sick Texan. "We are sitting so comfortable by a beautiful American cheminée fire, by Lager beer, thinking of you and take a big mouth full. L. Kugner."

"Dear Friend" . . . "My dear old chap" . . . "Hello" . . . the other notes were none too interesting, until the last one, written by a fading Danish countess, a fabulous flirt in the days when Montreux was a giddy little town full of gamblers and royalty. She had stayed on after all the others left, because her husband was there in a private insane asylum. She always had lovers, attracted by her enormous income and her great reputation for wifely devotion. And she was a gay charming creature, as well.

"Dearest Court," she wrote. "If you believe or not . . . we give a damn, but we thought more on you as you probably believe. Every think we took . . . thinking on poor old Court . . . enjoying the food, so sorry that Court can't taste. It is rested two inches below the heart a pear with kirsch, so take my love. Eva."

Yes, the suppers by the American cheminée were nice, now and then, but in the summer it was really better. When the terrace was too cool or breezy we set a long table in the living room in front of the open French windows, and if the lake seemed too wide, the Alps too high, we could look into the great mirror opposite and make them more remote, less questioning of us.

In the summer there were always a lot of people; Vevey was on the road to almost any place in Europe, and Le Pâquis was such a *pleasant* little stop, everybody said. Sometimes Chexbres and I wanted to run away . . . but we were proud of where we lived, and like many hospitable people we were somewhat smug about being so. Sometimes there were complications, political, national, religious, even racial, but in general we managed to segregate the more violent prejudices. Only once did Chexbres have to take three men who were on their way to join the Spanish Loyalists to Cully for filets of perch while I served supper at Le Pâquis to several charming but rabid Fascists from Rome, one of them a priest and all of them convinced that Communists were their personal as well as national enemies.

And once we were sitting on the terrace drinking sherry before a rather elaborate dinner, all of us dressed in our best bibs in honor of an old English lady who had arrived trailing chiffon, diamonds, and monkey fur, when down the path from the road came the clanking of a cowbell, and behind it the great hulk of a Princeton halfback.

He had walked and hitchhiked that day from the French Alps, and he was burned magenta-red and wore nothing but shoes, slacks, and the cowbell around his neck. There was nothing in the house big enough to cover his shoulders except a blue and white striped milking jacket from Fribourg, the kind with silver buttons and embroidered edelweis and little puffed short sleeves. We stuffed Princeton into it somehow, after a quick shower, and sat him next to the dowager at dinner.

At first she was frankly scared of him, and looked at him sideways. The two people down from the village to serve dinner were timid too, and held dishes precariously on the very ends of their hands when they got near the boy. Chexbres and I despaired.

But Princeton was such a kind simple person, and the dowager was in her own way so much simpler even than he, that halfway through the second course she was beaming at him and shrieking to all of us, as if he could not understand her, "But *listen* to him! He's *amazing*! Poor poor lad . . . he's *hungry*!"

He was indeed, and thanks to his unannounced arrival there was less leeway than I'd planned on, so that when he said to me, in a slow benevolent drawl that could not possibly offend, "The trouble with this piece of meat, ma'am, is that it's too small," I felt only gratitude to have the old Englishwoman plop the rest of her course onto his plate.

It was probably the most unconventional thing she had ever done in her life, and her son looked at me as if he had just seen one of the family Romneys thumb its nose.

I nodded solemnly to him. He needed reassurance: the night was young, and before it was over he was going to sit calmly by while his mother, in one of the most abrupt and vivid little love affairs I've ever watched, put a big white daisy behind Princeton's ear and watched him do the Lambeth Walk for her, and then patted his enormous red arm in its silly little puffed sleeve when he said solemnly to all of us, "Gee, I *like* this old lady!" We did too.

Once, that same year, we had a queer dream-like dinner, and a sad one too, in a muted wordless way.

My brother David was there, resting after a summer course at the University of Dijon which he had managed somehow to follow from the fairly distant beaches of Cannes and Monte Carlo. His fatigue was understandable, but it melted like mist in the sun when he learned that his favorite prom-date was in Geneva, and from then on he spent most of his time catching and riding on trains to see her. Finally, in order to see something of him before summer ended and his boat sailed for America, I suggested that he invite her to Le Pâquis for a day.

He seemed pleased, in a casual way. Perhaps inside he was nervous, wary, as I would have been at his age to bring a stranger before the eyes of my family, but it did not show. Le Pâquis was full then . . . Chexbres' sister Anne, my sister Norah, three or four friends . . . and all of us loved David and were curious in our various ways about any girl who was more attractive to him than our combined company. She was the first woman any of us had seen him with, in the real male-female way, and suddenly he seemed even younger than he was, and terribly vulnerable. We tried to keep from watching, from listening for false tones, from protecting with our older tact and knowledge and jealousy.

The girl was a very pretty pale limp one. She was about seventeen, I suppose, and world-weary the way children that age are often caricatured or satirized as being. It comes from a great shyness, and

I knew it, and tried not to feel any mockery or amusement or pure exasperation at her manners.

She drooped everywhere, her eyelids, her little pink mouth, her slender shoulders. She murmured occasionally in an exhausted way, but never anything more than Yes or No, and never turned her head or even her eyes toward anyone else who talked. That was disconcerting; we all talked a lot that summer, and sometimes quite well.

She smoked one cigaret from another, and whenever it was time for a new one she did not reach for it or even ask for it, but instead let her smooth white arm drop slowly along the chair or the table toward David. Then she would let her fingers uncurl one by one, and he would watch like a hypnotized hen, so that there was almost a balloon above his head, funny-paper style, with the words in it, "Her tiny hand is like a flower, like an unfolding lily bud . . ." It was ghastly.

She came after lunch, and by teatime we were all of us so nervous, waiting for that precocious sensual thing to happen again, that we did not dare look at one another. We felt hysterical, and deeply embarrassed in a queer personal way that was mixed up with loyalty to David. And there was nothing to do about it: he was a hopelessly gone gosling; his nimble tongue was tied; his quick flashing mind was full of smoke.

In desperation we all went up back of the vineyards to a little bowling alley in a mountain meadow. The late summer sun slanted across the piney slopes, and the air was full of fragrance, and the click of the ancient hand-turned balls made an easy music. A big farm woman brought us tea and bread, and pots of wild green honey. It was one of the most idyllic moments I have ever known, very sharp, like a Breughel painting.

But the little blonde girl did not make a part of any of it. The game was too much for her, and the food was boring. She drooped wearily against the long crude table beside the alley, and whenever David seemed for a minute to forget her, she let her hand fall slowly toward him, let her soft pink fingers uncurl. It was wordless, and it was like the crack of a whip. He would drop anything . . . his bread and honey, the pins he was setting up, and come dazedly to watch her lift the fresh cigaret to her mouth and wait for him to light it.

Back at Le Pâquis we all bathed and dressed. By that time we were meeting one another secretively in rooms and hallways, whispering like conspirators. "Isn't it awful?" we'd hiss despairingly. "But we *mustn't* let David know. Poor David! We mustn't let him see what we think!"

We felt that we were betraying him, in a way, to be so consummately bored and annoyed by the girl he seemed to worship; we felt we must protect him from our own betrayal.

We all met as usual on the terrace for sherry. David's girl never drank sherry, he interpreted for us when she languidly shook her head at the glass Chexbres gave her. Apparently there was nothing in our cellar, which was a fairly interesting one at that time, that appealed to her, and we felt definite relief when she dragged herself to her feet, took David's arm, and broke all our habits of pre-dinner behavior by leading him off toward the orchard. She looked like a delicate drifting moonbeam in her long skirt, with her gold hair blowing long about her throat . . . and I felt as if her lily-hand on David's arm weighed five thousand pounds.

We could at least talk with the two of them gone; her weary murmurs and her dead drooping face stopped our mouths . . . from anything, that is, except words we would not say because we loved David. We sat happily with our sherry, and chattered in an easy peaceful way, while we watched the lake darken far below us.

Once from the garden we heard the girl say clearly, in the clipped flat drawl that was a badge of her expensive school, "*Who* did you say these people are, darling? I suppose I'll have to send a thank-you note. . . ."

"*Well!*" Chexbres' sister sounded crosser than I thought possible, and Norah remarked casually to me, "She can talk, after all. Maybe you'd better write out your name, with Hostess after it . . . pin it on your shoulder . . . it would be a pity to have her keep all that on her mind."

It seemed very funny, suddenly, and we had a little more sherry and let ourselves simmer in a kind of irritated merriment.

I was proud of the dinner. I had spent a lot of thought on it, because even before I saw the girl I felt an exaggerated loyalty to David, a kind of pity for the ordeal he might possibly be going through to bring her there to Le Pâquis before our curious inspection.

First we drank a delicate broth made of chicken stock and white wine and fresh tomato juice, the three iced and mixed together just before we sat down. Then there were little hot cheese tarts, made in Vevey that afternoon. With them we drank a three-year-old Faverges from the vineyard across the road, a high thin white wine like all those of the coast we lived on. Then there was a tray of cold roast pigeons lying on a bed of herbs from our garden, and a big earthen tureen of all the small summer vegetables we could find, cooked whole and separately and then tossed together with sweet butter. There was bread, fresh and crusty.

And we drank one of our best wines, a Corton 1929 sent from the Château for a present the year before. It was beautiful with the strong simple food. We all raised our glasses before the first sip, and then for a few seconds we could but stay silent, with its taste under our tongues. I looked down the long table through the candlelight and saw Chexbres, and all was well with me.

The little blonde girl smiled patiently at him now and then, but even he, charmer of all women, could not rouse her to more than an occasional murmur of response to his calculated nonsense. She smoked all during the meal, which none of us was doing, and once when she let her pretty arm fall toward Chexbres and the fingers unfold commandingly, I saw him pick up the cigaret box and offer it to her, so that she had to lift her hand again and choose one for herself, and I knew that he was deeply angry with her, in spite of his wisdom and his tolerance.

The rest of us were disjointing our little brown birds and eating them in our fingers, as is only proper on a summer night among friends in a friendly room. But the girl cut one little piece off one side of the breast, one little piece off the other, and then pushed the plump carcass almost fretfully away. She picked a few late-summer peas from the vegetables on her plate, and ate a little bread, and then asked Chexbres for coffee.

I saw him disappear into the pantry, where François, the village gravedigger and our self-appointed chaperon-houseman, was standing guard over hot plates and such for us, and in a few minutes she had a cup, made with a little filter because the big pot was still at work on what we planned to drink later. Chexbres raised his wine reassuringly to me, and I looked at David, to see whether his girl's supine disdain of all our ways, and of me as her hostess, and of most of the rules of so-called polite behavior, had hurt him.

But he seemed oblivious of any lack in the perfection of his own young world, content to leave his love to Chexbres' attentions while he bent adoringly toward Chexbres' sister. She too was tiny, and golden-haired . . . but she had the gem-like vigor of a humming bird about her, and her mind flashed in the same otherworldly light, so that I felt proud whenever I saw her with David, because of his good fortune.

All of us were recovering, too, from the first numbing effect of the girl. We found it easier to talk, to brush past her stony lethargy. The wines lay lightly in us, and sent fine vapors high into our palates and our brains, so that our conversation was perhaps almost as delightful as it seemed then. We ate fruits that had lain all day on ice in their blended juices and Tokay, and little crisp *gaufrettes* baked in the village by François' witch-like mother. The candles flickered, and cast the same transient lovely shadows on our faces as what we said did on my mind while I listened.

I saw the girl look, with her eyes almost open this time, at David as he bent away from her toward the other little blonde woman, the one so vital, so different. Then, as if she had a plan, she smiled faintly before she lowered the heavy lids over her beautiful flat blue eyes, and let her arm fall slowly again toward Chexbres. Again he offered her the whole box of cigarets, so that she had to pick up one herself. "Stuffy Old Uncle," I thought with amusement, "Peppery Old Colonel. . . ."

We were talking about swimming then, and drinking coffee at the table because it was too pleasant to leave, even for the terrace. Suddenly the girl spoke. Except for once in the garden, it was the first time any of us had heard her real voice, and we turned to watch her, almost shocked.

"Oh, yes," she was saying in a high deliberate way to Chexbres, "I adore swimming." Then she turned to look full at David, and I knew that in some way she was going to give back the hurt he had dealt her with his casual forgetfulness. "Didn't I tell you . . . don't you remember my letters from San Sebastian, darling? Don't you?"

David lowered his head and drank what was left in his coffee cup nervously. He looked terribly young, and she, with her head tipped back and her small mouth smiling strangely, was as old as an old mountain. She laughed softly.

"It was marvelous," she said to all of us, while we sat looking at her and listening in a kind of dream-like dumbness. "We used to flock to the beach, simply flock, every afternoon, because the more of us there were, the more chance there was of an escape."

David pushed back his chair. He knew what was coming, I suppose, and didn't want to hear it. But she went on lightly, chattily, as if we were intimates. "*You* know . . . refugees trying to swim past the border into France, pretending they were summer people. It was simply breath-taking! The guards always spotted them, because they couldn't help swimming too hard."

She laughed again, and lowered her eyes.

"And what then?" Chexbres' sister spoke gently, with the impersonal sternness of a doctor taking the last clips from a healing wound.

The girl leaned across David, who still sat with his head bent, and answered her, "Why, then there was always shooting. It was exciting. We'd dash for shore, of course, and there'd be the man, trying to escape, swimming all alone. It was easy for the guards then. They never missed. It was all right, though . . . the tide always carried the bodies farther along toward Bordeaux, where they'd wanted to go anyway."

There was nothing to say, but the silence did not seem clumsy. I felt that if I tried to start another kind of talk it would be cruel to my brother. I did not look at him but, perhaps mistakenly, I suffered for him as I would have suffered for myself if I had been eighteen or so and in love the way he was.

François came in with more coffee. Then David stood up.

"I'm sorry," he said to me, and when I looked at last at his face, it was smooth and meaningless, the way I can make mine too. "I'm afraid we'll have to go, if we make the last train."

I knew he was lying, because there was time to catch at least three more, but I thought he was right, and I felt better when Chexbres said, "Why don't you take the car? I don't need it until tomorrow noon. That would give you plenty of time to get back in the morning."

"I'll be coming back tonight," David said noncommittally. "I'd like to take it. Thanks."

And he made his manners and the little girl got her things from upstairs and they were gone.

We still sat around the table. The candles were low. We heard François tiptoe along the terrace, leaving. Chexbres and Norah went down to the cellars and brought back a very old bottle of Armagnac, and we sat for a long time with our elbows on the table and glasses in our cupped hands, gradually coming to life again, gradually recovering from the shyness we had felt when David walked with such dignity from the room, and from the helplessness we'd felt, too, knowing that in some way we, with our love, had made the little blonde girl do what she did to him.

That was perhaps the strangest meal we ever ate at Le Pâquis, Chexbres and I, with other people. But there was another time that was strange, too, in a different way.

It was at Easter. A young American was staying with us, on a vacation from Oxford. He was very easy to have in the house; every morning he piled twenty or thirty books around him, in the corner by the fire, and sat there like a somnolent young bull or stallion, storing up strength in ways of his own. Now and then, wordlessly, he would climb out of the big chair and over the books and get himself some bottles of beer from the cellar. A few times a day someone would bring food to him, sandwiches and such. Then at night he ate with us, and sang and drank and talked enormously.

He was stimulating, and we knew that he would be almost as important by now as he already is, but one night we ran away from him.

We all ate dinner together, and talked for a time, and then Chexbres and I sneaked away, blushing probably through our lies. He did not care; he was playing all the Russian records we had, and we made sure before we deserted him that there was firewood, and that the wine was ample.

I hurried to my room. That afternoon I'd found a big sheet of drawing paper on my desk, heavy with scrolls and banners and phoenixes: I was invited to Chexbres' studio at midnight, for an Easter supper. I made myself look as beautiful as I could, and then as a non-existent clock chimed twelve I went on tiptoe up the stairs to the attics where Chexbres lived, carrying a nest I'd made of grasses, with some painted eggs in it. They were very pretty, and I knew they'd please him.

Inside the studio there were many candles, and the upper part where the big bed and the *armoires* and such things were had meadow flowers everywhere. We stayed in the lower part.

He had hung all my favorite pictures, and there was a present for me on the low table, the prettiest Easter present I have ever seen. It was a big tin of Beluga caviar, in the center of a huge pale-yellow plate, the kind sold in the market on saints' days in Vevey, and all around the tin and then the edge of the plate were apple blossoms. I think apple blossoms are perhaps the loveliest flowers in the world, because of their clarity and the mysterious way they spring so delicately from the sturdy darkness of the carved stems, with the tender little green leaves close around them. At least they were the loveliest that night, in the candlelight, in the odd-shaped room so full of things important to me.

Chexbres was dressed as I was, very specially, and we whispered as if our friend two thick stone floors below us might at any moment suspect our skulduggery and march furiously up the stairs, and pound on the door to shame us.

There was a bottle of smooth potent gin, unlike any I'd ever tasted. We drank it in glasses Chexbres had bought for then, shaped like crystal eggs almost, and with the caviar it was astonishingly good. We sat whispering and laughing and piling the pungent little black seeds on dry toasted bread, and every swallow of the liquor was as hot and soft as the candle flames around us.

Then, after we had eaten almost all of the caviar and drunk most of the gin, and talked as Chexbres and I always talked, more and better than we ever talked with anyone else, I stood up, thanked him very politely for the beautiful surprise, and walked toward the door to the stairs.

For a minute he was too startled to do anything. Then he leaped to his feet, and got there in front of me.

"You are leaving now?" His voice was as polite as mine had been.

"Yes," I said. "Goodnight, and thank you."

"Goodnight," he said calmly, and I knew as I went silently down the stairs to my own room that he was watching me with incredulity.

I felt amazed myself; but suddenly there in the softly lighted studio with the two of us in our best clothes and the formal secret invitation still in my mind, I'd seemed to become a timid young girl watching her behavior in the apartment of a man of the world. I was unchaperoned, shy, flooded with a sense of propriety that had nothing to do with my real years, my real life with Chexbres. That is why I stood up and walked so primly past the upper part of the room, the part with the big bed and the clothes presses and such intimacies. That is why I said goodnight with such politeness to the only man in the world I knew. And that is why, long after I had lain me down in my small austere room, I heard from upstairs the sound of Chexbres' long gusts of laughter.

In the morning it was all right, except that by then both of us had recovered from the shock of my gauche flight, so that whenever we looked at each other we would grin and then laugh. We probably puzzled our young Oxonian, but no more than I had puzzled the two of us the night before . . . and as long as Chexbres lived the sight of caviar, of tender virginal apple blossoms, made us feel helpless with amusement.

Once I Dreamed

1938

CHEXBRES had awakened me, but I lay in bed watching the sky full of fast clouds. I heard him call to me, "Here is a fine cat, probably from the farm across the road—a lovely cat. It looks hungry."

That is nice, I thought: we need a cat.

In a few minutes I got up, and was somewhere in a bigger dressing room than my real one, washing my teeth, when I heard a scuffling in the wardrobe. It too was bigger than my real one. I knew that the strange cat had got in there under my clothes.

I heard a soft gentle laugh from the door—François the houseman stood watching.

Then, just behind the cat, Chexbres too came out from between the long silk dresses, looking proud.

The cat, which did not frighten me, was a young lioness, with the big bones of any kitten, and the cinnamon-and-coffee coat of a puma we once saw in Zurich.

"Look, Mary! She's caught a mouse!"

At that the great cat began to caper, and held up her paw; and caught on one of the long claws was a tiny bright-blue field mouse.

She came to my side, and laid the mouse on one of my bare feet while she curled herself, crouching, around my legs. I looked down at her beautiful rippled brownness. I felt tender and loving, as I knew she did, and I understood the gentility of her hunger.

She drew the little blue mouse onto her tongue, and crunched delicately once, and on my foot was a cool feeling from a spot of soft cerulean blood.

I Remember Three Restaurants

1936–1939

I REMEMBER three restaurants in Switzerland with a special clearness: one on the lake near Lausanne, another behind it in the high hills toward Berne, and the last on the road to Lucerne, in German-speaking country.

When we went back, in June of 1939, to pack our furniture and bolt the shutters, we drove toward Lucerne one day. Children were selling the first early Alpine roses along the roads . . . tight ugly posies, the same color as the mottled purple of the little girls' cheeks.

At Malters, one of the few villages of that part of the country not almost overpoweringly quaint and pretty, we stopped at the Gasthaus zum Kreuz. We wondered if Frau Weber would remember us, and if her neurasthenic daughter Anneli would be yearning still to be a chambermaid in London, and if . . . most important . . . if there would be trout swimming in the little tank of icy water that stood in the dining room.

Frau Weber, looking more than ever like a virile Queen Victoria, did indeed remember us, discreetly at first, and then with floods of questions and handshakings and general delight. Anneli was there, fat, pale, still yearning, but this time for Croydon, where she hoped to exchange her Cockney accent for a more refined one. And the trout darted behind glass in the bubbling water.

We stayed there for many hours, eating and drinking and remembering incredulously that once we had almost driven past the Kreuz without stopping.

502

That was several years ago, when we were roaming about the country with my parents. The chauffeur was sleepy after a night spent in a hotel filled with unusually pretty kitchen maids, and he lost the way. We went confusedly along roads that led where we did not want to go at all; and we all got very hungry and perhaps a little too polite.

Finally we said to stop at the first *gasthaus*, no matter what it looked like. We could certainly count on beer and cheese, at the least.

Pierre stifled a yawn, and his neck got a little pinker; and in perhaps a minute we had come to an impressive stop in front of one of the least attractive buildings of German Switzerland, in the tight village of Malters.

The place had a sharp peaked roof and many little windows; but there were no flowers on the wooden ledges, and a smell of blood came from the sausage shop on the ground floor. Dark stairs led up from the street through a forbidding hallway.

We wanted to go on. It was late, though; and we were hungry and cramped and full of latent snarls. I told Pierre to see what the place looked like.

He yawned again, painfully, and went with false briskness up the dour, dark stairs. Soon he was back, beaming, no longer sleepy. We crawled out, not caring how many pretty girls he had found if there was something in their kitchen for us, too.

Soon life looked better. Frau Weber herself had led us solicitously to ancient but sparkling toilets, and we had washed in a porcelain bowel enameled with swans and lavender chrysanthemums, and were all met again in a little piney honey-colored room full of family photographs. There was a long table with chairs primly about it, and cupboards and a beautiful rococo couch. We felt happy, and toasted one another with small glasses of a strange, potent bitters.

"Whatever you have," we said to Frau Weber, and sat back complacently waiting for some sausage from her shop and maybe a salad. We watched the trout swimming in a tank by one of the windows, and thought them an odd, enormous decoration.

Anneli came in. She was pretty, in a discontented way; and we knew Pierre would have a pleasant lunch. We talked to her about England, which she apparently loved as some women love men or some men the bottle. She set the table, and then came back with a net and a platter. She swooped up a trout, held it by the tail, and before we could close our ears or even wince, had cracked its skull smartly on the sideboard.

My mother lay back farther on the couch and gulped wanly at her bitters; and Father muttered with a kind of sick admiration, "That's the way! By George, that's the way!" as Anneli whacked the brains loose in some ten trout.

She smiled and said, "You 'aven't long to wite naow," and hurried from the room.

By then we were eating slices of various strange sausages, surprisingly light, and drinking cold, thin white wine of the country. Nothing else much mattered.

Frau Weber and her daughter came in carrying a long shallow copper pan between them. They set it down carefully; and Anneli stood back puffing while the older woman lifted the lid, her white hair bristling upward in a regal pompadour, and her face flushed and dewy.

The trout lay staring up at us, their eyes hard and yet somehow benevolent. Our heads drew nearer to the pan, willy-nilly, pulled by one of the finest smells we had ever met. We sniffed and murmured. Frau Weber beamed. She scolded at the girl, who ran from the room for little white potatoes and a great bowl of hot buttered peas from the garden. The mother served the fish herself, and then disappeared proudly.

It was, of course, the most delicious dish that we had ever eaten. We knew that we were hungry, and that even if it had been bad it would have been good . . . but we knew, too, that nevertheless it was one of the subtlest, rarest things that had ever come our way. It was incredibly delicate, as fresh as clover.

We talked about it later, and Frau Weber told us of it willingly, but in such a vague way that all I can remember now is hot unsalted butter, herbs left in for a few seconds, cream, a shallot flicked over, the fish laid in, the cover put on. I can almost see it, smell it, taste it; but I know that I could never copy it, nor could anyone alive, probably.

Finally we were eating large, fragrant strawberries and drinking quite a lot more wine. It amused Anneli that we wanted our coffee in the tall porcelain goblets we saw in the cupboard. But it is the trout that really mattered. They were more important than getting to Lucerne, or than the pride of Frau Weber, or than the girl Anneli, frustrated and yearning. They were, we felt, important like a *grisaille* window or the coming of spring.

And we went back many times to the Kreuz, and the trout were always that way . . . important.

The second restaurant I remember now was near our old home, in Châtel St. Denis, where the Army used to send its ski-learners to use the fine, easy slopes all around. It was called the Hôtel des XIII Cantons.

We knew Mademoiselle Berthe there. She was tall; she had a thin, spirited face; and her dark hair was rolled in odd corkscrews behind each ear, in the disappearing fashion of her village. She had hips that were wide and firm, hung low on her legs; and her feet, on which she always wore exotic beach sandals, were very long and flat. She flapped about on them, and was the best waitress that I have ever known, in Europe or America.

The upstairs room held perhaps fifty people on market days and times like Easter; yet Berthe was always alone and always unruffled. Sometimes in winter, when Army officers were there, teasing and flirting and barking, she got more taciturn than usual. But no matter what kind of people she served, she was always skillful and the most impersonal woman I have ever watched.

She never made mistakes; and no matter how many people were tapping their empty glasses and calling, she would always see that plates were hot and platters properly bubbling above her innumerable alcohol lamps before she left one table for another. She sped about, flat-footed, heavy-hipped, unruffled, waiting for the day when her mother would die and she could renounce the dining room for the glories of the kitchen.

In the meantime, Madame reigned on the other side of the wide stairs which led to the square pine dining room, with its mirrors and white linen curtains and window ledges heavy with hideous, meaty begonias.

Madame Mossu was famous for her trout, her frogs' legs, and especially her shrimps. I have eaten them all many times. Some sticklers for gastronomic etiquette have criticized what she called *truites meunières* because the fish were always curled like *truites au bleu*. Once I asked Berthe why that was. She shrugged and said, "What of it? A trout dead not a minute curls with agony in hot butter. One can flatten him, I admit it. But Maman prefers to let him be as comfortable as possible." There was nothing more to be said.

The season for shrimps is short, and Madame Mossu paid well for all the boys and old men could find in their hundred icy streams. But there were never enough; so diplomats from Geneva and Bernese politicians and horny shepherds on their annual gastronomic bender in Châtel would make appointments in advance for cold shrimps in their shells, or in a *court-bouillon* or a *bisque*.

There was a general who always had to unbutton his tunic, and at the bottom of the table a lieutenant with a gleam in his eye that meant, by God, some day he too would be a general. Once, on All Saints' Day, there were three peasants in full black-linen smocks, and two sat smiling quietly while the third stood up and sang a little mountain song. None of us listened, and yet we all heard; and probably we all remember his serious, still face flushed with feast-day drinking, and the way he sat down after the song, and wiped his lips and put a piece of trout between them with complete un-self-consciousness. Then, besides all the diplomats and such, there were *pensionnaires*; a tall, beautiful girl dressed like a Paris man-nequin, who played cards every night with the butcher and young Mossu, and then went away without a word; the lame pharmacist, who had widowed himself four times by his own vitality; a dried, mean, sad old woman who might have been the librarian if there had been a library.

One night a little woman with a black wig came in. She went straight to the long table usually reserved for the military and seated herself. Then a strange party of domestics sat down facing her. One was a woman who looked as though she took dictation daily from 10 until 2. Her hair was like mud, and she was probably a "com-panion." One was a flirtatious man with a mouth too sensitive; two others were poor, beaten-down maids with mean eyes and stringy skins; and last was a young, healthy, arrogant chauffeur. Berthe scuttled with her usual dexterity around this motley table. First of all, as if she well knew what to do, she brought one glass and a large dusty bottle of the finest Cognac to the old woman, who poured it out hastily for herself, all her dirty diamonds a-tremble. Then Berthe brought cheap wine for the others, who did not speak, but drank thirstily without looking at their mistress.

An enormous platter of twisted trout Berthe carried in next and put down before the old woman, who drained her glass for the fifth or sixth time and started shoveling fish on to the plates the others held out to her. While we all tried not to watch, the poor souls slashed and poked at the fish until each plate held its neat pile, with bones tidily put on a side dish. The clatter stopped.

Old Wig lifted her glass again, and tossed the brandy down. The servants stood up; and she looked at each plate with its heap of the best trout in Switzerland, boneless and delicate. She nodded finally; and the companion, the weak-mouthed secretary, the two maids, the chauffeur picked up their plates obediently and went out the door and down the stone stairs.

Berthe's long face was expressionless, but her little ear-curls vibrated gently.

"Curiosity grips my bowels . . . excuse me," my husband said. In a few minutes he was back, full of news: the five servants, solemnly, as though they were serving some obscene Mass, had filed out into the little square before the Soldiers' Monument, and had stopped by three immense and antiquated limousines. In each car were three or four tiny feeble Mexican dogs, the shuddering hairless kind, yapping almost silently at the windows. The humans fed them, and then stood in the cold thin air for a minute, silent.

They came back to the dining room and ate well. The secretary flirted dispassionately with the companion and the less dreary of the maids, and the chauffeur stared arrogantly about. Old Wig ate little; but as the evening went on and the brandy warmed her, she smiled occasionally, and spoke to Berthe once about how cold she had been for the thirty years since she left Guatemala.

She makes me think of Monsieur Kuhn's sister, in the last of the three Swiss restaurants I remember so well.

Monsieur Kuhn ran the Hôtel de Ville et du Raisin at Cully, near Lausanne on the lake. He was quiet, with sad eyes and a long face. The only things in the world he cared about were fishing for perch and cooking his haul.

The inn itself was strange and secretive, like its keeper, with cold, high halls, dank air, and an enormous kitchen which never showed anything like a live fire or a sign of bustle. There was a gaunt dining room, always empty, and the café where we sat, a long, queer room with a big stove in the middle, local wine advertisements on the murky walls, and a paper rose in the vase that topped the elaborate coffee machine.

From that dead kitchen into that bleak, smoky room Monsieur Kuhn would send his wonderful filets. He ripped them from the live, stunned fish, as they were ordered. The filets were perhaps three inches long, always with a little crisp point of the tail left on.

Monsieur Kuhn would creep shyly into the dining room, after we had come to his café for a year or more, and bow and shake hands and smile painfully when we thanked him. His long, lined face was always sad and remote and we felt that we were wrong to distract him.

His sister and his wife were different, and grew to like us almost too much. At first we thought they were blood sisters: they both looked so virginal that we could not believe that one of them was married to Monsieur Kuhn, even though he himself looked quite beyond such bothers as co-habitation. It took us some time to learn that the taller of the two women was his wife.

She was very thin, and something about her was out of a drawing, out of an El Greco. Her eyes were bigger than human eyes, and slipped upwards and sideways; and her mouth was pale and beautiful. She was shadowy . . . a bad liver probably . . . but mysterious-looking. She wore black always, and her long hands picked up sizzling platters as if they were distasteful leaves from a tree. She had a light voice; and there was something good and fine about her, so that I always warmed to her.

Her husband's sister Mitzi was quite different. She was short; and although she had a thin face, she looked puffy, with a white, thick skin, the kind that would bend a hypodermic needle. She wore her mole-colored hair in an elaborate girlish mass of curls, and her hands were small and pretty. She, too, dressed in black; but her sweaters had gold threads in them, and her skirts were broadcloth.

Madame Kuhn adored her more plainly than is often seen, and saved all the easy work for her, and did all the ugly jobs herself.

One time we took Michel to the Raisin. He was the kind of short, virile, foxlike Frenchman who seems to have been born in a beret, the kind who is equally ready to shoot a wild boar, make love, or say something which seems witty until you think about it. He was unconscious of Mademoiselle Kuhn.

She, on the other hand, was completely upset by him. She sidled and cooed, and put down our plate of bread as such a thing had never been put down before, and smiled again.

We finished our celestial filets, and drank more wine. Madame Kuhn hovered in the cold darkness near the kitchen, agonizing with her great dark eyes for the poor tortured sister. We paid the bill, cruel and wrapped in our own lives.

As we got into the car, Mademoiselle ran out with a knot of the first wild narcissuses, and thrust them loosely into Michel's hand.

"Some are for you, Madame," she cried, but she looked only at him, and his neat aristocratic bones and the power in his flesh. Then she ran back into the cold glare of the doorway and stood close against the stone, saying, "Oh, you are adorable, adorable . . ." in her bad Swiss-French.

Michel suddenly broke into a sweat, and wiped the flowers across his forehead. *"Mon Dieu!"* he cried.

We drove away as fast as we could, leaving the poor soul there against the stone, with Madame watching her through the colored-glass door, and the smell of the little filets all around.

But when we went back, that June of 1939, things were changed. Madame stood with a plate of bread in her long hands, and tears ran down her face. Mitzi was in a clinic. "Ah, she is not the same. My little dear will never be so sweet, so innocent again," the woman said. And her eyes, as dead and haunted as something from a Spanish portrait, stared at the wine posters on the murky walls. "Nothing is the same. Nothing will ever be the same."

She walked toward the cold, dank kitchen, truly grief-stricken; and we, sitting there in the café, felt lonely and afraid. The filets, though, were the same as always; and when Monsieur Kuhn came from the kitchen and smiled proudly at us, we forgot his foolish sister and why we were there at all, and remembered only that some dishes and some humans live forever—remembered it thankfully, as I do now.

Sea Change

1937–1939

AND the eighth and ninth, the tenth, eleventh, twelfth trips? What have they to do with me, the gastronomical me? What sea changes were there, to make me richer, stranger? I grew older with each one, like every other wanderer. My hungers altered: I knew better what and how to eat, just as I knew better how I loved other people, and even why.

I came back alone to America, to tell my family that I was going to get a divorce from Al. Chexbres said, "Why not write it?" I had no answer; I felt I must do it myself, a kind of castigation for hurting good people.

The first three days aboard the large Dutch ship were rough, but not enough to make me feel as I did. I was prostrated . . . not seasick the way the stewardess wanted me to be, but flattened, boneless, with despair at having gone away from Chexbres. It was the strongest physical reaction I had ever felt, and I was frightened and dazed.

I lay shivering in my berth, but my mind was full of feverish plans, which I knew were unreasonable even while I worked on them: I would fake a contagious disease, one so awful the captain would turn back rather than approach New York . . . that sort of thing. I think now that my instincts were right. I should have turned back, not in the middle of the Atlantic as my brain was trying to make me do, but certainly as soon as I reached port. Something inside me stronger than my stubbornness was punishing me for leaving Chexbres, when there was to be so little time for us together.

It was a bitter period I spent there, alone in my neat chintz-curtained cabin. And when I finally got up and looked at the rest of the ship, and at the people on it, I found myself plunged into an atmosphere so much more tortured than mine that it was almost as sickening as my private woe had been.

Almost everyone aboard was fleeing. There were a few Dutch-American business men, and a few stiff racial snobs who ate and sat and gambled apart. The rest were Jews. Most of them had gone from Austria to Holland. Then, as things grew worse, they had finally managed to leave Holland for America. They were doctors, many of them, wondering how they could pass state examinations after thirty or forty years of practicing and sometimes months of cruel stagnation in labor camps.

In First Class they walked quietly up and down with little dictionaries, or stood, not speaking to anyone, watching the swift gray waters. There were a few who talked with me. One was a short tired old man, who shyly drank beer with me and asked about Texas, where he had a grandniece who might welcome him.

I helped him with his dictionary words, and the day we docked he said, "You must have children soon. Here is my address in Texas. I want to deliver them for you . . . free, for friendship."

The other was a lean white-haired editor from Berlin. He had owned one of those slick revues that after the last war made German photographic technique famous . . . especially pictures of nude girls with long jade cigarette holders, and apple blossoms trembling against spring skies. He prowled restlessly about the ship, like a man in great pain, and occasionally sat in the chair next to mine and talked very wittily in French about the reasons for the New Order in his country.

In Second Class the people were poorer and younger. They were less resigned, and their eyes, even while they played chess or deck tennis, were ferociously resentful. Most of them were doctors or lawyers, many with girls they had married in Holland. The blonde wives spoke quite freely and even calmly about their flight, but the dark repressed men said very little, and played games and smoked.

They had cameras and fine medical tools, which they hoped to sell in America because they were allowed to bring so little money with them. And like all the others, they must go to stay with unknown relatives. . . .

In Third Class (the differences were rigid on that ship, with luxury on top, plainness in the middle, and stark clean poverty below), the people were small, bent, furtive, true products of the pogrom and the ghetto. I knew that somewhere in them beauty and love and even hate still lived, but they were the Victims, malnourished for centuries into these silent shivering little creatures.

That voyage was the one that made me most mistrust myself, alone to face sea change. I was full of a slow misery of loathing for what was happening to make all the people around me act as they must. It mixed, there on that proud stiff-necked ship, with my own perturbation at the hurt I was causing people I loved, and with my realization that leaving Chexbres even for a few weeks was one of the stupidest things I had ever done.

I saw clearly for the first time that a woman traveling alone and behaving herself on a ship is an object of curiosity, among the passengers and even more so among the cynical and weary officers. I developed a pattern of behavior which I still follow, on ships and trains and in hotels everywhere, and which impresses and undoubtedly irritates some people who see me, but always succeeds in keeping me aloof from skulduggery.

There are many parts to it, but one of the most important is the way I eat; it not only surrounds me with a wall of awe, but makes my private life more interesting and keeps me from boredom.

I discovered, there on the staidly luxurious Dutch liner, that I could be very firm with pursers and stewards and such. I could have a table assigned to me in any part of the dining room I wanted, and, best of all, I could have that table to myself. I needed no longer be put with officers or predatory passengers, just because I was under ninety and predominantly female. It would never again matter to me that the purser looked oddly at me for my requests, and that people stared and whispered when I walked alone to my table; I had what I needed to bolster my own loneliness, a sense of strength.

And once seated, I could eat what I wanted, and drink what I wanted. I could spend all the time I needed over a piece of *pâté*, truly to savor its uncountable tastes; I could make a whole meal of little lettuce hearts and buttermilk, or ask for frogs' legs *provençale* and *pêches* Victoria—and get them.

And if I felt like it, I could invite another passenger to dine with me, and order an intelligent thoughtful meal, to please the chef and the wine steward. That was enjoyable occasionally, but in general I preferred to eat by myself, slowly, voluptuously, and with an independence that heartened me against the coldness of my cabin and my thoughts.

It has always been that way since, so that in a Hollywood "bachelor" with a pull-down bed, or on a plane pointed any which way, or even in my own hollow house with death at my shoulder, I can protect myself with that same gastronomic liberty, and eat quietly, calmly, and with a special dignity. It has often saved me, and my reason too, as it probably did when I first found it, on that trip away from Chexbres.

There was a great deal of whoring all about me. It had none of the perverted vileness I felt on the German ships, and was in general good-natured, except for the one fact that some of the most outspokenly anti-Semitic of the small group of business men in First Class were the hottest after the beautiful Jewish girls. It is equally unpleasant that they were very successful.

The two most discreet girls on board were what was spoken of quite casually by the officers as "water babies."

They were married, both of them, to men in concentration camps. They seemed to have plenty of money, and for safety and probably from habit they had not set foot on land since they escaped from Germany. Instead, they went back and forth from Europe to America, sometimes for months on a single ship, making one trip as the First Officer's girl, the next as the Second's, and so on.

The men seemed genuinely fond of them, and apparently had a strict code of behavior in deciding whose turn was next and in respecting it.

The girls were pretty, and very well behaved. They danced and drank beautifully, and must have grown equally accomplished in more intimate matters. I asked one of them what she did while the ship was in port, and she said she read all the newspapers and then bought new clothes by telephone. Sometimes if she read that another ship was near by with one of her girl friends on it, they talked to each other and made plans for the next few voyages, always by 'phone.

I wondered if that strange sea-borne life was in its own way like the one I was evolving for myself, and if it protected them from thoughts of their men in Dachau as mine did shield me from my own grim dreamings. It was based on hungers, all of it. . . .

11

I went back to Switzerland as soon as I could. I found when I changed my reservations that the only other ship at that time was one with six hundred German youths and maidens on it, returning from a Good Will tour, of course. So I went Second on the *Ile de France*, probably the coldest, most unattractive luxury liner I ever saw.

My system of public independence was working well, partly because I was headed in the right direction and full therefore of secret joy. I ate alone usually, and well . . . but almost every night I went with two Frenchmen named Jacques and Pierre to First Class, where the officers were impressed with Jacques because of his title and all of us because we were actually traveling in Second.

They were bitter men, the officers, in a gruesome laughing way, and always spoke of the line they sailed on as *La Compagnie Générale Tragique*.

We would sit in the bleak fantastic bar, perhaps only ten of us or twelve awake on the whole ship, and at eleven the waiters would set up one of the most lushly extravagant buffets I have ever seen, and we would drink champagne and have the maître d'hôtel cut one sliver of breast from a grouse, or dig one spoonful of *pâté* from a great yellow terrine.

"Please accept more," he would beg, and piled caviar on our plates, while we talked quietly, wearily, against the rhythm of the great ship, about Laval and Blum and which way France would fall when she fell. . . .

III

About two years later Chexbres and I came back. We wanted to be on the *Champlain*, because he had often enjoyed it, but it was retired. The *De Grasse* was a sister ship, I think. There were only twenty passengers, and I was the only woman, which made the seating easy for the Captain's Dinner.

I don't know how we ever got to New York. Chexbres was dying, really, and in revolt at the whole cruel web of clinics and specialists and injections and rays we had run away from in Europe, as if we knew that nothing could be worse than what was happening there to us. We were without nurses, for the first time in months. It was a very rough crossing, and I still wake up shaking sometimes to remember how I prepared hypodermics between rolls of the ship. . . .

We were bolstered by the wine of freedom, really, and I don't think anything could have daunted us.

We went to meals whenever the motion permitted, and Chexbres would invent dances down the empty corridors on his one leg and the crutches, so that when we went into the dining room we were always laughing wildly.

The chef, bored almost insane, pounced on us via the wine steward, and we were sent dishes such as I had only read about before. We seldom did them justice; the motion perhaps and our state of mind made it hard to eat. But we were appreciative, and we heard that the chef was happy.

The only passenger I can remember was a tall fat man, ringed and heavily perfumed in spite of his Brooks Brothers tweeds, who ate by himself and flew into rages when he saw anything being served to us that was not on the menu. Finally he pulled off the linen and all the dishes, one day, and ran from the room crying.

After that his waiter, with many apologetic eyebrows at us, served him small editions of our masterpieces, always with a polite mockery about him that would have reduced me to more than tears. The fat man beamed and giggled with pleasure, and lifted his glass magnanimously to us. . . .

He was a milliner. "The most expensive chippies in New York wear my hats," he said candidly to us. He told Chexbres that he was in great demand socially, but that his deepest pleasure was to stay at home, take off all his clothes, and let his cat sleep on his naked stomach. The purring made him feel creative, he said. Chexbres had another drink.

The captain sent me flowers once or twice, because he knew Chexbres was so ill, and after I thanked him for having caviar at his dinner, he presented me with a large tin of it when we left the ship. He was always polite and impersonal, but the note with the caviar said, "Pain cannot touch the loving-hearted." I thought of his eyes, dark, tired, intelligent *French* eyes. *Compagnie Générale Tragique* . . .

IV

Then, in half a year or so, eleven and twelve.

I was with Chexbres. We knew what was happening, and how to cope with it as long as he lived, and we were like two happy ghosts, I really think. We were charmed, so that doors opened and people smiled shyly, and everywhere there was decency and cleanliness and light. It sounds fatuous to say that, but it was so.

We had to go back to Switzerland, to close our house forever and sell many of our goods, and to get medicine for him, figured coldly to last as long as he did. And that sounds, not fatuous, but grim and ugly. It never was . . . we were immune to everything, that summer, that could hurt us.

We went to France and back again on the *Normandie*, both times in the same beautiful room which was in First Class but right next to the door into Second. Second was easier for Chexbres, smaller and with fewer stairs and such.

The *Normandie* was the loveliest ship I ever saw. It wasn't a ship the way the little Dutch one had been, but at the same time there was nothing vulgar or pretentious or snobbish about it, like some of the others.

We spent the time either in bed (it was a big room with real beds in it, the first I had seen on a ship except in movies), or in the Smoking Room or Lounge or whatever it was called: an airy place, all glass walls but not frightening, with comfortable places to sit and a wonderful waiter. He reminded us with his sad hollow eyes of François, our Swiss houseman.

His dream was to save enough money to send himself to a mountain sanatorium, and there die. We knew the one he had picked out, a glum barracks in the Savoy Alps. But he had read fine things about it. We agreed with him that it would be a peaceful way to end. He was only about thirty, but his mind was made up and his lungs were obviously rotting.

We drank to his plan, the night before we landed back in New York . . . and then the next time the *Normandie* docked, it was to burn, and that poor man was cheated. He liked us very much, sensing perhaps a companionably fateful air about us, and he approved highly of our well-organized and thoughtful drinking.

We got up late, and went after bathings and shavings to the Lounge, where we sat in soft chairs by the glass wall and looked out past the people sunning themselves to the blue water. We drank champagne or sometimes beer, slowly, and talked and talked to each other because there was so much to say and so little time to say it.

I have probably talked more to Chexbres, and he to me, than to all the other people put together in both our lives. We often wondered about it: how we could talk so much and never bore each other. The wine served perhaps as a kind of delicate lubricant . . . but without it, it would have been the same.

Then we went slowly down to lunch. We had a table near the door, easy for Chexbres, and there we watched the people coming in and out, and drank more beer or a good wine . . . whatever we had started with. The *sommelier* liked us, of course, and stopped often to tell us strange things about people or his bottles.

We ate lightly but well; by then we knew just about what Chexbres needed and could stand, and although I ate more than he, it was in the same way, not grimly because we must still live, but with much enjoyment always.

After lunch we rested. That sounds silly . . . but the way we had to move about, and even sit down or sneeze, was a great deal of work for both of us. In order to stay self-controlled and blissful, the way we were, we had to rest a great deal.

About four o'clock we would go up to the Lounge again, and turn our backs on the ocean to watch a movie. We had never liked movies, but this time, sitting in the slowly rolling gently shaking body of the great ship, watching the artful foolery unwind on the screen, they seemed a natural part of the whole trance-like voyage we were making. We sat in great soft chaises-longues, with little tables beside us on a kind of private balcony, and for the first time in my life I drank Pernods.

If there was one film we each drank one, in small sips until the end, and if there were two films we drank two. I cannot imagine drinking them any place else, but then they were perfect, in a quiet comforting way, and very clean in the throat.

And before dinner we drank more champagne, watching the sun set through the thick glass walls, and after dinner, which we sometimes ordered at noon to please our waiter who was convinced we were starving to death, we drank still more, or sometimes cognac. Then we went to bed again, and two or three times in the night we would start talking, and eat a few of the little sandwiches the worried waiter sent down to us, and drink some hot consommé or more brandy.

Even when New York loomed near us, we felt outward bound. I bit gently at my numb fingers. I seemed beautiful, witty, truly loved . . . the most fortunate of all women, past sea change and with her hungers fed.

The Lemming to the Sea

1938

MORE often than not people who see me on trains and in ships, or in restaurants, feel a kind of resentment of me since I taught myself to enjoy being alone. Women are puzzled, which they hate to be, and jealous of the way I am served, with such agreeable courtesy, and of what I am eating and drinking, which is almost never the sort of thing they order for themselves. And men are puzzled too, in a more personal way. I anger them as males.

I am sorry. I do not like to do that, or puzzle the women either. But if I must be alone, I refuse to be alone as if it were something weak and distasteful, like convalescence. Men see me eating in public, and I look as if I "knew my way around"; and yet I make it plain that I know my way around without them, and that upsets them.

I know what I want, and I usually get it because I am adaptable to locales. I order meals that are more typically masculine than feminine, if feminine means whipped-cream-and-cherries. I like good wines, or good drinkin'-likka, and beers and ales. I like waiters; I think the woman who said that waiters are much nicer than people was right, and quite often waitresses are too. So they are always nice to me, which is a sure way to annoy other diners whose soup, quite often, they would like to spit in.

And all these reasons, and probably a thousand others, like the way I wear my hair and what shade my lipstick is, make people look strangely at me, resentfully, with a kind of hurt bafflement, when I dine alone.

Sometimes the results are more tangible. I think now of Jacques.

He was on the *Ile de France* when I went back to Switzerland. By then I had fairly well developed my system of public behavior, but

518

the ship was a hard test, bleak, rattling, stuffy in Second, and heart-breakingly pretentious in First. Jacques and I were in Second.

I saw him soon, and enjoyed the way he moved quietly about the decks and halls, like a Spanish dancer, very self-contained. He was small and dark, and made me think of a fox, not because of the cunning a fox is supposed to have, but because of a smooth fine brown-eyed potency about him.

He was looking at me, and admiring me too, but I did not realize it: my whole reason for being lay ahead of me, on the lake near Vevey in the canton of Vaud, and I was hurrying there as irrevocably as an Arctic lemming hurries to the sea cliff, through poisoned fields and fire and flood to what he longs for.

Jacques watched me in the dining room, where I sat alone and ate judiciously, with amiable concentration. And he watched me in the Smoking Room, which was the only warm place to sit. I read, and drank without ever showing anything but a self-contained enjoyment, and seemed not to want better company than my own. All this was puzzling to Jacques, and because he was a man it was annoying too.

Finally we met, and when he told me his name and asked me teasingly if I could spell it, I amazed him by doing so, because I had learned it in a history course in Dijon, years before.

He was a Norman. There were seven sons and six daughters in his family. Some of the boys went to the colonies or to Canada, like Jacques, and some of the girls went into nunneries. There were a few of each sex in private insane asylums. The rest were very important in Paris, or the Foreign Service. Jacques showed me pictures of his home, a great grim place with its own church, its own village, and of his stubborn handsome mother.

He was a very simple man, almost childish, and did not talk much at a time. Sometimes we drank cognac together after dinner, and once he ate at my table, with a kind of charmed jealousy at the good meal we had, and the good wine.

He was very modest, but always there was in his bones, in every hair on his fine dark head, the assurance of his great name, so that one night when he was trembling with nervousness at having to officiate at the ship's concert, and I said, "Why not get someone else to, then?", he dismissed the idea and me with it by saying, very simply, "But it is expected of me."

That night, in honor of the concert and perhaps of taking me up to dine in First with the captain, he wore a beautiful little satin waistcoat, I remember, of the most delicate shell-pink, with flowers embroidered on it in petit-point. It was perfect on him, for some reason I cannot tell.

Only twice did he ever say anything personal to me. Once he said he liked to look across the dining room and watch me eating there, so thoughtfully and voluptuously, because I was the only woman he had ever seen except a Chinese, the wife of a great leader, who could do it. I knew very little about her, but I asked if it might not be our smooth hair. No, he said, and did not have words for more.

And another time, just before we landed, he stood twirling his beret on one finger, not confusedly but with real grace, and asked me if I had ever thought what it would be like to marry a trapper and live in the Canadian forests. I never had, but when I looked at him I realized he was planning something in his slow simple brain, and I said, "It would take strength."

"Yes," he said, looking impersonally at me, as if I were a horse.

I don't know how or why I told him what hotel I would stop at in Paris, on my way to Switzerland. Certainly I never thought to see him again. My mind was fixed on tomorrow, on being once more with Chexbres.

The boat train was late, and by the time I had tidied myself for dinner and got to Michaud's, a boy was putting up the shutters. I felt depressed and tired, and went past him anyway, thinking I could get a good glass of sherry, and then go to bed. But when Madame Rollo saw me she shrieked for her brother, and a dash to the kitchen proved that there was enough heat left in the ranges to make me a little omelet, and would I consider eating a few spiced mushrooms first, and yes, by God, there was one portion of *crème au kirsch* left, after a little salad . . . and for this time of night and this cold month a small bottle of Montrachet '23, with my permission. . . .

It all made me feel warm and human, sitting there with those kind voluble quarrelsome people behind the shutters, knowing that tomorrow I would be with Chexbres again, and my long journey over.

When I got back to the hotel and saw Jacques sitting by the desk, I could hardly remember who he was. He was very nice, and asked me to forgive him for being importunate . . . but two of his brothers were in Paris, and anxious to meet me, and . . . and he looked so fine-boned and simple and honest that I left my key on its hook, and went out with him to a waiting car.

We went to the little upstairs-bar at Weber's. It was the first time I had been there. People were sitting quietly, drinking champagne and eating vanilla ice cream, which one of Jacques' brothers told me was chic at the moment.

They were taller than he, and handsomer, but they did not have his *good* look. They were much more intelligent, and treated him with a kind of affectionate scorn that older members of a large family often seem to feel for the young ones. He was a yokel home from Canada, and they were Paris diplomats, and even if he had been articulate he would have said very little.

They were politely startled when I ordered a very good cognac. One of them drank scotch, and the other champagne, and Jacques ordered a bottle of Perrier water.

I had told them when I first met them that I was very tired and must go back soon to the hotel, but as I listened to them I wanted to go even sooner. I was speaking good French that night, probably because their accents were so perfect, but very quickly I knew there was nothing I could say that would be truthful. They were the most cynically weary men I had ever met, like the young officers on the *Ile*, but with more force . . . not physically or religiously or sexually, but in their patriotism. They were complete defeatists.

I sat there listening to them, hardly able to swallow for the revolt and horror I felt. They were betraying France, two men as old as France herself, and strong and intelligent enough to fight for her. They were selling her, there in Weber's little bar, as surely as they were selling her on the Bourse and in the embassies.

I looked at Jacques, to see if he understood what had happened to his brothers, but it was impossible to tell. He was tired and obviously bored by them.

They kept on talking, charmingly, wittily, and I realized that all around me there was the same kind of conversation. Hitler and Tardieu and Laval: these aristocratic Frenchmen were discussing them blandly, as if they were unpleasant but humble menials, to be handled puppet-like at their own discretion.

I could stand no more of it, and asked to be taken to my hotel. I was shocked, so that I could hardly keep from shaking.

Jacques took me to the desk from their car, and when he kissed my hand he looked and me and said, "I should have stayed in Canada. I understand trapping animals better."

His poor simple mind was full of misery, I could tell, and I said goodnight gently, as if I would see him tomorrow, to comfort him.

A few weeks later I got a strange letter from him. "I am just back in Paris for a couple of days," he wrote. "I find the country place most depressing, dreary, and terribly damp. I can hardly tell you how much unpleasant it was to stay there, in consequence of the wet and my sister who has returned to the château after twenty-one years in a convent, to expect the world to have been stopped during that time. However, my dear, I shan't bother you with all that . . . how are you getting on, working hard, do you?"

Here Chexbres, who knew as much as I did about Jacques, said rather stuffily, "I thought you told me his English was good." I could only laugh. I thought the letter was funny.

He wrote about going south. He wanted to go to Corsica and buy an old farm. "I don't want to stay home too long. I will fill too depressed. Do you know Marie Françoise how happy I will be if it were possible for you to take that trip with me?"

"The bastard," Chexbres said softly.

The letter told me that it might help my writing to go on such a trip in that interesting island, and then, "Please let me know how foolish it all sound to you. I won't get *fâché*. Excuse this awful writing. The pen is a poem! Hoping to read you soon and have my life worth living, *à bientôt*."

I felt confused, to have to read this in front of Chexbres. He would think I had flirted. . . . Then I began to laugh again. It was such a simple proposition, just like Jacques.

But Chexbres, for a time, was almost hateful toward me, feeling a kind of brotherhood with Jacques against all women. "You can't do things like that to men," he said resentfully.

"But what?"

"Whatever it is that makes them write letters like that," he muttered, hating me. "That chap's suffering. . . ."

How could I say it was because I ate in a dark cold miserable ship as if I enjoyed myself, and drank without getting silly . . . because I behaved myself in public?

I wrote to Jacques and thanked him for his invitation, and told him that if ever he was near Lausanne, Chexbres and I would be so glad to see him. It was a very polite letter.

And in a few days I was called up to the village (it was before we had a telephone), to reverse a call to Evian from the Café de la Grappe, and it was Jacques. I had sat trembling, thinking awful thoughts of runaway relatives and such, and when it was only Jacques, so matter of fact, I felt almost glad to hear him. He wanted to stop to see us on his way south.

I was rather ungracious, and told him our houseman had influenza, which was true, but he ignored that. I knew Chexbres would look grim, and he did.

Jacques came that afternoon, and that night we went to dinner at Cully and ate piles of perch filets on a big platter in the café. I don't think Jacques had ever eaten so simply that way, with a lady and gentleman in a common-man's place.

Later we dressed and went dancing at Montreux, and drank a lot of champagne. Jacques danced almost as well as Chexbres. And that night his only personal remark was, very close to my ear in a tango, "But who is Chexbres?"

I told him, as well as anyone could ever tell who that strange man was, and he said, "Oh."

The next day we went all over the neighboring vineyards with Jules, our own *vigneron*, and it was wonderful to see Jacques with those cautious careful Swiss.

They had always been cordial with us, and seemed to like us, but with him it was different. They frisked about like stiff colts in the spring, and I have never heard such delight and laughter from them. They boasted and sang, and brought out bottles of wine that we had only learned about in whispers, and invited us all to festivals months away. It was fun, although Chexbres and I felt a little jealous of what we had thought was our own solid friendship with the vine-yardists.

That night we drove up through the snow to Châtel, and ate trout at the Treize Cantons. We had a nice enough time, but Jacques was really hard to be with for very long, because he was too simple. He had only a few reactions to things, and almost no words to de-scribe them. And besides, there was the feeling underneath that he had written asking me to go to Corsica with him. . . .

We were glad when he said that he must leave the next day at two o'clock. He told us that a sister-in-law was staying at Glion, and that he was very anxious to have her meet me. Would that be all right with Chexbres? Chexbres looked strangely at me, and said of course.

So I drove Jacques up the winding road behind Montreux, and was presented to his sister-in-law, who as wife of the oldest son was representing the mother of the tribe. She was a beautiful thin Englishwoman, resting while her husband took one of his periodic vacations in a private asylum. She inspected me in a completely cold-blooded and charming way.

And then we drove down the mountain again. Jacques looked depressed.

"Denise is enchanted by you," he said glumly. "My mother will be enchanted by you too. It is very important that you go see her. She is old, and hates Paris now, or she would be glad to meet you in Paris."

I felt a little hysterical.

"Jacques, we have time before your train," I said. "Let's go eat something. We need some lunch."

"Undoubtedly you know just where you want to go," he said politely, and if I had not known his denseness I'd have suspected him of sarcasm.

We sat in the station restaurant, and ordered a *fondue*, because it was a cold day and Jacques said he had never tasted one.

It was not very good: too thin, and then suddenly stringy like cool rubber. Jacques ate two or three polite bites of it, and drank a little of the Dézaley and ate some bread crumbs.

We made conversation about regional dishes, and all the time he looked glummer and sadder. He wrote out his mother's address for me, and said, "I have showed you her picture, haven't I?"

"Yes, yes," I said. I didn't think I could stand much more.

"She will be enchanted by you," he said again.

We still had twenty minutes or so. I picked up a piece of bread, and dabbed at the cold gluey *fondue* on my plate. Suddenly Jacques began to speak very rapidly, standing up and reaching for his hat and coat on the station rack behind the table.

"Go on eating. Go on sitting there with your food and your wine. I saw you first that way, alone, so god-damned sure of yourself. This is right. I'll leave now. Do this last thing and stay as you are, here at the table with the wine in your hand."

"Oh, Jacques, I'm so sorry," I said. I looked up at him, and his eyes were very black. Then he moved swiftly among the tables, like a dancer, and the door swung behind him.

I must get home, I thought. I feel awful, like crying or being sick. I must get back to Chexbres.

I drove as fast as I could. I didn't know what I would do when I got there, but I must get home. I wanted never to be alone again, in a restaurant or anywhere.

The house was full of a fine smell. Chexbres was in the kitchen.

"Hello," he said. "Did that poor bastard give you his address? He left his pajamas. I've invented a new way to make *fondue*. It's absolutely foolproof. Here . . ."

We sat by the fire for a long time, and the *fondue* was indeed delicious, and by the time we had finished it and the bottle of wine and written the new recipe, Jacques was well on his way to Corsica, and I felt all right—sorry, but all right.

The Flaw

1939

THERE was a train, not a particularly good one, that stopped at Vevey about ten in the morning on the way to Italy. Chexbres and I used to take it to Milano.

It had a restaurant car, an old-fashioned one with the agreeable austerity of a third-class station café about it: brown wooden walls and seats, bare tables unless you ordered the highest-priced lunch, and a few faded advertisements for Aspirina Bayer and *"Visitez le Maroc"* permanently crooked above the windows.

There was one table, next to the galley, where the cooks and waiters sat. In the morning they would be talking and sorting greens for salad and cutting the tops off radishes for the *hors d'oeuvres*, and in the early afternoon they would eat enormously of some things that had been on the menu and some that certainly had not. There was always a big straw-wrapped flask of red wine with them.

Sometimes the head chef smoked while he drank, or read parts of a newspaper aloud, but usually he worked with his helpers. And if one of the two waiters sat there, he worked too.

We liked to go into the restaurant partly because of the cooks, who after a polite salute ignored us, and partly because of the waiters, who were always the same ones.

Of course, it is impossible that they were on every train that went to Milano through Vevey at ten in the morning. But they were on that train every time we took it, so that very soon they knew us and laughed and even patted Chexbres' shoulder delightedly when we appeared.

We always went into their car a few minutes after we started . . . after we had been seen by the conductor and what few travelers

526

there were on the unfashionable train. The restaurant would be empty at that hour, of course, except for the table of amiably chattering cooks.

We would order a large bottle of Asti Spumanti. That delighted the waiters, whether it was the young smooth one or the old sour withered one. We would sit drinking it, slightly warm, from the thick train-goblets, talking and watching the flat floor of the Valais grow narrower and wilder, waiting as always with a kind of excited dread for the first plunge in to the Simplon.

The champagne would stay us, in that familiar ordeal. We'd drink gratefully, feeling the train sway, knowing a small taste of death and rebirth, as all men do in swift passage through a tunnel.

When we came out finally, into the light again and the high mountains, we'd lift our glasses silently to each other, and feel less foolish to see that the cooks too had known the same nameless stress as we.

Then people would begin to come in for lunch, and we'd go back to our compartment. The younger waiter would always call us when there were only a few more people to serve, in an hour or so.

Usually both waiters took care of us; they seemed to find us strange, and interesting enough to crack their cosmic ennui, and in some way fragile, so that they protected us. They would come swaying down the aisle as we ate, crying to us, "There will be a few bumps! Hold tight! Hold tight, M'sieu'-'dame! I will help you!"

Then they would grasp the wine, and usually my arm, and we would, it is true, make a few mild grating noises over some repairs in the road. Then they would gasp with relief, and scuttle away . . . one more crisis safely past.

It made us feel a little silly, as if we were imbeciles of royal blood, or perhaps children who only *thought* they had gray hairs and knew how to survive train trips alone. It was fun, too; almost everyone likes to feel pampered by public servants.

The young waiter with the smooth almond face was more given to the protective gestures, equally lavished on Chexbres or me to avoid any sexual misunderstandings, but the older one, whose body was bent and whose face was truly the most cynical I have ever seen, was the one who watched our eating.

He hovered like an evil-visaged hawk while we ordered, and we soon found that instead of advising changes then, he would simply substitute in the kitchen what he preferred to have us enjoy that day. After the first surprise it was fun, but we always kept up the bluff of looking at the menu and then watching him pretend to memorize our order.

One thing he permitted us: simplicity. The people who traveled on that train were the kind who liked plain food and plenty of it. The menu might or might not list meat or fish, but it always had *pasti* of some kind, and lentils or beans cooked with herbs, and of course fine honest garden salad. Then there would be one or two *antipasti*: the radishes we had watched being fixed, and butter for them in rather limp and sooty curls, and hardboiled eggs and sliced salami. There would be cheese for dessert, with fruit . . . fat cherries or peaches or grapes or oranges, according to the season, and always green almonds in the spring.

The people ate well, and even if they were very poor, and brought their own bread and wine into the restaurant, they ordered a plate of beans or a one-egg omelet with dignity which was no rebuke to the comparative prodigality around them. The two waiters served them with nonchalant skill, and everyone seemed to agree that Chexbres and I should be watched and fed and smiled at with extra care.

"Why are they like that? Why are they so good to us, all the people?" we would ask each other. I knew reasons for him, and he knew some for me, but for the two of us it was probably because we had a sort of palpable trust in each other.

Simple people are especially conscious of that. Sometimes it is called love, or good will. Whatever it was in us, the result was mysterious and warming, and we felt it very strongly in places like the restaurant car to Milano, always until the last time.

That was in the summer of 1939.

We were two ghosts, then. Our lives as normal living humans had ended in the winter, in Delaware, with Chexbres' illness. And when we got word that we should go back to our old home in Switzerland and save what we could before war started, we went not so much for salvage, because possessions had no meaning any more to us, but because we were helpless to do anything else. We returned to the life that had been so real like fog, or smoke, caught in a current of air.

We were very live ghosts, and drank and ate and saw and felt and made love better than ever before, with an intensity that seemed to detach us utterly from life.

Everywhere there was a little of that feeling; the only difference was that we were safely dead, and all the other people, that summer, were laughing and singing and drinking wine in a kind of catalepsy, or like cancerous patients made happy with a magic combination of opiate before going into the operating theatre. We had finished with all that business, and they had it still to go through.

They looked at us with a kind of envious respect, knowing that war was coming to them, but that we were past it; and everywhere we went, except the one time on the Milano train, we moved beatifically incommunicado, archangels on leave. None could touch us, just as none could be harmed by our knowledge of pain yet to be felt.

The train was the same. By then we had grown almost used to miracles, and when the young almond-faced waiter stood in the door of the compartment and gaped helplessly at us, we laughed at him. He stammered and sputtered, all the time shaking our hands and laughing too, and it was plain that he had buried us long since.

When he saw what had happened to Chexbres, he turned very red, and then said quickly, trying not to stare, "But the Asti! At once! It will be very chic to drink it here!"

And before we could tell him how much we wanted to drink it in the old restaurant car, and look once more at the faded aspirin signs and listen to the cooks, he was gone. It was necessary for him to disappear; we were used by then to having people do impetuous things when they first saw us, ghosts come back so far. . . . We sighed, and laughed, because even that seemed funny.

The boy brought the champagne, wrapped elegantly in a red-checked napkin for the first time. He was suave and mischievous again, and it was plain that he felt like something in a paper-bound novel, serving fair wine that way at eleven in the morning in a first-class compartment. He swayed with exaggerated grace to the rocking of the car, and flicked soot from the little wall table like the headwaiter at the Café de la Paix, at least, with his flat black eyes dancing.

We saluted him with our first taste, hiding our regret at having to be "gentry" and drink where it was chic. The wine was the same, warm and almost sickish, and we looked quietly at each other, with delight . . . one more miracle.

But at Sion, before the tunnel, three Strength-through-Joyers got on, bulbous with knapsacks and a kind of sweaty health that had nothing to do with us. We huddled against the windows, not invisible enough, and I wondered how we could ever get past all those strong brown hairy legs to the corridor.

But there in the doorway, almost before the train started again, stood the little waiter. His face was impassive, but his eyes twinkled and yet were motherly.

"*Pardon, pardon,*" he murmured. "*Entschuldigen Sie, bitte . . . bitte . . .*"

And before we knew it the German tourists were standing, trying to squeeze themselves small, and the boy was whisking us expertly, nonchalantly, out of the compartment, down the rocking aisle, and into our familiar hard brown seats in the restaurant.

It was all the same. We looked about us with a kind of wonder.

The old waiter saw us from the end of the car. His face did not change, but he put down his glass of wine and came to our table. The boy started to say something to him in an Italian dialect . . . it was like Niçois . . . but the old man motioned him bruskly aside.

His face was still the most cynical I had ever seen, but his eyes were over-full of tears. They ran slowly down his cheeks for a few minutes, into the evil old wrinkles, and he did not wipe them away. He stood by the table, flicking his napkin and asking crankily if we had made a good trip and if we planned to stay long in Milano. We answered the same way . . . things about traveling and the weather.

We were not embarrassed, any more than he was, by his tears; like all ghosts, I suppose, we had grown used to seeing them in other people's eyes, and along with them we saw almost always a kind of gratitude, as if people were thanking us for coming back and for being so trustful together. We seemed to reassure them, in a mysterious way . . . that summer more than ever.

While the old man was standing there, talking with his own gruff eagerness about crops and storms, flicking the table, he had to step in behind my chair for a minute while three men walked quickly through the car.

Two were big, not in uniform but with black shirts under their hot mussy coats, and stubble on their faces. The man between them was thinner and younger, and although they went single file and close together, we saw that he was handcuffed to each of them.

Before that summer such a thing would have shocked us, so that our faces would be paler and our eyes wider, but now we only looked up at the old waiter. He nodded, and his own eyes got very hot and dried all the tears.

"Political prisoner," he said, flicking the table, and his face was no more bitter than usual. "Escaped. They are bringing him back to Italy."

Then the chef with the highest bonnet saw us, and beamed and raised his glass, and the others turned around from their leafy table and saluted us too, and the door slammed behind the three dark men.

We got through the tunnel, that time, without feeling our palms grow sticky. It was the only difference: the train was the same, the people were the same. We were past the pain and travail, that was all. We were inviolate.

We drank the rest of the Asti, and as people began to come in to lunch, we made the signal to the suddenly active boy that we would be back later.

Just then there were shouts and thuds, and the sound of shattering glass. A kind of silence fell all about us, in spite of the steady rattle of the train. The old waiter ran down the car, not bumping a single table, and the door at the end closed sharply behind him. People looked strangely at one another.

Gradually the air settled, as if the motors inside all the travelers had started to hum again, and the young waiter took orders for lunch. When he got to us he said without looking at us, in his bad French, "I suggest that M'sieu'-'dame attend a moment . . . the restaurant is not crowded today."

As a suggestion it had the icy command of a policeman or a guardian angel about it, and we sat meekly. There was no more champagne. It did not really bother us.

Finally the old man came hurriedly back into the car. His face was furious, and he clutched his shoulder. The travelers stared at him, still chewing. He stopped for a minute by our table. He was panting, and his voice was very low.

"He tried to jump through the window," he said, and we knew

he was talking about the refugee. "The bastards! They tore my coat! My only coat! The dirty bastards . . . look at that!"

He flapped the ripped shoulder of his greasy old black jacket at us, and then went madly down to the galley, muttering and trembling.

We stood up to go, and the smooth almond-faced waiter hurried toward us, swaying with the downhill rush of the train under a big tray of hot vegetables. "I am bringing M'sieu'-'dame's order at once," he called.

We sat down obediently. We were being bullied, but it was because he was trying to protect us, and it was kind of him. He brought two glasses of a dark vermouth, and as he put them in front of us he said confiding, "A special bottle we carry for the chef . . . very appetizing. There is a little muss on the platform. It will be swept up when M'sieu'-'dame have finished. Santé!"

As we lifted our glasses, willy-nilly, he cleared his throat, and then said in English, "Cheerio!" He smiled at us encouragingly, like an over-attentive nurse, and went back to serving the other people. The vermouth was bitterer than any we had ever tasted, almost like a Swiss gentian-drink, but it tasted good after the insipid wine.

When we went through to our compartment, there was indeed a neat pile of broken glass on the platform between the cars, and the window of the door that opened when the train stopped was only half filled: the top part of the pane was gone, and the edge of the rest curved like ice in a smooth fine line, almost invisible.

The Strength-through-Joyers leaped politely to attention when we got back to our compartment, and subsided in a series of small waves of questions in English . . . did smoke bother me, did we mind the door open, did we feel a draft. . . .

I forget the name of the town now where the train stops and the passport men come on. Is it Domodossola? How strange, not to know! It is as if I have deliberately wiped from my mind a great many names. Some of them I thought would stay there forever, whether I wanted them or not, like old telephone numbers that suddenly come between you and the sound of a new love's voice. I never thought to disremember this town, that man, such and such a river. Was it Domodossola?

That day we were there a long time. There seemed more policemen than usual, but it was always that way in Italy. We got the questions of visas and money straightened out; that used to upset me, and I'd feel like a blushing diamond-smuggler when the hard-eyed customs man would look at me. This time it was easy, unimportant.

I kept thinking it would be a good idea to walk back to the restaurant car while the train was quiet, but Chexbres said no, we should wait for the boy to call us.

Finally we started, very slowly. We went past a lot of roadwork. Men were building beds for new tracks with great blocks of gray stone, and the Germans looked at them with a grudging fascination, leaning over us to see better and exclaiming softly.

We were glad when the young waiter came to the door. "Your table is ready, M'sieu'-'dame," he announced loftily, and the men stood up hastily to let us out.

When we got to the end of the car, the boy turned back. "Take care, please," he said to Chexbres. "There is a little humidity on the platform."

And the place was wet, right enough. The curved piece of glass was still in the window, but it and the walls and the floor were literally dripping with water. We went carefully through it, and into the almost empty restaurant.

The chef rested at the end, reading a paper, but got up and went back to the galley as we came in. Our table was nicely laid, with fresh linen, and there were two or three little square dishes of pickled onions and salami and butter. We felt very hungry, and quite gay.

The boy brought us some good wine, a fairly expensive red Chianti we always drank on that train, and we began to eat bread and salami with it. I remember there were some of those big white beans, the kind Italians peel and eat with salt when they are fresh and tender in the early summer. They tasted delicious, so fresh and cold. . . .

It was good to be eating and drinking there on that train, free forever from the trouble of life, surrounded with a kind of insulation of love. . . .

The old waiter came through the car. He was going to pass our table without looking at us. Chexbres spoke to him. "Stop a minute," he said. "Your coat . . . how is it?"

The man turned without answering, so that we could see the

neat stitches that held his sleeve in place. I said something banal about the sewing . . . how good it was . . . and Chexbres asked quietly, "The man . . . the prisoner . . . did he get away?"

The old man suddenly looked at us, and his eyes were hateful, as if he loathed us. He said something foul, and then spat, "It's none of my business!" He hurried away, and we could not turn to watch him.

It was so shocking that we sat without any movement for quite a time. I could feel my heart beat heavily, and my throat was as if an iron collar hung around it, the way it used to be when Chexbres was first ill. Finally I looked at the few people still eating, and it seemed to me as if they met my eyes with a kind of hatred too, not as awful as the old man's but still crouching there. There was fear in it, and fear all around me.

Chexbres' face was full of pain. It was the first time it had come through for weeks, the first time since we started to drift like two happy ghosts along the old current of our lives together. The iron collar tightened to see it there. I tried to drink some wine, but I couldn't swallow more than once.

The young waiter hurried past us without looking, and Chexbres stopped him firmly. "Please," he said. "What is wrong? What has happened?"

The boy looked impassively at us, and for a minute I thought he was going to be rude. Then he whispered, still protecting us, "Eat, M'sieu'-'dame. I will tell you in a minute." And he hurried off to the galley, bending supplely under the last great tray of emptied plates.

"Yes, you'd better eat something," Chexbres said coldly to me. "You've drunk rather a lot, you know." He picked up his fork, and I did too. The spaghetti was like ashes, because I felt myself coming to life again, and knew he did.

When we were the only ones left in the car, the boy came back. He stood leaning against the table across the aisle, still swaying with the motion of the train but now as if he were terribly tired, and talked to us so softly that we could hardly hear him. There was no friendliness in his voice, but not any hatred.

He said that when the train stopped at Domodossola, or wherever the border was, the political prisoner was being taken off, and suddenly he laughed and pressed his throat down on the edge of broken windowpane. The old waiter saw it.

"That was probably the plan in the first place," the boy said. "The poor bastard was chained to the cops. There was no escaping. It was a good job," he said. "The border police helped clean up the platform. That was why the train stopped so long.

"We're making up time now all right," the boy said, looking admiringly at the rocky valleys flash past us. "The old man keeps fussing about his coat. He's nuts anyway."

By the time we got to Milano everything was almost all right again, but for a few minutes the shell cracked. The world seeped in. We were not two ghosts, safe in our own immunity from the pain of living. Chexbres was a man with one leg gone, the other and the two arms soon to go . . . a small wracked man with snowy hair and eyes large with suffering. And I was a woman condemned, plucked at by demons, watching her true love die too slowly.

There in the train, hurrying across the ripe fields, feeling the tranced waiting of the people everywhere, we knew for a few minutes that we had not escaped. We knew no knife of glass, no distillate of hatred, could keep the pain of war outside.

I felt illimitably old, there in the train, knowing that escape was not peace, ever.

The Measure of My Powers

1941

FOR several months after Chexbres died I was in flight, not from myself particularly nor of my own volition. I would be working in my little office and suddenly go as fast as I could out the door and up the road, until I had no breath left. Or my sister Anne would look at me and say, judiciously, as if I were a vase of flowers to be moved here and there, "You must go to Mexico." Then she would buy a ticket for me, and a new hat, and she would take care of visas. It seemed all right. I doubt if it did much good, except to pass the time with as little damage as possible. But that too was all right.

People thought I was in a state of shock at the dying, but it was more one of relieved exhaustion after the last three years. It dulled parts of me, so that although I looked quite normal I walked into chairs and doors, and was covered with dreadful bruises without feeling any hurt.

But other senses were bright and alive in me. I saw things like rocks and mouse-prints clearly at last. I heard almost too much. I ate, with a rapt voluptuous concentration which had little to do with bodily hunger, but seemed to nourish some other part of me.

"She needs people around her," the people themselves would say. It was not they, but the chance to feed them that was good for me. I planned and cooked really beautiful meals for them, and when I was alone I did the same thing for myself, with perhaps even more satisfaction. Sometimes I would go to the best restaurant I knew about, and order dishes and good wines as if I were a guest of myself, to be treated with infinite courtesy.

I still kept walking into things, though, and after I side-swiped a parked car with the same cold immunity to violence, Anne said,

536

"Mexico." That was all right. All I needed was time, and while it was passing I could look and hear and taste in Jalisco as well as California, and with my new acuteness.

I was late getting to Guadalajara, where Norah and David and his new wife Sarah were to meet me. The plane was to stop overnight at Mazatlan, the officials told us at three in the morning: the fog was too thick, and ice would form on the wings. I didn't care.

I stood aimlessly about for a few more minutes with the other passengers in the drear shoddiness of the airport offices. Then we went our twelve or thirteen separate ways to benches and folded overcoats and even one or two hotel beds. I rented a room, and turned down the bed, and then spent the rest of the night riding up and down in the elevator with the Filipino boy who ran it. We said very little, but he seemed to enjoy my sitting there with him, and we ate Lifesavers and smoked amicably now and then. It was quite a natural thing to do, although it seems a little strange now, in the telling.

At five or six we were back at the port again. The plane would perhaps take off in two hours. Some of us sagged back, bag-eyed and grimly polite, onto the benches; and others stumbled toward the newly lighted coffee shop, where a pale waitress flicked last night's crumbs off the counters and laid out last year's menu cards.

I saw four of the middle-aged men-passengers brighten as they dug into their eggs and meat and toast, and sucked their coffee. It was queer, in that gray waiting room, to look in past the shrouded cigaret counter to the harsh glare of the eating place, and watch the sleepy men revive. It was like watching a speeded-up movie of flowers opening, or of a foetus changing into a human in nine minutes instead of nine months.

I felt almost indecent, looking at them, and walked away toward the baggage office, where two colored men were chatting and snoozing on the pile of suitcases. I stood near them for a few minutes, listening to their soft snickering voices and feeling comfortable, the way I had in the elevator with the tiny clean brown boy. Then maybe I went into a little dream standing up, because when I awoke we were flying over puckered hills and unnaturally straight rivers without apparent banks, and I realized that everybody on the plane but me was eating breakfast. Especially the men who had eaten breakfast in the coffee shop were eating breakfast.

Of course, I could see only the two people across from me (I knew already that he was a dentist from Monrovia), and maybe one-third each of three people in front of me, but I watched the little dapper steward flicking his tail up and down the aisle, carrying trays and trays.

The women were for the most part drinking cups of coffee and eating one piece each of dry toast and then, as far as I could see, devouring everything their husbands would let them snatch from the more robust masculine trays, saying as they did so, "Just one bite!" Sometimes, but not often they said, "Just one bite, dear!"

The men, though, paid small attention. They looked beamingly at their well-filled laps, their brimming knees. It would not have mattered much if the air were rough, for not only was every cup and plate sunk into its own well in the tray, but each tray was clutched as if the poor men had never seen such good food before.

There was coffee, of course. It was properly steaming. There was orange juice. Besides that there was a large orange rolling slightly between the two cups, with more than enough publicity stamped on the skin in purple ink to make us realize that the state fruit-exchange was only too glad to add to the happiness of the airline's passengers by this little added surprise.

On the less liquid side there was, tucked among the expected array of stiff cardboard cutlery and paper napkins, a pair of oddly obscene envelopes made of cellophane. They were printed in bright blue ink with the name of a caterer, and his trademark of jolly little Dutch girls and windmills masked too inadequately the hot limp contents.

In one envelope was a generous slice of grilled ham, complete with its juice and what looked like an overgenerous supply of condensed steam. The men speared impotently for a minute at the horrid containers, and then their paper forks went in, and the whole inside slipped onto the plates. It must have looked good to them, because someone behind me said, "Oh boy!" Or maybe it was, "Golly, that looks fine, all right!"

The other of the two envelopes was filled with pale yellow, creamy, hot scrambled eggs.

I felt unusually well. There were purplish clouds underneath us, that really had no color at all when I looked down on them and thought about them. I had pulled out the little aircock above me, and thin sweet air poured in on my face, and made my eyes feel cool. Perhaps I needed food. But I thought that those limp cellophane envelopes of hot egg and meat were the most disgusting things I had ever seen. I kept watching the clouds and feeling a little ashamed for acting snobbish or persnickety, while the steward looked resignedly at me, sure that I had made up my mind to be sick, and the other men and most of the women tucked into their good hot food and enjoyed themselves in their own ways, as I was doing.

Lunch, which followed almost immediately, was very interesting. It was already packed in paper boxes, which folded open and back into trays. Of course, there were two or three cups of water and fruit punch and hot consommé and such, and the paper and napkins, and an enormous pear and an enormous apple tucked into little couches of shaved lavender paper.

Then there were two closed paper cups, each with a little spoon sticking out of it like a stiff umbilical cord. One held a canned pear with cottage cheese under it, and was undoubtedly called a salad, and the other was filled with fruit jelly, the kind that is bright yellow and has pieces of banana and pineapple in it.

Then there were three sandwiches, each wrapped and sealed separately in cellophane: one chicken on white bread, one cheese on white bread, one ham on rye. The fillings were generous, and there was good butter between them and the bread, which was perfect and tasteless, being American.

I called the neat lizard-like little steward and asked him to empty most of my drinking water. He looked puzzled, but almost before I could shift my tray enough to lean down to the floor for my hand-bag he was back with the half-filled cup. I poured in a good shot of bourbon from my flask, looked out of the window and toasted a cloud that had a big nose much like my father's, and almost at once felt even better than I had before.

The dentist and his wife looked queerly at me, or perhaps jealously. I sipped at my drink until there was one swallow left, and then went to work on the tray.

The cheese in one sandwich was the processed gluey kind, cut from a block, and I ignored it. I undid the ham and the chicken packages, and put all the insides of one sandwich on all the insides of another, and then telescoped the outsides, so that I had a thick ham-and-chicken sandwich put together with half white and half rye bread.

Then I poked around among the napkins and fruit wrappings and sandwich papers until, sure enough, I found a minute pair of salt and pepper shakers, and I fairly well plastered the chicken with salt and the ham with fine black pepper. Then I put the two pieces together, and ate them.

It turned out very well. It was a pleasant lunch, small yet nourishing, and I concocted it with a neatness and intense dispatch impossible anywhere but high above the earth, so that it was not ridiculous or gross or even finicky while I did it.

When I had finished I drank the *bonne bouche* of water and bourbon in my cup, rolled up all the odds and ends of paper into a little plug for one of the elaborate number of holes in the tray, and put all the cups and plates and uneaten things of food as best I could into the remaining places. Then I asked the steward if I might steal the tiny shakers, black for pepper and white for salt.

He looked completely thrown off the track of his Berlitz lessons for a minute, and then flushed and giggled and said, "Oh, but of course it will be serious jail for the Señora, with your permission!" He disappeared down the aisle, staggering slightly under the impact of his own waggery, and I put the shakers in my purse and as far as I can remember never saw them again.

Underneath there were dry black mountains, sharper than pins. Around me people sat back, literally full, eased by the action in their bellies from the secret fears of all men in the air. Their glands ticked on, whipped by the altitude and occupied and preoccupied by digestion, so that even if the plane had faltered and hiccuped they would not have minded.

The shadows on the black mountains grew impossibly acute, with the going down of the sun. Before long we would land. The flying was rougher . . . the cooling air flowing up or down the hot earth, maybe.

The little steward pretended to adjust the thermometer, forward in the cabin, and gave us all a sharp look. And before we knew it he was putting queer cellophane hat boxes on our laps, tied with bright blue rayon ribbon like something for Easter; and inside each one, very pretty indeed, were waxy pears and fine grapes and little packages of extra-fancy raisins and I think a few nuts, the washed-looking kind that come in gift packages.

In a moment what pale cheeks there were had flushed, and the

fretting women were gay, and the tired men looked more mildly at the dour savage land beneath us, or forgot it entirely. People munched and exclaimed, like happy infants.

I took out my flask, drank a mature-sized sip, and opened my little hat box dutifully as the steward looked obliquely at me.

There was a slip of imitation vellum laid across the top of the beautiful fruit, which two hungry people might have eaten during a whole day, and on the slip was printed in old Gothic the name of the company so happy to donate this small token to the airline. Then it said, still in Gothic, "You may eat this with carefree abandon, for it has been washed and scrubbed and rub-a-dub-dubbed."

Good, I thought. That's fine. Me too.

I ate a few grapes, which were tasteless but enjoyable, and then carefully tied the bright ribbon about the box again and asked the steward to give it to me when we landed. It would be a nice little surprise for Norah and Sarah and David: they must be hungry for fruit that had not been dipped in anti-typhoid anti-malaria anti-dysentery water. This had been rub-a-dub-dubbed.

We were almost at Mazatlan. I saw coconut trees, poisonously impossibly green in the last sunlight, and then the blank silver bay and the black boats on it. We sloped over the port, and as I tightened my landing belt I suddenly felt very hungry, especially for something not wrapped or bedded or boxed in cellophane. And at the same time I was grateful to the air company for trying to take my mind off the troublous certainty that for several hours I, a little wingless human, had been much higher than a kite. A kite in flight, I thought, and the earth moved up to touch my foot . . .

II

It seemed as if we made a lot of noise when we walked into the high darkening coolness of the hotel. The Mexicans at the doorway, sitting under the arcade, talking and watching the sea across the road, looked curiously at us, thinking perhaps that we had been rescued from a plane accident; and the people inside bustled softly about, allotting rooms and carrying bags and being temporarily energetic.

All the other passengers stood in a clot by the desk, asking for the best. I leaned against a pillar, not caring whether my room had a view, nor if I had a room at all. The hotel smelled nice, and I could see a great sloping staircase without steps going up one side of the patio, and a mighty splash of purple flowers clinging to the stone wall. I felt good.

A pleasantly aloof man, an American-German Jew who ran a clothing factory in Mexico and flew a great deal, asked me if I would have a drink with him, while we waited until the other passengers stopped being sure that on this, their first stop in a foreign country, they were not robbed, cheated, and insulted. It seemed like a fine idea.

He knew his way to the bar, a dim quiet room behind the *cantina* that opened off the street. The barman knew him, too, and with my permission the man said, "Two of the same, Charlie," in Mexican slang.

The same was a tall cool drink with rum in it. The man was nice, because he was so impersonal and seemed to enjoy the same thing in me. We talked about smuggling, and rum, and a drink made with tequila and tomato juice called, appropriately, *un sangre*. Then I thanked him and we went into the hall again, feeling better.

At the desk the three or four men behind it exclaimed "Ah!" loudly and with a kind of coy theatrical relief, and a little boy laden with four bags and an enormous ring of keys trotted ahead of us up the long incline of the stairless stairs and through some halls, and after a bit of breathless finagling flung open a door. It was a beautiful room, with two great double beds, as high and four-postered as something in *David Copperfield*, and the sound of the sea everywhere.

The boy put the bags inside. I stood there without any embarrassment, waiting to be alone, smelling the air and feeling light and warm.

The man flushed a dark red. "These bags are mine," he said quickly to the boy.

He put his hand on the knob of the door, bowed with a stiff movement never learned since he left Germany, and said very quietly, "I hope you will forgive this. It is a stupid mistake."

I looked at him, and his nice brown eyes were full of misery. But before I could tell him how little it mattered to me, and how sorry I was for his confusion, he had closed the door. He must have dined away from the hotel, because I saw him only on the plane the next morning, and then he did not speak.

The room was wonderful, austere and airy the way I like a bedroom to be. I decided which of the two beds I would climb into, later, and put my slippers beside it and my nightgown on it, with the waist pinched in the way the maids used to do at the Ritz, or at the Trois Couronnes in Vevey.

The bathroom was like a big box of hand-made tiles, colored a vile yellow that seemed lovely to me, with occasional smears of purple under the glaze, as if the people in the pottery work had grown bored with one color and plainness. There was, besides the washbowl and moderately regal throne, a fine large tub. And one corner of the floor sloped a little, with a grill in it and a pipe overhead, and that was the shower.

It is fine to take a bath standing up with no tight walls around, when the room is warm. I felt fresh and self-contained, in spite of sleeplessness and being up so high, but still it was pleasant to bathe again. I dressed slowly, wandering about in a kind of distracted contentment, leaning every now and then on the deep sill of the open window.

A sunset breeze pushed the long white curtains back against me, and filled my nostrils with the male smell of kelp on tide-rocks. Underneath, in the arcade of the hotel and on the roadway, people talked and walked softly, and past the low wall the waves broke, like the regular breathing of something known, familiar. The water in the harbor, beneath the fading brashness of the sunset, was as hard and colorless as gunmetal, or an old engraving.

Finally I was dressed, in a clean blouse under my gray jacket, but without a hat. I went down slowly, stilted in my high heels along the steep slope of the stairway, like a horse trotting downhill.

I went out on the quai or esplanade or whatever it was. Under the arcade of the hotel lights were on over the café-tables, but along the sea-wall it was dark now, and cool. Couples already strolled silently, or young men alone, looking at me and murmuring.

I went back, and five or six of the passengers at a table asked me to sit and have a drink with them. I was surprised, in a dispassionate way. Probably they felt sorry for me, all alone: most people are so afraid of that for themselves that they assume it is the same for others. I ordered a tequila and a small beer, and listened to them talking about the exchange and tipping and how you had to watch the Mexicans every minute. They were not bad people, but shy and on guard against everything, especially everything that did not speak good American.

Then I asked if they would not have a drink with me. They said no, no, one was plenty thank you, and laughed daringly. I was sorry to be obligated to them but there was nothing to do about it.

They were making plans for "seeing the town" after dinner, and asked me to go with them. I said I was going to bed, and they looked strangely at me. "You've been here before, then?" they asked, and when I said no, they laughed again, daringly, and said *they* weren't going to waste any time in bed; *they* weren't going to miss a trick. Then one of the women asked me if I'd sit with them at dinner, after I'd got my hat, and I told them I was very tired, and thanked them for the drink and went into the hotel. I knew they felt hurt and snubbed, and in a blind way angry at me for being alone and hatless and self-sufficient enough to go to bed when I was tired. But there was nothing to do about it that seemed worth the changes I would have to make, even for a few minutes, in the way I was.

The dining room, like hotel dining rooms all over the world, was large, bleak, dull. I walked through it as far as I could, past a few tables of almost silent people who stared for a second and then dropped their eyes to their food again.

A waiter appeared at the end of the room, chewing and looking surprised to see me so far from the safe company of the other diners. I smiled at him, and he smiled back, and I sat down at a little table by the open door into the patio, dark and strange now like a cave.

I ordered a bottle of beer, and drank slowly at the first little glass of it until the food started coming. I asked for only a few things on the pretentious menu, but even they were too many. The stuff was abominable: a tasteless *sopa de pasta*, a salad of lukewarm fish and bottled dressing, some pale meat . . .

I felt very sorry, but I simply could not eat it. And all the time delicious smells came from the kitchen when the waiters went past me, not from what they carried but from something they had just left. And I could hear laughing and talking, so that the stilted silence of the dining room was painful.

Finally the waiter brought me a little dish of bread pudding . . . *poudingue inglesa*, the menu said. There must have been something about my face that broke him then, in spite of my being an uninvited unexpected diner there. He leaned over me and whispered some-

thing very rapidly. I understood only, "There is an American kitchen and there is a country kitchen, side by side out there . . ."

Then he disappeared. It seemed to me the smells got better as I waited for what would happen next. They were like a farm kitchen in the south of France, but with less garlic and more pepper. I was almost alone, waiting peacefully, sipping my beer. The passengers who had bought me a drink came and went, stiffly looking away from me. I felt mildly sorry to have hurt them by staying apart.

Then the waiter came back, and he was smiling and breathing hard in a pleasant excitement. He brought me what he and the others were eating in the kitchen, and it was even sitting in their dishes: a brown clay bowl and plate, with green and white birds under the thin glaze.

The bowl had beans in it, large light-tan beans cooked with some tomato and onion and many herbs. I ate them with a big spoon, and now and then rolled up a tortilla from the plate and ate it sopped in the beans.

And the feeling of that hot strong food going down into my stomach was one of the finest I have ever had. I think it was the first thing I had really tasted since Chexbres died, the first thing that fed me, in spite of my sensuous meals always. I ate everything . . . enough for three or four probably . . . and finished the beer while the waiter peered paternally at me occasionally from the kitchen door.

Then I paid him, and thanked him more than he could know, and went up to my sea-filled room. I slept like a cat all night, dreaming good dreams in my well-being, but hearing the waves when I wanted to through the dreams.

III

The little house in the fishing village was fairly new, built to rent to summer-people who came for the lake and the quiet. It had a bathroom upstairs, fed from a tank on the roof which a man came every night to fill by the hand-pump in the tiny patio. The tub did not work, but that was all right because Norah and Sarah and I were helping David paint murals in the municipal baths, and spent several hours every day neck-deep in the clear running water of the pools, walking cautiously on the sandy bottoms with pie-plates full of tempera held up, and paint-brushes stuck in our hair.

(The lavatory and toilet worked well, though, except occasionally when the water-man did not feel strong enough to come, after a fiesta. Then David would go next door to the bar, and Norah and Sarah and I would have a convenient beer in the lobby of the Hotel Nido on the plaza, where there was plumbing almost as good as ours.)

Our house was about thirty steps from the little square, which was very correct, with a wooden bandstand in the middle and a double promenade around it under the thick green trees, so that the boys could walk one way to the music and the girls the other . . . until the boys found courage or centavos enough to buy flowers and join their loves.

The flower-women sat at one end of the plaza on concert nights, the dark end, and candles or little lamps shone like magic on the blossoms lying on clean cloths in front of them. There were camellias and tiny gardenias, and sometimes spidery jewel-like orchids, and plainer garden-flowers, all glowing in the soft light on the earth while the women crouched darkly behind, deep in their shawls, and the band wheezed bravely for the innocent concupiscent strollers on the paths.

There were two or three bars, with juke-boxes when the orchestra got tired, and a little kiosk sold bright pink and yellow ices and Coca-Cola.

In the other direction from our house, and around the corner was the market. It was a sprawling wandering collection of stands, some of them elaborate, with counters for eating and stoves in the center, and some of them a piece of cloth on the ground with two little heaps of dried peppers and a bruised yam or a pot of stew waiting to be bought. Of course there were *serape* merchants and sandal-makers on Sundays, and piles of thin pottery everywhere and always because it broke easily after it was bought.

There were hungry dogs and cats near the one meat-stand, where flies buzzed so thickly over the strange strips of hanging bony flesh that we could hear them before we even turned the corner.

Some days, and perhaps for a week at a time, there would be almost nothing to buy except one thing, like tomatoes, at every stand . . . little pungent tomatoes no bigger than pigeon eggs. It was the wrong season for avocados when I was there, but now and then we found string beans, or a rotting papaya.

It was hard to get enough food for our meals, even though we probably had more money than most of the marketers. I'd have liked to take bowls to the open kitchens, the way the people did, and buy them full of hot beans to eat with a stack of tortillas . . . but perhaps that was because I had not been in Mexico as long as my sisters and brother. Perhaps it was because I remembered the beans in Mazatlan, too.

Whenever any of us went to Guadalajara we bought lettuces and butter and bread there, and whatever else we saw.

The little house, besides the bathroom, had three sleeping rooms upstairs and two rooms and a kitchen downstairs. I wanted very much to cook something, to fold myself in the comfortable cloud of mix-baste-and-boil. But there seemed very little to cook, and the kitchen itself was baffling. I think I could soon have learned to handle myself in it. But I was a guest.

The room was very small, with a window and door into the stub-end of the patio, by the pump, and another door into the shelf-lined hallway to the dining room. There was a small table, almost a tabouret, with a deep clay pot of supposedly sterile water in it, for drinking and rinsing vegetables, and on the long side of the room a kind of ledge of red tile, waist-high.

I can't remember whether there was a little sink in the ledge, with a cold-water tap. I think so. Then there was a sunken place for a charcoal fire, with a grill over it, and room for the little two-burner kerosene stove David had bought in Guadalajara after all of them had tried miserably to learn how to fan charcoal enough to cook anything in less than several hours. Above the ledge there were five or six clay pots and an iron saucepan on a shelf, and some wooden spoons and a knife hung above the grate.

In the little hallway one of the shelves had a screen door to keep flies away from food, and there was a tiny ramshackle icebox, that held about four kilos of ice when there was any to be had.

And that was where we got our meals, when we got them.

A square ageless woman, not quite a dwarf, came every morning to get breakfast and do the cleaning. For some reason we made a point of not knowing her name. I think it may have been because we were all so big and she was so little, and she did all the dirty work for us, so that we felt basically ashamed of ourselves and tried to hide it by keeping her anonymous. David ordered her to be called

Big Lige, as if her name were Elijah. Little Lige was her daughter, who worked there before I came and did our laundering, and she was almost normal in size.

Big Lige worked harder than her child, and had a very strong unpleasant smell, not foul but stifling. She was one of the most courteous people I have ever been with. When we left she wore her Sunday *rebozo*, and wept. I would like to have her near always, like a little dark stone to anchor me, except for that smell.

She admired the kerosene stove deeply but always used the charcoal one. When she worked it, it made a nice thin smoke, not at all like the black clouds we could draw from it so easily, and the toast had the same delicate smokiness to it, delicious with butter. She learned quickly how to make coffee the way my family liked it, and seemed especially happy when Sarah or David would ask her to go to the corner for an egg to boil for them. Canned tomato juice was more than she felt worthy of coping with, though, and David always had to open and pour that himself, while she held her shawl over her eyes shyly.

We used to sit in the little dining room a long time at breakfast, eating and talking and listening to Big Lige fan patiently at the embers, waiting for us to command her.

At noon, when we collected from the baths or walks or our own workings, we could sit in the small high living room on the floor, because there were only a few stiff chairs, and drink for a time . . . beer or tequila. The others liked Coca-Cola for a mixer, and a little lime juice, but I liked tequila alone, and then beer afterwards.

The room was like a glorified bath, all of stone and tile, so that our voices echoed wonderfully, and sounded full and rich, and clearer than ever before. David played his guitar, and sometimes Norah, and we sang in our various ways, but all beautifully because of the resonant walls and the tequila we were drinking. I heard myself doing *vocalizes* that amaze me even to think on . . . like a robust flute I was.

Then Sarah or Norah or I, or all of us, would go to the kitchen while David kept on like a rooster, strumming and crowing until the hens came back.

We ate bread and butter and what we wanted from a plate as big as a table-top covered with tomatoes and hard eggs and whatever other things like radishes we had been able to find. Sometimes we had a jar of red caviar from the grocery in Guadalajara. We drank some more, and ate and sang.

At night we usually went to one of the little restaurants. They were very plain, and it was best to stop by in the afternoon and ask what there would be for four people. Most of the people ate in them or ordered food to be cooked there and taken home, even if they were quite poor. It was because the kitchens were so bad, I suppose, and charcoal and water and food so scarce. Always at meal times boys would be walking through the streets with food on their heads, from the little eating-places . . . pots of stew and beans, piles of tacos, sometimes a boiled chicken steaming naked on a platter if it was for a family feast-day.

We would order little white lake-fish if we could: they were like the perch I used to eat at Cully, on the Lac Léman, but not so knowingly prepared. Then there were thick porridges of rice and herbs, "not running and not standing," like Elizabethan soups. And tortillas.

And unless you liked beans, which none of my family seemed to, that was all: the meats were repulsive and poorly cooked; there were no salads and almost no vegetables; none of us liked the violently colored stiff sweet pastes that were called desserts.

There was one place, a bare room with two tables in it and a stove at the end, that made nothing but tacos. I liked them very much . . . hot limp tortillas filled with chopped herbs and lettuces or whatever you wanted. We went there often, and watched the pretty woman swirl two big oval pans slowly over the embers, just enough to wilt the tortillas without burning them.

Always the *mariachi* players would find us, whether we had any pesos left for them or not, while little children squatted listening delightedly on the sidewalk, and cats waited under the table for our crumbs. The music followed us everywhere, like something in a dream.

A few times, in spite of my shyness about the kitchen, I made supper. It took a long time, and involved scuttling all over the village for supplies, the way I used to in Dijon before I learned how to market there. I found there was very little I could cook, partly because of the lack of food and partly because I could do nothing with it but boil it.

I scrambled eggs a few times. But it was hard to find more than two or three at once, and there was no cream or cheese in the village.

One night I produced a very fine sauce, which we ate with toasted tortillas. It used up most of the kerosene to cook it enough, and took almost a day, and kept me occupied agreeably. I stirred and stirred, there in the little kitchen.

I remember it was after dark when I heard the pump clanking. I looked out the window, past the steam from my pot of sauce, and saw the white eyes of the water-man going up and down, up and down, never leaving my face as he rode the stiff handle. His face was very thin.

I tasted the sauce, and stirred, and put in more things, and all the time the man looked at me, but so that I could not tell if he saw me.

Finally I got a little glass of tequila and rolled some of the dark rich juice in a tortilla, and took it out to him. I knew that it was more work to start the pump once it had stopped, but I felt wrong there in the light and flavor and comfort, unless I took some of it to him. It was always like that in Mexico: I felt wrong to be clean and nourished among those fine people who could not be . . .

He was very nice about it, and stood holding the glass and the taco while the pump slowed itself silent.

We exchanged a few phrases, the kind printed in conversation-books which people really say by instinct in every language, and then I went into the kitchen again, feeling a little foolish before his poised gentility.

I started to take a drink. The man tapped on the window, waiting for that, and held up his little nip, bowing to me from the darkness. I bowed to him. We smiled. Finally he ate the taco, politely, in three bites instead of one. I felt a little better about stirring all that sauce . . . but not much.

One morning we were sitting after breakfast around the big cluttered table, when there was a strange dreadful sound outside on the street, and a wailing cry.

We looked silently at one another, pale because of the sickening finality of the noise, and before David got up unwillingly to see what had happened, I thought of a book I'd read long ago in France, in which a pregnant girl jumped from a window and "split open on the pavement like a ripe melon." It sounded like that.

When he came back he said, with a kind of relief but mournfully too, that a woman from the hills with a big pot of boiled beans on her head had stumbled, there in front of our house on her way to sell them in the market. She had probably walked most of the night. And they were probably her whole crop, David said.

He moved restlessly about, and we all got up and went away from one another, in a kind of pain.

I looked down from Norah's room. The beans, pale and nasty, were spread on the stones, all mixed with broken pottery and already half-eaten by the starved dogs of the village and a few beggar-children. People walking to market made a wide silent circle, or hurried past sadly, impotently. And the hill-woman sat folded into her shawl, with her face on her knees, never making any sound after her first wail.

She sat there all day, not moving even her shoulders, with one closed hand beside her on the cobbles.

The beans were soon gone, and someone picked up the broken clay into a little pile, so that the street looked cleaner than before, where the dogs had licked around her.

At lunch we could not eat or sing or talk. We did not speak of the woman sitting there, but each of us would go secretly from the others to the upper windows, on tiptoe, and peek to see her. None of us knew what to do, in the face of such absolute stillness.

David told me, long after we were all in California again, that he tried once to put some money into her hand, and shook her a little. He had a very gentle way with women when he wanted to, or thought he was alone with one, but she did not hear his voice at all, and the money rolled away from her fingers. The man who ran the bar next to us saw, and said, "It's no use, Señor. Come in and have a drink."

And at sundown she was gone. None of us saw her go. She took all the pieces of clay with her, back to the hills. We could go out past the place where she had been, then, to eat some supper. We went to the Nido, and spent a lot of money, and drank cocktails first by the lake, still feeling shocked by the sound of the pot falling on the stones, and her long silence. It was her own kind of flight, as good perhaps as mine . . .

Feminine Ending

1941

How can I write the love-story of a woman I don't know? There must be more than cerebration, more than the skillful plotting of my thoughts. A song, a drunken look, a light remembered along Juanito's fingers . . . but will the blended brew have flavor?

Recollection is not enough. Perhaps I must pound the table, be harsh, be loud-tongued, to make what never happened assume its own reality.

What shall I hate, then? Shall I hate something beyond hatred, something like the Church, the tawdrily solid Church in that village on the Mexican lake, where the young long-nosed priest wore his cassock short, as if his trousers' virile proof would reassure him?

Shall I hate myself, as part of the life that molded us all, my brother, my sister Norah, the sloe-eyed Sarah, so that we went there in our white skins, with our vocabularies of suffering and hunger and our soft light hair, and lived among the courteous people of Jalisco as if anyone could live anywhere in such pale immunity?

Shall I get drunk on hatred, or sit back tranquilly, listening to the quiet voices of the long and newly dead, peacefully now as I should have been on the lake?

I heard Juanito singing almost as soon as I came to earth in Mexico. I did not know it at first. I was like a sea-plant, with a thousand ears out on little stalks, but only to hear what I was listening for.

Norah and David met my plane at Guadalajara. How tall, how insolently beautiful they were, moving within their fine skins and their clothing and the world about them like creatures from another planet, and yet shyly. We drove through the edge of the city and

552

then out over the long gaunt plains, talking a great deal and listening tentatively to one another, not asking questions for a time. Then we came to a break in the wavering flatness, and started to go down, with the lake below us and the air changing. The little car stopped rattling and swooped smoothly toward the shore.

Norah got out at the gates of a place where her picture was being painted, and walked with a kind of cool assurance along the path toward the villa, as if she liked going there. David and I stopped talking. The road was very bad. And we were thinking of the next stop, where I would meet Sarah, my new sister-in-law, all three of us nervous and educated not to show it, all three wanting things to be easy and friendly long before we'd had the time to make them so.

I was the oldest child, and David was the youngest, and between us there were years of dependence and resentment and love and ruthlessness, and now the knowledge that he had married sooner than we'd hoped for him, and in a far country, to an unknown girl. It was a cautious moment . . .

We stopped in front of a door a few steps off the leafy plaza, and David beeped the horn and jumped out to fuss at the back of the car, in self-protection.

Sarah came out. She had a true share of dignity. I liked that and her fine unlacquered fingernails and the sloping contours of her very quiet face. I suppose she was nervous, like me, but probably neither of us showed it much. We went into the little house, and soon she left, without any fuss or explanation, to market or sit by the lake, and to leave David and me to get used to each other. It was well done.

The house was a good one, with simple bones to it. A stair went up two sides of the living room to the bedrooms, so that the ceiling was high. It was wonderful for singing, or for any sounds from the street, which rang clear and full and rich. There was almost no furniture, and the tile floor looked as clean as a plate.

David took me up to my room: I felt foolish in high heels and a hat and a flannel suit, with jet in my ears and my traveling face still on. The room for me had a wide window, with white curtains tied back with pink candy-box ribbons, and there were two narrow beds in it, one soft and lumpy and the other a real Mexican bed with boards instead of a mattress. After one or two nights, I always slept on that one. There were beautiful *serapes* for blankets, and some of David's pictures on the wall, and the three children had bought me a little silver comb, and a pair of Spanish *alpargatos*. David said they had been imported for the refugees, but the refugees liked leather sandals better.

I put on slacks, and the soft blue cotton shoes, and the comb in my hair, and went down the stairs again. It was like going down into a clear white well, and David was at the bottom, sitting on the floor, with a guitar on his knees and a drink on either side of him. We talked for a while, not about Sarah, nor anything that had happened to any of us. The drink was very good.

I was glad to be there. I felt welcome, but not as if it would have mattered if I had flown north instead of south, and that was the way I wanted to feel.

David was waiting for something. Maybe it was Sarah, I thought. He tapped on his glass and on the belly of the guitar, and I noticed how his knuckles had thickened in his long pale hands. His face had changed too, but I could not yet tell how, except that it looked much older than he was.

"Why don't you play?" I asked.

"No, wait," he said, and his eyes were mischievous, and wary, far back in his skull. "Wait. You'll hear some real music pretty soon."

So we went on drinking, and I told him about our parents, and he asked me if people at home were wondering much about war . . . things like that.

Then, far away, I began to hear the music. It came upon us quickly, so that before I could think about it the whole tall white room was full of sound, beating insistently like an excited heart all around us. David's worn look vanished, and he stared delightedly at me, but with a sideways slant to his vision, as if he were seeing the music, too. It was the first time I ever heard such sounds. I knew there were musicians outside in the street, but I had no idea yet of what they looked like, or how they could make such wild nagging sounds. There was a steady strumming, but it had no *thump* to it, no *plunkety-plunk*. There was some sort of wind instrument, but I didn't know what. And the men were singing, in a kind of rollicking wail.

"It's a *mariachi*," David said, under the beat of the music. "There are two bands here, in spite of the god-damned juke-boxes. They're disappearing, though. This one is Juanito's, the good one. Juanito is the falsetto. You'll hear."

The men kept on playing, about three songs, I think, and then they began one that made David lean back voluptuously against the cool wall. It was a kind of duet with sometimes one or two or three singing against all the rest, and always the chorus in a high single voice, piercing and sweet, with the strings beating against it. It was a passionate song, and at the end the two male voices singing under the high one sobbed like children, in thirds.

Then the band went away, and we could hear it faintly at the far end of the plaza. It seemed, though, as if the whole house, and we in it, were still throbbing, almost with fatigue. I felt shaken. Perhaps it was because I had been so high in the air that morning, then drunk the long good drink: I knew that, but still I felt strange.

David finally stood up, and stood looking down at me tenderly. "The high one was Juanito," he said. "That was *La Malagueña*. There's a good *mariachi* band at the hotel bar in Guadalajara, but nobody can sing like Juanito. It gets you, doesn't it?"

He stood leaning against the wall, as if he wanted to say more.

"I thought I'd heard plenty of recordings," I said, "but I never heard Mexican music like that."

"There are some records . . . but it's Jalisco music, and there aren't good recording stations down here, maybe. Or the *mariachi* bands don't like to leave their own villages. I don't know. They're getting scarcer. God-damned juke-boxes . . ."

Norah came in then, and Sarah just after her, with a big purple eggplant in her hands.

"I see you had some music. We met them," Norah said in her noncommittal way.

She and Sarah stood looking at me, so that suddenly I felt awkward and asked, "Is it all right to wear slacks here?"

"Of course," Norah said.

"You look fine in them," David said, as if he were soothing me. "You look fine in slacks. I don't like slacks on women, but you . . ."

"Did she see Juanito?" Norah interrupted. I felt like a backward child, or like a hermit who has forgotten how other people communicate with one another.

"No, I didn't see him," I said impatiently. "He's the falsetto, though. Did you want me to see him?"

"Well," Norah said, "you will. Tonight, probably. He plays all the time . . . if Dave's there."

"Yes," Sarah said in her soft light voice, "Juanito is so young to have his own band."

Then David said, "Let's have a little drink before lunch, shall we?" And that was really the only thing I understood in the whole conversation.

They all stopped looking at me with their blue and brown and green eyes, big and little and flat and deep eyes, speculating eyes, cool and full of question. I sat there on the floor, waiting for lunch, and waiting too, for the next time I would hear that music, and not the ghost of it that still throbbed in my head.

II

There was a bar on the lake, under a kind of roof. It was too expensive for the village people, but enough tourists and weekenders from Guadalajara came to keep fine silk dresses and heavy bracelets on the fat widow who ran it. She was a white-faced woman with a sly flashing smile, and welcomed me warmly. I ordered the kind of cocktail the children told me they always drank there, and I could see her smiling toward a prosperous future as she stirred the liquors.

It was beautiful and peaceful under the roof by the quiet water. Little islands of hyacinths nudged and drifted against the half-flooded quai, and across the lake a few lights winked already in the clear darkness of November twilight. The air was warm and sweet. I thought of another lake, with Saint Gingolphe under the shadow of the Savoy Alps, cold and familiar, instead of these lower, stranger Mexican highlands. But the lake was the same. All lakes are alike when they are quiet . . .

The widow called to David, and then snapped on the lights under the roof, so that we were walled in from the darkness suddenly, and as suddenly were glad to be secure against it.

I looked at my fine-boned brother walk with the wary slouch of a tall man to the bar and pick up the tray of drinks, and I saw that there was a man on the other side of the bar, who fell silent as David approached, and watched as I was doing.

He was a small man in a tight Spanish beret and thickly horn-rimmed spectacles, with the thin shoulders and half-fed bravado of a ghetto-boy. It was almost startling to see, as my eyes got used to the hard light, that he wore a very short priest's cassock, so that his trousers and brightly striped socks in brown shoes showed below the hem. It was plain that he and David knew each other, although they did not speak, but as David came back silently toward us I was thinking more of the trousers than of that.

The only frocked priests that I saw much in my life were in Dijon, and there they wore long underwear and on very cold days flannel petticoats. If there were ordinary trousers anywhere, they were well-hidden by the long full cassocks, even on windy days. And now these flagrant inches of pin-striped masculinity astonished me. I was still pondering when David put the four glasses gingerly on the table.

We all toasted each other, and my coming, and the invisible lake so near us. The drink was good, like a Martini in Southern France, with a strong taste of herbs to it. The widow stopped her quiet laughing talk with the priest to put a waltz on her phonograph, and Sarah and David danced silently to it. They danced well. David bent over the small blonde woman with a drowsy smile.

"Norah," I said, touching my glass to hers as if I could reach her more quickly that way, "the little priest keeps staring at us. Don't you know him?"

She looked slowly at me with her large brown eyes, as if she were thinking. Oh yes, I remember you . . . Sometimes there is not even that recognition in them, which must be more disconcerting to men who love her than it is to me, who also love her and rubbed olive oil on her before she even had a navel.

She turned toward the bar without answering me, and bowed cordially to the priest. He bowed to her, and his face was very sweet and kind when he smiled. I saw the widow whisper something to him and then they both looked at me, still smiling. So I bowed too.

"Why doesn't he come over here?" I asked Norah. I was still warm from the way his face changed, and thought I would like to talk with him.

It was almost the end of the waltz. Norah said quickly to me, "It's because of Dave. I'll tell you . . ." And then Sarah and David were back again, and he said, "What about ordering another drink and I'll go up to the hotel and tell them ten more minutes."

The widow was delighted when David told her we wanted more, as he walked past the bar, but the priest was looking the other way.

The whole thing was so queer and rude and exciting, there in the little pavilion by the Mexican lake, with everything so new around me, that I stopped treading lightly, and said, "What's going on? Tell me. Is Dave fighting a one-man battle against the Mother Church?"

But Sarah looked cautiously at me from her tilted myopic eyes, and Norah said, "Not exactly. You know Dave. He shoots off his mouth a lot about what the Church has done here in Mexico. But it really isn't that. It's about Juanito."

I could hardly believe the thoughts in my head. But I had to ask more: our little house was like an echoing cave, impossible for confidences, and I felt I must know why my brother was so discourteous to a little Jewish priest, and what Norah meant about the *mariachi* singer.

"But Norah," I said angrily, "are you saying that Dave and this man are in love with . . . are having an affair with . . . I mean jealous of . . ."

It was such a strange thing to ask in front of the unknown little silky woman David had just married that I floundered clumsily, until both girls began to laugh at me, Sarah blushing under her mop of yellow hair.

"Oh, *no*," Norah said. "It's not that at all! We'll tell you about it. But you must see Juanito first."

"Yes," Sarah said earnestly, "we want you to see Juanito."

Just then the widow brought us the new drinks, and the priest walked past our table toward the village. He bowed again, but not smiling, and we answered him silently.

David came padding back on his big silent feet grinning at us. He loved ordering dinners.

"Everything is ready! The entire hotel holds its breath. Tonight," he said, turning to me, "you're going to eat *pescados blancos* from the lake and wild hill-birds no bigger than a fig, as many as you want . . ."

"*Salud, pesetas, y amor*," we all said, and the second drink tasted better than the first, and we felt very happy to be there together, the four of us alone in the brightness beside the still lake, while the woman watched casually and any other lives seemed far away.

III

The other *mariachi* band, not Juanito's, came to the inside door of the hotel while we were eating, and played three or four songs. The big plastered room, which went up to the glass ceiling, with bedrooms opening onto galleries around it, and the tables at the bottom like pebbles, made the music almost unbearably loud. But still I liked it.

"Yes, it's good," the others said. "But not as good as Juanito's. We'd better go back to the widow's for a while . . . this is a party, anyway . . ."

There was a wind blowing from the water, when we had finished our long dinner. Under the widow's roof the lights on long cords swung a little, so that strange shadows jumped and stretched around the tables. There were a few people now, drinking beer or coffee, and the phonograph played loudly from somewhere under the bar. We drank little glasses of a poor brandy.

"They'll stop the music when Juanito comes," David said.

"How are you so sure he'll come?" Norah asked, but there was no more malice in her voice than there was smugness in his when he answered.

"Oh, everybody in the village knows where we are. He'll be here."

I was beginning to feel bored with the whole noncommittal mystery. All right, *mariachi* music was fine. All right, I loved my family for entertaining me. But it had been a long day, and suddenly I wished I were all alone somewhere, maybe back at Mazatlan with the sea in my ears and a big white bed for me and nobody in the world to wait for.

Then the music came to the end of a record, and the widow did not put on another one, because up near the plaza was the sound of the band, whuddering in the wind, but with the underbeat strong and sturdy, like a pounding heart.

More people came silently in from the darkness where they had been watching us and listening to the records. They sat against the steps, so that the widow would not serve them anything, and waited, and while the music got nearer a few beggar-children flitted toward us, and then obediently away as David waved his long hand at them and said, "Later."

I felt that he liked them, maybe for being citizens in the world

already, feeding themselves in their own way . . . so tiny, so big-
eyed . . .

Then the band was there, standing in a little group on the street
at the edge of the light. There were eight or nine men, some short
and old-looking, a few big fat-bellied ones. The fattest man played
a cornet, in a harsh, triumphant way, and when he played the others
sang in unison, letting it take the melody to their thirds. Other
times they all sang, always in thirds, and the insistent beat of the
music was six-eight time, I guess. It never stopped. There were two
violins, and two guitars and the rest plucked and strummed at big
curved things like cellos or flat ones like mandolins.

The horn-player wore a pink silk shirt, but he and all the other
men had their small *serapes* over one shoulder, and their straw hats
with the embroidered bands and the wide black strings knotted at
the back and hanging down like pigtails.

David and two or three others gave pesos to the fattest one after
songs, but Norah whispered to me, "Juanito's the boss. He's there at
the back. He won't come out because of David."

As if she had dropped a stone in a pool, people all around us
began to say, "Juanito, Juanito," and finally call and clap and whistle.
David called too, and Sarah put her hand quickly on his arm in
protest, and when he did not notice her, but went on with the other
people, she and Norah looked strangely at each other, in a kind of
female amazement.

Finally a small figure stepped out from behind the men, and while
everyone shouted names of songs, and Juanito smiled a little and
waited, his eyes cast down, touching the strings of his instrument,
I solved the mystery for myself.

I knew that the three others were looking at me, even David in
spite of his absorption in the band, and I kept my face as still as
plaster. I was remembering, while I looked at the stooped slender
little man who was the leader.

He had a pale dirty skin and hair that was rusty black, like a
half-breed's, and there was a dry old look about him, as if he slept
in the dust. His hair was almost shaved off, under the Jalisco hat,
and his face was young and very weary. His hands on the guitar
and his sandaled feet were like claws.

He stood waiting in the light, and then began to sing one song alone, without his men, a raw wild yelling song like Flamenco music, but with the *mariachi*-beat to it.

I was hearing it all, and watching him, and I was remembering one day when I was maybe sixteen. I was filled with eagerness, then, partly romantic and partly hereditary, to know more about my father's newspaper office. He humored me, but only a little: I was a woman, and he wanted to save all that for David. One day, though, he took me through the Back Room, and I watched the linotypists and then went over to the job-presses. The men did not seem to mind my watching their finicky work, but Father was in a hurry, and we went on through to his office.

At supper that night we were talking about the little presses, and Father said, "There's one chap there . . . I should have pointed him out to you. He does the finest work in the shop. He made a little trouble a few years ago . . . tried his hand at agitating. All right now. But he spends all his spare time illuminating . . . the real thing. Churches and big companies wanting rolls of honor . . . that sort of thing. I should have pointed him out. He uses real gold leaf."

"Do you mean the short fat one, with white hair?"

Father stared at me. "That's the one. Always has a cigaret in his mouth. He never says much, but he's the best man in the shop."

Before I thought, I said, "But, Father . . . that's not a man! It's a woman!"

Father was really upset. He was sure I was teasing him for some obscure reason: the chap had been there for years, he used the men's toilets, he'd even been in some labor-scare, he had a good reputation. And anyway, how in hell did I know?

I tried to tell Father that I had looked at the worker, and suddenly she had looked right into my eyes, and I had known . . . but that was no answer to him.

And the next day he was so disturbed by this strange thing that might have been going on for so long in his own place that he called his foreman, who laughed in his face. So Father called the worker, and she said, "Yes. Do you want me to quit?"

He didn't, but she stopped work for a few days, and talked to a minister, and after that she worked all week as a man, and then on Sundays she dressed in tailored dresses and went to church. I always felt badly about it, although the minister's wife said things were much happier for her. And once in a while at home Father would shake his head and say to me, "You certainly called the trick . . . I don't see . . ."

I knew, while I sat listening to the harsh music, with the shadows jumping in the wind, with my brother and sister and even Sarah watching me. I felt bewildered and timid. If they already had the answer, why did they wait for my confirmation? Was I going to hurt anything?

I saw the young priest on the edge of the light. He was watching me, too. I could not see his eyes behind their thick glasses, but his big nose and all the lines of his thin face were sneering, sardonic.

Then Juanito finished, and melted in among the men again, smaller than even the bent old fiddlers, and the priest disappeared. People started to leave.

"How about one more song? How about *La Malagueña?*" David's eyes were bright, and his face fresher and younger than I had seen it for years, as if the music had filled him, just under the skin, with some kind of magic wax.

But Norah said, "No!" very sharply, and we all stood up. We said goodnight and thank you to the band, and they bowed so that the front fringes of their *serapes* touched the ground.

The streets were dark and uneven, and we walked arm in arm. I felt so tired I could hardly move my legs. I was full of little roasted birds and alcohol and a kind of heavy impatience with the world, so that when David said, "Well, what about Juanito?" I could hardly drag an answer through my lips.

"Well?" I said angrily. "Why 'o'? Why this bluff? It's Juanita, of course, feminine ending . . . 'a.'"

David laughed delightedly, as if he had pulled off some sort of *coup,* and I knew he had been boasting to Sarah, just the way Father might have, about the time I saw the woman at the job-press.

"What of it, what of it?" Norah murmured wearily, and I felt her fingers tighten on my arm as if she were comforting me in some way that must for a time more be wordless.

IV

It took a long time for me to find out more about Juanito than I discovered that first day. Once the three children had it settled for them that I knew the little worn boy was a girl, they seemed to avoid talking about her.

It was impossible for me to question David: he was, in those last months of his life, turned in upon himself with a concentration I had seldom seen, in a hard, furious devotion that was at once tragic and admirable. It was beyond selfishness, beyond cruelty, so that his marriage, his imperious gentleness with Sarah and his sisters, even the intensity of his eating and drinking had a remoteness about them impossible to assault.

The only thing that seemed to reach him, and then as a kind of reassurance, was the *mariachi* music. It had a visible effect on him, so that while he listened to it, I could see his skin change from a strange jaded gray to the fresh firmness rightful in a young man. No. I could not ask him questions.

And, as I say, once he knew that I recognized the little musician, his interest in the whole thing stopped, and she was simply a part of the *mariachi* band. Even when she sang *La Malagueña*, she was not Juanito, a mysterious human with a passionate voice: she was a voice, passionate because David willed it, singing to David for David. At least, that is the way it seemed to me, and I withdrew in a kind of timidity from such ferocious self-concentration.

With Sarah and my sister the reasons were different, but it was hard still to ask about Juanito. Sarah I did not know well, and behind her soft dignity I sensed a kind of resignation that would make such questions seem impertinent. Gradually from Norah I learned what she could tell me, but there was an unwillingness about her, as if she too felt mixed up with Juanito, and resented it.

I used to walk along the rutted road to the villa with her, and sit under the queer heavy twisted trees while her picture was being painted, and on the way back to the village again and our house she would talk sometimes.

Once we met a handsome man in a black suit. He looked like a lawyer in a provincial French town, with sad eyes and a smirking dissipation in his face.

"That's the doctor," Norah said. "He's a snob, and thinks he is condemned to this village because in a bigger place people would look down on him for his Indian wife. But he says he's a liberal. He and the priest are the intellectuals. He pierced my ears for me. We both got a little drunk. I was scared and I don't think he'd ever touched a white woman's ears before. He did a bad job. He was with the priest the night David and Sarah came back from their honeymoon."

That was the way she talked, but before I came back to California I knew all there was for me to know about Juanito. And what I knew made me sorry that any of us had ever gone to that village, and ashamed that we were so big, so pale, so incautiously alive.

If we had gone somewhere else, though, it might have been the same . . . not for Juanito, but for some other creature. Or, if stars and bodies had been different, it might have been Juanito who with an innocence even greater than ours could blast our lives . . . But how can you know, when you walk through a room, that you have made such havoc? Must you hide always, for fear of the damage you may or may not cause?

Juanito came down from the hills as a boy, alone. That was not strange: there were many children who lived that way, begging when they had to, running errands, sleeping where there was the most shelter. Some of them disappeared, into another village, or into the lake, like stray cats, but Juanito stayed because that village still had real *mariachi* music in it.

He used to go everywhere with the bands, and finally he was singing with them in his wild cracked voice, and playing the instruments with his claw-fingers while the men rested between songs. In a year or so he was the leader: all the best men went with him, and his band was the one people called for when they got married or wanted to go out onto the summery lake for eating and singing and love-making.

Juanito grew a little, but not much, and lived with the children of the cornet-player. After the priests could wear cassocks again in that part of Mexico, and the young Jewish Father came to the village to stay, Juanito went regularly to confession . . . but only the two of them ever knew that he was anything but a proud local possession, a fifteen-year-old boy who had his own band, and could play and sing for three days running, at fiestas.

That is how it was when David and Norah came.

They were odd strangers to the small dark village-people, as they moved with their naïve insolent assurance through the stony streets. Everywhere they went eyes watched them politely, acutely, and as soon as it was seen how they smiled and looked peaceful when the bands played, they lived in an almost constant storm of music. It beat and whimpered and nagged insistently outside their home, whether they paid for it or not, and at night when they ate in the little open restaurants, the men seemed to know where they would go before they did themselves. They loved it.

David got Juanito to come to the house sometimes, to teach him new words to the songs, and better ways to hold his fingers. Perhaps that is what started Juanito to change, but I doubt it. Juanito's eyes, downcast and far back under his wide-brimmed hat, saw every time he played how David's queerly exhausted face grew younger, and Juanito saw that as a woman would see it, with tenderness and probably a purely physical stirring inside.

And then, instead of going away to do it, she changed right there in the village into a girl.

She had to stop playing with her men, and stop wearing trousers. The cornet-player's wife got her a dress, which hung slackly on her thin body, but no more so than it would have on any other malnourished girl there in that hungry village. She let her hair grow, but it kept its dusty spiked look, and hung incongruously over her large eyes in her small sallow face, like a monkey's.

She went to church with the other women, instead of all alone to confession, and the young priest watched over her anxiously, gently. Perhaps he felt that religion had brought Juanita to her true life at last. Perhaps he simply felt relieved that someone he knew to be female was no longer living as a male.

As for the villagers, they seemed to accept the change without much surprise. Keeping themselves alive took most of their energies, and what little was left over they spent, with native wisdom, on fiestas to make them forget their hungers and sicknesses. They missed Juanito the *mariachi*-leader; there was no doubt of that.

Two or three men tried to hold the band together, and then it melted slowly into the rival one or went to other parts of Jalisco.

Norah told the doctor how much she and David missed the good music, one day when she was having the little holes in her earlobes disinfected, and he smiled and said the priest would be interested to hear that. Had she heard, he asked her, swabbing and poking, that in Guadalajara there was a *mariachi* band much better than the little Juanito's had been? It played in a few bars . . .

My brother and sister began to go oftener to the city, especially after Sarah came.

Then David and Sarah were married, and went away on their honeymoon, and Norah went to stay at the villa with the big gates until they came back. She said she saw Juanito in her ugly dress a few times in the market, and they always smiled shyly at each other, the way women do when they have nothing to say but feel friendly.

The Saturday David was to bring his new wife home, Norah moved back to the house to have it ready for them and ordered a fine dinner at the hotel, and warned the widow to have the cold drinks waiting.

Everybody in the village knew about it, and there was an almost visible shimmer of excitement behind the courteous faces everywhere: the young American was coming back with a wife . . . not a friend, a *wife* . . .

Things went off beautifully. The flowers in the little house did not wilt much, and the flies under the high dome in the hotel dining room did not settle as hungrily as usual on the dinner Norah had commanded. And afterwards at the widow's the brandy seemed almost as good as the cocktails had before, and a moon spread smoothly over the windless waters of the lake.

The little beggar-children came giggling and grinning to look at Sarah, and when the lone *mariachi* band rolled up to play, people came as always from the shadows and smiled and even nodded timidly as they watched the three strangers and listened to the music.

Norah saw the priest on the edge of the light that night. He seemed searching, and soon hurried off, without bowing to her. There were a lot of people still on the streets when the three went home, because it was Saturday, and on the plaza the little tequila-joints were full. Norah said that on a bench outside of one of them, the worst one, which was often closed for days while its proprietor lay drunk on the floor, the priest was sitting.

She was surprised to see him. Even though he was so young, and wore striped sport socks under his short cassock, he was still a priest, and Saturday night on the plaza was not right for him.

Then she saw . . . they all saw . . . that he was holding up Juanito.

Juanito was a boy again, since that very morning. His hair was shaved roughly from his head, and his white face and closed eyes made him look like a saint, somehow. He was drunk, dead-drunk, and the little priest was holding him around the shoulders, like a mother, to keep him from rolling to the ground.

Norah said they walked over, shocked, intuitively thinking they could help. David was big . . . maybe he thought he could carry the little unconscious Juanito away from the foul air in front of the bar. But when the priest saw who it was coming toward him, the three tall compassionate strangers, David and his pale-haired wife and his grave-eyed sister, he stood up slowly.

Juanito felt softly along the bench. The priest took off his thickly rimmed glasses. He kept staring at David, and Norah thought, "There's trouble! There's trouble!" And then the little man, with a look of complete scorn on his pinched, pale, hook-nosed face, spat in the dust in front of him.

"Hey!" David said in the slow way big men say it when their stomachs are tightening and they are going to fight.

There were some people watching, but not with much interest, and all the time music from the juke-boxes in the bars whined and bellowed, three or four tunes at once, while the two men stared at each other and the boy Juanito lay on the bench, dead-drunk.

As I think about it now, I feel almost as if David and the priest were the same man. Even their bodies were alike: tired, big-nosed, sunken-eyed. One had grown higher and fuller, because of good food and freedom from oppression. One had grown wiser, perhaps from hunger and slavery. And they met, there in the plaza.

The doctor came swiftly down from his pharmacy on the corner. Maybe someone had told him . . . one of the beggar-children. He said in a fast low voice, almost without stopping as he passed my family, "Go home. Hurry. This is not your affair."

The priest stared for a few seconds longer up into David's eyes, and then he put on his glasses again, and as the three strangers turned and walked toward their house, they saw him help the doctor lift Juanito, and head toward the church with her.

It took a long time for me to find out what had happened, and instead of feeling that it had stopped, to me it was still going on. I knew it whenever I saw the priest. He always walked past the widow's, or the restaurants, when Juanito was playing and we were listening. If David was not there he bowed to us, and I wanted to know him better, and knew that I never would.

And I knew something was still going on when I watched the faces of my family, and saw how David's always grew younger and simpler to the music, and how sometimes Sarah's and Norah's looked tight under the smooth beautiful well-bred skin. Sometimes when David would call out "*La Malagueña*," and clap and smile, Sarah would permit herself one small movement of protest, as if she had been jabbed with a goad, or she and Norah would look at each other in a kind of wonder, as if David were beloved but imbecilic.

I was the one who would say, "No more, I'm tired. No more tonight." It was because sometimes I felt as if I could not stand another note to beat into my body, the way they all did in those insistent *mariachi* songs, until they were like blood in a fever, or a wild heart.

The strangest thing, maybe, was that after Juanito came back, David took it for granted the lessons would go on. He asked her one night why she had not come as usual on the set day, to finish teaching him a song interrupted when she left her band. She said she would come the next afternoon, and David was annoyed when she did not.

One of the cornet-player's children tapped on the window, and shouted in that Juanito was sick, but would come in two more days. Perhaps Juanito got drunk again. When she finally came, she looked more than ever like a little monkey, or a ghost.

Norah and Sarah went away that afternoon, and every time the lessons happened, and I stayed up in my room, lying in a kind of helplessness on my wooden bed, listening to David and the singer in the patio. The stone house sent their voices up to me with a clear intensity.

David treated him as if he were the boy who led the *mariachi* band, and who was giving him lessons at so much per hour. I think what had happened about Juanito, and my brother's knowledge that she was really a girl, had gone completely from his strange mind. He was too concentrated on his own existence to be conscious of any others, except as they could help him. I am sure, certain-sure, that it never occurred to him that he had anything to do with Juanito's behavior. He thought of her, if he thought at all, as an instrument who played music that pleased him.

It was the priest who thought of Juanito as a human, the priest who seems mixed now in my mind with David, as if they were parts of a whole.

v

Finally it was time for us to go. Norah and I were going to fly, from Guadalajara, and we all went up there for a few days before the plane left. Then David and Sarah were starting out in the little car.

We went to the bull fights, and took showerbaths and drank beer. There were many Germans in the city then: they seemed to own all the big groceries and pharmacies and such, and the best restaurants were very much like ill-kept beer-halls. People ate sauerkraut and sausages around the big tables, and played backgammon or read old Berlin newspapers. But there was good Mexican food, too. It goes well with beer, bottled or in steins.

We would rest after the bull fights, and bathe, and then in the twilight, ride in a carriage to an oyster-bar, and eat pink oysters, black oysters. Sarah hated that part, but she was patient. Then we would go to a plaza where there was a restaurant named, I think, Valencia's. Valencia was the chef, and he fixed chicken with herbs and oil, the way I have often eaten it in Italy. We would sit under the trees in the plaza, while other swells in carriages ate all around us, and the drivers flicked goodnaturedly at raggamuffins with their whips.

Or we would have a drink or two in the bar of the hotel, where the good *mariachi* band played high up against the ceiling in a little alcove, and go afterward to one of the beer-halls for supper.

The night before Norah and I were to leave, we decided to do that.

We went into the noisy little bar, where most of the local bloods crowded about six at night and a few hard-faced genial American business men were well known by the barman. He was a eunuch. By now he knew us, too, and he greeted us shrilly, and made us each a double-Gibson with a special flourish. We felt gay and taut, the way you always do when you know you are ending one part of your life on a high note.

Men and a few women were talking all around us, and the band was beating it out up near the roof, yowling in thirds that would never sound anything but exciting to us. I think we had finished the drink and started another when we looked at each other and knew that Juanito was singing up there. It made us all feel strange. The village was behind us, we had thought . . .

David got up and asked the barman, and came back looking as pleased as a child. It was Juanito, all right. He was well known, and any time he wanted to, the barman said, he could leave his own band for this one. He came in just before the music started. We could not see up into the alcove, but his voice was as familiar as our own.

I felt disturbed, in a passive way. There was nothing to do or say about it. Sarah seemed as withdrawn and silky as ever, and Norah would not look at me, and David was obviously happy. To him it was probably one more bit of good luck, one more augur of the gods' special interest in him, in David . . .

We went on to the beer-hall. I forget its name. It was a good one, dark and smelly, with old Coca-Cola ads on the walls and an agreeable disinterested hum from all the other people. We had a table in a kind of booth. We had often sat there, and the waiter was pleased to see us. We started in drinking dark beer, from fine big steins.

When the food came, it was delicious. We ate a lot of enchiladas, some with herbs and cheese in them and some with chicken. Then there were beans, of course, and a rather despondent ·guacamole in our honor, though it was long past time for avocados.

I think all of us but David were deliberately liking everything, the way people do when they are trying to push down in their minds the insistent knowledge that never again, never again will they be together and young and free and all the other things they may think they are at that moment. No matter how many times you have said goodbye to yourself in the presence of others you will assume something of the same resolute gayety. It is a form of armor.

We were perhaps half-finished with our supper, eating slowly because it was the last one, when a little *mariachi* band came in. The men were tired and tipsy, but they were playing like demons, and Juanito was leading them, not singing far back as at the bar. He stood boldly in front of his few recruits, and struck at the guitar slung over his suddenly strong-looking little shoulders with a vigor that was uncompromising. He looked straight at us, not shyly any more, and his eyes were all black, like a squirrel's . . . no pupils, no whites.

We listened, while they played for us and then moved slowly around to other tables. When they came back, David asked them if they would not like a drink. Juanito bowed, and said in his cracked sweet voice that they would come back soon, and then if the Señoras permitted . . . He bowed smilingly again to us and marched out, tiny in front of his tired meek band.

We kept on rolling tortillas into pencils and dipping them in a bowl of hot brown sauce, and drinking beer. Sarah wanted to go back to the hotel. But we felt we must stay a little longer, in case Juanito came back. The chairs were hard.

Finally the music came again, and Juanito was standing by our table, with his men swaying from weariness and a few more shots of tequila, and playing as I have never heard a band play anywhere. They were hoarse by now, but they sang with a muted savagery, and Juanito's clear wailing rose and fell against the strumming like a voice from a dream.

It did not matter that we were too full of beer, too full of regrets and presentiments: we sat there like dry trees in the rain. The music washed over us, and it hurt, but it was good.

The men drank some more, and Juanito too, and then Sarah said, "I'm going."

She said it almost violently, and slapped her hand on the table. It was the first time I had ever known her to be like that, and I was glad to see it. Her oval face with its odd oblique blue eyes was flushed, and she started to stand up.

Norah said, "Yes."

But David said, "Wait. One more thing. Let me ask them one more thing. I want to see . . ."

He spoke to Juanito, before we could protest. "Señor," he said in his fluent bad Spanish, "will you do us the favor of playing for us the song you think is the most beautiful in Jalisco?"

Juanito looked at him for a moment, as if to decide something in a language never spoken. The men straightened, waiting, with their hands on their bows and strings. And Juanito, with his full black eyes moving easily from one face to another, in a new assurance, sang *La Malagueña*.

It was so beautiful, and the high passionate woman's voice rose so wildly above the whimpering men, and the strings beat so rhythmically into our hearts, that all over the beer-hall people fell silent, and put down their steins and their newspapers, and turned to watch, as if that could make them understand what the music was meaning.

It was a different song for each of us, of course. Sarah looked very peaceful, suddenly, and there were the same tears in Norah's brown deep eyes that I had seen there when the first bull dropped proudly to his knees, that afternoon in the arena. David's face was calm and drowsy, remotely voluptuous, like a Chinese carving.

And for myself, as Juanito sang the last bars to us and the weeping voices rose against hers over the rhythm, I felt a kind of humility and a thankfulness that we were leaving. Juanito would be free again, as much as anyone can be who has once known hunger and gone unfed . . .

1949

An Alphabet
For Gourmets

FOR HAL BIELER, *who taught me
more then he meant to about the
pleasures of the table.*

Foreword

It is apparently impossible for me to say anything about gastronomy, the art and science of satisfying one of our three basic human needs, without involving myself in what might be called side issues—might be, that is, by anyone who does not believe, as I do, that it is futile to consider hunger as a thing separate from people who are hungry.

That is why, when I set myself to follow anything as seemingly arbitrary as an alphabet, with its honored and unchanging sequence and its firm count of twenty-six letters, I must keep myself well in hand lest I find *A Is for Apple, B Is for Borscht*, and *C Is for Codfish Cakes* turning into one novel, one political diatribe, and one non-fiction book on the strange love-makings of sea monsters, each written largely in terms of eating, drinking, digesting, and each written by *me*, shaped, molded, and, to some minds, distorted by my own vision, which depends in turn on my state of health, passion, finances, and my general glandular balance.

If a woman can be made more peaceful, a man fuller and richer, children happier, by a changed approach to the basically brutish satisfaction of hunger, why should not I, the person who brought about that change, feel a definite and rewarding urge to proselytize? If a young man can learn to woo with cup and spoon as well as his inborn virility, why should not I who showed him how feel myself among Gasterea's anointed? The possibilities for bettering the somewhat dingy patterns of life on earth by a new interest in how best to stay our human hunger are so infinite that, to my mind at least, some such tyrannical limitations as an ABC will impose are almost requisite.

The alphabet is also controversial, which in itself is good. Why, someone may ask, did I scamp such lush fields as *L Is for Lucullus, G Is for Gourmet*? Why did I end the alphabet with a discussion of the hors d'oeuvres called zakuski, surely more appropriate at the beginning of any feast, literary or otherwise, and ignore the fine fancies to be evoked by the word zabaglione, with all its connotations of sweet satisfaction and high flavor?

I do not really know, but most probably because I am myself. This ABC is the way *I* wrote it. There is room between its lines, and even its words, for each man to write his own gastronomical beliefs, call forth his own remembered feastings, and taste once more upon his mind's tongue the wine and the clear rock-water of cups uncountable.

A *is for dining* Alone

... AND SO am I, if a choice must be made between most people I know and myself. This misanthropic attitude is one I am not proud of, but it is firmly there, based on my increasing conviction that sharing food with another human being is an intimate act that should not be indulged in lightly.

There are few people alive with whom I care to pray, sleep, dance, sing or share my bread and wine. Of course there are times when this latter cannot be avoided if we are to exist socially, but it is endurable only because it need not be the only fashion of self-nourishment.

There is always the cheering prospect of a quiet or giddy or warmly somber or lightly notable meal with "One," as Elizabeth Robins Pennell refers to him or her in *The Feasts of Autolycus*. "One sits at your side feasting in silent sympathy," this lady wrote at the end of the last century in her mannered and delightful book. She was, at this point, thinking of eating an orange[1] in southern Europe, but any kind of food will do, in any clime, so long as *One* is there.

I myself have been blessed among women in this respect—which is of course the main reason that, if *One* is not there, dining alone is generally preferable to any other way for me.

Naturally there have been times when my self-made solitude has irked me. I have often eaten an egg and drunk a glass of jug-wine, surrounded deliberately with the trappings of busyness, in a hollow Hollywood flat near the studio where I was called a writer, and not been able to stifle my longing to be anywhere but there, in the company of any of a dozen predatory or ambitious or even kind people who had *not* invited me.

That was the trouble: nobody did.

I cannot pretend, even on an invisible black couch of daydreams, that I have ever been hounded by Sunset Boulevardiers who wanted to woo me with caviar and win me with Pol Roger; but in my few desolate periods of being without *One* I have known two or three avuncular gentlemen with a latent gleam in their eyes who understood how to order a good mixed grill with watercress. But, for the most part, to the lasting shame of my female vanity, they have shied away from any suggestion that we might dally, gastronomically speaking. "Wouldn't dare ask *you*," they have murmured, shifting their gaze with no apparent difficulty or regret to some much younger and prettier woman who had never read a recipe in her life, much less written one, and who was for that very reason far better fed than I.

It has for too long been the same with the ambitious eaters, the amateur chefs and the self-styled gourmets, the leading lights of food-and-wine societies. When we meet, in other people's houses or in restaurants, they tell me a few sacrosanct and impressive details of how they baste grouse with truffle juice, then murmur, "Wouldn't dare serve it to *you*, of course," and forthwith invite some visiting potentate from Nebraska, who never saw a truffle in his life, to register the proper awe in return for a Lucullan and perhaps delicious meal.[2]

And the kind people—they are the ones who have made me feel the loneliest. Wherever I have lived, they have indeed been kind— up to a certain point. They have poured cocktails for me, and praised me generously for things I have written to their liking, and showed me their children. And I have seen the discreetly drawn curtains to their family dining-rooms, so different from the uncluttered, spinsterish emptiness of my own one room. Behind the far door to the kitchen I have sensed, with the mystic materialism of a hungry woman, the presence of honest-to-God fried chops, peas and carrots, a jello salad,[3] and lemon meringue pie—none of which I like and all of which I admire in theory and would give my eyeteeth to be offered. But the kind people always murmur, "We'd love to have you stay to supper sometime. We wouldn't *dare*, of course, the simple way we eat and all."

As I leave, by myself, two nice plump kind neighbors come in. They say howdo, and then good-by with obvious relief, after a polite, respectful mention of culinary literature as represented, no matter how doubtfully, by me. They sniff the fine creeping straightforward smells in the hall and living-room, with silent thanks that they are not condemned to my daily fare of quails financière, pâté de Strasbourg truffé en brioche, sole Marguéry, bombe vanille au Cointreau. They close the door on me.

I drive home by way of the corner Thriftimart to pick up another box of Ry Krisp, which with a can of tomato soup and a glass of California sherry will make a good nourishing meal for me as I sit on my tuffet in a circle of proofs and pocket detective stories.

It took me several years of such periods of being alone to learn how to care for myself, at least at table. I came to believe that since nobody else dared feed me as I wished to be fed, I must do it myself, and with as much aplomb as I could muster. Enough of hit-or-miss suppers of tinned soup and boxed biscuits and an occasional egg just because I had failed once more to rate an invitation!

I resolved to establish myself as a well-behaved female at one or two good restaurants, where I could dine alone at a pleasant table with adequate attentions rather than be pushed into a corner and given a raw or overweary waiter. To my credit, I managed to carry out this resolution, at least to the point where two headwaiters accepted me: they knew I tipped well, they knew I wanted simple but excellent menus, and, above all, they knew that I could order and drink, all by myself, an apéritif and a small bottle of wine or a mug of ale, without turning into a maudlin, potential pick-up for the Gentlemen at the Bar.

Once or twice a week I would go to one of these restaurants and with carefully disguised self-consciousness would order my meal, taking heed to have things that would nourish me thoroughly as well as agreeably, to make up for the nights ahead when soup and crackers would be my fare. I met some interesting waiters: I continue to agree with a modern Mrs. Malaprop who said, "They are *so* much nicer than people!"

My expensive little dinners, however, became, in spite of my good intentions, no more than a routine prescription for existence. I had long believed that, once having bowed to the inevitability of the dictum that we must eat to live, we should ignore it and live to eat, in proportion of course. And there I was, spending more money than I should, on a grim plan which became increasingly complicated. In spite of the loyalty of my waiter-friends, wolves in a dozen different kinds of sheep's clothing—from the normally lecherous to the Lesbian—sniffed at the high wall of my isolation. I changed seats, then tables. I read—I read everything from *Tropic of Cancer* to *Riders of the Purple Sage*. Finally I began to look around the room and hum.

That was when I decided that my own walk-up flat, my own script-cluttered room with the let-down bed, was the place for me. "Never be daunted in public" was an early Hemingway phrase that had more than once bolstered me in my timid twenties. I changed it resolutely to "Never be daunted in private."

I rearranged my schedule, so that I could market on my way to the studio each morning. The more perishable tidbits I hid in the water-cooler just outside my office, instead of dashing to an all-night grocery for tins of this and that at the end of a long day. I bought things that would adapt themselves artfully to an electric chafing dish: cans of shad roe (a good solitary dish, since I always feel that nobody really likes it but me), consommé double, and such. I grew deliberately fastidious about eggs and butter; the biggest, brownest eggs were none too good, nor could any butter be too clover-fresh and sweet. I laid in a case or two of "unpretentious but delightful little wines." I was determined about the whole thing, which in itself is a great drawback emotionally. But I knew no alternative.

I ate very well indeed. I liked it too—at least more than I had liked my former can-openings or my elaborate preparations for dining out. I treated myself fairly dispassionately as a marketable thing, at least from ten to six daily, in a Hollywood studio story department, and I fed myself to maintain top efficiency. I recognized the dull facts that certain foods affected me this way, others that way. I tried to apply what I knew of proteins and so forth to my own chemical pattern, and I deliberately scrambled two eggs in a little sweet butter when quite often I would have liked a glass of sherry and a hot bath and to hell with food.

I almost never ate meat, mainly because I did not miss it and secondarily because it was inconvenient to cook on a little grill and to cut upon a plate balanced on my knee. Also, it made the one-room apartment smell. I invented a great many different salads, of fresh lettuces and herbs and vegetables, of marinated tinned vegetables, now and then of crabmeat and the like. I learned a few tricks to play on canned soups, and Escoffier as well as the Chinese would be astonished at what I did with beef bouillon and a handful of watercress or a teaspoonful of soy.

I always ate slowly, from a big tray set with a mixture of Woolworth and Spode; and I soothed my spirits beforehand with a glass of sherry or vermouth, subscribing to the ancient truth that only a relaxed throat can make a swallow. More often than not I drank a glass or two of light wine with the hot food: a big bowl of soup, with a fine pear and some Teleme Jack cheese; or two very round eggs, from a misnamed "poacher," on sourdough toast with browned butter poured over and a celery heart alongside for something crisp; or a can of bean sprouts, tossed with sweet butter and some soy and lemon juice, and a big glass of milk.

Things tasted good, and it was a relief to be away from my job and from the curious disbelieving impertinence of the people in restaurants. I still wished, in what was almost a theoretical way, that I was not cut off from the world's trenchermen by what I had written for and about them. But, and there was no cavil here, I felt firmly then, as I do this very minute, that snug misanthropic solitude is better than hit-or-miss congeniality. If *One* could not be with me, "feasting in silent sympathy," then I was my best companion.

1

Probably the best way to eat an orange is to pick it dead-ripe from the tree, bite into it once to start the peeling, and after peeling eat a section at a time.

Some children like to stick a hollow pencil of sugarcandy through a little hole into the heart of an orange and suck at it. I never did.

Under the high-glassed Galeria Vittorio Emanuele in Milan before the bombs fell, the headwaiters of the two fine restaurants would peel an orange at your table with breath-taking skill and speed, slice it thin enough to see through, and serve it to you doused to your own taste with powdered sugar and any of a hundred liquors.

In this country Ambrosia is a dessert as traditionally and irrefutably Southern as pecan pie. My mother used to tell me how fresh and good it tasted, and how pretty it was, when she went to school in Virginia, a refugee from Iowa's dearth of proper *fin de siècle* finishing schools. I always thought of it as old-fashioned, as something probably unheard of by today's bourbons. I discovered only lately that an easy way to raise an unladylike babble of protest is to say as much in a group of Confederate Daughters—and here is the proof, straight from one of their mouths, that their local gods still sup on

AMBROSIA

6 *fine oranges*	1½ *cups sugar*
1½ *cups grated coconut,*	*good sherry*
preferably fresh	

Divide peeled oranges carefully into sections, or slice thin, and arrange in layers in a glass bowl, sprinkling each layer generously with sugar and coconut. When the bowl is full, pour a wine glass or so of sherry over the layers and chill well.

2

Crêpes, approximately Suzette, are the amateur gourmet's delight, and more elaborately sogged pancakes have been paddled about in more horrendous combinations of butter, fruit juices, and ill-assorted liqueurs in the name of gastronomy than it is well to think on.

A good solution to this urge to stand up at the end of a meal and flourish forks over a specially constructed chafing dish is to introduce local Amphytrions to some such simple elegance as the following, a recipe that was handed out free, fifteen years ago in France, by the company that made Grand Marnier:

Dissolve 3 lumps of sugar in 1 teaspoon of water. Add the zest of an orange, sweet butter the size of a walnut, and a liqueur glass of Grand Marnier. Heat quickly, pour over hot, rolled crêpes, set aflame, and serve.

3

The following dish has almost the same simplicity as the preceding ones, but where they are excellent, this is, to my mind, purely horrible.

It is based on a packaged gelatin mixture which is almost a staple food in America. To be at its worst, which is easy, this should be pink, with imitation and also packaged whipped milk on top. To maintain this gastronomical level, it should be served in "salad" form, a small quivering slab upon a wilted lettuce leaf, with some such boiled dressing as the one made from the rule my maternal grandmother handed down to me, written in her elegantly spiderish script.

I can think of no pressure strong enough to force me to disclose, professionally, her horrid and austere receipt. Suffice it to say that it succeeds in producing, infallibly, a kind of sour, pale custard, blandly heightened by stingy pinches of mustard and salt, and made palatable to the most senile tongues by large amounts of sugar and flour and good water. Grandmother had little truck with foreign luxuries like olive oil, and while she thought nothing of having the cook make a twelve-egg cake every Saturday, she could not bring herself to use more than the required one egg in any such frippery as a salad dressing. The truth probably is that salads themselves were suspect in her culinary pattern, a grudging concession to the Modern Age.

B is for Bachelors

. . . AND the wonderful dinners they pull out of their cupboards
with such dining-room aplomb and kitchen chaos.

Their approach to gastronomy is basically sexual, since few of
them under seventy-nine will bother to produce a good meal unless
it is for a pretty woman. Few of them at any age will consciously
ponder on the aphrodisiac qualities of the dishes they serve forth,
but subconsciously they use what tricks they have to make their
little banquets, whether intimate or merely convivial, lead as subtly
as possible to the hoped-for bedding down.

Soft lights, plenty of tipples (from champagne to straight rye),
and if possible a little music, are the timeworn props in any such
entertainment, on no matter what financial level the host is operating.
Some men head for the back booth at the corner pub and play the
juke-box, with overtones of medium-rare steak and French-fried potatoes. Others are forced to fall back on the soft-footed alcoholic
ministrations of a Filipino houseboy, muted Stan Kenton on the
super-Capeheart, and a little supper beginning with caviar malossol
on ice and ending with a soufflé au kirschwasser d'Alsace.

The bachelors I'm considering at this moment are at neither end
of the gastronomical scale. They are the men between twenty-five and
fifty who if they have been married are temporarily out of it and are
therefore triply conscious of both their heaven-sent freedom and
their domestic clumsiness. They are in the middle brackets, finan-
cially if not emotionally. They have been around and know the
niceties or amenities or whatever they choose to call the tricks of a
well-set table and a well-poured glass, and yet they have neither the
tastes nor the pocketbooks to indulge in signing endless chits at Mike
Romanoff's or "21."

In other words, they like to give a little dinner now and again in

584

the far from circumspect intimacy of their apartments, which more often than not consist of a studio-living-room with either a disguised let-down bed or a tiny bedroom, a bath, and a stuffy closet called the kitchen.

I have eaten many meals prepared and served in such surroundings. I am perhaps fortunate to be able to say that I have always enjoyed them—and perhaps even more fortunate to be able to say that I enjoyed them because of my acquired knowledge of the basic rules of seduction. I assumed that I had been invited for either a direct or an indirect approach. I judged as best I could which one was being contemplated, let my host know of my own foreknowledge, and then sat back to have as much pleasure as possible.

I almost always found that since my host knew I was aware of the situation, he was more relaxed and philosophical about its very improbable outcome and could listen to the phonograph records and savor his cautiously concocted Martini with more inner calm. And I almost always ate and drank well, finding that any man who knows that a woman will behave in her cups, whether of consommé double or of double Scotch, is resigned happily to a good dinner; in fact, given the choice between it and a rousing tumble in the hay, he will inevitably choose the first, being convinced that the latter can perforce be found elsewhere.

The drinks offered to me were easy ones, dictated by my statements made early in the game (I never bothered to hint but always said plainly, in self-protection, that I liked very dry Gibsons with good ale to follow, or dry sherry with good wine: safe but happy, that was my motto). I was given some beautiful liquids: really old Scotch, Swiss Dézelay light as mountain water, proud vintage Burgundies, countless bottles of champagne, all good too, and what fine cognacs! Only once did a professional bachelor ever offer me a glass of sweet liqueur. I never saw him again, feeling that his perceptions were too dull for me to exhaust myself, if after even the short time needed to win my acceptance of his dinner invitation he had not guessed my tastes that far.

The dishes I have eaten at such tables-for-two range from home-grown snails in home-made butter to pompano flown in from the Gulf of Mexico with slivered macadamias from Maui—or is it Oahu? I have found that most bachelors like the exotic, at least culinarily speaking: they would rather fuss around with a complex recipe for

Le Hochepot de Queue de Boeuf than with a simple one called Stewed Ox-tail, even if both come from André Simon's *Concise Encyclopædia of Gastronomy*.[1]

They are snobs in that they prefer to keep Escoffier on the front of the shelf and hide Mrs. Kander's *Settlement Cook Book*.

They are experts at the casual: they may quit the office early and make a murderous sacrifice of pay, but when you arrive the apartment is pleasantly odorous, glasses and a perfectly frosted shaker or a bottle await you. Your host looks not even faintly harried or stovebound. His upper lip is unbedewed and his eye is flatteringly wolfish.

Tact and honest common sense forbid any woman's penetrating with mistaken kindliness into the kitchen: motherliness is unthinkable in such a situation, and romance would wither on the culinary threshold and be buried forever beneath its confusion of used pots and spoons.

Instead the time has come for ancient and always interesting blandishments, of course in proper proportions. The Bachelor Spirit unfolds like a hungry sea anemone. The possible object of his affections feels cozily desired. The drink is good. He pops discreetly in and out of his gastronomical workshop, where he brews his sly receipts, his digestive attacks upon the fortress of her virtue. She represses her natural curiosity, and if she is at all experienced in such wars she knows fairly well that she will have a patterned meal which has already been indicated by his ordering in restaurants. More often than not it will be some kind of chicken, elaborately disguised with everything from Australian pine-nuts to herbs grown by the landlady's daughter.

One highly expert bachelor-cook in my immediate circle swears by a recipe for breasts of young chicken, poached that morning or the night before, and covered with a dramatic and very lemony sauce made at the last minute in a chafing dish. This combines all the tricks of seeming nonchalance, carefully casual presentation, and attention-getting.

With it he serves chilled asparagus tips in his own version of vinaigrette sauce and little hot rolls. For dessert he has what is also his own version of riz à l'Impératrice, which he is convinced all women love because he himself secretly dotes on it—and it can be made the day before, though not too successfully.

This meal lends itself almost treacherously to the wiles of alcohol: anything from a light lager to a Moët et Chandon of a great year is beautiful with it, and can be well bolstered with the preprandial drinks which any bachelor doles out with at least one ear on the Shakespearean dictum that they may double desire and halve the pursuit thereof.

The most successful bachelor dinner I was ever plied with, or perhaps it would be more genteel to say served, was also thoroughly horrible.

Everything was carried out, as well as in, by a real expert, a man then married for the fifth time who had interspersed his connubial adventures with rich periods of technical celibacy. The cocktails were delicately suited to my own tastes rather than his, and I sipped a glass of Tio Pepe, properly chilled. The table, set in a candle-lit patio, was laid in the best sense of the word "nicely," with silver and china and Swedish glass which I had long admired. The wine was a last bottle of Chianti, " 'stra vecchio."

We ate thin strips of veal that had been dipped in an artful mixture of grated parmigiano and crumbs, with one of the bachelor's favorite tricks to accompany it, buttered thin noodles gratinés with extra-thin and almond-brown toasted noodles on top. There was a green salad.

The night was full of stars, and so seemed my eager host's brown eyes, and the whole thing was ghastly for two reasons: he had forgotten to take the weather into his menu planning, so that we were faced with a rich, hot, basically heavy meal on one of the worst summer nights in local history, and I was at the queasiest possible moment of pregnancy.

Of course the main mistake was in his trying to entertain a woman in that condition as if she were still seduceable and/or he still a bachelor: we had already been married several months.

1

Two of the three proper recipes in Monsieur Simon's useful as well as delightful volume on meat in his *Concise Encyclopædia of Gastronomy* recommend soaking the sections of ox tail in either hot or cold water. For ox-tail soup this is a good idea, but I myself do not like it for stew because it robs the texture of that almost glutinous thickness which should be one of its chief characteristics, and which when correctly brought about should obviate the use of flour in thickening its ample gravy. (I say this humbly but positively.)

One of the three recipes in Simon's *Meat*, typical in all its practical common sense of the *farmhouse fare* from which it is culled, says in italics something that wins my heart and my approval, something true of every kind of stew I ever made: *"It is always better to start cooking this dish a day before it is wanted."*

Here is my recipe, subject to unbasic change of course, following the season and the vegetables thereof:

OX-TAIL STEW

3 *ox tails, cut in joints and discarding the smallest ends*

3 *tablespoons butter*

3 *tablespoons olive oil (or bacon fat)*

salt, pepper, bay leaf, what you will

1 *quart (or more to taste) of either tinned consommé, stock, vegetable juice, or even beef cubes in water*

8 *or* 10 *small peeled onions*

8 *or* 10 *peeled potatoes*

1 *small bunch celery, with its leaves, in* 1-*inch pieces*

6 *or* 8 *thickly sliced carrots*

handful of chopped parsley

1 *clove chopped garlic*

6 *chopped peeled fresh tomatoes (or* 1 *No.* 2 *can)*

Brown the clean ox-tail joints in the melted butter and fat. Season. Add the stock. Cover tightly and let simmer until tender, adding the vegetables for the last 40 to 60 minutes of cooking. (Pressure-cooked vegetables with their juices can be added when the meat is completely done.) Mix well, put to one side, and serve the next day, first tasting to "rectify," as some cooks say. Seasonings and texture will have set, and red wine, more salt, even a judicious thickening may seem necessary.

C *is for* Cautious

... THE kind of dinner at which there is an undercurrent of earnest timidity, of well-meant and badly directed eagerness to do well, and absolutely no true feeling for what can best be described as Fun at Table.

A complete lack of caution is perhaps one of the true signs of a real gourmet: he has no need for it, being filled as he is with a God-given and intelligently self-cultivated sense of gastronomical freedom. He not only knows from everything admirable he has read that he will not like Irish whisky with pineapple chilled in honey and vermouth, or a vintage Chambertin with poacned lake perch; but every taste bud on both his actual and his spiritual palate wilts in revulsion at such thoughts. He does not serve these or similar combinations, not because he has been *told*, but because he *knows*.

But there are some would-be gastronomers who live only by the book. Most of them are happily unconscious of their loss. Many of them acquire a basic knowledge of the pleasures of the table that is often astonishingly broad, and that gives them countless fine moments of generosity and well-being: what is much better in life than to be hospitable and to know by your guests' faces that you have proved a noble host indeed?

Then again, there are some people who never in a century of Sundays can hide their underlying confusion and caution. They subscribe to *Gourmet* and its satellites, and even submit incredibly complicated recipes to the sub-editors, which are discreetly rearranged before publication in some such dutiful department as "Letters to Our Chef." They belong to local food-and-wine groups or their reasonable facsimiles, and bring back packages of musty filé powder from New Orleans, and order snails (packed as a special inducement with the shells wrapped separately) from a former maître d'hôtel who lives next to the airport in Lisbon. They have Grossman's *Guide* on their shelves, and Saintsbury and Schoonmaker, and they serve the proper wines at the proper times and temperatures. They know Escoffier's basic sauces. Their dinners march formally from start to finish.

And over everything, over all the thought and the earnest planning, lies a weight of uncomfortable caution. It is invisible of course and cannot even be identified except by the gastronomically wary, but it shows with damning clearness in the polite faces of the guests, in the genteelly labored tempo of the conversation, and in the well-bred avoidance of any direct mention of the pleasures of the table.

The guests eat well, drink like kings, and go their separate ways unsatisfied. The tired host lies puzzled on his bed, unable to tell himself why he has had no fun, no fun at all, in spite of the thought and effort that went into his little celebration. Why do other people give such amusing dinner parties, he wonders. I tried and *tried*, and did *just* what they all do. . . .

That is the thing: the cautious host's need to follow, to rely on other people's plans. That is what spreads such faint but inescapable vapors of timidity and insecurity over his fine plates and glasses and whatever lies upon and in them. He does not trust himself—more often than not with some justification.

The art of dining has settled upon a basically sound pattern in the last hundred years or less, so that in an instinctive progression of textures and flavors a good classical meal goes from hors d'oeuvres through soup and fish and meat and cheese to the final "sweet conceits" of some dessert designed to amuse rather than excite appetites already more than satisfied. Anyone who wishes may follow this traditional pattern, and his success will be the greater if he is willing to admit, as do present-day princes of gastronomy, that he may occasionally slip into a heretical habit which must be corrected. (A delightful example of this was the decision, made in Paris late in 1947 at the Third International Congress of Gastronomy, that pâté de foie gras must henceforth be served in its proper place at the beginning of a meal, and not later with the salad as has increasingly become the custom!) It shows no caution, no lack of self-assurance, to lean on this classical schedule, for it is the most natural one in modern Western living.

Damning timidity, which can dampen any fine gastronomical fires at table, springs, I suppose, from the fact that the cautious host is incapable of enjoying himself. I know one nationally famous "gourmet" who has absolutely no innate good taste, whose meals are incredibly and coarsely and vulgarly overelaborate and rich, but who presents them with such contagious high spirits that they are unfailingly delightful.

I also know at least four people who have plenty of money for the more Lucullan tidbits of cookery, as well as a devouring desire to be good hosts, whose banquets are dreaded and, more often than not, bluntly shunned. I sit through them now and then because I admire their dogged earnestness. I always wish desperately, compassionately, that my hosts could summon enough gastronomical courage to turn their backs on rote and plan a meal dictated by no matter what faint glimmer of appetite within them rather than by other men's rules.

A supper of two or three ample and savorous courses, with two honest wines to be honestly enjoyed, would do more to kill caution in a good host's soul than all the elaborate menus indelibly engraved in gourmets' history books because of their extravagance and preciosity. I have never met anyone who dined with George Saintsbury, but I am confident that one of his meals could be duplicated, except for the years of the wines, by almost any eager would-be gourmet with enough money, and that it would be a ghastly ordeal for everyone concerned if it were not carried out with the good Professor's zest, his joy of living and eating and drinking and talking in good company.

Here is a dinner served by him in Edinburgh at the end of the last century. It has at worst a horrid fascination to the modern and emasculated palate, but could be, and assuredly was, enjoyable, because the host was not a cautious man:

Clear soup and then fillets of whiting with a sherry (Dos Cortados, 1873); calf's head à la Terrapin[1] and then oysters en caisses with Château La Frette, 1865; then in proper succession an aspic of tunny, braised beef, roast Guinea fowl, apricots in jelly, velvet cream, anchovies Zadioff,[2] and ices, accompanied by Champagne Giesler 1889, Château Margaux 1870, a La Tache Burgundy of 1886, and an 1870 Port.

This menu is impossible except in its correct classical pattern,

and impossible except purely in theory to almost any of today's gastronomical children. But it has a kind of dashing enthusiasm about
it. It was not a cautious dinner! It was fun!

1

I cannot find a recipe for this. But perhaps Saintsbury's Terrapin is
a cautious Scotch equivalent of à la Tortue.

From what I know of terrapin, most of it vicarious, I would say
that Escoffier's Tortue garnish, which includes eggs fried almost without benefit of their whites, comes close to it. The rest of the recipe
is interesting in a completely un-Scotch and extravagant way, and
it hints at the pains a chef will go to in order to coax his diners to
eat a boiled calf's head!

In the Tortue sauce are small quenelles of veal forcemeat with
butter, cock's combs and kidneys, pitted stuffed poached olives, slices
of truffle, and gherkins cut to the shape of olives. Separate from
the "sauced" garnishes are slices of tongue and calf's brain, small
trussed poached crayfish, little croutons fried in butter, and the
trimmed near-whiteless fried hens' eggs!

To my mind the best recipe for this fantastic hodgepodge of
flavors which Professor Saintsbury *may* have served to his guests
is the one from Francatelli's *The Modern Cook*, published in London in 1846. It is a tribute to Victorian staunchness.

CALF'S HEAD À LA TORTUE

*Bone, blanch, and trim a calf's head, cut it up into large scollops,
keep the ears whole, neatly trim the pieces, and toss them in the
juice of a lemon; put them in a stewpan, with carrot, onion, celery,
garnished-faggot, cloves, mace, and a few pepper-corns; moisten with
half a bottle of Madeira or sherry, and two large ladlefuls of good
stock; cover with a well-buttered stiff paper, and put on the lid; set
the whole to braize on the stove for about two hours. When the
pieces of calf's head are done, drain them on a napkin, and afterwards dish them up, in the form of a close wreath, round the base
of a fried bread croustade; place the ears at the ends and on the
flanks: if the party be large, two extra ears should be procured, as
the four make the dish look much handsomer: next, place the tongue,
cut down its centre, and spread out on top of the croustade; on this
put the brains, which must be kept whole and white, and round
these, on the croustade, should be stuck six ornamental silver skewers,*

garnished with a double cocks-comb, a large mushroom, a quenelle, a truffle, and a large crayfish; sauce around with a well made sauce à la Tortue; garnish the dish round between the spaces of the ears with four larded and glazed sweetbreads, and eight decorated quenelles, and send to table.

2

I have searched through several cookbooks which might have been used by Professor Saintsbury, and I am defeated: no oysters en caisses, no savory called anything even approximating anchovies Zadioff. Perhaps they were staring at me, and I was too dazed by all the other Victorian dishes to see them.

But I can remember once in England, in a fairly Victorian household and in spite of the year (1936 or so), being served, at the end of a dinner which began with plovers' eggs, a kind of cold appetizer-tickler, rather a change from the usual hot overspicy British fillip to a good meal. They were little coffins, as Elizabethan manuals would have named them, of rich pastry, generously filled with black caviar and with one trimmed handsome oyster resting upon each dark bed. What a strange and intrinsically stimulating flavor at the end of the rococo menu!

D *is for* Dining *out*

. . . AND its amenities.

A great deal has been written about the amenities of dining, but few writers have seen fit to comment on the very important modern problem of eating in a public place.

I had a happy beginning in this neglected art and much abused privilege, one that has sheathed it in unfading pleasure for me when it is done well. When I was no more than five or so my father and mother would begin to prepare my spirits for Easter, or Christmas, or a birthday, and when the festival rolled around, there I would be, waiting to greet it in my wide hat with ribbons, on the pink velvet seat of the region's best restaurant.

At first it was called Marcel's, I believe. By now Hollywood and its New York refugees have widened the choice if not the choiceness, and there are several eating houses within a hundred miles of me in which I am delighted to be seen. I have friends who feel the same way. The problem, given that situation, is now most smoothly to combine our presences at the same public table.

I admit that I am prejudiced about it. I seldom dine out, and because of my early conditioning to the sweet illusion of permanent celebration, of "party" and festivity on every such occasion, I feel automatically that any invitation means sure excitement, that it will be an event, whether it brings me a rained-on hamburger[1] in a drive-in or Chicken Jerusalem at Perino's. The trouble is, I am afraid, that I expect the people I dine with to feel the same muted but omnipresent delight that I feel.

They seldom do. More often than not they eat out (and what a dreadfully glum phrase that is!) several times each week. They have business lunches: in a small town, service clubs and Chamber of Commerce meetings and so on; in a city, conferences with colleagues

594

they must quickly dominate. In both cases, no matter what type of food is served, they are tense, wary, and gastronomically bored to the point of coma. As for their dinners, those too are at best a frank mixture of business and pleasure. The attitude seems to be that all humans must eat, and all humans must make money in order to eat, and therefore the two things might as well be combined.

The result of this is a common sight in any restaurant from the Black Kat on South Main to Mike Romanoff's on Rodeo Drive: carefully dressed women are very polite to other carefully dressed women while their male companions walk in invisible circles around one another, sniffing out the chances of anything from laying a new plastic tile floor in the bathroom to trading top stars for two hundred grand.

Such luncheons and dinners are the reason, fairly obviously, that successful people have gastric ulcers. I, on the other hand, may be less successful, but I have never been menaced by that dreadful burning sensation, which is laughingly called occupational but is more likely to be known in the future as merely twentieth-century. I refuse, almost categorically, to dine out. I refuse to have my childhood dreams of fun and excitement turned into a routine and ungracious feeding, to the tune of wifely chitchat and the clink of unmade dollars.

However, there are occasions on which one must do so, and one of these was the time I took a Very Important Person to dinner. He had often entertained me and various glamorous groups with lavish simplicity in his home, with its electrically shaken cocktails, electrically lighted swimming pool, and electrically rotated spit. I thought it would be a compliment to him to cook dinner for him myself, as soon as I got a place to cook it in. But no: I was tipped off with elaborate tact by his wife, his secretary, and the secretary of his immediate superior in the studio, that he felt bad, in fact terrible, that I had not "entertained" him. All right, I said, all right, forgetting my disappointment in a deliberate campaign to do the thing as nearly as possible as I thought it should be done in a public eating place.

I telephoned the restaurant the day before and asked for a table in accord with my friend's local importance. This obviated standing in line, which is ignominious no matter how diplomatically the line may be spread through the bar by a good headwaiter.

Then I ordered the meal, to be served to four people. It was dictated by what I could remember of my honored guest's tastes, just as it would have been in my home. He boasted of being a meat-and-potato boy, a hater of fancy sauces, a lover of Scotch in moderation, and a shunner of any but chilled pink wine. Very well: smoked salmon, a small rack of lamb, potatoes Anna, Belgian endive salad, and a tray of Langlois Blue, Rouge et Noir Camembert, Wisconsin Swiss, and Teleme Jack cheese; Scotch or sherry first, and then Louis Martini's Gamay Rosé. It was not my idea of a perfect meal, but it could be eaten with no pain.

By ordering in advance I avoided another horrible barrier to decent dining out: the confusion that inevitably follows the first showing of menu cards to more than two people at once.

The waiter waits. The diners ponder, stutter, variously flaunting their ignorance or their pretensions to knowledge. They mutter and murmur into the air, assuming Godlike clarity of hearing on the part of the poor harried servant and disregarding entirely the fact that they are guests at a table. The men usually blurt some stock familiar order. Women hum, sip their cocktails, and change their minds at least twice after the waiter has scrawled on his pad. There is a general feeling of chaos, and nobody seems to realize that if the same human beings were invited to any normal home they would not dream of giving their orders so confusedly and arbitrarily, nor would the hostess dare leave her guests thus tenderly exposed. No, a good meal inside or outside the private circle should be ordered in advance (or at least ordered with great firmness by the host at table in a restaurant), to avoid this distressing welter of words and the resultant unrelated odors, plates, servings, when a group has gone helter-skelter through a menu.

The third thing I did was to see the headwaiter and tip him. And since I knew the restaurant and the good relations therein between the various professional levels, I left another tip with him for the man who would take care of us come eight o'clock.

The final step: I arranged for the bill to be mailed to me. There are few things more boringly painful about public dining, to my mind, than the obligatory plunging and grabbing and arguing that are taken as a matter of course at the end of a meal. If men are present they look on it as an insult to their virility to let a woman pay. If women are eating together, they simply outshriek one another, and the noisiest bears off the check in expensive but curiously rewarding triumph. I feel rebuffed, when I have invited anyone of no matter what sex to dine with me, to have the bill snatched gallantly from me, just as I would feel insulted if after dining in my home a guest slipped a bill under his plate for the groceries I had used.

When I walked out of the restaurant I felt that I had done everything I could to assure my friend of a meal which I could have given him for one-fourth the cost and about one-eighth the bother at home, but which he would, because of his peculiar importance in a very peculiar industry, enjoy a hundred times as much because it was in this peculiar town's smartest eating place.

Everything went beautifully. The table was the "right" one socially, the Scotch was from the proper dimpled bottle, the waiter scudded on velvet, other Very Important People nodded and smiled. The slices of salmon were *so* thin, and the wine came and the rack of lamb, a masterpiece, the headwaiter cool as a surgeon above it.

My guest turned to me, for the first of many times that night, and said, "Do you know, in my whole life nobody has ever ordered a meal just for me?"

"Nonsense," I said, thinking of all the dinners that people had served him, people who for one reason or another wanted to please him—as I did.

"No," he said—by the end of the evening tearfully—"no, never! And I hate menus. I hate them. I go to places where they know what I want just so I don't have to look at menus. If I pretend to look, I have something memorized to say. If my doctor has told me to eat tomatoes I say, 'A fresh tomato omelet'—something like that to make them pay a little attention to me. Now and then I get peeved at all the French and I say, '*Spécialité de la maison*'—how's my accent? But, do you know, this is the first time anyone ever realized that I hate menus and having to order and—do you know, this is just like a party!"

It would be easy here for me to indicate that at this somewhat maudlin point my guest slid under the table. He did not. It was a good evening, with good talk, even in Hollywood where the fact that we were enjoying ourselves in public proved us embarrassingly out of line. It had about it something, no matter how faint, of the festive ease, the latent excitement, of my childhood celebrations—a reward to me for having observed the basic principles of decent dining out. I had treated my guest as much as possible as if he were in my home, and "miracles occurred."

1

A recipe which was whispered awesomely to me as being the authentic one used by a famous restaurant was a strange, sloppy mixture of ground sirloin, raw egg, salt and pepper and mustard, Worcestershire sauce, and an impossible quantity of rich chicken broth. Perhaps it is authentic. Perhaps if this quasi-soup is mixed and allowed to stand, it will thicken itself enough to be made into cakes fit to broil. Cynically I say no.

It is easy to make very good hamburgers, given the same ingredients in more realistic proportions, and given, of course, the acceptance of the modern American meaning of hamburger: chopped meat formed into cakes, cooked, and served on or in a split bun.

When I was much younger and proportionately hungrier and less finicky, a minor form of bliss was going to a drive-in near school and eating two or three weird, adulterated combinations of fried beef, mayonnaise, tomato catsup, shredded lettuce, melted cheese, unidentifiable relish, and sliced onion. These concoctions were called "Rite-Spot Specials," in dubious honor of the place that served them. They seemed wonderful then. Now I gag.

Now I prepare, from time to time, an austere and fine adaptation of this adolescent dream. It is as much better than the old as being my age is than being that age—and that is a lot! Served with some sourdough bread, a bowl of fresh celery or plain green salad, and some simple red wine or beer, it is good.

HAMBURGERS (*à la Mode de Moi-même*)

1½ to 2 lbs. best sirloin, trimmed of fat and coarsely ground (or finely chopped)

1 cup ordinary red table wine

3 or 4 tablespoons butter

1 cup mixed chopped onion, parsley, green pepper, herbs, each according to taste

4 tablespoons oyster sauce (Chinese or American) or 2 tablespoons Worcestershire sauce

Shape meat firmly into four round patties at least 1½ inches thick. Have the skillet very hot. Sear the meat (very smoky procedure) on both sides and remove at once to a hot buttered platter, where the meat will continue to heat through. (Extend the searing time if rare meat is not wanted.)

Remove the skillet from the fire. When slightly cooled, put the wine and butter in it and swirl, to collect what Brillat-Savarin would have called the "osmazome." Return to heat and toss in the chopped ingredients, and cover closely. Turn off heat as soon as these begin to hiss. Remove from stove, take off cover, add oyster sauce, swirl once more, and pour over hot meat. Serve at once, since the heat contained in the sauce and the patties continues the cooking process.

E *is for* Exquisite

. . . AND its gastronomical connotations, at least for me.

When I hear of a gourmet with exquisite taste I assume, perhaps too hastily and perhaps very wrongly, that there is something exaggeratedly elaborate, and even languidly perverted, about his gourmandism. I do not think simply of an exquisitely laid table and an exquisite meal. Instead I see his silver carved in subtly erotic patterns, and his courses following one upon another in a cabalistic design, half pain, half pleasure. I take it for granted, in spite of my good sense, that rare volumes on witchcraft have equal place with Escoffier in his kitchen library, and I read into his basic recipe for meat stock a dozen deviously significant ingredients.

Such deliberate romanticism on my part can most easily be dismissed as the wishful thinking of an amateur cook who scrambles eggs very well but only reads, these days, about filets de sole Polignac and pâté de foie truffé en brioche. Or perhaps it is Freudian: subconsciously I might murder, or even seduce, by means of cookery, and therefore I ascribe such potentialities to someone whose culinary freedom I envy! Whatever the reason, in my private lexicon of gastronomy I continue to see the word exquisite ringed about with subtle vapors of perversion.

Most of the great historical and literary gourmets, in the sense of their being exquisites, have had the unlimited money, like Des Esseintes in Huysmans' *Against the Grain*. The very fact that they can command no matter what incredible delicacy adds to their satiety, and that in turn gives just the fillip of distortion to their appetites which satisfies my definition of their exquisiteness.

Huysmans' sad young man, for instance: his "farewell dinner to a temporarily dead virility," as the invitations shaped like bereavement notices called it, was a masterpiece of jaded extravagance. He needed to be a millionaire, as well as a determined exquisite, to serve—in a black-draped room lighted by green flames, attended by nude black virgins wearing silver slippers and stockings trimmed with dripping tears—a dinner beginning with blackest caviar and ending with black-heart cherries. He needed to be at least a demi-millionaire to fill his fountain with ink for that one dubious feast, and to line his ash-covered paths with funereal pine trees.

He needed, above all, to be sublimely indifferent to the taint of vulgarity, for his earnest efforts at eccentricity were indeed vulgar, and ridiculous too, in a basically shameful and extravagant way. All that saved him from oblivion was his dignified disregard of anything but his own kind of pleasure.

It is the same with some of the dishes we still read about with a strange fascination, those cooked for the most dissipated of the Romans two thousand years or so ago. Doubtless many of them tried to astound their sycophants by serving whole platters of the tongues of little birds that had been trained to talk before they went into the pot. We do not remember the names of these men, nor anything more than the vulgarly idiotic waste. But what if one of those epicures, greatly in love with a proud lady named Livia, had taught a thousand birds to sing her name, Livia, Livia, to the moment of most perfect diction, and then had served forth to the lady a fine pie of their tongues, split, honeyed, and impaled on twigs of myrrh? *Then,* I think, that fat lover would still be known to us for what he was, an exquisite—a silly one perhaps, extravagant certainly, but with his own dignity about him.

I remember deciding once, long ago and I believe after reading Elwanger's *Pleasures of the Table* for the first time, that the most exquisite dish I had ever heard of was a salad of satiny white endive with large heavily scented Parma violets scattered through it. It meant everything subtle and intense and aesthetically significant in my private gastronomy, just as, a few years earlier, a brown-skinned lover with a turquoise set in one ear lobe epitomized my adolescent dream of passion. It is a misfortune perhaps that not many months ago the salad[1] was set before me in a bowl.

That it was not very good was relatively unimportant: the dressing was light to the point of being innocuous, and it was unable to stand up under the perfumed assault of the blossoms. What disappointed me, finally and forever, was that it was served neither exquisitely, nor by an exquisite, nor with an exquisite disregard of the vulgar.

Instead it was concocted and presented with both affectation and awkwardness and was at best an attempt at that insidious decadence which is a prerequisite of my definition. It suddenly became ridiculous.

I blushed for my long dream of it and felt a hollowness, for where again will I know so certainly that such and such a dish is it? What will it be? Expense is not enough, for sure, and no intricate silverware, no ritual of serving and compounding, can guarantee the magic. There must, for me at least, be a faint nebular madness, dignified no matter how deliberate, to a dinner that is exquisite.

1

Eastern Americans find it an all-too-easy gastronomical gambit to sneer, no matter how genteelly, at the Western habit of serving a salad before a main, or meat, course at dinner.

I used to do this in a kind of reverse snobbism. I learned in Northern California why I was wrong.

There people know how to drink table wine better than anywhere else in the United States, and there they are much influenced by fellow countrymen of French and Italian descent who would never cut into a good wine's attack on human taste buds by adding vinegar or lemon juice or even mustard to the battle.

There they are not afraid to lead up to the triumph of a heady entrée and its accompanying bottle by such sturdily subtle flavors as a fresh tomato can give, or garden lettuce touched with a garlic bud, or a morsel of anchovy. In Napa or Livermore or Sonoma a roadside boarding-house will serve such an antipasto as would please any finicky gourmet strong enough to meet the wine he wanted.

There an approximation of the classical tossed green salad may well be part of any laborer's daily fare, as a prelude to the meat and the wine that must mainly nourish him, and not as a routine sourish aftermath, tackled without appetite or interest simply because it has become traditional elsewhere to serve the salad after the roast.

The nearest I ever came to the fresh, crude before-meat salads of Northern California was in Venice, in 1940, when an extraordinarily keen porter at the hotel found us a gondolier who was possessed of the gourmet's "curious nose" if ever I did hear of it.

Vittorio, whom we hired by the week, paddled us dreamily from one *trattoria* to another, and we would jump bobbily from the gondola into its dappled garden-restaurant and then two or three hours later sag carefully back again into our little ship, full of a number of good things, none of which I can remember except the omnipresent scampi, the little shrimps of foul repute which Casanova's mother cried out for the night before his birth, and the salads. (The coffee was fine too.)

The salads stood in common white kitchen bowls and platters for the most part, in two or three linen-covered tiers upon a table at one side of the garden. Every vegetable had an immediate life to it, so that the tiny potatoes boiled in their skins *almost* crunched, but not enough to repel; the dozen different kinds of artichokes were *almost* tough; the celery poached in chicken broth *almost* felt raw between the teeth. It was somewhat like Chinese food, fresh but purified, and my husband remarked casually that this, as well as the untoward delicacy and flavor of everything, was probably because of the Venetian night-soil it was grown in. I continued to delight in it, and to point like a happy child at this bowl, that platter, and then watch my waiter toss the little morsels together in a salad that may be well known to every traveler but me. It served as a fine introduction to whatever followed rather than as a dutiful tonic afterward.

I continue to find many people, especially Englishmen and Americans, who because of their early gastronomical education (or lack of it) cannot enjoy a fresh salad before the entrée. Then I serve it after the entrée, but I try to suit the seasoning to what has gone before and make it bland in proportion to the wine being drunk. One thing I do not do is use lemon juice when we are drinking anything good—which to my mind is any honest wine ever bottled, of no matter what year or price. I use a good wine vinegar: I do not hold much with the fancy bottled tarragon vinegars and such, although herb vinegars have their own place in seasoning. Sometimes I cheat, silently of course, and use no vinegar at all, but an extra dash of soy, or of oyster sauce after lamb, for instance.

I almost never serve such fundamentally sharp things as tomatoes in a salad after meat, feeling that they, like vinegar, cut into the wonderful action of wine upon the tongue. Now and then I put in a pinch of good curry powder, or fresh minced anise, to baffle people. (I have yet to try hard enough to astonish them by using Paul Reboux's trick of tiny matchsticks of carrot and an equal quantity of tiny matchsticks of orange peel, which are of identical color but such different tastes!)

Mostly I depend on oil, the best I can buy. I like a heavy, greenish, very strong olive oil, from California or Spain. I do not like the highly refined oils I have been served, with such elation, from Italy: my palate is probably too crude for them. A few times in France I have eaten salad made with the now rare walnut oil . . . delicious! I truly dislike American vegetable oils, but on the other hand I grew to enjoy the huile d'arachides, rather like our kosher peanut oil, which I used in Dijon and Switzerland between wars.

Now and then I like to put tomatoes, sliced onions (preferably those pretty rose-blue ones), garden greens, fresh chopped herbs, some anchovy fillets or a boiled sliced potato or a hard-cooked egg, into a bowl, sprinkle them with salt, freshly ground pepper, vinegar, and oil, and toss them around lightly, the Italian way, the way hungry Venetian waiters on their days off from the big restaurants in San Francisco do it for themselves at places like La Tosca, while the juke-boxes throb "Return to Sorrento" and "Now Is the Hour."

Occasionally I read, with sick fascination, the ads for elaborate household gadgets in the slick-paper magazines. The last one I saw said, in ten varying types to astound me, "The New Salad-master! Make salads you will be proud of! This new all-purpose, marvelous, revolutionary, indispensable kitchen aid will make *you* a cook! It chops, peels, waffles, grates, strings, shreds, crimps, cuts, and slices lettuce in a second! Free wonderful salad recipes!"

Could the people in Venice have been wrong with those forthright bowls of little whole poached potatoes, scalded whole beans as thick as a needle, whole peas fragrant as flowers?

F is for Family

. . . AND the depths and heights of gastronomical enjoyment to be found at the family board.

It is possible, indeed almost too easy, to be eloquently sentimental about large groups of assorted relatives who gather for Christmas or Thanksgiving or some such festival, and eat and drink and gossip and laugh together. They always laugh: in Norman Rockwell magazine covers and in Iowa novels and in any currently popular variation of "I Remember Mustache Cups" there is Gargantuan laughter, from toothless babe to equally toothless Gramp. Great quantities of home-cooked goodies are consumed, great pitchers of Uncle Nub's hard cider are quaffed, and great gusts of earthy merriment sweep like prairie fire around the cluttered table. The men folk bring out their whittling knives in postprandial digestive calm, the women (sometimes spelled wimmin to denote an inaudible provincialism) chatter and scrape and swab down in the kitchen, and the bulging children *bulge*.

The cold truth is that family dinners are more often than not an ordeal of nervous indigestion, preceded by hidden resentment and ennui and accompanied by psychosomatic jitters.

The best way to guarantee smooth sailing at one of them is to assemble the relatives only when a will must be read. This at least presupposes good manners during the meal, if the lawyer is not scheduled to appear until after it. Funeral baked meats have perhaps been more enjoyed than any christening cakes or wedding pottages, thanks largely to the spice of wishful thinking that subtly flavors them, as yet untouched by disappointment, dread, or hatred.

My own experience with family dinners has fallen somewhere between this facile irony and the bucolic lustiness of popular idealization. I remember that several times at Christmas there were perhaps twenty of us at the Ranch for a lengthy noon-dinner, to which none of us was accustomed. I always had fun, being young and healthy and amenable, but I do not recall, perhaps to my shame, that I had any *special* fun.

To be truthful, I was conscious by my eleventh or twelfth year that there was about the whole ceremony a kind of doggedness, a feeling that in spite of hell and high water we were duty-bound to go through with it, because my grandfather was very old and might not live another year, or because a cousin had just lost her abominable but very rich husband, or because another cousin was going to Stanford instead of Yale at Yale's request and so would be with us, or something like that. It was tacitly understood that the next day would find my sister Anne droopy and bilious, my mother overtired, and the cook crankily polishing glasses and eying the piles of the "best" Irish linen that had to be laundered. My father, on the other hand, would still be glowing: he loved any kind of party in the world, even a family one.

I seem, and I am thankful for it, to have inherited some of his capacity for enjoying such intramural sport, combined, fortunately, with my mother's ability to cope with it. In spite of my conviction that a group of deliberately assembled relatives can be one of the dullest, if not most dangerous, gatherings in the world, I am smugly foolhardy enough to have invited all my available family, more than once, to dine with me.

The last time was perhaps the most daring, and it went off with a dash and smoothness that will always bulwark my self-esteem, for it was the happy result of many days of thought and preparation.

Parents, cousins, new generation—all came. It meant hotel reservations in the near-by town, and great supplies of food and drink for a long holiday during which the stores were closed. It meant wood stored under cover for the fireplace in case of rain (it poured), and Band-Aids and liniment (my nephew and my two-year-old daughter fell off a boulder into the pond), and considerable self-control (my favorite male shot several of my favorite quail).

It meant a lot of work: I was cook, and before the festival I had food prepared or at least in line for an average of twelve persons a meal, three meals a day, for three days. And the right good wines. And the other potables, right, good, and copious. That, I say smugly, is no mean feat.

It was exciting and rewarding and completely deliberate. Nothing, to my knowledge at least, went wrong. There was an aura of gaiety and affection all about us—and that too, with people of different ages and sexes and beliefs, political and religious *and* social, is also something of a feat to attain and to maintain. The whole thing, for a miracle to bless me, went off well.

This is most often the case in planned celebrations, I think. Now and then there is a happy accident in families, and brothers and cousins and grandparents who may have been cold or even warlike suddenly find themselves in some stuffy booth in a chophouse, eating together with forgotten warmth and amity. But it is rare. Most often it must be prearranged with care and caution.

It must not simply be taken for granted that a given set of ill-assorted people, for no other reason than because it is Christmas, will be joyful to be reunited and to break bread together. They must be jolted, even shocked, into excitement and surprise and subsequent delight. All the old routine patterns of food and flowers and cups must be redistributed, to break up that mortal ignominy of the family dinner, when what has too often been said and felt and thought is once more said, felt, and thought: slow poison in every mouthful, old grudges, new hateful boredom, nascent antagonism and resentment—why in God's name does Mother always put her arm *that* way on the chair, and why does Helen's girdle always pop as she lifts the denuded meat platter up and away from Father, and why does Sis always tap her fingers thus tinnily against the rim of her wine glass? Poison, indeed, and most deeply to be shunned!

It takes courage to give a family party, and at least once I had enough to do it, being mightier in my youth than I am now. I was almost stony broke, unable to take no matter how judicious a collection of relatives to a decent restaurant. So . . .

I summoned my father, mother, brother, and sisters to a supper in the Ranch dining-room, to celebrate nothing at all. I managed to pay for it, almost to the least grain of salt: silly, but a sop to my proud young soul. I set the table with the family's best silver and china and crystal (especially the iridescent and incredibly thin wine goblets we have always had for "party").

I went to Bernstein's on the Park in Los Angeles and bought beautiful fresh shellfish: tiny bay shrimp in their shells, crab cooked while I waited, and lobster claws too, pink prawns, little mussels in their purple shells. I went down behind the Plaza and bought flat round loaves of sourdough bread and good spaghetti and sweet butter. I bought some real cheese, not the kind that is made of by-products and melted into tinfoil blocks. I bought Wente Brothers' Grey Riesling and Italian-Swiss Colony Tipo Red, and some over-roasted coffee blended on Piuma's drugstore counter for me. There, in short, was the skeleton of the feast.

The flesh upon this bony structure was a more artful thing, compounded of my prejudices and my enthusiastic beliefs. It is true that my comparative youngness made me more eager to do battle than I would be now, but I still think I was right to rebel against some of the inevitable boredom of dining *en famille*.

To begin with, I reseated everyone. I was tired of seeing my father looming against the massive ugliness of the sideboard, with that damned square mirror always a little crooked behind his right ear. I assumed, somewhat grandly, that he was equally tired of looking down the table toward my mother, forever masked behind a collection of cigarette boxes, ash trays, sugar shakers left there whether needed or not, a Louis Quinze snuff box full of saccharin, several salt shakers, a battered wooden pepper-mill, and an eternal bouquet, fresh but uninspired, of whatever could be gleaned from the garden. With never a yea or nay to guide me I eliminated this clutter from the center of the table—it had been on my nerves for at least fifteen years—and in a low bowl I arranged "bought" camellias instead of a "grown" bunch of this-or-that from the side yard.

My parents were rocked on their bases, to put it mildly, and only innate good manners kept them from shying away from my crazy plan like startled and resentful deer whose drinking place has been transferred.

Those were my first and most drastic attempts, clumsy enough, I admit, but very successful in the end, to break up what seemed to me a deadly dull pattern. Then I used the sideboard as a buffet, which had never been done before in our memory. I tipped off my siblings beforehand, and we forced my father to get up and get his own first course of shellfish, which he enjoyed enormously after he recovered from the first shock of not having someone wait on him. He poked and sniffed and puttered happily over the beautiful platters of shrimp and suchlike and made a fine plate of things for my mother, who sat with an almost shy smile, letting the newness of this flood gently, unforgettably, into her sensitive mind and heart.

My brother poured the cold Grey Riesling with a flourish, assuming what had always been Father's prerogative. Later I served the casserole of spaghetti, without its eternal family accompaniment of rich sauce, and it was doubly delicious for that flouting of tradition.[1]

The Tipo was good. The Tipo flowed. So, happy magic, did our talk. There we were, solidly one for those moments at least, leaning our arms easily along the cool wood, reaching without thought for our little cups of hot bitter coffee or our glasses, not laughing perhaps as the families do in the pictures and the stories, but with our eyes loving and deep, one to another. It was good, worth the planning. It made the other necessary mass meals more endurable, more a part of being that undeniable rock, the Family.

1

There is an inevitable ritual about serving and eating spaghetti. Sometimes when I have endured the pompous stewings and simmerings and scrapings and tastings of an amateur chef's performance (for it can be called no less), I have felt that nothing at all would be preferable. But, fortunately for me, I like good spaghetti too well to forego it.

The first time I ever saw it eaten as it should be, in varying degrees of longness and a fine uniformity of writhing limpness and buttery richness and accompanying noisy sounds, I was fairly young, fourteen or so. I was old enough to be conscious of wearing my best manners, for I was upstairs in Los Angeles' one elegant restaurant, and the fact that it was Ignace Paderewski I watched with such fascination did nothing to alleviate my priggish horror at the spectacle. That he was obviously enjoying himself could not, at my tender age, mean much: I still thought in terms of being sent away from the table for glupping and spilling, both of which he did nonchalantly. For a long time I pondered on the whole strange sight.

What undoubtedly made it stranger still to me was the way spaghetti was always served at home. There it was, and still is, the cook's easiest choice for using leftover beef or lamb. In spite of the mediocrity of inspiration, we loved its soft texture and its warmth, the little broken lengths of pasta, the various bits of meat crumbs and tomato and cheese, and the crust that formed on top of it in the baking. We still do, and no matter what life has done to our taste buds, when we are home for a week end or a week, we hope there will be enough fried chicken or pot roast left for Helen to make spaghetti.

My natural revolt against this uninspired, misbegotten pattern filled me, when I left the nest, with overenthusiasm for the gymnastics of the amateurs, and I hate now to think of the sticky lukewarm messes I have happily downed, sitting, ah, *vie bohème,* upon a dirty studio floor with a glass of red ink beside me. But, come to think of it, I do *not* hate that thought! I look back on it, relieved both to be able to look back and to have its unthinking youthful liveliness to look back *on.*

I prefer, I add with no haste, the present. I prefer, infinitely, my own routine for making and serving spaghetti, for I have come to admit that no matter how simply it is done, it involves enough calculation and timing to qualify as a real performance, like any theatrical routine. There is an apt description of it, by James M. Cain, in Merle Armitage's *Fit for a King.* What he says about the quickness and the hotness of everything is what I too would say. He gives typically virile recipes for two sauces to be served with the plain cooked spaghetti, according to taste. Then he writes, "There is always one peculiar fellow, the same one who always puts salt in his beer, who likes his with butter only, so a little butter on the table won't hurt."

Now I never put salt in my beer, nor do I ever plan to. But I am one of Mr. Cain's "peculiar fellows" in that I like not only spaghetti but every other form of pastasciutta without a trace of the popular and indeed socially requisite sauces that always coat them or swim alongside. I go so far as never to serve them at my own table, and I can add smugly that many a confirmed sauce-man has left my table converted to my theory that nothing helps fresh hot spaghetti as much as a plenitude of sweet butter, freshly ground pepper, and good grated Parmesan cheese, all added at top speed and tossed and mixed regardless of fourteen-year-old stares like the one I gave the innocent Paderewski, the whole washed down with a good Chianti or a Tipo Red.

I must confess that it is in a way harder to achieve my seeming simplicity, hew to my chastity of design, than to ask some one of my eager food-and-wine club acquaintances to come in and devastate the kitchen in the creation of one of his Famous Spaghetti Dinners. I can remember all too many weighty pinches of saffron and thunderous hints of sweet marjoram, in the name of this gastronomical oddity, and cannot help feeling, in all cynicism, that a quantity of preprandial highballs had more to do with the half-famished guests' acclamations than did any real goodness in the dish itself.

I have watched a great many off-the-record culinary shows, nonprofessional of course, and I think that the production of a large platter of spaghetti in its sauce calls forth more of the prima donna in the average amateur cook than anything, except, perhaps, crêpes Suzette. One otherwise sober friend of mine goes so far as to assemble all the guests, let them watch a few simple but dramatic processes such as searing the chopped beef and then dousing the blue-black choking fumes with red wine, and immediately afterward makes his invited spectators leave the kitchen, at once, peremptorily, and bound to silence, while he bends tensely over a secret packet of spices he has procured at great expense and brought, seemingly, to the noisy staccato of gunfire from rival chefs who would kill him for his treasure and the proportions therein.

Here is the way, ridiculous anticlimax, that I myself serve spaghetti and prefer that it be served to me. I am, to quote Mr. Cain again, "peculiar."

Have a bowl of grated Parmesan, genuine and sandy and unadulterated by domestic packaged stuff; a large pat of sweet butter; a good salt shaker and a freshly filled pepper-mill; as many hot plates as there are people, and a big, hot casserole with a lump of butter melting in the bottom.

Cook good spaghetti rapidly in plenty of boiling water. (If the spaghetti is really reputable I do not salt the pot.) When half cooked add a lump of butter or a tablespoonful of olive oil; this keeps the water from boiling over and seems to eliminate the danger of sticking. When a strand of the spaghetti (of course not broken beforehand) can be pinched between my thumb and forefinger, I think it is done, somewhat more than *al dente* but not too soft. Then pour it, throw it almost, into a big colander, dash very cold water thoroughly through it and then boiling hot water even more thoroughly (I know this is a heinous procedure to some gastronomical purists), and shake it furiously to dry it off a little. Pour it, blazing hot, into the almost sizzling casserole, and serve it immediately on the equally hot plate of whoever is hungry for it.

The next step precludes any so-called table manners: it must be carried out with rapidity, a skill easy to enlarge by pleasurable practice, and undaunted enthusiasm. Put a generous lump of sweet butter on top of the pile of spaghetti (first served first come . . .); shake and twist on the salt and pepper, also generously; pile Parmesan on top, and with your fork mix the whole into an odorous, steamy, rich, Medusa-like tangle.

All that is left is to eat it. That, according to the general air of *bien-être* and relaxation which should by now have spread through the company, is perhaps best left undescribed. Let us say that Paderewski did it beautifully.

G *is for* Gluttony

. . . AND why and how it is that.

It is a curious fact that no man likes to call himself a glutton, and yet each of us has in him a trace of gluttony, potential or actual. I cannot believe that there exists a single coherent human being who will not confess, at least to himself, that once or twice he has stuffed himself to the bursting point, on anything from quail financière[1] to flapjacks, for no other reason than the beastlike satisfaction of his belly. In fact I pity anyone who has not permitted himself this sensual experience, if only to determine what his own private limitations are, and where, for himself alone, gourmandism ends and gluttony begins.

It is different for each of us, and the size of a man's paunch has little to do with the kind of appetite which fills it. Diamond Jim Brady, for instance, is more often than not called "the greatest glutton in American history," and so on, simply because he had a really enormous capacity for food. To my mind he was not gluttonous but rather monstrous, in that his stomach was about six times normal size. That he ate at least six times as much as a normal man did not make him a glutton. He was, instead, Gargantuan, in the classical sense. His taste was keen and sure to the time of his death, and that he ate nine portions of sole Marguéry the night George Rector brought the recipe back to New York from Paris especially for him does not mean that he gorged himself upon it but simply that he had room for it.

I myself would like to be able to eat that much of something I really delight in, and I can recognize overtones of envy in the way lesser mortals so easily damned Brady as a glutton, even in the days of excess when he flourished.

Probably this country will never again see so many fat, rich men as were prevalent at the end of the last century, copper kings and railroad millionaires and suchlike literally stuffing themselves to death in imitation of Diamond Jim, whose abnormally large stomach coincided so miraculously with the period. He ate a hundred men like "Betcha-Million" Gates into their oversized coffins simply because he was a historical accident, and it is interesting to speculate on what his influence would be today, when most of the robber barons have gastric ulcers and lunch off crackers and milk at their desks. Certainly it is now unfashionable to overeat in public, and the few real trenchermen left are careful to practice their gastronomical excesses in the name of various honorable and respected food-and-wine societies.

It is safe to say, I think, that never again in our civilization will gluttony be condoned, much less socially accepted, as it was at the height of Roman decadence, when a vomitorium was as necessary a part of any well-appointed home as a powder room is today, and throat-ticklers were as common as our Kleenex. That was, as one almost forgotten writer has said in an unforgettable phrase, the "period of insatiable voracity and the peacock's plume," and I am glad it is far behind me, for I would make but a weak social figure of a glutton, no matter to what excesses of hunger I could confess.

My capacity is very limited, fortunately for my inward as well as outer economy, so that what gluttonizing I have indulged in has resulted in biliousness more spiritual than physical. It has, like almost everyone's in this century, been largely secret. I think it reached its peak of purely animal satisfaction when I was about seventeen.

I was cloistered then in a school where each avid, yearning young female was allowed to feed at least one of her several kinds of hunger with a daily chocolate bar. I evolved for myself a strangely voluptuous pattern of borrowing, hoarding, begging, and otherwise collecting about seven or eight of these noxious sweets and eating them alone upon a pile of pillows when all the other girls were on the hockey field or some such equally healthful place. If I could eat at the same time a nickel box of soda crackers, brought to me by a stooge among the day girls, my orgiastic pleasure was complete.

I find, in confessing this far-distant sensuality, that even the cool detachment acquired with time does not keep me from feeling both embarrassed and disgusted. What a pig I was!

I am a poor figure of a glutton today in comparison with that frank adolescent cramming. In fact I can think of nothing quite like it in my present make-up. It is true that I overeat at times, through carelessness or a deliberate prolonging of my pleasure in a certain taste, but I do not do it with the voracity of youth. I am probably incapable, really, of such lust. I rather regret it: one more admission of my dwindling powers!

Perhaps the nearest I come to gluttony is with wine. As often as possible, when a really beautiful bottle is before me, I drink all I can of it, even when I know that I have had more than I want physically. That is gluttonous.

But I think to myself, when again will I have this taste upon my tongue? Where else in the world is there just such wine as this, with just this bouquet, at just this heat, in just this crystal cup? And when again will I be alive to it as I am this very minute, sitting here on a green hillside above the sea, or here in this dim, murmuring, richly odorous restaurant, or here in this fishermen's café on the wharf? More, more, I think—all of it, to the last exquisite drop, for there is no satiety for me, nor ever has been, in such drinking.

Perhaps this keeps it from being gluttony—not according to the dictionary but in my own lexicon of taste. I do not know.

l

The word *financière*, for fairly obvious reasons, means richness, extravagance, a nonchalant disregard of the purse, but I sometimes suspect that I use it oftener than it warrants to denote anything Lucullan. I need only reread some Victorian cookery books to reassure myself and justify my preoccupation with the word.

I imagine that now and then, in the remotest dining clubs of London and Lisbon, in the most desperately spendthrift of *nouveaux-riches* private kitchens, quails are still served *à la financière*, and unless I am much mistaken they are prepared almost to the letter as Queen Victoria's kitchen contemporaries did them. Her own chef Francatelli scamps on the sauce but elaborates with pardonable smugness his method for the whole entrée, and his rival Soyer of the Reform Club makes up for it by giving a recipe for the sauce alone that would stun modern gourmets.

Herewith I present them both, *chefs-d'oeuvres* of two dashing culinary kings, flashing-eyed, soft-lipped prancing fellows if the engravings printed at their own expense in their two cookbooks are even half true.

SOYER'S SAUCE À LA FINANCIÈRE

Put a wineglassful of sherry into a stewpan with a piece of glaze the size of a walnut, and a bay-leaf, place it upon the fire, and when it boils add a quart of demi-glace; let it boil ten minutes, keeping it stirred; then add twelve fresh blanched mushrooms, twelve prepared cock's-combs, a throat sweetbread cut in thin slices, two French preserved truffles also in slices, and twelve small veal forcemeat quenelles; boil altogether ten minutes, skim it well, thin it with a little consommé if desired, but it must be rather thick, and seasoned very palatably.

This is of course from *The Gastronomic Regenerator*, which the famous Reform Club's even more famous chef dedicated to the Duke of Cambridge in 1847. It can be assumed at our safe distance that the Queen's cook needed no lessons from the Club's, but even so Francatelli's sauce recipe is less interesting. His detailed method, though, for preparing the quail with and for the sauce is a fine prose poem to the God of Gastronomical Surfeit, and I give it here for modern pondering.

FRANCATELLI'S QUAILS À LA FINANCIÈRE

Remove the bones entirely from eight fat quails, reserve the livers, and add to them half a pound of fat livers of fowl, with which prepare some force-meat, and stuff the quails with part of this; they must then be trussed in the usual manner, and placed in a stewpan with layers of fat bacon under them, a garnished faggot of parsley in the centre, and covered with layers of fat bacon; moisten with some wine mirepoix, and braize them gently for about three-quarters of an hour. Prepare a rich Financière sauce, which must be finished with some of the liquor in which the quails have been braized. When about to send to table, warm the quails, drain and dish them up, garnish the centre with the Financière, pour some of the sauce around the entrée, and serve.

This recipe is rather reminiscent of Brillat-Savarin's method for pheasant à la Sainte Alliance, although less pure, gastronomically speaking. He would, I think, have shuddered at applying it in no matter how simplified a form to quails, of which he wrote, "A man betrays his ignorance every time he serves one cooked otherwise than roasted or *en papillote,* for its aroma is most fragile, and dissolves, evaporates, and vanishes whenever the little creature comes in contact with a liquid."

It has always astonished and horrified me that this pretty wild bird, which Brillat-Savarin called "the daintiest and most charming" of all of them, should be so thoroughly unpleasant to clean, once killed. Its innards, supposedly nourished on the tenderest of herbs and grains, send out a stench that is almost insupportable, and hunters dread the moment when they must cope with it, in order to savor somewhat later one of the finest tastes in all the world.

The best of these that I have ever eaten were in Juárez, Mexico, in two shoddy, delightful "clubs" where illegal game was cooked by Chinese chefs, the quails grilled quickly over desert-bush coals, split open flat, and brought sizzling and charred to the table, innocent of grease or seasoning, and served with a dollop of strangely agreeable cactus-apple conserve. They were superb, thus unhampered.

A recipe I would follow if I could is the classical one for Quails in Ashes, *Cailles sous la Cendre,* a true hunters' rule, whose prime requisite is a fine log fire!

Each clean, emptied bird is wrapped in thickly buttered grape leaves and good bacon. (This is supposedly late summer, when the grain-fattened birds have fled before the guns to the high fertile meadows, just before the vineyards begin to turn gold.) Then they are enclosed in sturdy, buttered "parchment" paper, put in the hot ashes, and left there for a half hour or a little more, with fresher hotter cinders raked over them from time to time. When ready to be served, the paper is cut off, and the inward-reaching layers of bacon, grape leaf, and tender quail send out such a vapor, I know, as would rouse Lazarus.

H *is for* Happy

... AND for what kind of dinner is most often just that evanescent, unpredictable, and purely heaven-sent thing.

In general, I think, human beings are happiest at table when they are very young, very much in love, or very lone. It is rare to be happy in a group: a man can be merry, gay, keenly excited, but not happy in the sense of being free—free from life's cluttering and clutching.

When I was a child my Aunt Gwen (who was not an aunt at all but a large-boned and enormous-hearted woman who, thank God, lived next door to us) used to walk my little sister Anne and me up into the hills at sundown. She insisted on pockets. We had to have at least two apiece when we were with her. In one of them, on these twilight promenades, would be some cookies. In the other, oh, deep sensuous delight! would be a fried egg sandwich![1]

Nobody but Aunt Gwen ever made fried egg sandwiches for us. Grandmother was carefully protected from the fact that we had ever even heard of them, and as for Mother, preoccupied with a second set of children, she shuddered at the thought of such grease-bound proteins with a thoroughness which should have made us chary but instead succeeded only in satisfying our human need for secrets.

The three of us, Aunt Gwen weighing a good four times what Anne and I did put together, would sneak out of the family ken whenever we could, into the blue-ing air, our pockets sagging and our spirits spiraling in a kind of intoxication of freedom, breathlessness, fatigue, and delicious anticipation. We would climb high above other mortals, onto a far rock or a fallen eucalyptus tree, and sit there, sometimes close as burrs and sometimes apart, singing straight through *Pinafore* and the Episcopal Hymn Book (Aunt Gwen was

618

British and everything from contralto to basso profundo in the Whittier church choir), and biting voluptuously into our tough, soggy, indigestible and luscious suppers. We flourished on them, both physically and in our tenacious spirits.

Lone meals, which can be happy too, are perhaps the hardest to put on paper, with a drop of cyanide on their noses and a pin through their guts. They are the fleetingest of the gastronomical butterflies. I have known some. We all have. They are compounded in almost equal parts of peace, nostalgia, and good digestion, with sometimes an amenable touch of alcohol thrown in.

As for dining-in-love, I think of a lunch at the Lafayette in New York, in the front café with the glass pushed back and the May air flowing almost visibly over the marble tabletops, and a waiter named Pons, and a bottle of Louis Martini's Folle Blanche and moules-more-or-less-marinières but delicious, and then a walk in new black-heeled shoes with white stitching on them beside a man I had just met and a week later was to marry, in spite of my obdurate resolve never to marry again and my cynical recognition of his super-salesmanship. Anyone in the world could dream as well . . . being blessed . . .

Group happiness is another thing. Few of us can think with honesty of a time when we were indeed happy at table with more than our own selves or one other. And if we succeed in it, our thinking is dictated no matter how mysteriously by the wind, the wine, and the wish of that particular moment.

Now, for no reason that I consciously know of, I remember a lunch at the Casino at Berne, in Switzerland. I was with my father and mother, my husband, and a friend deep in his own murky moods but still attainable socially. We had driven there from Vevey, and we sat in the glass-enclosed bourgeois sparkle of the main dining-room with a fine combination of tired bones and bottoms, thirst, hunger, and the effect of altitude.

I do not recall that we drank anything stronger than sherry before lunch, but we may have; my father, a forthright man who had edited a paper in the hard-liquor days when his Midwest village had fifteen saloons and three churches or thereabouts, may have downed a drink or two of Scotch, or the Bernese play on words, *ein Gift*, aptly called "poison" and made of half sweet vermouth and half any alcohol from vodka to gin.

Then, and this is the part I best remember, we had carafes of a rosé wine that was believed to be at its peak, its consummateness, in Berne, and indeed in that very room. Zizerser it was called. It came in the open café pitchers with the Federal mark at the top, naming the liquid content. It was a gay, frivolous color. It was poured into fine glasses (they were one of the many good things about that casino) from a height of two feet or so, and miracle! it foamed! It bubbled! It was full of a magic gas, that wine, which melted out of it with every inch of altitude it lost, so that when I took down a case of it and proudly poured it lake-side, in Vevey, it was merely a pink pretty drink, flat as flat. In Berne it was champagne. We drank deep.

So did our driver, François, and later when a frenzied-looking mountaineer waved back our car, we drove on with nonchalance along a cliff road above fabulous gorges, singing "Covered all over with Sweet Violets" and "Dir Heimat" (ensemble) and "Rover Was Blind but Brave" (my mother), until finally a rock about half as big as our enormous old Daimler sailed lazily down in front of us and settled a few feet from the engine.

We stopped in time.

Another mountaineer, with tiny stars of gold in his ear lobes to make him hear better, dropped into sight from the pine forest. Go back, go back, he cried. We are blasting a new road. You might have been killed. All right, all right, we said.

He lingered, under the obvious spell of our happiness. We talked. My father introduced my mother as the sweetest singer in Onawa-iowa, which she once was. My husband breathed deeply, as if in sleep. My friend looked out over the plumy treetops and sighed for a lost love. François blinked in a surfeit of content. We all sat about, on felled branches and running boards, and drank some superlative cognac from an unlabeled bottle which my father had bought secretly from a Vevey wine merchant and brought along for just this important moment.

A couple more boulders drifted down and settled, dustily and noisily but without active danger, within a few feet of us.

The mountaineer sang three or four songs of his canton. Then, because of the Zizerser and mostly and mainly because we were for that one moment in all time a group of truly happy people, we began to yodel. My father, as a small-town editor, had the edge on us: he had practiced for years at the more unbridled of the local service-club luncheons and banquets. My mother found herself shooting off only too easily into *Aïda* and the more probable sections of *Parsifal*. My husband and even my friend hummed and buzzed, and I too buzzed and hummed. And François? He really yodeled, right along with the man from the mountains.

It was a fine thing. Whatever we had eaten at lunch, trout I think, went properly with the Zizerser, and we were full and we were happy, beyond the wine and the brandy, beyond the immediate danger of blasted boulders and cascading slides, beyond any feeling of foolishness. If we had lunched on milk and pap, that noontime in the Casino, we still would have felt the outer-world bliss that was ours, winy and full, on the Oberland mountainside that summer day.

It happened more than ten years ago, but if I should live a hundred and ten more I would still feel the freedom of it.

1

AUNT GWEN'S FRIED EGG SANDWICHES
INGREDIENTS (*Physical*)

½ to 1 cup drippings	12 *slices bread*
6 *fresh eggs*	*waxed paper*

The drippings are very English, the kind poured off an unidentified succession of beef, mutton, and bacon pans, melted gradually into one dark puddle of thick unappetizing grease, which immediately upon being dabbed into a thick hot iron skillet sends out rendingly appetizing smells.

The eggs must be fresh, preferably brown ones, best of all freckled brown ones.

The bread must be good bread, no puffy, blanched, uniform blotters from a paper cocoon.

The waxed paper must be of honest quality, since at the corners where it will leak a little some of it will stick to the sandwich and in a way merge with it and be eaten.

INGREDIENTS (*Spiritual*)

These have been amply indicated in the text, and their prime requisite—Aunt Gwen herself would be the first to cry no to any further exposition of them. Suffice it that they were equal parts of hunger and happiness.

METHOD

Heat the drippings in a wide flat-bottomed skillet until they spit and smoke. Break in the eggs, which will immediately bubble around the edges, making them crisp and indigestible, and break their yolks with a fork and swirl them around, so that they are scattered fairly evenly through the whites. This will cook very quickly, and the eggs should be tough as leather.

Either push them to one side of the pan or remove them, and fry bread in the drippings for each sandwich, two slices to an egg. It too will send off a blue smoke. Fry it on one side only, so that when the sandwiches are slapped together their insides will turn soggy at once. Add to this sogginess by pressing them firmly together. Wrap them well in the waxed paper, where they will steam comfortably.

These sandwiches, if properly made and wrapped, are guaranteed, if properly carried in sweater or pinafore pockets, to make large oily stains around them.

Seasoning depends on the state of the drippings. As I remember Aunt Gwen's, they were such a "fruity" blend of last week's roast, last month's gammon, that salt and pepper would have been an insult to their fine flavor.

PRESCRIPTION

To be eaten on top of a hill at sunset, between trios of "A Wandering Minstrel I" and "Onward Christian Soldiers," preferably before adolescence and its priggish queasiness set in.

I is for Innocence

... AND its strangely rewarding chaos, gastronomically.

There is a great difference in my mind between innocence in this gourmand interpretation, and ignorance. The one presupposes the other, and yet a truly innocent cook or host is never guilty of the great sin of pretension, while many an ignorant one errs hideously in this direction.

Almost any man who is potentially capable of thus cheating his guests is also incapable of telling the truth to himself and will sneak a quick look into a primer of wine names, for instance, and then pretend that he knew all along to serve red wine with red meat or some such truism. His lie will betray his basic insecurity.

An innocent, on the other hand, will not bother to pretend any knowledge at all. He will, with a child's bland happiness, do the most God-awful things with his meals, and manage by some alchemy of warmth and understanding to make any honest gourmet pleased and easy at his table.

The best example of this that I can think of happened to me a few months ago.

I know a large, greedy, and basically unthinking man who spent all the middle years of his life working hard in a small town and eating in waffle shops and now and then gorging himself at friends' houses on Christmas Day. Quite late he married a large, greedy, and unthinking woman who introduced him to the dubious joys of whatever she heard about on the radio: Miracle Sponge Delight, Aunt Martha's Whipped Cheese Surprise, and all the homogenized, pasteurized, vitalized, dehydratized products intrinsic to the preparation of the Delights and the Surprises. My friend was happy.

He worked hard in the shop and his wife worked hard at the stove, her sink-side portable going full blast in order not to miss a single culinary hint. Each night they wedged themselves into their breakfast-bar-dinette and ate and ate and ate. They always meant to take up Canfield, but somehow they felt too sleepy. About a year ago he brought home a little set of dominoes, thinking it would be fun to shove the pieces around in a couple of games of Fives before she cleared the table. But she looked hard at him, gave a great belch, and died.

He was desperately lonely. We all thought he would go back to living in the rooming-house near the shop, or take up straight rye whisky, or at least start raising tropical fish.

Instead he stayed home more and more, sitting across from the inadequate little chromiumed chair his wife had died in, eating an almost ceaseless meal. He cooked it himself, very carefully. He listened without pause to her radio, which had literally not been turned off since her death. He wrote down every cooking tip he heard, and "enclosed twenty-five cents in stamps" for countless packages of Whipperoo, Jellerino, and Vita-glugg. He wore her tentlike aprons as he bent over the stove and the sink and the solitary table, and friends told me never, never, *never* to let him invite me to a meal.

But I liked him. And one day when I met him in the Pep Brothers' Shopping Basket—occasionally I fought back my claustrophobia-among-the-cans long enough to go there for the best frozen fruit in town—he asked me so nicely and straightforwardly to come to supper with him that I said I'd love to. He lumbered off, a look of happy purpose wiping the misery from his big face; it was like sunlight breaking through smog. I felt a shudder of self-protective worry, which shamed me.

The night came, and I did something I very seldom do when I am to be a guest: I drank a sturdy shot of dry vermouth and gin, which I figured from long experience would give me an appetite immune to almost any gastronomical shocks. I was agreeably mellow and uncaring by the time I sat down in the chair across from my great, wallowing, bewildered friend and heard him subside with a fat man's alarming *puff!* into his own seat.

I noticed that he was larger than ever. You like your own cooking, I teased. He said gravely to me that gastronomy had saved his life and reason, and before I could recover from the shock of such fancy words on his strictly one-to-two syllable tongue, he had jumped up lightly, as only a fat man can, and started opening oven doors.

We had a tinned "fruit cup,"[1] predominantly gooseberries and obviously a sop to current health hints on station JWRB. Once having disposed of this bit of medical hugger-muggery, we surged on happily through one of the ghastliest meals I ever ate in my life. On second thought I can safely say, *the* ghastliest. There is no point in describing it, and to tell the truth a merciful mist has blurred its high points. There was too much spice where there should be none; there was sogginess where crispness was all-important; there was an artificially whipped and heavily sweetened canned-milk dessert where nothing at all was wanted.

And all through the dinner, in the small, hot, crowded room, we drank lukewarm Muscatel, a fortified dessert wine sold locally in gallon jugs, mixed in cheese-spread glasses with equal parts of a popular bottled lemon soda. It is incredible, but it happened.

I am glad it did. I know now what I may only have surmised theoretically before: there is indeed a gastronomic innocence, more admirable and more enviable than any cunning cognizance of menus and vintages and kitchen subtleties. My gross friend, untroubled by affectations of knowledge, served forth to me a meal that I was proud to partake of. If I felt myself at times a kind of sacrificial lamb, stretched on the altar of devotion, I was glad to be that lamb, for never was nectar poured for any goddess with more innocent and trusting enjoyment than was my hideous glass filled with a mixture of citric acid, carbon dioxide, and pure vinous hell for me. I looked into the little gray eyes of my friend and drank deep and felt the better for it.

He had not pretended with me nor tried to impress me. He knew I liked to eat, so he had cooked for me what he himself enjoyed the most. He remembered hearing somewhere that I liked wine with my meals, so he had bought "the mixings," as he knew them, because he wanted me to feel gay and relaxed and well thought of, there in his dear woman's chair, with her radio still blasting and her stove still hot. I felt truly grateful, and I too felt innocent.

l

My father, who was born within shouting distance of the back room of his parents' small-town newspaper office, and was making up forms on a tombstone when he was nine, and has been a small-town news-paperman for a good sixty years since, claims to have been served more fruit cup than any man alive.

He may well be right: he has gone to an unaccountable number of Chamber of Commerce Semi-Annual Luncheons, Get-Together Suppers, and service-club Annual Banquets, not to mention Father-Daughter Feeds, and gastronomical assemblies to Let-Us-Caponize-Our-Pullets Week, Be-Kind-to-the-Walnut-Pickers Month, and Better-Butter Year. And at a probable nine out of every ten of these feasts he has sat down, cold (unless previously warmed by a discreet stirrup cup *chez lui*), to a short-stemmed glass filled with a seemingly patented and changeless mixture of overcooked tinned fruits, always with a cherry lurking somewhere between its recommended place on top and the watery bottom.

Father mentions this dubious honor, world's champion of fruit-cup contemplaters, with a quiet, fatalistic pride. He says, when pressed, that he feels none the worse for the long siege, and that he infinitely prefers this gastronomical test to any other he can think of in the lexicon of small-town feastings.

Soups are impossible. The Ladies' Guilds and suchlike, which most often agree to serve the local merchants for a set weekly fee, are incapable, either in equipment or skill, of presenting a hot palatable broth to their contracted numbers, which may range from twenty to five hundred, always with a proportionate ten per cent of unexpected delegations from neighboring towns.

Salads are universally shunned: the Ladies dislike them because they wilt and don't look pretty, and diners dislike them because the Ladies don't seem to know how to make them fit to swallow.

Any such outlandish and foreign appetizer as an inexpensive and stimulating canapé of something is rife with political, religious, and cultural suspicion, and therefore best left unconsidered.

There remains the fruit cup. It can be put on the tables anywhere from half an hour to half a day before the feast, depending on the weather. It looks, the Ladies say, "nice," no matter how long it has stood, and the best local cooks know to a fine drop how much of the canned liquid to allow to each cup so that it will stay moist but not too soupy. It comes in gallon tins, much cheaper and more generally successful than any fussy mixture of fresh local fruits. What is more, housewives who want to please husbands who have grown used to it in their business lives can make it just as well at home, from a can marked with some faintly varying version of the following: "diced Bartlett pears, diced yellow peaches, pineapple tidbits, best gooseberries, artificially colored, artificially flavored modified cherries in heavy syrup."

Almost any of these mentioned edibles (if indeed considered edible —there is some question about gooseberries) is worth a passing query, but I think the modified cherries have the finest ring of fantasy to them. What has modified them? And how?

To be truthful, I have no great enthusiasm for fruits as an appetizer, as a prelude to higher flavor (unless tomatoes be considered a fruit, which technically they are). I have eaten chilled slender slices of melon in the summertime, in Europe and in California, that were delicious, but no temptation to continue to anything else, which they were meant to be. Rather, I would have stopped with them, and sipped cold wine an hour longer with none but their own delicate flavor upon my tongue. In Italy I have eaten figs, as well as melons, served with prosciutto, ripe, seedy, overpowering figs warring with the salt challenge of the ham, and I have liked them very much. And Escoffier gives as an appetizer a recipe for chilled figs served peeled on a bed of green leaves and ice.

I still rebel.

Perhaps it is a latent hereditary revolt, handed on to me by my well-mannered, incredibly tolerant father. Perhaps if he were laid out on a psychoanalyist's couch, he would babble of fruit cups, gooseberries as green as the mayor, pineapple sharp as the advertiser who cut off his account last week after Father printed the story of his son's drunken-driving fine, peaches and pears and syrup as bland as the small-town diplomacy my sire has practiced for so long —and all of it served, and then eaten, with a common compassion, the good women in the kitchen, the good men bending over the banquet trestles, considering flood control, and rent control, and pest control—and fruit cup.

J *is for* Juvenile *dining*

. . . AND the mistakenness of adults who think that the pappy pabulum stuffed down their children's gullets is swallowed, when and if it is swallowed, with anything more than weak helplessness and a bitter if still subconscious acceptance of the hard fact that they must eat to survive.

I myself was fascinated witness to the first bite of so-called "solid food" my elder daughter took.

Quite aside from my innate conviction that she is unusually subtle and sensitive, I considered her at that moment undeniably *normal,* and felt that I was watching a kind of cosmic initiation to what, if I had anything to say about it, would be a lifetime of enjoyment of the pleasures of the table. I was depressed, then, to see such a thorough, bone-shaking, flesh-creeping shudder flash through her wee frame when the spoonful of puréed green beans touched her tongue, as I had known before only in the tragicomic picture of a hung-over bindlestiff downing his morning shot of red-eye. She shook from top to toe in a real throe of revulsion. Then she looked at me, and speculation grew in her wide gaze.

I wondered in a kind of panic if perhaps true papillary bliss lay in a lifetime of bottle-feeding. While the child stared at me I ate a spoonful of her stuff, not to goad her into taking more of it but to see if I too would shudder. I did: it had a foully metallic taste, even to me whose tongue was perforce much duller than her innocent uncalloused one.

But she must eat puréed green beans, I thought, if I want her to flourish and go on to better things. So I took what was left in her silver porringer and put it in a porcelain bowl, feeling somewhat helplessly that thus I might curb the nasty taste of metal.

628

Perhaps I did; I'm not sure. I know that when I brought the dish back to my babe she opened her mouth, poker-faced, and ate everything with only a faint sigh to show her helplessness.

Since then, over some five years, she has progressed with a mixture of common sense and emotion through several stages of appreciation. She likes things with salt on them, feeling instinctively the stimulus of that abused flavoring (which I seldom allow her), and this morning when I asked her with clinical interest what she most loved to eat she told me without hesitation that it was potato chips. As far as I know she has never eaten one in her life. But she has heard me say how salty they are, and that, combined with the fact that she has also heard me say that I adore them (but don't eat them because they are hellishly fattening), made her answer like a flash that she adored them too.

She does not want *fat* things, too much sweet butter on her bread and such. She hates, with a real intensity, pepper; and I suppose she would react in the same clear-cut way to other hot seasonings, curry, for instance.

She does not like whisky or brandy for the same instinctively protective reasons, but she enjoys an occasional apéritif of Dubonnet or white wine with soda water (proportions about one to fifty, I would say), which she clicks against my glass with the proper *Salud* or *Santé* or *Na Zdarovia*.

She has the waistline of an especially slim bee and eats about six minuscule meals a day, for lack of space I suppose, and almost every day I give her one taste of something from the grown-up board, to prepare her, toughen her, indoctrinate her.

One time it is a nibble of Wisconsin Cheddar as big as a pinhead. She likes it. Another time it is a microscopic smear of Camembert or Liederkranz. She pulls away, shocked by its fine odor of putrescence, too decadent for her simplicity. I let her taste a Coke, knowing fatalistically that she must inevitably absorb them for social reasons. And it is the same with candy bars and grocery-store cakes and all that: I feel that I must harden her to their packaged onslaught rather than shield her from it, since she is to be a good, well-balanced American citizen.

So far the only thing in this category of preventive nutrition that she yearns for is a popsickle, which she was once given by a well-meaning ranch hand and which in retrospect has acquired all the nostalgic beauty that I myself attribute to a truffled pâté I ate too many years ago during the Foire Gastronomique in Dijon.

As for the Cokes and cookies I use experimentally on her to accustom her to them, she is polite but largely uninterested; she will eat them, but ho-hum is the word. It is a different thing with "bought" bread. Most of the stuff that comes already sliced and in waxed paper she picks up, occasionally smells, and then puts quietly down again, no matter what strength of hunger gnaws at her.

Fortunately I can buy, more often than not, a brand of bread that is not only edible but good. It is brown as the ripe earth, nutty, moist, and inescapably honest. My daughter feels this honesty the way she would feel terror at a madman's leer, with an intuitive knowledge. When she has not known I was watching, I have seen her sniff a crust of this good stuff and smile, unthinking as a puppy but absolutely right.

And I have thought sadly how far we have come from our forefathers in Latvia or Sicily or Cornwall who once so honored bread that if they dropped a piece of it on the floor they begged its pardon. In our country today it is in a sorry wax-bound servitude, so weak that it must be reinforced with chemicals, so tricked-out that a hungry dog or cat will not eat the puffy stuff unless it is actually starving.

My child likes a kind of pattern to her meals: I put raisins in rows, instead of willy-nilly, on a slice of buttered toast, or rounds of banana in an X or an A over the top of her applesauce[1]—A is for Anne, and X is, but naturally, for X-citing! Now and then, pure gastronomical fillip, there is a faint dash of cinnamon, a touch of nutmeg.

In five years she has been sick only once, in the good old English sense of the word, and that was psychosomatic rather than digestive, when a brush fire threatened us.

She seems to have a constant and lively speculation about taste and a truly "curious nose," which reassures me when I remember her first instinctive shudder, and which keeps me watching, trying, testing, and always using my wits to avoid havoc. I want her to have a keen palate, inquisitive but never tyrannical. I want her to be able to eat at least one taste of anything in the world, from Beluga caviar to porcupine grilled with locusts, with social impunity and a modicum of inquisitive gusto.

I want her to shun such gluttonous excesses as those of two small boys we know who, like half-starved beasts, wait with an unhealthy intensity for the aftermath of their parents' cocktail parties and then drain every glass and strip the messed hors d'oeuvres trays of every crumb of shriveled anchovy and withered olive.

I want her, on the other hand, to avoid such back-to-the-earth gourmandism as is betrayed by the earnest addicts of stone-ground, hand-trampled, nature-cured (and inevitably mildewed and weevilly) buckwheat groats and such, who, I find, are pretty dull once they have been fed—and/or eaten.

I am doing all I can to turn Anne into a sentient, intelligent, voluptuously restrained gastronomer, with a clear recognition of the odds of modern "improvements": pasteurization, dehydration, *et al.*; with firm resolves never to make her eat anything, from oatmeal gruel to escargots à la mode de Bourgogne,[2] and never to hurry her; and with a constant excitement and a growing conviction that I am giving her something much more precious than Great-Aunt Jennie's topaz parure.

l

My mother used to make the best applesauce I have ever eaten, and the only recipe I have found that uses her "trick" is in Marion Harland's *Common Sense in the Household: A Manual of Practical Housewifery*, which was published in 1871 and which by a completely unstrange coincidence belonged to my mother's mother.

My mother's trick, thus obviously passed on to her, is to stir in a plump lump of honest butter just as the mixture is to be removed from the stove. It is, to my knowledge, infallible—that is, if you like applesauce that is somewhat lumpy, never, never, *never* puréed, never, never, *never* flavored with vanilla or lemon-zest as if it were a sissified pudding; it is a lightly cooked mixture of pared apple quarters and brown sugar, doused, once in its bowl, with a bit of powdered cinnamon, no more.

But, ah, that rich Victorian touch of the butter pat! Ah, the good, almost grainy texture, and the forthright ugly color of it in a sauce dish, with milk alongside or a slab of hot gingery molasses cake! Ah, nothing but *applesauce*—even if Mrs. Harland did put her recipe among the Meat Garnishes and say, with her habitual firm authority, "It is the invariable accompaniment of roast pork—or fresh pork cooked in any way."

2

Many people eat snails, in every fashion from the most primitive one of burning the bushes upon which they feed and then sucking them hot and roasted from the ashy shells, to the most intricate, complete with specifically shaped brushes for scrubbing the involuted little houses and special forks for plucking them, correctly starved, fed, starved, washed, cooked, sauced, and finally broiled, from those same lovely shelters.

I cannot decide whether the idea of eating a snail is intuitively repulsive: by the time I myself was confronted by a plate of them, *chez* Crespin in Dijon, in about October of 1929, I had been conditioned by enough other gastronomical tests to be able to meet them with equanimity. I looked around the plain, pleasant little room, and at the end of it crossed glances with a visiting provincial, a woman about sixty with the full, coarse, ribald, moody face of a real Burgundian, happy that night at least. We looked at one another, and as we looked she slowly picked up three or four shells from the sizzling plate in front of her, tipped the hot garlicky juice from each one into her mouth, and then swabbed at it with a morsel of her crusty bread. I felt very young and glad for the lesson, and did likewise, with only a faint and final nod to whatever nascent prohibitions against the beasts themselves might have stayed with me.

Since then I have eaten snails prepared in perhaps five or six other ways and have not really liked them; they are basically a tough bite and need some such heady treatment as the one they get in Burgundy to interest me. Oddly enough I cannot find a recipe, à la bourguignonne, that sounds quite the way it should to produce those tender-green shimmering things that used to be piled in Dijon store windows in cool weather, prepared with such skill and patience to sell for a penny or so apiece, and then be taken home and heated on their special little dimpled platters to please the Côte d'Or gourmandizers and gourmets.

The nearest I can come to it is in, of all things, a collection of Bordeaux recipes! And it calls for minced mushrooms, which I feel pretty sure the Dijon snails did not have, and "a pinch of garlic" where they were dizzy with it.

But the slow, finicky preparation of the snails, the fasting, the washings, the boiling with a little sack of charcoal in the water—

all that sounds correct; and then the final aromatic mixture of herbs and sweet butter, which is packed smoothly over the snail, by now returned to its clean shell—that too has the rightful ring.

I know, though, that my young daughters would not like it—yet. They must wait many more years. It took me twenty or so, California being so far removed from France, and they perforce cannot have the indoctrination that made my friends Doudouce and Plume such seasoned tasters at the ages of ten and twelve, when I helped them pluck the snails from twigs and suffered with them through the tedium of preparation, in Dijon so long ago. Plume is now buried, and Doudouce disappeared, but the aura of true gastronomy that surrounded them is still strong in my mind and heart. I hope that my own children will know a little of it.

K *is for* Kosher

. . . AND for a few reasons that the dietary laws laid down by Jehovah to Moses in 1490 B.C. have rightly been called "one of the best economic regimes ever made public," gastronomically as well as otherwise.

These interdictions, which except to the orthodox Jews have come to mean very little beyond borscht and blintzes in any restaurant which displays the Star of David, are puzzling mainly because so few people really know them (including a great many modern Jews, who are astonished to learn that they can read them easily in Leviticus, the Third Book of Moses in the Old Testament—and very good reading it is, for anyone with a gourmet's "curious nose").

The complex rituals for the butchering and inspection of meats by properly trained men need bother no one, since these are taken care of by experts before food is bought and prepared for the table; but the ancient, sensible, good rules for cookery, to be followed or at least pondered on, are best told as Moses told them to his people more than a thousand years before the greatest Jew frightened the Romans in Jerusalem and then, after the Passover feast, died, perhaps to save them.

Pragmatism, of course, often triumphs over religious principles, as when, in G. B. Stern's *The Matriarch*, Babette Rakonitz inadvertently discovered the excellence of ham and managed to enjoy it for many a long year by pretending not to know what she was eating. It is easy to reason as Babette did, when wealth and wanderings have turned people willy-nilly into tolerant cosmopolites like the Rakonitzes. And there are many Jews like them.

It is the poorer ones, the oppressed, who have held fiercely and loyally to the ceremonial laws bound round and round them, who centuries after their nation disappeared, to rise again, stand un-

634

shakable as a people of great religious faith. It is an astonishing and moving thing that after so many flights from terror, after so many vigils in strange lands, many Jews still feast and fast as Moses told them to.

It is exciting, gastronomically, to recognize the influence of their wanderings in their wealth of dishes: olives and oil from Spain and Portugal; German sweet-and-sour stews; cucumbers, herrings, butter cakes, and grain rolls called bolas from the hospitable Dutchmen; fishes stewed and stuffed, and fremal soup made with goose drippings, from Poland; from Russia and Rumania the blintzes, the buckwheat groats called kasha and puddings called Kugel, the sweet heaviness of fruit compotes and preserves, and borscht thin or thick, hot or cold, any time of the clock or calendar.[1]

But it is not the international flavor of the Jewish cuisine that makes it really exciting; rather, it is the fact that many dietary and ceremonial laws have of necessity evolved a peculiar art of substitution, disguise, and even trickery (a trickery which has nothing to do with dishonesty, as was the case in rich Babette's delicate gluttony, but which is one solely of flavorings and spicings).

Fish is a much used dish of the Jews because of the many prohibitions about preparing and eating meats. Highly seasoned salmon, for instance, is one of the main dishes for the Sabbath, when all cooking is forbidden, since it can be made the day before and served delectably in a hundred ways when it is cold. Fish is convenient too, because there is no prohibition against cooking a cold-blooded animal with cream or cheese or any other milk products.

Meat is usually served only once daily in Jewish households that can afford it at all, but even so, relatively few vegetables are eaten in most orthodox homes, since they cannot be prepared with butter or cream at any meal containing meat, and the cooks are therefore not educated to cope with them. They are eaten more by the poor people in soups than by the wealthier classes, although salads are more in favor than they were even a few years ago.

In a city like New York the number of children from strict Jewish families is enormous and the public-school teachers have to adjust many of their courses to that fact. In Domestic Science, for instance, where little girls are taught the rudiments of cooking, it can become a serious emotional problem if kosher rules are violated, even unwittingly. The same is true in school cafeterias, where children face alienation from their parents if they "forget" and eat both meat and ice cream at lunch.

Fortunately there are a great many feasts to be observed by good Jews, but there are also alarming numbers of strict fasts. A few of them, like the Fast of Esther which precedes the Feast of Purim, are observed now only by the very religious, but Yom Kippur, the Day of Atonement, will be a period of purification and reflection as long as the world rolls, wherever a Jew may find himself.

There are semi-fasts too, such as a nine-day period in the summer heat when no meat should be eaten: a simple, dietetically sound rule to protect any wandering or ill-housed people, whether in the desert of Arabia a thousand years ago or in a New York tenement next August!

The rules for keeping Passover properly are many, and to a Gentile are mysterious as well as very confusing. The most bothersome prescription is the one that no utensil which has touched even a crumb of leavened bread can be used for eight days. This means that separate sets of dishes are needed, and that all the table silver and cutlery must be sterilized.

To "kasher" correctly (which means in Hebrew to make right or fit), red-hot stones are plunged into a kettle of boiling water and the various articles also immersed in it. They can be used when Passover has finished for that year, but must be kashered again before the next holiday. The special sets of table dishes are usually carefully wrapped and stored in a place where there is not even the faintest danger of their being polluted by the presence of leaven.

As a result of this and other kasher rules a strict orthodox family should have four complete sets of tableware: duplicate Passover sets, one for meat meals and one for dairy meals!

As for the house, it is scrubbed to the tinest mousehole before Passover, to avoid such dangers as even a forgotten cake crumb might cause.

Passover dishes are probably the most interesting of any in the Jewish cuisine because of the lack of leaven and the resulting challenge to fine cooks. There are all kinds of torten and almond cakes and puddings, and an infinity of uses for mazzah or matzos: matzo klos, or dumplings, cakes and puddings of the matzo meal. Everything is doubly rich, as if to compensate for the lack of leaven, and

clarified goose and chicken fat, and beef drippings carefully ex-
cluding suet, are used most artfully.

And it is thus that old Moses looked after his children, as well as in
his bluntly realistic attempts to protect them from pollution and
decay, dietetic as well as spiritual, in their wanderings through
the hot, filthy countries of the ancient world: he made them see to
it that the vessels for their feasting were sterile, freed from most
of their omnipresent bacteria by the ceremony, at once mystical and
practical, of kashering.

He forbade them to eat any kind of leaven, that fine proving
ground for digestive bubbles.

He let them soothe their starved nerves and muscles at least
once yearly with a wise unguent of fat, fat from the goose and
even, most carefully, from the cow . . . and as any refugee from
today's Europe knows, that is balm indeed, for hungering people
who have had no fat at all for too long a time become moody,
shiver easily, and grow sick.

Moses let his people lie back, now and then, upon whatever kind
of couch they could find, and eat and eat. Even today, at Passover,
they eat well if they eat at all, and woes are forgotten in the pleasures
of the table, for if the Mosaic laws are rightly followed, no man
need fear true poison in his belly, but only the results of his own
gluttony.

l

The taste for borscht and the prejudices thereof can involve as many
personal quirks as a recipe for hang-overs. I have ceased to take
them very seriously, for, after years of listening worshipfully to
one famous comedian swear that he would eat borscht at only one
restaurant in the whole world, where it was prepared magnificently
and as it *should* be, I went to that restaurant, ordered that borscht,
and found it a pale, watery, and indeed completely dishonest shadow
of what I myself, unfamous un-comedian, think good borscht should
be.

I believe that it is one of the best soups in the world. It can be hot,
cold, thick, thin, rich, meager—and still be good. It can be easy or
intricate to make.

Some people like it hot, with boiled beef in it, or quarters of cabbage (the variations on cabbage alone are almost infinite: chopped, minced, quartered, whole, on and on).

Some people like it cold, with chilled sour cream, poured over a steaming hot boiled potato in the middle of the plate.

Some people like grated fresh beets in it, and some like nothing at all, just the clear red consommé, and of course the cream.

Some people like little poached forcemeat balls in it.

Some people, apparently, like my comedian-friend, like it bad.

And then again there is the aspect of its sourness. Should it be fermented beets that give it its own peculiar sharpness, or fresh sliced beets in honest vinegar? Is it a heinous gastronomical sin to use the handier fresh lemon juice or vinegar instead of citric acid crystals from the corner drugstore? Should you spit it out and stalk from the table if it contains no sour taste at all, but rather the bland smoothness of a Little Borscht that can only be Polish if you are Russian, Russian if you are Finnish, and so on?

Well, I like it two ways the best, and these are they, one cold and easy to make, the other hot and comparatively complicated:

COLD SUMMER BORSCHT

1 *quart vegetable juice*	½ *to ¾ cup good vinegar*
1 *pint strong stock (canned con-*	1 *thinly sliced onion*
sommé is all right)	*salt, pepper, and so on*
1 *can sliced beets with juice*	

I say "and so on" because some people like a touch of clove or kümmel. The vegetable juice can be tinned or what is saved from pressure-cooking.

Pour the liquids into a casserole containing the canned sliced beets, their juice, the sliced onion, and the seasoning. Chill for 12 hours or more. Strain off the liquids and serve very cold with sour cream —and hot potatoes if desired.

HOT WINTER BORSCHT

16 *young beets*	*handful of parsley sprigs*
2½ *cups good vinegar*	2 *bay leaves*
3 *tablespoons butter or*	*salt, pepper*
chicken fat	3 *tablespoons flour*
2 *sweet onions*	3 *quarts rich beef stock*
4 *young carrots*	

Scrape and wash the beets and put 12 of them through the coarse meat grinder. Cover with the vinegar for several hours. Melt the fat, add the onions and carrots which have been coarsely ground, the chopped parsley, the bay leaves, and seasoning. Stir until golden, add half the flour, brown all well, then stir in the rest of the flour. Drain the ground beets thoroughly, saving ½ to 1 cup of the vinegar, and add them to the braised vegetables. Add the stock. Let simmer a half hour or until the vegetables are tender. Grate on a cheese grater the four remaining beets, mix them with the vinegar, and add to the soup five minutes before serving. Little sausage balls poached in boiling water can be added, and of course an accompanying bowl of sour cream is necessary.

L *is for* Literature

. . . AND the banquets it can serve forth, from the gorgeously photographed Spamola sur Bun à la mode de Fourth-of-July of a present-day advertisement to the phosphorescent elegance of a courtesan's memoirs, in which every dish at her table possesses, at least in legend, a special phallic importance.

There is no question that secondhand feasting can bring its own nourishment, satisfaction, and final surfeit. More than one escaped war prisoner has told me of the strange peacefulness that will come over a group of near-famished men in their almost endless talk of good food they remember and wish to eat again. They murmur on and on, in the cells or the walled yards, of pies their sisters used to make for them, and of the way Domenico in Tijuana grilled bootleg quail, and of the pasta at Boeucc' in prewar Milan. They swallow without active pain the prison's maggotty bread and watery soup, their spiritual palates drowned in a flood of recalled flavor and warmth and richness.

If they had books, they would be reading their banquet. For want of them they talk it, voluptuously repetitious, unconsciously fighting against the death of their five senses, without which they would indeed be death-condemned.

The men outside the walls are not so immediately menaced, but there are many of us who have found something of the same sensuous relief from our invisible and private prisons in gastronomical literature.

Given the fact that almost every gastronomer has some kind of literary predilection, it is amusing and interesting to speculate on the whys and whens of such a love. I know one man, for instance, who for fairly obvious reasons collects only political menus, from Julius Caesar's to Harry Truman's; and another who for equally

640

obvious reasons has little curiosity about any meal that has been served outside a brothel, to anyone but a whore or a whorer.

As for me, I sometimes think wistfully that it would be pleasant to be able so completely to limit myself! I have too much to read.

I have a fat pile of menus, actual ones dating from 1929 and book ones for the past five thousand years. Among them are the last dinner served *chez* Foyot, the ink already very faded, and an illuminated parchment limned by George Holl in San Francisco, the gold still bright although the round, witty gourmet is now gone, and a smudged paper from a Nazi *Bierstube* in Mexico, and another from a Loyalist café in Zurich where we drank out of bottles like udders, in squirts from the little glass dugs, as in a Hemingway story.

And there are so many books!

Why can I not limit myself to gastronomical novels, to *Hotel Imperial* by Arnold Bennett and *Work of Art* by Sinclair Lewis and all the stuff about hotels by Ludwig Bemelmans; or Huysmans and Saltus and Petronius and all those boys, new and old, who wrote of the excesses; or . . . or . . . or Virginia Woolf who wrote perhaps better than anyone in the Western world about the feeling of being a little drunk, or of being a hostess, in books like *The Waves* and *To the Lighthouse?* Why not make it that simple?

Or why not just cookery books? Why do I not just have what I think are the best work manuals and read them carefully when I need them (which I do constantly)? But no: I have everything from Mrs. Simon Kander's *Settlement Cook Book*, through all of Sheila Hibben, to the latest throwaways from baking powder and refrigerator companies, with their flossy culinary triumphs in full Kodachrome. I have them in rows and piles. Fortunately I also have the common sense to limit my working manuals to a maximum of twelve inches of shelf space. But the rest![1]—they go on for countless feet, through European titles and Hawaiian and regional, through Suzanne Roukhomovsky and Trader Vic and André Simon, some of them good and a lot of them absolutely phony except for perhaps one invaluable recipe or hint.

And then the other books, the ones I have kept because they are bound in shagreen or mottled with age or smudged with the adolescent gorgings of boarding school! All have a gastronomical significance, some of them to no other human being but myself. They mean exoticism, or respect, or gluttony. Perhaps they should be shed at regular intervals, like a skin. But they sit safely on my shelves, a strange company bolstered by nostalgia, curious indeed, and a dead giveaway to anyone equally curious to know their owner.

I do believe sincerely that a gastronomical library, if it is sternly limited, is more significant than mine could ever be. That is, I think a collection of menus from the Regency to the First Republic or vice versa, as served in one town or one district, say Dijon or Seine-et-Oise, might prove to be intensely interesting to gourmets of the whole world. It might even have a fine building erected around it, and provide bookwormish nourishment for a score of dyspeptic curators. As for my own magpie collection, it can do little but bewilder.

Few but I can ever know, or care, why this particular frayed paper-bound edition of Paul Reboux's *Plats du Jour* means high zest and adventure in Burgundy in 1930. Perhaps no man in the world speaks truthfully who says he knows where my one-shilling copy of *Farmhouse Fare* came from, and why its recipe for Butter Brine brings me close to weeping. And how about *Notes on a Cellar Book* and why I keep this new shiny vulgar edition rather than the "first" I gave away? George Saintsbury would know. I know. But it does not matter in the least that no one else does, not at least to me.

I look at my crammed shelves and feast with artful reflection, for no meal is good that cannot be reflected upon with pleasure. It comforts me to know, in this distracted world, that thanks to my motley library I could be well fed in the worst of this world's distracted prisons.

1

There is no better antidote for me, when I have perforce read too many modern recipes, quasi- (or should I say queasy?) practical or purely fluffy, than a quiet backward look.

The English and American receipts of a hundred years ago, in Mrs. Beeton or Marion Harland, are hardly less removed from today's standards of goodness than Elizabethan formulas, and even the proper order of service at mealtime sounds strange, and proportionately refreshing and stimulating, in the middle-class cookery books I have mentioned, and in the higher flying lexicons like Soyer's *The Gastronomic Regenerator* and Simpson's *System of*

Cookery, destined for aristocratic kitchens but most certainly peeked at by many a modest housewife of the early nineteenth century.

The jump back from Victoria to James the First is easy enough, once having taken the greater one between today's manuals and Marion Harland's and Soyer's and suchlike. There, fortunate accident, opens *The Closet of Sir Kenelm Digby, Knight,* one of the most tantalizing and robust and in a way mysterious cookbooks ever written, except, perhaps, *The Deipnosophists* of Athenaeus.

Digby was an arch-romanticist, the "special friend of queens," an experimenter from his youngest days in the connection between what people eat and what they die of, from plague to poison. And the recipes, starting with "Take one Measure of Honey" for his Metheglin and ending ". . . it is a beautiful and pleasant Liquor" for his Conserve of Roses, are full of weird delight. The one quickest to hand, of countless such, is called

A HERRING-PYE

Put great store of sliced onions, with Currants and Raisins of the Sun both above and under the Herrings, and store of Butter, and so bake them.

I read this cookery rule and then sit back, trying to taste with my mind's tongue the fantastic product of it (to me here and now, that is fantastic), a baked dish of onions, raisins, butter, and fish. I cannot. And then I go still further back, as far as the plumed decadance of Rome, remote from such Elizabethan vigor as Sir Kenelm Digby always showed, and yet blunt as his.

I read of sauces and bird-pyes, or of the intricacies of perfumed roasted fig-pecker breasts, or of pâté made from almond-stuffed white geese, or of

GARUM (400 B.C.)

Place in a vessel all the insides of fish, both large fish and small. Salt them well. Expose them to the air until they are completely rotted. Drain off the liquid that comes from them, and it is the sauce garum.

This recipe, ugly and simple, is in its own way salutary against the onslaughts of marshmallow-vegetable-gelatin salads and such which smile at me in Kodachrome from current magazine advertisements. It can act, and indeed it does, as a kind of gastronomical purge, and I find myself turning much oftener than I need to, and perhaps with much more relief than I am justified in feeling, to the bygone receipts, the flummeries and syllabubs and pastes, of cooks now comfortably past hunger.

M is for Monastic

. . . AND for what happens when men become monks—at table, I hasten to add!

It seems to me that too much has been written about the dogged pleasures than can be savored by any knowing gourmet who sits down alone to his own idea of culinary excellence. Lucullus is called on far too often to bolster such solitary morale, and many a man who secretly yearns to join the nearest roistering group has smugly comforted himself by remembering how, one rare time when the great Roman general dined alone, he chided his chef for a slight feeling of hit-or-miss slapdashery in the menu. "But My Lord" (or Your Excellency or however anyone as rich as Lucullus was addressed some two thousand years ago) "has no guests tonight," the poor dolt stammered, "and therefore . . ."

And then enough was said, for the fabulously skilled gastronomer shrugged coldly and remarked, "But tonight—tonight Lucullus dines with Lucullus!"

Yes, what comfort that cruel reproach has been to countless lonely but still normally hungry souls! They have sat back, in world-wide beaneries called everything from Le Roy Gourmet to Ye Kat's Meow, and hoped devoutly that they looked as blandly gourmandish as they wished they felt.

Some cities make this solitary public act much easier to accomplish than do others. It is apparently impossible for a man to dine alone with dignified enjoyment in Los Angeles, for example, except perhaps at a Thrift-i-Save drugstore counter, which automatically cancels out the dignity if not the enjoyment. I have yet to see any normal Southern California male go willingly by himself to an eating house and consume an intelligent meal easily and pleasurably.

On the other hand San Francisco has many restaurants where men seem to go not merely to staunch the wounds of their immediate appetite, but to sit alone and savor without chit-chat what has been set before them. There are places like Sam's and Jack's and Tadich's, often with mousy-looking curtained booths upstairs which in the main are *not* filled with the expected willing damsels and their sexually hungry escorts, but with calm-faced lawyers and bankers and vintners and sea captains, sitting miraculously by themselves, reading Elizabethan sermons and sonnets over the intricacies of a cracked crab's shell.

When I was last in Paris and London, they were like that, and will be again, I think.

But no matter how much help a place may give, men dining alone in public do not often find the ease and elegance they wish for. And as for their private gastronomical patterns, they are fantastic! For one famed celibate whose Filipino houseboy understands not only the intricacy of a soufflé au Grand Marnier but the precise and utterly precious moment at which to serve it, there are a hundred, a thousand, myriad men who are caught in the drab toils of modern moneys, and cannot afford such escapism.

They must live alone, for one reason or another. They learn countless ugly little tricks for such an existence, which add to the hateful pattern. They gradually forget Lucullus and lean on one good meal a week, with the rest filled in by snatched bottles of milk and grabbed drugstore ham-on-ryes. Now and then they let a girl grill them a steak in her kitchenette, which they would not let her pay for in a restaurant for obtusely virile reasons. But in general they prefer to survive in solitude.[1] Quite often they find themselves in a position similar to that of a friend of mine, who is aptly named Monk.

He was then about twenty-eight, which sounds young to some of us, but he was much older than most of the other students at the university where he was writing his doctor's thesis. He had very little money, and thanks to family troubles and an occasional irresistible urge for pretty girls, he found himself living on a food purse which had dwindled within a few months from seventy-five cents a day to about twelve. This happened to him in 1939, when it meant twice as much cash as ten years later, but even so he was hard put to it to sleep for the way his guts cried out and warbled to him in the night.

He was not alone in his hunger: there have been many such students who later grew fat as college presidents, and they tipped him off to such timeworn tricks as serving at fraternity banquets

and eating the scraps. But Monk was finicky, and out of pure finickiness his belly protested at such untidy snatchings.

Then he made a deal with a hash house for one meal a day, everything he could eat, in return for washing plates. It was not right: the
black greasiness underfoot wiped out any pleasure he may have
found in the sparkling countertops of the little joint, and again he
was racked with sickness.

It seemed to color not only his immediate eagerness for life but also
his politics and even his love-making, and he realized that he must
ignore the common ways of such poverty as his and devise his own
plan. He was an intelligent man, although dulled and warped by
hunger, and he deliberately lived another week on scraps in order
to save a dollar or so to buy himself one pot, one plate, one spoon,
and one fork. He did not need a knife, recognizing fatalistically that
he would never cook anything that needed to be cut, anything like
a steak . . . a chop. . . .

He arranged to use the back of his landlady's stove two or three
times a week. She would have been more than glad to see him in
her kitchen every day, but by now his monastic approach to life
had spread from the table to the bed, and he withdrew with discreet
relief from many such snag-toothed and fumy invitations.

He made himself a stew on Saturdays and Wednesdays. It had
good things in it, which he bought just at closing time in the big
public markets. It smelled good. It tasted good. He did not languish
on it, he grew strong and sparkling.

The important part of the story is not that he continued to flourish,
but that he stopped. One day he realized, alone in his odorous
little back room with his empty plate before him, that he had at
first, a few weeks earlier, eaten nicely from it with his fork. Then
for a few weeks he had spooned up his food. And then one day
he found himself very neatly, very thoroughly, licking the plate
clean to save the bother of washing it three flights below!

He was flabbergasted. He sat back and thought about it. In
some ways this licking was a logical act: no other soul but him would
eat from the plate and therefore it was not contaminated by his
doglike behavior. Also, it saved some of his jealously husbanded
strength for his studies. Moreover, such secret washing protected him
from the sly-eyed woman in the kitchen, which also kept some
energy for other things. But he was horrified nevertheless.

Quietly he took the plate up and broke it over his knee. He went down to the kitchen and gave the rest of his stew to a family of blue kittens which had lately emerged from the back alley.

Then he took three dollars and eleven cents, which he had counted on for the rest of the month, gastronomically, and he called his favorite girl, who was majoring in Dramatic Diction but enunciated his own language with great clarity on at least one important subject.

And the next morning he felt so much more energetic than he had for several months that he applied for, and immediately got, a fat job as a laboratory assistant. What happened to him later really should not happen to a rising physicist, but at least it had very little to do with monasticism, culinary or otherwise!

1

The things men come to eat when they are alone are, I suppose, not much stranger than the men themselves. I myself have concocted more than one weird dish when I felt I was unobserved and therefore inviolate.

A writer years ago told me of living for five months on hen mash. He said he felt fine at the end and was fatter in his purse than he could possibly have been otherwise, and that the only eggs he had laid were on magazine editors' desks. And if you study, instead of a cookbook, the requisite ingredients of any packaged food that is supposed to keep furred or feathered creatures in good shape, and even increase their usefulness, you will see the fantastic lengths to which cooks go, whether they be purveyors to hens and puppies or, at the other end of the gastronomical scale, royal chefs nourishing princes and prime ministers. Where one will specify three dozen ortolans, twelve large fresh truffles, and sauce Espagnole, the other will require calcium carbonate, bone meal, and fish liver oil in even fussier proportions.

I do not know what political reactions might ensue if a good honest dog biscuit were served, no matter how tricked out with this and that, at a state banquet, but from what little I have seen most animals would turn away from the overspiced mixtures put upon regal or diplomatic plates.

Myself, if I must choose, I would take the hen mash, the dog meal, for every day, with promise of a respite now and then, rather than daily ordeals of rich tricky nothingness. My palate might faint, but my bones would not, and, being alive, I must consider those bones and their uses, and the flesh thereon.

The phosphorescence that lurks upon the very breath of well-fed sophisticates, subtle mélange of Béchamel, seconal capsules, and bismuth, is not for me. I would, having measured my powers and my capacities, settle for many a monastic feeding of my physical cells, and then in the resultant glow of well-being sample a very occasional snail, truffle, pâté, pheasant Souvaroff, bombe Trocadéro, diplomate au kirsch. A time-to-time savoring of Lucullus's choicest fare, the kind he would serve in his Apollo room, has never harmed anyone who knew enough to sight his landmarks and recognize where he was. And on the other side of the medal, a "scouring of the maw" is something that Lucullus himself would recommend, a ritual not necessarily painful, which the most devout gourmets recognize as healthful.

Perhaps the best of such refreshers that I know, at least in its obvious results, is one described to me by a man who lives a life of innumerable Scotches at the Ritz, uncountable bisques and pâtés and tournedos, too many bottles of Château Lafitte (if that be possible), and all for reasons more professional than voluptuous. His antidote is good: once a month, or oftener if he can, he retires, in the full sense of the word, to his own privacy, in this case a two-room hotel apartment. He bathes slowly, covers himself softly, and lies back upon a couch, the inevitable manuscripts at one side of him for possible scanning (but with the telephone turned off), and at the other side a little table upon which waits the following medicine, to be taken slowly:

STRENGTHENING PRESCRIPTION FOR MONASTIC SUPPER

1 *small loaf crusty sourdough bread*

1 *fresh but ripe piece of Gorgonzola or blue cheese*

1 *stick sweet butter, a quarter pound or so*

1 *bottle Chianti or Tipo Red*

This menu presupposes a certain ease and dictates a definite peacefulness. Better that than madness, digestive as well as social, and no more unattainable!

N *is for* Nautical

. . . AND inevitably for nostalgia, in my own alphabet. Dinners aboard ship have a special poignancy for me, partly because I have not sailed anywhere since I went with the *Normandie* on her last fateful crossing, but mostly because I have always been in love at sea, so that each bite I took was savored with an intensity peculiar to the moment. I think I am not alone in this particular juxtaposition of two words for *N*.

The first time I ever rode a ship it was deep down in the shuddering guts of it, so that dining-room silver and china jangled tinnily on the calmest day—another coupling of two letters: *S* for Student Third rather than Steerage. It was smart to hop the Atlantic thus cheaply and uncomfortably in 1929, and a great many bored travelers who could afford A-deck accommodations titillated themselves by rubbing elbows with errant priests and broken-down fan dancers and even students in the renovated holds of a dozen enormous liners (mine was the *Berengaria*).

I myself was happily dazed with love, but I do remember one priest, one dancer, three medical students, and most of all one incongruously proper middle-class plump Englishwoman who had nothing to do with anyone at all and seemed non-existent except three times a day in the dining-room. Then it was that she became immortal, at least for me. With one blind regal stare she picked up the large menu, handed it to the apparently hypnotized waiter, who hovered over her and almost ignored the seven other passengers at our table, and said "Yes."

It seems to me, when I try to be reasonable about it, that she must surely have said, "Yes, pastries," or "Yes, soups." But all I can remember is "Yes." All I can remember is sitting for long periods watching her, when I should rightly have been playing shuffleboard or any other of the games connected with my first honeymoon, while she ate slowly, silently, right through the menu.

650

Surely it must have been all the soups one meal, and all the roasts another: no human being could eat every dish mentioned on a ship's carte du jour, not even in Student Third where kippered snacks and spiced onions took the place of First Class caviar and bouchées à la Pompadour. But as far as I can say, that woman did. What is more, the waiter seemed to enjoy it almost as much as she; he would hover breathlessly behind her with a dish of apple trifle and a plate of plum heavies while she chewed on through her chocolate sponge with one hand and cut at the crust of an apricot tart with the other.[1]

One day of comparative roughness, when the silver and china clashed noisily to the ocean's roll instead of jingling to the engine's shudderings, I sat almost alone in the room with this relentless eater, feeling that for once in my life I was in the presence of what Rabelais would have called a Gastrolater; insensitive to the elements, unthinking of ordinary human misery, uncaring of the final end to such appetite, she was wrapped in a worship of her belly. "Yes," she said simply and sat back for her priest to attend her.

I was awed. Naïve as I was then in the ways of transatlantic liners, I knew our fare was nothing compared to what was served six or seven decks higher up. I wished with a kind of horror that I would meet this immortal again—in First.

I was to learn, somewhat regretfully, that the more people paid for their fares, the less they ate of the fare's fare and the fewer times they strolled biliously into the luxurious dining-room on B-deck to peck at the fantastically generous and rich food provided for their amusement. Instead they paid even more than they would on dry land, once having got onto the most crowded and therefore most desirable ships, for the privilege of avoiding almost all of their fellow passengers by dining in some small and quite often stuffy and viewless restaurant called a club. It was ridiculous, but I must admit it could be fun.

One ship I crossed on several times boasted a tiny room where each day a luncheon was devoted to a country: Monday it would be Sweden, Tuesday China, and so on. I have never since eaten such good national dishes in my life, anywhere. I have never since eaten so much either. The sea change worked its magic, and I sat for three or four hours every midday, savoring everything with a capacity which is unknown to me now, but which in the elegant little dining-room had nothing gluttonous about it, nor gross. Smoked eel and aquavit, Hung Yuen Gai Ding and tiger-bone wine—what was in the glasses tipped ever so slightly this way and that, and our hearts felt the tide's pull.

And in the main dining salon dully benighted souls ate their way stodgily, or so we believed in our own tight supercilious little sea-going island, through one endless meal after another, while decks below them still other human beings, less moneyed, less well aired, but in some cases equally blessed by good digestion, had to forego caviar for kippers in what was, even so, a gastronomical spree.

The truth is that no matter what cabin a passenger pays for on a luxury liner, he feels that he has simply bought his passage and is getting his meals free. And when he is confronted with a dinner card as big as the front page of his home-town paper, with no prices visible, he can only treat it according to his lights—his liver and lights, to make a carnal and abattoirish pun.

Perhaps he has known slow true hunger. Then he does one of two things: he either shudders away from such a vulgar show and asks for dry toast and tea, or he does in his own limited way what my Gargantuan fellow passenger did on the *Berengaria*—he eats imperturbably from the "free" Radis et Céleris Frais to the "free" Café Turque. If he is somewhat further removed from the pangs and passions of his belly, by politics or the stock market or even marriage, he becomes more exacting.

And now I think of one of the worst times I ever had on a ship, when I was finagled into introducing a Very Rich Passenger to my friends the Purser and Master Chef, and then was invited to a few exquisite little dinners with this Very Rich Passenger, arranged of course with great to-do by the Purser himself and the Master Chef himself, the kind of dinners for which, almost literally, one bird was stuffed inside another and another and roasted and then we ate the innermost truffle-stuffed olives, with my two friends beaming and gleaming proudly; and then at the last I had to listen to the miserable story of how the Very Rich Passenger skipped ship, on the harbor tender, and did not pay a single tip. I wanted to evaporate with embarrassment, since I am a firm believer in friendship and in tipping, and I am a practitioner of both. I still dread meeting my two friends again.

I comfort myself with the thought of countless other people who have gone back and forth on ocean liners, reveling with far from innocent pleasure in the somewhat decadent excesses of the transatlantic fare, and paying proper fees for those excesses to the servitors who made them possible.

I see them emerging from bedrooms lined with rare woods and heavy with the scent of jungle flowers, in fair gowns and knife-sharp creases, only a little tipsy-crazy from the sea's roll and that last cocktail. I see them happily wandering the length of long buffets set with tubs of caviar in snow, and thick yellow casseroles of truffle-black pâté from Strasbourg. I see them ordering from a hundred knowingly selected ocean-going wines.

It is a shame that I must confess I seldom figured in this pretty picture: early in my travelings I found that for my own peace of mind I must shun most of my fellow passengers. I could not cope with their behavior, there at sea level where so many social inhibitions went overboard, with the protocol of stuffiness on one hand, the licentious whoring on the other.

I worked out my own pattern, dictated by my glandular condition of the moment, and it was something like this when in 1940 I ceased for a time my interurban voyages:

I slept and read, rolling like a delicately balanced log with the ship, until noon. Then after various sybaritic dabblings I went to the bar, not the main one but a tiny place familiar with leather chairs and peanuts in bowls and a discreetly gossipy man named some variation of Fritz who poured fine beer or made impeccable Martinis. I took beer, and I could have been in the Lausanne-Palace, or the Ritz, or . . . or. . . . There was dignity about the very banality of the place. I sensed it and sat back, watching Fritz's ears prick to gossip and his busy eyes flicker cynically over the sleep-fattened faces in front of him.

Then I went to lunch, not in the dining salon but in a little restaurant where I had engaged my table before the ship sailed. I ate and drank and ate and drank, and in a drugged way it was fun.

I always skipped tea, just as I skipped breakfast and the mid-morning consommé and crackers, even though tea had a ghoulishly interesting "concert" with it, at which the captain now and then tangoed carefully with one of the three richest women present, and then, even more carefully, with the current femme fatale. I hated teas, tangos, and in a lesser way the lethal women, and went instead to the movies, where I lazily watched ten-year-old-and-to-morrow's cinema seductions and sipped a mild Pernod with water.

The ritual of "dressing" is a pleasure so removed from the present that I look back on it with much the same helpless emotion that I feel about a ten-pound tin of caviar a friend brought me to Dijon from Moscow in 1931: I can only dream of its present impossibility, as I do of the hot water and the countless towels and the dreamy leisure.

Before dinner, ordered in advance from a sheet which had nothing to do with the vulgar printed menu of the main dining salon, I drank either champagne or two very dry Martinis, depending on whether the captain's chart marked the wind velocity at 3 or 7. The little bar (I *never* went into the main bar!) was full and amusing.

Dinner in the club, which suddenly might sprout orchids on its walls or pine branches from the Black Forest behind which tired, invisible cabin boys tootled bird whistles, dinner was indeed exquisite.

And then, after dancing perhaps, or talking in the bar, *my* bar, came the best part of the pattern, when I went to my cabin and there, in the soft light by my bed, was the same curiously exciting and satisfying thing each night: a split of my favorite champagne in a little silver bucket, and a silver plate of the thinnest sandwiches in the world, made knowingly of unbuttered fine bread, slivered breast of chicken, and a generous amount of cayenne pepper. I really do not understand what chord it was in my nature that always vibrated at this sight, but hum and twang it did, inevitably, and still does, in my mind.

I forget what it used to cost, in those happily vanished days, to lunch and loll and sup thus fatuously, but it was one-tenth of what it cost the steamship company to put on such a rich-bitch show —one-tenth or one-fiftieth. And I wonder now what it would cost to make me young enough again to love it, and all the silken extravagance it meant. I think back on it with no regret, but still with a real nostalgia.

And in some ways also I would like to be a lithe, eager twenty and sit across from an immortal big-bosomed implacable Gastrolater who could say "Yes!" and mean it.

I would, but less so, like to be a suave thirty—the caviar was so good then and so plentiful, and I do so love caviar.

Nostalgia hits all my five senses, and colors and perfumes my thoughts. Still I remain upright and cogent, in the face of such a backlog of remembrance, knowing that I, like many another honest gastronomer, can safely lean in secret, now and then, on such things as the word nautical.

1

There is for me a special lure in the names of English puddings: the Steamed Spotted Dog my Aunt Gwen used to make for our delectation, and the Chocolate Mud. They have a realistic ugliness about them which sums up my whole finicky adult approach to something inseparable from the unquestioning, lusty appetite of childhood.

When I was little I was happy in the presence of unlimited Treacle Sponge. Now I would pull away from it and agree with the old proverb, "Cold pudding settles one's love"—right to the pit of one's stomach, I could add.

My interest in even the most bluntly named sweets is largely clinical by now. I can produce one when visiting adolescent nephews make it seem advisable, something like a rich caramel mousse piled with whipped cream and shaved toasted almonds (!), which vanishes almost before it has been set upon the table. I can taste and admire some such daintier masterpiece as was made for me lately in a San Francisco restaurant, a poached fresh peach in chilled zabaglione, very delicate and, as far as any dessert can be, refreshing. (Another one, just as pretty to the eye, was beyond my capacity even to admire after a long winy dinner: a coeur à la crème aux fraises.)

I continue to be baffled by such gastronomical somersaults, but I must acknowledge their necessity to many finer palates than my own, and can even serve forth, here on the page, two of my favorite infallibles, as English as Suet Mould.

NORTH COUNTRY TART

short pastry
gooseberries, or any fruit in
    season

sugar
thick cream

Line a deep baking dish with the pastry and cover with fruit and ample sugar. Put in a layer of the pastry that is a little smaller than the dish, then more fruit and sugar. Repeat this. Then cover the dish with a top layer of pastry, pinch it well around the top, cut a little hole in the center, and bake in a hot oven for about 45 minutes. The fruit and sugar will make a fine rich syrup for the two floating layers of pastry. Serve hot in the winter, cold in the summer, and always with a jug of thick chilled cream.

This is a really heavenly sweet, as even I will swear to. It should obviously come at the end of a simple and not too heavy family supper rather than a proper party dinner, but I have occasionally used it as a kind of titillation, a gastronomical gambit, in an otherwise more sophisticated menu.

A suaver pudding, still very, very British indeed, is my version of a recipe served at the famous Hind's Head, which I have found versatile and apparently pleasing to less limited palates than mine. It seems more like a tart than a pudding to my American mind, just as the North Country Tart is more like a pie or a pudding.

DUKE OF CAMBRIDGE PUDDING

short pastry
1 cup chopped candied or
    heavily preserved fruits
brandy, enough to moisten
    fruit (kirsch is good with
    cherries)

6 tablespoons butter
6 tablespoons sugar
2 or 3 egg yolks, depending on
    size

Line 9-inch baking plate (pie pan!) with crust, making a good, firm, pinched rim. Soak fruit in liquor about an hour, so as to be soft but not mushy. Melt butter in double boiler; add sugar, mix well, stir in egg yolks, and stir gently until thickened. Lightly drain fruit, spread over crust, and pour the cream over it. Bake in hot (425°) oven until the top browns and crinkles. Serve hot or cold.

Of course nothing could ever be quite as good as Aunt Gwen's Muds and Sponges, but as I look back over the spiritual recording of these English sweets, I suddenly feel that perhaps the best one I ever ate, which served as a kind of psychological bridge, was at Simpson's on the Strand, in 1935 or '36. It came as the summation of all such puddings and led me gracefully from childhood hunger to maturity. It came in the springtime after a long, dour London winter, the kind in which I was photographed on Easter Sunday, without my knowing, battling my way across Hyde Park in a whirl of enormous snowflakes. "Visiting Yankee Feels at Home in Unseasonable Blizzard" was one of the newspaper captions. And lunch at Simpson's was a daily ritual, a kind of amiable stoking of my overworked human furnace.

I ate happily through a monumental cut off the joint, with its accompanying "two vegs.," and then a "winter salad," composed largely of pickled beets as I remember, and then, ah, then, came the plum tart, hot, bathed in a flood of Cornish cream, steaming and flowing in the ample plate! How rich it was, how sweet and revivifying to my cold and enervated and above all *young* body! How its steam and savor engulfed and comforted me!

Yes, that was the best pudding of my whole pudding life, and Aunt Gwen would understand my betrayal of all others for it, even her Christmas Bun, when we could play Snap around it with raisins burning in the holiday bath of rum.

O *is for* Ostentation

. . . AND how dignity is most often lacking in it but need not be, at table or anywhere.

While it is very true that rich Amphitryons (and that is indeed an ostentatious way of saying hosts!) are more apt to strut and attempt bedazzlement than poor ones, I think it quite possible for a bowl of soup and a crust of bread to be served with the pompous affectation that in any social milieu spells real ostentation.

In a subtle reversing of the law, it is a poor man who might most easily be ostentatious if he pretended riches and served forth a truffled turkey rather than a stew, to impress me for no matter what venal reason; but a rich man who with great show invited me to sup on pottage would be equally suspect. In either case my gastronomical suspicions, dormant somewhere between my heart and my stomach, would be roused to the lasting damage of my innocent appetite. Why, I would ask, is the stage thus set for me? Why has the delicate peace of a friendly table been thus threatened?

More often than not, ostentatious dining has little dignity about it, although the combination is possible. I can think of one good literary proof of this apparent contradiction: the unforgettable dinner in *Alice Adams* by Booth Tarkington. That Mrs. Adams served wilted canapés of caviar, without cocktails in that Prohibition day and without even warning her husband what to call them, could be a perfect example of undignified ostentation if it were not for her true nobility, her enormous generosity in wishing, by this puny attempt at worldliness, to work a miracle for her daughter. She failed, in a masterpiece of misery-at-table, but her innate goodness kept her effort from vulgarity.

The other side of the medal, to my mind, is the supper that the two protagonists in *Hotel Imperial* by Arnold Bennett ate in an oyster bar in London: one of the richest girls in the world and the manager of one of her world's most luxurious hotels. Their enjoyment of

658

simplicity, while artfully told as if with sympathy, is a good example of gastronomical pomposity. They are slumming. They are carried away by their own God-like sharing of food with mortal men. They are being infinitely more undignified than if they had walked out in a huff because the oyster bar did not carry the brand of caviar their hotel could produce so easily and quickly.

A queen can, if she indeed be queenly, serve forth a ghastly meal with as much dignity as Mrs. Adams. If I were Disraeli, for instance (one of the few people I would not mind having been, although if I had been he I would most probably have minded the being, a fine but obvious distinction), I would think nothing of a dinner with Her Majesty Victoria something on this order, as served, say, in the summer of 1841 by her dashing Chief Cook and Maître d'Hôtel Francatelli.

There were two services—the first consisted of four soups; four fish dishes; four different hors d'oeuvres of lobster claws; four "removes" (truffled pullets, ham in aspic, stuffed leg of lamb, beef fillets larded with anchovies); sixteen entrées ranging from turtle fins with a Madeira sauce through roasted pigeon breasts; and a "sideboard" of venison, roast beef, roast mutton, and what was in 1841 called "vegetables," an overcooked, overseasoned, and usually ignored collection of turnips, potatoes, and Brussels sprouts.

The second service, after a recess which with the Queen present was apt to be more bluntly digestive than wittily revivifying, began with six roasts—two each of quail, young hares, and chickens. Then came six different kinds of puddings, a strange remnant of Elizabethan days when baked honeyed dishes made in part of eggs were as liable to be based on cabbage as on vanilla cream. Two main edible ornaments and four minor ones accompanied these horrendous sweets: they were monumental, minareted, and buttressed with a thousand elaborate swirls of nougat, caramel, and almond paste, and they were, from the evidence of Victorian menu cards, a variation of the sixteenth-century "set-piece" essential to any honest-to-God dinner party.

Next, and finally, came sixteen side dishes, or entremets, which in another fifty years or so were to turn into the present British idea (or better, dream) of a savory. Today that means, at least in memory, a small, would-be appetizing and usually hot nibble of highly seasoned cheese and/or fish and/or pâté (a classic example is John

Fothergill's recipe for Little Cat, which includes grated cheese, anchovy or curry, cayenne pepper, scraped onion, chutney). When Disraeli was dining, more or less at the helm of state, the future savory included a kind of reverse Russian-buffet of everything from truffles to gooseberry jelly, a macédoine of fresh fruits, new green peas à la française, string beans in butter, strawberry tarts, artichokes, a chicken aspic, whipped cream with sugared almonds. An incredible hodgepodge!

Disraeli, like most of the other familiars at the Queen's board, thought little of this meal, if anything. He chose what he wanted, sent away what did not please him, asked for and was poured the drinks he fancied, in an elegant confusion which was routine, scheduled, and even mildly enjoyable. And there at Buckingham it was removed from any slightest hint of undignified ostentation, either gastronomical or social.

Anywhere else? No matter how wealthy a brewer or duke or shipbuilder might find himself in that time of rolling Victorian riches when many a merchant-prince could have bought out the Crown, he would have been damned indeed if he had tried to imitate this royal show. Anywhere else it would have been too smug, too long, above all too undignified, for even Disraeli to choke down.

The Queen's fantastic dinners, like poor Mrs. Adams' heat-wracked party for her daughter, had a rhythm of nobility about them; they were unconscious of such nonsense as the capacity of the human belly or the perquisites of local custom. If the Queen or Mrs. Adams had known better, and had still put on their shows for reasons for low cunning known as state, Disraeli (and I) would have spat out the nourishment rather than be sickened by the lies. As it was, the countless dishes of the one and the sad little curling canapés of the other had the same regal disregard of men, weather, and history, while any such self-conscious little feast as the one eaten in a London oyster bar by two refugees from velvet has an uncomfortable condescension about it.

Few of us can honestly admit that at some time in our lives we have not swanked, gastronomically: at school, when we pretended cookies made by our mother and sent in the weekly laundry box were really baked by a non-existent cook (or vice versa and just as ostentatiously); in business, when we have ordered truffled quail at Romanoff's instead of a Number Nine at Lindy's to please a possible client (or vice versa!); in love, most of all perhaps, when we have put on a painful show of utter sophistication or of complete simplicity in order to win a sexual prize who, if worth its basic ration of good honest salt, would recognize such flummery and cast it out.

All of that is ostentation, familiar to the human animal. It need not be expensive, although usually it is: a show of opulence has always been fashionable, but a gutter-rat can be ostentatious if necessary, in his own way, with the butt-end of a dead cigar. In other words, it is relative and as varied as the men who practice it. The one thing it most often lacks, although that too can be a part of it, is the one thing that can redeem it: at least a modicum of un-self-conscious dignity.

1

A recipe from an unidentifiable cookery book published in London in 1814, dedicated to a duke as they all had to be, gives a formula that makes a pretty contrast to what I myself do to fresh zucchini, the nearest decent gastronomical counterpart to those overgrown pithy garden monsters called vegetable marrows in England:

VEGETABLE-MARROW À LA POULETTE

Cut the legumes, according to their size and age, into sections of four, six, or eight, like oranges; peel them thoroughly, trim them neatly, and put them into a basin with ample salt and vinegar, and steep for several hours. Pour off the resultant liquid, and put them into a deep sautapan thickly spread with butter, and season well with nutmeg, mignonette-pepper, salt, and a large spoon of powdered sugar. Moisten with half a pint of white broth, and set to boil gently over a stove-fire until they become quite tender; this will require a half-hour or an hour. Then boil them down in their glaze; it must then be poured off, and a gravy-spoon of Velouté added; finish by simmering the vegetable-marrows over the lively fire for a few minutes, and incorporating with them a leason of four yolks of eggs, mixed with half a gill of cream, a spoonful of chopped and boiled parsley, and the juice of half a lemon; dish them up with a border of short fleurons and serve.

This in its own fantastic pre-Victorian way is a kind of frittata. Today's pressure-cooking takes the place in a few seconds of the hours of soaking and simmering the old cooks needed, or so they thought, to make a vegetable soft enough, and enough drained of its own forthright flavor and worth, to set before a duke.

When I can buy zucchini not over four inches long and preferably with the little withered blossom still clinging to the umbilicus, I lightly brush them under cold water, cut off both ends, and cook them for something less than two minutes in my Presto. I drain them at once, saving the fine green juice for everything from midmorning broth to borscht, and then what I can salvage from my children's avid fingers I sprinkle with grated Parmesan, and bake whole and quickly, five minutes or so in a hot oven in a buttered casserole, and serve forth, unadorned by nutmeg or powdered sugar or even salt and pepper! They are sweet, somehow nutlike, infinitely fresh.

And now and then I make a frittata, an honest, delicate concoction, which will be honestly but very indelicately loathed by anyone honest enough to confess to a basic loathing for zucchini (it can be made with any fresh cooked vegetable, such as green beans).

FRITTATA ALLA ANYTHING-AT-ALL

½ cube butter (4 or 5 tablespoons)
1 green pepper, coarsely chopped
3 tablespoons chopped parsley
2 tablespoons minced shallots, scallions, or chives, or/and herbs

1 to 2 cups-freshly cooked vegetables in small pieces (zucchini, eggplant, cauliflower, plain or mixed)
6 to 8 eggs
1 cup good cream
4 to 6 tablespoons grated Parmesan
salt, fresh grated pepper

Brown butter in casserole in hot (450°) oven. Add green pepper, onion, and herbs and mix well. Reduce oven heat to about 350° and let mixture get partly cooked. Add cooked vegetables, mix well, and let reach bubbling point. Stir (do not beat) eggs gently with cream, cheese, and seasoning, and pour into the very hot casserole. Turn off oven, return casserole to it, and bake the mixture slowly in the heat, taking care that it does not bubble and pulling it away once or twice with a fork from the sides to the center of the dish. Serve as soon as fairly firm in center; otherwise it will be overdone by the time it reaches the table. For a more pungent frittata use olive oil rather than butter and increase the herbs and ingredients according to taste—garlic, anchovy fillets, that sort of thing.

P *is for* Peas

... NATURALLY! and for a few reasons why the best peas I ever ate in my life were, in truth, the best peas I ever ate in my life.

Every good cook, from Fanny Farmer to Escoffier, agrees on three things about these delicate messengers to our palates from the kind earth-mother: they must be very green, they must be freshly gathered, and they must be shelled at the very last second of the very last minute.

My peas, that is, the ones that reached an almost unbelievable summit of perfection, an occasion that most probably never would happen again, met these three gastronomical requirements to a point of near-ridiculous exactitude. It is possible, however, that even this technical impeccability would not have been enough without the mysterious blending, that one time, of weather, place, other hungers than my own. After all, I can compare bliss with near bliss, for I have often, blessèd me, eaten superlative green peas.

Once, for instance, my grandmother ran out into her garden, filled her apron with the fattest pods, sat rocking jerkily with a kind of nervous merriment for a very few minutes as she shelled them—and before we knew it she had put down upon the white-covered table a round dish of peas in cream. We ate them with our spoons, something we never could have done at home! Perhaps that added to their fragile, poignant flavor, but not much: they were truly *good.*

And then once in Paris, in June (what a hackneyed but wonderful combination of the somewhat overrated time-and-place motif!), I lunched at Foyot's, and in the dim room where hot-house roses stood on all the tables the very month roses climbed crazily outside on every trellis, I watched the headwaiter, as skilled as a magician, dry peas over a flame in a generous pan, add what looked like an equal weight of butter, which almost visibly sent out a cloud of sweet-smelling hay and meadow air, and then swirl the whole.

At the end he did a showy trick, more to amuse himself than me, but I sat open-mouthed, and I can still see the arc of little green vegetables flow up into the air and then fall, with a satisfying shush, back into the pan some three or four feet below and at least a yard from where they took off. I gasped, the headwaiter bowed faintly but with pride, and then we went about the comparatively mundane procedure of serving, tasting, and eating.

Those petits pois au beurre were, like my grandmother's, à la crème mode d'Iowa, good—*very* good. They made me think of paraphrasing Sidney Smith's remark about strawberries and saying, "Doubtless God could have made a better green pea, but doubtless He never did."

That was, however, before the year I started out, on a spring date set by strict local custom, to grow peas in a steep terraced garden among the vineyards between Montreux and Lausanne, on the Lake of Geneva.

The weather seemed perfect for planting by May Day, and I had the earth ready, the dry peas ready, the poles ready to set up. But Otto and Jules, my mentors, said no so sternly that I promised to wait until May 15, which could easily be labeled Pea-Planting Day in Swiss almanacs. They were right, of course: we had a cold snap that would have blackened any sprout about May 10. As I remember, the moon, its rising, and a dash of hailstones came into the picture too.

And then on May 15, a balmy sweet day if ever I saw one, my seeds went into the warm, welcoming earth, and I could agree with an old gardening manual which said understandingly, "Perhaps no vegetable is set out in greater expectancy . . . for the early planting fever is impatient."

A week later I put in another row, and so on for a month, and they did as they were meant to, which is one of the most satisfying things that can possibly happen to a gardener, whether greenhorn and eager or professional and weatherworn.

Then came the day with stars on it: time for what my grandmother would have called "the first mess of peas."

The house at Le Pâquis was still a-building, shapes of rooms but no roof, no windows, trestles everywhere on the wide terrace high above the lake, the ancient apple tree heavily laden with button-

sized green fruit, plums coloring on the branches at the far end
near the little meadow, set so surprisingly among the vineyards that
gave Le Pâquis its name.

We put a clean cloth, red and white, over one of the carpenters'
tables, and we kicked wood curls aside to make room for our feet
under the chairs brought up from the apartment in Vevey. I set out
tumblers, plates, silver, smooth, unironed napkins sweet from the
meadow grass where they had dried.

While some of us bent over the dwarf-pea bushes and tossed the
crisp pods into baskets, others built a hearth from stones and a couple
of roof tiles lying about and made a lively little fire. I had a big
kettle with spring water in the bottom of it, just off simmering, and
salt and pepper and a pat of fine butter to hand. Then I put the
bottles of Dézelay in the fountain, under the timeless spurt of icy
mountain water, and ran down to be the liaison between the har-
vesters and my mother, who sat shelling peas from the basket on her
lap into the pot between her feet, her fingers as intent and nimble
as a lacemaker's.

I dashed up and down the steep terraces with the baskets, and my
mother would groan and then hum happily when another one
appeared, and below I could hear my father and our friends cursing
just as happily at their wry backs and their aching thighs, while the
peas came off their stems and into the baskets with a small sound
audible in that still high air, so many hundred feet above the distant
and completely silent Léman. It was suddenly almost twilight. The
last sunlight on the Dents du Midi was fire-rosy, with immeasurable
coldness in it.

"Time, gentlemen, time," my mother called in an unrehearsed
and astonishing imitation of a Cornish barmaid.

They came in grateful hurry up the steep paths, almost nothing
now in their baskets, and looks of smug success upon their faces.
We raced through the rest of the shelling, and then while we ate
rolled prosciutto and drank Swiss bitters or brandy and soda or
sherry, according to our various habits, I dashed like an eighteenth-
century courier on a secret mission of utmost military importance,
the pot cautiously braced in front of me, to the little hearth.

I stirred up the fire. When the scant half-inch of water boiled, I
tossed in the peas, a good six quarts or more, and slapped on the
heavy lid as if a devil might get out. The minute steam showed I

shook the whole like mad. Someone brought me a curl of thin pink ham and a glass of wine cold from the fountain. Revivified, if that were any more possible, I shook the pot again.

I looked up at the terrace, a shambles of sawed beams, cement mixers, and empty sardine tins left from the workmen's lunches. There sat most of the people in the world I loved, in a thin light that was pink with Alpen glow, blue with a veil of pine smoke from the hearth. Their voices sang with a certain remoteness into the clear air, and suddenly from across the curve of the Lower Corniche a cow in Monsieur Rogivue's orchard moved her head among the meadow flowers and shook her bell in a slow, melodious rhythm, a kind of hymn. My father lifted up his face at the sweet sound and, his fists all stained with green-pea juice, said passionately, "God, but I feel good!" I felt near to tears.

The peas were now done. After one more shake I whipped off the lid and threw in the big pat of butter, which had a bas-relief of William Tell upon it. I shook in salt, ground in pepper, and then swirled the pot over the low flames until Tell had disappeared. Then I ran like hell, up the path lined with candytuft and pinks, past the fountain where bottles shone promisingly through the crystal water, to the table.

Small brown roasted chickens lay on every plate, the best ones I have ever eaten, done for me that afternoon by Madame Doellenbach of the Vieux Vevey and not chilled since but cooled in their own intangibly delicate juices. There was a salad of mountain lettuces. There was honest bread. There was plenty of limpid wine, the kind Brillat-Savarin said was like rock-water, tempting enough to make a hydrophobic drink. Later there was cheese, an Emmenthaler and a smuggled Roblichon . . .

. . . And later still we walked dreamily away, along the Upper Corniche to a café terrace, where we sat watching fireworks far across the lake at Evian, and drinking café noir and a very fine *fine*.

But what really mattered, what piped the high unforgettable tune of perfection, were the peas, which came from their hot pot onto our thick china plates in a cloud, a kind of miasma, of everything that anyone could ever want from them, even in a dream. I recalled the three basic requisites, according to Fanny Farmer and Escoffier . . . and again I recalled Sidney Smith, who once said that his idea of Heaven (and he was a cleric!) was pâté de foie gras[1] to the sound of trumpets. Mine, that night and this night too, is fresh green garden peas, picked and shelled by my friends, to the sound of a cowbell.

l

Conveniently, P is for pâté as well as peas, and I continue to feel near enough to Sidney Smith, my long-time ideal of a charming person, to agree with him that the former can be as heavenly as the latter, with or without the sound of trumpets!

I used to think, and perhaps still do, that I can never really have enough pâté de foie gras. I spent almost a half a year in Strasbourg once and could eat it at will, or at least whenever I could justify splurging from twenty to forty American cents for a generous slice of it, which seemed to be more often than not.

There was a "patriotic" *brasserie*, reputedly run by the French government at a hideous financial loss in order to indoctrinate Gallic gaiety into the morbid confused basically Germanic citizens, and there we could eat delicious, well-served pâté in aspic for six francs, as I remember, which would rightly have cost three times as much in any café less bent toward propaganda.

Once in a while we went to a very pompous, small, elegant restaurant, Prussian as a slashed cheek, and ordered pâté de foie gras truffé en brioche, a culinary trick that has always fascinated me, like the Baked Alaska of my adolescence. How does the rich goose liver stay whole and fresh while the dough bakes? And how did the ice cream stay cold and firm while the magic white mound of meringue turned gold? (I prefer to remain puzzled over the former, and leave the latter to my wide-eyed children.)

I used to go, now and then in Strasbourg, to the Doyen offices and choose little or big pots, according to my purse, to be sent back to America. The eighteenth-century Doyen, the founder, is said to be the man who first put truffles into his paste of fat goose livers and spice and brandy, and he or whoever else it may have been who consummated this celestial wedding of high flavor should be tendered some special gastronomical salute, it seems to me, just as should the brave soul who first ate a tomato, and the equally hardy one who first evolved a Camembert cheese from a fermenting pudding of old cream. There is nothing much better in this Western world than a fine, unctuous, truffled pâté, and I suspect that when next I taste one, packed and shipped from Strasbourg itself, I shall be hard put to it not to shed a tear of impious nostalgic bliss upon it.

Meanwhile I look back with no great difficulty to many a pâté maison I have enjoyed, most of which had never even seen the shadow of a fat goose liver. They were delicious.

In general, from Paris to New York, the smaller the maison of which it was the pâté, the better it tasted: an inverse attempt to be important, I suppose, made the little restaurants exert themselves to produce an honorable substitute for the real thing, while the big ones simply took it for granted that anyone who could afford them would of course order nothing but genuine pâté de foie gras de Strasbourg.

Whatever the materialistic reasons for this triumph, I have eaten many unheralded pâtés that almost, if not quite, comforted me for the unavoidable realization that they were but substitutes. I have often made them myself, not always with as good fortune as some of the professional chefs whose loaves I have cut into, but still passing well—passing damn well. I have found that it takes time to make them properly, that they improve with aging, that they must hold only the best of whatever ingredients they call for (no cheap butter, for instance, no "cooking" brandy), and that they must be quietly but sternly heady with the fumes of freshly ground pepper, fine smoky bacon fat, sweet butter, honest booze. If properly served, cold and smooth from their casseroles or terrines, with good crusty bread and good red wine, they need touch the lock to none.

The best of these pâtés that I have ever tasted, but not made myself, was one sent to a friend in Dijon from Brillat-Savarin's town of Belley, and kept on a ledge in the wine cellar all summer. Then, one of the first nippy days of fall, Monsieur Ollagnier lifted it down from its cobwebs. While we all leaned, noses to windward, over the table, he broke open the hard flour crust that was the seal. He lifted it off delicately, in one fine piece, mildewed on top and closed impregnably, underneath, with yellow, cold, chaste fat. He plunged his knife sharply, surely, into one end of the casserole.

Madame Ollagnier clashed the plates roughly toward him, as if afraid to lose one crumb upon the cloth, and their son stood up pontifically, for nineteen that is, and prepared to pour the Nuit-St.-Georges Grands Suchots, with which we planned to drink to countless unpresent souls.

The pâté itself was truly a hunters' dish, worthy of Belley and its mighty ghost, a heady, gamy mixture, laced as tight as an 1880 belle with the best local brandy, high as a kite with spices and forest herbs, a true pâté de gibier à la mode de whoever made it, like this one of mine:

PÂTÉ FIN (*pour Fêtes*)

1 *hare (or equivalent bulk of quail, pheasant, duck, what you will), the best parts*
equal weight of lean bacon in thin strips
3 *or 4 thinly sliced truffles, if possible*
brandy

1 *pound good meat from hare or whatever meat is being used (scraps)*
6 *ounces pork*
6 *ounces veal*
1 *pound bacon*
1 *egg*
1 *scant cup brandy*
bay, nutmeg, etc., as desired

Bone the best parts of the hare (assuming you are making a pâté de lièvre), and put them with an equal weight of bacon and the sliced truffles into a casserole. Marinate in brandy to cover.

Make a forcemeat of the clean scrapmeat, pork, veal, and bacon, and run through a fine meat grinder twice. Mix well with the egg and brandy and put through a fine sieve.

Line an oval or round terrine carefully with the marinated bacon strips, and then fill it with alternating layers of hare, forcemeat, and bacon, scattering the precious truffles judiciously. Cover with bacon. Put on bay, etc., as desired. Cover with a heavy lid, set in a pan of water, and bake in a slow (325°) oven. When the ample grease that rises to the top is quite clear, the pâté is done, and not before.

Remove from oven, cool, and then let chill at least two days before serving. If care is taken to use only the best ingredients, and to see that the top "butter" is absolutely clear before removing from the stove, this pâté will last in a cold place for many months, and it will be worth the guarding of it.

I would, if I could, send a pot of it, in Heaven surely, to Sidney Smith himself.

Q is for Quantity

. . . AND for The Case of the Hindu Eggs, as well as the case of some people, many of them gastronomical as well as human, who honestly believe that if a recipe calls for two cups of butter it will be twice as good if they use four.

If Escoffier, or Mrs. Mazza, or Henry Low, asks for one teaspoon of Béchamel, one teaspoon of chopped basil, or one teaspoon of soy sauce, these mistaken searchers for the jewel of perfection will double the dose, and in so doing wreck themselves. The ones who thus continue assaulting the palates of their intimates deserve rather than mercy a good stiff lecture on the pleasures of the table as opposed to the wounds of an outraged tongue, and if that fails they should be, quite bluntly, crossed off the gastronomical list.

There is no hope for a cook who will not learn his own as well as other gourmets' limitations, and a man who has made one good Béchamel by rote, one good minestrone, or one good Yat Gai Mein, and then goes on to make impossible ones because of his lack of balance, perspective, and plain common sense and modesty, is, to be blunt again, past recall.

Of course it must be added here that many a clumsy amateur who early believed in all good faith that enough of a good thing could never be too much has later turned into a chef of subtlety and breeding, just as many a man who later learned to judge the points of a setter picked out, in his first dog-days, his own early puppyhood, a male because he was big, or a bitch for her pretty eyes. It takes some people a long time to realize that there are rules which have filtered into our life-patterns in a near perfect state, just as it takes other people to act as a kind of ferment, forever questioning these rules or others like them, in rich rebellion.

Gastronomical precepts are perhaps among the most delicate ones

670

in the modern arts. They must, in the main, be followed before they can be broken: that is, I can do something with five given ingredients that Escoffier perhaps never dreamed of, but in order to do it well I must follow his basic rules for white stock, glaze, and poaching, which he and all his kind perfected in a grueling devotion to their métier.

A rebuttal to this hidebound theory could be that gastronomical accidents often give birth to beauty: a chef forgets the fried potatoes, pops them out and then into the fat, and has pommes soufflées; another cook adds a raw yolk quickly to a portion of scrambled eggs when he finds it is to serve two people instead of one and has a new nutlike flavor on his conscience and his reputation. There are uncountable anecdotes of such chance discoveries.[1] Basically they have nothing to do with the fact that certain rules must be followed in order to reach certain results, in the sublime chemistry of food. They must, as Brillat-Savarin pointed out in his quasi-solemn little lecture on the art of frying, spring from a knowledge of natural laws.

My own rude forcing in the school of obedience to them came, perhaps fortunately for myself and certainly with great good luck for my intimates, when I was about nine.

I had already learned to follow recipes and could, I say now with a somewhat smug astonishment, make pan gravy, blanc-mange (cornstarch pudding), jelly roll, and other like requisites for my maternal grandmother's diet, and a few stolen delicacies such as mayonnaise, which we ate hungrily when she went away to religious conventions. I felt at home in the kitchen, at least on the cook's day off, and could poach eggs with the best of them, standing tiptoe on a needlepoint footstool beside the gas range.

But there was, as always, a salutary come-uppance. It happened one time when my father and mother went away for a Sunday and I was appointed to make a nice little supper for my sister and myself. I read a recipe in one of the smudged kitchen stand-bys. Hindu Eggs,[2] it said, and it was not the exotic title but the fact that curry powder was among ·the ingredients that decided me. The procedure was simple, quite within my skills, and as I boiled eggs and made a cream sauce I thought happily of that half-teaspoonful of curry, and of all the other delicious curried dishes of lamb and suchlike that we had sneaked when Grandmother was, as she was that very day, in Long Beach or Asbury Park.

The eggs peeled miraculously smooth. The sauce was a bland velvet dream. The casserole was buttered. And then I chose destruction: in a voluptuous maze of wanting to see again upon my sister's face the pleasure she always showed when we sneaked a curry, and in my own sensual need for more spice, more excitement, than Grandmother would allow us in our daily food, I put in several tablespoons of the nice yellowish-brownish powder.

The rest of the story is plain to any cook, no matter how amateur, but it conditioned at least two potential gastronomers to look up and murmur "Hindu Eggs!" whever ignorance or stupidity shows in the seasoning of a dish.

It is fortunate that an obedience to the laws of nature is quite often an inherent thing in a good cook. I know at least one, a woman, who could not possibly say why she adds ice-water rather than tap-water to her superlative pastry; she can neither read nor write, and indeed can hardly talk, and if she is asked she will say grudgingly, "Kinda makes it set right." She knows what all good cooks do, but not why.

Anyone, though, who wants to make pastry, or any other perquisite of gourmandism, can comfort himself with the certainty that if he is not born with this inarticulate knowledge he can acquire it. He can read, try, observe, think. He can, after a period of trial and inevitable error, somewhat like beginning to skate, turn out a pie as good as my friend's—maybe better. He may be like another chef I know, a dentist, who for his own amusement has translated every one of his heavenly recipes into purely chemical terms and formulas, an occupational whimsy far beyond most people; or he may be content, as am I, to leave "1 c. milk, 3 t. flour," and so on. But if he is honest, he will not tamper with any of the basic rules.

Myself, I have read so many recipes in the past thirty years or so, for both love and hunger, that I can and mostly do separate the good ones from the bad at a glance. What is more, I have followed so many of them, both actually and in my culinary brain, that I unconsciously reword and reorganize most of them, and am rebuffed and made suspicious by anything clumsy in them. For instance, I think a good recipe lists its ingredients in the order of their use, and there are a dozen other such rules I like to see followed.

And one thing I do, always and every time, is to wonder about the pepper in a new récipe. Me, I like pepper. Me, I find that every professional rule, say in *The Settlement* or *The Boston*, puts in about one-half what I want. On the other hand, most amateur recipes call for too much. Always and every time, therefore, my pepper-conscious mind (or palate?) questions the seasoning, and with one eye on what I already know about cooking and the other on what I think I know about the people who will eat my food, I alter the indicated proportions—as far as pepper goes, that is.

Much further than that I do not stray, at least in the basic requirements of fat and flour, flour and liquid, liquid and temperature, and so on. I have learned in my own laborious workshop the culinary laws of nature and by now can fairly well adjust them to the stove at my command, the weather and passions at whose command I am.

I know enough, in other words, not to double the lemon juice in a Hollandaise sauce: it will be too sour and it will probably curdle and it will, in short, be a flop. I know it won't help at all to make a custard of whipping cream instead of milk: it will flop. I know a salad won't be twice as good if I put in two tins of anchovy fillets instead of one. It, and the salt-killed lettuce in it, will flop, and dismally.

On the other hand I can, and do, double the butter or chicken fat when I make kasha,[3] and treble the wine in aspic, and cut the cooking time in half for almost any fish—all these are personal tricks which time has verified for my own taste, once I admit, as heaven knows I do, that I must first obey what the great cooks have found out for me.

What Brillat-Savarin said in 1825 about frying is still true, because it is based on nature's laws, and the same holds for a master like Escoffier on sauces and roasting, for any thoughtful cook, derivative or not, who bows to law and does not wildly say "Twice as much butter, or garlic, or zubzubzub, *must* be twice as good . . . If a pinch of nutmeg picks up this dish of spinach, *two* pinches . . ." and so on.

We who must eat such well-meant messes can do no better than refuse them and then beseech all such misguided cooks to stop and consider, to ponder on the reasons as well as the results, and to decide for themselves and also for our stomachs' sakes to follow the rules based on common sense and experience, the rules set down by great chefs, whatever their sex and in whichever of these last two centuries they have worked.

We must hold out the torch to these taste-deafened friends of ours and promise them that they too can throw away a few, if not all, of their gastronomical hearing aids; they too, once they have learned how to walk among the pots and pipkins, can add saffron where Escoffier said thyme, or put kirsch instead of maraschino into a soufflé—once they have rightly learned what saffron tastes like, and what a soufflé is.

1

The following accidental result of a flustered surmise that the juice of a whole lemon must certainly taste that much better than the skimpy teaspoonful the recipe demanded is to my mind a typical Bachelor's Delight, the kind that in its originator's hands can become almost a psychological drama of just-so stirring, a soul-tearing ordeal of finickiness, but that in more nonchalant, calloused hands, culinarily speaking, is almost as easy to make as what the *Ladies' Aid Manual* calls "Plain Sauce."

The rule for it, coaxed with some skulduggery from a highly successful Benedict, is truly one of those gastronomical monstrosities, The Happy Accident: it should be nasty, holding so much flour; it should be inedible, especially when served upon its destined breast of chicken with rice, with so much lemon juice in it; it is not a Hollandaise, not a cream sauce, not anything identifiable. But it is good.

SAUCE HAPPY ACCIDENT

½ cup sweet butter
½ cup flour
2 cups strong chicken consommé

salt, white pepper, cayenne
1 egg yolk
juice of one lemon

Gently blend butter and flour over boiling water in double boiler. Heat the strained consommé, add slowly, blend, and stir over simmering water for ½ hour. Season to taste. Five minutes before serving stir lemon juice into egg yolk, pass through fine strainer into sauce, and blend carefully.

This should be very good with something like poached fillets of sole or perch, but I have not tried it. I know that it is rather startling and fresh on properly boiled chicken. My one quarrel with it is that it is too sharp for the white wine that I like to accompany such a dish.

2

It may seem strange thus to return to the scene of the crime, but often since that far-off horrible day, that basically *blessed* day, I have made a more knowing version of this dish. Then it was nothing but sliced hard-boiled eggs covered with a rich cream sauce lightly (or so it said in the recipe!) savorous of good curry powder. Here is my mature adaptation of it, pleasant in hot weather, curry's natural climate, with a green salad and some beer.

HINDU EGGS, 1949

12 *peeled hard-boiled eggs*	1 *tablespoon finely minced*
½ *cup mayonnaise*	*onion*
1 *tablespoon curry powder*	1 *tablespoon finely chopped*
salt, cayenne pepper	*parsley*
1 *tablespoon soy sauce*	3 *to 4 cups heavy cream sauce*

Cut the eggs once lengthwise and then mix their yolks well with all the other ingredients except the cream sauce: that is, make a good recipe for the deviled eggs of any proper picnic, but adding curry powder. Stuff the eggs, put them together in their proper shape, and let stand several hours or overnight, to bring out the heat of the curry. Place in shallow buttered casserole, cover with hot bland sauce, place in a medium oven until almost bubbling, and serve. Use more cream sauce if it is to be served with rice. The eggs should have a strong curry flavor, in contrast to the gentle sauce, so some experimentation with your brand of curry powder is a good idea.

3

The patriotism of gastronomy has always caused emotional havoc, and who can know if my avowal here that I think Russian kasha one of the world's best dishes may not breed trouble for my children? I hope not. My devotion to the food as such is one of animal satisfaction rather than iron-curtained boundaries, and I feel quite safe in saying that as long as I can buy whole, unadulterated buckwheat groats I shall not only do so but shall prepare them in a fashion predominantly Slavic, even though I may stoop for reasons of family security to dubbing it Greek or Latvian (or Japanese?).

Most kosher delicatessens in this country carry one form or another of uncooked kasha. It is increasingly bad, thanks to the wave of

precooking and even predigesting that has swept away good packaged cereals in the last few years: it turns into an ugly mush, not
fit to soil the pan.

Unless you are sure of your market and your brand, the best thing
is to go to a "health food" store ("My God," a friend exclaimed,
waiting outside one while I bought raw sugar for the children and
eying the rows of natural-remedy cathartics in the window, "my
God, I didn't know *everybody* was so constipated!"). Such stores,
once you work past the sugarless candies and the sucrose-less sugars
and such, have very good honest things like stone-ground oatmeal—
and kasha. It should be *whole*, unprecooked, unpasteurized, unvi-
taminized, and so on, and so on.

Once having got it (and it will be worth the fuss), prepare it more
or less according to the following recipe, remembering that if you
are like me you will agree to most of the additions I shall make later:

BASIC RULE FOR KASHA

2 cups whole grain buckwheat
1 large or 2 small eggs
½ teaspoon salt

2 to 4 cups hot water
2 tablespoons butter or chicken
fat

*Put buckwheat in cold, ungreased, heavy skillet. Break in egg and
stir until each grain is coated. Heat gently, stirring often, so that the
grains become separate, glossy, and pleasantly odorous. Season. When
skillet is hot, add water to cover grains and stir in fat. Put on heavy
lid and reduce heat to minimum (or cook covered in 350° oven).
Steam for ½ hour to 45 minutes, checking now and then and adding water if too dry. Use as you would rice.*

Now here is where I branch off, as an old kasha-hound sniffing
my way along ruggedly individual trails!

To begin with, I like to use kasha, made my way naturally, as a
light stuffing for anything from old hens to wild turkeys: its straightforward flavor is more unexpected than that of the customary (and
delicious) wild rice—and much less expensive. I like it as it comes
from the pot, hot with butter or sour cream, and it is one of my
daughters' favorite meals, cold in a bowl with cream and brown
sugar. I like it mixed lightly with hot sliced mushrooms, or under
mushrooms in sharply seasoned sour cream. I like it alongside any

gamy meat, from venison to sauerbraten, in or near or quite without a sauce. It seems that I like it.

As for my own rich changes to ring: I do more than dry out the groats in the raw egg—I toast them to the nutty stage, very carefully, as if they were almonds. Then, instead of adding water, I use either good meat stock (tinned consommé is good) or vegetable juice from my pressure-cooker stock. I heat this, pour it on carefully so that it does not leap right out again with the heat, put double the advised amount of good butter or chicken fat or goose fat in the middle of the puddle, and batten down the heavy lid. I let it cook at something below a simmer, so that no fine steam is lost. I add more hot liquid if it seems wise, and every time I do this I put another tablespoon or so of butter into the middle and shake the pan gently without stirring it. It is rather like making a risotto.

When the kasha is fairly dry, cooked but not soft, I stir it, taste it, season it mildly with salt, take it off the fire, and leave it uncovered to air for an hour or more. Then I put what I'll need into a well-buttered casserole and put the casserole in the oven, to heat through at about 350°, usually with another dollop of butter (once I had some high-flavored drippings from wild pheasants I had cooked the week before, a superlative heady flavor, melted through the kasha!).

This is admittedly a blatant example of rich-bitch deviation from a basically "poor" recipe. I know that I could be grateful for a handful of the beneficent grains, boiled in a little water. I know that some day I may want them that way, desperately. But meanwhile I like them in a cloud of added richness and savor and have no shame in saying so. However they may come, they will be good.

R *is for* Romantic

... AND for a few of the reasons that gastronomy is and always has been connected with its sister art of love.

Or perhaps instead of reasons, which everyone who understands anything about digestion and its good and bad endocrinological effects will aready know, I should discuss here, with brief discretion, a few direct results of the play of the five senses, properly stimulated by food upon human passion. The surest way, if not the best, is to look backward.

Passion, here at least, means the height of emotional play between the two sexes, not the lasting fire I felt for my father once when I was about seven and we ate peach pie together under a canyon oak, and not the equally lasting fire I felt for a mammoth woman who brought milk toast to me once in the dusk when I was seventeen and very sick, and not the almost searing gratitude I felt for my mother when she soothed me with buttered carrots and a secret piece of divinity fudge once when I had done wrong and was in Coventry, and not the high note of confidence between two human beings that I felt once on a frozen hillside in France when a bitter old general broke his bread in two and gave me half.

This other kind of passion that I speak of, romantic if ever any such brutal thing could be so deemed, is one of sex, of the come-and-go, the preening and the prancing, and the final triumph or defeat, of two people who know enough, subconsciously or not, to woo with food as well as flattery.

The first time I remember recognizing the new weapon I was about eight, I think. There was a boy named Red, immortal on all my spiritual calendars, a tall, scoffing, sneering, dashing fellow perhaps six months older than I, a fellow of withdrawals, mockery, and pain. I mocked back at him, inadequately, filled with a curious tremor.

He followed me home every afternoon from school, a good half-block behind, and over the giggles of my retinue of girl friends came his insults and his lewd asides to a train of knee-britched sycophants.

We must have looked very strange to the relics of the Quaker settlers of our little town, who pulled aside their parlor curtains at our noise, but if our pipings were audible to their ancient ears they would not have felt too shocked, for as I recall it all we said, in a thousand significantly differing tones, was, Oh, yeah? Huh! Oh, *yeah?*

My friends gave me advice, as doubtless Red's gave him, and our daily march continued until February 14 that year without much variation. Then Red presented me with the biggest, fanciest, and most expensive Valentine in the class box: we knew, because it still said "50¢" on the back, in a spidery whisper of extravagance marked down thoughtfully in indelible pencil by the bookstore man and left carefully unsmeared by my canny lover.

I stalked on sneeringly every afternoon, virginal amid my train of damsels, the knights behind, hawking and nudging.

I was won, though, being but human and having, at eight as now, a belly below my heart. Red, through what advice I can never know, a few days later slipped into my desk the first nickel candy bar I had ever seen, called, I think, a Cherriswete.

It was a clumsy lump of very good chocolate and fondant, with a preserved cherry in the middle, all wrapped up in a piece of paper that immediately on being touched sent off waves of red and gilt stain. It was, to me, not only the ultimate expression of masculine devotion, but pure gastronomical delight, in a household where Grandmother disapproved of candy, not because of tooth decay or indigestion, but because children liked it and children should perforce not have anything they liked.

I sniffed happily at the Cherriswete a few times and then gave each girl in my retinue a crumb, not because I liked her but because of her loyalty. Then I took it home, showed it to my little sister, spun it a few times more past her nose to torture her, and divided it with her, since even though young and savage we loved each other very much.

My heart was full. I knew at last that I loved Red. I was his, to steal a phrase. We belonged together, a male and female who understood the gastronomical urge.

I never saw him again, since his father was transferred by Standard Oil from Brea to Shanghai that week end, but he has had much more influence on me with that one Cherriswete than most men could have in twenty years of Pol Roger and lark tongues. Sometimes

I wonder if he is still tall, freckled, and irreverent—and if he remembers how to woo a woman. Often I thank him for having, no matter how accidentally, taught me to realize the almost vascular connection between love and lobster pâté, between eating and romance.

1

That kind of milk toast is part of the unwritten cookery book engraved, almost without conscious recognition of it, in the mind of anyone who ever tended the young, the weak, the old. It is a warm, mild, soothing thing, full of innocent strength.

There is no recipe for it in even my homeliest kitchen manuals, in their generally revolting lists under such titles as "Feeding the Sick" and "Invalid Receipts." It is, in other words, an instinctive palliative, something like boiled water. But since some human beings may by dire oversight have missed the ministrations of their grandmothers, or of such a great hulk of woman as cared once for me when I was low in body, I shall print an approximation of the rule, to be adapted naturally to the relative strength or weakness of the person to imbibe it.

MILK TOAST for the Ill, Weak, Old, Very Young, or Weary

1 pint milk, part cream if the person is not forbidden that	sweet butter, if butter is allowed
4 slices good bread, preferably homemade	salt, pepper, if not a child or very ill

Heat the milk gently to the simmering point. Meanwhile have ready 4 freshly toasted slices of bread. Butter them generously. Heat a pretty bowl, deeper than it is wide. Break the hot buttered toast into it, pour the steaming but not boiling milk over it, sprinkle a very little salt and pepper on the top, and serve at once.

It can be seen that compromise lies in every ingredient. The basis for the whole is toasted bread soaked in warm milk. The sweet butter, the seasoning, the cream and the milk—these are sops indeed to the sybarite in even the sickest of us.

I have used this bland prescription more than once upon myself, recognizing a flicker across my cheekbones, a humming near my elbows and my knees, that meant fatigue had crept too close to the fortress walls. I have found partaking of a warm full bowl of it, in an early bed after a long bath, a very wise medicine—and me but weary, not ill, weak, old, not very young!

And I remember going one night to a famous restaurant, the quiet, subtly lighted kind like the Chambord, for instance, with a man who was healthier than almost anyone I ever met, because he had just emerged from months of dreadful illness, the quiet, subtly mortal kind. He still moved cautiously and spoke in a somewhat awed voice, and with a courteous but matter-of-fact apology he ordered milk toast for himself, hinting meanwhile at untold gastronomical delights for me.

I upset him and our waiter, only temporarily however, by asking for milk toast too, not because of my deep dislike of a cluttered table, but because I suddenly wanted the clear, comforting feel of the brew upon my tongue.

While I drank a glass of sherry an increasing flurry surrounded us. It took me some minutes to realize that probably never before in the fifty or so years the restaurant had been there had anyone ordered milk toast—nothing but milk toast. I began to feel as if screens would be whisked up around us, like two unfortunate or indiscreet athletes on a football field. There was a mounting air of tension among the waiters, who increased gradually in our corner of the room from three to about twelve. By the time the silver chafing dishes had been wheeled before us, we had three captains, all plainly nervous, eying the maneuvers from near-by vantage points.

The thing began: butter sizzling here, toast smoking delicately there, rich milk trembling at the bubbling point but no further, a huge silver pepper-mill held ready, salt, rock-salt, in a Rumanian grinder, paprika in a tin marked "Buda-Pesth." Helpless, a little hysterical under our super-genteel exteriors, my friend and I waited. The flames flamed. The three captains surged into action. And before we could really follow the intricate and apparently well-rehearsed ballet, two mammoth silver bowls, just like the nursery ones but bigger and more beautiful, steamed before us, and we sat spooning up the most luxurious, most ridiculously and spectacularly delicious milk toast either of us had eaten in our long, full, and at times invalidish lives.

It was a small modern miracle of gastronomy, certainly not worth having illness for, but worth pondering on, in case milk toast might help.

S is for Sad

. . . AND for the mysterious appetite that often surges in us when our hearts seem about to break and our lives seem too bleakly empty. Like every other physical phenomenon, there is always good reason for this hunger if we are blunt enough to recognize it.

The prettifiers of human passion choose to think that a man who has just watched his true love die is lifted above such ugly things as food, that he is exalted by his grief, that his mind dwells exclusively on thoughts of eternity and the hereafter. The mixture of wails and wassail at an Irish wake is frowned upon as merely an alcoholic excuse by the sticklers for burial etiquette, and the ancient symbolism of funeral baked meats is accepted, somewhat grudgingly, as a pagan custom which has been Christianized sufficiently by our church fathers to justify a good roast of beef and some ice cream and cake after the trip to the family burying ground with Gramp.

The truth is that most bereaved souls crave nourishment more tangible than prayers:[1] they want a steak. What is more, they need a steak. Preferably they need it rare, grilled, heavily salted, for that way it is most easily digested, and most quickly turned into the glandular whip their tired adrenals cry for.

A prime story of this need is the chapter in Thomas Wolfe's *Look Homeward, Angel,* just after Ben has died, when his two racked brothers begin to laugh and joke like young colts, and then go in the dawn to Ben's favorite all-night beanery and eat an enormous, silly meal. Another good example is in D. H. Lawrence's *Sons and Lovers,* as I remember. There are many more, all of them shocking, and yet strangely reassuring too, like some kinds of music.

Perhaps that is because they are true, far past prettiness. They tell us what we then most need to be reminded of, that underneath the anguish of death and pain and ugliness are the facts of hunger and

682

unquenchable life, shining, peaceful. It is as if our bodies, wiser than we who wear them, call out for encouragement and strength and, in spite of us and of the patterns of proper behavior we have learned, compel us to answer, and to eat.

More often than not, in such compulsory feastings, we eat enormously, and that too is good, for we are stupefying ourselves, anesthetizing our overwrought nerves with a heavy dose of proteins, and our bodies will grow sleepy with digestion and let us rest a little after the long vigil.

I tried to say this once to a man who, being well raised and sensitive, was in a state of shock at his behavior.

It was late at night. He had been driving up and down the coastal highway, cautiously and in a numb way almost happily, ever since a little before noon that day when his love had died. She was one of the most beautiful women in the world, and one of the most famous, and he loved her for these reasons and even more so because she loved him too. But he had to watch her die, for two nights and a day.

When she was finally at peace he walked from her bedside like a deaf, blind man, got into his car and headed for the coast, and in the next hours he must have stopped at four or five big restaurants and eaten a thick steak at each one, with other things he usually ignored, like piles of French-fried potatoes, slabs of pie, and whatever bread was in front of him. He had a flask of cognac in the car but did not touch it; instead he drank cup after cup of searing black coffee, with or without food, in a dozen little joints along the road, and then left them humming and whistling.

By the time I saw him he was literally bulging and had loosened his belt futilely to make room for the load in his middle. He put his head in his hands and shuddered. "How could I?" he said. "How could I—and she not yet in her coffin!"

It was a helpless protest, and I, more plain-spoken than usual, tried to cut through his digestive fog, to tell him how right he had been to let his body lead him on this orgy, how it would tide him over the next hours, how his hunger had made him do what his upbringing had taught him was gross, indelicate, unfeeling.

He soon went to his bed, staggering, hardly conscious, certainly uncaring for a time at least of his own or the world's new woe. But years later, so strong was his training, he would think back on that day with a deep embarrassment, no matter how candidly he admitted the basic wisdom of his behavior. He would always feel, in spite of himself, that sadness should not be connected so directly with gastronomy.

1

Going to a funeral is perhaps even more wearing than watching someone die, and I know of at least one candid admission of this ugly fact. An old French marshal, returning from the elaborate rites for his last contemporary, let servants and his family strip the heavy decorations from him and then said with great dignity, "You may serve me with two roasted pigeons. I have noticed that after eating a brace of them I arise from the table feeling much more resigned."

I imagine, since this happened many years ago, that the birds were braised in good butter, covered closely, and allowed to fret in their own juices until done. (Some, scorning the meat as so much crow, say a pigeon is *never* done. But crow, to yet others, is good.)

Old pigeons, except stewed in a pie, are barely mentioned in kitchen manuals, and even squabs, their tender little chicks, are in none too good gastronomical odor. I agree heartily with the great Escoffier that this is a crying shame, "since when the birds are of excellent quality, they are worthy of the best tables."

I grew interested in them, roasted of course, when I was fairly young. My mother was in the throes of several years of child-bearing, which I watched interestedly from the side lines. My father seemed, except at certain moments quite beyond my youthful understanding, to be quite as ineffectual as I was, and when it was found that grilled squabs might satisfy the troubled, peckish woman, he and I bent with mutual ardor, and an enthusiasm on my part which I do not think he yet recognizes, to satisfy her need.

He bought pigeons. He read books. We discussed the less romantic aspects of mating and breeding. I helped, even more realistically, to maintain the impeccable cotes. We had very fine birds. We even had a few babies, thanks to my father's jealous watchings, waitings, and pigeon-wise suspicions.

But by the time the eggs hatched Mother had lost her yearning for roast squabs: quite plainly it sickened her to hear them named. As for the increasing roar of early-morning cooings from the cotes, it drove her nearly frantic.

My father moved the birds down to a ranch in the country and kept on studying, perhaps with vicarious delight, the intricacies of pigeon fidelity. He was always buying new birds, handsome puff-throated males, shimmering sweet little matrons.

As far as I can remember I never ate a single squab. All that remains with me, at least about the edible part of the lengthy experiment, is looking at the little roasted birds that came downstairs untouched on Mother's tray, feeling ready to pounce on them, and hearing her nurse say, "Nupnup*nup*! Mizz Fuss-budget may want it later!" I still don't really know who ate those plump juicy little morsels, but I can guess, so appetizing did they look as Nurse flicked them through the door into the darkened kitchen. There was anticipation in every starched crease of her.

A friend of mine who was on the municipal council in a provincial French town studded with architectural gems has told me that there used to be daily battles, every springtime, over whether the pigeons roosting in the church façades and on the statues' heads should be netted and made into a kind of brothy pie for the poor, or left yet another year in their disfiguring filth. The latter alternative always was carried, mainly because it would take more men than the town could muster to kill the birds and clean up their accumulated droppings, and then there would be more pigeon pie than a town of five times that size could eat, poor and rich together, if by some miracle all the birds flew properly into the traps held out for them. The town, thanks to time's unceasing labors, remains just about as limy and beautiful as ever, and its poor are hardly hungrier than they would have been if they had sat down once annually before a Gargantuan pie of an origin so obviously more practical than charitable.

To be truthful, I do not know what I would do if I were presented with, say, twenty-four tough stringy pigeons to make edible. I suppose I would put them in a pie, like the blackbirds, but anything that involves plucking, cleaning, boning, simmering, seasoning, this and that, somewhat discourages me. Perhaps it would be best to make a soup of them, a good heartening broth, with a little sherry in it.

No. Gastronomically undaunted, I would do this, given not twenty-four but four healthy birds: clean them properly, rub them well with a cut lemon and then a little cloth wet with decent brandy, brown them evenly and well in a mixture of sweet butter and olive oil, and simmer them closely covered for about a half-hour, or until tender.

If I felt fussy and ready for more fussiness, as often happens after a funeral, I would remove the birds to a shallow casserole, put a little brandy over them, and set them alight, to rid them of some of their fat gaminess; and I would reduce the braize and a cup of good red wine to a fine sauce to pour over them, and I would serve them on toasted buttery slices of decent bread.

It sounds good. It does not need a burial to make it so. All it needs, oh, dreadful practicality, is some pigeons!

T *is for* Turbot

. . . AS well as trout, and for me at least these two gastronomical delights will be forever one.

Do I mean turbot, what dictionaries call "a large, flat fish esteemed as food," or do I mean trout, leering up, twisted and blue, from its pan? My confusion, spiritual at least, springs from an experiment with pressure-cookers, which started some time around 1820 near the little French village of Villecrêne, and ended in 1948 near the little American village of Beverly Hills.

One of the pleasantest stories, I think, in one of the pleasantest books ever written, Brillat-Savarin's *Physiology of Taste*, is the anecdote called, very simply, "The Turbot." In it he tells, with a ruminative smugness which he was indeed entitled to, how he saved the day as well as the menaced domestic bliss of two of his dearest friends.

They had invited a group of "pleasant people" to lunch at their country place at Villecrêne on a Sunday, and when Brillat-Savarin arrived on horseback from Paris on Saturday night, as their privileged guest, he found them at polite swords' points over what to do with a magnificent turbot which was, unfortunately, too enormous to fit into any cooking pan.

It would be another hundred years or so before the great Escoffier was to state sternly, "It is of the greatest importance . . . that the turbot not be cooked too long beforehand, since it tends to harden, crumple, and lose its flavor," and the young French couple, happily unconscious of blundering, plainly planned to boil their catch whole and then serve it the next day in its own jelly, with some such sauce as a mayonnaise, probably garnished with little tomatoes and cucumbers from their garden.

Madame stood up stoutly against the chopper which her exasperated husband was threatening to use. The tactful Professor

687

insisted, in spite of feeling ravenously hungry, that the whole household help him immediately in coping with this domestic crisis. He sniffed through the establishment like an eager hound, until in the laundry, of all places, he found exactly what he needed: the copper wash boiler, which of course was solidly a part of its own little furnace. He marshaled the servants into a solemn procession, himself at the head bearing the turbot, the doubting cook and his skeptical friend in the rear, and proceeded to carry out his first dramatic assertion that the fish must, and indeed would, remain in one piece until its final appearance.

While the maids built up a fine fire, and the cook assembled onions, shallots, and highly flavored herbs, he devised a kind of hammock from a large reed clothes hamper. He laid the fresh herbs in a thick layer on the bottom, then the cleaned and salted fish, and then a second layer of herbs.

"Then the hammock was put across the boiler," he wrote, "which was half full of water, and the whole was covered with a small washtub around which we banked dry sand, to keep the steam from escaping too easily. Soon the water was boiling madly; steam filled the inside of the tub, which was removed at the end of a half-hour, and the hammock was taken out of the boiler with the turbot cooked to perfection, white as snow, and most agreeable to look at."

The next day all the guests exclaimed at its handsome appearance, and ". . . it was unanimously agreed that the fish prepared according to my system was incomparably better than if it had been cooked in the traditional turbot-pan . . . [for] since it had not been passed through boiling water it had lost none of its basic qualities, and had on the contrary absorbed all the aroma of the seasoning."

This is so obvious a result of his method that it surprises me to find some such master as Escoffier ignoring its principles and continuing, a century later, to advise his followers to boil turbot in the classical mixture of seven parts salted water to one of sweet milk.

The Professor himself hoped that his system would be followed and developed for the inexpensive and wholesome feeding of large numbers of people, as in armies and institutions, and I should think that hotel cookery as understood by Escoffier would fall somewhere into these categories. Perhaps it did not because pressure-cookers, as we casually know and use them today, were still too risky a utensil when the master-chef died in 1934. Whatever the reasons, there can be no doubt that the boiled and/or poached fish generally served in even the best restaurants suffer from too much water and too little taste—too much Escoffier and not enough Professor.

The only real mass harnessing of steam to the pleasures of the table that I know about is done by the Chinese, and I can, in my mind, be at this very minute in the alley doorway of a Cantonese restaurant just off Plymouth Square in San Francisco, watching the exciting rhythm of the steam cookery there.

Ducks and cabbages and bean sprouts and a curled carp are all under the one bell-like top, and a fine vapor rises from it, not mingled, not blurred in savor, as the helper raises and lowers it on a long rope according to the hissed, hectic directions of the cook. The hot room has an airiness about it unknown to most public kitchens, in spite of, or perhaps because of, the controlled clouds of steam.

There is a steady chopping sound: everything edible seems to pass from the shelves to the steam-stove by way of the chef's incredibly skilled knife, and fish, fowl, celery, and a hundred other things turn, almost too fast to watch, into the strips, sticks, and mouth-sized morsels proper for eating with chopsticks. It is perhaps the freshness of these foods that sends up such a salutary vapor, like the bottled chlorophyll we buy to sweeten our stale household air. Certainly the high speed at which the food is cooked keeps it still sending off its gases when it is done—and I prove that a dozen times a week when, mouselike compared to the elephant of a Chinese steam-stove, and like an *écrivisse* to the Professor's fish, my four-quart Presto turns out vegetables for my ever-hungry children.

It interests me to watch their instinctive love of the good smell of the pot just after it has been opened: they cluster like bees around a jam jar, and sniff and smile, and pop into their mouths the beans or zucchini or whatever I have fixed when it is almost too hot to touch. The next day, inevitably, there is much less interest in what is left, since its first fresh flavor has been tainted by time's passage, and I myself, more jaded in palate, find that salt and soy and butter are necessary, where for the first minutes nothing could possibly have been wanted to accentuate the indescribable freshness of the food.

There are a dozen books and a hundred booklets on modern pressure-cookery. I think most of them dull, after the first simple principles have been laid down and shown to be foolproof, to the timid and the superstitious, with a series of artful photographs and charts. Perhaps it is because I can attain such comfortable forgetfulness of my life's problems in the construction of a stew (as some women do in baking bread) that I do not wish to cut the time for it from four hours to forty minutes. And I am not particularly interested in "tenderizing" inferior cuts of meat, being intransigently of the school that would choose one good dinner of prime beef rather than six of thinly disguised chuck.

But for succulent, almost melodramatically delicious vegetables nothing can equal a modern Presto; and since my children live mainly upon the earth's plants, to strengthen them for keener if less nourishing delights, I sharpen their palates thankfully with what comes in a seemingly endless flood from my steam-cooker.

At times, I confess gastronomically, I grow damned bored. And that is when I call up the Professor's ghost, and with a bow to him I make, much more timetakingly than any modern recipe would tolerate, my own modest version of his turbot.

I could not duplicate his, of course, even if I did have the turbot—and an ancient copper boiler in a laundry house. Given the fish (and my Bendix!), where would I find the herbs? But there is the Presto. And there are, thanks to fast trains and efficient fish farms, beautiful almost instant-fresh rainbow trout. And there is my postmaternal necessity for something besides beans and zucchini. There is, finally, my sentimental feeling about Brillat-Savarin himself.

The recipe which I have devoutly evolved,[1] assumes that I have two fresh trout, handsome and alike—a somewhat impertinent assumption on the side of a sage-covered desert hill, but not so much so near the fine markets of Beverly Hills where I first assumed it. Two trout, unfortunately, are all that my cooker will hold. But the best thing about the recipe is that it can be repeated endlessly, and a dozen or so pretty fish, side by side in their clear jelly upon their couch of herbs, is a sight worth any coping, especially when it can be saluted, while the Professor's ghost smiles just over my left shoulder, with a bottle of Wente's Pinot Chardonnay or, dryer and just as cold, Grey Riesling.

Then I can feel, almost as justifiably smug as the old Frenchman when he wrote about his turbot, that I have bolstered my own self-esteem as a cook, if not saved such domestic bliss as he fought for.

I can forget the sometimes tiresome routine of nourishing my family, and sit back happily, in the company of One, and eat as artful a combination of fresh natural flavors as ever lay upon a plate. I can compliment myself unashamedly that I have dared ponder on what a gaffer wrote down more than a hundred years ago and have adapted it to such an anachronism-in-reverse as a little aluminum pot with a gauge sticking up, a far cry from the boiler at Villecrêne.

"While my ears drank their fill of the compliments which were showered upon me," Brillat-Savarin wrote contentedly, "my eyes sought out other even more sincere ones in the visible post-mortem verdict of the guests, and I observed with secret satisfaction that General Labassée was so pleased that he smiled anew at each bite, while the curé had his chin stretched upwards and his ecstatic eyes fixed upon the ceiling, and . . . Monsieur Villemain leaned his head with his jaw tipped to the west, like a man who is listening. . . .

"All of this is useful to remember," he went on. And I know how right he was, for though no general has tasted my little offshoot of the famous turbot, and no curé, another good man has—and with me—and I shall remember the usefulness of the recipe many times again, and the magic of its flavors, when I may, being human, have become boresome.

1

TROUT BRILLAT-SAVARIN

(who said [Aphorism IX], "The invention of a new dish adds more to the happiness of mankind than the discovery of a star.")

⅓ cup water
1 small head lettuce
4 scallions
    parsley, other fresh herbs at discretion
2 fine trout
    wine vinegar

2 packages plain gelatin
1 cup fish stock (add water if necessary, to make full cup)
½ teaspoon salt
    tabasco sauce
2 cups dry white wine
¼ cup wine vinegar, optional

Put water in pressure-cooker. Put in the rack. Shred lettuce, mince scallions (tops and all), chop parsley and choice of fresh herbs— enough to make about 4 cups when lightly tossed together. Put mixed greens on rack and lay properly cleaned trout, bellies together and fins affectionately intertwined, on this soft bed.

Follow the procedure that is correct for the make of pressure-

cooker being used, and when gauge is at Cook *keep it there for 2½ to 3 minutes, no longer.*

Put cooker under cold-water stream at once, remove cover as soon as possible, and take out rack holding trout and greens.

Put all juice, strained, into a measuring cup, adding enough cool water to make one full cup. Carefully slide trout on their bed into a shallow oblong casserole or a fish platter. Sprinkle generously with good wine vinegar.

Dissolve the gelatin in the fish stock. Add salt and 2 or 3 drops of tabasco (and the ¼ cup of wine vinegar if a sharp aspic is desired). Bring the 2 cups of dry white wine to the boiling point, no more, and mix well with the stock-gelatin. Allow to cool to the thickening point. Spoon ⅓ of it gently over the trout and shake a little to let it penetrate the herb bed. Place casserole in refrigerator for five minutes or so, then repeat 2 or 3 times, so that the fish will be well covered with a clear jelly. Chill well. Serve with a freshly made and very simple mayonnaise.

Lemon juice can be used instead of wine vinegar, but it may war with the wine, as well as with the delicate nutlike quality of the fish itself. For luncheon it is amusing (I can never use this word, no matter how straightforwardly I mean it, without wincing at the ever-present memory of an early Thurber cartoon in *The New Yorker*, in which two pompous people were apparently awing two timid ones by yammering of "an amusing little wine of the country," or something like that) to use in the aspic a rosé wine rather than a white: it turns it into what more than one good chef calls "a ladies' dish," and the rosé, from Louis Martini or Beaulieu for instance, can be served with the meal.

You must take care not to overcook the fish by even ten seconds or it will "crumple," as Ecoffier says of turbot. But in spite of his dictum, this dish can be made the night before it is to be served, although the trout lose something of their shimmer in such a wait, as perhaps the Professor's turbot at Villecrêne did not.

U is for Universal

... AND for a fleeting discussion of bread and salt, which remains man's universal meal in spite of the understandable assumption that it may instead be restaurant sauce, as served from Singapore to Buenos Aires and back again in any upper-class chophouse.

There is a special and unmistakable liquid, a staple of the chef who must maintain his so-called standards but still is too busy to start afresh for each patron which at this very moment is being doused indiscriminately upon veal cutlets, fillets of beef, and even slices of salmon in uncountable kitchens all over the world. It is thinner than thick, browner than red, a consummate mixture of mediocrity that baffles and impresses the ignorant and nauseates the knowing. Its sparing use denotes a clever restaurant cook, its prodigality a reckless one, for even the dullest diner will in the end revolt and go elsewhere if every entrée he orders swims in the same questionable flood.

It may serve one good purpose: any homesick wanderer can, with one mouthful of it in Detroit, be back in any almost identical eating house in Plymouth, Bombay, or Lima, snug in his nostalgic memories of other steaks or cutlets that tasted just the same!

Perhaps gastronomers of a few hundred years from now will consider it the Universal Food of our century. Meanwhile I prefer to think of an older and much simpler one: the bread that has been broken, for countless years, and the salt that has been eaten with it, as well as sprinkled over the doorsteps of our ancestors and offered with incense to the gods, even unto now.

Salt, sodium chloride, NaCl, is perhaps too much a part of today's table, or so at least many of our doctors feel,[1] and rightly when they can point to patients with hardened arteries and palsy, and less often but with equal poignancy to the palate-deadened children and travel-

693

ing salesmen and such who whip themselves at every meal the way
a cow must in the spring, licking at salt to stimulate her glands.

It has always been vegetable and cereal eaters, cows and human-
kind alike, who most crave the taste of salt, and men who live on
roasted meat, like the Bedouins, need never touch it, for natural
flavors can appease them without any help. But once meat is boiled,
with its goodness in part drained from it, salt must be added to
make it decently palatable. There is a sensual satisfaction about the
rough bitter crystals of rock-salt that are sprinkled over a true pot-au-
feu or bouilli, at least as I used to eat it in Burgundy, that no grilled
kid could equal, and yet I have never put salt on beef to be seared
and roasted over the coals in my patio barbecue, and people who in
restaurants would automatically reach for the saltcellar eat it blissfully, incredulous when at the end they learn what they have done.

I was taught when very young that it is an insult to the cook to
salt a dish before it has been tasted, and in spite of my adult knowledge of the reasons for such an unthinking gesture I still resent it
when anyone at my table seasons something as soon as it is put before him. I know that his tongue is jaded, calloused even, by restaurant sauces and a thousand dinners that have had to be heightened
with anything at hand in order to be swallowed at all. Still I wish,
silently most of the time, that he would take a chance and eat just
one bite before he sprinkles the ubiquitous salt and pepper upon
whatever has been prepared for him. I have great pride in my culinary knowingness, and feel, with good proof, that some things need
salt and some do not. Green beans, for instance, as opposed to my
patio steak: the first needs an ample touch of salt, ample sweet butter, and then an ample grind of fresh pepper, while the second never
sees anything but herbs and wine.

Bread is another thing again, a cereal which in one way or another
carries itself most easily with salt somewhere about it. I know a man
of parts who, when he eats reddish-brown Russian rye bread, will
spread it thickly with sweet butter and then, to my own private horror, coat the whole with an impossible load of table salt; he likes
the odor, texture, taste; it makes him feel good to eat this honest,
enriching fare.

Bread made without salt has a strange sweetness about it, almost
a nutmeg taste, much more of a chemical difference than the one
small omission would be expected to make. And in the making it

does not smell as yeasty and irresistible somehow. It is worth the bother, if indeed it can be called bother to mix the whole and then pound it and let it rise and pound it, in the age-old ritual of "baking."

It is too bad, I think, that fewer and fewer people try its classical rhythm. It brings a mysterious satisfaction with it, which I saw not long ago when a fine woman was told never to touch salt again, and suddenly her whole house became more peaceful, all because the cook had to make salt-free bread twice weekly.

The cook herself was drunk less often, for having to concentrate and remember: breadmaking is not a quarter-hour task like pie crust or dumplings.

The fine woman's fine husband came home oftener, and sniffed happily at the round pan of dough, a clean linen napkin laid lightly over it, rising on a dining-room chair near the furnace register.

People too, not just husbands, came in on baking days and sat, and no matter what their financial brackets, they leaned back gladly to eat a slice or two or three of the warm delicious fresh-baked loaf, and taste its strange sweetness, and never miss the salt that supposedly should make it palatable.

The fine woman told me that the accident of being forbidden ever to taste salt again had made her very happy, because of the bread-baking, and I know what she meant. Few people now are forced, as she was, to make their own loaves, and even fewer to forego the seasoning which has become a modern gastronomical necessity but should still be, according to the laws of nature, a privilege dictated by position, the priests, and the time of year.

A cook who must rely upon his own skill to make something edible, rather than toss in an impossible load of salt in the hope that it will stupefy if not soothe the outraged palates of his guests, can count himself fortunate indeed, for there is no culinary challenge quite as demanding as salt-free food in the modern diet. It can be good food, as I know. It can in the end wreak a strange revenge and make most other dishes in most other dining places taste ghoulishly pickled and cadaverous, like warmed-over slices of zombie.

There are a thousand tricks at hand, of course, to make saltless food full enough of natural flavor to be satisfying. The most helpful one in present-day kitchens is the pressure-cooker, which if intelligently used can turn out such things as garden peas with a God-given flavor unfamiliar to most modern tongues.

In general the simplest procedures are the best, and a cook who finds himself by force or his own choice in a salt-free kitchen will soon revert to an almost primitive way of roasting, basting, and poaching. He will also, if he is worth his forbidden salt, think back on his own more ornate skills and dream of a perfect Soubise the way some men dream of virgins. And he will, and this I can swear to, next make that Soubise with a tenderness and respect unknown to him in the old days when he did it daily, and at times overcasually, assuming with most of his clients that too much of a good thing might be a sin but was still more desirable than not enough of it.

I am convinced that coping with a saltless regimen should be part of every good chef's schedule, at least once a year or so, to sharpen his dulled appreciation of food's basic flavors and make him consider them with caution before his routine boiling and peeling. In a strange kitchen-fashion some such penance as this might act as a kind of purification, connected in its own way with the religious significance that has always cloaked bread and salt.

Having made honest bread again,[2] with or without salt, and recollected its mysterious moving fragrance; having grilled meat again,[3] untainted by the chemistry of salt, the cook would be able to sense fundamental flavors that are quite beyond too many of us, and would be refreshed, strengthened, able once more to make his cunning sauces without stooping, as he has found it increasingly easy to do, to the universal brew, the one served in so many restaurants, the one recognizable from here to there.

He would, knowing it or not, remember that salt and bread are to be honored, not turned into dull necessity and the puffed packaged furnishings of any corner grocery. He would be a better cook.

1

When I was younger, and less set in my sensory patterns than I am now, I was impatient of people who rebelled, more or less helplessly, at a doctor's dictum that they must forego cigarettes, or desserts, or, most especially, salt.

Although it is something I myself could be told never to taste again and still manage to live pleasurably, I am more tolerant today of diabetics who risk sure death for a secret orgy of banana cream pie, or heart cases who fret and even weep a little at the ghastly flatness, or so it seems to them, of a salt-sodium-free diet. My sympathy, as I approach the stiffer years, grows more compassionate.

One reason most people protest so passionately against giving up salt is that they, like morphine addicts, have set up an almost miraculous tolerance, thanks to its indiscriminate use in modern cookery, to the lack of natural flavor or to camouflaged carelessness.

It is impossible to conceive of average-to-good restaurant food, say, some completely simple thing like scrambled eggs with spinach, which would be much more than edible without a double dose of salt, the one slapped in automatically by the chef, the other sprinkled in almost as automatically by the diner. As for home-cooking, too often food is drained of its inherent goodness by overcooking, by throwing away its natural juices, by a hundred things which could be remedied with a little thought.

And thus it is that when, as in the case of a fine friend of mine, the outraged human body cries no, no to such cumulative excess as we take for granted, there is a rebellion of the palate, as drastic in its way as the violent battle of nausea and agony that a dipsomaniac puts up, or a cocaine-sniffer, and in spite of himself too, when he is deprived of his poison.

The substitutes for salt are many, and pathetically interesting. They come in powder or liquid form, to be sprinkled at will upon the food which is at first so tasteless, and which will remain that way if unintelligently prepared. They have a dozen different names, most impressive, and although the powder form, for instance, can easily be put into a regular salt shaker and used without comment, I have noticed that most heart patients prefer to keep it in its dramatically blunt little bottle, with the elaborate formula marked plainly if cryptically upon it, and to say with self-pitying resignation to their nurses or husbands or dutiful daughters, "Please pass me my Ceo-Nurtasode" instead of ". . . the salt."

The plainly printed ingredients of such a gastronomical stopgap are equally soul-satisfying psychologically. Instead of sodium chloride, which is about all that would be mentioned on a pharmacist's label for plain table salt, there is a handsome list of mysterious and at times unpronounceable chemicals: ammonium and potassium chlorides, calcium and potassium formates, magnesium citrates, on and on, increasingly polysyllabic.

It is fun, in a sad way, to cloak monotony in such giddiness. This bottled powder, though, makes vegetables taste bitter; that colorless liquid, a teaspoonful to a loaf, makes bread taste no better than if it were blankly saltless. Hohum, the salt-free sufferer finally murmurs, hohum, enough of *that*!

There is, it seems, no substitute for NaCl. There is no faking its fine stimulus, its artful aid—except to use it with more respectful attention to its basic powers and dangers; except, perhaps, to taste it for a change, instead of taking it for granted.

2

There are as many good recipes for bread as there are good cookbooks, a statement not quite as equivocal as it at first sounds, for there are indeed formidable numbers of honest collections of the basic rules of cookery: Fanny Farmer's, Mrs. Simon Kander's, Mrs. Rombauer's, Louis de Gouy's, Louis Diat's, and on and on, just here in America.

Of course national and racial differences are at times in conflict, and an Italian recipe for bread, or a French one, will astound and amuse a housewife in Kansas who has learned the weekly rhythm of the baking from her Great-Aunt Maggie. I have watched polite Mexicans almost gag on the "American bread" my brother brought down to Chapala from Guadalajara's one fancy grocery as a special treat for them, as an exotic as well as optimistically healthful change from their tortillas, so flat and sandy-dry.

Breadmaking, I have found, is a very personal thing, and what one cook does another cannot or will not do because it does not feel right. Fortunately for the cook's vanity as well as the consumer's appetite, *good* bread can never be anything but that, whether the dough rose twice or thrice, whether the yeast worked in a Yorkshire buttery or on a California cellar shelf. *Good* bread will forever send out its own mysterious and magical goodness, to all the senses, and quite aside from all the cookbooks, perhaps the best way to learn how to make it is to ask an old, wise, and, above all, *good* woman.

3

This recipe is anyone's for the taking. It presupposes a simple outdoor grill, but can be followed in a kitchen (also presupposing inevitable clouds of almost-choking but still-delicious blue smoke).

The kitchen grill should be *very hot*. The outdoor fire should be reduced to a good bed of lively, glowing coals. The ingredients are simple, as is the practiced routine which pulls them into focus. The result is, inevitably, a happy one, at least for Occasions: it is not the kind to expect too often, having something magnificent and sacrificial about it in a primitive way.

INGREDIENTS (for 5-pound sirloin steak)

1 steak, at least 2 and prefer- ably 3 inches thick. (Sir- loin is best; fillet is too ten- der.)

6 cloves garlic

¾ cup good olive oil

¾ cup soy sauce

½ pound unsalted butter

2 cups finely chopped scallions, green pepper, celery, pars- ley, fresh basil if available

3 cups good plain red table wine

METHOD

Remove meat from refrigerator at least 4 hours before you need it. Cut off almost all fat, otherwise it will catch on fire. Slash edges ¼ inch deep, every 2 inches, to avoid curling. Skewer tail of steak firmly around bone to insure even broiling, and if it is still loose-looking, bind it around with stout twine. (This will burn off, but by the time it does the meat will have taken its final shape.)

Rub sturdily with peeled and halved garlic cloves on all surfaces, including the bone and what little fat is left.

Put meat into shallow casserole, lying flat, and rub half of soy sauce thoroughly into the upper side. Let stand uncovered. In about an hour turn over and rub the other side. This makes a tough-looking dark coat. Then pour the olive oil on the steak and turn it over two or three times before dinner. (The soy souce may seem a concession to salt-lovers but is not: it acts as a kind of innocent tanning, and is wonderful on fish, used in the same way.)

Put the chopped vegetables and herbs, the butter and the wine, into a bowl over a very low flame about an hour before dinner, or at the back of the outdoor grill. (¼ cup oyster sauce or Worcester-shire sauce can be added at end—not necessary, but good.)

About 20 minutes (rare) to 35 minutes (well-done) before dinner is to be served (this takes a bit of practice in outdoor cookery, to time the right combination of intense heat minus any flame), put the steak on the grill, near which you are standing ready in asbestos or very thick gardening gloves, armed with a whisk broom and a bowl of water to douse the flames (very exciting).

Pour the heated sauce into the casserole containing the remaining oil and soy sauce and put near the coals to bubble.

Turn the steak once or twice by hand, so as not to pierce the shell of seared meat.

When done, lift into the hot casserole of sauce. Slice in fairly thick (about ½ inch) slices into the sauce and douse each one well in it before serving. Slices that are too rare will cook if left in the sauce a minute or so.

This somewhat primeval dish is easy to prepare, once practiced. I always serve it generously, with equally generous baskets of lightly toasted sourdough bread (for sopping), piles of fresh watercress in wooden bowls, platters of thickly sliced tomatoes (innocent of anything but a possible sprinkling of chopped fresh basil), and ample Tipo Red or ale. I used to have cheeses later, for what was left of the bread, but I have found that a basket of cool fresh fruit and cups of strong "Louisiana" coffee are more welcome to the pleasantly stimulated and at the same time surfeited diners.

V *is for* Venality

. . . AND for the mixture of gastronomical pleasure and corruption that helps senators and actresses pounce with such slyly hidden skill upon their prey.

Wherever politics are played, of no matter what color, sex, or reason, the table is an intrinsic part of them, so much so that Brillat-Savarin asserted, enthusiastically if not too correctly, that every great event in history has been consummated over a banquet board. Though I may question his statement, I still admit the loose rightness of it and bow to the companion thought that history is indeed largely venal, no matter what its ultimate nobility. Surely many a soldier has been saved from death because his general slept the night before the battle with Ottilia instead of Claudia, and more than one pretty creature in a Hollywood restaurant has missed stardom but kept her female balance because a producer did not like the way she ate asparagus.

Wherever politics are played, then, which means wherever in the world more than five men foregather, venality sits at table with them, corrupt, all-powerful. In every city from Oskaloosa to Madrid, there is one meeting place which above all others furthers and comforts the inevitable progress of the evil-bent, and the ghost of a Paris senator who last lunched at Foyot's in 1897 would find itself perfectly at home in a certain air-conditioned restaurant in Washington, this year or next, or in some such place as Mike Romanoff's[1] in Beverly Hills.

Some of the best food in America can be, and occasionally is, found at his eating place, although architecture rather than gastronomy seems at first glance to be what makes it a necessary part of the nourishment of Hollywood politicians.

The perfection of a rack of lamb served from Mike's overpoweringly beautiful silver meat cart is unimportant; it is where that lamb is consumed that matters. And the interior of this all-important chop-house is so cunningly arranged that its zigzag windowed partitions change it from a long dull store building into a series of rigidly pro-tected social levels.

There are the few tables by the bar, known as Stockholders' Row, and with much of the well-padded comfortable aura of an exclusive club. Probably fifty people in the whole world are qualified to sit at them, and any slight deviation from the twice-daily pattern of familiar paunches causes as much local speculation as a mysterious drop in the market.

Then there is the Reinhardt Room, named for its professorial and omnipotent head-captain. It was rightly ignored at first because of its unbecoming pink sides and its dull isolation, until large peepholes were cut in the wall nearest the bar and a celebrated columnist was prevailed upon with true Romanoff tact to make it the center of her sharpest operations. Now anyone in Hollywood is glad to lunch or dine there, in order to catch her eye, and nod and smile, and guarantee himself one more kind printed word.

Off Reinhardt's stronghold and down a step or two, but still with low partitions so that no Keneth Hopkins hat, no famous toupée, need be missed by a quick-eyed loiterer at the bar, is a small quiet room where big deals are made. There fading stars form independent companies with other people's fortunes and themselves as writer-director-producers. Story editors buy unwritten masterpieces for a quarter of a million. Agents murder other agents with invisible bloodshed.

In spite of the fact that the silver meat cart is too luxuriously weighty to go down the steps, rack of lamb tastes better in the quiet little room, temporarily at least, than anywhere except Stockholders' Row. Certainly it would taste infinitely better there, basted with cyanide and laced with strychnine and garnished with Paris green, than it ever could if by some trick it were served plain and un-poisoned to the star or the story editor or the agent in the Back Room!

The Back Room, quite simply, is suicide. It used to be the whole restaurant, and a few old-timers smile fondly if discreetly at the remembrance of its early days, when Romanoff had not quite enough money to buy chairs and tables for it, and it was cut off from the half-deserted bar by long, gloomy curtains that flapped dismally in the draughts of debt and insecurity and emptiness. That was before Prince Mike and his loyal architect, in mutual desperation, had evolved their fantastically successful scheme of separating the local dukes, cabinet ministers, and lesser nobility into their proper groups, and their fair ladies into the correctly improper ones. Now the room, the dread Back Room, is reserved for a few miserable people whose options have just been dropped and a blissfully ignorant flow of Eastern visitors who do not realize that they are actually enjoying what to a local inhabitant would mean social death.

Well-groomed matrons from the hinterland chatter brightly over excellent cocktails and down great quantities of delicious pastries served with skill and tact, never suspecting that from the Row, and the Reinhardt Room, and even from the far-west quiet corner where big deals are made, any glances that may come their way are heavy with scorn, boredom, or at best a faint pity.

Producers shudder at the thought of ever stepping over the sill of that airy pleasant limbo. Producers' girl friends in very new mink coats shudder at the chance that some crowded day they might have to sit two tables in. Ambitious and "promising young" writers of no matter what age recognize the ugly truth that in a pinch they might penetrate as far as the third small table to the left, but pray that it will never be necessary. And meanwhile the happy visitors from Iowa and New York sip and chatter under the same artful roof with countless movie-great, oblivious of their wretched lot—and of one other room, which perhaps even the aristocracy up front might envy: a cool trellised garden off the kitchens, where one day I saw waiters and cooks and the lowliest busboys sitting at a long clean table in the dappled light, eating amicably together without benefit of silver meat cart but from bowls and platters that looked well laden.

Mike Romanoff and his architect had built exceedingly well, I thought with my own kind of snobbism. And I wondered if there, and at the Chambord still, and once at Foyot's, and once at the place in Amsterdam where there were, before the bombs fell, strawberries served two by enormous two upon white damask napkins, and at a hundred other great restaurants around the globe, venality and all its hugger-mugger of intricate play upon the senses did indeed work maggot-like through the kitchens as well as the bar and the Reinhardt Room. I looked at the men and boys eating with such seeming friendliness and pleasure under the vine leaves, and wondered if, for them, cuts of smuggled venison and truffles en papillote took the place of red-haired actresses, of senators of the Opposition, to be manipulated and wooed in the full sense of the word venal. It was harder to believe, there in the sunlight, than it could have been elsewhere.

1

Royal kitchens have always been great ones, gastronomically speaking, although the monarchs themselves have seldom been reputable gourmets. Their power, their more or less ill-gotten means, have made them a mecca for ambitious culinary artists, and there is, in most classical cookbooks, a fairly high level of dishes named after the various kings to whom masterpieces must from time to time be dedicated. Fortunately many such regal dishes are quite simple concoctions, perhaps because the rulers smiled on them in blessed relief after too many headier ones presented to them as a matter of course.

There is, for instance, the delightful dessert named Raspberries Romanoff, which as far as I know has never been served in Prince Mike's Beverly Hills chophouse, nor even in the Winter Palace in St. Petersburg. And there is riz à l'Impératrice: probably I should know for what empress it was presumably first made, but I suspect, being culinarily cynical, that some fair version of it has existed through many a European reign, fresh-named for each, since rice first appeared in the regal cupboards.

There are many good recipes now in circulation for this dish, varying slightly according to the whims of their editors. Fundamentally they follow so closely the nostalgic description given to me by a man to whom riz à l'Impératrice was inextricably a part of great family festivals, with his grandparents' old-school German cooks at the helm, that I can do no better than repeat what he has said.

It was very pretty indeed he said, a not-too-sweet, indescribably light ring of molded rice, vanilla flavored and very suave with custard and whipped heavy cream, with a hint of kirschwasser and tiny bits of minced candied fruits. When the stiff but delicate mold was tipped out upon its platter, there was, magically to a hungry child, red currant jelly on the top, which flowed down over the rich creamy pudding. Ah, it was pretty, the man sighed, not feeling at all silly in his rush of infantile delight.

There may have been a taste of apricot in the rice, he added slowly, evoking from so far back the perfection upon his tongue. (He was right: there should be equal parts of apricot jam and chopped candied fruits stirred into the vanilla-flavored rice before adding the thick custard and the beaten cream.)

But it was the delicate tartness of the currant jelly, opposed to the bland sweetness of the rice, that haunted him most powerfully and made him in the end look so far backward upon his own gastronomical self that I left him, an intruder. . . .

As for the raspberries loftily called Romanoff, they are one variation, and to my mind the best, of a hundred more or less complicated ways of combining fresh fruits and fresh cream. Many other fruits will do, but raspberries seem perfect, when they are indeed fresh and dead-ripe and preferably not touched by water, as they can be when grown in a country garden, whether in Russia, Connecticut, or Savoy (where I first tasted them this way).

RASPBERRIES ROMANOFF

1 *pint carefully sorted rasp- berries*	¼ *cup powdered sugar*
	¼ *cup kirsch*
1½ *cups heavy cream*	

Chill berries. Beat cream stiff, gradually adding sugar and kirsch. Mix lightly with berries, chill thoroughly, and serve in tall thin glasses, with thin unsugared wafers if desired.

W *is for* Wanton

... AND the great difference between the way a man eats, and has his doxy eat, when he plans to lead her to the nearest couch, and the way a woman will feed a man for the same end.

A man is much more straightforward—usually. He believes with the unreasoning intuition of a cat or a wolf that he must be strong for the fray and that strength comes from meat: he orders rare steak, with plenty of potatoes alongside, and perhaps a pastry afterward. He may have heard that oysters or a glass of port work aphrodisiacal wonders, more on himself than on The Little Woman, or in an unusual attempt at subtlety augmented by something he vaguely remembers from an old movie he may provide a glass or two of champagne, but in general his gastronomical as well as alcoholic approach to the delights of love is an uncomplicated one which has almost nothing to do with the pleasurable preparation of his companion.

A woman contemplating seduction, on the other hand, is wanton, and a wanton woman, according to the dictionary, is unchaste, licentious, and lewd. This definition obviously applies to her moral rather than her culinary side. Considered solely in connection with the pleasures of the table, a wanton woman is one who with cunning and deliberation prepares a meal which will draw another person to her. The reasons she does so may be anything from political to polite, but her basic acknowledgment that sexual play can be a sure aftermath of gastronomical bliss dictates the game, from the first invitation to the final mouthful of ginger omelet.

It is an agelong rumor, apparently fairly well founded, that the great procuresses and madams have always been the great teachers in *"la cuisine d'amour."* Such proficient pupils as Du Barry and the Countess of Louveciennes bear out this theory, and recipes ascribed to both of them are reprinted annually in various undercover publications dedicated to the somewhat dubious encouragement of libertinage.[1]

Most of the culinary secrets told in them, at a high price and "in plain wrappers for mailing," lean heavily on the time-worn knowledge that dishes made with a great deal of mustard and paprika and other heating spices, and ones based on the generous use of shrimps and other fish high in phosphorus, are usually exciting to both human sexes but particularly to the male. Sometimes a more complicated significance, straight from Freud, is given to recipes thought of long before his day. The dish of eel innocently prepared for a gathering of good pastors by a former brothel cook, which Brillat-Savarin describes so lightly in his *Physiology of Taste*, is a perfect example of this: there is a phallic rightness about the whole thing, visual as well as spiritual, which has more to do with the structure of the fish than the possible presence of a mysterious and exotic spice.

In general, however, the great courtesans have paid less attention to the Freudian appearance of their kitchens' masterpieces, from what I can gather, than to the temperaments of the men they have willed to please. They have studied the appetites of their prey.

This is, in a way, a paraphrase of the old saying, "First catch your hare, then cook him": wolf or even goose can be substituted for the little wild rabbit.

Once caught, a human male is studied by the huntress as thoroughly as if he were a diamond. She looks at his ear lobes and his fingernails after he has eaten of rare beef, and if the former are plump and ruddy, and the latter rosy pink, she knows his glands to be both satisfied and active. She analyzes his motor reflexes after he has downed a fair portion of jugged venison, and if instead of showing a pleasurable skittishness he yawns and puffs and blinks, she nevermore serves that gamy dish. She notes coldly, calculatingly, his reactions to wine and ale and heady spirits, as well as to fruits, eggs, cucumbers, and such; she learns his dietetic tolerance, in short, and his rate of metabolism, and his tendencies toward gastric as well as emotional indigestion. And all this happens whether she be a designing farm girl in Arkansas or a slim worldly beauty on the Cap d'Antibes.

Now I myself am neither of these. I have met a few famous

madams, but for one reason or another have never discussed the gastronomy of love with them. I have read a great many books. I have watched a great many people, and fed them too. And here is how I would go about it, as of today, if I wanted to ensnare an average man and lead him, with proper discretion, to the marriage bed. (I say average. The truth is that I do not know a really average man, gastronomically or otherwise. A further complication is that I would quite probably be uninterested in one if ever I met him.)

Given the fact that I have found a male of about my own age, healthy, not too nervous, fairly literate, in other words, one I would like to have cleave unto me for reasons of pleasure if not reproduction: I would soon discover his likes ("First catch your wolf . . ."), and more gradually his dislikes, the deep-seated kind based on the fact that his grandmother made him eat cold turkey one day when it thundered, and his father once called stuffed goose's neck rattlesnake meat, and that sort of thing.

By then I would know what he thought he admired and what he *really* did. If he fancied himself as a bored diner-out I would gradually tease and excite him by bewilderment, and serve him what he thought he hated, in a quiet, lonely room. If he thought he could not possibly eat anything with onion in it I would prove my own control of the situation without his knowing it and prepare a few artful dishes to lead him to realize that he now loved what he had most abhorred. If he hated company I would insinuate two or three or even five arresting characters into his prandial pattern.

In other words I would quarrel with him, on a celestially gentle plane.

I would placate his early inhibitions, and flatter his later ones, and in the end I would have educated him without pain to the point where some such menu as the following would culminate in the flowering of mutual desire, whether social, financial, or impurely intramural:

Good Scotch and water for him, and a very dry Martini for me.
    A hot soup made of equal parts of clam juice, chicken broth, and dry white wine, heated just to the simmer.
    A light curry of shrimps or crayfish tails. The fish must be peeled raw, soaked in rich milk, and drained, and the sauce must be made of this milk, and the fish poached for at best six minutes in the delicately flavored liquid. This is a reliable trick.

Rice for the curry, and a bland green salad—that is, with a plain French dressing containing more than its fair share of oil.

A dessert based on chilled cooked fruits, with a seemingly inno-cent sauce made of honey, whole cinnamon, and brandy, poured over and around them at boiling point and allowed to chill.

By preference I would serve a moderately dry champagne, from the curry on through the last course. If I had no champagne I would produce a bottle of some light chilled wine like a Krug Traminer, since it would be stimulating without going dead once swallowed, as most of the beers and ales do which might superficially seem more de-sirable. I would serve coffee in great moderation, to put it bluntly, lest it dampen the fire with cold reason.

Thus, depending on the man, the surroundings, and the general conditions of light and shade, I would go about my business—in a time-honored gastronomical fashion which indeed has much of the wanton and therefore unchaste about it, more in the telling than in the dreamed performance, but which still need not be either lewd or vulgarly licentious, at least in one woman's lexicon.

1

Here it seemed a good time, and place, to consult a few friends whose amorous experience was admittedly wider than my own. Instead of asking their opinions on aphrodisiacal gastronomy, how-ever, I managed to astound them by demanding the reverse side: the dishes, meals, drinks, which had proved most likely to dismay them, couchward.

It was agreed, and in my own timid way I must concur, that there is no true whip to love except the need itself, which needs no whip. That is, if two people wish, hope, plan, to be together, they need have no fear of what they must eat first, and indeed no interest in it. Provided they do not eat and drink too much, which there is little risk of their doing if the other hunger be urgent and strong enough, they are as it were impervious to the throes of postprandial digestion. They can eat lobster, rarebit, oysters, tenderloin, and even cold pudding, and will arise undismayed.

On the other hand, flickering passion that must be fanned by a deliberate conglomeration of spices, perfumes, shaded pink can-delabra, muted gypsy music, and stretched satin underpinnings, is in a delicate state, most easily nourished and strengthened by the frank admission that autosuggestion is more important than proteins, temporarily at least. This form of hypnosis, no matter how delicious its results, was not what interested me in my naïve census-taking: I wanted to know what would most quickly and completely down my aides.

One said overeagerness for something too long wanted, which I pointed out to him had no necessarily gastronomical connotation, to which he replied that when he was nine he yearned for a Christmas orange more than ever he had since for a woman, and that when he finally got it and bit into it he was as sick as a little pig.

I had no answer to this Jesuitry, so I turned with genteel determination toward a more forthright lover of fair ladies. He supported the theory that nothing can stop true passion, but that an unfortunately chosen dish can form a distinct hazard in the smooth path toward its consummation. When urged, he sketched in with discreet brevity the picture of a male invited by a female to sup with her; he arrived shaved and laved, dallied hopefully over a predinner drink or two, and then was sat down before the one thing in the world he most actively loathed the thought of eating, in his case okra (another and another of my helpers spoke up: avocados, one said in vicarious anguish, kidneys said another). Love hopefully turned to lust, and then lust itself dwindled.

Early training forbade my further questions, but as I am somewhat impatient of such sad, adamant prejudices, I cannot help wondering if a strong enough passion might not surmount even a detested flavor, the okra or avocado, even the kidneys en brochette or in a crisp little artful pie. It seems to me that if a mature, otherwise sensible man turned resolutely from me because he was served with something his mother or his governess had shuddered away from a generation earlier, I would feel myself none too irresistible and would, quite candidly, look elsewhere.

Such surmises, happily, are neither my meat nor my poison, and I can only hope, with all possible philosophy, that fewer and fewer of my fellow men will need to retreat from battle with some such excuse as the look, taste, or smell of a dished overture to another equally basic form of nourishment. I have watched youths and maidens, physically beautiful no matter how boring otherwise, lap up with catlike wisdom a few loathsome hamburgers at a drive-in before going bluntly into the hill country under the moon. I have also watched, perhaps with more curiosity because of the perverse quality of the outcome, producer and star,' who would eagerly consent to being billed as satyr and nymph but would more aptly qualify as tired-old-dyspeptic and faded-dope, seat themselves in a good restaurant with all the refined smirks, pattings, and ocular caresses of an expurgated page from *Nana*, and then nibble this, sip that, with the deliberate sly caution of children who have been promised that if they wash the front steps every Saturday they will get their heart's desire for Christmas.

I doubt that they ever do, and a dingy hint of suspicion in even the most amorous, oysterish eye, the coyest café smile, strengthens that doubt.

No matter what shrewd compound from an old whore's cookery book might be produced for them, or for their likes in any walks of life; no matter what revivifying wine or tonic water could be poured for them; no matter, in the end, what spiced essences they spilled upon themselves in the hope of future flames, it would be futile if there was no hunger or lust stronger than their physical ennui, their worldly exhaustion. Something beyond gastronomical boundaries must then take over: the pharmacopoeia of passion.

This special medal has its other side. A wanton woman who could knowingly lead a man toward bed might just as easily, according to my talkative advisers, turn him away from it; and perhaps a whole dictionary of non-love should be written, about how to prepare this and that food most sure to stem desire—kidneys, okra, and avocado, all of them sur canapés d'hier-soir. I myself, imagining one man I would like to woo, can easily invent a menu that would floor him like a stunned ox, and turn him, no matter how unwittingly on his part, into a slumberous lump of masculine inactivity. It is based on what I already know of his physical reactions, as any such plan must be.

I would serve one too many Martinis, that is, about three. Then while his appetite raged, thus whipped with alcohol, I would have generous, rich, salty Italian hors d'oeuvres: prosciutto, little chilled marinated shrimps, olives stuffed with anchovy, spiced and pickled tomatoes—things that would lead him on. Next would come something he no longer wanted but could not resist, something like a ragout of venison, or squabs stuffed with mushrooms and wild rice, and plenty of red wine, sure danger after the cocktails and the highly salted appetizers. I would waste no time on a salad, unless perhaps a freakish rich one treacherously containing truffles and new potatoes. The dessert would be cold, superficially refreshing and tempting, but venomous: a chilled bowl of figs soaked in kirsch, with heavy cream. There would be a small bottle of a Sauterne, sly and icy, or a judicious bit of champagne, and then a small cup of coffee so black and bitter that my victim could not down it, even therapeutically.

All of this would be beautiful fare in itself and in another part of time and space. Here and now it would be sure poison—given the right man. I would, to put it mildly, rest inviolate.

What a hideous plan!

It could be called:

HOW TO UN-SEDUCE

(recipe above)

X is for Xanthippe

... AND the sure way any shrewish woman can put poison in the pot for her mate, whether or no he be as wise as Socrates and call her Xanthippean or merely Sarah-Jane-ish or Francescan, routinely vituperative or merely undergoing "one of her bad days."

Probably no strychnine has sent as many husbands into their graves as mealtime scolding has, and nothing has driven more men into the arms of other women than the sound of a shrill whine at table. Xanthippe's skill at being ill tempered is largely legendary, and I do not know how much of her nastiness took place over the daily food she served forth to Socrates, but I am convinced that there is no better culture for the quick growth of the germs of marital loathings than the family board. Even the bed must cede position to it, for nighttime and the occasional surcease of physical fatigue and langour can temper mean words there. Nothing alleviates the shock of nagging over an omelet and a salad.[1]

Brillat-Savarin has said as much, and most straightforwardly. But each of us has the right to add his own version of it, and as a two-time widow, both grass and sod, I can vouch for the fact that every man who ever confided in me, as all men eventually will to a seemingly lone woman, that he has not been well understood by his wife, has in the end confessed that try as he would to come home patient and kind for dinner, Sarah-Jane or Frances would serve it forth to him with such a mishmash of scowls and scoldings that he must, to save himself, flee from her.

There are, of course, many sides to this problem, as to all, and I can and do understand Xanthippe's. The main thing to do, in my way of thinking, is to strike an amicable if not truly easy relationship, with full admission that the husband may be basically weary of his wife and the wife fed to the teeth with him. I know several

713

such arrangements, questionably right from a moral point of view (or sentimental!) and made for a hundred reasons from the most venal to the vaguest, and if they be done intelligently they can and do succeed.

The reason I advocate this tacit admission of extramural satisfactions and intramural tolerance is that people must eat. It is true that they must also make love, and in order to do so must in one way or another make money. But the most important of these functions, to my mind, is the eating. Neither of the others can be done well without it: an impoverished man is hungry, and a hungry man, as too many dictators have proved, is not a reproductive and perforce sexually keen fellow. That is why I think that food is the most important of our three basic needs, and why I do deplore its poisoning, its deadly contamination, by anything as vicious as bad temper.

Socrates escaped from Zanthippe in ways impossible to modern man, no matter how philosophical. Today a lesser thinker must hide in his Third Avenue pub and snatch a tough steak and worse potatoes to nourish him if he cannot bear to go home and face the sour woman he is commanded by law to live with. Indigestion is the inevitable aftermath, not so much from the rank victuals he has stowed away as from his basic sorrow that he and she have come to such a pass.

But if he does go home, his stomach will curse even louder, thanks to the acids of anger and hatred that he can counteract in the pub with aloneness and a couple of short ryes. He sighs, gulps, and looks over the bar at his own mirrored face, bitterly thankful that he does not see there the pinched, ruined beauty of his woman, the Sarah-Jane, the Frances, who forced him here.

And she? Women have more ways than men for lone survival, so Xanthippe may drink too much, or exhaust herself in a whirl of club meetings with her like, or sit weeping and moaning in a darkened movie house. She may long for her husband . . .

. . . and then when he does come home, heavy with fatigue and forced joviality, she forgets her longing and slaps ill-cooked food upon the table, a kind of visual proof of her boredom at his dullness and her hatred of his dwindled lust, which she, poor soul, was genteelly raised to mistake for love. She may even try hard to be patient, and not to mind when in subconscious pain at the sight of her sharp face he hides it from him with a spread-out sheet of news about pugilists and midget auto-racers. She may hope that he will notice the cherry she has, with synthetic optimism fed by radio commercials and monthly magazines, placed upon the top of his canned peach.

But he reads on, with the instinct of a cornered toad pretending courage, and in desperation the woman, who has sworn not to do it again, begins to talk.

The rest is too familiar, a pattern used tastelessly by comic-strip writers, modern literary giants, and psychiatrists: she whangs, he scowls back, suddenly the food in their bellies feels intolerably sour and dreadful, he returns in a furious rush to his pub and she to her bitter, teary pillow, and finally they end according to accidents of time and place and money in the relative asylums of death, insanity, hypochondria, or the law courts.

A good answer to this Xanthippean formula must start practically with the cradle. A child, male or female, who has been raised to eat in peace, and has never gulped to the tune of scolding or anger, stands a better chance of knowing the pleasures of the table when he is full grown than one who has listened with fright and final callousness to endless bitter arguments and rows, who has bolted his food to escape them, who has at last come to think them a part of family existence and to expect, with a horrible resignation, that his wife will turn out to be the same noisy, bickering shrew his mother was at mealtime.

I think that it is a good thing, for many reasons, to have children eat at least half their meals at their own table, at the hours best suited to them, and removed from sight or sound of older people whose natural conversation would be as boring to the young ones as theirs would be to their elders.

But if, as was true when I was little, the children must have dinner with their parents, some such rule as the one my family followed should be law: business was never mentioned in any way, nor money problems, nor grown-up worries. And if any of us children had grouses to air, or peeves, we did it earlier or later, but never at the table. There we were expected to eat nicely and to converse with possible dullness but no rancor, and, being expected to, we did—or else were excused from the room.

My father, because of the endless evening meetings he had to go to as a small-town newspaper editor, had to dine early, and my mother, dependent on unskilled "help," could not arrange separate dinners at different hours for the children and for herself and him, but I have often thought it a pity that they had to refrain from any of the rich quiet talk that a husband and wife should indulge in over their evening meal, in order to teach us children one more rudiment of decent living. The only place where they could converse properly was in bed, and I can remember hearing their low voices going on and on, far after the house slept.

Even so long ago I used to think how dull it must be for my father to come home after the paper was off the presses and well onto the streets to find my mother deep in the unavoidable and noisy routine of getting four or five or six children washed and brushed and ready to be fed, with never a chance to sit down together and breathe.

Perhaps that is why, now in my own life, I feel that the quiet drink I have before dinner with my husband, after the children have been tucked away, is one of the pleasantest minutes in all the 1440. It makes the meal which follows seem more peaceful, more delicious. Physically it smoothes out wrinkles of fatigue and worry in both of us, which could, especially if we had been conditioned differently by wrangling parents, lead us inevitably into the Xanthippean tragedy of nagging, and bitterness, and anger. And that, I know because I have seen it happen, would be the world's surest way to send my husband from my table and my life—an ugly prospect indeed, and one rightly to be avoided, just as is the poison it would take to do it, brewed to the tune of a woman's shrewish voice and served, quick death to love, at the family table . . .

1

. . . and it may be said here that no omelet can withstand the spiritual battering of a bad-tongued shrew. It will look delicious, certainly, but turn to gravel between the teeth no matter what its creamy texture or its fine ingredients.

I know how to make scrambled eggs that to my own mind are, quite frankly, the best I have ever eaten, and they would taste like old minced carpet and stick in my throat if I had to try to swallow them while Xanthippe hacked at Socrates, or anyone else for that matter: a son, a relative of either sex. I have, in public places, watched women suddenly turn a tableful of human beings into scowling tigers and hyenas with their quiet, ferocious nagging, and

I have shuddered especially at the signs of pure criminality that then veil children's eyes as they bolt down their poisoned food and flee.

My recipe, guaranteed to gripe a man's vitals if served with hate, and to soothe him like pansy petals if set down before him with gentle love, varies somewhat with the supplies to hand, but is basically this, and, as will be evident, it is quirky:

SCRAMBLED EGGS

8 *fresh eggs*
1½ *cups rich cream (more or less)*
salt, freshly ground pepper

4 *tablespoons grated cheese, or finely minced fresh herbs, if desired*

Break eggs into cold, heavy iron skillet, add cream, and stir gently until fairly well blended. Never beat. Heat very slowly, stirring occasionally in large curds up from the bottom. Never let bubble. Add seasoning (and/or cheese and herbs) just before serving. This takes about half an hour—poky, but worth it.

This concoction is obviously a placid one, never to be attempted by a nervous, harried woman, one anxious to slap something on the table and get it over with. Its very consistency, slow and creamy, is a deterrent to irritation, and if it were attempted by any female who deliberately planned to lean over it, once on its plates, and whang at her guests (for a lover, a husband, a father, or a child is indeed the guest of any woman who prepares the food they must eat), I would rather have my scrambled eggs turn into hard, fanged snakes and writhe away. I love this recipe, for its very gentleness, and for the demands it makes upon one's patience, and the homage it deserves from its slow tasting.

I can suggest a good recipe for a shrew, to take little time, be very indigestible, and imply frustration, outrage, and great boredom by its general air of hardness and tough, careless preparation:

4 *eggs*
4 *tablespoons water*

cooking oil or fat
salt, pepper

Beat eggs angrily until they froth. Add the water. Season without thought. Heat oil quickly to the smoking point in thin skillet, pour in egg mixture and stir fast. Scrape onto cold plates and slam down on carelessly laid table.

This is of course a travesty, rather grim, rather too recognizable. What usually happens with Xanthippes (and I have heard several of them confess to it, with a strange perverted smile) is that they "just open a can of beans, if Harry takes it into his head to come home on time for a change!" I have even heard some of them add, with a yet stranger smile of sadistic (masochistic?) bravado, "No fancy stuff! If he wants all the trimmings, he can get it from *her!*" (Or, "at the Brass Kettle!")

The recipe here is unprintable, but with merciful briefness I can say that it consists of one can of baked beans, one can-opener, one plate, and, as a special Lucullan touch, one cloggy bottle of old catsup.

Now I know myself to be guilty of many a sin, but I feel fairly safe in saying that Xanthippean gastronomy is not among them. And yet I confess to a great liking for canned baked beans, as well as to a sociological admiration for them and what they stand for. Perhaps the worst I ever ate were in a pub in Cornwall, the locality's fanciest, where an open can of them stood proudly at one end of the bar, surrounded by good honest slabs of freshly baked bread, as snacks for the regular patrons. Cold, sluggish, a hideous tone of mud-gray-brown, they were served forth to us by the publican as a true Yankee delicacy, and I gulped down my share with a rewarding glow in my soul for the interested friendliness of everyone around me, and no thought of the horrid taste and the texture of what I gulped.

Quite aside from any and all such sentimental connotations, I think American canned beans are wonderful. They are quite (and I use the word "quite" in its proper sense of "utterly," "completely") inferior to home-prepared beans, which send out from a winter's oven a warm, rich smell unlike anything else on earth. (My mother used to put a pot of them on the farthest-off ledge of the furnace for five days or so, when she was a bride in Michigan, and her father-in-law would say gently, chopping his way down to the edible parts, "A peck of charcoal a year never hurt a good man, my dear.")

I have a fine recipe for them, in which the beans must cook gently, covered and in the slowest oven, for at least eight hours, and which toward the end, say a couple of hours before supper, should have hot bacon drippings poured drop by odorous drop over their top crust. It is, indeed, fine.

But I can also make a good thing out of two cans of ordinary beans—like any woman who will consent to earn her just reward by the happy palate rather than the acid tongue:

2 or 3 No. 2 cans pork and
    beans, any reputable brand
½ cup molasses, "black strap" if
    possible

1 teaspoon dry mustard (or 3
    of prepared)
6 strips sliced bacon or ½ cup
    melted bacon drippings

Mix beans, molasses, and mustard thoroughly in generous casserole or baking dish, put bacon across top or dribble melted fat evenly over it, and bake in moderate oven (350°) until bacon is almost crisp or top is crusty. Serve with toasted sourdough bread (or steamed Boston Brown Bread if you must), and crisp celery . . . and beer.

Y *is for* Yak

... AND the steaks that may possibly be carved, now and then, by hungry visitors to the plateaus of Tibet if they can sneak one of the great black oxen far enough from its native owners ... as well as for other peculiar steaks, stews, and soups which have nourished men, for one reason and another, within my own knowledge.

To be truthful, I have never met anyone who would admit to tasting yak. Perhaps these bisonish beasts are too valuable as vehicles to end in the pot. Perhaps there are religious scruples against devouring them, as with the sacred cows of India. Perhaps it is simply that I do not move among the gastronomically yak-minded.

But whale, now: I can discuss whale, at least vicariously enjoyed. I was married for a time to a man whose father, a most respectable Presbyterian minister, once spent a large chunk of the weekly budget on a whale steak and brought it home gleefully, a refugee from respectability for that one day. Who can know how many memories of unutterably dull prayer meetings the exotic slab of meat wiped from his mind? It may well have been opium, moonlight, orchids to his otherwise staid soul.

Whatever the escapism of his purchase, it threw his harried wife and his four habitually hungry children into a pit of depression. They had no idea how to cook it, and stood looking helplessly at it, wishing it were a good honest pot roast.

What finally happened to it completed the dismal picture: it was treated as if it were indeed chuck beef, and the minister, his wife, and the four children ladled off cup after cup of blubber oil, which rose high in the pan for hours while they waited, futilely, for the meat to grow tender enough to eat.

It was possibly the first, and certainly the last, attempt the minister made to flee from his proper routine of prayers and pot roast, pot roast and prayers.

The only successful dish of whale I know about was the result of a Machiavellian plot, carried out quite successfully too, by more or less Machiavellian but certainly hungry people. To begin with, a young oceanographer was given a piece of whale by the captain of a hush-hush government ship, which, it may be deduced, had been exploring far northern waters. This was in the deepest days of meat rationing, and the oceanographer brought home the great slice of ruddy meat with both pride and jubilation.

His beautiful blond wife admired it properly, but she was a scenario-writer, not an Eskimo, and the three cookbooks she owned said nothing, less than nothing, about what to do with whale. She was very resourceful, however, and her quick brain lit upon the fact that a producer-friend had lately married a Hungarian girl who was supposed to be able, and indeed could, make two old riding boots and an onion into a dream dish—given plenty of paprika of course.

The whale steak went into the oceanographical laboratory "cool rooms," the producer and his new wife were invited for the next week end, and, the blond writer added casually, "We have a simply fabulous and fantastic surprise for you!"

The Andrássys, for such was approximately their name, drove hungrily down the long coast on Friday after the studios in Hollywood closed, he thinking, "Food! I am starved for something that doesn't taste like lunch in the Commissary and dinner at Mike's!" and she thinking, "Food! I am starved for something I never saw before, something I haven't had to buy and cook, for other people to rave about."

The whale steak, but lately removed from the lab, so that it was stiff as a granite cemetery stone and of almost the same gray color, lay on the kitchen table as the supreme welcome to them.

The next few minutes have never been described to me by my well-mannered friends, at least not to my satisfaction, but the end of the evening is very clear. It seems that some five hours after the Andrássys arrived, and bolstered by beneficent libations, they and the blond scenario-writer and the oceanographer sat down to a truly delectable and beautiful dish, which, naturally, tasted exactly like Hungarian goulash, complete with paprika and without a trace of whalishness about it. Even Mrs. Andrássy enjoyed it.

There is a creature something like a whale, for he lives in the cold northern waters as whales often do, and something like an elephant, for he has two ivory tusks, one of which grows long and curved and handsome. He is called a narwhal, and although fewer men have tasted him than have tasted either whale or elephant, his skin is reported to be delicious, crisp as celery and tasting of nuts and mushrooms—and looking like half-inch thick linoleum, which for me at least would prove an esthetic handicap.

As for elephant meat, many human beings have enjoyed it, mostly in jungles, but also, it is admitted, within walking distance of the local zoo. One man I know who was the most skilled butcher in his district had a standing agreement with the zoological gardens near him that he might do a bit of sub-rosa carving "in case of accident" to any of the more exotic guests, and he assured me over several bottles of Tavel that elephant trunk is one of the most succulent meats ever swallowed (except perhaps crocodile).

Certainly some such menu of the Siege of Paris in 1870 as the one which can now be seen at Voisin's in New York is ample proof of the gruesome legend that Castor and Pollux, the two elephants of the zoo, ended nobly in the soup kettle after everyone in the city who could afford to had supped from them.

The Voisin menu, to celebrate Christmas on the ninety-ninth day of the Siege, is an unpleasantly fascinating example of what people will eat if they are hungry enough. Besides the consommé d'éléphant it boasts stuffed donkey head, roasted camel, kangaroo stew, rack of bear, leg of wolf, cat garnished with rats, and antelope pie—a far cry from the first timid use of anything extraordinary *chez* Voisin, when Bellenger consulted with his chef and grudgingly devised a menu around the meat course of saddle of spaniel!

The degree of exoticism is dictated by both time and place, of course. One winter in Strasbourg I ate wild boar as if it were commonplace beef, but in Southern California I would feel strange indeed to find it set before me. And when I was a child I dried kelp leaves over our evening beach fires and ate them happily, quite unconscious of the fact that probably nowhere else but along the shores of northern Japan were children doing likewise, and all because my Aunt Gwen had been a child there herself and was now helping to raise me in the only pattern she knew.

I have always believed, perhaps too optimistically, that I would like to taste everything once, never from such hunger as made friends of mine in France in 1942 eat guinea-pig ragout, but from pure gourmandism. The first time I ever felt this compulsion of gastronomical curiosity over instinct was when I was about fourteen and was confronted with my first shrimps. (I do not understand how it took me that long to meet one; perhaps my grandmother's rigid Midwestern ideas of what was fit and proper to put on the table kept me from that pleasure.)

I was immediately repelled by what now delights me, and the little curled pink things, lying in whorls upon the mayonnaise, with snow packed around the bowl as only "Victor Hugo" could do it so long ago in hot Los Angeles, seemed horrible to me. I looked about the airy charming room, with the canaries singing in their golden cages and soft lights glowing behind their incredibly fancy chiffon shades, and I recognized the fact that I was facing a test: I must eat at least one shrimp, and *then* die or be sick.

It was the first of uncountable more, from many a bay and stream, of every color from dank gray to rose, every size from bee to field mouse. Once I saw a corpse fished from a Louisiana bayou, and it was three times its size for the shrimps sucking at it; and another time I saw another corpse, off Brittany, stripped by lobster claws; and still I think without any qualm at all that shrimps, and all their cousins, make one of the sweetest things in this world to put between my teeth.

The next hardest test I passed, at table, was my first oyster, an overlarge and rather metallic one, in the dining-room of The Bishop's School in La Jolla, a few years after the shrimp.

I found it dangerously disgusting for several minutes, but since that memorable day I have eaten oysters whenever I could, including one very bad one in Berne which, my husband told me, would prove to have been all right if I did not die within six hours. I did not, although the last hour had me waiting with ill-concealed anxiety, my eyes on the clock and one hand lying expectantly upon the bedside bell.

I later learned, from no less an authority than Henri Charpentier, that the best thing to do if a bad oyster has been swallowed is to drink generously of coarse red wine, whose tannic content will counteract the acid in the rotting mollusc. I have never had a chance to prove this, I add almost regretfully, for since I learned the trick I have not been in oysterish places.

Imagination tells me that probably the hardest test I could face would be to eat live maggots which had lived in a cheese, like the dish Charles Reade wrote of in *The Cloister and the Hearth.* But I am quite sure I would try, without too much squeamishness, the white termites in Africa, which must be snapped at skillfully before they bite the tongue, and which, more than one gastronomer reports, tastes very much like pineapple. For some reason the thought of them does not repel me, nor, at least theoretically, does the story of the tiny live fish which are swallowed by some South Sea tribes during feasts, to flop around in their bellies and make room for more food.

As for roasted locusts strung on twigs over a fire and basted with camel butter, I think they sound very good indeed, since I react well, gastronomically, to things that are crisp and not sweet, and I might find them almost as irresistible as my peak in this category, the potato chips in the bar of the Lausanne Palace, which were hideous to any kitchen purist, tasting one time of chicken fat, another time of lake perch, but so fresh and so crisp and so salty that ten years after I last ate one I can enjoy it still, and will ten years from this present vicarious enjoyment.

I have found that people, when questioned about the strangest things they ever ate, are vague, and I myself am so. One man to whom livers-and-lights are anathema will say that the worst experience he ever had was finding himself halfway through a grilled kidney before he realized what he was eating. Another will go dreamily into the story of the time William Seabrook picked up what was presumably an ox-tail bone and announced to his well-fed guests that it was the best human coccyx he had been able to buy for a long time. Personally I can murmur no such ghoulish titillations at the proper or improper moments. But although none of my acquaintances has eaten yak, one man I know, who has become a bishop, told me, long ago, of the time he went to a savage Oriental village and was served, by the head man, a stew of what he knew at a glance was boiled newborn baby. The Christian pretended to eat it, feeling souls at stake, and later confessed he was not overly relieved to learn that it was little monkeys, not children, he had nibbled at.

So, limited as I am to shrimps, oysters, and wild boars, I still do talk with people, now and then, who have known stranger flavors: monkeys and crocodiles, the ordinary whale, the extraordinary innard of a calf.[1]

1

To many a man who has never heard the forthright British term "offal" in connection with livers-and-lights, they are still just that.

Gastronomical prejudices have a fleeting vagueness about them, a mysterious, shadowy equivocation. If you ask anyone why he shudders away from grilled calf's liver, he will murmur a seemingly haphazard excuse, usually drawing, to prove his point, on childhood shock, racial traits, and what his grandmother told him once. And yet he purrs like a happy cat when confronted with a fine jar of truffled liver pâté! Or if you demand a reply to your question about his almost pathological horror of kidneys, the most direct thing he can say is that he refuses categorically to eat a critter's innards, and then wonders why he isn't served smoked tongue once in a while!

(This happened to me not long ago, and my fastidious but confused friend was more than annoyed, indeed almost insulted, by my bland remark that a calf's tongue is as much a part of his innards as his brains, cheeks, head, heart, kidneys, liver, muzzle, palate, sweetbreads, and those enigmatic delicacies known to some Western cattlemen as "mountain oysters."

(Indeed, I added cruelly, even an ox tail can be considered as what a *nice* butcher calls "a tidbit." My friend turned gray-green, as heavy prejudices, acquired God knows where and how, made all the delectable soups and stews heave dangerously in his spiritual belly. I formed, and then as quickly discarded, a pettish resolve to serve forth no ox-tail stew until a fine skewer of kidneys and tomatoes had been pronounced bliss rather than anathema. But why fight? Such inner battles are part and parcel of a lifetime's story, and perhaps one more facet in the jewel's perfection.)

I know of countless ways to make nourishing and delicious dishes from kidneys, tripe, brains, and yet not only must I not serve them in my own home for reasons of marital stability, but I could not buy the supplies in the village near us if I needed them, because I would be the only person for miles around who would countenance having them in her house.

Even here in the United States, where most hundred-per-centers don't know tête de veau exists, and if they did would be horrified by it, there are dozens of good cookbooks with dozens of good recipes for such extraneous delights. But butchers say sadly that more and more shoppers, young and old, seem incapable of ordering any-thing but lamb chops, sirloin steaks, and an occasional roast.

I don't know what the answer is. Quite aside from such unreason-able and intrinsic prejudices against sweetbreads and kidneys and such as I can recognize in many of my friends, there seems to be a powerful combination of snobbery and culinary laziness that makes most cooks avoid them. And since an increasing number of people do their own cooking, the prospects for eating a good cervelle au beurre noir or tripes à la mode de Caen a half-century from now look very slim indeed. I myself need not worry over-much about the gastronomical pleasures of that far time, but stubbornly I could wish to prepare my children for them.

The only gesture left to me is to pass on to them, from a great sheaf, one of my favorite recipes. The very mention of its main ingredient sends their father grimly from the room. I copy it secretly, rather as a prisoner whittles at his cage, rather as if it were to be a tiny sign, fifty years from now, that hunger for more than T-bone and French-fries gnawed at one woman's gastronomical conscious-ness.

It stems (all my pet rules *stem*) from a page of Ali-Bab:

KIDNEYS ALI-BAB-ISH

2 *pairs fresh kidneys*	*salt, pepper*
3 *tablespoons butter*	1 *cup thick (or sour) cream*
brandy	1 *teaspoon horseradish sauce*
sherry	*(optional)*
1 *cup sliced mushrooms (fresh or*	
canned)	

Slice kidneys nicely and brown in very hot butter (this is a good chafing-dish recipe). As soon as brown, set aflame in glass (about ½ cup) brandy. When flame dies completely, add same amount good dry sherry. Add sliced mushrooms, cover, and simmer about 10 minutes. Season to taste and add the cream (and horseradish if de-sired). Bring quickly to boil, then serve on crisp toast (or with rice).

Z *is for* Zakuski

... AND for a few reasons that I think a discussion of hors d'oeuvres is a good way to end an alphabet as they themselves are to begin a banquet.

The main trouble with them, almost a legendary one, is that if they are enjoyed to the hilt, the meal that follows is, can be, and usually must be more or less ignored—except by real trenchermen, that is. The variety, the tempting spicy smells, the clashing flavors, all lead even jaded appetites to a surfeit that destroys what is to follow, no matter how simple or how Lucullan.

Gastronomically this may well be thought a pity, at least by the sad hosts who have commanded a feast thoughtfully and then found their balanced courses almost painfully shunned by their too satisfied guests. Even so, it is fun now and then to roam uninhibited and un-hurried through a smörgasbord, a buffet russe, hors d'oeuvres variés, however it may be called. Myself, I like the name zakuski, although I don't know why, for I have never had them in the classical way, countless bowls and dishes and platters set out upon a long table, to be tasted as and how I wished, and swept down with frequent little glasses of vodka.

The nearest I came to that was when I used to go to a small cellar-restaurant behind the Russian Church in Paris, after Sunday morning services. I always stopped in the bar and drank one or two vodkas and ate pressed caviar, the black at about eight francs if it had been a flush week, the red at five francs if it had been a thin one.

And I felt much too shy to go into the next room where everyone standing around the long table was speaking Russian with a liveli-ness that to me still seems part of the zakuski ritual. I remember how thin most of the people looked, and how handsome: that was not long after Paris had filled with refugees from the Revolution, and

727

although I was innocent of the average American awe at having princes for taxi-drivers, I could not help admiring the way most of the people in the café-cellar held their heads.

I do not know quite how they paid for the things they nibbled so avidly and gaily: whether there was a flat fee for this little post-churchly spree, or whether some sharp-eyed waiter totted up their various mouthfuls. As I say, I was too timid and too far out of my lingual element to investigate, and instead stayed in the bar, absorbing by a kind of gastronomical osmosis the high spirits in the other room.

My time was far from wasted though: I learned the lasting delight of pressed caviar, which I found to be best when it was most removed from freshness, when, in fact, the barman hacked it off the mother lump as if it were a piece of rubber, and it had to be chewed and mumbled over in the mouth. Then it went down in a kind of gush of pureness, caviar in essence.

One day I staggered into the bar, dizzy from the most beautiful *a capella* singing I had ever heard in my life or in my dreams, and the barman, who by that time recognized me, put down before me on the counter a tough slab of the red and a little brimming glass, and for an instant I felt very lonely and wished that I might be in the other room, where people milled merrily after the strain of standing and kneeling and then standing all morning. But next to me I suddenly saw a big man drinking vodka from a water tumbler, and he too was eating pressed red caviar, holding it like a slice of bread in his hand, and he was joking with the barman. Something about the vibrations of his voice made me recognize that it was Feodor Chaliapin who spoke, and that it had been he, no other in the world, who had sung in church that morning with the choristers.

I must have looked the way I felt, awe-struck and flabbergasted and naïve, for the barman said something and they both glanced at me and smiled, and then Chaliapin clicked his glass against mine and said, "*Santé!*" and they went on talking in Russian.

It was a strange moment in my life, as strong and good as the taste of caviar on my tongue and the bite of vodka in my throat. I walked straight out, past the door to the other room, where the gaiety and the countless zakuski no longer lured. Everything was in shadow beside the almost brutal glare of the voice that had so uplifted me in church and then had said *"Santé!"* to me. Even now I blink a little, spiritually, thinking of it.

Caviar, of course, is only one zakuska. (Personally I think it is the best one and would willingly forego almost any other gastronomical delight for it—*enough* of it, which I have never had, even though once I slowly and happily ate a pound of it by myself, over a day or so in time and unlimited distances in voluptuous space.) It has for many centuries been thought the most luxurious of all hors d'oeuvres, too good for ordinary diners or dinners. Even Shakespeare used it as a simile: "Caviare to the general . . . ," he wrote in *Hamlet* about a play which pleased not the million—and indeed it is reported that British soldiers stationed on the Caspian Sea after one of the last wars complained angrily about being fed too much of "this 'ere fish jam."

I moan at the thought and wonder if they would have liked any better the lowest form of it, a futile imitation called Peasant Caviar, made of eggplant and various seasoning. I myself think it utterly delicious, no matter how far removed from what it tries to counterfeit, and would gladly eat it spread thick and cold upon black bread every summer noontime of my life. It is another zakuska, seen more upon poor sideboards than rich ones, of course.[1]

Then there are all the pickled mushrooms and tomatoes and eggplants, usually flavored with dill in one degree or another; and the pickled smelts and boned pickled anchovies, the smoked salmon and sturgeon, the little fried or poached cheese pats called tvorojniki, the pirojki stuffed with a dozen things like game, fish, cheese, cabbage, mushrooms; and bowls of mushrooms in sour cream; and, of course, the vodka (this and tequila are the two most appetizing fire-waters in the world, I think, although I learned from one of Arnold Bennett's books to find good dry gin[1] a fortunate substitute for either of them).

That, all that and much more too, will make an honest side table of zakuski. Anything that follows is incidental, obviously, although at Easter time, in Russian households all over the world of whatever political hue, it is obligatory to stay upright if not completely sober for the main table of baked ham and ducks and suckling pigs, and the high baba and the cone-shaped paskha, and the painted eggs all nested in their grass and blossoms.

A man I know who spent his boyhood in St. Petersburg has told me that never in his life, anywhere else in the world, did he see such Gargantuan, near-insane gourmandizing as on Easter at his home, when he was about twelve. He cannot forget it, nor how the still merry people fell back like walruses into their chairs, for the gentlemen had visited several other houses for a nibble of the special zakuski and a nip of vodka, and then had met with their women and children at his parents' house for the rest of the traditional celebration. He shakes his head now, with a half-incredulous, half-envious look in his eyes that says, too recognizably, There were giants in those days. . . .

I have never seen such a rite, raised as I was prosaically if with less digestive danger in a small California town, but I remember the first time I ever went to the Brasserie Universelle in Paris, which was notable then for its hors d'oeuvres variés, a great favorite with provincials like me. I was young and hungry, with a commensurate capacity and sturdy bodily functioning. I had never beheld so many tempting dishes in my life, and the waiters who brought, in a seemingly endless procession, hot, cold, spiced, bland, scarlet, green, black things to set before me apparently enjoyed my pleasure.

"Hold back," one would advise tensely. "Wait! There will soon come a truffled pâté one must taste!"

Or another would say, "Now just a tiny little morsel of this, it is not too distinguished, to save place for the cèpes which are next."

And so it went, I sitting back in happy helplessness, like a queen ant being nurished by her husbands, feeling myself grow great with sensuality.

As I remember, this happened several times, only by virtue of my youth and general good health, and at the end of each meal I toyed languidly with a Coupe Jacques. I could face neither the hors d'oeuvres nor the dessert today, but it is somehow pleasant and reassuring to feel that I was not always thus ascetic, and also that I have known more exciting things than the tray of canapés which is considered the American equivalent of zakuski, in whatever language it is said.

What emasculation they have undergone, these pretty and minuscular appetizers! What a far cry, no matter how artfully made and served, they are from the generous bowls and tubs and boats of a buffet russe, a smörgasbord, a table of hors d'oeuvres variés! And for that matter, how far from the straightforward and tonic thrust of vodka or aquavit is the genteel stimulation of no matter how fine a Sidecar or Manhattan, the vulgar and happy wallop of even the best Martini!

I cannot ponder upon a Gargantuan Easter in St. Petersburg, but I can succor my hungry memory with thoughts of pâté and mushrooms and suchlike in an upstairs restaurant in Paris; and perhaps better than any of this with thoughts of the simplest zakuska ever eaten, when Feodor Chaliapin ate it too and touched his tumbler to my little glass.

What better way could there be, to begin a meal or end an alphabet?

1

Peasant Caviar, somewhat ironically named in my opinion (I have known a few so-styled *paysans*, but never any who either could afford to or would want to make such a mishmash), can have its own strata of richness, extravagance, and giddiness. I know and use three different recipes for it, depending on both my purse and my patience, and I suppose that whoever makes it has a somewhat different version from any of mine.

They fall roughly into the following kinds: 1) cheap, easy, and refreshing; 2) fairly expensive and finicky; 3) expensive, dark, rich, and fancy-fine.

The first I keep in a covered jar in the refrigerator, a kind of private restorative which I usually manage to do away with single-forked for lunches, with perhaps some Ry Krisp but more often nothing at all. It is not pretty, but like many another dish of whom and/or which the same has been said, it is good:

NUMBER ONE

1 *large or 2 small eggplants*	½ *chopped fresh green pepper*
1 *minced onion*	*(optional)*
1 *mashed garlic clove*	¼ *cup fresh herbs chopped*
1 *peeled chopped tomato*	*(also optional)*
or	3 *tablespoons vinegar*
½ *cup tomato sauce or catsup*	3 *tablespoons olive oil*
	salt, pepper

Boil the unpeeled eggplant in ample water until tender. Cool, peel, cut into small pieces, and stir vigorously with the rest of the in-

gredients, added slowly, until it is a well-blended mush. Chill well
for at least a day before serving. Use with thin black bread as an
appetizer, or as an accompaniment to cold meat.

The second recipe is perhaps the best of the three, but I am too
lazy to make it very often. It was taught me by a Honey-colored
Actress along with a lot of other gastronomical jewels. It is, given
her strange patience, perhaps more like real caviar than anything
could or should be, because the trick of slow baking disposes of
much of the vegetable's pulpiness and leaves only the dark little
egglike seeds.

NUMBER TWO

*Put three or four mature eggplants in a pan (they will dwindle
astonishingly) and let them stay all night in the lowest possible
oven heat, around 225°. In the morning scrape the pulp from the
withered and blackened skins and put it, and any black juice that
may have accumulated, into a big bowl. Beat strongly as you add
minced onion, garlic, herbs, seasonings, and vinegar and olive oil,
rather like a salad dressing. It should be a heavily flavored mixture,
according to your own tastes and distastes. Put in a cold place for
at least 24 hours before serving.*

The third rule is a fruity concoction, to quote my father. It is
rich in color and texture and a little overpowering in flavor, so that it
needs crude black bread to be eaten with it, and vodka or jolting Gibsons or some such drink alongside it. People who have been in Algeria
and Turkey and such localities say they have often eaten something
that looks and tastes pretty much the same.

NUMBER THREE

1 *large onion*
4 *tablespoons olive oil*
2 *small or* 1 *large eggplant
(about 6 cups, cubed)*
2 *cups diced peeled tomatoes
  or*
1 *cup tomato sauce*

½ *cup (scant) good vinegar
salt, pepper*
2 *tablespoons oyster or Worcestershire sauce*

Chop the equivalent of about 1 *cup of onion, brown it well in the
oil, and add the peeled, cubed eggplant. Stir carefully until nicely
brown. Then add the tomato, the vinegar, and the salt and pepper.*

Mix well. Cover and simmer for about 1½ hours, stirring occasionally. Add the oyster or other hot sauce, mix well, and allow to cook slowly with the cover off until it begins to look thick and dryish. When the eggplant is thoroughly done, remove from fire, beat well, and pack in jars, to store in a cool place for at least 24 hours.

A chapter about hors d'oeuvres at the *end* of a banquet book might just as well retrogress one step further and make its final bow with a short and appropriately dry discussion of what has become the American equivalent of vodka, aquavit, and other such whips to the human appetite: the Martini.

The first one I ever drank was strictly medicinal, for threatened seasickness, and in spite of a pure enjoyment of them, which may be increasing in direct ratio to my dwindling selectivity of palate, I must admit that I still find them a sure prop to my flagging spirits, my tired or queasy body, even my overtimid social self. I think I know how many to drink, and when, and where, as well as why, and if I have acted properly and heeded all my physical and mental reactions to them, I have been the winner in many an otherwise lost bout, with everything from boredom to plain funk. A well-made dry Martini or Gibson, correctly chilled and nicely served, has been more often my true friend than any two-legged creature.

On the other hand the tipple can be dangerous, and I, when about to drink one, make sure of several things, but mainly how soon after it I can expect to sit down to a decent bite to eat. If things look grimly as if they would drift on; if my host has a glint of predinner wanderings and droppings-in in his eye; if my hostess seems disarmingly vague about how to get a meal on the table; if all this obtrudes no matter how quietly into my general enthusiasm, I firmly say no, to no matter how masterly a mixture of gin, vermouth, and lemon-zest.

If, on the other hand, I see plainly that I can relax, confident of tangible nourishment within the hour, I permit myself the real pleasure of a definite alcoholic wallop.

There is no less vulgar way of expressing what a dry Martini gives me. It is as warming as a hearthfire in December, as stimulating as a good review by my favorite critic of a book I have published into a seeming void, as exciting as a thorough buss I have yearned for from a man I didn't even suspect *suspected* me.

There are two classes of non-professional Martini-makers, those who are rudely convinced nobody in the world can make one quite as well as they, and those who shy away from the bar and say with melodramatic modesty that they can ruin *anything*. The second, when pressed, usually make much the better drink.

My own rules for Martinis fall, like those for Peasant Caviar, into three somewhat loose groups: the safe, the perfect, and the intimate (and therefore pluperfect).

The first is the mild kind I give to people I don't know well, which means, truthfully, that they are not close enough to me to betray how many or what kinds of drinks they have had before they knock on my door, and that I want to serve wine with the dinner I have carefully prepared for them and do not care to have them turn mussy and maudlin and monotonous. It is made of two parts of good gin to one of dry vermouth, and is stirred with ice, poured into chilled stemmed glasses holding not more than two ounces, and served with a green olive stuffed preferably with a pearl onion but passably with a bit of pimiento or almond-meat, and the oil from a twisted lemon peel on top. It is mild, generally safe enough, and can be very good.

The second type is the one I ask for on my occasional sprees in the region's best restaurant, wherever I am. If I do not know the barman, I try a single Gibson. If it is good, I know that I can ask for a double one with equanimity, and from then on not bother with the first puny sample known as a bar drink. (I was raised to accept Gargantuan glasses as my just due by my extra-tall, extra-lusty father, and I am incapable of feeling that anything but a double-sized drink is potable in public places.)

Given the fact that a barman understands what I want, I like, then, on my rare and deeply savored debauches, to precede the luncheon or dinner with one double Gibson, to be served to me in a chilled champagne glass, with the lemon peel twisted once lightly over it. My favorite Bacchus gives me a little dish of salty pearl onions, impaled properly on tiny sticks, lying in a bed of snow. I never touch them, but we respect each other for this sop to custom, a compromise on his part with putting onions into the drink itself, and on mine with wishing that they not appear at all.

Perhaps the best bar Gibsons I ever drank were made by a man in Colorado Springs, in the old Antlers Hotel, I think. They were about four parts of gin to one of vermouth, and after stirring them he put a tiny spoonful of the pickled-onion liquor into each portion. I have tried this, but I suspect that the so-called cocktail onions we have produced, since war made life "so dreadfully difficult" for us drinkers, do not have the correct Dutch kick to them. Certainly the trick has not worked any too well for me, which is one reason why my second category of Martinis is arbitrarily professional, and why I myself no longer try to duplicate what Bacchus can so deftly and beautifully flick before me.

The third kind, which I have dubbed intimate, is something which should never be served in public, nor to any but the one or two people you know in the world. It should never be drunk when weariness or the moon's tides or the press of worldly business are too evident, nor when red wine is to follow. But given an easy, airy evening, a pleasurable quitting of the day's chores, and the prospect of uninterrupted and peaceful communion with One, it can be a fine thing indeed.

My recipe sounds like a parody of Robert Benchley's apocryphal dictum which electrified early Martini-bibbers: three parts of gin and enough vermouth to take away that ghastly watery look. Mine says four parts of dry gin and one eyedropper of vermouth! It must be served very cold indeed, in generous wine goblets, and it is, in truth, a version of what is still much better than *it* can ever be, for such things: vodka, aquavit, tequila. . . .

It seems improbable that my hint of herby wine, the tonic quality of a drop of vermouth, could possibly turn straight dry gin into a quick-working apéritif, but it does: chilled gin has nothing in common with this ridiculously delicious cocktail, and unless it be colored with a drop of bitters, or poured from a cold stone flask of real Geneva, it is a poor way to precede a meal. Given the silly fillip of a scant driblet of vermouth, icy-cold gin can make a private and soul-satisfying drink indeed, and one not to be indulged in lightly, too long, or oftener than the stars dictate.

It is a special thing. It, like other more subtle assaults upon our senses, can bring peace with the pain, and a kind of surcease, gastronomical and therefore spiritual, from the world's immediate anguish. Palliative or poem, it is good.

From A to Z

THE PERFECT DINNER

Once while I was walking in a leisurely but not dawdling way from Vézelay to Avallon (it was only about sixteen kilometers, but I managed to spend a good five hours covering the gentle empty roads), I discussed, with an intensity seldom given to any conversation and very rarely sustained without boredom for so long a time, the subject of The Perfect Dinner.

Everything was in favor of such a quietly passionate entertainment. The weather was heady, an April day of breath-taking clearness after days of rain, so that the earth steamed and quivered a little in its pushing fertility, and birds in the air and hares along the ground and moles and earthworms underneath it sent out an almost tangible excitement. I myself was young but not too young, healthy and free-limbed. And my companion was not only my true love, but also a man I knew to be the most charming talker in a world largely peopled by the stiff-in-tongue, so that quite apart from our shared physical emotions we could speak together, tirelessly, any time at all, of no matter what, and find it good.

All this conspired to make our nonsensical deliberations on The Perfect Meal as celestially enjoyable as such communion possibly could be, and although I have by now forgotten most of what we did decide upon, the slow steady murmur of our voices, thoughtful one minute and mocking or purely silly the next, echoes unquenchably in my mind's ear. It was a kind of contest, and as we walked on and on toward Avallon we fought with all our wiles to win, one from the other, the palm for perfection.

We decided, after some fumbling and confusion, that time, place, weather, and, above all, people, were as important to the gastronom-

736

ical consummation as the food itself. We settled on six as the perfect number of guests, including our two selves of course.

I remember that I named Colette (I might not today, feeling that in her powerful old age she would monopolize the conversation, never a good thing at such a feast as I wanted then and can still dream of), and the Prince of Wales (whose impossibly attractive person had not yet been dimmed in a million women's minds by Mrs. Simpson's svelte shadow and who, I thought, would, because of his great social skill, make a proper table companion, amusing if not witty, charming if not overly intelligent). I cannot remember what two other people were my guests, nor any of my love's, and I have forgotten every other detail of his plan, which by mutual agreement won the palm from mine.

I know that I wanted my meal to be served at the cool end of a hot August day, while there was still light in the sky for the first part, with candles to come later, on a wide studio-balcony on the top of a house on the Quai Voltaire in Paris, the whole glass wall of the apartment open that night, with dusk-colored gauze curtains moving faintly in the air rising upward from the Seine, and the pink lights of the Tuileries coloring the sky. (That is all I wanted!)

Food I have forgotten, except for one detail I insisted on, enthusiastic even so long ago in my belief that unexpectedness and a modicum of astonishment enliven any good dinner: I stipulated one course of small, fairly peppery enchiladas, using real tortillas and slivers of chicken breast, obviously a prodigal version of this delicacy but coming fortuitously at the end of the hot, enervating day—or so I thought then, and still suspect.

And that is all that is left in my conscious mind of the long, solemn, ruminative discussion—all that can be made tangible. Colette has withdrawn, and so has the Prince, and so, even further has my good companion. And I am less capable of nonsense and find reality easier to think upon, more probable. I can still plan perfection, but I am impatient of not attaining it, where on the road to Avallon I could contemplate any fantasy with seriousness.

It seems to me now that for my own satisfaction I must divide Perfect Dinners into three categories, none of them too improbable. And I need not depend, as I did that far day, on perfect synchronization of the weather, the place, the décors; time's passage has made me willing to compromise a little.

I feel now that gastronomical perfection can be reached in these combinations: one person dining alone, usually upon a couch or a hill side; two people, of no matter what sex or age, dining in a good restaurant; six people, of no matter what sex or age, dining in a good home.

Three or four people sometimes attain perfection either in public or in private, but they must be very congenial, else the conversation, both spoken and unsaid, which is so essential a counterpoint to the meal's harmony, will turn dull and forced. Usually six people act as whets, or goads, in this byplay and make the whole more casual, if, perhaps, less significant.

The six should be capable of decent social behavior: that is, no two of them should be so much in love as to bore the others, nor at the opposite extreme should they be carrying on any sexual or professional feud which could put poison on the plates all must eat from. A good combination would be one married couple, for warm composure; one less firmly established, to add a note of investigation to the talk; and two strangers of either sex, upon whom the better-acquainted diners could sharpen their questioning wits.

All six should be congenial in their vocabularies—that is, they should be able to converse in one or more commonly understood languages, and the words they use should be neither too simple nor too elaborate for comprehension.

As for social hurdles, they should not exist, but if by chance one otherwise intelligent and charming guest would, because of early training or later worldly compulsions, prove incapable of dining with pleasure in the company of a butcher or a nuclear physicist, the latter should be invited some other time, or vice versa: it is ridiculous to threaten an evening's possible perfection in the name of democracy, gastronomical or otherwise.

Some such dinner party, then, for six carefully chosen people, should not be given in a public place: a large table in a restaurant, unless it is isolated in a salon privé, is awkward to serve and to manage conversationally. If the noise of the other diners is heavy enough to cover the sound of six people's talk, it is also loud enough to reduce all the talking to twos. And if a subject is interesting enough to lure the six into discussion of it, their voices will be forced to a shout that is unattractive and in the end uncomfortable. No, six are too many for anything but a private room, and a family dining-room, no matter how ornate or simple as long as it is fairly small, is the best place.

There they can be served easily and smoothly by one servant or by the host or hostess. They can attain, in the intimate quiet, an effortless familiarity impossible in public. They can spend as long or short a time over every course as their pleasure and the spiritual climate dictate, without thought of the unavoidable rhythm of restaurant service. They can also, and this is perhaps most important after their basic congeniality, eat dishes impossible to command in no matter what large kitchen, things shunned by busy professional chefs for reasons of snobbism, economy, or unadulterated ignorance.

It is advisable, to my mind, to avoid serving foods that are too exotic, too highly spiced; one of the less familiar guests may be actively nauseated at the mere mention of escargots à la mode de Bourgogne, or be sent toward death's door by a Bombay curry. On the other hand, I think it a pity to serve a sirloin steak, no matter how good: that has become almost an obligatory order, nine times out of ten, when people go to restaurants as a routine thing.

If beefsteak is to be eaten, it should be in some such incredible form as tournedos Rossini, which hardly any chef will bother to prepare properly (if he can afford to), and which will please the guests by its luxurious unexpectedness.

If chicken, perhaps the second-most-ordered food in public eating places, seems indicated for whatever reasons, it should not be fried or roasted as any restaurant will present it: it should remain chicken, plainly and honestly, and comfortably recognizable in order not to scare away the skittish; if fried it should perhaps be placed with mushrooms in a casserole of cream, and if roasted it should perhaps have a dressing never tasted before by any of the guests, of kasha and minced clams.

In other words, the usual should be made unusual; extraordinariness should cloak the ordinary. So long after my decision to serve enchiladas on a Paris roof to Colette and the Prince, I still believe firmly in the attributes of the unexpected! I still believe, perhaps stubbornly but with a satisfying list of proof to back me, that hidebound habits should occasionally be attacked, not to the point of flight or fright, but *enough*.

A guest, for instance, who boasts (stupidly or not as it may seem) that he is a meat-and-potato man, should be given just that. But the meat should be a little gigot of lamb, with a clove of garlic tucked into it and a quick douse of brandy and flame to cut the sticking fatness, cooked in an almost tepid oven until the juice runs clear, and no more. A casserole of peas and mushrooms would walk in with it most happily. And the potatoes? They'd follow, making the next course noble and alone, beaten until cloudlike with cream and butter and then piled into a dish, dusted with Parmesan, and put for one moderately searing moment under the oven flame. The meat-and-potato man would thus have his accustomed fare, but just enough out of focus, standing just honestly enough on its own various pedestals, to astonish him, and please him too, if the cook had St. Teresa on her side to admit that God walks among the pots and pipkins as well as in the cloisters and the marts.

A meal which might be perfect for six well-chosen guests to enjoy and linger over in a small room amply candlelit would perforce depend upon the hundred aspects already hinted at, of place, weather, temperament, and such. Hunger and fair-to-good health are basic requirements, for no man stayed by a heavy midafternoon snack or gnawed by a gastric ulcer can add much to the general well-being. Given, then, six people (two beautiful, one intelligent, three of correlated professions such as architecture, music, and photography); a cool autumn evening with perhaps enough wind outside to make the dining-room sound more like a haven than usual; a good cook . . .

I am that all-powerful being, tonight at least, with Black Bea in the kitchen to cope with the order I fight for but do not always maintain. I have slyly kept last-minute preparations to their minimum, so that I appear uninterested in anything but my guests. We have Martinis or sherry before we enter the dining-room, and red caviar in a generous bowl, it being easier to be generous with the red than the black or gray just now. There is thin dark bread, with a pat of sweet butter and cut lemons; no hidden economy of chopped onion, chopped egg, to stretch out the primitive goodness of the taste.

The dining-room table is set with warm colors, this being autumn: reds, brown-handled knives, strong plates and sturdy goblets, pink and purple grapes in the center—a very blunt decoration indeed.

First we drink a hot consommé double, of equal parts of clam juice and veal stock, to carry the fish taste over to the coming meat taste, and laced with dry vermouth instead of sherry to interrelate the Martinis and the wine to follow.

That will be a firm, rich Burgundy type, too heavy for anything but celebrations, in this case a Paul Masson Pinot Noir, standing three bottles deep on the sideboard, handsome indeed in its thick green-glassed pomposity.

Next comes an almost medieval platter of rump roast baked artfully with prunes and then smothered in a sauce that might be dubbed sweet-and-sour by the unknowing. It falls under the knife in hearty slices, and there is a casserole of wide noodles in butter, to go with it and take up some of the heady juices.

The wine flows down happily. The six people talk, move with a new ease upon their seats and in their skins, feel a new zest, Breughel-ish.

Then there is a large but bland green salad ("to scour the maw," Rabelais would say), made with the minimum of good wine vinegar so as to leave unassaulted the strong tannic impact of the wine, and gently toasted sourdough bread, which stays on the table for the next course of a hand-count of cheeses on a board: buttery Gorgonzola, Camenbert "more running than standing," impeccable Gruyères, Cheddar with a bite and a crumbling to it, and double-cream as soothing as a baby's fingertip.

The wine improves, especially in the third bottle. The candles begin to flicker. There is bitter black coffee, sitting carelessly beside the last bits of cheese, the last freckled crumbs of bread upon the cloth. There is, above all, a kind of easiness, which at this point in my life, both social and private, I find more valuable than rubies, for waily-waily, too often now the world's woes press in like a tumorous growth upon our hearts, like a relentless balloon upon our tables, like a sword upon our beds. If, in the alchemy of hospitality, some such ease as I have told of may be attained, it is to our general good and devoutly to be wished for, and while better, wider-traveled wines and rarer viands might be substituted for my menu based on local possibilities and my own purse, no happier result could follow, to my thinking.

The question of what to do with four people is a different one, and as I have already said it depends dangerously upon the keen mutual interest of the four. It can too easily turn into a business conference or, in the case of two men who meet for dinner together with their doxies, a complete rout. When necessary, it should be held in private.

Two people who dine together are a different thing again. They separate themselves into two more kinds, the ones in love sexually and the ones in love.

In the latter class I think of myself dining with my father, such a strangely relaxed, amicable meeting after the years of family confusion at table; of several meals I have had, at noon and at night, with women who for one reason or another attracted me—their brains, their creamy cheeks, the way they talked about their lovers; a dinner in the back room of a shoe-repair shop with the cobbler, the two of us in a kind of gastronomical communion, tasting and sniffing without a thought of the sheets that are supposed to cover invisibly any such male-female encounters: I was in love with all these people, and richly rewarded for being so.

But the other kind is more demanding. It can and should be disciplined. The best place to indulge in it, when two people are sexually caught and still must eat, is in public, granted of course that they are well in hand and able to observe the amenities of combining such a basically physical act with the one they already have committed, may soon again commit, and now wish they were committing. Anything else is unthinkable, and I dislike the memory I have of countless couples mooning at each other over good food gone to waste.

I think a delicately chosen, artfully presented, lingering, and languorous meal, indulged in publicly, can be one of the most successful fillips to a love affair, but only when it is done with some intelligence. The presence of the other near-invisible diners makes the promised isolation seem even more desirable. The waiters float in a conciliatory cloud. The food—but there is no need to give details of that in such an amorous pattern: almost anything in a good restaurant will be tinder to the flame, breath blown on the ash.

The love feasts that perhaps need, and merit, more thought, are the ones between father and daughter, mother and son, sister and sister. My reason for making these rendezvous apparently adulterous is that in a proper family its various members seem able to attain an easiness of soul together, not known by most other people. But I have lunched once with my literary agent in an airy women's club in New York; I have sat once on the chair that Somerset Maugham had just stood up from, and spent three hours there, beside a beautiful woman who was my husband's wife before I was; I have been with a lanky, handsome secretary in a Hollywood Strip restaurant eating cottage cheese and fruit, which I loathe—and always I have reached a peak of contentment, satisfaction, fulfillment, which is a special virtue of sharing food in a public place with one other human being, of no matter what sex, who for that moment at least is naturally close.

Perhaps the most limited, and at the same time most intricate, form of the perfect dinner is the kind eaten by one person. Then food takes strange forms, and so indeed does the position it is eaten in.

Where in a restaurant with his loved one a man might order his accustomed pattern of oysters and a dry Riesling, little roasted squabs to nibble at with wild rice, and a watercress salad with chilled fruit to follow, a Château Neuf du Pape and brandy of the best, alone at home he will lie back in his deepest chair, a low table handily beside him, and eat a series of unforeseen concoctions.

One man may want a cold plate, and upon it a cold, topless tin of salmon—no mayonnaise, no toast, no nothing—and a stiff Scotch and water. Another may putter and simmer over his electric hot plate and produce a strange dish of tinned shrimps, slightly blinky cream, wilted scallions, and too much tabasco, which he will pour happily over a piece of yesterday morning's toast and eat languorously, one hand holding the latest pocket-edition of *Blood Fell on the Corpse* and the other piloting his fork to his mouth with deep satisfaction and a feeling of culinary triumph. There may be anything from Pilsner-Urquell to the tail end of a bottle of Wente Mourestel in his glass, and indeed drinking is something of an interruption in such a feast.

Then again there is the studied, deliberate dining alone, not accidental but arranged for in a kind of purgative sense, which I and most other thinking people (I use the word "thinking" in a non-philosophical but gastronomical connotation) have practiced.

I figure that the peace and requisite relaxation of sitting by myself in front of a little fire, or in a shadowy patio in summer, are worth the effort they take, occasionally. They are in a way a kind of retreat. I balance my day to their accomplishment. I arrange them as if I were sending a posy to Jenny Lind, with all the proper bows to protocol. Finally I am there, alone, upon a chaise longue, or a tuffet. I have, according to the season, my mete and proper meat.

In the winter, if I am indeed alone, I drink some *good* vermouth, which seems increasingly hard to come by, and eat a little thinly sliced smoked salmon (this is a dream, of course, winter or summer), and then a completely personal and capricious concoction, shrimps or lobster tails or chicken in a thin, artful sauce, very subtle indeed, the kind that I like to pretend would be loathed by anyone but me. I eat it with a spoon and fork. I have a piece of good toast at hand, but hardly touch it. And I sip, from a large, lone Swedish goblet, all its mates being long since shattered, a half-bottle of well-chilled fairly dry white wine; there is something delicately willful and decadent about drinking all alone no matter how small the bottle. And then, after one ruminative look at the little zabaglione I have painstakingly made for myself sometime earlier that day (I enjoy desserts in theory, but seldom can come to the actuality of eating them), I close the refrigerator door firmly upon it and go to bed, bolstered by books to be read and a hundred unattended dreams to be dreamed.

The slightly depraved ramifications of dining alone are plainly limitless. I have savored many of them and do not feel myself the loser. In the main, though, I prefer the category of Two: a white-maned literate male who is past wanting me, a beautiful woman who would not want, a man who would . . . above all the company of One other, making the rarest kind of Two . . . and for lack of that, granted that in my own time I can gracefully eat alone if I am meant to do so, I would choose, at spaced deliberate intervals, the excitement and the whetting, the conflict and the intricate patterns, of a Perfect Dinner for the Six of us.

Index

BREADS

Addie's Quick Bucket-Bread, 250
butter crackers for oyster stew, 132
Canelloni, 274
crackling bread, 263
flowerpot bread, 249-250
Hot Loaf, 249
milk toast, 680
oyster loaf, 168-169
pain d'huitres, 167
sausage or sardine pie, 274
Southern spoon bread, 293
to keep fresh, 240
white, 247-249
zwieback, 203

CHEESE

as dessert, 319
cauliflower casserole, 441
ham and cheese casserole, 203
in polenta, 294
in scrambled eggs, 238
in wartime, 340-341
Potage Mille Fanti, 222
Swiss supper, a, 286-287
with Canelloni, 274
with minestrone, 217
with spaghetti, 292, 610

DESSERTS

ambrosia, 581-582
applesauce, 631
baked apples, 202, 314
Canelloni with jam, 314
cheese, 319
colonial dessert, 348
crêpes suzette, sauce for, 582
Date Delight, 317
Diplomate au Kirsch, 82
Edith's gingerbread, 204, 315-316
    uses for, 204
fruits aux sept liqueurs, 348-349
maple sugar bowl, 319
nectarines, grilled, 315
pain d'épice (gingerbread), 81
peaches and gingersnaps, broiled, 315
pineapple with kirsch, 348
Pudding, Duke of Cambridge, 656
Raspberries Romanoff, 705
Rice and Spice, 318
rice desserts, 289
riz à l'Impératrice, 319
sweet potato pudding, 317
Tart, North Country, 655-656
tomato soup cake, 314
Turkish cake, Sabri's, 47
walnuts, roasted, 203
War Cake, 205, 313
    with wine sauce, 205

DRINKS

beer, 332-333
Cock Ale, 54
coffee, 312
    Italian over-roast, 312
Gaspacho, for hangovers, 215, 216
Half-and-Half cocktail, 332
Infusion of Ladies' Slipper
    Root, 311
Martinis, 734-735
Old-timer's Highball, 331
Prairie Oyster, 230, 239
sherry, 331
    and egg, 230
tisanes, 311
vegetable juices, 205, 297-298
    for pets, 307-308
vodka, homemade, 334
wine, 332

EGGS

Eggs in Hell, 236-237
Eggs Obstaculos, 237
egg yolk sandwich, 230
Equator Plus North Pole, 110

foo yeung, basic, 232, 235-236
fried, 232
fried egg sandwiches, Aunt Gwen's,
  621-622
frittata
    alla Anything-at-all, 662
    of zucchini, 234-235
greet-the-dawn eggs, 237
hard-boiled, 231
Hindu Eggs, 675
omelet
    basic French, 232, 233
    basic soufflé, 232, 233-234
    filled, 233
Potage Mille Fanti, 222
Prairie Oyster, 230, 239
raw
    for pets and children, 307
    with sherry, 230
scrambled, 232, 238, 717
    made by a shrew, 717
    to stretch, 200
shrimp and egg curry, 227
skirled, 232
to boil, 231
to preserve, 230
to prevent cracking, 231
to stretch a soufflé, 200-201
to test freshness, 229
with anchovies, 345-346

FISH AND MOLLUSCS

anchovies with eggs, 345-346
broiled fish, **224**
catfish, 225
fish balls in potato soup, 222
fried fish, 224-225
Hawaiian shrimps, 225
Herring-Pye, a, 643
hors d'oeuvres, 225
oysters
    à la Bazeine, 143
    à la Foch, 142
    and onions, 183-184
    as aperitifs, 145
    baked, 140
    bisque, 172, 173
    catsup, 148-149
    cream of oyster soup, 171
    Doylestown Stew, 132-133
    dressing for turkey, 147

oysters (continued)
    dried, with vegetables (ho tsee
      soong), 149-150
    French creamed, 153-154
    fried, 140
    grilled, 155
    gumbo, 141-142
    Hang Town Fry, 183
    in mushroom sauce, 141
    loaf, 168-169
    oyster-crabs and whitebait, 160
    pain d'huitres, 167
    roasted, 154
      sauce for, 155
    Rockefeller, 152
      sauce for, 152
    rolls, 168
    soup, 172, 173
      bisque, 172, 173
      cream of, 171
      gumbo, 141-142
      with consommé, 174
    stew, 129-134
      Doylestown, 132-133
      fundamentals for, 130, 131,
        133
      without milk, 131
    stuffing, 147-148
    to make a pearl, 164
salmon pancake, 226
sardine pie, 274
shrimp
    and egg curry, 227
    Hawaiian, 225
    pâté, 344
snails, 34-39
    les escargots d'or, 36-37
    to prepare, 37-38, 632-633
    to starve, 36
tartar sauce, 141
tinned or glassed fish, 225-226
Trout Brillat-Savarin, 691-692
tuna
    baked with mushrooms, 227
    pancake, 226
with soy sauce, 224

FOWL AND GAME

capon and pig, 110
chicken
    Apicius' sauce for boiled, 33
    in sauce with polenta, 284

chicken (continued)
  pollo in umido, 284
  poulet à la mode de Beaune, 347
  to prepare, 284
jugged hare, 281
  accompaniments for, 281
live goose, 284-285
oyster dressing, 147
oyster stuffing, 147-148
partridge with sauerkraut, 282
pheasant
  Normandy, 282
  with sauerkraut, 282
pigeons, 685-686
  roasted, 279
quails
  à la financière, Francatelli's, 616
  in ashes, 617
rabbit
  in casserole, 280
  to prepare, 280

FRUIT

ambrosia, 581-582
apples, baked, 202, 314
Date Delight, 317
fruits aux sept liqueurs, 348-349
juices, 205
nectarine-halves, grilled, 315
orange and carrot salad, 110
peaches and gingersnaps, broiled, 315
pineapple with kirsch, 348
tangerine sections, radiator-dried, 26-28

HORS D'OEUVRES

anchovies with eggs, 345-346
caviar
  in pastry, 593
  Peasant, 731-733
fish in lemon (or lime) juice, 225
Pâté Fin, 669
shrimp pâté, 344

HOUSEHOLD HINTS

basting rack, 260
can openers, 220-221
food mills, 240
four burners from one, 301
Hot Spots, 300-301
mortar and pestle, 219

steam-cookers, 205, 297, 688-690, 695
temperatures for roasting beef, 260
tin cans, 225
  for heat, 301
to boil water, 208
to hide food fumes, 327-328
to keep bread fresh, 240
to keep olive oil, 201
to make a haybox, 200
to put out fires, 301
to save bacon fat, 201
to stretch preserving sugar, 201
to stuff pincushions, 304
to use iceboxes wisely, 201-202
to use old tea leaves, 304
to use ovens sensibly, 202-205

MEATS

baked ham
  in cream, 267
  with chutney, 266-267
  Baked Ham Slice, 203, 266
beef
  dumplings in consommé, 221-222
  filet, 258
  heart, stuffed, 272
  left-over, 259-260
  Moreno, 346-347
  pan-broiled, 264, 598-599
  prune roast, 268
  roasted, 260-261
    gravy for, 261
  Tartare, 259
  y-Stewed, 55
Calf's Head à la Tortue, 592-593
calves' brains, 272
calves' hearts, 272-273
cheap cuts, 261
Cold Shape, Aunt Gwen's, 270
crackling bread, 263
English curry, an, 275
gravy for a roast, 261
ground round steak, 262-264
ham See also baked ham
  and cheese casserole, 203
  and mushroom casserole, 204, 290
hamburgers, 264, 598-599
heart loaf, 272-273
kidneys
  Ali-Bab-ish, 726
  in sherry, 273

kidneys (continued)
  on skewers, 273
lambs' hearts, 272
liver, 271
mock duck, 267
ox-tail stew, 588
pig and capon, 110
prune roast, 268
roast beef, 260-261
sausage and yam casserole, 204
sausage pie, 274
Sludge, 240-243
  for pets, 307
steaks, 261-262
  filet, 258
  flank, 267
  sirloin, 699-700
stew, 265-266
stuffed beef heart, 272
Tête de Veau, 270-271
to make tough meat tender, 261,
  262
Turkish hash, 275
with Canelloni, 274

MISCELLANEOUS

How to Unseduce, 711-712
Monastic supper, strengthening prescription for, 649

PETS

canned food, 307
ideal diet for dogs, 307
milk and vegetable juice, 307-308
raw eggs, 307
Sludge, 240-243, 307
yeast, 307

POTATOES

baked, 203, 287
boiled, 286
chowder, 213
history of, 22-25
new, 206, 287, 299
soup
  cream of (Vichysoisse), 214-215
  quick, 287-288
  with fishballs, 222
stuffed, 287
sweet potato pudding, 317
sweet potato and sausage casserole,
  204

Swiss supper, 286-287
Venetian salad, a, 206

SAUCES

Apicius', for boiled chicken, 33
brown sugar sauce, 316
canned meat gravy, 340
cinnamon milk, 315
for Calf's Head à la Tortue, 592
for crêpes suzette, 582
for Oysters Rockefeller, 152
for polenta, beef, 294
for roast oysters, 155
Garum, 29-33, 643
gravy in salad, 261
hard, 316
herb butter, 264-265
oyster catsup, 148-149
roast beef gravy, 261
Sauce Happy Accident, 674
soy, 224, 262
Soyer's sauce à la financière, 616
spaghetti, 291-292
  Napolitana, 292
tartar, 141
wine, 316

SOUPS

borscht, 637-638
  cold summer, 638
  hot winter, 638-639
broth, 202
canned, 221-222
Chinese consommé, 211
chowder, 213
cold buttermilk, 217
Consommé Talleyrand, 222
garden lettuce, 220
Gaspacho, 215
green garden, 219
liaisons for, 222
minestrone, a basic, 218
oyster, 172, 173
  bisque, 172, 173
  cream of, 171
  gumbo, 141-142
  with consommé, 174
onion
  Parisian, 212
  Peculiar, 212
Potage Else, 220

Potage Mille Fanti, 222
potato
    cream of (Vichysoisse), 214-215
    quick, 287-288
    with fishballs, 222

SPAGHETTI, RICE, AND SO ON

Boeuf Moreno, 346-347
boiled rice, 288
broth, 202
Chinese rice, 289
English curry, an, 275
foo yeung with rice, 236
Hawaiian shrimps, 225
instant rice, 289
Kasha, 278, 676-677
left-overs, 289, 290
noodles
    with ham and cheese, 203
    with ham and mushrooms, 204,
        290
polenta, 293-295
    sauce for, beef, 294
Rice and Spice, 318
rice desserts, 289, 317
risotto, 290
riz à l'Impératrice, 319
shrimp and egg curry, 227
spaghetti, 291, 611-612
    with honey and almonds, 202
to cook economically, 202
to keep from boiling over, 202, 288
Turkish hash, 275

VEGETABLES

baked beans, 719
bean sprouts, 299, 581
canned, 298
cauliflower
    and cheese casserole, 441
    buttered, 299
Chinese consommé, 211
chowder, 213
foo yeung, basic, 232, 235-236
frittata
    alla Anything-at-all, 662
    of zucchini, 234-235
frozen, 298
garden lettuce soup, 220
Gaspacho, 215

green garden soup, 219
hash, 299
herb butter, 264-265
herbs for, 298
juices, 205, 297-298
    for pets, 307-308
minestrone, 218
mushroom and ham casserole, 204,
    290
Napolitana sauce, 292
onion soup
    Parisian, 212
    Peculiar, 212
peas, 665-666
    petits pois à la française, 296-297
    with potatoes, 286-287
polenta sauce, 294
salad, 202, 206, 602-604
    carrot and orange, 110
    Romaine, 346
    Venetian, a, 206, 602-603
    with gravy, 261
sauerkraut with partridge, 282
Sludge, 240-243
    for pets, 307
social status of, 111-115
stew, 265-266
to cook in a haybox, 200
to cook sensibly, 205-206, 297, 298
tomato soup cake, 314
Vegetable-Marrow à la Poulette,
    661
with herbs, 206, 298
yam and sausage casserole, 204
zucchini
    baked, 662
    frittata of, 234-235

"WRINKLES FOR THE COOK"

Monkey Soap, 303
mouth wash, 302
to cure bruised withers, 304
to keep hair sweet-smelling, 327
to make soap, 303
tooth powder, 302
to stay soft-handed, 325
to stay sweet-handed, 324-325
to stuff pincushions, 304
to wash dishes, 326

M. F. K. Fisher, who was born in Michigan on July 3, 1908, grew up in the town of Whittier, California. After attending a variety of schools in California and Illinois, she spent three years in France at the University of Dijon. Her first book, *Serve It Forth*, was published in 1937 and established her as a gastronome and writer of note, a reputation reinforced by her subsequent writings—among them *Map of Another Town* and *A Considerable Town*, both of which recapture the periods she spent in Provence. She has also won acclaim for *Among Friends*, a memoir of her early years in Whittier, and for several collections of essays, including *As They Were* and *Sister Age*, and her brilliant translation of Brillat-Savarin's *The Physiology of Taste*.

In her later years, her home in Glen Ellen, California, became a mecca for aspiring culinary writers and her many friends, and she continued to work on three collections of journals and essays that were published posthumously. Shortly before her death on June 22, 1992, she was elected to the American Academy and National Institute of Arts and Letters.